W9-CLJ-009

HOLLYWOOD Celebrity PLAYGROUND

HOWARD JOHNS

BARRICADE
BOOKS

FORT LEE, NEW JERSEY

DISCLAIMER AND AUTHOR'S NOTE

Hollywood Celebrity Playground is intended for entertainment purposes only. Although every effort has been made to insure the accuracy of its content, some minor discrepancies may have occurred. For instance, while I've tried to identify any house or building that has been razed or rebuilt, a few of the addresses mentioned no longer exist.

Finally, the identification of the homes of celebrities, living or dead, and their published addresses, does not mitigate the privacy laws that protect homeowners. Trespassing on private property is prohibited, and violators can be prosecuted.

Published by Barricade Books Inc.
185 Bridge Plaza North
Suite 308-A
Fort Lee, NJ 07024

www.barricadebooks.com

Library of Congress Cataloging-in-Publication Data
A copy of this title's Library of Congress Cataloging-in-Publication Data
is available on request from the Library of Congress.

ISBN 1-56980-303-X

10 9 8 7 6 5 4 3 2 1

Manufactured in the United States of America

Contents

Acknowledgments

HOLLYWOOD LOVES sequels! That is not the reason, however, why I wrote this star-studded follow-up to *Palm Springs Confidential*, which proved to be something of a bombshell when it was published in 2004.

Several socially prominent friends and acquaintances, whose personal addresses had been printed in that mildly scandalous tome, were so taken aback by my effrontery that I was excommunicated from their lives, and my name was deleted from invitation lists.

The reason for this condemnation, they informed me, was that I had violated the code of silence and told what I had seen and heard. Their sharp criticism, I learned, was motivated out of resentment and jealousy.

Conversely, many thousands of homeowners, real estate agents, and tourists, for whom I had written the book with the intention of broadening their knowledge of important people, places, and events, were genuinely appreciative of my efforts.

These loyal curiosity seekers, together with long lines of customers that greeted me at book signings and luncheons, all wanted to know which movie stars lived elsewhere in the Coachella Valley, in cities omitted from the first book. The most frequently asked question was invariably, "Did so-and-so live in such-and-such a place?" And if so, where were those homes located and in what cities within the proximity of Palm Springs?

Those questions were the reason I planned to write a sequel; I always wanted to round up all the celebrities that, for one reason or another, had been excluded from the first book.

It turned into a long and strenuous journey into uncharted waters, but one full of unexpected delights. Like a fisherman trawling the ocean, I was extremely pleased by the different species of vibrant creatures that landed in my net, dazzling me with their odd shapes and colors. Apart from the usual quota of actors, singers, and comedians, there were many politicians, corporate titans, and sports heroes splashing about in the shallows, and quite a few gangsters hiding in deeper waters.

Unlike *Palm Springs Confidential*, which was a valentine to the past, this book aims to focus on more recent events.

But its pressing need as a record of modern times soon evolved into a much larger project than I had originally anticipated. The sheer number of cities in the Coachella Valley, and the long distances between them, made it impossible to provide a full guided tour of each neighborhood.

I was also stumped by the logistical problem of maintaining a correct sequential order for the confounding maze of streets, only to retrace my steps because of the desert's circuitous geography.

Ultimately I decided to adopt a less formal approach and allow the voices of this teeming populace, whose lives are intricately woven around the thousands of palm trees and modular homes that flourish in this harsh paradise, tell their own stories without superfluous commentary.

Perhaps the biggest challenge was the new book's dramatic change of locale. I had to shift from accessible streets in Palm Springs, where homes are within comparatively easy reach of each other, to gated country clubs patrolled by armed security guards. I don't recommend trying to skirt their boundaries unless you want to take a bullet or wind up in jail.

Fortunately I had been admitted to a large number of these regal addresses on prior occasions, so I was able to recall important details from notes as well as from memory. Nevertheless, the contributions of valley residents who provided me with useful information, or helped to clarify long-held misconceptions about these homes and their occupants, must be acknowledged.

At the top of my list is the staff at the Palm Springs City Library, undoubtedly the greatest repository of paper files in the desert. Reference librarians Shelly Thacker, Sastri Madugula, and Jeff Clayton welcomed me—if not with open arms, then at least with smiling faces and willing dispositions—when I showed up for hours of newspaper and microfiche searches.

Ray Kelley at the First American Title Company in Riverside obtained records of grant deeds and title conveyances that irrefutably confirmed the celebrity ownership—or lack thereof—of several hotly disputed homes. Sometimes it is difficult to know exactly who owns what, since many homes have been put in family trusts or are held by dummy corporations for tax purposes.

Murders, suicides, and other violent crimes have been fully documented whenever possible. Police reports and autopsy findings about the deaths of well-known individuals such as Arthur Lake, Irene Roosevelt, Jilly Rizzo, Georgia Skelton, and Al Adamson were obtained from the Riverside County Sheriff Coroner. Other death records came from the Riverside County Recorder's office.

Palm Springs Life, a prestigious monthly magazine for which I have contributed numerous columns, articles, and interviews over the past decade, afforded me the opportunity to interact with numbers of people whose names appear in this book, and observe them in close quarters.

Actor Brad Dexter, whom I interviewed several times, was unflinchingly honest about his broken friendship with Frank Sinatra, the details of which he asked not to be published in his lifetime. A few of Dexter's colleagues, who had been ostracized from the singer's life, also commented off the record about their unfair treatment by Sinatra.

Bandleader Les Brown, whom I interviewed regarding his half-century association with Bob Hope, discussed the big band era and the involvement of organized crime in the entertainment industry, a prevalent theme in these pages. Brown's observations were extremely helpful in forming a picture of old-time Hollywood.

Singer Joy Hodges, whom I first met at a cocktail reception at the Racquet Club and later saw on a number of occasions, shared her remembrances of former co-star Charles "Buddy" Rogers, who was married to Mary Pickford. Hodges also described her close friendship with President Ronald Reagan, whom she had known when they were both young radio performers in Des Moines, Iowa.

Producer William T. Orr, who attended a number of cocktail parties at which I was present, along with his trusted friend Kem Dibbs, chatted with me about the Hollywood studio system, his father-in-law Jack Warner's involvement with the Mafia, and various movie stars with whom he was intimately acquainted.

President Gerald R. Ford, whom I previously interviewed for an extensive profile of Kirk Douglas, was effusive about both his love for the desert and his wife's enduring legacy, the Betty Ford Center. The world's leading alcohol-and-drug-treatment clinic, the Center plays a significant role in the stories of this book.

There were many inspiring conversations. Ron Chaney got me excited about horror movies. Ethel Hyde-White told me quaint stories about her husband, Wilfrid Hyde-White. Randall James lamented the passing of his father, Dennis James. Bill Marx commended his loving parents, Harpo and Susan Marx.

Robert Mitchum laughed at my blunt questions but answered them anyway. Joanna Moore was flattered that I wanted to meet her and said she missed Hollywood. Joseph Pevney cried at the memory of his deceased wife, Mitzi Green. Over lunch, Terry Moore recounted her life with Howard Hughes.

Other contributions both large and small were equally appreciated. Jill Maya of Two Bunch Palms furnished information about the Al Capone legend—one of the desert's enduring mysteries. Shirley Quake of Desert Memorial Park identified the correct locations of cemetery burial plots. Sara Harper of La Quinta Resort & Club indulged my questions about Hollywood director Frank Capra and offered to show me his typewriter.

Bill Waring of Dyson & Dyson in Palm Desert discussed the life of his father, the bandleader Fred Waring, who was one of the founding members of the Bermuda Dunes Country Club. Craig Conley of Coldwell Banker in La Quinta gave me vintage sales brochures that shed light on the tantalizing history of the Fountains estate, once the home of Floyd Odlum and Jacqueline Cochran.

Time and space regrettably did not permit complete histories of the prosperous desert cities mentioned in this book. But they still merited the overviews that I have included for atmosphere and authenticity. Toward that end, former Cathedral City mayor Bob Hillery was very helpful for clarifying the exact whereabouts of the city's former illegal casinos. Guy Hann of the Desert Hot Springs Historical Society faxed me the names of many people who contributed to that city's early development.

Dan Callahan and Anne Tuttle of the Historical Society of Palm Desert provided descriptions of many residents from that city, which now rivals Palm Springs. Significant details about the visits of President Dwight D. Eisenhower to La Quinta and General George Patton to Indio were furnished by Louise Neeley of the La Quinta Museum and Carolyn Cooke of the Coachella Valley Historical Society.

Lois Ware of the City of Palm Springs, Sylvia Borrego of the City of Rancho Mirage, and Dan Taylor of the Inland Empire Film Commission alerted me to the sites of pertinent filming locations that have been used throughout the valley.

Rare photographs, the majority never before published, were obtained from various public facilities and private collections. Sally McManus and Jeri Vogelsang of the Palm Springs Historical Society made available many archival snapshots of the desert in its heyday, when it was less crowded and infinitely more glamorous.

In Hollywood, Pete Bateman at Larry Edmunds Bookshop, and Sabin Gray at Backlot Books & Movie Posters, helped me track down scene stills and original portraits of movie stars. Additional photographs came from Cinema Collectors in Las Vegas and Hollywood Memories in Yucca Valley.

Journalist Michael Fessier, Jr., allowed me to use excerpts from his exclusive story about murdered film director Al Adamson, which was published in *LA Weekly* in 1996. The Betty Ford interview, in which she confessed her alcoholism, first appeared in *Parade* magazine in 1983. Quotations and excerpts from other interviews are from *The Desert Sun*, *The Hollywood Reporter*, *The Los Angeles Times*, the *New York Times*, and *Variety*.

Additional thanks go to Jacque Becker, Chuck Caldwell, Ric Delateur, Daniel Finnane, Gloria Greer, Maggie Hickman, Bruce Houston, Stephanie Ince, George Jacobs, Steve Kiefer, and Mark Miller, for their colorful reminiscences; and to Steven Biller, Lee Ann Blythstone, Donna Curran, Stuart Funk, Peter Hollister, Carolyn Moloschko, Martin Rotondi, Sam Schenkl, John Thompson, and Ron Young for their kind and varied assistance.

HOLLYWOOD CELEBRITY PLAYGROUND

I am very appreciative of Michael Arnold for his computer technical support during the critical writing phase of the manuscript. Greg Gray served as my unofficial muse for one month of much-needed bliss in Puerto Vallarta, Mexico, where a sizable portion of this book was written while I gazed out of his fifth-story condominium apartment at the pelicans flying across Banderas Bay.

In the same way as a movie cannot be made without a producer, so a book cannot exist without a publisher, in this case my champion, Carole Stuart, and the staff at Barricade Books, who are to be commended for their ongoing commitment to this project.

I was extremely fortunate to have a wonderful editor in Alexis Greene, whose smart Broadway sensibility humanized many of the characters in this book and gave them style, shape, and, most of all, substance.

Lastly but most important, I extend the highest praise to my loyal friend and colleague Craig De Sedle, who is well known to many readers for his unstinting faith in me during the last eight years. Without his gentle prodding and constant encouragement, I would never have completed the first book, let alone undertaken the second one.

Palm Springs, California
January 2006

Introduction
That Big One!

Hollywood, California. The rumbling started precisely at 4:31 A.M. on Monday, January 17, 1994. The frightening thump came from deep within the earth's core, as though a colossal beast were unleashing its pent-up aggression.

Soon a subterranean moaning shook the ground beneath the three and a half million inhabitants of Los Angeles. It tossed thousands of people out of their beds and pelted them with heavy objects and broken glass.

The low growl echoed through basements, attics, and garages, and as its strength intensified, water pipes burst, electric power lines snapped, freeways buckled, and buildings collapsed.

One hundred miles away, in the fashionable vacation resort of Palm Springs, retired businessmen, movie stars, and politicians were jolted from their slumbers by a deafening roar, as the invisible poltergeist hurtled through their homes. The ground beneath their houses rolled, doors banged, and windows rattled.

In the surrounding hills and canyons, nervous quail took flight, and bighorn sheep scampered out of the path of falling rocks. Everywhere, the air resonated with the cacophony of impending destruction.

No sooner had this hellish chorus reached a crescendo than it abruptly stopped, and the unseen behemoth, which had triggered fires and countless accidents, retreated to its lair.

The magnitude 6.7 earthquake left 57 victims dead and another 1,500 seriously injured. Portions of the Santa Monica Freeway lay in pieces, and insurance companies were swamped with thousands of claims from residents whose homes were either seriously damaged or totally destroyed.

It wasn't The Big One, as millions feared—merely a prelude to that oft-predicted catastrophe about which scientists have been warning Southern Californians for more than 30 years.

But it was big enough. Scared homeowners, especially those close to the quake's epicenter in Northridge, put their houses up for sale and relocated to coastal beaches, or fled into the mountains and outlying desert.

Palm Springs, long considered a sanctuary where believers in divinity came to regenerate and rejoice, found itself welcoming a flood of urban refugees. Some observers even compared this exodus from L.A. to a modern reenactment of Moses leading the Jews out of Egypt.

The leader of this procession wasn't a bearded law-giver, however, but a pop star-turned-mayor: Sonny Bono. And the Promised Land lay not beyond the impassable Red Sea, but across the San Andreas Fault.

From the air, the jagged San Andreas Fault resembles an ugly suture—a rupture hiding a wound of incalculable trauma. This immense gash in the earth's crust extends from the Gulf of California and zigzags in a northerly direction across fields, roads, and cities, all the way to the San Francisco Peninsula.

Along its hazardous 600-mile journey, the fault cuts like a rusty knife through the Coachella Valley, an isolated gorge revered for its Native American totems and modern engineering marvels, a place where man coexists with an abundance of wildlife.

This oasis of dates, grapefruit, and other desirable crops occupies a 45-mile stretch of irrigated desert that was once a prehistoric seabed. The valley's unusual name, in fact, is derived from the Spanish word *conchella*, meaning seashell, and hard, round fossils can still be found at the base of low-lying hills where water once lapped the shore.

The valley's precious resources are protected by three massive mountain ranges—San Bernardino, San Jacinto, and Santa Rosa—which guard against the elements and are said to possess a powerful aura that fosters creativity and dispels harmful energy.

Nestled in this cradle of life—"like a necklace of emeralds on an ancient, parched chest," wrote Bob Colacello in *Vanity Fair*—lie the sparkling cities of Palm Springs, Cathedral City, Rancho Mirage, Palm Desert, Indian Wells, La Quinta, and Indio.

Strung along the valley's lifeline, Highway 111, these jewels represent the spoils of human conquest, from when indigenous tribes hunted for food to when European settlers prevailed during centuries of colonization. The wide avenues, terraced buildings, and bronze statues that stand in glorious tribute to their founders, who fought for supremacy of their adopted land, are both reminders of victory and monuments to self-aggrandizement.

Because Palm Springs looms at the gateway to this seemingly blissful paradise, it is often compared to Shangri-La, the mystical city of James Hilton's utopian fable, *Lost Horizon*. Precipices guard this modern Valley of the Blue Moon, where everyone who pledges loyalty and obedience is rewarded with eternal youth, and where spiritual pilgrimages are often won and sometimes lost.

The magnet that drew Sonny Bono and other ambitious leaders to rule this desert empire has also lured treasure-hunters and seekers of fame, aristocrats and philanthropists, and shameless provocateurs of controversy.

After all, in this golden cocoon of perpetual sunshine and clear skies, the lines between reality and fantasy have been blurred by the intoxicating pursuit of pleasure. Greed and temptation manifest themselves as kindness and generosity, and new arrivals are quickly seduced by the promise of everlasting happiness.

Topping the roster of distinguished personages who have dined at the valley's sumptuous banquet are royals such as Queen Elizabeth II and Prince Charles of England; sports idols Arnold Palmer, Rod Laver, and Don Drysdale; and Hollywood legends Frank Sinatra, Kirk Douglas, Paul Newman, and Elizabeth Taylor.

Indeed, consummate performers from every facet of show business have thrived in this place of enchantment, where each person basks in the glory of their own accomplishments. The list includes Gene Autry,

Lucille Ball, Carol Channing, Bing Crosby, Clark Gable, Merv Griffin, Goldie Hawn, Howard Keel, Gavin MacLeod, the Marx Brothers, Julia Roberts, Ginger Rogers, Kurt Russell, Telly Savalas, Dinah Shore, Red Skelton, Danny Thomas, Andy Williams, Jane Wyman—and keeps going.

The valley's wealthiest and most influential residents include Bill Gates, Walter Annenberg, Leonard Firestone, Marvin Davis, Lee Iacocca, and Joan Kroc, whose money cascades like silver waterfalls, splashing envious onlookers with riches.

But like the Tibetan temple in Hilton's story, where worshippers wrestled with the forces of good and evil, there is a dark side to such extravagance. Over-consumption is an inherent danger of the valley's pleasure-seeking lifestyle. Saturated by excessive intakes of alcohol and drugs, many unfortunate individuals have withered like rotting grapes on a vine. Some have died from self-inflicted gunshot wounds or by taking poison. And others have been murdered in their sleep.

To avoid such awful consequences, more resilient members of the community have embarked on health-food and fitness regimes to improve their minds and bodies.

The promise of physical renewal is not without its own risks, however. Plastic surgery has been called "the aspirin of Palm Springs," because everyone takes it sooner or later. Obsessed with looking good, men and women submit to a surgeon's scalpel or consume youth-enhancing drugs to improve their appearance and enjoy a better quality of life. They undergo painful facelifts, tummy tucks, liposuction, breast implants, and penis enlargements.

And if all else fails, these restless souls find the desert a convenient place to indulge their romantic passions, even changing their sexual preferences to spice up humdrum love lives.

Such expressions of desire are commonplace among the valley's 300,000 full-time residents and numbers of foreign visitors, called "snowbirds," who maintain second and third homes in enclaves where millionaires are, if not quite literally, a dime a dozen.

At present there are 70 country clubs, 120 golf courses, and 239 hotels serving the well-heeled of the valley. These glistening resorts are served in turn by three airports—Palm Springs, Bermuda Dunes, and Thermal—and on any given day more private jets land than commercial flights.

Money has always played a major role in the desert's development. Before the legalization of gaming on Native American reservations, high rollers would cram into stifling card halls and bingo parlors, where illicit gambling prospered in an uneasy alliance between Hollywood and the Mafia. No one was immune from the corrupting influence of mob bosses such as Anthony Accardo and Sam Giancana or of their watchdogs, Mickey Cohen and Johnny Roselli, who took part in shakedowns of bars, restaurants, and nightclubs.

Today, gamblers can choose among six modern casinos, the latest of which, the Morongo Casino Resort and Spa, boasts a 27-story hotel that rises like a neon-lit domino above Interstate 10. There's also the Fantasy Springs Casino Resort, a 12-story, 250-room luxury hotel in Indio, where players can bet their bankrolls in air-conditioned comfort.

As for politicians, every American president since Harry Truman, with the notable exception of Jimmy Carter, has visited the Coachella Valley, often for memorable weekends of party-going and occasional bed-hopping.

Once, after a late night on the town, Truman caused a ruckus when Secret Service men tried to hustle the feisty Democrat out the back door of the Racquet Club. "I came in the front door and I'm going out the front door!" he roared.

In a quieter vein, President Dwight D. Eisenhower's first visit to the desert in 1954 changed its image forever.

The valley's outdoor charms had usually been reserved for hardy folk who saddled up at dawn and went horseback riding over mountain trails and arroyos. But televised images of Ike and Mamie strolling along a golf course in brilliant winter sunshine sent desert real estate prices through the roof and started a tourist stampede.

That stampede continues to this day. The valley's heavy consumption of liquor, food, and entertainment is a constant source of fascination for planeloads of bewildered tourists, who take guided bus tours of stars' homes and snap pictures of busy intersections that are dedicated to luminaries of stage, screen, and television.

Similarly, the valley's tradition as a place to rest and recuperate continues to attract a wide spectrum of local and foreign dignitaries, who relax poolside or engage in private conferences behind closed doors.

California Governor Arnold Schwarzenegger spends so much time strategizing in the desert that many people erroneously believe he owns a home here. In fact, the muscle-bound movie star has only visited, usually to take part in celebrity golf tournaments.

While tourists ogle and heads of state confer, the valley's reputation as a rapacious hot spot keeps growing, as does its population of political dissidents, flagrant lawbreakers, and social nonconformists.

Although the desert has always appeared outwardly conservative, that status quo is being challenged by a new generation of liberal-minded thinkers, who are striving for a more egalitarian way of life. It remains to be seen if this new generation will sway popular opinion; old habits die hard.

In the meantime, this is the amazing story of world-famous celebrities and their desert playground, where a blessing can be a curse—and the truth, more often than not, lies buried in the sand.

Boys' Night Out

"I came to Casablanca for the waters," grumbled
Humphrey Bogart.
"The waters?" Claude Rains asked, raising an eyebrow.
"What waters? We're in the desert."
"I was misinformed."

IT WAS A defining movie moment: the cynical American expatriate Rick Blaine and his friendly adversary Louis Renault, the corrupt French police captain, sharing a drink in a Moroccan café filled with political refugees, thieves, and con artists.

The year was 1942. The film, of course, was *Casablanca,* which won three Academy Awards and was rapidly installed in Hollywood's pantheon of classic films.

Supporting players such as Sydney Greenstreet and Peter Lorre, who helped bring this tale of love and intrigue to life, whiled away their free time by drinking and gambling, much as their characters did on the screen. Only the actors were doing it in a completely different desert.

At the start of every weekend, usually late on Friday nights or in the early hours of Saturday morning, a quiet caravan of shiny Chevrolets, Plymouths, and Oldsmobiles, driven by some of Hollywood's most recognizable faces, wound its way east from Los Angeles and motored through Riverside and San Bernardino toward Indio.

Six miles east of Palm Springs, the cars came to a long dirt road, turned down an unmarked driveway, and parked side by side behind rows of oleander bushes and tamarisk trees. The drivers retrieved their keys, lit fresh cigarettes, and walked the short distance to a seemingly deserted tile-and-stucco building, where they knocked on the front door.

And there, beyond the restrictions of any legal authority, the Hollywood contingent entered a sumptuous private gambling club called the Dunes—a rambling, Spanish-Colonial *casa grande* that looked inconspicuous from the outside but glittered like Aladdin's cave within.

The Dunes was not Hollywood make-believe, however. It was the real thing.

"The Dunes had it all," remembered real estate agent Tony Burke, "beginning with an aperture ingrained in the massive door through which the guard on duty could give the visitor the once-over and inquire as to the person's interest of the moment."

Oscar, the head doorman, was a darker-skinned version of actor Dan Seymour, who had played Abdul, the 300-pound bouncer who guarded Rick's Café in *Casablanca*. Except this muscle-bound gent didn't wear a fez; he wore a tuxedo.

Inside, beyond a glittering, chandeliered foyer, was a highly polished mahogany bar, its mirrored glass shelves stacked with expensive liquor. Several feet away, in a circular dining room, uniformed waiters carrying gleaming silver trays served twelve-ounce Kansas steaks and whole Maine lobsters to well-dressed patrons.

Instead of listening to *Casablanca's* Dooley Wilson play "As Time Goes By" on an upright piano, this restaurant's customers heard a gleeful Russian-born violinist named Irwin Rubenstein and a ten-piece orchestra.

Indeed, unlike the gloomy atmosphere of Rick's Café after the Nazis took it over, the mood was distinctly upbeat. At the Dunes, there was always noisy chatter and spontaneous laughter from a vibrant show-business crowd: Brylcreemed studio executives accompanied by pampered wives or mistresses, widowed socialites and their handsome escorts, and smooth-talking bachelors with roving eyes.

Overlooking the candlelit room were ornate "boxes"—elevated balcony tables where Marlene Dietrich, Eddie Cantor, Errol Flynn, and Sophie

Tucker held weekly reservations, and where industry moneymen like Darryl Zanuck and Joseph Schenck, who lived in Palm Springs, entertained starlets.

"Schenck," wrote *Variety* columnist Frank Scully, "was the Republican picture producer who had been clinked for a year for tossing a hundred thousand dollars to labor racketeers and failing to report the gift in his income tax report."

Few people at the Dunes cared.

"Here, Joe," said Zanuck, reaching into his shirt pocket. "Have a cigar."

After dinner, couples listened to swing music and danced the samba. The Ritz Brothers might put on an impromptu floor show or vaudevillian Ned Sparks might start a drunken conga line that kicked its way past the bandstand and around the white linen tables amid bursts of applause.

Everyone knew the Conga line was merely an excuse to move the party to the next room. There, behind an iron grille and a red-velvet curtain lay the real attraction: poker, blackjack, craps, and roulette, all attended by smiling dealers and croupiers in dinner jackets.

Fifty dollars a chip was a lot of money to lose on a bet in those days, but Hollywood's elite didn't care. They had driven more than 100 miles to have a good time, whatever the cost, and each of them spent freely on food, drinks, and conversation. It was not uncommon for some moneyed players to drop between $100,000 and $200,000 each season—or $1,000 a day.

The club's proprietor, **Al Wertheimer**, fawned over the latest big star, providing complimentary French champagne in the hopeful expectation that the celebrity would bet everything against the house and lose.

Wertheimer didn't like to schmooze if he could avoid it, but he had to keep up appearances. There were whispers that the tall, somber host was being shaken down by the mob and had to pay protection money. Another rumor had Wertheimer bribing Sheriff Carl Rayburn with a bankroll from the office safe, in order to stay open.

Wertheimer certainly was a man of many secrets. Reportedly he had once been a member of Detroit's infamous Purple Gang, which controlled Michigan's illicit bootlegging and hijacking operations during Prohibition. Described by disgruntled storekeepers as being "off color" (which is how the group got its distinctive name), the Purple Gang not only ran the

Detroit rackets, and plotted jewel heists and other crimes, but also was responsible for 500 contract killings throughout the city's lower east side and waterfront districts.

When the gang's reign of terror finally ended, Al Wertheimer beat a hasty retreat to Southern California and started a new life in the safety of the desert. In 1934, he cleared a road on ten acres of land and opened the **Dunes** (now Sam's Club) at 35–780 Date Palm Drive.

Perhaps an event in Wertheimer's colorful past had affected the way he walked. He had a terrible limp and dragged one foot after the other like a beggar in a silk suit. So he preferred to stand completely still, a burning Chesterfield cigarette dangling from his mouth. That's when some people said he looked like Bogart and others remarked he even talked like Bogie.

With his swarthy, lined complexion, Wertheimer could easily have passed for the frowning actor on a moonlit night. Both men also possessed an arrogance which, in Wertheimer's case, occasionally made him a target. That's why he also carried a loaded gun.

Wertheimer wasn't being nervous—just careful. He had needed to be cautious ever since the cold night of November 20, 1937, when he offered to drive an unescorted woman home. The pretty blonde he befriended at the Dunes that fateful evening was none other than the estranged wife of Edgar Mannix, vice president and general manager of Metro-Goldwyn-Mayer.

Now MGM, as it is commonly known, was the most prestigious of the Hollywood movie studios, with a galaxy of stars that included Norma Shearer, Spencer Tracy, Joan Crawford, Clark Gable, Nelson Eddy, Jeanette MacDonald, the Marx Brothers, Judy Garland, and Mickey Rooney.

But there was nothing prestigious about Eddie Mannix, a former amusement-park bouncer with a foul mouth and a fierce temper who was prone to use fisticuffs to settle an argument. His crude features and strong physique had earned Mannix an unflattering nickname: the Ape.

Terrified of being his next victim, Bernice Mannix had instituted divorce proceedings against her physically abusive husband, charging him with cruelty and infidelity. She was also seeking $4,000 a month in alimony and half of his estate, which was valued at $1 million. The divorce papers included accusations of beatings so severe, it was alleged that Mannix had broken a vertebra in her back, causing Bernice to be in constant pain.

Well, Eddie Mannix was so furious at having his authority challenged, especially by a woman, that he took a kitchen chair and smashed it. The thuggish MGM executive then drank half a bottle of whisky and decided to wipe his hands of his wife once and for all. He picked up the telephone, called some underworld friends, and asked them to take care of the problem.

"Do it," he barked.

At 2:30 A.M. on November 20, as Al Wertheimer drove his sedan along the two-lane highway to Palm Springs with Bernice Mannix nestled beside him, another car sped up from behind and ran them off the road. Wertheimer's sedan flipped over several times and landed in a steep ditch.

Wertheimer was in so much pain he couldn't move: his shoulder, ribs, and pelvis were broken, and his bladder was ruptured. The smells of burning rubber and leaking gasoline eventually brought the injured casino owner to his senses, but when he tried to move his legs, they were crippled. Then he looked across the empty passenger seat and saw Mannix's wife lying dead on the ground. Her neck had been broken.

Wertheimer thought he heard voices calling to him in the darkness, but his eyes fluttered, and he lost consciousness. He awoke two days later in a hospital bed after receiving four lifesaving blood transfusions.

The following week's *Desert Sun* informed its concerned readers:

WERTHEIMER RECOVERING;
MRS. MANNIX DIES IN AUTOMOBILE WRECK

The California Highway Patrol launched an immediate investigation into the unfortunate "accident," but the perpetrators were never apprehended. Wertheimer thought he knew who had caused the deadly crash but wisely kept his mouth shut—he didn't want to tempt fate twice.

Fortuitously for Wertheimer, the year he opened the Dunes, Hollywood actors Charles Farrell and Ralph Bellamy started the Racquet Club in Palm Springs, which attracted more big spenders than Wertheimer had ever dreamed of. People literally lined up to gamble at his spot and spend their money on booze and broads.

All the fancy local hotels had direct telephone lines installed to the Dunes, so guests could place bets on horse races at Santa Anita Park or Aqueduct. "All the bartenders were bookies," said bandleader Bill Alexander. "Christmas week all the hookers came to town and they stayed until Easter."

Milton Hershey, the founder of Hershey's Milk Chocolate, was a regular at the Dunes, where he liked to play roulette. The rotating wheel had a curious effect on the elderly candy mogul, however; entranced by the spinning ball, he would promptly fall asleep at the gaming table. When he awakened, the old man would be staring at $15,000 worth of markers. Then, alerted by a solicitous phone call from the Dunes's staff, Hershey's chauffeur would make out a personal check to cover his employer's losses and take him home.

If the house couldn't always win, Wertheimer believed it should at least protect the odds; thus the constant presence of the Dunes's stickman, George "the Greek" Zouganiles, who had an iron grip like an Olympic discus thrower. If a craps player was enjoying a profitable hot streak, Zouganiles would calmly substitute a pair of crooked dice, until the player lost his nerve and crapped out. The Dunes soon developed a reputation as a clip joint and in 1943, following growing accusations of bribery and corruption, it burned down.

In those days the Dunes wasn't alone in attempting to separate well-heeled players from their bulging wallets. Shortly after Wertheimer arrived in the desert, Los Angeles bookmaker Jake Katleman and his business partner Carl Cohen—who went on to run two Las Vegas gambling institutions, El Rancho and the Sands—leased a corrugated metal garage on Andreas Road and Indian Avenue in Palm Springs and installed crap tables.

When police armed with nightsticks showed up and broke the doors and windows, Katleman moved his operations five miles east to Cathedral City, outside their jurisdiction. That's when Frank Portnoy, a Purple Gang alumnus who previously ran the gambling at the Dunes, was tapped by Katleman and Cohen to front a new club called the **Cove**, which opened in Cathedral City in 1941.

This unrestricted nightspot (now Elks Lodge #1905) quickly became a haven for out-of-town gamblers and stars with deep pockets. Actors such as William Powell and Paul Lukas, along with spirited producer David Selznick, whose Civil War epic, *Gone with the Wind,* was the most popular film of all time, were among the gambling night owls seen munching on thinly sliced ham sandwiches and drinking beer drawn from ice-cold kegs.

In the late 1940s, Frank Sinatra could often be seen at the Cove, smoking nervously and fiddling with his pinky ring. "He used to come down on weekends," said former manager Bobby Garcia. "At that time he was married to Nancy. He owed the joint a marker for about $5,800." It was a large sum for the beleaguered singer, who was then in the middle of a career slump; his records weren't selling and his marriage was in trouble.

Gangster Mickey Cohen was also into Sinatra's pocket, for money to subsidize a magazine called *Hollywood Nightlife.* Garcia realized Sinatra was on a losing streak and told him that, if the singer quit lending money to Cohen, the club would tear up his marker. "You got yourself a deal," Sinatra grinned. It was good public relations, and Sinatra never forgot the gesture. "I like Palm Springs," he told his friends back in New Jersey. "They got class."

■ ■ ■

LOCATED A HALF mile away from the Cove stood the **One Thirty Nine Club**. Originally a private residence that stood at 139 Broadway, the fortified brick-and-concrete bunker had slits lined with boilerplate cut into the sides of the windows and a second-story gun turret. There, after a few glasses of Kentucky Bourbon, you could imagine that James Cagney might hold police at bay in a violent shoot-out.

The club's owner, Earl Sausser, was a short man with a penchant for wearing multicolored vests and carrying a gold pocket watch and chain. Guests were admitted to the club through a heavily guarded front door; once inside, they removed their fedoras and fur coats at a hat-check stand, then proceeded into the 80-foot-long main lounge. Contrary to what has been alleged, there was no bar. Players were served glasses of gin or whisky and bowls of homemade chili—on the house.

But finally it didn't matter whether these were high-class venues or not. What mattered was that they catered to people's pecuniary needs in the years before the Las Vegas casino boom. After all, there wasn't much to choose from in those pre–World War II days. The only alternative for most hardcore gamblers were places like Hollywood's Clover Club, where high rollers conferred on the neon-lit Sunset Strip.

That's why most stars headed for the desert.

■ ■ ■

IN TRUTH, CATHEDRAL City was little more than a glorified truck stop at that time. Its main street consisted of grimy gas stations and fly-specked roadside diners.

The name Cathedral Canyon first appeared on U.S. geographical survey maps in 1904, although the description had reportedly been intoned as early as 1852, when Colonel Henry Washington, under contract to Samuel King, the surveyor general of California, made the initial survey of Colorado Desert land.

According to local folklore, Colonel Washington, resplendent in his officer's uniform and with an army pistol at his side to dispatch troublesome rattlesnakes, paused his steed at the top of a canyon bathed in orange sunlight and likened the dramatic rock formations below to a vast, ruined cathedral.

In 1928, a group of land-developers intent on honoring Washington's memory succeeded in establishing a post office named Cathedral City, around which a variety of small homes and businesses sprang up. The four developers' names—Jack Grove, George Allen, Glenn Plumley, and Mont Van Fleet—were preserved for posterity as local streets.

By 1941, the town only contained a few hundred people, most of whom lived in whitewashed cottages along A, B, C, and D Streets, or along intersecting First, Second, Third, Fourth, and Fifth Streets.

Still, Cathedral City, often derided as the poor relation of Palm Springs, had one undeniable attraction: illegal gambling.

■ ■ ■

ONE OF THE town's most unexpected and incongruous inhabitants was **Raymond Chandler**, the pipe-smoking author of *The Big Sleep, Farewell My Lovely,* and *The High Window.* Hoping to cure his sinus problem in the desert air, he leased a two-bedroom bungalow there at the outbreak of World War II.

"This place bores me," Chandler wrote to his New York publisher, Alfred Knopf. "But I've just about been talked into sticking out the mountains and the desert for another year. After that to hell with the climate, let's meet a few people."

Chandler's gripe, as usual, was the lack of culture: no decent shops and nothing to do. His one diversion was to buy meat at a grocery store on First Street, cook a rib roast for his wife, Pearl Hulburt, whom he called Cissy, and feed the leftovers to their cat.

Just why one of America's most popular crime writers was content to spend his days holed up like a fugitive in the middle of nowhere says a lot about either his low self-esteem or his low finances.

A former oil company executive with a serious drinking problem, Chandler routinely moved several times a year, renting homes in Echo Park, Silver Lake, Pacific Palisades, Brentwood—an apartment in Santa Monica, a log cabin at Big Bear Lake. He had, in fact, bounced around the greater Los Angeles area for two decades.

According to his biographer, Tom Hiney, who followed the misanthropic writer's nomadic wanderings, "Chandler's wariness about being ripped off by Angelino real-estate brokers and landlords was partly born of paranoia about being poor again, and partly a reaction to the scam-ridden local economy."

Chandler's personal frustration was translated into the pages of his fourth detective novel, *The Lady in the Lake*, which was published in 1943. This bleak tale of private eye Philip Marlowe's relentless search for a missing woman, whose body, he eventually learns, lies in a watery grave, had the best sales of any books Chandler had written so far.

After that, Hollywood beckoned with big bucks, and he sat at his typewriter, a bottle at his elbow, and pounded out the screenplays for *Double Indemnity, The Blue Dahlia,* and *Strangers on a Train.*

After Cissy died in 1954, Chandler was heartbroken and, afflicted with a painful nerve disease, relied even more intently on grog. His writing suffered, and he attempted suicide. But he proved to be a bigger bungler than his fictitious killers and survived his own sorry attempts.

Despite unhappiness with his adopted surroundings, Chandler

returned periodically to the desert, and in 1956 he could be found at one or more of the city's watering holes, filling his pipe with cut tobacco and ordering a scotch and soda.

In his novel *Poodle Springs,* published posthumously, Chandler incorporated details of the nights he had spent at gambling outposts looking over people's shoulders. In that book, which pitted Marlowe against a money-grubbing land developer, the Dunes served as the model for a joint appropriately called the Agony Club.

Chandler, finally released from his own agony, died of pneumonia in 1959 at the age of 70.

Thirty years later, Cathedral City still looked pretty much as it had in Raymond Chandler's day. The only difference was the number of full-time residents, which by 1981 had reached 14,000. By 2001, that figure would exceed 46,000, and almost a quarter of them would be gays and lesbians.

■ ■ ■

RESTAURATEUR **MICHAEL ROMANOFF** had experienced all manner of degradation in his youth. A former stowaway, jailbird, check bouncer, escapee, and thief, he became, through sheer will and determination, the owner of Romanoff's, for 23 years the most fashionable restaurant in Beverly Hills—a restaurant patronized by the crème de la crème of Hollywood.

It was at Romanoff's that Spencer Tracy, Clark Gable, Humphrey Bogart, and Frank Sinatra routinely drank each other under the table, and where Marilyn Monroe, Jayne Mansfield, and Sophia Loren competed with each other for having the best photographs taken of their ample cleavage. "'Star-studded' was the term that gossip columns invariably used to describe Romanoff's," commented society writer Dominick Dunne, who frequented the place.

The Rat Pack, which was founded by Bogart, held its first meeting in the upstairs dining room. Sinatra was named pack master, Judy Garland was the first vice president, and her husband, Sid Luft, was dubbed cage master. Swifty Lazar was appointed secretary, Nathaniel Benchley became the historian, and Lauren Bacall the den mother. Bogart himself was in charge of public relations. Their motto: "Never rat on a rat." After Bogart died from esophageal cancer in 1957, the torch passed to Sinatra, who claimed the pack as his own.

These and their headline-making antics were watched over by the mustachioed restaurant owner with the basset-hound face, jug ears, and brush haircut. Everyone called him "Prince Michael"; the self-styled aristocrat insisted on it.

To make himself appear more regal, Romanoff affected an English accent, wore tweed jackets, and carried a Malacca cane. And if he really wanted to make an impression, he'd inhale smoke through a cigarette holder and wear a polished monocle.

In reality, he was a Jewish orphan from Illinois. But his stories, which he invented and embellished with total dedication, overtook Romanoff until he became the biggest bullshit artist in the world. Still, for all his lies, he was an honest man, unimpressed by people's affectations and given to heartfelt generosity.

The original Romanoff's opened for business in 1939 on North Rodeo Drive and remained at that address for eleven years. The atmosphere was part New York speakeasy, part Russian tea room. When the restaurant moved to bigger premises down the street, architect Douglas Honnold envisioned a palace fit for a king, with terrazzo, marble floors, gold-plated fixtures, and tufted leather upholstery. A sculptured archway with a short flight of steps created a grand entrance to the main dining room, which was a hexagonal "fish bowl": twenty-four padded booths surrounded by private dining alcoves. There were banquet rooms on the second floor, and a penthouse and rooftop garden.

Romanoff's name was spelled out on the new façade in stylized wrought-iron letters, with the "R" topped by a crown.

The total cost was $400,000.

In 1959, Sinatra, who played innumerable practical jokes on Romanoff during their frequent jaunts to London and Paris, talked his princely friend into opening a second restaurant, **Romanoff's on the Rocks**, at 67–399 E. Palm Canyon Drive in Cathedral City.

But Sinatra wasn't joking this time. He was genuine in his encouragement and counted on the patronage of their desert friends to help make the restaurant a success. (A third restaurant, Romanoff's on Nob Hill, had already opened in San Francisco.)

Flattered by the singer's good intentions, Romanoff went all out to attract the well-tailored likes of Bob Hope, Liberace, and of course the

Rat Pack, which ate culinary delicacies in the glass-walled dining salon while tapping their toes to Paul Whiteman and his Orchestra.

But underneath the bonhomie was a sense of desperation. The champagne lacked fizz, and the caviar tasted sour. The magic that had endeared the phony Russian prince to Hollywood's in-crowd was somehow missing from this latest endeavor. "I would see Elvis Presley driving around aimlessly in his pink Cadillac convertible, looking for action he was never going to find," recalled Frank Sinatra's valet, George Jacobs, about the lack of club patronage.

Romanoff had hoped to cash in on the Palm Springs nightclub boom, but he had misjudged the clientele's level of sophistication, possibly because he put an inordinate amount of trust in Sinatra—normally his good-luck charm.

Whoever was to blame, the crowds stayed away. Faced with a rotten egg instead of a tasty omelet, Romanoff sold his eatery for $185,000 in 1962 to Los Angeles restaurateur Milton Kreis, who changed the name to Rim Rocks. "I paid them too much of a compliment by opening up in Palm Springs," Romanoff haughtily declared. "There just didn't seem to be too much interest there but that's their fault and my mistake."

After reincarnating as various failed nightclubs—Pompeii, Club International, and more recently, Escape (a fitting description considering its subsequent fate)—the restaurant remained a white elephant more than 45 years after it first opened. It is now permanently closed and covered with gang graffiti.

The phony Russian prince died in 1971 at the age of 78.

■ ■ ■

IN THE TWO decades since Michael Romanoff bid Cathedral City a less-than-fond farewell, the town's popularity took a dramatic nosedive. Many folks refused to go there; those that did maintained they were just passing through on their way to someplace else. "It was the kind of town you drove out to for shoe repair," said author Gregory Hinton, "to get your vacuum cleaner fixed; to poke around in thrift stores—or maybe to have a drink with a whore."

One of the few places doing any real business during the 1980s was the **Pink Lady** at 67–990 E. Palm Canyon Drive, a rowdy topless bar where male customers stuffed five-dollar bills in female strippers' thongs. Its major competition was a stretch of neon-lit dance clubs along industrialized Perez Road—better known as "The Gay Mile"—that attracted a roving crowd of homosexuals who watched swimsuit contests, whipped cream wrestling, and female impersonators.

It was an all-too-familiar scene, especially at Happy Hour, when drinks were half-price. There were "men in white mesh tank tops or Hawaiian shirts. Old men swathed in gold chains and tennis bracelets buying rounds of drinks for drifting, muscular, sun-beaten younger guys," wrote Gregory Hinton.

The most patronized of these flashy discothèques, Choices and C.C. Construction, where sweaty couples in leather chaps and boots danced the night away under strobe lighting, are now passé. New generations of mild-mannered drinkers prefer karaoke contests at Club Whatever (formerly Ground Zero) or billiards at Sidewinders, located uptown.

A few of these nocturnal hangouts, such as **Daddy Warbucks**, which stood at 68–981 E. Palm Canyon Drive, and piano lounges where smiling men in tight-fitting pants cruised each other at night, were tolerable meeting places. But the majority, including Wolf's Den (now the Barracks) and the aptly named Gravel Pit, were only for the lonely or for seekers of cheap thrills.

One regular customer seen ogling pretty boys at these noisy bars, where pink triangles and rainbow stickers were affixed to the windows, was the Reverend Jim Bakker, who was a part-time valley resident with his wife Tammy Faye. "Jim was not only gay," recalled hotel owner Bob Canon, "but he was openly so, and known to be gay within the homosexual community in Palm Springs."

Bakker was not alone in his lascivious prowling. Many well-known actors and TV talk-show hosts, who passed for straight but in fact led double lives, were among those patrons whose expensive cars were spotted outside these seedy establishments.

■ ■ ■

JUSTIFIABLY DESCRIBED AS a midcentury desert landmark, the architecturally noteworthy **Desert Palms Inn,** at 67–580 Jones Road, has always been a fun place, thanks to its "anything goes" atmosphere and frisky all-male clientele.

The inn's reputation dates back to the sophomoric 1963 romantic comedy *Palm Springs Weekend,* which starred Troy Donahue, Connie Stevens, Robert Conrad, and Stefanie Powers. The 29-room hotel doubled for the film's hitching post, La Casa Yates, where clueless cowboy Ty Hardin sang "Bye Bye Blackbird" with Jerry Van Dyke, and eight-year-old Peeping Tom Bill Mumy put soap suds in the swimming pool.

During the busy tourist season, the "D.P" is a popular cruising spot, and you can see butch men in G-strings having water fights with drag queens wearing cha-cha heels. But the once notorious garden maze, where naked men disappeared for moonlit trysts, has been removed in the interest of public safety.

■ ■ ■

AT 67–670 CAREY Road, a short trek through groves of date palms leads you to the **Villa Resort**, a collection of historic, whitewashed adobe buildings. This was the site of the Butterfield Overland Mail's stagecoach route, which once transported dusty passengers between Yuma, Arizona, and Los Angeles.

Stout, waist-coated husbands and their corseted wives had no idea that, in little more than a hundred years, this isolated coach stop would become a favorite gay destination called Dave's Villa Caprice, with 44 deluxe bungalows where tangled male bodies writhed in passion.

Prior to its "men only" occupancy, the Elizabeth Arden Company developed the site as a beauty farm. Here, overweight women ate low-calorie meals served on pink linen tablecloths and bone china. Matronly ladies sweated in steam cabinets and infrared baths, and underwent massages or a whirl through a giant contraption of wooden cylinders designed to "smooth" the pounds away.

Today, the Villa is the oldest of the more than 40 gay-owned resorts in the Coachella Valley. The hotel recently received a makeover from its new proprietors, who bought the historic lodging in 2003 and performed much needed cosmetic enhancement on the Arden property.

■　■　■

VISITORS TO PORN star Will Clark's annual Bad Boys Pool Party, at **Wally World** at 67–698 Carey Road, probably don't know or care about the history of this lushly landscaped estate, which was cultivated by local pioneer **Raymond Cree**. They prefer to sip cocktails and frolic nude in the water.

The clerical-looking Cree was superintendent of schools for Riverside County for twelve years. He was also a prominent Palm Springs land developer, who subdivided Vista Santa Rosa Tract, Winterhaven Manor, Warm Sands Park, Palm Canyon Mesa, and Las Palmas Estates. In 1915, Cree acquired 65 acres of unfarmed land and began planting grapefruit and Deglet Noor date palms.

Eventually he sold off most of the acreage, but he kept the original homestead. Known as the Old Cree Ranch, this impressive seven-bedroom estate served as Cree's main residence from 1932 until a few years before his death at 92 in 1967. A decorative pillar outside the front door is inscribed "Dar Essalaam 1933"; it refers to the seaport in Tanzania on the East African coast where many of the home's imported trees originated.

In 1990, investor Walter Magnuson purchased the two-and-a-half-acre property, which he renamed Wally World. The sprawling resort was the scene of much sexual frivolity, even when Magnuson died five years later of a heart attack at a party celebrating his seventy-third birthday. "His partner Mark Rose came out and told all the guests that Wally had died, which was a big shock to all of us," recalled Chuck Caldwell. "But the party went on. That's what he would have wanted."

Successive owners have restored the home's faded magnificence and up-graded the property. Among the enticing features: two huge black-bottomed swimming pools equipped with a swim-up bar, two Jacuzzis, a cascading waterfall, and a tennis court.

In 2001, cherub-faced actress Christina Applegate, who played promiscuous teenager Kelly Bundy on TV's *Married . . . with Children*, tied the knot there with hunky actor-model Johnathon Schaech in a wedding ceremony attended only by immediate family and friends.

■　■　■

FANCY A WALK on the wild side? **Cathedral City Boys' Club**, better known as CCBC, at 68–369 Sunair Road, advertises itself as the largest clothing-optional resort in the desert. It's a fetishist's paradise: naked gay men take Viagra and other chemical stimulants, have group sex, or enjoy mutual masturbation and oral copulation.

There are plenty of secluded pathways and alcoves to explore, especially after dusk, when the majority of intoxicated guests have rested up for a night of non-stop partying. Leather freaks can choose from several mock-correctional facilities, including Danny's Jail and the Dungeon.

Some of the most wicked and depraved X-rated gay movies, starring waxed muscle-boys enjoying these libidinous delights, have been filmed against this suburban tropical jungle.

It's fortunate that these sexual encounters take place among consenting adults on private property. There are inherent risks associated with habitually cruising public parks and restrooms—mugging, gay bashing, arrest for indecent behavior, and much worse.

■ ■. ■

IN 1998, THE district attorney for Riverside County was asked to file manslaughter charges in connection with the 1996 death of national AIDS activist and philanthropist **Edward "Ed" Gould**.

Openly HIV-positive, Ed Gould had been a member of President William J. Clinton's HIV/AIDS Advisory Council. He also had served on the board of the Los Angeles Gay & Lesbian Center, where he helped raise money and awareness for people living with HIV and AIDS.

Unfortunately he didn't always practice what he preached. On November 8, 1996, Gould met another man for sex at **Club Palm Springs**, an infamous bathhouse at 68–449 Perez Road. Moments after inhaling the contents of a bottle of video head cleaner, Gould went into cardiac arrest and died. He was 53.

The toxic liquid, commonly known as "poppers," is used by gay men to heighten the intensity of orgasm. Gould had purchased the chemical substance at Black Moon Leather, which sells dildos, lubricants, and gay erotica.

■ ■ ■

THE DEPLORABLE ACTIONS of **Father Paul Shanley**, a renegade "street priest" who advocated sex between men and boys, threatened to disgrace two Catholic dioceses when allegations of sexual abuse were leveled at him during the summer of 2002.

That's when Shanley, who previously was a tenant at the Ocotillo Place Apartments at 69–155 Dinah Shore Drive and owned the Cabana Club, a gay hotel in the Warm Sands neighborhood of Palm Springs, was arrested. He was charged with ten counts of child rape, and six counts of indecent assault and battery involving four boys.

According to his male accusers, the defrocked priest had pretended to give them medical examinations, but instead he played strip poker and raped them anally. The allegations went back more than 20 years and involved boys as young as six years of age. The boys said they had been molested in church rectories, bathrooms, and confessionals.

Many of Shanley's sexual assaults had occurred in the former Palm Springs home of actor Tony Curtis, which Shanley and another gay priest, Jack White, leased in 1991 for all-male sex parties. Behind locked doors, unsuspecting males were served a potent brew of alcohol and pills, after which Shanley violated them.

By the time the law caught up with him, Shanley had ditched his clerical collar and bolted from Cathedral City for San Diego's gay Hillcrest district. There he was promptly arrested by police and extradited to Massachusetts, where, in January 2005, his case went to trial.

An anonymous accuser testified that Shanley had repeatedly raped him, all the time warning the terrified boy not to tell anyone about the crime, including his parents, because no one would believe him.

Looking feeble and wearing a hearing aid instead of a silver cross, the 74-year-old child molester stood in front of the judge and meekly proclaimed his innocence. But a jury of seven men and five women were unmoved by his ploy. Three months later they returned a verdict that made front-page headlines in *The Boston Globe*:

JURY CONVICTS SHANLEY OF RAPING CHILD

For Cathedral City's law-abiding community, fighting this scandal became a difficult challenge. They had always strived to distance themselves from such vulgarities, believing that they could do little to stop this sort of indecency anyway. Then they found an unlikely savior in the relationship between church and state—real estate, that is!

Aware that Cathedral City needed a new image, local business leaders set out to change the face of its aging downtown. They turned it from a shambling collection of peeling clapboard storefronts, with broken windows and missing roof tiles, into a vibrant, pedestrian-friendly entertainment plaza. They even planted 100 palm trees along Date Palm Drive.

The first controversial step involved replacing obsolete street names with more significant ones. In 1997, Second Street became Buddy Rogers Avenue, in deference to the 92-year-old silent film star and longtime desert resident, who made hefty monetary contributions to the city's redevelopment program. "I love you all," cooed Rogers, outfitted in a red jacket and waving to enthusiastic fans outside Cathedral City's new $40-million Civic Center.

The rebuilding of downtown could not have been accomplished without Rogers's help or the encouragement of his wife, Beverly Ricono. Through her work in Los Angeles charities, Ricono had met the mother of real estate developer Robert Selleck, Jr. (brother of Tom Selleck of *Magnum P.I.* fame). Robert, Tom, and a third brother, Dan, were partners in Selleck Properties, and with Beverly Ricono's encouragement, the Sellecks erected the new Mary Pickford Theatre on Pickfair Street, next to the Civic Center Park and the Fountain of Life.

Three years after Rogers saw his name above an avenue it was Monty Hall's turn. The smiling host of TV's perennial game show *Let's Make a Deal,* a longtime resident, was honored with his own street sign in recognition of his outstanding charity work.

Other newly dedicated streets included George Montgomery Trail, which saluted the Hollywood cowboy star and former husband of singer Dinah Shore, and Avenida Lalo Guerrero, which was named after the father of Chicano music. All of them lived at one time or another in Cathedral City.

■ ■ ■

AS CATHEDRAL CITY cleaned itself up, it rediscovered the local homes of the rich and famous. Some houses, such as the one belonging to silver-haired actor **William Boyd**, were reclaimed by the Cathedral City Redevelopment Agency.

Boyd, who was discovered by the great Hollywood showman Cecil

B. DeMille and played robust roles in many silent screen epics, including *The Volga Boatman* and *Two Arabian Knights*, occupied the house at 68–941 Second Street with his fourth wife, the actress Grace Bradley.

With the coming of sound to the movies, Boyd won a whole new generation of fans playing the clean-living, two-fisted Western hero Hopalong Cassidy, who spent 66 features chasing bad guys aboard his trusty white steed, Topper. Boyd eventually bought the rights to Cassidy's name and parlayed this kindly character, who didn't smoke, drink, or swear, into an early television phenomenon, netting himself an estimated $25 million.

After Boyd retired from acting, he went into the hotel business and managed the Trip Along Apartments in Palm Desert, where he could be found at his new home at 73–498 Joshua Street, grinning and waving to fans who were delighted to meet Hopalong Cassidy in person.

In 1968, Boyd underwent surgery to remove a tumor from a lymph gland, after which he refused all interviews and photograph requests. He died of Parkinson's disease in 1972 at the age of 77.

■ ■ ■

ASCENDING THE HILLSIDE from which Colonel Henry Washington once looked down into the valley, it's impossible not to notice the abstract steel spire of **St. Louis Catholic Church** at 37–220 Glenn Avenue. The generous donations of Natalie "Dolly" Sinatra, the elderly mother of singer Frank Sinatra, helped build this church, and here Oscar-winning actresses Jane Wyman and Loretta Young attended weekly mass.

Here, too, Nancy Sinatra, Frank's oldest daughter, married her second husband, Hugh Lambert, in 1970. Nancy's first marriage, to singer Tommy Sands, had been a disaster; after five years, he walked out on her, unable to live in the shadow of the Sinatras' fame and wealth. So Nancy hoped that she would find true happiness in her marriage to Lambert, a tall, sensitive choreographer who had worked on Bob Fosse's *How to Succeed in Business without Really Trying*.

Their traditional wedding took place on a Sunday. Frank Sinatra was in an unusually magnanimous mood and allowed the general public, most of them poor Mexican families, to watch the wedding ceremony. Sinatra himself was in attendance, as were his best friend, Jilly Rizzo; son

Frank, Jr.; and daughter Tina, who caught her sister's bouquet.

Sinatra gave the bride away, and everyone cheered the happy nuptials. The marriage produced two daughters and lasted 15 years, until Lambert's premature death from cancer at the age of 55 in 1985.

■ ■ ■

CATHEDRAL CITY COVE is protected on three sides by the Santa Rosa Mountains, one reason why, until recently, the only people who knew about this bucolic place were those with a special reverence for the locale's natural landlords: bighorn sheep, bobcats, and coyotes.

Did I mention the possibility of werewolves? "Whoever is bitten by a werewolf and lives becomes a werewolf himself," intoned an old gypsy woman at a campfire, sealing the fate of Lawrence Talbot, who turned into a hairy beast in *The Wolf Man.*

Actor **Lon Chaney, Jr.**, who played the tortured central character in this 1941 horror film and several snarling sequels, was cursed in real life, but not by a wolf bite—by a succession of bad movies.

He had one good crack at stardom when he played the mentally retarded farmhand Lennie in the critically acclaimed film *Of Mice and Men.* But the movie was not a commercial success, and ever after Chaney was typecast as a freak. He spent the remainder of his Hollywood years in limbo, despite scaring the beejesus out of movie audiences acting rampaging monsters in *The Ghost of Frankenstein, The Mummy's Tomb,* and *Son of Dracula.*

Decades of heavy drinking and smoking took its toll on Chaney's health and, like many down-and-out actors before him, he found himself the victim of producers and directors who had little concern for his welfare. All they cared about was selling tickets to movies that would have made his legendary father, Lon Chaney, Sr., spin in his grave.

In 1973, at the age of 67, Lon Chaney, Jr., died of a combination of illnesses, including beriberi and liver failure.

But all good monsters have a strange way of coming back to life.

In this case it was the wolf man's offspring who did the lycanthrope's bidding from his mist-shrouded casket. Grandson **Ron Chaney**, a long-time resident of 38–825 Elna Way, and the custodian of numerous family heirlooms, tried to right some of the wrongs done to Chaney, Jr. He's had his grandfather's films reappraised and in the process has restored much-needed luster to the actor's dulled reputation.

Ron has a treasure-trove of collectibles from both his grandfather and his great-grandfather, Lon Chaney, Sr., the "Man of a Thousand Faces" who was the original black-cloaked star of *The Phantom of the Opera*. In 1992, Ron and his brother, Gary, who also lives in Cathedral City, formed Chaney Enterprises to preserve the family name and market licensed products. Their proudest moment thus far was having *both* famous ancestors honored on a set of five commemorative U.S. postage stamps. Issued in 1997, the stamps were appropriately titled "Famous Movie Monsters."

■　■　■

ONE OF CATHEDRAL City Cove's earliest residents was famed American cartoonist **James Swinnerton**, whose weekly comic strips in William Randolph Hearst's *San Francisco Examiner* helped boost that newspaper's circulation.

Swinnerton's longest-running creation was "Little Jimmy," a strip about the adventures of a forgetful boy that Swinnerton started in 1904 and drew for the next 54 years. He also created the playful characters "Mr. Jack" and "Canyon Kiddies." From 1920 on, his cartoons dealt increasingly with aspects of desert life, with which he first became enamored when he traveled to Arizona to recover from tuberculosis. But in 1959, after Swinnerton moved to the Cove for his health, he lived at 68–437 Treasure Trail. He died from complications of a broken leg in 1974, at the age of 98.

Another early resident of Cathedral City Cove was veteran radio comedian **Charles Correll**, who played the role of vociferous Andy Brown on *Amos & Andy,* the first entertainment program to depict the working lives of African-Americans, albeit characterized for comic effect. Correll was caught in a tug-of-war between the successful series and pressure from black activists to curb its mocking humor, which was considered disrespectful in many communities.

Despite its racial stereotypes, the weekly radio show, which co-starred Freeman Gosden as Amos Jones, was extremely popular. More than 40 million Americans regularly tuned in and kept the show alive for 32 years.

Four years after the landmark program's final broadcast in 1960, Correll retired to 38–132 Charlesworth Drive, where he kept in touch with actor-friend Gosden, who lived in Indian Wells. Correll passed away in 1972.

■ ■ ■

BURLY CHARACTER ACTOR **Simon Oakland**, who brayed and bullied his way through more than 100 films and TV shows, playing streetwise cops and explosive military commanders, resided at 39–521 Bel Air Drive.

Formerly a New York City concert violinist, Oakland's coarse features and intense manner were perfectly suited to the bossy roles in which he was frequently cast. He acted the hardened journalist who goes to bat for convicted murderess Susan Hayward in *I Want to Live!*, the court psychiatrist who explains Anthony Perkins's cross-dressing in *Psycho*, and the police captain who cuts Steve McQueen some slack in *Bullitt*.

But it was Oakland's humorous turn in *The Night Stalker*, where he played the apoplectic newspaper editor who butts heads with monster-chasing crime reporter Darren McGavin, which put his face on the movie-star map. After that, he could always be seen in a variety of roles, especially in TV series such as *Toma, Baa Baa Black Sheep*, and *David Cassidy—Man Undercover*.

Oakland died in this house in 1983 after a long battle with cancer, one day after his sixty-eighth birthday.

■ ■ ■

AS NAÏVE PEGGY Jones, who inspired the hit song "Have You Met Miss Jones?" singer and dancer **Joy Hodges** became the toast of Broadway in the electric 1937 musical *I'd Rather Be Right,* starring George M. Cohan. In Hollywood, Hodges played the role of Gale Rogers in the comedy *Personal Secretary* and co-starred opposite Vincent Price in his film debut, *Service Deluxe*. But it was Hodges's crush on an unknown actor that inspired his rise to fame and put her name in the history books.

In 1937, Hodges met and befriended a shy, bespectacled Des Moines sports announcer named Ronald Reagan. The actress was so smitten by his wholesome good looks that she made him take off his glasses and arranged for a Warner Bros. talent agent to hire him at $200 a week.

"I also got Ronnie his first set of contact lenses," she remembered. "He was the first leading man in Hollywood to wear lenses and would take them out on a regular basis to show all his friends." But romance between the energetic hoofer and the novice actor was not to be, although they remained close friends throughout Reagan's political career as Governor of California and the nation's fortieth president. Once, when Hodges was a guest at the White House, she sat next to Soviet leader Mikhail Gorbachev at dinner.

Hodges continued to work in films, television, and on Broadway, most memorably in *No, No Nanette*, replacing her ailing desert neighbor, Ruby Keeler, and in a revival of *Babes in Arms* directed by longtime friend Ginger Rogers.

Still, throughout her extensive career and busy private life, which included three marriages, Hodges's most cherished possessions were boxes of personal letters from President Reagan that recounted their 60-year friendship. One, written in 1982, reminded her that "You started it all." Their last meeting occurred in January 2001, seven years after Reagan was diagnosed with Alzheimer's disease. "He looked at me and all he remembered was that I was once Miss Jones," she cried. It was a bittersweet parting for the woman who had inspired Reagan's acting career and the man who had brought an end to the Cold War.

In 1994, Hodges moved to 69–455 Las Begonias in the Date Palm Country Club, where failing health required her to use a wheelchair. She died at a Palm Desert nursing home of a stroke in 2003, at the age of 88.

■ ■ ■

ANOTHER WELL-KNOWN homeowner who resided at the Date Palm Country Club was portly radio and TV announcer **Don Wilson**, who lived at 465 Cerritos Way. Wilson was Jack Benny's favorite foil for 33 years ("Oh, Don!"), as well as the subject of innumerable fat jokes on *The Jack Benny Program*.

It seems Benny was always making fun of Don's weight, and in between pitching the show's sponsors, Lucky Strike cigarettes and Jell-O pudding, Wilson would get his revenge by mentioning Jack's receding hairline.

Wilson also played the role of Mr. Chubby in the Jerry Lewis comedy *Sailor Beware* and was Marilyn Monroe's nosy neighbor in the thriller *Niagara*. Wilson was 81 when he collapsed and died of a heart attack in 1982.

■ ■ ■

SHAPELY **CARROLL BAKER** was a star-struck kid who always wanted to be in the movies.

The sexy blond actress suddenly got her wish when she was plucked from virtual obscurity and groomed to be the next Marilyn Monroe. Not that Baker was a total unknown—in 1949 she had been crowned with the tempting accolade "Miss Florida Fruits & Vegetables"—and she had played small roles in films and TV.

Baker's potent charms were thrust on moviegoers when she played the thumb-sucking teenage bride who drives men crazy with lust in *Baby Doll*. "She's 19 years old and married ... but not really!" teased newspaper ads. The offensive film was condemned by the Catholic Legion of Decency, and Baker, who received an Oscar nomination for Best Actress, was pilloried in the nation's churches for playing a magnolia-scented virgin.

Undaunted, she tried to regain favor in popular, Western-themed family films such as *Giant, The Big Country,* and *How the West Was Won*. But once people (men mostly) clapped their amazed eyes on her beautiful body, everything else seemed irrelevant.

Raped by her first husband, pawed by studio boss Jack Warner, and degraded by producer Joseph Levine (he screamed, "I piss on you!"), she eventually suffered two nervous breakdowns that left the young actress terrified of sex.

Ironically, Baker's meltdown occurred when her stardom was at its raunchiest, in films such as *Something Wild, The Carpetbaggers,* and *Harlow*. Commenting on her platinum sex-goddess image, Baker said, "The more I exposed myself and played available, the more I turned off personally. That flagrant, unnatural whorishness I was pretending seemed to harden my own state of frigidity."

It didn't stop her from posing nude in *Playboy* magazine, however, and winning a $1 million breach-of-contract suit against Paramount Pictures. Her sex appeal was so in demand that, while she was on location for the 1965 movie *Mister Moses,* an African Masai chief reportedly offered to buy her for 150 cows, 200 goats, some sheep, and $750.

Not surprisingly, she refused.

Baker then fled to Italy, where she took a succession of handsome male lovers, including actor Franco Nero, whose patient lovemaking restored her damaged libido. She finally found lasting happiness with British actor **Donald Burton**, whom she married in 1982.

Eight years later, the Burtons purchased a three-bedroom home at 35–315 Calle Sonseca in Cathedral Canyon Country Club, where they spend the winters. But their enjoyment has been tempered of late by Burton's worsening emphysema, caused by heavy smoking. His last major role was Alfred, the malevolent butler in the Bruce Willis spy thriller *Hudson Hawk*. His wife's last good role was in *Kindergarten Cop* with Arnold Schwarzenegger.

■ ■ ■

TELEVISION GAME-SHOW HOST **Monty Hall**, who invited throngs of excited contestants on *Let's Make a Deal* to choose between doors 1, 2, or 3, has lived at 68–065 Seven Oaks Place since his retirement in 1986. Hall's emceeing talents weren't just limited to asking tough questions such as "Do you want what's in the box or what's behind the curtain?" He could also be extremely generous: "I'll give you $50 for a hard-boiled egg!"

But it wasn't all funny business.

A native of Winnipeg, Manitoba, Hall was awarded the prestigious Order of Canada for his humanitarian work with Variety Clubs International, which helps underprivileged children. In 2002, the grinning 80-year-old, who hosts a yearly three-day fund-raiser for diabetes, fell and broke his hip while visiting his doctor at Cedars-Sinai Medical Center in Los Angeles. He recovered from the accident but now walks with the assistance of a cane.

Hall's deal-making days are officially over, but the indefatigable product spokesman has participated in several short-lived revivals, most recently in 1990 and 2003.

■ ■ ■

THOM RACINA BOASTS an impressive list of screenwriting credits, including 4,000 broadcast hours of bitchy, backstabbing television, for which he received five well-deserved Emmy nominations. Racina was the head writer on some of TV's favorite daytime soap operas. He planned Luke and Laura's wedding on *General Hospital*, caused Bo and Hope to get hitched on *Days of Our Lives*, and made Donna and Michael tie the knot on *Another World.*

A full-time resident of 2851 Calle Loreto, this talented man is also the author of supercharged romance novels, an achievement that gives him the greatest satisfaction. Racina's books have included *Snow Angel, The Madman's Diary,* and *Deadly Games.* His most recent novel, *Deep Freeze,* was published in 2005.

True story: Brad Pitt, who has made frequent trips to the desert, once stayed at Racina's house for the weekend. "He came up to my bedroom one night and asked if I had a good book to read. He returned it two weeks later, saying he didn't care for it much." The book was *Interview with the Vampire,* which was later made into a hugely successful film—starring Pitt and Tom Cruise.

■ ■ ■

THE PANORAMA NEIGHBORHOOD is home to hundreds of Spanish-speaking families. One of the area's most honored residents was Mexican American folksinger **Eduardo "Lalo" Guerrero**, who lived at 31–750 Avenida Ximino.

Hailed as "the father of Chicano music," Guerrero kicked off his 60-year performing career with the pachuco hits *Marijuana Boogie* and *Vamos a Bailar*—songs that appealed to 1940s teenagers from the barrios of East Los Angeles. He effortlessly mastered rancheras, corridos, boleros, mambos, cha-chas, rhythm and blues, Latin pop—even rock 'n' roll.

Even more important, this native of Tucson, Arizona, was the first musician to blend American swing with traditional Mexican music. Several of his original compositions, including *Cancion Mexicana* and *El Chicano,* are considered classics. He also performed protest songs for California farm workers and wrote clever parodies of American pop tunes, which he variously titled "I Left My Car in San Francisco," "Tacos for Two," and "Mexican Mamas, Don't Let Your Babies Grow Up to Be Busboys."

Long before pop sensation Ricky Martin arrived on the international music scene, Guerrero pioneered the art of singing lyrics in both English and Spanish. Indeed, he has influenced many performers, including concert singer Linda Ronstadt, comedian Cheech Marin, and Louie Perez of the rock band Los Lobos. In 1996, President William J. Clinton awarded Guerrero a National Medal of the Arts, saying, "He still has his salsa!"True to form, this original Chicano hepcat was playing the guitar and singing at age 87 in 2004. Sadly, it was his last hurrah.

Guerrero's death one year later merited front-page obituaries in Tucson and in Palm Springs, where he had been institutionalized at Vista Cove Senior Living in Rancho Mirage. The musical void left fans of both nationalities crying "There's No Tortillas"—the title of one of his beloved songs.

■ ■ ■

WILFRID HYDE-WHITE NEVER met a movie camera he didn't like and vice versa! The hammy British character actor shuffled his way with eccentric aplomb through more than 120 films, including *The Third Man*, *The Million Pound Note*, *Northwest Frontier*, *Carry on Nurse*, *Two Way Stretch*, *My Fair Lady*, and, finally, *The Toy*, which starred Richard Pryor and in which Hyde-White played Jackie Gleason's doddering butler.

A classically trained veteran of the London stage, Wilfrid was often cast as aristocrats, dubious businessmen, and clergymen with mischief on their minds. His greatest talent was playing dumb onscreen when most of the time the character wasn't dumb at all. Critics occasionally made fun of his horsy facial expressions, but Hyde-White always had the last laugh. A snappy dresser, he was in fact quite a ladies' man, and his first wife, Blanche Glynne, had to contend with his having a mistress. His second marriage, in 1957 to actress-stage manager Ethel Drew, fared better; they were together for 34 years.

How did a classically trained British actor end up with a career in American movies? "Dad had been brought out to California by George Cukor, the famous director, to film *Let's Make Love* [1960] with Marilyn Monroe," recounted the actor's son, Alex Hyde-White, who followed his father into show business.

In his late fifties, when most actors were approaching retirement, Wilfrid found himself inundated with offers, including co-starring roles in *On the Double* with Danny Kaye, *In Search of the Castaways* with Hayley Mills, and *Chamber of Horrors*, a ghoulish remake of *House of Wax*. The Hyde-Whites were so overjoyed, they decided to stay in the United States and in 1963 they bought a three-bedroom house at 67–157 Santa Barbara Drive, in the Dream Homes section of town. There Alex and his sister, Juliet, grew up. "But the area declined in the '70s," said Alex. "Some people even called it 'Nightmare Alley.'"

Alex is now a successful actor himself, having racked up impressive credits in films such as *Pretty Woman,* in which he played Ralph Bellamy's polo-playing grandson. Father and son finally were able to work together in several episodes of the TV series *Buck Rogers in the 25th Century.* For his part, Wilfred continued to play scoundrels and lecherous old men until he retired. He died six days before his eighty-eighth birthday in 1991.

■ ■ ■

A MUST FOR STARGAZERS is the **Palm Springs Mortuary and Mausoleum** at 69–855 E. Ramon Road, Cathedral City. The contemporary Spanish-style funeral home offers the only aboveground burial plots in the Coachella Valley. Among the celebrities interred here are:

Frantisek Daniel (1926–1996). Writer and director; he produced the Oscar-winning foreign film *Shop on Main Street.*

Alice Faye (1915–1998). Singer and actress; she was a popular star of Hollywood musicals, radio, and TV specials.

L. Wolfe Gilbert (1886–1970). Composer and lyricist; his songs include "Green Eyes," "Waiting for the Robert E. Lee," "Ramona," and "The Peanut Vendor."

Phil Harris (1904–1995). Singer and bandleader; he was a regular performer on *The Jack Benny Program*; married to Alice Faye.

Guy Madison (1922–1996). Actor; he starred in the TV series *The Adventures of Wild Bill Hickok.*

George Montgomery (1916–2000). Actor, director, writer, and artist; he was the first husband of Dinah Shore.

John Phillips (1935–2001). Singer and songwriter; he wrote "California Dreaming," "Monday, Monday," and "I Saw Her Again Last Night."

Todd Michael Rice (1970–2001). Gay adult-film actor; he also made films under the names Brett Ford and Joey Pagano.

Harold Robbins (1916–1997). Bestselling novelist; his books include *The Carpetbaggers, The Betsy,* and *The Lonely Lady.*

Charles "Buddy" Rogers (1904–1999). Actor and musician; he was the third husband of silent-screen legend Mary Pickford.

Dinah Shore (1916–1994). Singer, actress, television hostess; fondly
remembered for her long career on stage, screen, TV, and radio.
Ex-*Lizzy Borden* heavy-metal guitarist **Alex Nelson**, who was killed
in a head-on automobile collision, was cremated there in 2004.

■ ■ ■

A SHORT DISTANCE AWAY is **Desert Memorial Park**, located at
69–920 Ramon Road, near the intersection of DaVall Road. This quiet,
tree-lined cemetery is the final resting place for many of the desert's most
beloved celebrities. They include:

Rodney Bell (1915–1968). Film and television character actor; best
known for his recurring role as Marvin in the *So You Want to Be
a . . .* film shorts.

Busby Berkeley (1895–1976). Director and choreographer of
Depression-era "feel good" musicals such as *42nd Street, Dames,*
and *Footlight Parade.*

Sonny Bono (1935–1998). Singer and songwriter; his long partnership with Cher produced a number of hit songs, including "I
Got You Babe" and "The Beat Goes On."

Lorayne Brock (1901–1993). Actress and singer; a former member of the talented Brox Sisters trio.

Brad Dexter (1917–2002). Actor; he played tough guy roles in
Untamed, Violent Saturday, and *House of Bamboo.*

Alex Dreier (1916–2000). Emmy Award–winning broadcaster; he
had acting roles in *The Boston Strangler* and *The Carey Treatment.*

Jansci "Jolie" Gabor (1899–1997). The glamorous Hungarian
matriarch of the world-famous Gabor Sisters.

Magda Gabor (1918–1997). Actress and society hostess; younger
sister of Zsa Zsa and Eva; former wife of George Sanders.

Bill Goodwin (1910–1958). Radio announcer and comedic actor;
he appeared in *Spellbound, The Jolson Story,* and *Tea for Two.*

Josephine Hill (1899–1989). Silent film actress; played enticing
heroines in more than 80 Westerns and serials.

Eddy Howard (1913–1963). Singer and songwriter; he penned the
songs "Careless" and "A Million Dreams Ago."

Andrea Leeds (1913–1984). Actress; she played sentimental roles in *Swanee River, The Real Glory,* and *Earthbound*; also a racehorse owner and jeweler.

Diana Lewis (1919–1997). Actress; she co-starred in *Bitter Sweet, Go West,* and *Johnny Eager*; married to William Powell.

Frederick Loewe (1901–1988). Broadway composer; he and lyricist Alan Jay Lerner wrote *My Fair Lady, Camelot,* and *The Little Prince.*

George Burr Macannan (1887–1970). Character actor; played ghostly roles in *White Zombie* and *Supernatural.*

Bill Miller (1904–2002). Vaudeville entertainer and talent agent; he invented the lounge act that became a staple of Las Vegas.

Cameron Mitchell (1918–1994). Actor; played hot-tempered roles in *Love Me or Leave Me, Strange Lady in Town,* and *Carousel.*

William Powell (1892–1984). Actor; he is best known as Nick Charles in *The Thin Man* movies.

Marjorie Rambeau (1889–1970). Actress; she co-starred with Wallace Beery in *Tugboat Annie Sails Again.*

Pete Reiser (1919–1981). Major league baseball player; an outfielder for the Brooklyn Dodgers.

Jessica Schilling (1984–2003). Beauty contest winner voted Miss Teen Palm Springs and Miss USA International; died in a traffic accident.

Ginny Simms (1913–1994). Band singer and actress; appeared in the films *That's Right—You're Wrong, You'll Find Out,* and *Playmates.*

Frank Sinatra (1915–1998). Singer, actor; also a producer. In accordance with his wishes, Sinatra's body is buried in a family plot next to his parents, Martin and "Dolly" Sinatra; his uncle Vincent Mazzola; and his best friend, Jilly Rizzo.

Sid Tomack (1907–1962). Balding character actor; played Al, the next-door neighbor on the TV series *My Friend Irma.*

Bobbe Van Heusen (1900–1999). Singer and actress; the eldest sister of Lorayne and Kathleen Brock of the Brox Sisters.

James Van Heusen (1913–1990). Prolific composer; he wrote such indispensable love songs as "Swinging on a Star," "All the Way," and "Call Me Irresponsible."

High Stakes

2

$\mathbf{S}$UN-BLEACHED BILLBOARDS, their buckled corners signaling passing motorists like outstretched arthritic hands, say it all: "40 Resorts and Spas," "World's Finest Natural Hot Mineral Water." If it weren't for the nearly constant howling of the wind and the blowing granules of sand, these might be welcome invitations.

Desert Hot Springs, perched in the foothills of the San Bernardino Mountains and overlooking Palm Springs nine miles away, can be a pleasure seeker's delight. But when the wind kicks up, which its does frequently and without warning, paper bags, plastic crates, and other pieces of trash are sucked into the air by spinning funnels of dirt. Pedestrians seek shelter, cars pull over to the side of the road, and homeowners close their windows.

And that's only when it's windy. In the worst heat of August, Palm Drive, the city's main thoroughfare, meanders down the hillside like a dead snake at high noon. The pizza parlors, Mexican cantinas, and pool halls shimmer like mirages in the burning sun. The only signs of life are to be found in air-conditioned supermarkets, where security patrols keep a sharp lookout for shoplifters.

At such times, Desert Hot Springs is almost a cliché—a set for a Clint Eastwood movie.

There was a time, however, when the city was clean and friendly. But the days when everyone owned a piece of land and raised livestock without a care in the world are almost things of the past. Now there are high-speed car chases, robberies, and shootings. The city even has a new nickname: *Desperate* Hot Springs. But that's more a sad indictment of the town's social problems than a guaranteed belly laugh.

The official birth of Desert Hot Springs was recorded on July 12, 1941, when the Desert Hot Springs Mineral Baths opened its doors to the public for the first time. The bathhouse was located on a parcel of land at the southwest corner of Palm Drive and 8th Street.

But the real history of this ancient cluster of artesian wells, which comprises more than 40 establishments featuring hot mineral water pools and spa treatments, began many years earlier. The year was 1913. The scene resembled *The Treasure of the Sierra Madre,* in which a shabby, bearded prospector played by Walter Huston pulls a burro across the mountains in search of gold, braving hostile Mexican bandits in his relentless quest. Like him, **Cabot Yerxa** was a man pursuing a dream. Only in Yerxa's case, his journey didn't take him to Mexico; it took him to a placid land inhabited by peaceful Cahuilla Indians.

Here he staked a claim on 160 acres next to a desert oasis called Two Bunch Palms, so named because of two groves of giant palm tress that had been mapped by the U.S. Army Camel Corps. Eventually Yerxa moved to higher ground and excavated a permanent site for a massive Hopi-style pueblo made of stucco, wooden poles, and railroad ties.

Other notable personalities who helped shape the town over the decades were builder Lawrence Coffee and engineer William Tarbutton, real estate agent R.H. McDonald and county supervisor Robert Dillon. In 1991, tattooed actors Mickey Rourke and Don Johnson would ride their motorcycles along Dillon Road in *Harley Davidson and the Marlboro Man.*

There is one person whose name does not appear in the city's official history, however, and for good reason. Some people believe the individual was a phantom; others maintain the whole incident was a case of mistaken identity. Nobody knows for certain, but there are one or two people still alive who swear that what they saw in 1931 really happened.

As the story goes, it was a typically hot day. The dirt roads shimmered. A group of pallid-looking men wearing three-piece suits and snap-brim fedoras got off the train at Garnet Station, got into a car, and started driving across the desert, their automobile bouncing along unmarked roads and trails. The unlikely visitors eventually stopped to buy some oranges at a fruit stand. One of the men had a long scar on his face and was smoking a cigar. Dark glasses shielded his eyes from the sun's glare.

"Eddie," the man soon said through thick lips. "It's time to go."

"Yes, boss," replied the car's driver.

The group sped off in the direction of what is now Two Bunch Palms.

Cabot Yerxa was hauling cement bags up the hill when he glimpsed the telltale plume of dust one mile away. He watched the moving object come closer until he was nearly blinded by its reflection. When Yerxa looked again, the car had turned a corner, passed through a metal gate, and disappeared down a short road toward a newly constructed stone bungalow behind a thick green hedge.

The man with the scar and the thick lips calmly got out of the car and walked to the front door, where he shook hands with another unidentified man. Then they all strolled inside, talking among themselves. If Yerxa had been able to see that far, he would have witnessed an odd sight: there, in broad daylight, someone went from window to window closing all the curtains.

America's most recognizable gangster had been tracked like a grizzly bear for months prior to his disappearance, and then the trail had gone cold. This was not the first time that Public Enemy Number One had gone missing. But it would be the last time.

■ ■ ■

AT THE HEIGHT of his power, during Prohibition, **Alphonse Capone** was the single greatest symbol of law and order's collapse in the United States. He controlled speakeasies, bookie joints, gambling houses, brothels, horse races, race tracks, nightclubs, distilleries, and breweries—for an estimated tax-free income of $100 million a year.

A modern-day Robin Hood who liked munching on salami and provolone, he stole from the rich and gave to the poor. He financed enough soup kitchens, and bestowed enough food and cash on starving families, to make the oil billionaire John D. Rockefeller look like a miserly skinflint by comparison. But Capone's motives were anything but altruistic. A former street punk, he ordered dozens of murders and even killed with his own hands. He was arrested in 1926 for killing three people but spent only one night in jail, because there was insufficient evidence to connect him with the deaths.

This uncanny ability to stay one step ahead of his adversaries made him a folk hero to some and a cold-blooded outlaw to others. He relished the publicity, although he was finding out that most of it was detrimental to his image. The headline-seeking press played fast and loose with the truth, dubbing him a saint one day and a sinner the next, so that he was openly ridiculed in even the poorest Italian neighborhoods. He had no choice but to travel farther afield to protect his identity. "The farther from Chicago Al Capone went, the fresher the air, the cleaner the towns, the less likelihood that he would be recognized," said biographer Laurence Bergreen.

On one of his periodic absences, Capone visited Los Angeles. He toured a movie studio and even drove to Pickfair, the plush Beverly Hills mansion of Mary Pickford and Douglas Fairbanks, where he posed outside the main gates for a photograph. It wasn't until he returned to Chicago that police confiscated a .45-caliber revolver, a smaller handgun, and pocketfuls of ammunition that he had managed to conceal on his flabby person. If the feds had known what he was thinking up, they would have arrested him then and there. But he was always careful not to breathe a word of his business plans to anyone.

One day when he was feeling particularly elated, he bought a dozen red roses from a flower-seller and pinned one of the crimson buds on his lapel. "Be my valentine," he repeated over and over under his breath.

Was it a sick joke or just an unhappy coincidence?

No one will ever know. But Capone's most publicized killing turned out to be the St. Valentine's Day Massacre in 1929. On February 14, four of his gang—two of them dressed as policemen—entered the headquarters of rival bootlegger George "Bugs" Moran and fired 150 bullets from two shotguns and two machine guns, killing seven men.

Even then, the law couldn't touch the King of Crime. He had a perfect alibi: at the time of the murders, he was holed-up in Miami, Florida, in the 14-room waterfront villa once owned by Clarence Busch, of the St. Louis brewing dynasty that made Budweiser, the king of beers.

Capone's wealth also taunted the feds. By the decade's end, Capone's pampered lifestyle almost equaled that of European royalty. He traveled to and from a choice of luxurious residences, business headquarters, and hotel suites in sixteen-cylinder limousines, slept in $50 French pajamas, and ordered fifteen suits at a time, at $135 each.

But in 1931, the ax fell: Capone was indicted on 22 counts of income tax evasion. The criminal mastermind turned himself in, posted $50,000 bail—and left town. Would he flee the country, leaving federal law enforcers flummoxed?

For three months people speculated on his whereabouts. Then, as abruptly as he had left, Capone returned. "As usual, no one in Chicago, with the exception of a handful of intimates, knew where he had been during the late summer weeks, how he had spent his time, or how he had acquired his tan," said Bergreen.

If, in reality, Capone had stayed at Two Bunch Palms, it was a well-kept secret. The big mystery is why the wealthy racketeer agreed to stand trial when he could easily have vanished to South America or Europe. Apparently he thought he could win the case. His lawyers wanted to plea-bargain, but the judge would have none of it.

Capone was sentenced to 17 years in jail. He was shackled like a convict and transported to the federal penitentiary in Atlanta, Georgia. The heavily guarded prisoner was later transferred to Alcatraz and served out the remainder of his sentence at Terminal Island near Los Angeles. He was paroled in 1939, but his mind and body were wracked by syphilis. He died eight years later at the age of 48.

The sinister image of Capone blasting a Thompson submachine gun has since passed into American pop culture. In *The Man with the Golden Gun*, character actor **Marc Lawrence**, formerly a resident of 6666 Desert View Avenue, accidentally shoots the arms off a wax dummy of Capone that he encounters in a shooting gallery. "Hey, Al," he apologizes to the broken-limbed figure, "wherever you are, don't hold it against me!"

In 1965, Cabot Yerxa, possibly the last man alive to see Capone on that history-making visit to the desert, died of a heart attack at the age of 81. He had been reading the daily newspaper in the country-style kitchen of his recently completed adobe home at 67–616 Desert View Avenue. The Old Indian Pueblo, as it's called, is now a tourist attraction on Miracle Hill, across from Angel View Crippled Children's Hospital.

■ ■ ■

SEVENTY-FIVE YEARS AFTER Capone first set his polished leather shoes on the hot desert sand, **Two Bunch Palms Resort & Spa,** at 67–425 Two Bunch Palms Trail, is still doing brisk business, much of it because of the Capone legend. The clientele are no longer gangsters but top-lined celebrities: Oscar-nominated actor Leonardo DiCaprio and Brazilian supermodel Gisele Bundchen were once observed submerging their naked bodies in the tropical rock pools.

This is the same place, incidentally, where Tim Robbins and Greta Scacchi took a refreshing mud bath in Robert Altman's dark satire of Hollywood moviemaking, *The Player.* Another celebrity who's been spotted at Two Bunch Palms is vegetarian pop singer Madonna, who regularly has her urine, saliva, and blood measured to improve her vitality and well-being.

Health-conscious movie star Goldie Hawn, mom to *Raising Helen* actress Kate Hudson, has also vacationed here. And in 2003, Hollywood sweethearts Alyson Hannigan, of *Buffy-the-Vampire-Slayer* fame, and Alexis Denisof of TV's *Angel* were married at the resort's famed black grotto. The three-day wedding was attended by *Buffy* co-stars Anthony Head and Emma Caulfield, who cheered the outdoor nuptials with actor-friends Ted Danson, Mary Steenburgen, Josh Brolin, and Neil Patrick Harris.

■ ■ ■

LUCIEN HUBBARD WAS a highly disciplined Hollywood writer, director, and producer who made more than 100 films, many of them in the crime and mystery genres. He oversaw production of the trailblazing aviation epic *Wings,* the first film to win an Academy Award for Best Picture.

In 1927, Hubbard purchased 100 acres of land on the gently sloping plains ten miles north of Palm Springs, near Garnet, and began constructing a Western-style adobe hotel called the B-Bar-H Guest Ranch. The original archway is located at 18–850 Bubbling Wells Road.

There Hubbard's friends and coworkers—Mary Pickford, Bing Crosby, the Marx Brothers, Tyrone Power, Lionel Barrymore, Peter Lorre, Marlene Dietrich, Gary Cooper, and others—spent time riding horseback, playing tennis, and swimming. The summer after Harpo Marx married actress Susan Fleming, the happy newlyweds went down to the ranch for a second honeymoon. It was a hot night and there was nothing to do, Harpo once said, so she dyed his brown hair pink, then black, and finally he shaved it off.

But the B-Bar-H Ranch wasn't just a place for fun in the sun. This was where Hubbard, fueled by a pot of fresh coffee, typed two Oscar-nominated film scripts: *Smart Money,* about the perils of gambling; and *The Star Witness,* about a family forced to testify against the mob.

Journalist Frank Scully once related an amusing visit he paid to the ranch with Marx Brothers writer Morrie Ryskind and MGM studio publicist Si Seadler: "They relaxed with all the intensity of a football team awaiting the kickoff at a Rose Bowl game. From morning to night they followed a schedule and were on time for everything," he said. "God help a member who preferred to sleep in the sun at eleven-fifteen A.M. instead of playing table tennis."

Hubbard later sold the ranch when he enlisted in World War II as a correspondent for *Reader's Digest.* He wrote the propagandistic film script for *Gung Ho!* starring Randolph Scott, and appeared as himself in *The Story of G.I. Joe,* about the life of Pulitzer Prize–winning war correspondent Ernie Pyle.

After the war ended, Hubbard commissioned architect John Lautner to design the Desert Hot Springs Motel at 67–710 San Antonio Street, which consisted of four separate units, each with its own patio and cactus garden. The motel, which was completed in 1947, was Lautner's first concrete building. It is deemed architecturally significant for its mid-century modern design.

Hubbard died on New Year's Eve 1971 at the age of 83.

■ ■ ■

THE B-BAR-H GUEST Ranch brought a great deal of media attention to Desert Hot Springs at a time when this city-in-the-making was not as well-known as it is today. The little township on the hill not only welcomed movie stars and film producers but also gradually became an adopted home for reclusive writers and retired sports figures.

One such person was the springboard diving champion **Dorothy Poynton**, who became the youngest U.S. medalist in Olympic history when she won a silver medal at the 1928 summer games in Amsterdam. At the time of the competition, she had just turned 13.

Poynton went on to win a gold medal at the 1932 Olympics and a bronze at the 1936 games. Her participation in the latter event, held in Berlin, Germany, earned the teenage athlete some unwanted notoriety when movie footage of her well-toned physique turned up in the quasi-documentary *Olympia,* which was made by the Nazi propagandist Leni Riefenstahl.

Two decades later, Poynton opened an aquatic club in Los Angeles, where she taught swimming for 20 years. In 1975, the retired swimmer and her Hollywood musician-husband **Gerald Tueber**, who as Jerry Teuber scored the music for the popular TV series *McCloud* and *Quincy,* purchased property at 76–850 Dillon Road, where they spent their final years. She passed away at the age of 79 on May 18, 1995; Tueber died exactly one year later.

■ ■ ■

THE MAN WHOSE dream it was to build a prosperous city on the northwest edge of Desert Hot Springs would, had he lived, sanctioned a development to rival the world's greatest resorts. But history had other plans.

John Jakob Raskob was the vice president of General Motors and treasurer of the DuPont Corporation. But today he is best remembered as the man who spearheaded construction of the 102-story art deco Empire State Building, which rose from the sidewalks of Fifth Avenue in midtown Manhattan and stretched 1,455 feet into the sky.

A large measure of Raskob's genius lay in his original concept for the modern skyscraper. Raskob was fond of using jumbo pencils, the kind that can be found in elementary schools. One day he took a pencil, stood it on end, and asked architect William Frederick Lamb, "How high can you make the building so it won't fall down?"

When completed in 1931, the Empire State Building was indeed the tallest building in the world, and it remained the tallest building in New York City until the towers of the World Trade Center were constructed 40 years later.

Was Raskob playing God? He also strongly advocated that American workers invest their money in the stock market instead of savings accounts. Unfortunately, his suggestion came two months before the Wall Street market crash that precipitated the Great Depression, leaving millions of people destitute and suicidal. Luckily for Raskob, he was not among those unfortunate souls whose financial livelihood was destroyed. In 1938, on one of his frequent trips west, he purchased 2,500 acres of desert land with the intention of building his dream city.

But World War II curtailed those plans, and Raskob's dream was never realized. He died of a heart ailment in 1950 at the age of 71. The following year, Raskob's estate sold the Empire State Building for $34 million. The land he owned in Desert Hot Springs was bought by Palm Springs real estate developer Ray Ryan and now includes an 18-hole championship golf course and part of the Mission Lakes Country Club.

■ ■ ■

IF YOU WERE a news junkie in the 1930s, the byline of ace reporter **Adela Rogers St. Johns,** printed in bold type on the front page of William Randolph Hearst's *Los Angeles Herald,* promised you a tantalizing story about sex or murder. Billed as "the World's Greatest Girl Reporter," St. Johns helped break down the barriers within male-dominated journalism by proving that she could be every bit as good as a man and sometimes better. She worked for the Hearst newspapers for 43 years.

The spunky, no-nonsense daughter of prominent criminal lawyer Earl Rogers, she covered big stories such as the kidnapping of Charles Lindbergh's baby, the abdication of King Edward VIII of England, the assassination of Senator Huey Long, and many years later, the trial of Patty Hearst—the granddaughter of St. Johns's longtime employer.

Not surprisingly, Adela's inside knowledge of politics and moviemaking formed the basis of hundreds of her short stories, and of several novels involving sensational crimes and celebrity scandals. Her novels *The Girl Who Had Everything, Final Verdict,* and *What Price Hollywood?* became successful films. This tireless crusader had a nose for news like a bloodhound and was not afraid to speak her mind on subjects ranging from capital punishment to abortion. Equally blunt about herself, she refused to have a facelift; she said that she didn't want to look like a blank page.

In 1978, after fracturing her hip, St. Johns rented a deluxe suite at the Desert Hot Springs Spa Hotel, located at 10–805 Palm Drive. There she ordered up room service and wrote her autobiography. She died ten years later at the age of 94.

■ ■ ■

ON NOVEMBER 4, 1980, veteran screenwriter **Noel Langley**, who had written some of Hollywood's best-loved films, was found dead in his two-bedroom cottage at 15–785 Via Quedo. He was 69 years old and had recently suffered a stroke.

Tall, funny, and a lifelong nonconformist, Langley had relished adapting the 1939 film version of L. Frank Baum's children's classic, *The Wonderful Wizard of Oz,* although he was disappointed that censors wouldn't allow a scene where Dorothy and the Lion get stoned in a field of opium poppies. Langley also penned the screenplays for *Ivanhoe, The Prisoner of Zenda,* and *Knights of the Round Table.* In 1956, he wrote and directed *The Search for Bridey Murphy,* which showcased his avid interest in the occult.

But his proudest accomplishment was undoubtedly *The Wizard of Oz.* Langley's screenplay contained substantial alterations to Baum's book. For one thing, the ruby slippers that everyone remembers so fondly for their high-gloss sheen were originally silver shoes in Baum's tale. Langley made the change from silver to red to take advantage of the film's Technicolor palette. The major difference, however, was the film's ending, where Dorothy awakens from a dream. In the book, Oz is not a figment of her imagination, but a real place.

The film's six-month-long production schedule was not without stress and mishaps. Sixteen-year-old Judy Garland was put on a strict diet and forced to wear a binding cloth to hide her developing breasts. Buddy Ebsen, the actor first chosen to play the Tin Man, inhaled poisonous aluminum dust from his makup and was replaced by Jack Haley. Margaret Hamilton, who acted the Wicked Witch, was badly burned when her witch's hat and broomstick caught fire.

On the lighter side, the MGM commissary was overrun with Munchkins. Langley said the unruly dwarfs created such havoc that the studio was forced to provide armed guards to protect the chorus girls and dancers.

After the film's sneak preview in San Bernardino (a place where many movies were tested for audience reaction), several extraneous musical numbers, including Ray Bolger's wobbly "straw dance," where he bounced off fence posts, were deleted, and other scenes were shortened.

But the film's biggest surprise was that Langley was gay. Fancy that! He really was "a friend of Dorothy." This euphemism, used by thousands of closeted homosexuals to identify each other secretly, has since passed into the realm of gay pop culture.

■ ■ ■

ON THE SCREEN, **Janet Gaynor** was the vulnerable and naïve heroine who pledged eternal love to Charles Farrell, her knight in shining armor in twelve top-grossing films, including *Lucky Star*, *Sunny Side Up*, *High Society Blues*, and *Delicious*. Their romantic pairing was so popular, they were known as "America's favorite lovebirds," and rumors flourished that the two actors were having a secret affair, although Gaynor was always coy on the subject. (Years later these stories proved to be false: Farrell was supposedly gay, and his movie sweetheart a lesbian, according to documented sources.)

Gaynor was the first woman to win the Academy Award for Best Actress in recognition of her outstanding roles in a trio of memorable films—*Sunrise*, *Seventh Heaven*, and *Street Angel*—and her popularity continued unabated throughout the early sound era. She was nominated a second time for her portrayal of the innocent farm girl who becomes an overnight sensation in *A Star Is Born*. In 1934, she was voted Hollywood's top box-office attraction, and her cherubic face adorned the covers of hundreds of fan magazines. But Gaynor was not as fragile as the waiflike characters she portrayed. In real life she was an opinionated businesswoman, married to MGM costume designer Gilbert Adrian and the mother of their young son. When Adrian died of a heart attack in 1959, she forged on alone.

Upon her retirement, Gaynor bought the Singing Trees Ranch, an 80-acre farm on 20th Avenue near Mountain View Road, where she raised 10,000 pigeons, or squab, with her third husband, movie and theater producer **Paul Gregory**. She also took up painting, and in 1976 her still lifes were exhibited in a New York gallery.

While on a visit to San Francisco in the summer of 1982, to see her best friend and Palm Springs neighbor Mary Martin, a tragedy occurred. En route to a Chinatown restaurant with Martin, Gregory, and her business manager, Ben Washer, Gaynor was critically injured when the taxi in which they were traveling was broadsided by a drunken driver. The force of the collision killed Washer and wrapped the pulverized car around a tree. Gaynor suffered eleven broken ribs, a ruptured bladder, a broken collar bone, a bleeding kidney, and multiple pelvis fractures. Gregory's injuries included a bruised kidney, broken ribs, and whiplash. Martin sustained a shattered pelvis, two broken ribs, and a punctured lung.

Four months and many lifesaving operations later, Gaynor was released from the hospital and returned home to her beloved ranch. But her recuperation was hindered by two unforgiving enemies: time and old age. Although strong in spirit, the actress continued to grow weaker. She died from pneumonia at the age of 77, in 1984.

Deeply sad, Paul Gregory sold the ranch and moved into a contemporary three-bedroom house at 9900 Santa Cruz Road. There he tried to console himself with the framed photographs, paintings, and cherished memories of his favorite leading lady, who had left him three months before their 20th wedding anniversary. Gregory's loss was compounded by his own lingering physical pain from the accident, as well as the memories that he replayed in his mind. He grew bitter and remorseful. "What if we hadn't gone out to dinner that night? What if Mary hadn't been brushing Janet's hair and distracted the taxi driver?" he asked himself.

There had been a time when Gregory felt no such concerns. As a brash, young, MCA talent agent, Gregory had signed the petulant Charles Laughton to perform a series of Bible readings around the country. Staged in high school auditoriums and church halls, the one-man shows reactivated Laughton's sagging career—and made its producer a small mint.

Next, Gregory tackled Broadway. He produced *Don Juan in Hell,* an ambitious adaptation of the third act of George Bernard Shaw's play *Man and Superman,* and put his cast of highly respected thespians—Charles Boyer, Cedric Hardwicke, Agnes Moorehead, and Laughton—on a bare stage in formal evening dress. For his subsequent production, *John Brown's Body,* Gregory recruited Tyrone Power, Raymond Massey, and Judith Anderson to read Stephen Vincent Benet's evocative Civil War poem on a tour of 60 American cities. The tour sold out.

He followed *that* coup with *The Caine Mutiny Court-Martial,* which was based on Herman Wouk's bestselling novel, and starred Lloyd Nolan as paranoid Lieutenant Commander Philip Queeg and Henry Fonda as the naval prosecutor, Lieutenant Barney Greenwald.

As if those achievements weren't success enough, the first film Gregory produced became a classic. *The Night of the Hunter,* which was filmed in 1955, was a weird, hypnotic tale of religious obsession and sexual sadism. Robert Mitchum played a murderous priest who tattooed the words "love" and "hate" on his hands. Laughton, the film's director, spared no effort to tell this unrelenting story of adult greed and hypocrisy as seen through a terrified child's eyes.

Gregory was hailed as an intellectual genius. He was touched only once or twice by the whiff of scandal, mainly because of his association with Laughton, who was a notorious homosexual. In some people's eyes, Gregory was guilty by association with the repugnant actor, who had often been arrested for soliciting young men for unlawful sexual practices. But in truth, this was a friendship created out of mutual need, with each man helping the other in his artistic endeavors. Any scent of scandal evaporated quickly.

In fact, the most embarrassing incident during the filming of *Night of the Hunter* probably occurred at Gregory's two-story beach house on Ocean Front Walk in Santa Monica. *Confidential* magazine stated that Robert Mitchum, in a drunken stupor, stripped down to his socks, squirted himself with ketchup, and declared, "I'm a hamburger!" Intoxicated dinner guests were titillated by these antics, but the sober ticket-buying public was not amused. The case ended up in court after Mitchum filed suit against the magazine's publishers.

Gregory eventually returned to his true métier, the New York theater, where he continued to tour actors in hit plays and musical revues such as *3 for Tonight,* starring Harry Belafonte, and *The Marriage-Go-Round,* with Boyer, Claudette Colbert, and Julie Newman.

■ ■ ■

DESERT HOT SPRINGS has long been a favored retreat of bohemian artists like **Rudolf Friml**, who was a valley resident for two decades. A native of Czechoslovakia, Friml composed 33 operettas and hundreds of popular songs. Among his many compositions was the glittering operetta *The Firefly,* with lyrics by Otto Harbach, which introduced the song "The Donkey Serenade." "Friml was to Broadway what Babe Ruth was to baseball," commented Todd Sollis in *Opera News.*

Friml collaborated with Oscar Hammerstein II on the musical comedy *Rose-Marie,* which featured such stirring tunes as "The Mounties" and "Indian Love Call." He also wrote the music for *The Vagabond King,* to lyrics by P.G. Wodehouse, as well as the swashbuckling score for a 1928 production of *The Three Musketeers.* These light, cheerful works were often criticized for their old-fashioned sentiments—considered trite by modern standards. But they enjoyed many revivals and were made into successful films starring the singing duo of Jeanette MacDonald and Nelson Eddy.

In 1953, Friml moved to Palm Desert, where he maintained a winter home for 15 years. He was scornful of contemporary music, which he called "a bunch of high-paid rubbish," and was particularly vitriolic in his criticism of several well-known composers, including Irving Berlin. Friml once boasted that he had walked out on a London performance of *My Fair Lady,* and he thought *Hello, Dolly!* possessed "a terrible score." "If I had written that music, they would have thrown me out of the theater," he complained.

Despite his increasing age, he remained physically agile and played the piano for six hours every day. At 86, he completed a five-month European concert tour; at 90, he was still exercising by riding a bicycle and standing on his head for ten minutes each morning.

In 1969, he and his fourth wife, Kay Wong Ling, moved to a new home at 9250 Allegre Drive, on the crest of a hill overlooking the city. In 1972, at the age of 92, he died from a brain hemorrhage after being hospitalized for five weeks.

■ ■ ■

VETERAN RADICAL JOURNALIST and stand-up comedian **Paul Krassner** has been America's unofficial voice of discontent, speaking out on a variety of taboo subjects, for more years than the Bush family has held public office. A former child prodigy on the violin, Krassner bristled at social convention and decided to swap classical music for controversy. His musings first appeared in the 1950s counterculture publication, *Mad Magazine.*

In 1967, Krassner and Abbie Hoffman cofounded the Youth International Party, which became infamous for its prankster activism—not unlike that of the Dadaists, an early-twentieth-century group of subversive intellectuals and nonconformists whose intentions were to offend traditional moralists. Krassner created a stir when he printed the controversial drawing "The Disneyland Memorial Orgy," a mock-pornographic illustration of Walt Disney cartoon characters engaged in public sex and other improper behavior. He also edited Lenny Bruce's autobiography, *How to Talk Dirty and Influence People*, which was first serialized in *Playboy* magazine.

Today Krassner is happily installed at 9829 San Simeon Drive with his wife, Nancy, and their two cats, Puffy and Donny. The irreverent 74-year-old political satirist moved to the desert in 2001, after ceasing publication of his leftist magazine *The Realist*, which had pricked society's consciousness for more than 40 years. Arch conservatives can breathe a temporary sigh of relief at the periodical's demise, but liberals are more than likely saddened by the sorely missed absence of Krassner's regular and healthy dose of bad taste.

■ ■ ■

ACTOR **DONALD CURTIS** portrayed noble army lieutenants and sergeants whose cautious optimism brought a sense of authenticity to such films as *Bataan, Salute to the Marines, The Cross of Lorraine, See Here, Private Hargrove,* and *Thirty Seconds over Tokyo.* But he truly excelled in science fiction. Few could top him as space-suited Captain Ronal in the third entry of the Flash Gordon serials, *Flash Gordon Conquers the Universe,* starring Larry "Buster" Crabbe. And he gave one of his best performances in the 1955 monster movie *It Came from Beneath the Sea,* in which he played a courageous scientist who battles a giant octopus that climbs the Golden

Gate Bridge and terrorizes San Francisco.

The following year, he was back in uniform as a fearless army general who uses powerful antimagnetic rocket beams to fend off alien spacecraft that take over Washington, D.C., in *Earth vs. the Flying Saucers*. (Forty years later director Tim Burton plagiarized this film when he made the black comedy *Mars Attacks!*)

In 1967, Curtis sought a higher calling and left show business to become a clergyman. Ordained by Dr. Ernest Holmes, founder of the Science of Mind Church, Curtis lectured all over the world and received many awards for his inspirational works. A longtime resident of 65–910 14th Street, Curtis also wrote a bestselling self-help book, *Your Mind Can Keep You Well*, in which he espoused various psychological theories. "Relaxation," he explained, "means relaxing all concern and tension and letting the natural order of life flow through one's being." His advice was not only relevant to the process of acting but also useful in day-to-day living.

He died at the age of 82, in 1997.

■ ■ ■

BEGUILING ACTRESS **JUDITH Chapman** made a name for herself playing scheming women on some of TV's most-watched daytime soap operas. She also played seductive roles on *Magnum P.I.*, *Murder, She Wrote,* and *Silk Stalkings*. Viewers first felt Chapman's sting as the notorious Natalie Bannon Hughes on *As the World Turns*. She followed that acting triumph with the unforgettable Ginny Blake Webber on *General Hospital* and bitchy Anjelica Deveraux on *Days of Our Lives*.

A health and yoga buff, Chapman and her partner of 12 years, James Offord, are residents of 66–067 8th Street and co-owners of the fine-dining restaurant St. James at the Vineyard, in Palm Springs. In 2005, Chapman replaced Joan Van Ark as Gloria Fisher Abbott on *The Young and the Restless*. Commenting on her return to daytime TV, Chapman told *Soap Opera Digest,* "It's been wonderful."

■ ■ ■

ACTOR **JOHN BRINKLEY**, who played greasy teenage rebels in many cheap 1950s exploitation films made by American International Pictures, now lives in a mobile home at 64–050 Desert Sand Drive. Brinkley starred in four early box-office successes from cult film director Roger Corman, including the all-girl, drag-strip riot *Teenage Doll,* and the bloody gangster saga *I, Mobster.* His most famous film is the way-out black comedy *A Bucket of Blood,* which, according to the money-minded Corman, was shot in five economical days.

In 1959, Brinkley and actor-pal Tony Miller wrote and starred in the low-budget beatnik classic *T-Bird Gang,* borrowing many cinematic nuances from their mentor, Corman. Brinkley's last film, *Valley of the Redwoods,* teamed him for the sixth and final time with AIP alumnus Ed Nelson.

■ ■ ■

AMONG THE FAMOUS visitors to the home of avant-garde painter and sculptor **Bruce Houston,** at 17–102 Sanborn Street, was the late Hollywood writer and director Billy Wilder, who won a total of six Oscar statuettes for *The Lost Weekend, Sunset Boulevard,* and *The Apartment.*

Apart from being a prodigious filmmaker, Wilder was a talented amateur artist. In December 1993, he curated a one-man show of his best work at the Beverly Hills gallery of his longtime friend, the art dealer Louis Stern. The exhibition included a collaboration with Houston entitled "Variations on the Theme of Queen Nefertete I." Their pop art creation featured a lifelike bust of the ravishing Egyptian queen sporting a Campbell's Soup can on her head and a necklace of smaller red-and-white cans around her slender neck.

In 1989, Wilder sold most of his personal art collection for $32 million (he died in 2002). Houston continues to make tongue-in-cheek parodies of contemporary art, such as replicas of Frank Stella's paintings juxtaposed with toy trucks, and to exhibit at galleries in Hollywood and San Francisco.

■ ■ ■

ACTRESS **JOAN WOODBURY** played sultry bad girls in dozens of B-movies, her lacquered hair and distinctive bat-wing eyebrows helping to define classic Hollywood sex appeal.

Woodbury's career spanned 30 years and more than 80 films, many of which capitalized on her dusky beauty and skill as a dancer; invariably she was cast as a Spanish or Mexican *senorita* named Lolita, Conchita, or Maria. Very often she was in only one or two scenes, but they were this talented performer's bread and butter. Sometimes she appeared in more than 10 films a year. "You usually did everything in one take, and if you went over three takes, you got fired," she recalled.

Woodbury's first screen credit (as Nana Martinez) was in *The Eagle's Brood* in 1935, followed by *Anthony Adverse,* in which she played a half-caste dancing girl. Woodbury also acted an assortment of fetching saloon girls and hardened young women in semiclassics such as *Algiers*, *King of the Zombies, Paper Bullets, Confessions of Boston Blackie,* and *The Arnelo Affair.* In 1945, she won the title role in Columbia Pictures's 13-part serial, *Brenda Starr, Reporter,* which was based on the famous newspaper comic strip. The publicity blurb called her "the New Serial Queen," and the name stuck.

Woodbury continued acting in films until 1964. Her next-to-last role was Korah's wife in the Golden-Calf orgy scene of *The Ten Commandments,* which co-starred her actor-husband, Henry Wilcoxon, who also served as associate producer. After they were divorced, Woodbury settled in the valley, where she participated in local theater and wrote free-lance articles. She married KPSL-AM radio announcer Ray Mitchell and moved to Vista Grande Spa Mobile Home Park at 17–625 Langlois Road.

She died in 1989 at the age of 73, the victim of a rare form of avian tuberculosis transmitted by infected tropical birds.

■ ■ ■

DESPITE THE INFLUX of celebrities, in some ways little has changed in Desert Hot Springs since Al Capone held his secret rendezvous in 1931. For many decades, Desert Hot Springs basked in its enviable reputation as America's Baden-Baden. But now some people believe that the place is doomed. The city's dirty little secret is not the street violence that erupts between restless teenage gangs; it's the manufacture and sale of a harmful drug called crystal methamphetamine, better known on the street as crystal meth.

In addition, financial problems have plagued this city of 17,000 residents, many of whom scrounge to make ends meet. Trouble erupted in

1990 when the city council denied a proposal from a Los Angeles–based developer to demolish a mobile home park on Pierson Boulevard and replace it with 116 houses for low-income families. The developer got so angry about the bureaucratic stonewalling that he sued, launching the city on a costly legal battle.

Then in 2001, a U.S. District Court found the city's decision violated the Federal Fair Housing Act. The city had no choice but to declare bankruptcy to stave off creditors. Three years later it emerged from under a dark cloud with a plan to sell 40-year bonds totaling more than $12 million—more than half its annual budget—to raise much needed revenue. Hopefully, with these crises behind it, the city of Desert Hot Springs can move onward and upward.

Morongo Valley

Smog-free Morongo Valley, 15 miles from Palm Springs, is one of several townships, including Yucca Valley and Joshua Tree, that comprise the high desert. Here a relatively cool climate encourages the growth of California fan palms and Joshua Trees, named after the biblical prophet.

Actor **Guy Madison** never cared much for the artificial Hollywood lifestyle. That's why he lived his sunset years at 50–210 Aspen Drive in Morongo Valley. Born Robert Moseley, this fresh-faced hunk had both women *and* men chasing after him. He was barely out of his teens when Hollywood agent Henry Willson brought the navy sailor to the attention of producer David Selznick. They decided to call him Guy (the "guy" girls want to meet) and Madison (from a passing Dolly Madison cake truck).

Madison's screen career consisted almost entirely of fancy, big-budget Westerns such as *The Charge at Feather River*, *The Command*, *Reprisal!*, and *Bullwhip*. But it was TV that gave him his best starring role: buckskin-wearing *Wild Bill Hickok*. After the series ended, Madison's popularity never again reached such heights; he was relegated to low-budget, European-made films.

When there were no more acting offers, Madison packed a saddle bag and moved to the desert, where he indulged his passion for lake-fishing and gardening. But physical ailments, the result of a lifetime of heavy smoking, contributed to his declining health, and he was left to con-template a bleak future, comforted by his daughter, Bridget, who lived a few streets away. (In 1961, Madison's first wife, the actress Gail Russell, who had fought a long battle with alcoholism, died in her West Holly-wood apartment, apparently of a heart attack.)

Finally, unable to breathe because of his diseased lungs, Madison died from emphysema in 1996 at the age of 74. He had also been diagnosed with prostate cancer. Informed of the actor's passing, his close friend and neighbor, Rory Calhoun, said, "We shared a lot of campfires together. It is another empty saddle in the old corral, and I will really miss him."

■ ■ ■

RORY CALHOUN WAS proof that an ex-con really can go straight. As a youth, he was often in trouble with the law. He dropped out of high school and became a car thief, eventually landing in a federal peniten-tiary in Springfield, Missouri, where he served three years for his crimes.

That was all in Calhoun's dark past, however, when he grabbed the reins as Hollywood's newest cowboy star in *Way of a Gaucho*, *The Silver Whip*, *The Yellow Tomahawk*, and *Four Guns to the Border*. He made three films with Marilyn Monroe, including the exciting frontier adventure *River of No Return*. But he always denied they were lovers.

At one point, his career was endangered when blackmailers threatened to expose his prison record. But Calhoun beat them to the punch when he made the revelation himself, emphasizing how he had changed. The actor's confession did nothing to harm his popularity, which continued gathering steam on TV's *The Texan*. That program led to another decade of roles playing flinty renegades, sheriffs, and town-tamers, until hard liv-ing got the better of him.

In 1970, Calhoun's 21-year marriage to Spanish-born actress Lita Baron, who gave him daughters Cindy, Tami, and Lorri, came to an end. So did his long-running stardom. The next year, he married Australian journalist Susan Rhodes, who bore him a fourth daughter, whom they named Rory.

After Calhoun retired in 1992, the couple bought a home at 8929 Fox Trail. He spent his remaining years here salvaging what was left of his health, which had been ruined by excessive drinking and smoking.

Ironically, his nickname was "Smoke"—on account of his smoldering blue-gray eyes. His final days were a source of immense pride and satisfaction as he watched his wife breed and show pit bulls. Calhoun died in 1999 after being hospitalized with the advanced stages of emphysema and diabetes. He was 76.

Yucca Valley

Brooklyn-born character actor **Richard Lynch**, whose long mane of white hair and scarred features made him ideally suited to play some of filmdom's most deranged villains, owns the two-story home at 8426 Paradise View Road, where he is a familiar sight in nearby Yucca Valley.

Among the rogues' gallery of marauding bad guys he has portrayed are the crazed kidnapper chased through New York by Roy Scheider in *The Seven-Ups*, an insane terrorist who takes on Chuck Norris in *Invasion USA*, and a ruthless assassin who matches wits with Sidney Poitier in *Little Nikita*. He has also played evil potentates in fantasy films such as *The Sword and the Sorcerer*, *The Barbarians,* and *Merlin*.

Lynch's neighbor is bug-eyed actor **Don Calfa**, a full-time resident of Aztec Mobile Park at 7425 Church Street. This nervous-looking performer virtually cornered the market on playing double-crossing weasels and traitors whose foolishness was both a source of fear and hilarity. He was the bumbling medical worker who unleashes a horde of zombies in *Return of the Living Dead*, a deadly child molester in *The Star Chamber*, and a clumsy Mafia hit man in *Weekend at Bernie's*.

■ ■ ■

TALL, FAIR-HAIRED **WILLIAM Hopper**, who played private investigator Paul Drake on TV's *Perry Mason*, which co-starred Raymond Burr as the unbeatable defense attorney and Barbara Hale as his hardworking secretary, Della Street, once lived at 8572 Joshua Lane, Yucca Valley.

The son of venomous Hollywood gossip columnist Hedda Hopper, who was briefly an actress, young Bill appeared in more than 100 films, mostly in well-dressed supporting roles. He graduated to mature leads in the science-fiction classics *Conquest of Space*, *The Deadly Mantis,* and *20*

Million Miles to Earth. After *Perry Mason* ended its nine-year run, Hopper moved to the desert. A heavy smoker, he died in 1970 at the age of 55, of complications from heart disease and pneumonia.

■ ■ ■

GANGLING ACTOR **TED Markland**, who portrayed Reno, a singing ranch hand, opposite Cameron Mitchell on TV's *The High Chaparral,* is a full-time resident of 8115 Balsa Avenue, Yucca Valley. Markland co-starred in five films with Peter Fonda, including *Wanda Nevada,* in which he played Strap, the Be-Bop Killer. He has also played grizzled hit men and is often seen sporting long hair and a mustache in violent action films such as *Another 48 Hours, Eye of the Tiger,* and *Wild Bill.*

Pioneertown

Four miles north of Yucca Valley off Highway 62, at a fork in the road where cattle drives once stirred up thick clouds of dust, are the remnants of a grandiose real estate venture—and the man who made it all possible was **Roy Rogers**, who still owned several parcels of land there when he died at the age of 86 in 1998.

Rogers's career as a singing cowboy closely paralleled that of Gene Autry, another Palm Springs icon, except that he was better looking than Autry and talked a good deal more than he sang. Dubbed "King of the Cowboys" by his fans, Rogers took the money he made from entertainment and invested it in thousands of acres of supposedly worthless land, which he either developed or resold at enormous profit.

One of his early business ventures was **Pioneertown**, a permanent 1880s Western-movie set that also doubled as a real working town, complete with general store, saloon, livery stable, and hitching posts. Built in 1946, the hilly development was the brainchild of gun-toting, B-movie actor Dick Curtis, who smelled the project's potential but was unable to finance the deal himself.

Enter Rogers and 16 other investors, including the singing group Sons of the Pioneers, Hopalong Cassidy sidekick Russell "Lucky" Hayden, and glib comedian Bud Abbott, who each pledged $500 in the corporation.

Curtis reasoned that it would be cheaper for producers to rent his studio facilities than to truck equipment and supplies 130 miles overland from Hollywood. His assumption made sense, and soon the studio space was booked.

The cliffhanging movie serial *Cody of the Pony Express*, featuring Dickie Moore and Jock Mahoney, was filmed there. So was *The Cisco Kid* starring Duncan Renaldo, and several Gene Autry films, including *On Top of Old Smoky*. Fittingly, Autry's 93rd and final film, *Last of the Pony Riders*, in which he played a Pony Express rider who establishes a stage line to carry the mail and then rides off into the sunset, was also shot there.

When founder Dick Curtis died in 1952, some people felt that part of his dream died with him. But many of those salty pioneers who had staked a claim in his movie-made town refused to leave, and film crews continued to use it. Actor Clayton Moore, who filmed *Son of Geronimo* there, recalled that Russell Hayden had his own ranch just east of the town, up a dirt hill. "It was used mostly for Edgar Buchanan's television series *Judge Roy Bean*, but we shot there as well," he recounted. Among the show's famous sets was the old saloon where Bean kept a tattered portrait of the celebrated stage actress Lillie Langtry behind the bar.

Hayden's ranch, where "Lucky" lived with actress-wife Lillian Porter, gradually fell into disrepair after he passed away from pneumonia in 1981 at the age of 69. Porter memorialized her husband by keeping things as they had been in his lifetime, until the wallpaper was literally falling down. She followed him in death in 1997; she was 79.

Two years after she was laid to rest, actor Bryan Cranston, from the Fox TV sitcom *Malcolm in the Middle*, wrote and produced the independent film *Last Chance* there. Its production represented the last gasp for this weather-beaten outpost, now inhabited mostly by scorpions and chuckwallas.

■ ■ ■

THESE DAYS, PIONEERTOWN resembles a ghost town. There are no street lights, no gas stations—not even a 7-Eleven. But it hasn't stopped curious visitors from straying into town and, in some cases, moving there.

The case of gadfly and blues singer **Johnny Merle "Buzz" Gamble** was as poignant as it was pathetic. The tattooed, bourbon-sipping former jailbird lived in a timber-framed house, formerly part of a teetering movie set along empty Pioneertown streets named after William S. Hart, Tom Mix, John Wayne, and other long-dead cowboy stars.

Gamble's celebrity status stemmed from several run-ins with the law. He was immortalized by the late country music singer Johnny Paycheck, who is best known for his working class anthem "Take This Job and Shove It." Paycheck reportedly based his song "The Great Donut Robbery" on a real incident involving Gamble's theft of 169-dozen pastries from a Winchell's Donut House in Salinas. Gamble dined out—or drank out—on this amusing story for years, until his overworked liver ceased to function in protest. He died of complications from alcoholism in 2004.

■ ■ ■

PIONEERTOWN MOTEL AT 5040 Curtis Road is constructed of railroad ties and mortar and was originally built to accommodate sunburned stars and dehydrated extras. Room #9 was nicknamed "Club 9" by Gene Autry, because that's where he invited pals for drinks after a long day's filming. The clanking of metal spurs and the fizz of soda siphons was a normal sound there during production of *The Gene Autry Show*.

Room #10 was occupied by Gail Davis when she played TV's legendary Wild West sharpshooter *Annie Oakley*, who kept law and order in the little town of Diablo, assisted by kid brother Tagg, played by Jimmy Hawkins.

But not all guests were of such illustrious social standing, although the management can hardly be held responsible for that infraction.

John Barrymore, Jr., the alcohol-and-drug-addicted descendant of the famous Philadelphia acting dynasty, which included siblings Ethel and Lionel Barrymore, later took up residence in Gail Davis's former room, where he whiled away the hours looking at old photo albums.

The son of legendary actor John Barrymore, who played every conceivable louse from Doctor Jekyll to Don Juan, this youngest male heir squandered his good looks and talent on inconsequential roles and was frequently unemployable because of his drunkenness. His half-sister, Diana Barrymore, was likewise doomed; mind and body ravaged from alcoholism, she tragically committed suicide at the age of 38.

John, Jr.'s daughter, Drew Barrymore, and her dogs slept in Room

#11 when they visited. Unfortunately, she inherited the destructive genes of her forebears, and there was genuine concern that the family's newest thespian, who became a star at age seven in Steven Spielberg's *E.T.*, would follow in her father's footsteps. She began smoking cigarettes and drinking alcohol at nine, inhaling marijuana at 10, and snorting cocaine at 12. At 13, she attempted suicide by cutting her wrists with a kitchen knife.

But after much soul-searching, this talented young performer chose not to be a victim and she regained her sobriety. Nothing, however, could save her ailing father, whom she rescued from his self-imposed desert purgatory and institutionalized for his own safety.

When John Barrymore, Jr., passed away at the age of 72, on November 29, 2004, Drew Barrymore, accompanied by her boyfriend, the Strokes rock band drummer Fabrizio Moretti, and by character actor Ted Markland, scattered her dad's ashes at Joshua Tree National Park.

■ ■ ■

ONE BREATH OF fresh air in Pioneertown has been the presence of sophisticated song stylist **Nancy Wilson**, whose soulful hits, "Save Your Love for Me," "You're as Right as Rain," and the Grammy Award–winning Rhythm & Blues number "How Glad I Am," put her at the forefront of classic pop vocalists.

Wilson has resided at 54–101 Pipes Canyon Road in Yucca Valley with her husband, Reverend Wiley Burton, since 1978. The couple share their six-bedroom home with a menagerie of music-loving pets, including two horses, a buffalo, ostriches and emus, four dogs, a flock of peacocks, doves, and quail. If they could talk to the animals!

In 2005, Wilson won a second Grammy Award, for Best Jazz Vocal for her romantically inspired album *R.S.V.P.*

■ ■ ■

THE LIST OF talented musicians who have performed at Pappy & Harriet's **Pioneertown Palace,** at 53–688 Pioneertown Road, without the benefit of large-scale promotion, is a minor revelation. They include renowned singer-guitarist Leon Russell, the rock band Canned Heat, and French Canadian music guru Daniel Lanois, who has worked with Bob

Dylan and Peter Gabriel. Many other famous names have dropped in unannounced for jam sessions and live performances.

This roadhouse-style tavern's biggest draw, however, may be British-born singer **Eric Burdon** of The Animals, whose howling vocals of "House of the Rising Sun" and "We Gotta Get Out of This Place" resonate with capacity beer-drinking crowds, although they may startle the coyotes and the jack rabbits.

Burdon's popularity is no doubt due to his status as a 30-year resident of the desert, where he has communed with Native American spirits, smoked pipes, and imbibed with various artistic and musical demigods. In 2000, Burdon took the Irish rock band U2, whose lead singer, Bono, is a frequent desert visitor, to task over a local environmental issue. He wanted to know why the group, whose highly praised album *The Joshua Tree* sold 10 million copies, did not volunteer their assistance to help fight a proposed landfill development.

Burdon's second published autobiography, *Don't Let Me Be Misunderstood*, in which he declared he was finally clean and sober after decades of living it up, was compiled at his 8808 Rock Haven Road home in Joshua Tree. He formerly lived in Whitewater and La Quinta.

Joshua Tree

A consecrated place that is worshiped for its spirituality as much as its abundant wildlife, Joshua Tree, located six miles east of Yucca Valley, is as close to a Martian landscape as humanity is ever likely to encounter on its own planet.

Most people agree that Joshua Tree possesses an unearthly quality that demands humble reverence. It is truly amazing that so much creative energy can be found at the same time in one place. But it's not always a good thing.

The bizarre predicament of prize-winning assemblage artist **Noah Purifoy**, who was famous for his multicolored "junk art" sculptures and collages, is a prime example of an unearthly culture clash. His acclaimed exhibition "66 Signs of Neon," which traveled the country, was crafted from pieces of debris from the 1965 Watts riots in Los Angeles.

Purifoy lived in a Spartan mobile home at 63–015 Blair Lane in

Joshua Tree, surrounded by two-and-a-half acres of scrap metal, wood, and plastic. There he created his special brand of art from everyday objects—old window frames, glass bricks, bicycle parts, bowling balls— much the way that Doctor Frankenstein used pieces of dead bodies to make himself a monster.

In trying to bring his art to life, Purifoy may have predicted his own death. "When I'm done with a piece, I'm done with it," he explained. "I don't care what happens with it, it takes on its own life." On March 5, 2004, a 911 emergency phone call from a concerned neighbor alerted fire crews to Purifoy's home. When police arrived, they found the deceased 86-year-old sculptor sitting in a wheelchair with third-degree burns over 90 percent of his body. Indeed, according to San Bernardino County Fire Department officials, the blaze was confined to the artist's body.

It appeared that Purifoy had been incinerated from head to toe. Or was it spontaneous combustion? Incredibly, nothing else in the home was damaged. His art, unlike its obsessive creator, was spared a fiery destruction.

■ ■ ■

OTHER LOCAL RESIDENTS imbued with the spirit of creativity include rock 'n' roll musician **Mark Olson** (an ex-member of the Jayhawks) and his wife, and singer and songwriter **Victoria Williams**, both of whom relocated from Minnesota to a ranch at 5881 Saddleback Road in Joshua Tree. They now record independent albums under the name of the Original Harmony Ridge Creek Dippers.

The trend that saw rock stars communing with nature in this desert started in the mid-1960s, when stressed-out singers and their groupies stayed at the Joshua Tree Inn at 61–259 Twentynine Palms Highway—a hacienda-style hotel located five miles from Joshua Tree National Park, an 800,000-acre wilderness.

Because the surrounding area is so vast, Hollywood has dropped in from time to time to film scenes requiring symbolic bleakness or physical isolation. Many music videos and fashion shoots have also used the unique scenery as a desolate backdrop.

■ ■ ■

FOLK SINGER **GRAM Parsons**, who pioneered country rock music, often went to Joshua Tree with Chris Hillman of The Byrds. Parsons also stayed there with Rolling Stones guitarist Keith Richards; they took LSD and watched the sky for UFOs, sprawled out on the rocks and drinking from bottles of Jim Beam.

Unfortunately, the only flying objects seen by Parsons were caused by drug-induced hallucinations. On September 19, 1973, two days after checking into the Joshua Tree Inn, Parsons died in Room #8 from a morphine-and-alcohol overdose. He was 26.

That, however, was not the end of the singer's journey. His road manager, Phil Kaufman, and another friend stole Parsons's casket from Los Angeles International Airport, where it was awaiting shipment to Louisiana for burial. They drove the body in a borrowed hearse to Joshua Tree and set fire to it, attempting to fulfill Parsons's wish to be cremated at the park. The two men were later arrested, and the singer's partially burned remains were finally buried in a New Orleans cemetery.

Grieving fans later placed a marker in Parsons's honor at Joshua Tree National Park. His shrine is a concrete slab on the geological formation known as Cap Rock. It's inscribed "Safe at Home"—the name of one of Parsons's record albums.

■ ■ ■

A SHORT TIME after Parsons died, British folk musician **Donovan Leitch,** better known simply as Donovan, settled in Joshua Tree with his wife, Linda Lawrence (formerly she had been the girlfriend of ex-Rolling Stones guitarist Brian Jones, who mysteriously drowned in a swimming pool in 1969).

Donovan's plaintive voice, fisherman's cap, and psychedelic waistcoats had made him a hero to the "flower power" generation, and his catchy pop songs "Sunshine Superman" and "Mellow Yellow" had sold millions of copies. During their desert sojourn, the young couple raised their two daughters, Astrella and Oriole, as well as Lawrence's son, Julian, by Jones.

By 1983, Donovan had temporarily stopped producing records; he left California in 1990 and resumed his singing career in England. His son Julian Leitch still owns the home that Donovan purchased at 2077 Wamego Trail.

Twentynine Palms

The city of Twentynine Palms derives its name from an oasis of native fan palm trees that were discovered by Colonel Henry Washington during his survey of the Colorado Desert in 1855. This outermost region of high desert, located 35 miles from Palm Springs, was first settled by gold prospectors and by homesteaders who raised thousands of cattle on the fertile slopes. In 1952, the U.S. Department of Defense established an army base north of the oasis for glider training. It is now the Marine Corps Air Ground Combat Center, the world's largest marine training camp, which houses approximately 20,000 military personnel.

Speaking of palm trees, the tatty-looking **29 Palms Inn** at 73–950 Inn Avenue holds a special fascination for contemplative celebrity guests such as Michelle Pfeiffer and Nicolas Cage, who like to stare out the window and try to count the exact number of palm trees—26, 27, 28— that sprout in the mystical Oasis of Mara, once an ancient Native American spring.

Singer Robert Plant composed his post–Led Zeppelin hit "29 Palms" while staying here, and in the quirky film noir *29 Palms,* hit man Chris O'Donnell pursues a bag of stolen money across the same countryside.

■ ■ ■

MGM CHILD STAR **Jackie Cooper**, a Best Actor nominee for *Skippy,* which was directed by his uncle, Norman Taurog, retained vivid memories of his mother, Mabel Leonard, and her courtship by his future stepfather, Charles Bigelow. Their budding romance, Cooper recalled, took place in a Twentynine Palms hotel, which the couple barely left for six days in 1933.

"I was eleven or so, and I knew the facts of life, but the idea of my mother and Mr. Bigelow sleeping together never dawned on me," Cooper said. "We had a two-room bungalow, and when I woke up in the morning, my mother was always in the other bed in my room." Sun streamed through the curtains, and little Jackie would sit enthralled, oblivious to the previous night's lovemaking between consenting adults. Then, after Bigelow and Cooper's mom showered and dressed, they would all go riding horseback.

This early, peripheral awareness of sex no doubt contributed to his rapid development, and Cooper remarked that he never again saw the world through a child's eyes. That realization was made even more apparent when his mom died at the age of 40 in 1941.

■ ■ ■

ONE OF HOLLYWOOD'S forgotten heroes is silent film producer **Thomas H. Ince**, who was known as the "Father of the Western" for his popular films starring eagle-faced actor William S. Hart. An astute businessman, Ince was a partner with D. W. Griffith and Mack Sennett in the Triangle Film Corporation. He built the Culver City studios that later became MGM, and helped develop the production and business techniques that characterized the studio system.

But he would not live to see many of these achievements take place. In 1924, Ince died under mysterious circumstances aboard a pleasure yacht. The frolicking passengers included William Randolph Hearst; his mistress, Marion Davies; the actor Charlie Chaplin; and gossip columnist Louella Parsons. Officially, Ince suffered a heart attack from consuming too much alcohol. But after the public learned about sexual dalliances among the party guests, rumors quickly circulated of foul play. One supposition was that Ince had been shot and killed by Hearst in a lover's quarrel over Davies. Another theory had Ince being poisoned by Hearst for the same offense. Supposedly, his body had been hastily cremated to cover up the crime.

The controversy sent Ince's 16-year-son, William, on a path of self-discovery that eventually drove him away from Hollywood. Although he had received a sizable inheritance from his father's estate, the young Ince had no interest in moviemaking. He preferred to travel and eventually studied medicine in Vienna. If his father's death had been in vain, he vowed that his own life would not be wasted on frivolous pursuits.

In 1946, **William Ince**, his wife, and their three children moved to Twentynine Palms, and there, as a practicing osteopathic physician and surgeon, he established the Thomas H. Ince Memorial Hospital (now Faith in the Word Christian Center) at 5792 Adobe Road. The hospital was designed by Pasadena-based architect Wallace Neff, whose recreations of Spanish-style archways, courtyards, and patios adorn more than 200 famous homes in Los Angeles and Palm Springs.

For 20 years, Dr. Ince supervised the births of hundreds of babies in the hospital's wards. But one evening he was summoned to a most unusual case: an exploding military cannon had seriously injured several cast and crew members during the filming of an episode of *The Gene Autry Show* in nearby Pioneertown.

Because of the seriousness of the accident, there was no time to wait for help to arrive, so Autry, who was present that day, deployed his twin-engine Beechcraft to fetch the doctor. It was dark by the time the plane took off, so neighboring townsfolk were instructed by the local telephone operator to turn on their car headlights to illuminate the Twentynine Palms landing field.

Autry's pilot collected Ince and his medical bag from the hospital and flew him out to the remote set, where the carnage resembled a battlefield. Actor Pat Buttram had sustained horrible injuries from the red-hot shrapnel, which had lodged in his chest and jaw and had severed the arteries of his left foot. Autry's famous horse, Champion, had been hit by a piece of mortar, and the horse's trainer had suffered a broken leg. Ince applied a clamp to Buttram's dangling foot and worked quickly to stem the loss of blood, cleaning and stitching the wounds. The actor was perilously close to death by the time an ambulance transported him to the hospital.

Two more emergency flights were made in Autry's plane to collect blood plasma and find a second physician who could assist Ince in the operating room. Buttram's life was undoubtedly saved that day by the doctor's swift actions, and nine months later he made a full recovery and was able to return to work.

Ince, who resided in modest surroundings at 5778 Ocotillo Avenue, continued practicing medicine and performing surgery until his death at the age of 64, in 1972.

■ ■ ■

MORE THAN ONE old-time rock 'n' roller receives divine inspiration from the desert. **Debora Iyall**, former lead singer of the 1980s "new wave" band Romeo Void, whose punk-inspired hits "Never Say Never" and "A Girl in Trouble" landed them on *American Bandstand*, lives at 78–711 Indian Trail in Twentynine Palms. A member of the Cowlitz tribe of Native American Indians, Iyall also teaches art and music.

There's also **Dick Dale**, who pioneered the advent of the "surf rock" music that was all the rage in the early 1960s and got excited teenagers wet in the *Beach Party* movies. Dale's musical prowess on vinyl records and in concert with his backing band, the Del-Tones, earned him the title "King of the Surf Guitar." His fast-paced electric guitar solos influenced future performers such as Jimi Hendrix and Eddie Van Halen.

In 1994, Dale's feverish instrumental version of the traditional Middle Eastern folk song "Misirlou" was featured on the soundtrack of Quentin Tarantino's cult film *Pulp Fiction*. It was a huge monetary boost to Dale's career.

Nowadays, the 69-year-old, ponytailed musician sells his own CDs via mail order from his 80-acre ranch in Wonder Valley, a short distance from Twentynine Palms. Dale, who is also a licensed pilot, resides there with his wife, Jill; his son, Jimmy; four dogs, two horses, and a middle-aged Sulphor-crested White Cockatoo named Fred. "I love living here. I really do," said the free-spirited Dale. "If I want to ride my horse naked, I can. If I want to jump in the pool naked, I can. If the Marines want to fly overhead and say 'Hi,' then Jill and I can yell 'Hello' back in all our glory."

Star Feuds

ELABORATE COVER-UPS AND conspiratorial denials—they are at the core of Washington's and Hollywood's obsession with the desert as the perfect hiding place. Perhaps it is the terrain. The red granite humps and the blue-domed sky seem to render everything slightly mysterious, even dangerous. Add a pulsating city that looks, from certain vantage points, like a mirage, and you have a recipe for intrigue and deception.

■ ■ ■

THERE ARE FEW places on earth like Rancho Mirage. A ten-mile drive from Palm Springs, it is the permanent residence of some of the world's wealthiest, most influential, most glamorous individuals. This is the playground of presidents, the destination of retired actors, youthful pop stars, and seasoned powerbrokers, all of whom can be found swinging five-irons or posing side-by-side at charity golf events.

Rancho Mirage is a luxuriant dell of country-club homes and fairway condominiums, and its litter-free streets boast maroon signposts that proudly honor the rich and famous who have lived here: Bob Hope, Frank Sinatra, Dinah Shore, and Gerald R. Ford, among others. Lucille Ball was Rancho Mirage's first honorary mayor.

Here, the golf courses have been designed by some of the sport's most recognized names: Pete Dye, Arnold Palmer, and Ted Robinson. The Westin Mission Hills Resort houses the Reed Anderson Tennis School, one of the country's top training camps. Rancho Mirage's Ritz-Carlton Hotel, now The Lodge, made Condé Nast Traveler's list of the top five resorts on the U.S. mainland. Enticing words, these. Printed in glossy magazines and brochures, they attract millions of tourists every year.

But what the articles and ad campaigns omit are the addresses where complicit gatherings take place. The bulk of these smart-looking, California ranch-style homes, whose influential owners fraternize over golf games and catered dinner parties, are situated behind intimidating electronic gates equipped with closed-circuit TV cameras and defended by 24-hour security guards—all designed to keep tourists and other unwanted visitors away. "The most prevalent criminal activity in the area is conspiracy," concludes Kitty Kelley, whose unauthorized biography of Frank Sinatra, which revealed that the tempestuous singer consorted with hundreds of dubious individuals during his 40-year residency, sent shock-waves throughout the city.

In short, it's all a far cry from the days when Rancho Mirage was a city of only 15,000 people. It bears little resemblance to the place of hand-hewn adobe cottages and citrus farms, where the few inhabitants used to haul produce to market in their pickup trucks and ride horses along the unpaved roads.

MGM director **Clarence Brown** extracted superlative performances from Swedish superstar Greta Garbo in seven lavishly produced films, including *Flesh and the Devil, A Woman of Affairs,* and *Anna Christie.* He lived at 71–793 San Jacinto Drive.

A skilled craftsman, Brown's strength lay in his ability to tap into the emotions of stars such as Mickey Rooney and Clark Gable and urge them to scale new dramatic heights—something that required time and patience and often eluded less intuitive directors. The secret to Garbo's unusual acting technique, Brown once said, was that she expressed her emotions not with traditional gestures and movements but "by *thinking* them," which was harder to do, he explained, than it sounded. Their successful partnership culminated in the blockbuster historical films *Anna Karenina* and *Conquest,* after which her career went into a slump, and she withdrew from public life.

Brown, however, continued to work his storytelling magic for another decade. A six-time Oscar nominee, he brought his vivid pictorial style to 50 outstanding films, ranging from *The Human Comedy, National Velvet,* and *The Yearling* to *The White Cliffs of Dover, Intruder in the Dust,* and *Plymouth Adventure.*

Although he was a master at depicting Hollywood gloss, Brown had little use for such artifice in his own life and avoided the spotlight. At the peak of his popularity he retired from making movies and embarked on a teaching career. In 1971, Brown donated $300,000 to his alma mater, the University of Tennessee, for a performing arts center named in his honor. He died at the age of 97 in 1987.

■ ■ ■

"WE HAD FACES then!" exclaimed Gloria Swanson as the preening, silent-screen diva Norma Desmond in *Sunset Boulevard*. One of those unforgettable faces belonged to **Neva Gerber**, a leading star of the era who appeared in 110 films, the majority of them now lost. The smiling, bobbed-haired ingénue, who lived out her retirement in cramped quarters at 42–346 The Veldt, had been the wide-eyed heroine of actor Harry Carey in several crackling Western melodramas directed by John Ford, including *Hell Bent* and *A Fight for Life*. The movie's title would come back to haunt the pretty actress.

She divorced her first husband, actor Arthur Millett, in the hope of marrying the flamboyant actor William Desmond Taylor, who directed her in *The Awakening* and *An Eye for an Eye*. But the marriage never took place. In 1922, Taylor was shot dead in his Hollywood mansion by a single bullet through the heart, the outcome of a sordid love triangle that involved fellow movie stars Mabel Normand and Mary Miles Minter. The ensuing scandal ruined both women's careers; the killer was never found.

Neva Gerber, meanwhile, co-starred in 35 one-reelers, including *The Mystery Ship*, the first of many cliffhanging serials she filmed with matinee idol Ben Wilson, who died from a cerebral hemorrhage in 1930. Upon learning of Wilson's death, however, Gerber was so heartbroken that she retired from acting.

Two subsequent marriages, including one to a mining engineer, Edward Nolan, ended in divorce. In 1960, Gerber became a widow upon the death of her fourth husband, William Munchoff, a Palm Springs general contractor. She herself died from pneumonia at the age of 79 in 1974.

■ ■ ■

EVERYTHING ABOUT BLUSTERING actor **Frank Morgan** bordered on the eccentric, from his thick white hair and waxed mustache to his perpetually befuddled expression, which could be highly amusing in *The Cockeyed Miracle*, kindly in *The Shop Around the Corner*, or sad in *Courage of Lassie*.

As a result of his exceptional versatility, Morgan was offered a lifetime contract by MGM, where this professional scene-stealer shared billing with almost every big star on the lot. A two-time Oscar nominee for *The Affairs of Cellini* and *Tortilla Flat*, Morgan resided at 71–845 Sahara Road with his wife, Alma Muller, from 1936 until Morgan's unexpected death in 1949 at the age of 59. Their ranch-style adobe home, which had an iron door-knocker, and kerosene lamps to illuminate the pitch-black desert evenings, was where the well-read actor memorized film scripts and polished his gun collection.

Although he was happiest telling a joke, Morgan was at his best playing blowhards, gamblers, and politicians who were usually seen bending the ears of co-stars Clark Gable, Jeanette MacDonald, and Mickey Rooney. But it was not these defining moments that audiences remember so much as Morgan's roles in one particularly outstanding film: *The Wizard of Oz*. Morgan played five different characters in this much-loved movie. He was Professor Marvel, the Emerald City doorman, the cabby who drives the Horse-of-a-Different-Color, the uniformed palace guard, and finally the Wizard himself.

Now that's versatility! His talent was so prodigious it's amazing to learn that Morgan almost didn't get the role of the Wizard; bulbous-nosed comedian W.C. Fields was offered the part first. Thankfully, he turned it down.

■ ■ ■

ACTOR JEFF CHANDLER, who received an Oscar nomination for his performance as the Apache Indian leader Cochise, in the pro–Native American film *Broken Arrow*, owned the home at 71–543 Tangier Road, where
he lived with his wife of eight years, actress Marjorie Hoselle, and their
two daughters, Jamie and Dana.

Chandler's prematurely gray hair, deep voice, and heavily tanned features made him an unconventional sex symbol in an era of young, blond
athletes. It led to screen romances with Maureen O'Hara, Loretta Young,
Joan Crawford, Jane Russell, Kim Novak, and Lana Turner.

His pairing with Esther Williams in *Raw Wind in Eden*, which was
filmed in Italy, blossomed into a real-life romance for the well-built actor
and the former MGM swimming star, and they decided to divorce their
respective spouses in order to legitimize their love affair. But when
Chandler proposed to Williams, she turned him down. "He loved me passionately, and I loved him back—with unspoken reservations," said
Williams.

It turned out that Chandler had a dark secret, which he tried unsuccessfully to hide from her. One evening, Williams walked into the actor's
bedroom and discovered him standing in front of a full-length mirror
wearing a flowing chiffon dress, high-heeled shoes, and a red wig. "This
was no joke," she confessed. "He enjoyed that kind of thing. He was a
cross-dresser."

According to Williams, he had closets full of women's clothes: suits,
dresses, negligees, foundation garments, hats, shoes, gloves—even two-
piece bathing suits, although Chandler, with his hairy chest and torso,
could never have worn them. If the actor's sexual fetish was supposed to
turn Williams on, it didn't; she ran screaming from the room. Her parting words were "Jeff, you're too big for polka dots." He stood there crying like a sad clown, the tears ruining his makeup. "But I love you," he
sobbed.

It was the end of their affair, and probably just as well. Williams could
never have handled the resulting bad publicity if the words "Mermaid in
Love with Transvestite" had ever appeared in the press.

Chandler died in 1961 at the age of 42, not from a broken heart but
from blood poisoning following surgery for a herniated disc. A doctor

had accidentally cut a major artery during the operation, and 54 blood transfusions failed to save the actor's life. Chandler's family brought a lawsuit on the grounds of medical malpractice, and his daughters received a large settlement. Dana died in 2002, Jamie in 2003—both of cancer.

■ ■ ■

IF THE TERM "respectable sleaze" can be applied to anyone, it should be awarded to raven-haired actor **Michael Dante,** a longtime resident of 71–372 Biskra Road. Dante's jet-black curls, sensuous lips, and wicked gaze have made him a prime exponent of villainy in more than 50 films and TV series.

A former shortstop for the Boston Braves, he was spotted by bandleader Tommy Dorsey, who arranged for the handsome baseball player to receive a screen test at MGM, where he later appeared in several unbilled parts. Then, after signing with Warner Bros., Dante was offered more substantial scripts. He played outlaws in the television westerns *Sugarfoot, Maverick, Colt .45,* and *The Texan,* in which he acted the recurring role of gunman Steve Chambers. He graduated to big-screen appearances as quick-on-the-draw cowboys in *Fort Dobbs, Westbound,* and *Arizona Raiders,* one of two films he made with Audie Murphy.

No matter what the role, Dante has always stood out. A notable example: his impressive portrayal of Maab, a dark-suited tribal leader who is crushed to death by falling rocks in a memorable episode of *Star Trek.* And his oily charms were ideally suited to the French caper *Seven Thieves,* as well as the cult melodrama *The Naked Kiss,* co-starring his Palm Desert neighbor Anthony Eisley.

■ ■ ■

PRESIDENT FRANKLIN D. Roosevelt's family had several skeletons in its closet, and not the clothes closet or the broom closet either. The highly respected First Family lived in the shadow of tragedy and scandal before, during, and after Roosevelt's record-breaking four terms in office. The nation's 32nd president was physically disabled as a result of polio, and often had to use a cane, wear leg braces, and for much of his third and fourth terms be confined to a wheelchair. He died of a cerebral hemorrhage two months after attending the Yalta Conference in 1945, at the age of 63.

During this time, the president's wife, Eleanor Roosevelt, was having a well-documented lesbian relationship with Washington journalist Lorena Hickok, whom she had met in 1928. Their burgeoning romance forced Hickok to resign from her job to avoid being branded, and she went to work for the Democratic National Committee. They remained secret lovers until Eleanor's death in 1962.

Franklin and Eleanor had six children, and their eldest son, **James Roosevelt**, who resided at 71–530 Biskra Road, served in the U.S. Congress, where he proved a decent, hardworking legislator. But despite that record, Roosevelt was an unsuccessful Democratic candidate for governor of California and was extremely disappointed when the party failed to nominate him for mayor of Los Angeles in 1965.

Roosevelt divorced his third wife, Irene Owens, in 1969, and soon after he remarried and moved to Newport Beach. He gave Irene the house on Biskra Road, and she lived there in quiet solitude. But her life was far from happy; she still suffered from the drinking problem that had reportedly contributed to the breakdown of her 13-year marriage to Roosevelt.

On June 5, 1987, firefighters responding to a predawn blaze at Irene's home discovered her charred body lying facedown on the bedroom floor. She had apparently fallen asleep in bed while smoking, awoke several hours later to discover the mattress ablaze, and was overcome by smoke. Her cat also perished in the fire. An autopsy found that Roosevelt had taken sleeping pills. When questioned by police, her son, Delano, who had been trying to get power of attorney over his mother, denied it was suicide. He claimed that her death, at age 70, must have been an accident.

James Roosevelt died in 1991, at the age of 83.

■ ■ ■

OSCAR-NOMINATED BRITISH SCREENWRITER **Alec Coppel**, whose scripts for *Obsession*, *No Highway in the Sky*, and *Mr. Denning Drives North* blend stark terror and gallows-style humor, moved to 42–976 Ocotillo Drive in 1958—the same year that the morbid Alfred Hitchcock masterpiece, *Vertigo*, for which Coppel wrote the brilliant screenplay, was released.

This was the pair's finest collaboration, although not their first. The master of suspense had hired Coppel to contribute vignettes for the TV series *Alfred Hitchcock Presents* and to write scenes for *To Catch a Thief.* That assignment led to Coppel's work on *Vertigo,* a story of necrophilia that is universally regarded as the director's most personal film.

At their first meeting, Hitchcock outlined the key sequences that he wanted Coppel to fashion into a script. These included the memorable opening—a rooftop chase during which James Stewart nearly falls to his death—and the famous kissing scene between Stewart and Kim Novak in her hotel room, where the camera spins around them, creating a feeling of ecstasy.

Coppel structured Hitchcock's film expertly, but production was delayed when Hitchcock underwent a hernia operation and also required surgery for gallstones. Then, because of her prior commitments, there were difficulties obtaining Novak's services. All in all, the start of filming was pushed back almost one year.

In the meantime, as often occurs in Hollywood, Hitchcock had brought in a second writer. Samuel Taylor, who had written *Sabrina,* polished the film script and added a character named Midge, the hero's best friend, who was played by Barbara Bel Geddes. "The delays deepened and darkened the script," wrote film historian Patrick McGilligan. "For the first time, a Hitchcock love story would end pathetically, with the abject failure of the hero and the death of the leading lady." The shocking denouement totally surprised audiences and helped turn the film into a classic.

Coppel's literary talents weren't limited to plotting murders. He was also an accomplished dramatist whose plays became successful films in their turn: *The Captain's Paradise, The Gazebo,* and *The Bliss of Mrs. Blossom,* among others. He died at the age of 64 in 1972.

■ ■ ■

CLASSICALLY TRAINED BRITISH actor **Sir Cedric Hardwicke** was justly famous for two physical traits: his aristocratic profile and his plummy voice, which he effectively used in the nearly 80 films which required his special brand of quiet authority. Reputedly the favorite actor of playwright George Bernard Shaw, for whom he first starred in Shaw's comedy *Caesar and Cleopatra,* Hardwicke was revered enough to be knighted in 1934 by King George V. After that, he went to Hollywood.

Among his finely honed portrayals are Theotocopulos in *Things to Come*, Dr. Livingstone in *Stanley and Livingstone*, Frollo in *The Hunchback of Notre Dame*, Henry Cabot Lodge in *Wilson*, and King Arthur in *A Connecticut Yankee in King Arthur's Court*.

It was Hardwicke who provided the portentous opening narration for the 1953 science-fiction classic *The War of the Worlds*: "No one would have believed in the middle of the twentieth century that human affairs were being watched keenly and closely by intelligences greater than man's."

Like his friendly neighbor, Alec Coppel, who lived up the street, Hardwicke also worked for Alfred Hitchcock, playing pivotal roles in *Suspicion* and *Rope* and making two guest appearances on the great director's droll TV show. By the time this veteran came to 71–690 Magnesia Falls Road, in 1960, he was in the final throes of his brilliant career; a divorce was pending from his second wife, Mary Scott, and he was suffering from a lung ailment that would claim his life in 1964, when he was 71.

Despite his success and longevity, Hardwicke always remained cynical about Hollywood. "I believe that God felt sorry for actors so he gave them a place in the sun and a swimming pool," he stated. "The price they had to pay was to surrender their talent." Hopefully, Hardwicke was generously recompensed for his efforts.

■ ■ ■

WILLIAM RANDOLPH HEARST'S body was cold only ten weeks when his mistress of 30 years, the stuttering actress **Marion Davies**, married for the first time. She had been the American publishing tycoon's lover, confidante, and silent business partner, but she had been ostracized by Hearst's family because she was not his wife.

The gentleman whom she wed, all the while holding back tears for the departed soul mate she truly loved, was Horace Brown, a former sea captain and policeman. It was a marriage doomed from the start, and if this had been a movie or a play, it would have been called *Love on the Rebound*. In fact, if Hearst had been alive, he probably would have produced it.

Act One: Davies and Brown barely exchange wedding vows on Halloween 1951 when trouble starts. The couple holds their reception at the Racquet Club in Palm Springs, and Davies, hung over from a night of boozing, wears dark glasses to hide her bloodshot eyes.

Act Two: Minutes later, the sounds of breaking champagne glasses and raised voices fill the air as the newlyweds start bickering, then yelling, and finally screaming at each other.

Act Three: The argument is about money (his not hers), but by the final curtain they have kissed and made up.

Eight months later, the show closed.

Davies drove drunkenly down to the Santa Monica courthouse and filed for divorce. Her friends Kay Spreckels, Eleanor Boardman, and Mary Pickford saw it coming and would have reserved tickets for the matinee if it hadn't already sold out. But even flops have a way of coming back. Davies and Brown surprised the critics by patching things up, and they continued taking curtain calls for ten more years. She died in 1961 at the age of 64.

■ ■ ■

THROUGH ALL THIS turmoil, Marion's last surviving sister, **Rose Davies**, lived in a house filled with empty liquor bottles at 71–281 San Gorgonio Road. According to eyewitnesses, their relationship had overtones of *Whatever Happened to Baby Jane?* There they were, one good sister and one bad, both crying over a lost love and taking it out on each other.

It was Rose, staggering drunk, who nagged Marion to buy this estate for her in the first place. "You'll get it, so let's drop it," Marion slurred in her best Bette Davis imitation. The home was at one time occupied by both sisters, who reportedly got on each other's nerves to such a degree that they engaged in ferocious hair-pulling fights.

Rose survived her sister by two years and died in 1963 at the age of 60.

■ ■ ■

DEBONAIR LEADING MAN **Gene Barry** resided at 106 Mission Hills Drive located in Mission Hills Country Club, the veteran film and stage actor's second desert home after he moved from Palm Springs.

Barry's gentlemanly charms had won the affection of female TV viewers who tuned in each week to watch his legal maneuvering on *Burke's Law,* for which he received a Golden Globe Award. In 1994, the successful CBS series was revived with all-new episodes. But the show got knocked off its schedule by live news coverage of the murder of Nicole Brown Simpson and Ronald Goldman, and by murder suspect

O.J. Simpson's freeway car chase. Barry gritted his teeth and hoped for the best, but the series was canceled because of low ratings.

Barry returned to New York City for a two-week cabaret engagement at the famous Oak Room in the Algonquin Hotel. He also made a cameo appearance in the bitchy ABC movie-of-the-week *These Old Broads,* and in 2000 he also sold his Rancho Mirage home for $245,000. Then in 2003, his actress-wife of 58 years, Betty Kalb, died after a long illness, leaving him alone and depressed.

One minor consolation was Barry's attendance at the fiftieth anniversary screening of his most famous film, *The War of the Worlds*, at the Egyptian Theatre in Hollywood. But there was little resemblance between the dynamic young scientist who battled Martians in the science-fiction classic and the stooped, white-haired, 82-year-old man who greeted fans in the theater lobby. Still, Barry's deflated spirits were buoyed somewhat when Steven Spielberg asked the retired actor to make a token appearance in the director's 2005 remake of H.G. Wells's apocalyptic prophecy. Tom Cruise assumed the heroic starring role that Barry had played in his prime.

■ ■ ■

MINNESOTA BUSINESSMAN **PERCY ROSS**, whose syndicated advice column, "Thanks a Million," appeared every week in 130 newspapers in the United States and Canada, including New York's *Daily News* and *The Philadelphia Inquirer*, was a frequent visitor to son Steven's home at 517 Desert Drive West.

A self-proclaimed multimillionaire, Ross made a showy pretense of donating millions of dollars in cash and gifts to impoverished individuals and other worthwhile causes. These bequests ranged from $100 to $20,000 for each person, depending on the severity of their hardship. One of Percy's favorite gestures was to give shiny new bicycles to needy children, creating the impression he had bought the bikes, when, in fact, they had been supplied by the manufacturer for promotional consideration. He also boasted of paying for household repairs, hospital bills, and college tuition.

Unlike wealthy donors who make anonymous pledges, Ross eagerly sought public recognition for his good deeds, courting the media and gloating over his own generosity. Some people were impressed by these acts of chivalry; others questioned his motives. Photographs of Ross tossing fistfuls of silver dollars into the air, to be grabbed by eager crowds, were criticized for degrading impoverished people. So were his sneering replies to thousands of letters requesting money, which he refused to give because he felt the writers did not deserve his munificence.

Although it was widely promoted that Ross gave more than $20 million over 17 years to tens of thousands of strangers, the validity of these claims was challenged on more than one occasion. In 1988, an investigation by the Minneapolis *Star Tribune* found that Ross frequently exaggerated the amount of money he bestowed. When asked to substantiate his acts of kindness, he was unable to provide a full accounting.

In the end, Ross gained little satisfaction from his extravagant gestures, other than boosting his ego with reams of free publicity and raising the level of his income-tax deductions. He died at the age of 84 in 2001.

■ ■ ■

EFFERVESCENT TV TALK-SHOW host, actress, and singer **Dinah Shore** was a club resident from 1986 until her death from ovarian cancer in 1994, five days before her seventy-eighth birthday. Shore's former home, which is located at 600 Hospitality Drive, was tastefully decorated with Southwestern-style furnishings.

The eight-time Emmy Award–winning performer moved here so she could play golf, which had become a necessity ever since she endorsed the Colgate-sponsored Dinah Shore Winner's Circle Golf Championship, which made its debut in 1972. (Ten years later it was renamed the Dinah Shore Nabisco Championship.) When she was first asked to lend her name to the annual sporting event, which now attracts more than 100 of the world's best professional women golfers, Shore was seemingly confused. "That's fine," she responded. "It'll be tennis, won't it?" When told it wasn't, she broke into a big grin and sighed, "Oh, well!"

To get in shape, Shore relentlessly practiced a round of golf every day until she played like a pro. This dedication to self-improvement stemmed from a childhood bout with polio, which had left one of her legs shorter than the other. Her optimism inspired legions of women, many of them avid TV viewers, to take up the game, which she stressed was important for their fitness and health.

Today, the Nabisco Championship is one of four tournaments that make up the grand slam in women's golf. Each year, more than 5,000 lesbians from all over the nation converge on the desert during Dinah Shore Weekend in March, to celebrate the late entertainer's legacy and to sing and dance to the music of Melissa Etheridge, k.d. lang, and Whitney Houston. In recent years, there have been rumors that Shore was a lesbian, even though she was married twice, bore two children, and engaged in a long-running affair with actor Burt Reynolds, who was 20 years her junior. "I'm old enough to be your mother!" she chided him.

It doesn't matter. Female fans take photos of each other posing with a bronze bust of their much-loved "dyke" icon on the eighteenth hole of the Dinah Shore Tournament Course on Dinah Shore Drive (previously 34th Avenue). The life-size statue was sculpted by her first husband, the actor George Montgomery, who inherited Shore's home after her untimely death.

It may have seemed unusual for a wife's ex-spouse to move back in, especially after 32 years apart, but Montgomery was delighted to do so. "We stayed friends all the way to the end of her life," explained the retired actor, who also found himself the subject of homosexual gossip because of the impressive size of his sexual equipment. Montgomery continued sculpting, painting, and answering fan mail in Shore's home until he died at the age 84 in 2000.

There are two lasting reminders of this actor's fame: George Montgomery Way, near the Rancho 16 Theatres in Rancho Mirage, and George Montgomery Trail, near the Cathedral City Civic Center.

■ ■ ■

ANOTHER PERSONABLE CLUB resident was **Dennis James**, one of America's first TV game-show hosts and sports commentators, and the onscreen spokesman for Old Gold cigarettes. James resided at 742 Inverness Drive until his death in 1997 from lung cancer, the unfortunate result of years of exposure to deadly nicotine. He was 79.

This inimitable master of ceremonies helped pioneer the Q&A quiz show format, displaying a friendly but firm handling of contestants on fondly remembered half-hour programs such as *Cash and Carry*, *Two for the Money*, *Chance of a Lifetime*, and *High Finance*. On *People Will Talk*, he politely asked 15 contestants to vote on a range of issues, including "Is it all right to kiss in public?" and "Should bald men wear toupees?" James also hosted an updated version of *Name That Tune* and emceed the original syndicated nighttime edition of *The Price Is Right*.

But perhaps James's biggest satisfaction came not from the prizes that were awarded to contestants but from the vast number of worthwhile charities that benefited from his enthusiastic efforts. In recognition, President Dwight D. Eisenhower presented him with a Humanitarian of the Year Award.

Throughout his announcing career, James did double duty as a part-time actor, showing his vocal dexterity in such roles as wrestling commentators and beauty contest judges in a range of films and TV shows, including *Mr. Universe*, *Batman*, *Fantasy Island*, *The One and Only*, and *Rocky III*.

■ ■ ■

SONGWRITER AND LYRICIST **Buddy Kaye**, who wrote hits for Perry Como, Frank Sinatra, and Dusty Springfield, resided at 1 Oakmont Drive. His popular romantic ballads—written in collaboration with Ted Mossman—included "Till the End of Time," which Como recorded, and "Full Moon and Empty Arms," sung by Sinatra.

Kaye also wrote "A-You're Adorable," which became a #1 hit for Como and the Fontaine Sisters; "Old Songs," for Barry Manilow; and the Pat Boone novelty hit, "Speedy Gonzales." Other songs included "I'll Close My Eyes," which was recorded by Sarah Vaughan, Dinah Washington, and Ella Fitzgerald; and "Little by Little" and "All Cried Out," for Dusty Springfield.

Although he wrote more than 400 published songs in his lifetime, there is one that stands out, if only because it has been replayed more than 10,000 times in TV reruns. It's the catchy theme song of the Barbara Eden sitcom *I Dream of Jeannie*, which he cowrote with Hugo Montenegro.

Kaye died of a heart attack in 2002 at the age of 84.

■ ■ ■

ACTOR **SYDNEY CHAPLIN**, the handsome, brooding son of Oscar-winning actor, writer, director, and producer Sir Charles Chaplin, resides at 69–753 Camino Pacifico in St. Augustine, where he moved in 2000 with his third wife, Margaret Beebe.

Chaplin's father is universally regarded as the greatest comedian of his era. A derby hat, bamboo cane, and toothbrush mustache were his trademark in *The Tramp*, *The Kid*, *The Gold Rush*, *The Circus*, *City Lights*, and *Modern Times*. But the comedian's questionable morals, left-wing politics, and refusal to take the oath of American citizenship earned him widespread criticism during his lifetime. He was labeled a Communist and, forced to leave the country, he lived the remainder of his life in Switzerland, where he died at the age of 88 in 1977.

As a small boy, Sydney spent a lot of time on movie sets, where he watched his urbane father transform into a grubby tramp by changing into a pair of baggy pants, outsized shoes, and a jacket that was always too small for him. In the library of the family's Beverly Hills home, Sydney also witnessed his father's arduous process of composing film music and writing screenplays.

Sydney was not Chaplin's only offspring. He has three younger half-brothers—Michael, Eugene, and Christopher—and five younger half-sisters—Geraldine, Josephine, Victoria, Jane, and Annette-Emilie—all from his father's fourth marriage to 18-year-old Oona O'Neill, the daughter of playwright Eugene O'Neill. His older brother, Charles Chaplin, Jr., from his father's second marriage, to 16-year-old actress Lita Grey, died from alcohol abuse in 1968. They both appeared with their stepmother and three of their siblings in Charles Chaplin's very personal film, *Limelight*.

Sydney himself went on to a bright career on Broadway, winning a Tony Award for Best Featured Actor in *Bells Are Ringing* opposite Judy Holliday and co-starring with Barbra Streisand in *Funny Girl*, for which he received a Tony Award nomination for Best Actor. During his Hollywood glamour days, Sydney was romantically linked to snooty actress Joan Collins while they were both making *Land of the Pharaohs*. He later operated a restaurant called Chaplin's at 69–950 Frank Sinatra Drive. It attracted a broad clientele that dined beneath vintage photographs of the little tramp and ate meals on bone-china plates engraved with miniature black derby hats.

■ ■ ■

COSTUME DESIGNER **PAUL** **Zastupnevich** created the eye-catching outfits for all of Hollywood producer Irwin Allen's science-fiction and disaster films. Whether designing costumes for modern explorers attacked by prehistoric dinosaurs in *The Lost World,* or stranded partygoers battling roaring flames atop a skyscraper in *The Towering Inferno,* no job was too challenging for this creative genius, who was first hired to design Rhonda Fleming's revealing wardrobe in *The Big Circus.*

The man's outstanding work earned him three Oscar nominations for Best Costume Design on *The Poseidon Adventure, The Swarm,* and *When Time Ran Out.* Among the actors he dressed were Gene Hackman, Shelley Winters, Red Buttons, Paul Newman, Fred Astaire, Jennifer Jones, William Holden, and Faye Dunaway. Zastupnevich also designed the futuristic items worn by intergalactic space travelers, and the rubber-suited monsters that menaced them, in the TV programs *Lost in Space, The Time Tunnel,* and *Land of the Giants.*

Nicknamed "Paul Z" because his name was unpronounceable by most cast members, he measured, cut, and sewed literally thousands of yards of cotton, wool, nylon, velour, and other fabrics destined to be shrunk, ripped, or burned in the name of entertainment. But his greatest achievement was the stylish, V-shaped, multicolored tunics worn by the Robinson family, whose spaceship, Jupiter-2, crash-landed on a distant planet in *Lost in Space.*

Despite their long and successful collaboration, Zastupnevich often became frustrated by Allen's grandiose manner and penny-pinching ways. "I called him an 'I-gomaniac,'" he said, meaning, "I-this, I-that, I-want this, I-want this tomorrow." The love-hate relationship between the pompous producer and his talented tailor lasted 32 years, until Allen's sudden death of a heart attack in 1991.

Five years later, Zastupnevich retired to 2 Mission Palms West in Mission Pointe—a ray-gun blast from where his late employer had stayed, at Tamarisk Country Club. Unfortunately, the great Z-man had little time to savor his new surroundings; he died of cancer at the age of 75 in 1997.

■ ■ ■

BORSCHT BELT COMEDIAN **Stubby Kaye**, whom Broadway producer Cy Feuer once called "the tubbiest tenor around" for his show-stopping performance as singing gangster Nicely-Nicely Johnson in *Guys and Dolls*, resided at several addresses during his 20-year desert tenure.

Kaye was at the peak of his game when he was hired to play the strolling minstrel Sunrise Kid, whose partner, Professor Sam in the Shade, was being played by the amazing Nat "King" Cole in the comic Western *Cat Ballou*. The pair strummed the banjo and sang their ode to the film's vengeful female gunslinger, played by the delectable Jane Fonda long before she became an outspoken pacifist.

This movie, a cult favorite, won hammy, unshaven Lee Marvin an Oscar and contains the famous drunken-horse scene, among other memorable comic highlights, many of them involving Kaye's impish wit.

Cole unfortunately was a heavy smoker, and regrettably he succumbed to lung cancer four months before the film's release in 1965, leaving Kaye to mull his own uncertain future, for he too smoked incessantly, against his doctor's orders. In 1997, Kaye died at 106 International Boulevard in The Colony, also of lung cancer. He was 79.

■ ■ ■

MELODY-MAKING GENIUS **William "Bill" Marx**, the adopted son of comedian Harpo Marx, whose prodigious musical talent he somehow inherited through a strange osmosis, has been coming to the desert for as long as he can remember—nearly 50 years.

A Juilliard-trained pianist, composer, arranger, and conductor, Bill Marx demonstrated his rebellious humor when he wrote original music for the horror film spoofs *Count Yorga Vampire*, *Deathmaster*, *Terror House*, and *Scream Blacula Scream*. Nowadays he is often a performer at various snazzy venues around Rancho Mirage. He is also a trustee of the Marx estate. His mother was the actress Susan Fleming, who was married for 28 years to Harpo, the third Marx Brother. Harpo died in 1964; Fleming passed away in 2002 at the age of 94.

"Dad was a bachelor for 48 years, and when he married Mom it was the only marriage for both of them," said Marx, who lives at 7 Buckingham Way in Victoria Falls with his third wife, fashion model Barbara

Herzog, and their two Yorkshire terriers, Cappuccino and Maestro. Show business, it seems, runs in both families' veins. Barbara's father, Howard "Buck" Herzog, was entertainment columnist for the *Milwaukee Sentinel,* where he interviewed Katharine Hepburn and many other screen luminaries.

■ ■ ■

SHORT-HAIRED IMPRESSIONIST AND singer **Kaye Ballard**, who headlined in the Broadway shows *The Golden Apple, Carnival,* and *Molly,* but who is better known these days for keeping unofficial score of the best and worst independent films at the annual Palm Springs International Film Festival, is a 36-year resident of 41–475 Mashie Drive, in Desert Sun Ranch Estates.

Kaye shares her comfortable three-bedroom cottage with her female companion, Myvanwy Jenn; two Shih Tzus, Sally and Miss Emily; and a black Lhasa Apso named Miss Liliane (after popular stage actress Liliane Montevecchi). Kaye purchased the home from actor-producer Desi Arnaz, while he was directing Ballard and Eve Arden in the TV sitcom *The Mothers-in-Law.* Arnaz had been living there with his second wife, Edith Hirsch, whom he married in Las Vegas on his forty-sixth birthday. Like Lucille Ball, whom Arnaz divorced in 1960, Hirsch was a redhead, and like Lucy, she shared his passion for fishing and horses.

Coincidentally, Ballard's first movie, *The Girl Most Likely,* was the last film produced by RKO Radio Pictures before the studio was sold to Desilu Productions, which Desi and Lucy owned. Ballard became close friends with the pair, who were still married at the time. "Desi was a true romantic, who kept champagne and caviar in the icebox," Ballard has declared. As for Lucy, off-camera, said Ballard, she "was a very serious lady."

Many celebrity friends, including Hermoine Baddeley, Jack Cassidy, and Shelley Winters, have stayed at Kaye's home. Director John Schlesinger dubbed her "The Dolly Levi of the desert," because, like that match-making heroine, Ballard introduced him to his life partner, the photographer Michael Childers.

She also has a good sense of humor. One day Ballard was bicycle riding with Ball when a large barking dog appeared from a neighbor's yard and chased after them. "Get the fuck out of here!" yelled Lucy in her best baritone. The scared mutt turned and ran off with its tail between its legs. The two women laughed so hard, they nearly fell off their bicycles.

But behind Ballard's sense of frivolity was a serious performer who was determined to succeed in her chosen profession, even though she was not considered to be a classical beauty. Kaye got her start in show business as a comedy vocalist with Spike Jones and His City Slickers. Her impressions of Bette Davis, Judy Garland, and Martha Raye made her a popular nightclub attraction, and in 1954, on the verge of stardom, she was featured on the cover of *Life* magazine.

In her recent memoir, *How I Lost 10 Pounds in 53 Years*, Ballard confessed she had a brief affair with Marlon Brando when they were both young actors in New York. She refused, however, to have sex with Phil Silvers, who propositioned her during the run of his burlesque show *Top Banana*. Perhaps Silvers didn't have what it takes—or she wasn't interested in being his second banana.

In any case, Ballard's propensity for playing hot-tempered Italians, which she inherited from her parents, resulted in a two-year stint as Angie Palucci on *The Doris Day Show*. She also co-starred as Vivian Proclo in the 1976 film version of that campy bedroom farce, *The Ritz*.

In 1994 she was diagnosed with breast cancer and underwent a mastectomy. Always the trouper, Ballard has kept on working, most recently in the national tour of *The Full Monty*, the musical about a group of male friends who decide to put on a strip tease, and in a revival of *Nunsense*, in which she plays the mother superior.

Kaye was overjoyed when the street where she lives was renamed Kaye Ballard Lane in 2003. "This is a big, big thrill," she beamed, "and much better than having my own star on Hollywood Boulevard."

■ ■ ■

ACTRESS **ISABEL BIGLEY**, who portrayed Sister Sarah Brown, the prim-and-proper mission worker who loses her heart to gambler Sky Masterson in the original Broadway production of *Guys and Dolls*, lives at 34 Fincher Way in the Club at Morningside, where many retired actors, sports personalities, and influential businessmen own winter homes.

Bigley won a Tony Award as Best Featured Actress in a Musical for that performance. But it was a star-making event that almost didn't happen.

The show's composer, Frank Loesser, was so angered by Bigley's nervous giggling during rehearsals that he jumped onstage and slapped her in the face. The show went on, however, and so did the talented young actress. Although Bigley played the coveted role of Sarah Brown for 1,200 performances, opposite actor Robert Alda as Masterson, when it came time for the 1955 film, they both lost their parts to Jean Simmons and Marlon Brando.

These days, Bigley, who also starred in Rodgers and Hammerstein's *Me and Juliet,* can afford to smile over the loss. Her husband is Lawrence Barnett, formerly the president of Music Corporation of America, now MCA Universal.

■ ■ ■

EMMY AWARD–WINNING COMPOSER **Earle Hagen**, who wrote memorable themes for *The Dick Van Dyke Show, I Spy, That Girl,* and *The Mod Squad,* and scored a total of 3,000 television episodes, lives at 8 Johnar Boulevard. It was Hagen himself who whistled the opening and closing credits of *The Andy Griffith Show,* in which Andy Griffith and Ron Howard, then just a kid carrying a fishing pole, stroll along a river bank.

A former trombone player, Hagen is perhaps best known for his bluesy saxophone composition "Harlem Nocturne," which he wrote late one night, he said, on a portable pump organ and half a bottle of Cutty Sark. The bluesy jazz tune has been recorded more than 500 times and gained renewed popularity when a modernized version (played by Bud Shank) was recorded for the TV series *Mike Hammer,* which starred Stacy Keach as the gun-toting private eye.

But it is Hagen's ground-breaking, psychedelic score for *The Mod Squad,* played on an electric synthesizer, which occupies pride of place in this composer's canon. It ranks in the Top 10 TV themes of all time, close behind Lalo Schifrin's sizzling *Mission: Impossible* theme and Morton Stevens's brassy composition for *Hawaii Five-O.*

During a highly productive 10-year period at 20th Century-Fox, Hagen also orchestrated more than 40 feature films, including *When My Baby Smiles at Me, On the Riviera, With a Song in My Heart, Call Me Madam, Gentlemen Prefer Blondes, There's No Business Like Show Business, Daddy Long Legs,* and *Carousel.* And as if those credentials weren't enough, he is the author of three books, one of which is the widely read industry textbook, *Scoring for Films*.

■ ■ ■

AUSTRALIAN TENNIS CHAMPION **Rod Laver**, whose ferocious serves, swift volleys, and devastating sliced drives took the powerful, left-handed player to 47 professional titles in a 23-year career, once owned the home at 5 Eaton Court.

Laver made his fearsome reputation as the only tennis player to win the annual Grand Slam of tennis (the Australian Open, the French Open, the U.S. Open, and Wimbledon) not once but *twice,* first as an amateur in 1962, then as a professional in 1969. Acclaimed as one of the greatest tennis players of all time, his fast-paced topspin, which defeated many slower opponents, has influenced several generations of younger, more aggressive players, including Bjorn Borg.

Laver's success was hard-earned; he began playing tennis when the game only paid living expenses. But his accuracy and speed on the court quickly earned the red-haired farm boy the nickname "Rockhampton Rocket"— and a place on Australia's Davis Cup team. In 1960, he won the men's singles at the Australian championships, and in 1961 he took the men's singles title at Wimbledon, launching an impressive 10-year winning streak, which culminated in a total of 11 Grand Slam singles titles, a record that remained unbroken until Roy Emerson scored 12 and Pete Sampras claimed 14.

Laver participated in the Davis Cup competition again in 1973 and led Australia to another victory, finishing his Davis Cup career with a 16–4 win-loss record in singles matches and a 4–0 win-loss record in doubles matches. His combined victories, spread across three decades, placed him fifth among the top male tennis players in history, and he became the first player to set a record in lifetime prize money: $1,564,213. In 1981, Laver was inducted into the International Tennis Hall of Fame in Newport, Rhode Island. The Rod Laver Arena in the city of Melbourne, Australia, is named in his honor and hosts the Australian Open tennis tournament.

Laver's good fortune unfortunately turned bad when the 59-year-old athlete suffered a major stroke in 1998 while being interviewed by sports cable channel ESPN. Characteristically, tennis played an important role in his recovery, a great deal of which took place in Rancho Mirage, where Laver underwent extensive physical therapy. In 2002 his home was sold for $1.1 million.

■ ■ ■

AMERICAN CONCERT PIANIST **Virginia Morley** became a household name as one-half of Morley and Gearhart, the piano-playing team who were the darlings of 1940s high-brow audiences for their interpretations of both classical music and show tunes.

For more than a decade, the demure Morley and the handsome Gearhart made headlines crisscrossing the United States and Canada 26 times to play their concerts. Accompanied by two nine-foot Steinways that traveled in a custom-built van, they performed their contrapuntal piano harmonies to widespread critical acclaim and clamorous standing ovations, from Carnegie Hall to the Hollywood Bowl.

The musically gifted couple had met in Paris in 1937, when they were the students of classical piano teachers Robert Casadesus and Nadia Boulanger. Virginia replaced her maiden name, Clotfelter, with the more euphonious Morley, and in 1940 she became Livingston Gearhart's wife and business partner. At first the good-looking duo specialized in Gallic fare such as "Debussy En Blanc et Noir," but with their access to night-clubs and radio, Livingston used his expert training in composition from Boulanger, Stravinsky, and Milhaud to create innovative arrangements of Strauss waltzes, Chopin concertos, and Gershwin operettas. Morley and Gearhart's two-piano artistry, in which they demonstrated their intuitive understanding of great composers, predated the popularity of such latter-day teams as Ferrante and Teicher, who cornered the market in their successful recordings of Broadway and movie themes.

Inevitably, success turned their pretty heads, and Morley divorced Gearhart to marry bandleader Fred Waring, whom she had first met on NBC's weekly variety program, *The Chesterfield Hour*. They remained together for 30 years, until Waring's death in 1984. Five years later, she bought the home at 2 Camelot Court.

■ ■ ■

CASTING AGENTS ALWAYS tell actors not to get a haircut or a shave before auditioning for a prospective role, because that decision will be made by the producer or director. But that didn't stop Greek American actor **Telly Savalas**; he landed the coveted role of Pontius Pilate in *The Greatest Story Ever Told* by ignoring that piece of advice and shaving his head.

It's more likely he borrowed the suggestion from Yul Brynner, who had successfully shaved his own head for *The King and I*. Interestingly, neither actor was naturally bald. It was an affectation, like so many other things in Hollywood. Savalas with hair was a rarity. He did have a full mop as a private investigator in *Cape Fear,* but mostly he wore hats or just oiled his scalp, depending on his mood. Like Zorba, he lived for the moment. That was the secret of his success, or at least his happiness, and made Savalas, who resided at 8 Surrey Court, unique in Hollywood.

He was nominated for an Oscar for Best Supporting Actor after playing a death-row prisoner in his fourth film, *Birdman of Alcatraz.* The part had all the right ingredients for Telly's surly acting technique: underlying psychotic tendencies, a malicious sense of humor, explosive anger. Similarly he brought truth to *The Dirty Dozen,* as the vile rapist who drops hand grenades into a wine cellar full of people, and again as the criminal mastermind, Blofeld, who was bent on world domination in the James Bond adventure *On Her Majesty's Secret Service.*

An accomplished poker player, swimmer, and golfer, Savalas fit right in with the Palm Springs lifestyle and cut quite a swathe through the country clubs, where he mingled at tee times with other actors. His catchphrase "Who loves ya, baby?"—coined on the long-running CBS television series *Kojak*—stuck with him even when the Emmy Award–winning actor wasn't solving murders and kidnappings. And he sucked on the ubiquitous lollipop, another of his trademarks, because he was always trying to give up smoking.

He denied he was a tough guy, however, preferring to be known as a lover than a fighter. "The truth of the matter is that I cry a lot," he said. "I am the most romantic and sentimental man you have ever met." Married four times, with six children, he was catnip to the ladies, who followed him across the globe while he maintained an exotic lifestyle of yachts, champagne, and caftans. His reputed fear of flying did not stop him from making films in far-flung countries such as Germany, Australia, and Spain.

In 1994, Savalas died in his sleep of prostate cancer, one day after his seventy-second birthday. His funeral drew Karl Malden, Angie Dickinson, Ernest Borgnine, and Tony Curtis, among others. Two years later, the actor's home sold for $525,000; in 2004, at the top of the real estate boom, it fetched $813,000.

■ ■ ■

SONGWRITER **BILLY STEINBERG,** who collaborated with Tom Kelly to write some of the most successful pop songs of the 1980s, lived for seven years with his wife, Brigitte Lehnert, and his son, Maxwell, at 19 E. Torremolinos Drive in Rancho Las Palmas Country Club. It was here that Steinberg and Kelly compiled the title track of Pat Benatar's album *Precious Time.*

But their breakthrough hit was the provocative song "Like a Virgin," which turned punk singer Madonna into a sex symbol overnight. In 1985, her suggestive rendition, which she chanted while wearing push-up bras and lace bodices, spent six weeks at #1 in the United States and then became a worldwide hit.

Steinberg and Kelly's spate of hit singles continued with "True Colors," which was recorded by Cyndi Lauper; "So Emotional," performed by Whitney Houston; "Eternal Flame," sung by the Bangles; and "Alone," by Heart. The duo's other hit songs include "I Drove All Night," which was recorded by both Lauper and Roy Orbison; "I Touch Myself," sung by the Divinyls; Pat Benatar's "Sex as a Weapon"; and Tina Turner's "Look Me in the Heart." They also wrote several songs with Chrissie Hynde of The Pretenders, including the Top 10 single "I'll Stand by You."

Steinberg, who grew up in Palm Springs, is the son of prosperous Coachella Valley farmer and art collector Lionel Steinberg, who owned a 1,300-acre grape ranch in Thermal.

■ ■ ■

FOR TWO DECADES, **Sara Southern,** the widowed mother of Oscar-winning actress Elizabeth Taylor, resided at 37 Sunrise Drive, which her devoted daughter had purchased at Sunrise Country Club in 1975, following the death of Elizabeth's father, Francis Taylor. Surrounded by rose bushes, and with a view of the golf course and man-made lakes, the two-bedroom Sunrise Country Club condominium was a shrine dedicated to Taylor's cinematic achievements. Gilded wall units and ornate coffee tables were piled high with framed photographs and awards from Elizabeth's lifetime spent cavorting in front of the cameras.

Sara's hobbies included riding her oversized tricycle around the complex each morning and participating in a ladies' bridge group that numbered Jolie Gabor among its players. Frequently she went out for dinner and dancing with gay male escorts, whom she doted upon—as did her famous daughter. When not kicking up her heels, Southern presided over various club activities for senior citizens.

"Benevolently but persistently controlled by Sara from childhood through a protracted adolescence, Elizabeth had always acknowledged that her career was spearheaded by her mother's ambition, strategy and stratagems," wrote biographer Donald Spoto. Her mother's controlling influence, which Spoto said Taylor often resented, was typical of the love-hate relationship between overbearing stage mothers and precocious child stars. In fact, this may explain the star's overreliance on alcohol and painkillers, which contributed to her many health problems. Through the years, Elizabeth experienced no less than 73 serious illnesses, injuries, and accidents, including at least one suicide attempt that required hospitalization.

Southern lived to see every one of her daughter's career highs and personal lows, from Elizabeth's belated Oscar win for *Butterfield 8* and the tragic death of gay friends James Dean, Montgomery Clift, and Rock Hudson to her eight headline-grabbing marriages, all of which ended in disaster.

After a lifetime in her daughter's shadow, Southern, who had suffered declining health for two years, died in 1994 three weeks after celebrating her ninety-ninth birthday. Seven years later, her home was sold for $235,000.

■ ■ ■

SARA KARLOFF, THE mild-mannered daughter of hulking, gaunt-faced actor Boris Karloff, who reigned as the undisputed King of Horror in classic monster films such as *Frankenstein* and its sinister sequel, *Bride of Frankenstein*, currently resides at 34 Sierra Madre Way.

Boris Karloff became a father late in life; he was 52 when his second wife, Dorothy Stine, gave birth to their only daughter, Sara Jane, during production of *Son of Frankenstein*. It turned out to be the last time he would play the grimacing monster. Despite his menacing voice and penetrating stare, Karloff was the quintessential English gentleman. When not eliciting screams from the terrified victims whom he poisoned, strangled, or gleefully tortured in *The Mummy*, *The Black Cat*, *Tower of London*, and *Isle of the Dead*, he could be found sipping tea and tending his rose garden.

But his ability to instill fear served him well, for he made 170 films. "He was appreciative of his success, and grateful for being typecast because it kept him working and out of the bread line," recalled Sara Karloff. Although Karloff had a penchant for fearsome parts in films, he occasionally also relished both comedic and serious roles on the stage. These forays into theater included playing a bumbling murderer in the original Broadway production of *Arsenic and Old Lace,* and acting the much-feared pirate Captain Hook in the play *Peter Pan*.

Karloff even popped up (albeit in animated form) as the green-faced hermit in the TV special *How the Grinch Stole Christmas!* and he portrayed an eccentric scientist in the children's musical spoof *Mad Monster Party*. Unfortunately, Karloff suffered from emphysema and arthritis, and in later years he was confined to a wheelchair. He died in 1969 at the age of 81.

After his death, Karloff's likeness was often exploited without any financial remuneration to his estate. So in 1993, Sara formed Karloff Enterprises, to honor his memory and protect his reputation. Now, in addition to Karloff's movies, there are T-shirts, baseball caps, coffee mugs, calendars, wrist watches, and other licensed collectibles.

■ ■ ■

IRISH AMERICAN ACTOR **Dennis O'Keefe**, whose cheerful wisecracks enlivened scores of 1940s second features, including *Mr. District Attorney*, *The Affairs of Jimmy Valentine,* and *Brewster's Millions*, lived at 71–883 Vista Del Rio in the same club. He often said that he owed his screen career to fellow desert resident Clark Gable, who prevailed upon MGM to sign the unknown actor to a studio contract.

He was the unruly hero of the gritty crime melodramas *T-Men*, *Raw Deal*, and *Walk a Crooked Mile,* and the ambiguous title character of *The Leopard Man,* a nerve-wracking whodunit in the tradition of the original *Cat People,* an atmospheric thriller rarely shown today. Probably the film that best typified O'Keefe's hardboiled onscreen personality was *The Fighting Seabees,* a World War II propaganda piece about the Navy's Construction Battalion Unit that O'Keefe made with John Wayne and Susan Hayward.

A persistent smoker, he died of lung cancer at age 60 in 1968.

■ ■ ■

WHEN BROADWAY LEGEND **Carol Channing** purchased a condominium at 95 La Cerra Drive in 2000, the Tony Award–winning musical comedy star had no idea it would change her life. This, after all, was the woman with phosphorescent hair, saucer-shaped eyes, and a raspy voice whom some people have mistaken for a tall, skinny, drag queen. Nothing could be further from the truth. Miss Channing is anything but a drag.

First, she is that undisputed embodiment of matrimonial bliss, Miss Dolly Levi, the opinionated matchmaker Channing originated and played to perfection during 2,844 performances of the humming, toe-tapping, stage musical *Hello, Dolly!*

Second, she is the perfect example of youthful exuberance known as Lorelei Lee, whose signature, gold-digging tune, "Diamonds Are a Girl's Best Friend," Channing coyly delivered in the musical based on Anita Loos's captivating novel, *Gentlemen Prefer Blondes.*

Third, she is the recipient of an Oscar nomination for Best Supporting Actress for her giddy interpretation of the acrobatic Muzzy, whose favorite expression is "No raspberries!" in the campy film musical *Thoroughly Modern Millie.*

Time magazine has compared Channing's kinetic star power to an exploding nova.

However, Channing's adoring public didn't see the backstage drama that erupted between the unstoppable entertainer and her manager-husband, Charles Lowe. She sued Lowe for divorce, accusing him of squandering her fortune, abusing her mentally and physically, and having sex with her only twice in 42 years. Apparently she was unaware at the time they exchanged marriage vows that he was gay.

Two years after taking Lowe to court, Channing moved to the desert

(Lowe died of a stroke in 1999). In her new home, in between painting watercolors and driving to friends' homes in a golf cart, the star wrote her memoirs. Published in 2002, *Just Lucky I Guess* dropped another bombshell. The book revealed that Channing's father had been a light-skinned African-American—a secret the performer kept hidden to avoid discrimination. She also admitted that she harbored a lifelong crush on a high school classmate named Harry Kullijian, whom she hadn't seen in 50 years.

The good news is that Channing and the recently widowed Kullijian were reunited and finally married in 2003. Together at last, they now reside in a $260,000 home at 77 La Ronda Drive. One year after the wedding, the 83-year-old entertainer took the stage again and performed a rapping turn with LL Cool J at the 2004 Tony Awards.

■ ■ ■

MEDIATOR **JOSEPH WAPNER,** the stern-looking judge of TV's first real-life courtroom series, *The People's Court*, lives at 17 Haig Drive, which he purchased for $192,000 in 1997. The former Los Angeles County Superior Court judge, who tried thousands of civil cases, first donned his black judicial robes on the top-rated show in 1981, after serving 20 years on the California bench.

Today, there are ten court shows on the air, including *Judge Judy, Judge Joe Brown, Judge Mathis,* and *Judge Hatchett.* But *The People's Court* was the original and the best. When Wapner picked up his gavel and uttered those intimidating words, "You may be seated," plaintiffs and defendants alike sensed they were in a powerful presence and promptly broke out in cold sweats. Through it all, Wapner managed to keep his sense of humor—he had to in the face of some pretty lame cases involving unpaid loans, over-charging, and lovers' quarrels.

In 1997, Wapner came out of semiretirement to handle disputes between pets and their owners on *Animal Court.* It was an odd situation: well-behaved birds, cats, and dogs watching their angry masters growling and hissing at each other. No wonder the show lasted only one season.

Case dismissed!

■ ■ ■

IN 1956, BUG-EYED actor **Lester "Smiley" Burnette,** who played the stooge for Gene Autry, Sunset Carson, and Charles Starrett in more than 100 films, lived at 72–057 Clancy Lane—part of a ten-acre estate that was owned by Illinois rancher Leslie Clancy. This was one of several addresses Burnette used after leaving Hollywood to roam the country in a car and trailer.

A talented musician and songwriter, Burnette's friendship with Autry dated back to 1934, when they both drove out to Los Angeles from their respective homes in Illinois and Texas. The duo's first screen appearance was *In Old Santa Fe*, followed by such humdingers as *Back in the Saddle*, *Down Mexico Way*, *Heart of the Rio Grande*, and *Last of the Pony Riders*. Initially, Smiley was known by his cheerful screen character, Frog Millhouse; later he went by his real name.

"We rode a lot of trails together, on the screen and off, and most were happy," commented Autry. But behind the scenes there were frequent disagreements. Burnette never made the money Autry did, and this discrepancy reportedly caused a rift between them, although Autry always denied it.

When that new medium of television snuffed out the B-western, Smiley retired his scarecrow's hat and his white horse with the one black-ringed eye. To make ends meet, he charged fans one dollar for each signed photograph of his grinning face; he mailed them by the thousands.

According to Burnette's friends, he owned several mobile homes and trailers, and he would travel cross-country with his wife, Dallas Mac-Donnell, to make personal appearances. He died of leukemia in 1967 at the age of 55.

■ ■ ■

DIMINUTIVE **ALAN LADD** demonstrated his shooting and horse-riding skills in many classic westerns, notably *Shane*, *Drum Beat*, and *The Badlanders*. In 1960, he owned valuable property at 72–758 Clancy Lane, where he could be found polishing bridles and filing hooves for his stable of horses.

Ladd began his screen career playing Raven, the gloomy hit man in *This Gun for Hire*. He earned so much sympathy as the reluctant killer that he was offered heroic roles opposite some of Hollywood's prettiest leading ladies, including Loretta Young, Dorothy Lamour, and Shelley Winters. But with the exception of Veronica Lake, most actresses were so much taller than Ladd that he was forced to stand on a box and wear padded costumes to appear of equal height. That was one of many reasons that the introverted actor developed a severe drinking problem, which was not helped by his addictions to painkillers and the drugs prescribed to treat his depression. Ladd's life preserver was his wife and agent, Sue Carol, who negotiated his contracts and personal appearances.

Ironically, as Ladd's movie career spiraled down, his business investments skyrocketed. He owned one hundred acres in Palm Springs, which he planned to subdivide and use for building a TV station; he owned and operated a hardware store in Palm Springs; and he acquired an office building on Wilshire Boulevard. Through his company, Jaguar Productions, he invested heavily in films and television. He even struck oil on his ranch in Hidden Valley.

But Ladd would never live to see many of the dividends these investments paid. In 1964, he died from an alcohol and drug overdose at his Palm Springs home. He was 50 years old.

■ ■ ■

CONTROVERSIAL MAJOR LEAGUE baseball star **Darryl Strawberry**, once hailed as "the Black Joe DiMaggio"—an accolade he failed to deserve—put down $1.2 million on a home at 23 Clancy Lane South, where he moved with his wife, Charisse Simon, in 1994. The following year, Strawberry was suspended from professional baseball when he tested positive for cocaine. But all was forgiven when the muscular New York Yankees slugger, who had previously batted for the San Francisco Giants and the New York Mets, helped his team win the 1996 World Series.

The husky, six-foot-five outfielder seemed on his way to a brilliant career with the Yankees when he was diagnosed with colon cancer and subsequently developed a drug problem. He spent 28 days in the Betty Ford Center, where he was treated for cocaine and alcohol addiction. Then, in 1999, Strawberry was charged with possession of cocaine and soliciting an undercover policewoman who was posing as a prostitute. "How much you willing to spend?" she asked him. "Fifty dollars," he replied. The handsome sports star was read his legal rights and taken into police custody.

He was arrested again the following year on more drug charges and placed under house arrest. He was also charged with violating probation, driving under the influence of medication, and leaving the scene of a traffic accident. Shortly afterward, Strawberry announced his retirement from baseball.

■ ■ ■

BASEBALL HALL OF Famer **Don Drysdale**, who pitched for the Los Angeles Dodgers for 13 years, owned the five-bedroom home at 72–390 Morningstar in adjoining Mission Ranch.

In the 1960s, Drysdale was one of the game's most intimidating players. He and Sandy Koufax dominated the National Baseball League and set a season record for combined teammate strikeouts: 592. A fierce competitor, Drysdale wasn't afraid to hit a batter who crowded the plate. "I hate all hitters," he declared. "I start a game mad and stay that way until it's over." Living up to his promise, Drysdale won 25 games in 1962 and set a record with 58 consecutive scoreless innings in 1968. While pitching, he hit 154 men in the batter's box, a number that remains a National League record. Drysdale pitched his record-tying fifth shutout on the day of California's presidential primary and was congratulated by Robert F. Kennedy during the speech he gave just before he was assassinated.

After his retirement from baseball, Drysdale became a TV commentator with ABC Sports. In 1986, he married professional women's basketball player Ann Meyers, a Naismith Memorial Hall of Fame honoree. It was the first time that a husband and wife in professional sports were members of their respective halls of fame.

In 1993, Drysdale collapsed and died of a heart attack in a hotel room in Montreal, Canada, where he had been broadcasting a Dodgers game. He was 56. Ten years later, his home sold for $1.75 million.

■ ■ ■

POOR **TAMMY FAYE**—she just can't get a fair deal! This born again (and again and again) Christian survived the embezzlement scandal of her husband, the Reverend Jim Bakker, and his Praise-the-Lord ministry, and finally divorced him one year before he was released on parole, in 1994. The emotional stress caused by all this religious chicanery landed the teary-eyed Bible thumper in the Betty Ford Center to be treated for Ativan addiction. Then, claiming she had seen the light, Tammy married the ministry's building contractor Roe Messner, and they moved to 230 Lakeshore Drive in Lake Mirage.

But wonder of wonders, Messner suddenly found himself swept up in his own controversy when the holier-than-thou church carpenter received a prison sentence for federal bankruptcy fraud. Undeterred, Tammy vowed to stand by her man. She went into the celebrity-for-hire business, popping up on the TV sitcoms *Roseanne* and *The Drew Carey Show*, and co-hosting *The Jim J. and Tammy Faye Show*.

But her most bizarre career choice so far was to remove her makeup on VH1's reality TV series, *The Surreal Life*, so the world could see what she really looked like. Incredulous viewers were subjected to Tammy's midnight ranting in company with actor Erik Estrada, rap singer Vanilla Ice, and former porn star Ron Jeremy.

In 2004, Tammy was diagnosed with inoperable lung cancer, which in true tabloid tradition has been turned into yet another TV show. Now it's Messner's turn to stand by his woman. Amen!

■ ■ ■

STEVE MCQUEEN'S BUFFED, tattooed actor-son, **Chad McQueen**, who worked as a production assistant on his father's final two films, *Tom Horn* and *The Hunter*, owns the four-bedroom, California ranch-style house at 118 Calle De Los Rosas. He paid $545,500 for the newly built home in 2002.

Chad McQueen's connection with the desert is a long one: his famous dad and his mom, Broadway dancer Neile Adams, both lived in Palm Springs when he was a boy (his older sister, Terry, died in 1998 following an unsuccessful liver transplant). Adams, whom Chad's rambunctious father divorced after falling in love with Ali MacGraw during the making of *The Getaway*, now resides with her second husband, Alvin Toffel, a few miles away in Palm Desert.

Steve McQueen was a star, but his look-alike son has enjoyed a less than perfect film career, in spite of his best efforts to project the family's genetic coolness in the mostly straight-to-video exploitation films *Night-*

force, Martial Law, Firepower, Death Ring, and *Red Line.* Both McQueens trained in martial arts under Professional World Middleweight Karate Champion-turned-actor Chuck Norris. But like his much-lamented dad, who drove cars at breakneck speeds in memorable films such as *Bullitt* and *Le Mans,* the younger McQueen has a wild side that he has tried to tame on the racetrack.

In 2005, two years after he announced his decision to quit acting, McQueen took to the California Speedway in Fontana, driving a customized Ford Mustang to prove he had what it takes to be the world's next racing car champion, despite busting up his left leg in an earlier motocross event. His racing car prowess remains to be seen.

■ ■ ■

SINGER **ROBERTA LINN**, whose beauty and vivacious personality made her a favorite of concert audiences as the fifth smiling "champagne lady" with the Lawrence Welk Orchestra, owns a three-bedroom home at 72–472 Doheney Way in Wilshire Palms.

Linn was the first smiling hostess to be seen giggling with Welk when his long-running TV variety program, *The Lawrence Welk Show,* premiered at the Aragon Ballroom in Santa Monica and later when it aired from the studios of KTLA in Los Angeles.

In addition to her TV chores with Welk's bubbling dance orchestra, Linn had a small part in MGM's music-filled *Get Yourself a College Girl,* which starred Chad Everett, Nancy Sinatra, and a former Miss America, Mary Ann Mobley.

■ ■ ■

ON FEBRUARY 28, 1961, President John F. Kennedy's autocratic father, **Joseph P. Kennedy, Sr.**, the formidable Boston wheeler-dealer and former ambassador to Great Britain, was a houseguest of Marion Davies and her husband, Captain Horace Brown, in Rancho Mirage. He arrived at Palm Springs Airport in President Kennedy's private plane, a twin engine Convair 240 aircraft christened "The Caroline." He disembarked, and a limousine trailed by a police motorcycle escort whisked him to the Davies-Brown ranch at 1 Von Dehn Road for a two-week vacation.

Davies was a close friend of the Martin Von Dehns, whose vast real estate holdings included property in Bel Air and Palm Springs. Their son Hyatt Von Dehn, who was married for six years to singer Ginny Simms, founded the Hyatt Corporation, one of the largest hotel chains on the West Coast. Coincidentally, Von Dehn, who became a crony of Horace Brown, had once been Marion's suitor, and their mutual friends included Thunderbird Country Club neighbors Buddy Rogers and Mary Pickford. Once, during a drunken party at Pickfair, Brown tripped on the driveway while demonstrating a new gun. There was a loud "ping," and a bullet ricocheted off Mary's scalp.

The Kennedy clan had been encouraged by its aging patriarch to look upon Marion "as kin," said biographer Fred Lawrence Guiles. It was well known in social circles that "'Big Joe,' as she called him, genuinely admired her as a human being and the feeling was reciprocated," he said. Kennedy was not known for his generosity, so for him to look upon Davies with such affection showed the true measure of their friendship. It was almost as though she was part of the family.

Davies and Brown had attended the wedding of Kennedy's second daughter, Eunice, to Robert Sargent Shriver, Jr. (Their daughter, TV anchorwoman Maria Shriver, is married to Governor Arnold Schwarzenegger.) And they had also attended the wedding of John F. Kennedy to Jacqueline Bouvier in Newport. So Joe Kennedy's visit to see Davies was prompted by a strong desire to spend time with his friend. At President Kennedy's inauguration the previous month, Joe, like so many others, saw that Davies's plump features were shrunken from repeated cobalt treatments; he knew she was slowly dying of cancer. Indeed, by that spring of 1961, she was hospitalized, and by summer's end she was gone.

Several months later, Joseph Kennedy suffered a devastating stroke that left him paralyzed. He died in 1969, having seen three of his four sons—Joseph, Jr., John, and Robert—precede him.

■ ■ ■

SPIRO AGNEW, THE former governor of Maryland who became the nation's thirty-ninth vice president, but was forced to resign from office over a tax-evasion scandal, lived for more than ten years at 78 Columbia Drive, in the Springs Club—a much-favored address for retired politicians and actors.

Agnew was a controversial and much-lampooned public figure, known for his colorful phraseology. He criticized the media, calling them "negative nabobs of negativism," and denounced opponents of the Vietnam War as "an effete corps of impudent snobs." One phrase he apparently overlooked was the expression "People in glass houses shouldn't throw stones."

When the Republicans came to Palm Springs one month after winning the 1968 election, Agnew stayed at the Riviera Hotel, site of a celebratory dinner for 1,000 supporters. But even then he was disliked. "Agnew, deliberately excluded, was the butt of several jokes," explained political observer Christopher Ogden, "including smirks at the recollection of his opening remarks to the governors' conference when he expressed pleasure at being in 'Palm Beach.'"

Walter Annenberg, who threw a party for President Nixon, former New York governor Nelson Rockefeller, and Congressman Gerald R. Ford, had serious doubts about Agnew's qualifications. "I thought he was the bottom of the barrel; a nobody," said Annenberg, the former ambassador to Great Britain. "I was really shocked when he was picked because I had heard that he was a foul ball, a two-dollar thief."

Agnew resigned in 1973, charged with evading federal income taxes and accepting kickbacks from contractors. He fled to Baltimore and pled no contest in U.S. District Court, which allowed him to stay out of prison for bribery and extortion. But he could not avoid being disbarred by the Maryland court of appeals in 1974 or paying $268,482 to cover his kickbacks, plus interest. Incredibly, Agnew is the only Maryland governor without a portrait in the Maryland Governor's Reception Room.

As far as his relationship with Nixon was concerned, Agnew said he was railroaded out of office by the president who, beset by the Watergate scandal, "naively believed that by throwing me to the wolves, he had appeased his enemies." Agnew never spoke to Nixon again and reportedly laughed with glee when his boss resigned over Watergate. He attended Nixon's funeral.

In a scathing article on Nixon's administration titled "He Was a Crook," the late counter-culture writer Hunter Thompson called the disgraced vice president "a flat out, knee-crawling thug with the morals of a weasel on speed." But in Palm Springs, Agnew was treated more kindly, if not forgiven for his derisive remarks, partly because he and Gerald R. Ford, who succeeded him in office and then, as president, pardoned Nixon, were friendly neighbors. Both politicians were frequently seen together on the cocktail party circuit.

Agnew divided his time between the Springs, where he played in celebrity golf tournaments, and a summer home in Ocean City, Maryland, from where he brokered deals for an international clientele. He died of leukemia at the age of 77 in 1996.

■ ■ ■

CHUBBY CHARACTER ACTOR **David Huddleston**, who resides at 27 Colgate Drive in the Springs Club, has played smiling "good ol' boys" in more than 70 films, where his wide grin conveyed a mixture of both mirth and menace. Huddleston's characters often carried a gun but rarely used it, preferring to talk their way out of trouble when confronted by John Wayne in *Rio Lobo*, Dean Martin in *Something Big*, and James Stewart in *Fool's Parade*.

In Mel Brooks's raunchy spoof, *Blazing Saddles*, Huddleston showed his comic timing as befuddled mayor Olson Johnson, whose town is over-run with whores and bandits. He also played connivers in *Billy Two Hats*, *The Klansman*, and *Breakheart Pass*. In late middle age, Huddleston's impressive girth landed him the starring role in *Santa Claus the Movie*, where he drove a sleigh towed by reindeer and delivered toys that were made in his factory by elves.

More recently, he was seen as Grandpa Arnold in the TV series *The Wonder Years* and played the recurring role of Senator Max Lobell in *The West Wing*. In 1998, Huddleston achieved cult movie status as the corpulent millionaire who is the object of Jeff Bridges's clumsy search in *The Big Lebowksi*.

■ ■ ■

IT SOUNDS LIKE a movie-of-the-week on Lifetime Television: a troubled young woman marries a dirty old man for his money and then kills him. But this was fact, not fiction. The woman's name was **Andrea Claire**; the man was Robert Sand, a wealthy lumberman with an $800-a-week prostitution habit. They met when the 69-year-old millionaire, whose wife was suing him for divorce, had dialed an escort agency and requested a call girl for the evening.

The woman who rang Sand's doorbell was Claire, a perky model and part-time actress, age 39, who turned tricks in order to pay the rent. Under the name Samantha Scott, she had appeared in a half-dozen soft-core adult films that featured topless nudity and simulated sex, notably *The Head Lady*, *Brand of Shame*, *The Daisy Chain,* and *Wild Gypsies*. She also had a small role in Russ Meyer's X-rated camp classic, *Beyond the Valley of the Dolls*.

When Sand answered the door, Claire was wearing a low-cut blouse and skimpy underwear. She was surprised, because he was wearing thick glasses and sitting in a wheelchair. He told her he had multiple sclerosis and did not think he had long to live.

Little did he know how prophetic that statement was!

Sand was overcome with lust and a few months later asked Claire to marry him. After their wedding, Sand bought them a new three-bedroom condominium at 6 Brandeis Court, where Andrea took care of his every need. Although confined to a wheelchair, Sand was always horny and demanded sex two or three times a day; he enjoyed role-playing, spankings, and golden showers. He also had a big pornography collection and liked taking nude photographs. His favorite picture was of Andrea in a wet T-shirt, nipples protruding. He had the photograph blown up and placed above the toilet in his bathroom, so that when he defecated, he could look up and see her.

Their marriage quickly evolved into a series of rape fantasies, during which Sand would draw the blinds and instruct Andrea to simulate fellatio or anal intercourse with imaginary sex partners, while he masturbated. Whenever they went out in public, he would get aroused and tell her to take off her top or wiggle her ass to try and get the attention of another man. When they got home, he would tell her to bend over and play with herself until he ejaculated.

Whatever the sex lives of the club's other residents, the Sands were engaged in some decidedly odd behavior, and their sadomasochistic lifestyle took a dangerous turn, until the line between reality and fantasy became totally blurred. He forbade Andrea to leave the house, warning her that she would be raped if she went outside. Whether this was part of their kinky sex games or was genuinely meant to intimidate her is unclear, but it pushed her over the edge.

Shortly before dawn on May 14, 1981, two security guards at the Springs, "The most exclusive and expensive residential resort in the Palm Springs area," according to Aram Saroyan, responded to an alarm at Sand's address. The front door was ajar, and they found Andrea Claire standing in a bathrobe. She told the guards about an intruder, so they searched the home, and there, lying on the floor of the master bedroom, was the naked body of Bob Sand. He had been stabbed more than 25 times. The guards radioed for an ambulance and called the police.

The grisly crime was too shocking to comprehend. Blood was splattered all over the walls, a piece of skin was missing from Sand's ear, there was a small hole in his head and cut marks across his back. The killing looked like the work of a madman. Claire told the police she had heard her husband scream and had run to help him. But he was too badly injured to survive the attack, so she comforted him as he lay dying. Then she attempted to wash away some of the blood and, when her mind went into shock, she went back to bed.

Her story made no sense to police or horrified neighbors, many of whom were young women married to elderly husbands. "The joke at the Springs, where there were so many of these May-December alliances, was that the average age was fifty," commented Saroyan. "The men were seventy, and the women thirty."

But no one was laughing now.

Police searched for evidence and found a bent kitchen knife pushed under the living room sofa. It had apparently been hidden there by the killer before he fled the scene. Claire was not the least bit concerned that she might be under suspicion; she said she loved her husband and was upset the murderer had escaped. But nobody was buying her story.

While the investigation continued, Claire made an appointment for grief counseling with the chief psychiatrist at Eisenhower Medical Center. The therapist had interviewed many women whose rich older husbands had died, their demise hastened, he suspected, for their fortunes. He recommended that Claire hire a criminal attorney—a good one.

"But I didn't kill Bob," she protested.

Two months later, while police were preparing their case, the first of several bizarre calls requesting assistance at the Sand residence came into the Indio Sheriff's Department. Officers arrived to find Andrea Claire lying naked on the kitchen floor, her hands and feet tied with ropes, and the wooden handle of a knife protruding from her rectum. From then on, Claire called the police on a regular basis, usually claiming that her home had been burglarized and that she had been raped. She also reported that she was receiving threatening letters from the killer.

The ploys did not work. Investigators determined that she had written and mailed the notes in an attempt to exonerate herself. Police suspected Claire was the real culprit and put her under constant surveillance. Ten months after Sand's death, she was charged with first-degree murder. By this time, a new man had entered her life: Joe Mims, a lonely, 56-year-old widower whom Claire had met at a gathering of the Evangelical Free Church. They were married in 1982.

On a star-filled Halloween night, they made passionate love on a picnic blanket by the side of Highway 74. Then, after Mims reached orgasm, Andrea hit him over the head with a hammer, telling the frightened man, "I've got to knock you out so that people will believe I've been raped." Fearing for his life, Mims realized almost too late that his wife was a dangerous sociopath; he decided to end their marriage, though he later admitted that he still loved her. (He subsequently died of a heart attack.)

Claire's bail was revoked, and she was remanded to jail to await trial.

There were serious doubts about Claire's sanity, and while she was under medical observation at Riverside General Hospital, Claire twice tried to commit suicide by cutting her wrists. But were these attempts just another ploy? A court-ordered psychiatric evaluation found Claire competent to stand trial, and she went before judge and jury in 1984.

The prosecution argued that by killing Sand she stood to receive $150,000 in death benefits and $100,000 from the sale of their home. Claire pleaded insanity, claiming she had been driven crazy by the men in her life. Her first husband, she testified, had raped and beaten her; her fourth husband, Sand, had attacked her. When he came at her in the middle of the night, threatening to cut her with a knife, Claire had no choice but to defend herself, she declared. When he fell on the floor, she picked up the knife and tried to fight off his advances. Then she blacked out. By the time she came to her senses, he was dead.

After listening to three months of testimony, a compassionate jury of ten women and two men found Andrea Claire guilty of murdering her disabled husband and sentenced her to 25 years to life in state prison. Unable to control her emotions any longer, Claire finally told prosecutors what they had been waiting nearly three years to find out: the reason she did it. "I killed him because he called me a whore!" she yelled. "Why didn't you give me the death penalty?"

Despite numerous appeals to reduce her sentence, Andrea Claire has repeatedly been denied parole.

■ ■ ■

If Rancho Mirage has an unequaled reputation as a political playground, then its status as a sports haven, where players can rest on their laurels, is not far behind. One of those brilliant achievers is baseball legend **Willie Mays, Jr.**, who resides at 140 Yale Drive.

A former college football and basketball player, Mays joined the New York Giants in 1951, when black players were still a rarity in the major leagues. He played centerfield for almost his entire 22-year career, astonishing fans and fellow players with his amazing fielding skills. Joe DiMaggio, in fact, once said that Mays had the greatest throwing arm in baseball.

But he is better known as a hitter. Dubbed the "Say Hey Kid," Mays is among the few players to have hit more than 50 home runs in each of two or more seasons. He finished his career with 660 home runs, the fourth highest total on record. As if that wasn't enough, he won 12 consecutive Gold Glove Awards for his outfield defense and was also an excellent base stealer, swiping 339 bags.

Mays's baseball career was bolstered by Giants manager Leo Durocher, who never stopped singing his praises even when the team was in a slump. Mays returned the favor. After army service in the Korean War, he helped to carry the Giants to victory in the 1954 World Series, hitting four home runs against the Cleveland Indians. After the Giants moved to San Francisco in 1958, Mays continued to bring baseball crowds to their feet with his brilliant batting and timely home runs.

Although the Giants lost the 1962 World Series, Mays remained the team's star player, hitting his way into history. Ten years later, he joined the New York Mets, and in 1973, after playing his final season, he became a coach. Six years after that, Mays was inducted into the National Baseball Hall of Fame.

The strength and endurance that enabled Mays to perform his athletic feats have often been attributed to his abstemious lifestyle; he neither drank liquor nor smoked cigarettes, virtues that undoubtedly have also contributed to his longevity.

■ ■ ■

JUST BECAUSE YOU'RE dead in Hollywood doesn't mean you are no longer an industry player. Take the case of **Leo Jaffe**, a highly respected film executive who worked at Columbia Pictures from 1930 until his retirement in 1981. Along the way he was the studio's president from 1969 to 1973, and later was chairman emeritus.

Indeed, Jaffe oversaw Columbia's miraculous comeback from near-bankruptcy in the mid-1970s to renewed movie-making dominance, despite the embarrassing check-forging scandal caused by Jaffe's successor, David Begelman, who committed suicide in 1995.

Among the hugely successful films produced by the studio during Jaffe's tenure were *Easy Rider, The Last Picture Show, Shampoo, Taxi Driver, Close Encounters of the Third Kind, Kramer vs. Kramer,* and *Tootsie.* A philanthropist as well as a filmmaker, he was a recipient of the Jean Hersholt Humanitarian Award for his outstanding contributions to charitable causes. Jaffe resided at 154 Yale Drive until he died of natural causes at the age of 88 in 1997.

The strange thing was that, for three years following his death his name was listed as chairman of the American Cinema Awards Foundation, a tax-exempt, not-for-profit organization run by event coordinator and music producer David Gest, who became Liza Minnelli's fourth husband in 2002.

The couple's kooky wedding should have sounded warning bells. The best man was Michael Jackson, and the bridesmaid was Elizabeth Taylor; the official wedding photo resembled a group portrait of *The Addams*

Family. Sixteen months later, Gest and Minnelli separated, and in October 2003 he accused her of abusing him during their marriage and sued her for $10 million.

Gest may have had good intentions in keeping the memory of Leo Jaffe alive; the American Cinema Awards annual gala bestows glowing tributes on worthy peers. But Gest's tactics raised a few eyebrows. Indeed, what the deceased Jaffe had no way of knowing was that his name was being used as bait to entice hefty financial contributions from the soft-hearted showbiz community.

The kicker? Three years of ACA tax returns, all signed by Gest, listed Jaffe, whom he surely knew to be dead, as the Foundation's chairman. IRS returns for a two-year period showed that Gest's private firm was paid almost $400,000 in production fees—more than Jaffe, when he was alive, earned each year as president of Columbia Pictures.

According to a Fox News report in 2003 headlined LIZA'S HUBBY RETIRES DEAD MAN AT CHARITY, "Gest paid himself handsomely from the tax-free income of the group, which served as a sop to old Hollywood stars."

Jaffe need not worry; the jig is up. May he rest in peace.

■ ■ ■

SCOTS ACTOR **PATRICK Macnee** is living proof that fame is a double-edged sword. His self-effacing autobiographies, *Blind in One Ear* and *The Avengers and Me,* in which he trundled out skeletons from the family closet, read more like two volumes of psychoanalysis. Unsparingly honest, they confirm he is every bit as daft as the foppish British secret agent John Steed whom he portrayed on TV's *The Avengers*—and just as likeable.

Written during Macnee's self-imposed, three-decades-long exile in the desert, the books reveal his father's gambling addiction, his mother's latent lesbianism, and his own struggle with alcoholism caused by years of personal frustration and professional displeasure. But these candid admissions do nothing to detract from his extraordinary career, which began on the London stage, covered the early days of Canadian television, and took him to Hollywood.

Although it's been almost 30 years since Macnee last played the umbrella-bopping Steed, he is so identified with that bowler-hatted, bou-tonniered character, that even an actor as polished as Ralph Fiennes, who starred in the 1998 big-screen remake, was unable to improve upon Mac-nee's performance.

That should be sweet music to the one good ear of this Scotsman, who recently celebrated his eighty-fourth birthday. "At my age," he confessed, "the fact that I can talk at all is wonderful."

In 2000, Macnee and his third wife, Klara Sekely, gave up their home at 3 Furman Court and moved to a bigger one at 7 Mount Holyoke, so they could have more room to entertain Macnee's daughter, Jennifer, of Rancho Mirage, and his son, Rupert, who lives in Thermal.

■ ■ ■

TALL, SARDONIC **FRANK Marth** is one of a handful of surviving actors who left their mark on TV's gleeful Golden Age. A full-time resident of 4 McGill Drive, Marth played a variety of self-important characters on the classic TV series *The Honeymooners.* He was often seen portraying fumbling crooks and pompous businessmen, whose actions were cut down to size by exasperated star Jackie Gleason's snide remarks, leaving audiences shrieking with laughter.

Marth's talent for inviting mockery was ideally suited to playing the leather-wearing German officers constantly outsmarted by Bob Crane in *Hogan's Heroes.* But not until the age of 66 was he finally accorded star billing, as Major General Worth in the short-lived TV series *The Dirty Dozen,* one of his best dramatic roles.

His wife is blond actress **Hope Holiday**, who brought her slightly nasal voice to big-hearted floozies in two Billy Wilder films: *The Apart-ment,* in which she appeared in the famous bar scene with Jack Lemmon and Shirley MacLaine; and *Irma La Douce,* in which she played the Parisian streetwalker Lolita. In the 1980s, Holiday was linked romanti-cally to scowling actor Cameron Mitchell, who lived for a time in Palm Springs. She co-starred with Mitchell in *Texas Lightning, Raw Force,* and *Killpoint,* which she also produced. Mitchell continued working until his death from lung cancer in 1994, at the age of 75. Holiday and Marth are still together.

■ ■ ■

PAUL NEWMAN SLEPT here! That's right, the blue-eyed superstar, who was nominated eight times for an Academy Award as Best Actor but didn't win the gold trophy until *The Color of Money*, stays at the home of his older brother, **Arthur Newman, Jr.,** at 36 Duke Drive, during the actor's periodic visits to the desert. The highly competitive sons of wealthy retailer Arthur Newman, Sr., who owned the Newman-Stern sporting goods store in Cleveland, Ohio, Paul and Arthur Newman, Jr., initially had an uneasy relationship. The younger brother's desire for fame and fortune left the more responsible brother to run the family business after their father died in 1950.

The Newman boys went their separate ways: one followed his dream, and the other followed his duty. "Arthur, Jr., was better at sports, bigger, taller, seemingly everything Paul wanted to be in his father's eyes," according to biographer Lawrence J. Quirk. But the two strong-minded siblings finally worked out their differences, and Arthur became his younger brother's Hollywood production manager. Among his producing credits are the films *Winning, The Life and Times of Judge Roy Bean, The Drowning Pool,* and *Slap Shot.* Arthur also was the associate producer on Paul's directorial debut, *Rachel, Rachel,* which starred the actor's second wife, Joanne Woodward. The movie received Oscar nominations for best actress, supporting actress (Estelle Parsons), screenplay (Stewart Stern), and picture.

In 1978, Paul's only son, Scott Newman, the first of six children from his two marriages, took a fatal overdose of Quaaludes and cocaine. A self-acknowledged six-pack-a-day man, Newman, who had battled booze for most of his adult life, was so devastated by the loss that he went on a long Jack Daniel's bender. Friends, including Arthur and his wife, Patricia Murphy, a retired fashion industry executive who moved to the desert 24 years ago, reached out to save him. The family's support helped pull Paul back from the abyss that had engulfed his own son.

Today the Newman brothers are closer than ever. Newman's Own, the popular line of all-natural food products that includes salad dressings, steak sauce, salsa, popcorn, and lemonade, brings in around $7 million a year, and every penny goes to charity. In 1995, Arthur Newman became a Rancho Mirage council member, a post he held for more than five years, voting on issues that are as important to the desert as screenplays are to Hollywood.

■ ■ ■

IN 1990, SIX years after her best friend and neighbor, Janet Gaynor, died of injuries sustained in a horrific car accident, **Mary Martin** died of cancer at the age of 76. Martin had been one of the brightest lights of Broadway. She won five Tony Awards for her captivating performances in *Annie Get Your Gun, South Pacific, Peter Pan, The Sound of Music,* and *I Do! I Do!*

With her large ears and long nose, Martin was no classic beauty, but she had that ephemeral star quality that transcends all else. Her charisma was apparent as early as Cole Porter's *Leave It to Me* in 1938, when Martin, costumed in a cut-off lynx coat, performed a three-minute striptease to the song "My Heart Belongs to Daddy"—an attention-getting turn that she reprised in the film *Night and Day.*

After that racy show-stopper, Martin could do no wrong and rarely did for the next 40 years. She spent her happy retirement painting and reminiscing with friends at 82 Princeton Way, where she received regular visits from Larry Hagman, her actor-son from Martin's marriage to Ben Hagman, and from Heller, her daughter by her second husband, Richard Halliday, who had died in 1973. So in 1990, Martin's demise at Eisenhower Medical Center, drawn-out though it was, caught many people by surprise. Apparently nobody knew she was at death's door. A consummate actress, she had hidden her illness and her fears behind the sunglasses that covered the ever-darkening circles beneath her eyes.

The event was even more startling because, since 1986, Martin and Carol Channing had co-starred on the stage in a musical vehicle called *Legends.* "With Larry's direction, Mary and I played *Legends!* for over a year," recalled Carol Channing. "I never knew she had cancer. She never missed a performance." But in 1989, Martin's back pain became so severe it was clear there would be no more encores.

"When I walked into her hospital room a prominent television pastor was sitting on her bed, holding her hand and praying for her," recalled Hagman, who was in the 12th season of his role as vicious J.R. Ewing in the top-rated prime-time soap *Dallas.* "I made sure Mother didn't remember his church at all."

She quietly passed away the next day.

Punch-drunk from anxiety and lack of sleep, Hagman arranged to have his mother's body cremated but forgot the name of the mortuary, so he started calling up funeral directors out of the phone book to locate her missing ashes. Finally, he reached Palm Springs's oldest funeral home, Wiefels & Sons, and the ashes were delivered to the set of *Dallas*. The next day, Hagman and his family carried the urn on a charter flight to his mother's hometown of Weatherford, Texas. Among the mementos they placed in Martin's grave were assorted family photographs and a portrait of actress Linda Gray, whom she had adored, and a bottle of Kahlua, her favorite drink.

"It was a fitting memorial to a life well-lived," Hagman said.

Five years later, Martin's 63-year-old son was confronted with his own doom when acute alcoholism required him to undergo a liver transplant. To everyone's astonishment, including his own, J.R.'s hard-drinking alter ego made a miraculous recovery.

■ ■ ■

MAJOR GENERAL **THOMAS Turnage** was appointed by President Ronald Reagan to be the thirteenth head of the Veterans Administration, where he participated in congressional hearings about mismanagement of VA hospitals and became a target of Vietnam protesters over the devastating effects of Agent Orange. He resided at 72 Dartmouth Drive until his death at 77 in 2000.

A veteran of World War II and the Korean War, Turnage received two Combat Infantry Badges, the Distinguished Service Medal, the Defense Superior Service Medal, the Legion of Merit with Oak Leaf Cluster, a Bronze Star, a Meritorious Service Medal, and other service medals reflecting four tours of duty. He was even inducted into the French Legion of Honor. Turnage used his combat skills to reassert law and order in the Watts neighborhood of Los Angeles after the 1965 riots. He later became deputy commanding general of the California Army National Guard.

His wife of 55 years was petite, rosy-cheeked actress **Jane Adams**, who attained cult status for her convincing performances of frightened heroines in the classic horror films *House of Dracula* and *The Brute Man*. She now resides in Del Webb's Sun City, in Palm Desert.

■ ■ ■

AN INNOCUOUS NEWSPAPER story in *The Desert Sun* on November 21, 1998, touched off a heated round of name-calling and brought bitter memories for the woman who had been President Ronald Reagan's first wife. The occasion was the dedication of the Palm Desert branch office of the American Alzheimer's Association; the person officiating was the woman's daughter, Maureen Reagan. An overzealous reporter, rushing to meet her deadline for the next edition, wrote what she believed to be fact: ACTRESS JANE WYMAN DIED FROM ALZHEIMER'S DISEASE.

It certainly got people's attention. When the reporter's paper hit the streets the next morning, telephones from Palm Springs to Los Angeles and New York started ringing off the hook. The tabloids quickly dispatched reporters and photographers to get an exclusive of the pending funeral of the president's first wife. "Will it be a closed casket?" someone asked. "Cremation or burial?" inquired another.

The only problem: it wasn't true. "Wait," everybody was told. "It's all been a terrible mistake."

The paper, left with a bad case of egg on its face, printed a long-winded apology. But the damage had been done. Wyman's death was no longer considered breaking news; it had been scratched, like a horse from the fifth race.

And no one was angrier than **Jane Wyman** herself. Sitting on a sofa in the living room of her three-bedroom home at 56 Kavenish Drive, in Rancho Mirage Country Club, Wyman couldn't help but stare at the newspaper that lay tossed on the floor and react like a hissing steam kettle.

"How dare they!" she seethed, reminding anyone who might have been present that the 84-year-old actress had lost none of the vitriolic spark which characterized her portrayal of Angela Channing, the domineering matriarch who ruled over a Napa Valley wine-making family in the TV series *Falcon Crest*. The portrayal of that crafty virago won Wyman her fourth Golden Globe Award. Not that she needed to prove anything; her acting abilities were beyond reproach, even if her eight-year marriage to Reagan, which had ended in divorce, was not.

Five decades earlier, Wyman had won the Oscar as Best Actress for her astonishing performance as the terrified deaf-mute and rape victim who is rescued by a kindly doctor in *Johnny Belinda*. She was also nominated for her performances in *The Yearling, The Blue Veil,* and *Magnificent Obsession*. Along the way, Wyman had made the difficult transition from a brassy, wisecracking blonde to a stylish, brown-haired vixen who could wrap men around her little finger, both on the screen and off.

Wyman and Reagan had officially met in 1938 on the set of *Brother Rat*, in which they acted cute and flirted like teenagers between scenes. What was not publicized at the time was the little-known fact that Wyman had already been married and divorced *twice*—and one of those times included a short-lived marriage to a salesman when she was 16.

The Reagan-Wyman wedding in 1940 was talked up in the fan magazines as if it was virtually an act of God. But that was totally understandable; after all, the news of their pending union had been leaked by Hollywood gossip columnist Louella Parsons, at whose home their wedding took place. The newlyweds honeymooned in Palm Springs where, to Reagan's complete surprise, he learned that his bride couldn't swim, an area in which Reagan excelled but Wyman showed little interest. The differences multiplied from there. Whenever they disagreed on a subject, or Jane didn't get her own way, she reportedly joked, "Don't annoy me. Remember my ulcer." Reagan, for his part, always seemed unimpressed by his wife's success. His typical reply was "That's swell, Janie." Then he would return to his favorite subject: politics.

The state of the Reagan-Wyman marriage was always a topic of discussion. People speculated on the reasons for their mutual attraction or lack thereof and often remarked that the pair seemed to have little in common. They kept the cracks in their marriage well hidden. Maureen, who was born in 1941, became the most photographed child in Hollywood. They adopted a son, Michael, who had been born in 1945. But all of it was small consolation for a marriage that was headed for the rocks.

In 1947, Wyman gave birth to their third child. The baby was four months premature and died soon after it was delivered. The distraught husband and wife, their nerves already stretched to the breaking point, blamed each other. There was nothing left but to go their separate ways.

Reagan was often portrayed as the villain during their breakup. He supposedly insisted on showing his favorite film, *Kings Row,* over and over to dinner guests, until Wyman, who was no more interested in his career than he was in hers, eventually snapped. Fifty years later, former first lady Nancy Reagan offered her own explanation of the underlying problem in an interview with Reagan's biographer, Edmund Morris, which was published in *Newsweek*. "Ronnie was much too young, he was just playing around," she told Morris.

Then why did they get married in the first place? "She said she would kill herself if he didn't marry her," said Nancy Reagan. "So she sent him a suicide note and swallowed a whole lot of sleeping pills, and got herself taken to the hospital." Reagan gallantly rushed to her side and said, "Of course I'll marry you!" Sadly, it was for all the wrong reasons.

Two years after excusing herself from the final season of *Falcon Crest*, because of ill-health, Wyman was cast as Jane Seymour's mother in *Doctor Quinn, Medicine Woman*. Costumed in western-style bonnets and dresses, Wyman mustered all the courage of her shrinking bones to play what she intuitively knew would be her final acting role. She then signed off with only a faint whisper of publicity and retired to Rancho Mirage, where the former "good time gal" embarked on a post-Hollywood career as spokesperson for the Arthritis Foundation.

In 1998, Wyman was invited to attend the 70th Academy Awards. Her answer was a polite but firm "No!" The following year, the brittle actress moved to a new home at 205 Kavenish Drive in the same country club. She later sold the home for $514,000.

In 2002, one year after the death of her daughter, Maureen Reagan, from skin cancer, Wyman moved again, this time to a house at 14 Kavenish Drive that she bought for $435,000. It seemed Wyman was trying to escape the ghosts of her past. Or, as a fellow club resident opined, "She's playing the real estate market and profiting very nicely from it."

Members Only

IN NATIVE AMERICAN culture, the Thunderbird is a huge, winged creature that stirs up wind and creates thunder as it glides through the sky. Indian tribes cowered in deference whenever they saw the bird flying overhead, and they were careful not to anger this terrifying aerial beast and incur its wrath. How ironic, then, that the modern conquerors of the Coachella Valley adopted this fearsome totemic symbol as the mascot for their new settlement, which they named Thunderbird and located on the site of the future city of Rancho Mirage.

The original landowner, Raymond Cree, who purchased 663 acres from the Southern Pacific Railroad in 1927, may have realized his grievous error; he divested himself of the land, perhaps to regain godly favor. But Frank Bogert and his group of backers had little time to ponder the sanctity of their actions. In 1945, they bought Cree out for $34,000 and started clearing the land. They hired British architect Gordon Kaufmann, who had created enduring California landmarks such as the *Los Angeles*

Times building, Santa Anita Park, and Scripps College in Pomona, to design a ranch-style clubhouse and adjoining cottages. And when the rounded gateposts were sunk, and a large sign was fastened above the main entrance, there was no mistaking the name: Thunderbird Ranch.

So authentic looking were Kaufmann's Western-themed creations that, in 1948, Warner Bros. rented the newly opened dude ranch for location filming of *Two Guys from Texas*. Dennis Morgan, Jack Carson, and Dorothy Malone starred in the Technicolor musical comedy, which featured an animated dream sequence with Bugs Bunny. But two years later, Thunderbird's owners, having dumped tons of money into the costly venture without seeing a profit, sold the ranch to leading amateur golfer Johnny Dawson, who transformed it into the valley's first 18-hole golf course.

In 1951, the old sign came down, and a new one was erected with the more enticing name of Thunderbird Country Club. Real estate agent Tony Burke began offering homes for sale around its grassy fairways, instituting a tradition that continues to this day. It wasn't long before Hollywood luminaries jumped on the band wagon and the houses found plenty of takers.

Perhaps the wrath of the mythical aerial beast had finally been appeased. In 1954, the Thunderbird sports car, Ford's answer to General Motors's Corvette, was named in honor of Thunderbird Country Club. Ernest Breech, chairman of the board of Ford Motor Corporation, and Los Angeles Ford dealer Holmes Tuttle—both of them club members— sought permission to use its distinctive name.

Fifty years after the first Thunderbird rolled off the assembly line, however, the car that had been immortalized in song by the Beach Boys ceased production. Ironically, the decision was made at the same time that William Clay Ford, Sr., the only surviving grandson of the company's founder, Henry Ford, announced his retirement.

■ ■ ■

"WET SHE'S A star. Dry she ain't," kidded Fanny Brice about **Esther Williams**, whose apparent natural ability to swim upstream, dive from a great height into water-filled tanks, and smile underwater without oxygen were tests of physical endurance that few performers could accomplish—with the possible exception of Flipper. Williams and her second husband, Ben Gage, were among the first Hollywood couples to join the club, where they bought a home at 70–863 Fairway Drive.

The one-time Olympic hopeful, whose dreams of winning a gold medal for swimming were shattered by World War II, when the games were temporarily canceled, was offered a consolation prize as a featured water ballet performer in Billy Rose's Aquacade. Her success led to an MGM contract, and Williams, whose aquatic talents matched her voluptuous figure, was given the star buildup in the crowd-pleasing films *Bathing Beauty*, *Neptune's Daughter,* and *Dangerous When Wet*. During her 19-year film career, this buxom performer would eventually swim her way through 26 features and cover a distance of 1,250 miles.

It wasn't all fun, however. Williams's health was frequently jeopardized by being submerged for hours in both the salty ocean and chlorinated pools. She suffered skin and eye infections and ruptured her eardrums. While filming *On an Island with You* on location in Biscayne, Florida, Williams fell into a four-foot-deep pit covered in palm fronds. She sprained her ankle and had to finish the movie on crutches. A short time later, while shooting a scene for *Pagan Love Song* in Hawaii, she narrowly escaped serious injury when a freak wave tossed her from an outrigger canoe onto a sharp coral reef.

What eased the pain were the men she met. Muscular diving instructors and handsome Latin lotharios came to her rescue both in and out of the water, to massage her sore thighs. That's probably the reason the waterlogged star always had a big smile on her face. Palm Springs was a place where she could relax—or so she thought.

Williams's love of swimming propelled her to move here, but Gage's love of drinking was her undoing. As she struggled to regain her career after the trend for splashy Technicolor musicals waned, Williams found she was pulling her drunken husband out of bars, sobering him up, and working twice as hard to replace the money he gambled and lost in Las Vegas. It made her wish that someone would throw her out of a plane over the Pacific Ocean so she could swim away from her troubles.

It seemed Williams was always being tested by drunks: Busby Berkeley, who directed her in *Million Dollar Mermaid*, would sit naked in his bathtub drinking martinis while he fantasized about increasingly bizarre ways to show Williams jumping, leaping, and diving into the water. As a result of one such stunt, where she performed a 50-foot swan dive from a cascading fountain, she almost broke her neck. She spent six months in a body cast. By the time of *Easy to Love*, which Berkeley also chore-ographed, Williams had wised up. She agreed to water-ski in the nine-minute-long speedboat finale at Florida's Cypress Gardens, but she refused to be hoisted into the air by a helicopter and dropped from a tra-peze 80 feet into the sea. Instead, Williams's friend, platform diving champion Helen Crienkovich, performed the risky stunt in one take that used multiple cameras.

But dealing with Ben Gage, her constantly inebriated husband, was another story. A giant of a man, he stood six-feet six-inches tall and was big everywhere. After a few cocktails he'd get an uncontrollable erection. "He was extraordinarily hung and down would come his trunks and there it would be," blushed Williams. After they were divorced in 1959, Gage bought a marble quarry in Yucca Valley, and Williams started tak-ing LSD on the recommendation of Cary Grant. It was hardly a replace-ment for sex, but she got plenty of that anyway from her third husband, Fernando Lamas, who never wore underwear and was always hard. "Fer-nando had a way of thrusting his hips forward that made it very obvious what was in those pants, which was very substantial," she said.

Williams's life took a turn for the worse when she discovered that Gage had gambled away nearly all of her money. Hit with a $750,000 tax bill from the IRS, she was relegated to performing in carnival shows and sell-ing manufactured swimming pools to pay off her debt. It took her decades to become solvent again, but Williams refused to give up or slow down. In 1985, she married her fourth husband, actor Edward Bell. In 1993, she underwent knee surgery and had to use a walker, a temporary setback that didn't dampen her spirits or her sex drive.

En route to her 80th birthday, she fractured her ankle and was hospi-talized for a month. Still, she threw a birthday party and greeted guests from her wheelchair. Former MGM debutantes Margaret O'Brien, Glo-ria de Haven, and Betty Garrett, who knew her for the trouper she has always been, helped Williams blow out the candles on her cake. Amid the cheers and laughter you could hear the sounds of her grandchildren splashing in the pool.

■ ■ ■

IF SILENCE IS golden, as has often been proclaimed, then it had twice as much allure with the matrimonial partnership of **Mary Pickford** and **Charles "Buddy" Rogers**, two smiling, dimpled, porcelain-like movie stars of Hollywood's great silent era. Truly, their lives seemed to resemble a fairytale.

Pickford then was what Britney Spears is today: a phenomenon of youth, beauty, and sex appeal that aroused both male and female passions. With her bright eyes, delicately shaped mouth, and fluffy blond hair, which she often wore in sausage curls, she was a vision of childlike, unsullied innocence. Her immense popularity playing the weeping heroine in hundreds of silent melodramas, from *Tess of the Storm Country* to *Rebecca of Sunnybrook Farm* and *Pollyanna*, earned her the title "America's Sweetheart" and made her a multimillionaire.

But Pickford's off-screen life as the embattled wife of grinning, posturing swashbuckler Douglas Fairbanks, with whom she co-starred in a 1929 film version of Shakespeare's rambunctious comedy *The Taming of the Shrew*, told a different story. So it was little wonder that she flipped over a cheerful young man in knickerbockers who auditioned for the role of a cocky rich-kid in her last silent film, *My Best Girl*, in which she played a salesclerk at a five-and-dime. Pickford couldn't take her eyes off him. "The handsomest man I'd ever seen," she cooed. "He had blue hair," she said, referring to his jet-black waves.

Charles "Buddy" Rogers was handsome and more. He was a trombone-playing, raccoon-coat-wearing campus star with his own traveling musical band. They spent the entire production in a blur, holding hands and acting cute. When the film wrapped, Rogers reported to the set of *Wings*, in which he was playing a World War I army pilot vying for the affections of Clara Bow (when he wasn't engaged in deadly air-to-air combat). But his heart was with Pickford. Although the actress was eleven years older than Rogers, the age difference didn't bother either of them. They were head over heels in love and would remain devoted to each other throughout Mary's three-year separation from Fairbanks and her divorce, which became final in 1936.

Ten years after they met, Pickford and "America's Boyfriend," as Rogers was nicknamed by the press, were married in a simple garden ceremony. The wedding was followed by a lavish reception for 300 guests at Pickfair, the fabulous Beverly Hills mansion Pickford had once shared with Fairbanks.

Nearly everyone was overjoyed, but there were a few unsmiling faces. Some women were jealous of Mary's happiness; others suggested that Buddy was just after her money. In some circles, the marriage was viewed as Mary's revenge against the male chauvinistic Fairbanks, who had blatantly cheated on his wife. "If so, be it," she uttered. Pickford made no secret of her love for Rogers, who had promised to love and protect her in return.

In the coming years, his steadfast vow would be put to the test.

The first hint of trouble was the liquor bottles. Buddy noticed they were stashed everywhere. He wasn't much of a drinker himself, but he knew Mary liked to take a nip or two, sometimes three or four, each day. He assumed it was for medicinal purposes; he had no idea of its extent. "The little dickens," he used to chortle. "She gets to drinking and she just can't stop." Rogers was reminded that Mary's first husband, actor Owen Moore, and her brother, Jack Pickford, were heavy drinkers and had died of alcoholism.

In those days, the disease was understood less than it is now, and Rogers grew puzzled. He knew he was no great shakes as an actor, but he liked to meet people and play his music. Pickford seemed not to care. And when he looked at her perplexed, she would whisper, "You don't have to work." Then she would wink at him. He could only wonder why his wife had become so inactive, hiding from the public, sleeping until noon, and watching her old movies after dinner.

Their lives began to resemble *Sunset Boulevard*, the ominous story of a demented movie star who takes a younger lover while planning a non-existent comeback. Indeed, the grotesque story had originally been conceived as a vehicle for Pickford. The film's writer-director, Billy Wilder, had hoped the actress would consent to play batty Norma Desmond, who is so paranoid that she spies on callers through closed drapes. But Pickford was revolted by the morbid script and turned it down.

Now she was living Norma Desmond for real. The gold-plated Oscar that Mary had won for *Coquette*, her first talking picture and the one in which she had cut off her famous curls—as though to signify her belated

adulthood—gleamed in the wood-paneled study of Pickfair, next to photographs and other memorabilia from her silent-screen days. It was disquieting to see her, in middle-age, wandering around the house that was
once the scene of so many grand parties with Fairbanks, Charlie Chaplin, and other Hollywood luminaries. Visitors were shocked to find her
standing there, petticoats showing and whiskey on her breath.

When she'd had one too many, she would ramble on like a little boat
drifting downstream and then reach out her hands and cry "Douglas!"—
though he had died way back in 1939. Rogers often heard her little-girl
voice echoing in the hallways long after the servants had gone to bed.
The situation scared Rogers so much that he decided to get out of the
house. He'd always enjoyed a game of golf, so he bought a new set of
clubs and joined Thunderbird in 1956. His cottage was located at 40–990
Paxton Drive off the second fairway.

One weekend he managed to convince Mary to join him there. She
powdered her face, put on a pair of sunglasses, and they drove in her
chauffeured town car from Pickfair to Rancho Mirage. But no sooner
had they arrived than the telephone rang with an urgent message: Their
adopted son, Ronnie, had tried to kill himself by taking a drug overdose.
So they turned around and sped back to St. John's Hospital in Santa Monica, where the sedated boy lay in bed, weak from having his stomach
pumped. Rogers was sympathetic; Pickford was not. "This is terrible," she
blurted to the attending doctor. "I was resting in Palm Springs. It was a
rest I needed." Then she put on her hat and gloves and left. The doctor
was amazed by her callousness.

For the next 15 years, the woman once voted America's most popular
box office star, stayed at home—reading the Bible and drinking whiskey.
At night, she often roamed the house like a sleepwalker, which must have
unnerved Buddy to no end. She saw few people except her stepson, Douglas Fairbanks, Jr., whom she grudgingly put up in the guesthouse, and
silent-screen cohorts such as Lillian Gish and Colleen Moore. For other
potential visitors, she had a list of excuses, which Rogers, with the finesse
of a butler, had to deliver by phone or in apologetic letters. He didn't dare
tell them the truth: Mary, the chatelaine of Pickfair, was drunk in bed.

The last time anyone outside of the immediate household saw her alive was in a segment on the 1975 Academy Awards telecast, when she was presented with an honorary Oscar in recognition of her unique contributions to the film industry. The award was given to her at home, where she was photographed sitting down, swathed in pink chiffon, and made up like a china doll.

By the time she passed away, at the age of 85 in 1979, she was wearing wigs to conceal her baldness and was unable to walk because the muscles in her legs had atrophied. When she died, the first thing Rogers did was to clean away the used whiskey glasses before the press arrived.

For all the pain and suffering she caused him, Mary was good to Buddy in the end. She left him a yearly income of $48,000, valuable stocks, and real estate. She granted him a piece of land adjoining her famous moated castle, where Fairbanks had once rowed their boat, and where they had once held archery contests on the lawn. In addition, Rogers received a gift of $1 million from the probate court, intended to offset any future financial responsibilities entailed in the building of a new home, which he planned to furnish with items from Pickfair. The vine-encrusted chateau, with its leadlight windows and alabaster statues, would be sold in accordance with Mary's wishes, and the proceeds would go to the Mary Pickford Foundation.

In 1980, Jerry Buss, who owned the L.A. Lakers basketball team, paid more than $5 million for the Pickfair estate. The contents were sold at auction, where buyers haggled over items of furniture, clothing, and jewelry, including one of Mary's prized possessions, a Chinese, red- and gold-lacquered bed used for smoking opium. Eight years later, the house went back on the market. The new buyer was Meshulam Riklis, a junk bonds trader married to the actress Pia Zadora. They loved the house so much, the first thing they did was order it razed by a bulldozer until there was nothing left but a cloud of thick dust. In its place rose an extravagant marble monument.

Buddy Rogers couldn't bear to watch the painful denouement. He and his much younger bride, Beverly Ricono, whom he had married in 1981, bid Pickfair a sad farewell. They headed back to the desert, where she and Buddy embarked on the second phase of his charmed life as part-time residents of the Club at Morningside. He died in 1999 at the age of 94.

■ ■ ■

THERE WERE *TWO* **Ginger Rogers**: the gum-chewing, wise-cracking, peroxide-blonde chorus girl decked out in a sheath of gold coins in *Gold Diggers of 1933;* and the sophisticated, ladylike ballroom dancer courted by Fred Astaire in ten art deco film musicals. Neither character, however, was the real thing. They were both "put-ons," as Rogers might have said—a combination of her charming, tomboyish Midwestern self and her cultivated, worldly persona, which she emphasized with a well-placed hand on her hip and marbles-in-the-mouth.

It was Rogers's lifelong dream to be an actress, a dream she shared with her unrelenting stage mother, Lela Rogers, who pushed the freckle-faced little girl out in front of vaudeville audiences just as Mama Rose does with her offspring in *Gypsy*. But Ginger Rogers had much higher expectations than being one-half of a song-and-dance act or, heaven forbid, a stripper. "One day," she told her doting mother, "I'm going to be a very big star!"

Rogers eventually got the chance when she was put under contract by RKO Radio Pictures, which groomed the talented hoofer for major roles in *Stage Door, Vivacious Lady,* and *Fifth Avenue Girl.* But the high-point of her stardom occurred when she and Astaire, between whom there was intense rivalry, performed classic dance numbers such as "The Carioca," "The Continental," and "The Piccolino" in the most representative of their films together: *Flying Down to Rio, The Gay Divorcee,* and *Top Hat.* Their dancing prompted Katharine Hepburn to utter the now-famous remark: "Fred gave Ginger class and Ginger gave Fred sex."

Her profitable pairing with Astaire aside, she quickly shot to the front ranks of box office popularity with her no-nonsense portrayals of self-reliant young women, whose careers came before husbands or boyfriends. She was cute in *Bachelor Mother* opposite David Niven, sentimental in *Tom Dick and Harry* alongside George Murphy, Alan Marshal, and Burgess Meredith, and elusive in *Once Upon a Honeymoon* with Cary Grant.

Known for her conservative views, Rogers didn't smoke, didn't drink, and didn't have sex—or so the jokes went about this devoted Christian Scientist, who refused to take an aspirin or drink caffeine but had an unquenchable thirst for malted milkshakes. Her five marriages—to one-time dancing partner Jack Pepper, actor and conscientious objector Lew

Ayres, U.S. marine Jack Briggs, lawyer-turned-actor Jacques Bergerac, and director-producer William Marshall—were all dismal failures, casualties of her never-ending career obsession.

"I never depended on someone else to support me—the government, welfare, husbands, or relatives," Rogers declared. "Furthermore, I did not serve or drink alcohol, and I never felt this was a hindrance to my career in any way." A dedicated thespian, she demonstrated her propensity for melodrama in *Roxie Hart, The Major and the Minor, Lady in the Dark, Magnificent Doll,* and *Weekend at the Waldorf* (made on a rare excursion to MGM).

By 1945, after spending 15 years toiling in front of the movie cameras, and with more than 50 films to her credit, she was proclaimed Hollywood's highest paid movie star, and she seemed determined to hang on to that accolade at almost any cost.

The mantle of her home at 40–230 Club View Drive, where she retired in 1984, was the prideful place for the Oscar that Rogers had won 44 years earlier, for playing the plucky heroine in *Kitty Foyle.* Some of her co-stars claimed that the award gave Rogers a swelled head. But the gold statuette often gathered dust while its unflagging owner toured in *Hello, Dolly!* and *Mame,* or presented her one-woman show, in which, at the age of 65, she still looked stunning in a shiny top hat, black leotard, and sheer stockings. When she wasn't working, Rogers enjoyed playing tennis, swimming, and doing leg exercises each day to stay in shape. She was proud that, unlike many of her peers, both male and female, she never had a facelift.

She also purchased a small house where Lela, an avowed patriot and a founding member of the Motion Picture Alliance for the Preservation of American Ideals, lived until 1977, when she died at the age of 86. A few years after her mother's death, Ginger sold the house to President Gerald R. Ford, who used it to accommodate his Secret Service.

Rogers would probably have never retired permanently to Palm Springs—she was much too fond of her ranch in Eagle Point, Oregon. But health considerations prompted the move, and when she finally got herself settled, out came the scrapbooks, the photographs, and the awards. Relishing the task of putting things and people in their proper places, she wrote her candid autobiography, *Ginger: My Story,* while living here. Of course, as critics were apt to point out, it was *her* story. "I've made thousands of mistakes," she acknowledged, "but they've all been stepping-stones toward a better concept of life."

Unlike many other stars, she was not overly nostalgic about the past. She remained what she had always been: headstrong and defiant and apparently unwilling to accept the blame for much that had gone wrong in her marital life. At least she knew that time was not always going to be on her side. "There is still much I would like to do," she confessed. "For starters, I would like to pursue directing musicals. That has become a new dimension in my life. Painting in oils and sketching portraits in charcoal has been part of my repertoire for a long time. I would like to continue this."

She was mobile enough to attend the Kennedy Center Honors in Washington, to receive an award given for a lifetime of contribution to the arts—a moment of tremendous pride. In 1993, she also attended the local dedication of Ginger Rogers Road, previously 35th Avenue.

But eventually she became infirm and sedentary. Soon, she no longer had the stamina to get out on her own but had to be assisted by a female nurse. Because of her adherence to Christian Science, however, she refused medical treatment that might have prolonged her life and relied instead on a religious practitioner. In her final years, her closest male companion was Skipper, a miniature white poodle.

One of her last public appearances was at the wedding of neighbor Gary Morton to Susie McCallister, when they were married in an outdoor ceremony at the Lodge (formerly the Ritz-Carlton) in 1994. "At this time," said Peter Marshall, who was a guest, "Ginger had been very ill and was in a wheelchair."

At the time of her death in 1995, at the age of 83, Rogers had not been in a doctor's care, so the district attorney ordered an autopsy. The delay in issuing a death certificate prompted media speculation about the cause of death, but an investigation ruled out foul play. It did turn out, however, that she might not have been as wealthy as everyone supposed. Many of Rogers's costumes, wigs, and handbags eventually turned up for sale in a Palm Springs consignment store called Celebrity Seconds.

There were racks of her sequined dresses and feather boas, along with dancing shoes, wide-brimmed hats, and imitation jewels that Rogers might have preferred to see donated to a museum or performing arts charity. One disapproving shopper, looking over the goods for sale, remarked, "This would never have happened to Fred Astaire."

■ ■ ■

SHE WAS AMERICA'S favorite redhead, even though she actually was a blonde. But fans of the celebrated TV sitcom *I Love Lucy* prefer to remember **Lucille Ball** as a dark carrot-top, from the tip of her coiffed head to her bright red lipstick and painted fingernails.

Her hair color made for some not-so-amusing headlines when the feisty comedienne admitted she had registered with the Communist Party in 1936 but never officially joined. Her remarks set off a firestorm of media criticism about her politics. The allegations that she was a Communist threatened to destroy Lucy's top-rated weekly show, then in its third season in 1953, and prompted her husband and co-star, **Desi Arnaz**, who had escaped a political revolution in Cuba, to defend his wife and issue a strong denial.

Then, in a storybook twist not accorded many less-fortunate actors, all was forgiven. The accusations became retractions. The *Los Angeles Times* announced:

LUCILLE BALL NOT RED

Desi thought it was funny; Lucy didn't.

The couple's sense of humor, which endeared them to 60 million viewers, is what kept them laughing through good times and bad, from the days when Desi was a struggling musician and Lucy was a striving dancer, through their burgeoning movie fame in *Too Many Girls*, to their hard-won success as TV's most lovable husband and wife, Ricky and Lucy Ricardo.

Their fictional personas very much resembled their real selves, which were boisterous, sentimental, passionate, and stubborn. They frequently argued but just as frequently kissed and made up. Still, by 1954, the year of their 14th wedding anniversary, when *I Love Lucy* was the #1 program in the nation, fault lines were appearing in their marriage. So to help themselves relax, they decided to buy a weekend home where they could spend time away from the hustle and bustle of Beverly Hills, where they lived with their two small children, Desi, Jr., and Lucie.

Always looking for a bargain, Desi acquired land on the ninth fairway at Thunderbird. It's been claimed he won it in a poker game with Phil Harris and Buddy Rogers, and if true, it must have seemed like a very good deal. "There we built a low, one-story contemporary beige stone house with six bedrooms and six baths, a swimming pool, gardens, and tropical plantings both indoors and out," remembered Ball. The address was 40–241 Club View Drive, next door to the house that Ginger Rogers would one day occupy.

Only after the Arnaz family moved to the newly opened club, did they discover that Thunderbird was restricted. Apparently, nobody had bothered to read the sign FOR THOSE WHO QUALIFY AS MEMBERS, which stood in a clump of Aloe vera bushes. Only whites could join the club; no Jews, blacks, or Mexicans allowed. Desi, in spite of his celebrity status, could not play golf there. Today that sort of discrimination would hardly be tolerated, but in those days people didn't know any better—or they feigned ignorance.

That Arnaz was Cuban was both a help and a hindrance. Women liked him—no doubt about that—and men enjoyed his company. But his spicy Latin temper and extramarital dalliances got him into a lot of trouble.

When *Confidential* magazine, which was the scourge of Hollywood because of its lurid exposés, broke the story of a sordid "three-way" between Arnaz, a woman not his wife, and another man, Lucy hit the roof. And then she hit Desi. According to the publication, Arnaz had taken a prostitute to the Beverly Hills Hotel and shared her with an unnamed male relative, because—the article quoted him as saying—a man "should have as many girls as he has hair on his head."

Keeping her temper in check must have been extremely difficult for Lucy in the face of her husband's adulterous ways. She acknowledged his peccadilloes and tried to forgive him, but in the end his behavior brought only misery to their lives. "The Arnazes had fights, some of them physical ones in which Desi was hit with a hammer and bopped with a bottle, and all of them bitter," stated biographer Stefan Kanfer. Script supervisor Maury Thompson recounted Lucy taking careful aim with her foot and kicking Arnaz between the legs.

Their final showdown occurred at Desilu Productions in the former RKO studios. Once they had worked there; now they owned it lock, stock, and barrel. (That had been the ultimate revenge, Ball once said; "We bought the company.") That was all about to go up in smoke. In their last fight, Lucy called Desi every name in the book and then she pulled a gun on him. Arnaz stood there as Ball pointed the gun at his face and squeezed the trigger. It was an ornamental dueling pistol that was used as a prop on the show. A small flame ignited at the tip of the barrel, and Desi lit his cigarette with it.

But for once, Lucy wasn't joking.

Their divorce split everything down the middle. *Time* magazine made light of the situation, listing who got what: "For Lucy, their two children, half of their $20 million Desilu interests, the leaky mansion, two station wagons, a cemetery plot at Forest Lawn. For Desi: the other half of the $20 million, a golf cart, a membership in a Palm Springs Country Club, a truck, and several horses." Lucy kept the Thunderbird house, which had been designed by the esteemed African-American architect Paul R. Williams. Eventually she lived there with her second husband, stand-up comedian Gary Morton, who was 13 years younger than she.

Maybe because it was her second time around, she didn't try so hard to make an impression. As a result, there was hardly a cross word spoken between them, and they showered each other with gifts. Lucy bought Gary a Stutz Bearcat; he bought her a Chrysler LeBaron convertible out-fitted with wood-paneling and bucket seats, and she drove it to the super-market wearing dark glasses and a headscarf.

The club was still restricted, however, so Morton, who was Jewish, had to play golf at Tamarisk. Lucy never did take up the game, insisting she was no good at it. Gary enjoyed the sunshine and sociability, especially after 18 holes, when he would head to the clubhouse for a round of drinks.

Lucy's life was better without Desi. Even so, she found it hard to get him out of her mind completely, so they kept in touch. The two former rivals became platonic friends and often dined together. Lucy even approved of her ex-husband's new wife, Edith Hirsch, who was also a red-head. "She's a sweet woman and good for Desi," Ball said.

Desi preferred to take things easy in his semiretirement, but Lucy was happiest when working. Well into her fifties she could still make people howl with laughter. Her cavorting on *The Lucy Show* with expert farceurs Vivian Vance and Gale Gordon, and on *Here's Lucy*, where she co-starred with her grown-up kids, contained enough jokes to fill several sitcoms.

There was one major upset, however, and it almost derailed her big-screen comeback in *Mame*. She was skiing in Snowmass, Colorado, when another skier collided with her on the slopes, breaking Lucy's right leg in four places. After a 16-month postponement, the cameras finally rolled on Lucy as sequined, Charleston-dancing Mame Dennis. But the 62-year-old actress had aged so dramatically since the accident that she looked like a mummified version of her former self. When Ball's longtime makeup man, who used a Spackle-like liquid adhesive to conceal her heavy wrinkles, accidentally hurt her, Lucy slapped him, and he walked off the set. She should have walked too; the film was a dud.

By now, Lucy wasn't going to parties anymore. When longtime neighbors Bob Hope and Frank Sinatra sent her invitations to celebrate New Year's Eve at their respective houses, she turned them down, exclaiming, "What a bore!" She preferred to stay home, play backgammon with a handful of friends, and count down the minutes to midnight—a glass of bourbon and a carton of Pall Malls by her side.

Maybe it was the booze. Perhaps she was lonely or missing Desi. In any case, in 1988 she suffered a stroke that left her with a slight speech impediment and a crooked bottom lip. But she kept drinking—and sneaking a cigarette here and there. Her final public appearance was at the 1989 Academy Awards, in which she strolled onstage with Hope to a one-minute standing ovation. She looked remarkably firm and trim, and her dancer's legs were in perfect synchronicity.

Two months later, Lucy was admitted to Cedars-Sinai Medical Center, where she died from a ruptured abdominal aorta following open heart surgery. She was 77.

Gary Morton, who remarried after Lucy's death, survived her by ten years. He succumbed to lung cancer in 1999 at the age of 73.

As for Desi, his wild ways finally caught up with him. In 1986, he died of cancer, the result of smoking too many Cuban cigars. He was 69.

■ ■ ■

AN OBJECTIVE OF the rush to own a much-coveted address at this prestigious club was the home of **Earle Jorgensen** at 40–253 Club View
Drive, where the wily steel magnate, who wielded tremendous political
power, lived in moneyed affluence in 1955. Architect William F. Cody,
whose specialty was creating contemporary living spaces for the wealthy,
had designed Jorgensen's domestic showplace.

From the roaring 1920s to the corporate 1990s, Jorgensen made his
fortune selling steel to California's expanding oil, aircraft, and construction industries. He was that highly prized American commodity, a self-
made man who controlled every facet of his business empire. The son of
a Danish sea captain, he took advantage of the Southern California oil
boom, combing shipyards for scraps of steel and aluminum to sell to oil
drillers at below the cost of newly milled steel. The business grew from
a single rented desk into the Earle M. Jorgensen Company and eventually became one of the country's largest independently owned steel and
aluminum distributors, with sales of more than $1 billion a year.

Jorgensen and his second wife, Marion, were among the social elite of
Los Angeles. The couple was close friends with Ronald and Nancy
Reagan; they dined at each other's homes and took vacations together.
Indeed, Jorgensen, who had urged Reagan to run for governor and then
for the presidency, was a trusted political advisor of the former movie star
and a member of an informal but influential group that was dubbed Reagan's Kitchen Cabinet. This coterie included multimillionaire oil financier Henry Salvatori; Justin Dart, the head of Rexall Drugs (his wife,
actress Jane Bryan, had co-starred with Reagan in the *Brother Rat* comedies); Los Angeles automobile dealer Holmes Tuttle; and A.C. Rubel of
Union Oil, who, along with Herbert Hoover, Jr., and publisher Norman
Chandler, secretly controlled business and political administration in
Los Angeles.

On the night of each of his major elections, Reagan ate dinner at Jorgensen's home and watched the returns come in, and when he became
governor, Reagan appointed Jorgensen to the State College Board of
Trustees. When Reagan celebrated his seventieth and seventy-fifth birth-
days, in 1981 and 1986, the cost of his triumphant parties at the White
House was paid not by taxpayer dollars but by Jorgensen and other key

supporters, who chipped in each time to buy Ronnie a special gift and .his customary birthday cake.

After Reagan completed his second presidential term, a group of 20 influential friends, including Jorgenson, helped to raise $2.5 million to buy him and Nancy a retirement home in Bel Air. The steel magnate said he wanted nothing in return except their friendship.

In 1990, Jorgensen sold his company, with 28 plants in 24 cities nationwide, to a group backed by leveraged-buyout specialists Kelso & Co. He wouldn't say what he received from the $264 million purchase, but he had owned 32 percent of the company stock—worth about $84 million—and retained 13.5 percent for a Jorgensen family trust.

He remained active in the steel business he founded until just days before his death at age 101 in 1999. "I can't stop working," Jorgensen said in 1997, two years after he had heart bypass surgery. "I might not get started again."

■ ■ ■

SONGWRITER **HOAGY CARMICHAEL** composed some of the 20th century's most beloved songs, including "Georgia on My Mind," "I Get Along Without You Very Well," "Lazy River," "Ole Buttermilk Sky," "Rockin' Chair," "Skylark," and "Star Dust" (the most recorded song in music history). He received many accolades and awards, notably for his jaunty composition "In the Cool, Cool, Cool of the Evening," which Jane Wyman and Bing Crosby sang in *Here Comes the Groom;* the number won an Oscar for Best Song.

Carmichael was a Hoosier, which is parlance for a native of Indiana. He grew up within sight of steamboats, paddlewheels, fireflies, and fishing—a vision of America that had a profound influence on his songs. As an adult, though, he was very much the dandy, prone to slick-backed hair, an ascot at his neck, and the ever-present cigarette between his fingers. A regular visitor to Palm Springs, he had been coming to the desert since the late 1930s, when he and fellow composer Johnny Mercer used to hide out with their respective wives at the Racquet Club, drinking and smoking and having a good time. Carmichael even tried his hand at tennis, though he wasn't very good at it.

Approaching middle age, during the 1940s, he inexplicably found himself in demand as an actor. And why not? He had the slightly jaded, detached look that appealed to wartime movie audiences. So he was cast as match-chewing piano players who offered advice to the hero in *To Have and Have Not, The Best Years of Our Lives,* and *Young Man with a Horn.*

The first house Carmichael ever owned, for which he paid $100,000 in 1942, was located in the Holmby Hills section of Los Angeles. It had previously belonged to Philip "P.K." Wrigley, heir to his father's chewing gum fortune. But Wrigley had abandoned the ranch-style home shortly after the Japanese bombed Pearl Harbor (he feared an invasion). Wrigley's loss was Carmichael's and America's gain. These were productive and happy years for the composer. He and his wife, Ruth Meinardi, raised their two young sons, Hoagy Bix (named in honor of family friend and cornet player Bix Beiderbecke), and Randy Bob (named for Randolph Scott and Robert Montgomery).

But after 18 years of marriage, Carmichael was jolted out of his comfortable existence by a midlife crisis, and the shocking details made the rounds of spiteful tabloid magazines. One rag in particular suggested that, instead of taking a few piano licks, the dried-up composer had swapped stardust for wanderlust and was now sucking on a bourbon bottle. According to his biographer, Richard Sudhalter, Carmichael was spotted in a fashionable Manhattan restaurant in the company of two glamorous women, neither of them his wife. "The evening degenerated into a melee, glassware and epithets flying freely and the police arriving to break up what had become a small-scale brawl," reported Sudhalter.

In 1955, the Carmichaels filed for divorce. Hoagy purchased a two-bedroom apartment on Sunset Boulevard and started making telephone calls to the desert. He had a lot of friends here, including the film directors William Wyler and Howard Hawks, so it seemed natural for him to be near them.

Although the divorce cost him lots of money, he still had plenty of income from song royalties, which brought in around $300,000 a year. He also had invested in everything from oil deals to revolutionary inventions. Carmichael went to the bank, withdrew a large amount of cash, and drove to Thunderbird, where he bought two homes: one at 40–267 Club View Drive on the eighth fairway; the other not far from the third hole. By the end of the 1950s, he was as much a part of the golf course as its clubhouse and sand traps.

His retirement years as a self-confessed "loafer" were not entirely without purpose. He recorded a very successful album, *Hoagy Sings Carmichael,* and, while residing on the links, wrote the second of two autobiographies, *Sometimes I Wonder.* But those supposedly relaxing years were marred by professional loss and personal tragedy.

In 1961, his youngest sister, Martha Clayton, who worked part-time at Barbara Wells's interior design shop in Palm Springs, took a lethal dose of sleeping pills. Her death occurred 30 years to the day after the passing of Hoagy's good friend Bix Beiderbecke. Five years later, Carmichael suffered another blow when police notified him that his depressed ex-wife had killed herself. From living high on the hog, she had gone to slumming in a rented second-floor apartment, where she developed a fatal drug habit.

The one ray of sunshine in his hour of darkness came in the form of a B-movie actress named Wanda McKay, whose sense of humor he found refreshing. They became lovers, constant companions, and eventually husband and wife. Of course, he still liked his booze. Golfers could hardly fail to notice him propped up at the club's bar, a cigarette in one hand and a whiskey glass in the other. It got to be a running joke around the club: "Hoagy's Bar."

Carmichael was too ill to attend his seventy-fifth birthday party in Indiana; among other ailments, his eyesight was diminishing. Later, he was diagnosed with prostate cancer, and his health went rapidly downhill. He died at the age of 82 in 1981.

■ ■ ■

IF THE OLD adage "You can count the number of friends in your life by the number of enemies you've made" holds true, then television producer **Gloria Monty** can rest assured that she has more than her fair share of both groups. As the person who took over producing chores on the TV daytime soap opera *General Hospital,* which had become a ratings loser for ABC, Monty cut a less-than-friendly swathe through the studio, hiring and firing staff in an effort to reshape a lackluster show and stave off cancellation by the beleaguered network.

She immediately proved a formidable foe because of her strong opinions and take-no-prisoners approach to writing, casting, and directing. It was not, however, her first time at the rodeo, to borrow an expression often used by Joan Crawford, someone with whom Gloria had a lot in common. The two women had struck up a peculiar friendship when the temperamental *Mildred Pierce* star substituted for her ailing real-life daughter, actress Christina Crawford, on Monty's earlier soap, *The Secret Storm*.

The exaggerated goings-on among the fictional community of this dark, moody serial were perfect fodder for the highly mannered Oscar winner, who was reputed to be a big soap opera fan. Of course, even Monty had to admit that it was a stretch for viewers to believe the over-dressed, 63-year-old Crawford could substitute for her considerably less vain 28-year-old offspring. But the experience taught Monty a valuable lesson: never let the truth stand in the way of telling a good story.

For nine years she put the bounce into the *General Hospital* production staff. She may have raised eyebrows and upped people's blood pressure along the way, but she insisted on creating adventurous storylines that would keep audiences glued to their TV sets. Many of the incredible plot twists were the work of Gloria's sister, Norma Monty, whose overactive imagination caused beatings, kidnappings, and murders to be depicted onscreen with all the coldness of an ice cream sundae.

Moralists were shocked when lovesick Luke Spencer took out his sexual frustrations on Laura Webber and raped her at the Port Charles campus disco. Gloria dismissed them with a wave of her hand. As if to prove her point, in 1981 more than 30 million viewers tuned in to watch Luke and Laura's wedding, an audience that garnered Monty the highest rating in daytime television history.

Still, that soap opera marriage might never have taken place, except that Hollywood diva Elizabeth Taylor generously offered to appear on the show if the young lovers got hitched. Taylor's vamping as the evil Helena Cassadine was either the high- or low-point of the convoluted series. During one scene where the frumpy star was supposed to put a spell on the newlyweds, Taylor reportedly told the head writer, Thom Racina, "Oh, hex, schmex, why don't I just lift my leg and pee on them?" Unfortunately, Taylor's line never made it into the final script.

Feeling vindicated, and with four Emmy Awards to her credit, Monty took a well-earned sabbatical and didn't return to the popular show until 1991. This time, however, her tough, dictatorial actions were no longer tolerated by a new generation of network executives. After Monty recast some roles and axed others, the ratings began to suffer, and when stars such as Tristan Rogers, who played Robert Scorpio, refused to work with her, ABC fired the indomitable daytime-TV pioneer.

Her name subsequently appeared as executive producer on several prime time thrillers written by Mary Higgins Clark, including *Remember Me, Let Me Call You Sweetheart,* and *Moonlight Becomes You.* Monty's remaining days were spent driving a customized golf cart with a Rolls Royce grille from the fairway to her home at 71–305 Cypress Drive, which she purchased for $200,000 in 1988. She died of cancer at the age of 84 in 2006.

■ ■ ■

IF A WHITE dove really is the sign of peace, then flawless peaches-and-cream beauty **Billie Dove**, who reigned supreme throughout the early twentieth century as one of the world's most beautiful women—who was billed as "the Girl in the Moon" and literally put on a pedestal in *Ziegfeld Follies of 1917*—was appropriately named.

Her suitors (and there were many) included artist James Montgomery Flagg, who painted her heavenly portrait; Broadway impresario Florenz Ziegfeld, who showcased her in four stage productions; and billionaire Howard Hughes, who paid her first husband, filmmaker Irvin Willat, the princely sum of $325,000 to divorce her!

Dove took it all in stride.

Coy and clever (some even said she was crafty), Dove wielded sex appeal like a frozen meringue, doling out tiny pieces to male admirers to mollify their hunger, but never giving them the whole pie. By the time she was signed to a Hollywood contract by First National Studios, which aggressively promoted her as the All-American Beauty, Dove had her act down pat and played variations of her chaste, eye-batting heroines opposite stalwart leading men such as John Gilbert, Lon Chaney, George O'Brien, Tom Mix, Rod La Rocque, and Warner Baxter. Her cuddling in *The Black Pirate* with the screen's premier swashbuckler, Douglas Fairbanks, so rankled the grinning, muscle-flexing star's wife, Mary Pickford, that Pickford refused to let him kiss Dove on the screen.

Howard Hughes's attempt to woo the virtuous beauty away from director-husband Willat, after six years of marriage and four films, was a gauche attempt to control her life and career. (He would later try to exert his will over other actresses, including Katharine Hepburn.) But Dove wasn't seduced by his palaver. After appearing in two of his costly flops, she terminated her professional and personal contact with Hughes. She kept his expensive gifts, including a valuable engagement ring, but turned down his marriage proposal because she considered he had been unfaithful. (Many years later, Dove privately admitted the real reason she broke the engagement: she discovered that he had contracted syphilis from having sex with prostitutes.) Instead, in 1933 she married Robert Kenaston, a wealthy Minnesota rancher, and that year she also retired from the screen, after shooting her fiftieth film, *Blondie of the Follies*, a snappy comedy co-starring Marion Davies.

The Kenastons lived in Pacific Palisades and Palm Springs and later bought a third home at 71–362 Cypress Drive, which served as Billie's primary address for the rest of her life. There she took up oil painting and became part of the club's chummy social set, the "Thunderbird Girls," a clique that included Alice Faye, Ginger Rogers, and Ruby Keeler. Members of the Palm Springs Palette Club, the actresses took art classes and sat at their easels, brushes in hand, sketching and painting for hours at a time.

In 1970, after 37 years of marriage, Dove divorced Kenaston, who was a heavy drinker. He died three years later at the age of 64. According to author James Watters, she then took a much younger man for a disastrous third marriage. It, too, ended in divorce.

The diplomatic Dove, who outlived her first two husbands as well as a son, Robert Kenaston, Jr., who died in 1995, was always reluctant to discuss her personal life. "My husbands never knew my age," she said. Very few other people knew her correct age either. In her tenth decade, she sustained serious injuries from a fall at her home and had to be hospitalized. She succumbed to pneumonia on New Year's Eve 1997, at the advanced age of 96.

■ ■ ■

ALICE FAYE COULD easily have been called Hollywood's Most Reluctant Star. In a cutthroat business filled with shameless self-promotion, overblown egos, and rampant ingratitude, she was remarkably modest— a person who almost didn't give a damn about her elevated status as "Queen of the Fox Lot."

Faye's quiet off-screen lifestyle, in which she took pride in raising a family with her second husband, singer and bandleader **Phil Harris**, belied her captivating onscreen personality as the dreamy-eyed songbird who found romance in the arms of Tyrone Power, Don Ameche, and John Payne. She frequently locked lips with each of these handsome leading men in tuneful musicals such as *Alexander's Ragtime Band*, *Rose of Washington Square*, *Lillian Russell*, *That Night in Rio*, *Tin Pan Alley*, and *Weekend in Havana*.

A favorite of the great composer Irving Berlin, who was said to be smitten by her deep singing voice, Faye introduced a total of 23 Hit Parade songs. That's almost twice as many ballads as those introduced by each of her closest competitors—Judy Garland, Betty Grable, and Doris Day. Those hits included "I Feel a Song Coming On," "You Turned the Tables on Me," "I've Got My Love to Keep Me Warm," "Wake Up and Live," and "You'll Never Know," from her penultimate musical, *Hello, Frisco, Hello;* it won the Oscar for Best Song in 1943.

As for her beauty, Faye never looked more ravishing than in Busby Berkeley's giddy Technicolor extravaganza *The Gang's All Here*, in which she crooned another one of her hits, "A Journey to a Star." This evocative paean to the U.S. government's Good Neighbor Policy with Latin America also featured Carmen Miranda wearing her famous tutti-frutti hat, which was filled to the brim with oranges, strawberries, and bananas. The movie featured terrific music by the "King of Swing," Benny Goodman, and fabulous tap dancing by the Nicholas Brothers. Alas, it was Faye's last good film.

After she attended a disastrous sneak preview of her first nonmusical drama, *Fallen Angel*, in which her best scenes were cut by Fox boss Darryl Zanuck (in revenge, it was said, for her steadfast refusal to have sex with him), she angrily left the studio and vowed never to return.

"I'm a housewife, not an actress anymore," she huffed.

The first step in this transformation was learning to drive, something she had never mastered because she feared being behind the wheel. She also had to learn to do her own shopping, which meant frequent trips to the grocery store so she could feed her hardworking husband and their two infant children, Alice, Jr., and Phyllis.

Her fans were agog. Faye's devotion to her new job was admired by almost everyone except the moviegoing public, many of whom resented her defection. In their eyes, it was tantamount to treason. Alice didn't care. She was truly happy for the first time in many years, even if, in reflective moments, she admitted that it was lonely staying at home, doing dishes and folding laundry.

She was far from alone, as it turns out. According to biographer Jane Lenz Elder, "The Harris's sprawling property in the still-rustic San Fernando Valley boasted a fully occupied duck pond, chicken coops, fruit trees, a stable for two or three horses, a ram named Clyde, and a Malaccan Cockatoo."

After she left Fox, it was alleged that Faye even stopped wearing makeup. But this seems hard to believe, given her reputation for dressing fastidiously. Maybe she just grew tired of plucking her eyebrows and painting her face now that she no longer had to be in front of the cameras.

In 1952, the Harrises sold their Encino home to flat-top comedian George Gobel and moved to a new three-bedroom house at 71–388 Cypress Drive, where they whooped it up with desert neighbors such as Jack Benny and Bing Crosby, who liked to enter through the backdoor and taste Alice's freshly baked chicken or hearty pot roast. Faye called life on the links "sheer heaven," an understatement considering the amount of hard liquor that she and her husband reportedly consumed. Even though Alice had officially retired, she would gladly sing any number of songs for her inebriated friends at the drop of a cocktail napkin.

At one famous Thunderbird party, attended by their neighbors Hoagy Carmichael and Lucille Ball, Faye hoisted herself onto a piano stool while Phil pounded the drums, accompanying Carmichael at the keyboard and Buddy Rogers on the trombone. The all-night jam session was still going strong when the first round of golfers teed off shortly after dawn.

Faye's clowning around with Harris, usually after they were both completely soused, couldn't disguise that she and Phil didn't always get along. "I know they loved each other very deeply," admitted their daughter Phyllis, "but I don't think they always liked each other." They often chose to lead separate lives and eventually maintained two homes, so rumors were rife that the couple's marriage was on the rocks. But it proved a false alarm. If anything, their periodic separations brought them closer together.

As she grew older, Faye took satisfaction in having beaten the studio system that made mortal casualties of many of her co-stars, including Carmen Miranda, Tyrone Power, and Betty Grable. Alice and her husband had invested their money, so they did not have a lot of financial worries.

Then, at a time when most men Phil's age were being put out to pasture, his career suddenly received a second wind. He was hired in 1967 to provide the voice of Baloo, the bear in Walt Disney's animated feature *The Jungle Book*. He warbled the Oscar-nominated song "The Bare Necessities." Three years later, Harris followed up that stint with his performance as O'Malley, the alley cat in *The Aristocats,* and then with the jovial role of Little John in *Robin Hood*, a part that suited Harris's inebriated personality. When he wasn't working, Harris spent so much time hunting and fishing with Bing Crosby that Alice joked, "If I ever sue Phil for divorce, I'll name Bing co-respondent."

But Faye found that she was in demand again, too. As a nostalgia craze swept the country, Alice was tapped to play the lead role in a Broadway revival of the musical *Good News*. She later toured the production with former screen beau John Payne, who tried to conceal his true age by wearing silk cravats and a shaggy toupee.

Again, separate lives seemed to help the Faye-Harris partnership. Whatever their personal differences, the marriage outlasted its critics. In 1991, they celebrated their fiftieth wedding anniversary and seemed destined to go on telling jokes and singing at parties. Unfortunately, a half century of smoking and heavy drinking finally took its toll on Harris, who was forced to endure kidney dialysis. "If I'd known I was going to live this long," he once remarked, "I'd have taken better care of myself." He finally died in 1995 at the age of 91.

Faye's health declined shortly afterward. She developed arthritis, broke her ankle, and underwent vascular surgery. Then one day she fell at home and fractured her wrist. The following year her spleen was removed, and she was diagnosed with stomach cancer. She died in 1998, four days after her eighty-third birthday.

■ ■ ■

ALMOST 30 YEARS after leaving the White House, President **Gerald R. Ford** occupies a unique place in American political history: he is the only person to serve as both president and vice president of the United States without having been elected.

There are two schools of opinion on this subject. One believes that Ford was entitled to serve as the nation's thirty-eighth president, and the other maintains that he usurped the highest office in the land. To be fair to both Ford and his critics, he had virtually no choice in the matter. After the shock of Vice President Spiro Agnew's resignation in 1973, amid charges of tax evasion, Ford, who was minority leader of the House, was appointed by President Nixon to take his place. In another stroke of luck, Ford took over Nixon's job when the beleaguered president stepped down in the wake of the Watergate scandal in 1974.

Ford never held any grudges against his predecessors. Why should he? The appointments afforded him the chance to attain a position of executive privilege and power that he probably would never have acquired under normal circumstances. In fact, Ford was so grateful to Nixon for giving him the chance to run the country, that he went against the general consensus and officially pardoned "Tricky Dick," excusing him of any crimes he may have committed as president. Would Nixon have done the same for him?

Ford developed his sense of fair play when he was an all-star football center and linebacker at the University of Michigan. During World War II he served in the U.S. Navy and was nearly swept off the deck of an aircraft carrier during a typhoon. He was discharged after two years with the rank of lieutenant commander. Ford entered politics at the grassroots level, campaigning door-to-door in his hometown of Grand Rapids, Michigan, to win election to the U.S. House of Representatives, where he served 11 terms and was voted minority leader by his colleagues.

It was said that he won many friends in the house because of his fair leadership and inoffensive personality, qualities that confirmed he was a nice guy but also made him vulnerable to criticism during his presidency. Some pundits argued that, as president, he was unprepared to deal with serious economic problems, including the rising inflation that plagued the country throughout his three-year term. He also faced the crisis of an escalating war in Cambodia and presided over the withdrawal of U.S. troops from Vietnam.

Throughout this unrest Ford maintained a pleasant demeanor, although some comedians, including Bob Hope, enjoyed making fun of the president's apparent lack of physical coordination. The joke went that Ford "can't chew gum and walk at the same time." No one laughed, however, when a female follower of incarcerated cult leader Charles Manson aimed a gun at Ford while he was shaking hands with well-wishers in Sacramento in 1975.

Two weeks later, there was a second assassination attempt: a woman fired a gun at Ford outside the St. Francis Hotel in San Francisco. The quick response of a former U.S. marine named Oliver Sipple, who grabbed the woman's arm and diverted the shot, probably saved the president's life. In a strange postscript to this event, Sipple was later outed as a homosexual. It was alleged that his sexuality was the reason Ford never awarded him a medal for bravery. The crestfallen hero was found dead in 1989. He was 47.

Ford's hopes of winning the presidency in 1976 were dashed when Ronald Reagan ran against him in an abortive bid for the nomination and became a spoiler in that historic bicentennial election. Although Reagan lost the party's nomination by fewer than 200 votes, the real loser was Ford. Coupled with negative response to Ford's pardon of Nixon, Reagan's challenge took away much-needed enthusiasm for Ford and allowed Jimmy Carter, a peanut farmer from Plains, Georgia, to lay claim to the Oval Office. It took years for Ford and Reagan to mend their differences.

While Ford was vice president, he and his wife, Elizabeth "Betty" Bloomer, had attended a North Atlantic Treaty Organization conference in Brussels, where Leonard Firestone was the U.S. ambassador to Belgium. The Fords stayed with Firestone at the American embassy and developed a lasting friendship with the tire mogul and his second wife, Caroline Hudson. "After Ford became president," said golf historian Robert Windeler, "the Firestones were frequent overnight visitors to the

White House. When the Fords decided to make Rancho Mirage their permanent home, Firestone offered them the extra Thunderbird lot he had been holding for more than two decades, waiting for the right neighbor."

It was worth the wait. In 1978, Gerald and Betty Ford built a four-bedroom home at 40–365 Sand Dune Road. The green-and-white living room, which faces the thirteenth green, had gleaming tile floors and natural linen sofas. Ford's favorite chair, covered in faded blue leather, had once occupied the sitting room at 1600 Pennsylvania Avenue; now it was installed in the den. A needlepoint pillow on the seat was inscribed "I'm a Ford, not a Lincoln." A fervent golfer, Ford practiced his swing each day and became a highly visible competitor in yearly tournaments held throughout the valley—with his Secret Service agents close behind him.

If readjusting to civilian life was relatively pleasant for the easygoing former president, it proved difficult for his wife. Betty Ford took pills—as many as 25 a day—to cope with her loneliness. Finally, she checked herself into a hospital for drug and alcohol treatment, where she came face-to-face with other addicts. Out of this life-changing experience came the idea for the Betty Ford Center, which the former first lady founded a short distance from their home, at Eisenhower Medical Center.

The Fords grew so accustomed to desert living that they made Rancho Mirage their winter home, too. There they enjoyed regular visits from their sons, Michael, Jack, and Steven, and their daughter, Susan. In 1982, a major Rancho Mirage thoroughfare, Avenue 36, was renamed Gerald Ford Drive, a fitting monument to one of the city's most auspicious residents.

Well into his eighties, Ford was still making regular appearances at political fund-raisers and dedication ceremonies. Advancing age and a busy schedule took their toll, however, and he suffered a mild stroke at the Republican National Convention in 2000. Three years later, the 90-year-old statesman felt faint while playing golf on a hot summer day and was admitted to the hospital. Increasing frailty soon precluded him from air travel. "I don't have quite the endurance I had 25 years ago," he said.

As of 2005, Ford was the oldest living former president. The odds of anyone beating that record are slim, but Ford's place in history has been assured, if not by his own determination, then by default.

■ ■ ■

CAPITALIST **LEONARD FIRESTONE**, the son of tire mogul Harvey Firestone, who, with Henry Ford and Thomas Edison, revolutionized the American automotive industry with surefire inventions such as the assembly line and the electric light, owned the six-bedroom home at 40–555 Sand Dune Road. In his youth, Firestone was employed in sales positions by the $2 billion Firestone Tire & Rubber Company that his father had founded in Akron, Ohio. At the age of 28, the younger Firestone was appointed sales manager, and in 1939 he became a director. He was named the company's president in 1943.

Firestone was appointed U.S. ambassador to Belgium by President Richard M. Nixon and was reappointed by President Gerald R. Ford. He was a generous contributor to charities and served as president of the trustees of the University of Southern California and president of the World Affairs Council of Los Angeles.

In 1952, Firestone bought four undeveloped lots overlooking the thirteenth hole, but he didn't get around to building his own home there until six years later. Eventually he sold the excess land to Ford, his longtime friend, who constructed his own home on the site after he left office in 1977. (Because of its close proximity to Ford's house, the Firestone estate is also behind a Secret Service security gate.)

A good example of the fierce rivalry that existed between Firestone Tire & Rubber and its major competitor, Goodyear, occurred during the making of Blake Edwards's transcontinental comedy *The Great Race*, starring Jack Lemmon and Tony Curtis. Producer Martin Jurow found himself short the $100,000 needed to replicate several vintage cars for the film, which was to be shot in Austria and France. On an impulse, Jurow asked Firestone, with whom he was acquainted, to give him the extra money. "In publicizing our wonderful picture in its marketing and advertising," he teased, "would you like me to say 'It's a good year for *The Great Race*'?"

"What do you need?" Firestone asked.

Jurow smiled and laid out his plan. In return, Firestone's distinctive red logo appeared nine times in the film, and Goodyear was nowhere to be seen. It was, Jurow later confessed, product placement born of necessity. The film grossed $11 million at the box office.

Like other prominent industrialists, Firestone often found his business interests overlapping the worlds of politics and entertainment. For instance, he was among a select group of extremely wealthy Republicans who initiated, financed, and guided Ronald Reagan's political career, and Governor Reagan and Nancy were frequent guests of the Firestones in Palm Springs.

But politics and tires weren't Firestone's only money-making interests. In his retirement, Leonard established a family ranch and farm in the Santa Ynez Valley, where he supervised the plantings of wine-making grapes—an odd choice given his self-confessed problems with alcohol but one that, typically, Firestone shrugged off. In 1975, Firestone Vineyards celebrated its first harvest, which wine connoisseurs praised highly. The boutique winery is still run by his oldest son, Brooks, who served two terms as a member of the California State Assembly.

Firestone died of respiratory failure on Christmas Eve 1996, at the age of 89. His former home was bought for $1.6 million in 1999. Remodeled, it sold for $3.9 million in 2003.

■ ■ ■

WHEN TAP-DANCING ACTRESS **Ruby Keeler,** who rose from the rank of chorus girl to major headliner in the Depression-era films *42nd Street, Gold Diggers of 1933, Footlight Parade,* and *Dames,* died of cancer in 1993—six months before her eighty-fourth birthday—many people presumed, incorrectly, that she was already dead. After all, the timid, squeaky-voiced performer, who resided at 71–029 Early Times Road in Thunderbird Park, in a three-bedroom home decorated outside with copper lampposts, had been away from Hollywood for 50 years.

Much of that time she spent trying to obliterate the memory of her disastrous 11-year marriage to singer Al Jolson, who had been billed as the World's Greatest Entertainer but whom she privately called the World's Worst Husband. Poor Ruby. Jolson was such an overbearing, egotistical, pain in the ass that she had reportedly contemplated committing suicide—even murder. But finally she had settled on divorce to rid herself of this over-the-hill *schlemiel.*

Her friend and neighbor, Alice Faye, who co-starred with Jolson and Tyrone Power in *Rose of Washington Square,* couldn't stand him either. "Jolson thought he was the greatest thing that ever happened, and he was a big star," said Faye. "Nobody's that big, and he seemed to intimidate Ruby."

When Columbia Pictures offered Keeler a large sum of money to portray her as the loving wife in a sycophantic biography entitled *The Jolson Story*, she refused. Indeed, Keeler had become so bitter about the old days that she didn't even appreciate her own talent. "It's really amazing," she said. "I couldn't act. I had that terrible singing voice, and now I can see I wasn't the greatest tap dancer in the world, either."

The one bright spot in Keeler's life, after her second husband, Los Angeles realtor John Lowe, died in 1969, was her enduring friendship with director-choreographer Busby Berkeley, who was known for his brilliant staging of musical numbers. Surprisingly, he talked her into a comeback: the lead in the 1971 Broadway revival of *No, No, Nanette*. The show's highpoint was Keeler's stirring rendition of the bubbling song "I Want to Be Happy," a poignant reminder of her own resilience. She played 861 performances.

Four years later, Keeler's inner strength was put to the test when she blacked out from a stroke and lay comatose with a brain aneurysm for two months. Ruby's close brush with death necessitated a dramatic change in her lifestyle. She moved to Rancho Mirage, where this heavy smoker, who used to puff on several packs a day, took up golf. Physical activity, the desert climate, and a new circle of friends were the perfect healing balm, and when she regained her strength, she was a different person: still Ruby Keeler with the friendly smile, but no longer the innocent, wide-eyed girl in glistening tap shoes. "It was," as she said herself, "such a long time ago."

Perhaps that is why so many people referred to her in the past tense.

■ ■ ■

CURLY-HAIRED ACTOR **BRADFORD Dillman**, whose disturbing portrayals of psychopathic young men broke new ground in exalted films such as *Compulsion*, *Crack in the Mirror*, and *Sanctuary*, often visited the home of his father, Dean Dillman, at 40–780 Thunderbird Road in scenic Thunderbird Heights. The younger Dillman's ability to play flawed, egocentric characters had him snarling and sulking in front of movie and TV cameras for three decades, and led him to a sizzling performance as Willie Oban in the 1973 film of Eugene O'Neill's play *The Iceman Cometh*.

But much of the time he was stuck in low-budget horror films that embarrassed him. The harried-looking actor fended off giant cockroaches in *Bug*, resisted attacks by killer bees in *The Swarm*, and escaped carnivorous fish in *Piranha*. "I'm motivated by financial necessity," he said. "I'll accept just about everything I'm offered."

The older Dillman, who saw the full orbit of his son's career, passed away at the age of 90 in 1983; his widow, Alice, survived her husband by ten years. After she died, Hollywood set decorator **Jay Hart**, who received Oscar nominations for the period furnishings that re-created faded decadence in both *L.A. Confidential* and *Pleasantville*, purchased the nearly mint-condition home from Dean Dillman's estate.

Hart used his extensive knowledge to redecorate the house. He retained the home's mahogany kitchen cabinets but copied the house's original white-cotton Roman shades to replace outmoded drapes in the master bedroom. And, always, he was busy with films—*Wayne's World*, *Clear and Present Danger*, and *Terminator 3*—to help him pay for the costly refurbishing.

■ ■ ■

NANCY BELCHER WATSON, the Los Angeles County Superior Court judge who presided over the 1980 murder trial of the Alphabet Bomber, resided for ten years at 70–461 Placerville Road. At the conclusion of the eight-month trial, Watson sentenced the bomber, whose real name was Muharem Kurbegovic, to life in prison.

Kurbegovic was convicted of planting and detonating a bomb at Los Angeles International Airport in 1974, killing three people and injuring 36 others, including a Catholic priest who lost his right leg in the explosion. He was also convicted of trying to bomb the downtown Greyhound bus terminal and of firebombing the homes of several local officials. He had been dubbed the Alphabet Bomber because he claimed to news agencies that he planned to detonate explosives at places which spelled out the name of the terrorist group Aliens of America.

A Yugoslav immigrant, Kurbegovic was the first person in U.S. history to acquire and threaten to use chemical agents against federal officials and citizens. At one point he said he possessed four canisters of deadly nerve gas and was going to Washington, D.C., to kill the president.

Watson's patience and fairness throughout the dramatic, much-publicized trial earned respect from lawyers nationwide. At the time, she was one of only five women judges elected to the county Superior Court, where she presided until her retirement in 1984.

She died in 2004 at the age of 77.

■ ▦ ■

IN 2001, FORMER Pittsburgh Pirates baseball star **Ralph Kiner** paid $1 million for the house in which he currently resides, at 70–346 Calico Road. He must really like the desert; this is his third home in almost as many decades. Indeed, Kiner is no stranger to Thunderbird, where he has lived on and off since it first opened. He was one of the club's original investors and has always been an integral part of its success.

His was a spectacular but brief sports career. Until a painful back injury forced him from the ball field, ten years after joining the majors, Kiner had hit 369 home runs and had won or shared the National League home-run title in each of his first seven seasons. According to official baseball results, he topped 50 home runs twice, with 51 in 1947 and 54 in 1949. His ratio of 7.1 home runs per 100 at-bats is second only to the legendary Babe Ruth and, more recently, Mark McGwire.

Kiner's marriage to Nancy Chaffee, a nationally ranked tennis player who won the 1947 Girls Outdoor Championship and the Women's Indoor Singles for two years running, seemed like a match made in heaven. Regrettably, however, the two well-known sports figures were not compatible on the same court. Because Nancy had competed at Wimbledon, the British press, unfamiliar with Kiner's baseball prowess, took to calling him "Mr. Chaffee." The term did not sit well with Kiner, and the pair eventually divorced.

In 1975, the prolific home-run hitter was elected to the Baseball Hall of Fame, where he occupies a unique place in the game's colorful history. Chaffee died in 2000, but the couple's children—two sons and a daughter—all live in Palm Desert.

■ ■ ■

HIT PARADE VOCALIST **Ginny Simms**, famous for her lush rendition of "Flamingo" (composed by the late Rancho Mirage resident Ted Grouya), lived at 70–368 Calico Road. This was the second of four houses the throaty-voiced singer owned in the Palm Springs area, where she eventually retired.

In the early days of her singing career, Simms used to entertain thousands of GIs, outdoors on makeshift stages and indoors at veterans' hospitals. But her later years were spent performing in nightclubs or resting at home, where she lamented the failure of her film career. It had started promisingly, with significant roles in *Hit the Ice, Broadway Rhythm,* and *Night and Day.* Then it just petered out.

Simms blamed orchestra leader Kay Kyser, with whom she had reportedly slept in order to gain his favor; when their relationship ended, so did much of her public appeal. Marriages to hotel heir Hyatt Von Dehn and millionaire Bob Calhoun, and divorces from same, didn't help. The man that got away was, ironically, the one she never wanted. Louis B. Mayer, her boss at MGM, had pursued her like one of his prize fillies at the horse ranch he owned in Perris, California.

Mayer was reportedly so in love with Simms that he went down on bended knee and offered a bounty of $1 million if she would marry him. Simms turned him down—and lived to regret it. Years later, there she was, pouring out her heart to friends over cocktails, much the way Mayer had kicked himself for not offering her $2 million!

Drinking champagne in mixed company and then belting back a few glasses of Scotch at home soon became Simms's crutch, as it had for hundreds of other stars whose brightness dimmed all too quickly. Her third marriage, to real estate developer Donald Eastvold, didn't dull the pain either, although supposedly he was totally devoted to her and practically worshiped the ground she walked on. As far as her career was concerned, it was a case of much too late. In 1994, in her eighty-first year, she died of a heart attack.

■ ■ ■

BING CROSBY WAS at the top of his game as a recording artist, movie star, and golfer with a two handicap, when he owned the sprawling four-bedroom home at 70–375 Calico Road. Sometimes referred to as Mr. Music on account of his ability to elevate practically any tune from obscurity to prominence, his records sold in the hundreds of millions. Crosby's evocative rendition of "White Christmas," in which he captured the fireside charm of Irving Berlin's Yuletide song, is the most successful single recording of all time. It has outsold all other popular songs, both on records and CDs.

Better known for his crooning than his acting, Crosby still garnered enough votes to win the Oscar for Best Actor as a singing priest in *Going My Way*. He was even nominated two more times, for *The Bells of St. Mary's* and *The Country Girl*. His mocking sense of humor, combined with perfect phrasing and a breezy soft-shoe dance routine, often in partnership with Bob Hope, put him at the forefront of American wartime entertainers. He was in the Box Office Top Ten for 12 consecutive years and was voted its #1 attraction five years in a row.

Crosby was also one of Hollywood's wealthiest denizens. He had vast holdings in real estate, banking, oil and gas wells, broadcasting, and the Coca-Cola Company. His smiling image, complete with trademark hat and pipe, was almost as familiar to people around the world as Mickey Mouse. But appearances can be deceiving. Although Crosby professed gentle humility, he was made of much stronger stuff. His relaxed manner and soft-spoken delivery gave moviegoers and radio listeners the misleading impression that Crosby was a laid-back kind of guy. He was not.

In truth, he was a condescending, self-centered, manipulative cheapskate. And following the death from ovarian cancer of his alcoholic first wife, Dixie Lee, Crosby let his teenage children run wild while he escorted a bevy of beautiful women around town. After this short period of mourning, he went back to work and hit the golf links in Palm Springs. The house on Calico Road was the second of three residences the popular entertainer owned in the desert, not counting homes he also occupied in Pebble Beach, Holmby Hills, and Hayden Lake, Idaho.

It was at this white stucco house, where a gravel road weaved between tall palm trees, that Crosby put the make on Kathryn Grant, a pixyish reporter turned starlet who was 30 years his junior. He promised to marry her but kept the excited actress waiting three years for the big day.

Why did it take so long for the chivalrous Crosby, as he was portrayed in fan magazines, to take the hand of his fair maiden? "It was no secret that Crosby had a girl in every port," said a former business associate. "That was how he had lived his life since the very first record he ever made, and he expected his loved ones to accept that as part of the arrangement."

Eventually, however, his deteriorating health intervened on the side of Kathryn Grant. He drank to excess, possibly from a deep-seated dislike of himself that came across as bitterness toward others and resentment of his family. The constant boozing, along with nonstop smoking and a work schedule that involved films, radio, and golf, would have exhausted a buffalo, and it finally took its toll on Crosby. In 1954, he was sidelined with nervous exhaustion.

As if that wasn't trouble enough, his appendix had to be removed, and soon after that procedure, he re-entered the hospital for a kidney ailment—the onset of a lifelong problem with kidney stones. The resulting operation slowed him down, but it gave him and Grant a chance to get to know each other in the privacy of Crosby's Thunderbird home. There, protected by well-shaded surroundings, Crosby gradually recovered, although his bout with kidney stones left him severely weakened. He spent most of the days swimming and lounging in the sun. He was put on a strict diet and drank hot tea with milk and Sucaryl.

Crosby soon regained his strength and reported to the set of *Anything Goes*, his last Paramount film after 23 years at the studio. He and Grant were often seen dining out in Palm Springs at the Sea Cove, Don the Beachcomber's, or El Patio. Crosby's convalescence apparently had put him in better spirits and helped him make good on his intention to take Grant as his lawfully wedded wife. So, after much procrastination, he got up the courage to ask her before she lost interest.

When they finally tied the knot in 1957, in Las Vegas, Alice Faye was so overjoyed that she fed them an impromptu wedding dinner of quail and macaroni and cheese. The happy couple honeymooned at Crosby's newly completed Palm Desert home, which had been designed by architect Howard Lapham. Their arrival was a moment of both drama and high comedy.

"We were met in Palm Springs by the mayor, with several hundred townspeople and a band playing 'Here Comes the Bride,' " recalled

Kathryn Crosby, who promptly collapsed from all the excitement. Unde-terred, Bing milked the moment for all it was worth. "He flaunted me as if I had suddenly been promoted to queen of the universe."

But the chiming of wedding bells quickly took second place to the clack-clack of typewriter keys, as veiled newspaper reports surfaced that Crosby was having a stormy affair with actress Inger Stevens. Stevens attempted suicide in 1959 and, despondent over her failed relationship with Crosby, and unable to reconcile with the past, would die from an overdose of barbiturates 11 years later.

During the time he lived here, Crosby's four sons, who had all attained the legal age of 21, were involved in minor scrapes with the law. Appar-ently their father never warned them about the dangers of alcohol, even though excessive boozing had landed the singer in jail on several occa-sions and contributed to his sons' delinquency. Crosby's denial of his drinking problem and that of his children was rooted in his strict Catholi-cism, which made it extremely difficult for him, in his repressed emo-tional state, to address fundamental moral issues.

Typical of his lack of understanding was this insensitive remark he made regarding his drunken escapades: "They say I left a trail of broken hearts. Now I wouldn't do a thing like that," he grinned. "The fact is I left a trail of broken bottles and unpaid bills."

In 1953, Crosby crashed his Mercedes Benz sports car on the way home from a Hollywood party. He was accused of driving his car at a wanton, reckless speed, in violation of traffic controls and while under the influence of intoxicating liquors. Seven months later, Gary Crosby's car hit and killed a Mexican laborer near San José. Eight months after that appalling incident, Dennis Crosby was arrested as a drunken passenger in a motor vehicle (quite possibly he had actually been the driver).

Not to be left out of the family adventures, Phillip Crosby suffered three fractured vertebrae in 1955 when his car struck a pedestrian; he was later acquitted of drunk driving. Two years after that, Lindsay was arrested. The charge? Failing to pass a sobriety test after his car hit a parked vehicle.

You'd think the Crosbys could have afforded a chauffeur or that, at the very least, one of them could have put the squeeze on Bing for taxi fare!

■ ■ ■

ACTOR **BRAD DEXTER** was born to be a tough guy. This burly, walking piece of beefcake, who always seemed to have a gun in his hand and a cigarette in his mouth, was synonymous with villainous roles, which he played to bristling perfection in more than 30 classic films.

He was a crooked private eye in *The Asphalt Jungle*, a trigger-happy casino manager who menaced Robert Mitchum in *Macao*, and a ruthless bank robber in *Violent Saturday*. He even got to portray the smooth racketeer Bugsy Siegel in *The George Raft Story*. "I love playing heavies," Dexter once commented. "It's the best-written character. The hero is always bland." Perhaps that is why he never became a major star; he was always killed off before the end of the movie.

A typical example of Dexter's onscreen fate occurs in *The Magnificent Seven*, in which he played the seventh gunman and is accidentally shot while defending a Mexican village. He got to do a great death scene with Yul Brynner, but the reviews praised Steve McQueen, James Coburn, and Charles Bronson.

Brad who?

Dexter didn't care. He was too busy acting tough in *The Oklahoman*, *Last Train from Gun Hill*, and *Taras Bulba*, his second of four films with Brynner, to worry about what someone thought of him. Away from the screen, he was a smooth ladies' man who made a better friend than foe. His first of three wives was singer Peggy Lee and he was a confidant of Marilyn Monroe. As for male friends, he was a wartime buddy of Karl Malden and a personal and professional colleague of Frank Sinatra. In fact, he risked his life to save Sinatra from drowning in Hawaii and was rewarded with a co-starring role in *Von Ryan's Express* and a job as Sinatra's producer. But it was heavy-going protecting the scrappy singer from getting into trouble, what with hiding him from ex-wives and girlfriends and dealing with his violent mood swings.

Dexter witnessed firsthand how terrible Sinatra could be. They were filming *The Naked Runner* in London, and Sinatra didn't want to finish the movie and was throwing one of his tantrums. Brad wouldn't give in to the singer's petulant demands. It was a classic case of courage versus cowardice. When his job was done, so was Dexter. "I was the only guy who dropped Sinatra," he said. "I couldn't put up with his nonsense."

He produced three more films, all helmed by Sidney J. Furie: *Little Fauss and Big Halsy* with Robert Redford; *The Lawyer*, which became the basis for the TV series *Petrocelli*, with Barry Newman; and the Billie Holiday biopic, *Lady Sings the Blues*. The latter received five Oscar nominations, including one for Best Actress.

Dexter married his second wife, Star-Kist tuna heiress Mary Bogdanovich, in 1970. Twelve years later, they moved to the Club at Morningside, where he took up swimming and golf. In 1997, three years after Mary's death, Dexter married June Dyer, the widow of founding Thunderbird club member Joseph Dyer, and they set up house at 41–950 Tonapah Road. Even in retirement, he kept busy reading scripts and attending movie conventions. He died from emphysema at the age of 85, in 2002.

■ ■ ■

THE COPS-AND-ROBBERS GENRE is almost as old as the printed word itself. So it's hardly surprising that it took a real-life street cop to reinvent the storytelling wheel by putting on the record what had usually been left off.

That man was **Joseph Wambaugh**, a second-generation policeman and former U.S. Marine who joined the Los Angeles Police Department and rose from patrolman to detective sergeant. A poster-boy for law enforcement, Wambaugh's strong ethics must have rankled his less-than-honest fellow officers. But mostly his principles won him widespread approval.

When he wasn't in uniform, this conscientious public servant was taking notes and compiling stories, which he later molded into fact-based novels written in a hard-hitting style. His powerful prose set new standards for realism in detective fiction. *The New Centurions* traced the lives of a group of young recruits from their police academy training to the Watts riots. *The Blue Knight* was a telling indictment of police corruption seen through the eyes of a bad cop. *The Onion Field* re-created the true-life events surrounding the kidnapping and murder of two police officers, and *The Choirboys* was a bawdy treatise about cops and their sometimes hilarious, sometimes tragic off-duty behavior.

Wambaugh, to his credit, never pulled punches. He seemed to take delight in surprising his readers and even himself with a detailed, inside knowledge of the LAPD, which in recent years has drawn fire for mishandling high-profile investigations such as the beating of Rodney King and the murder of O.J. Simpson's wife and Ronald Goldman.

Wambaugh watched it all on television from his secluded, two-story mansion at 70–555 Thunderbird Mesa Drive, where he wrote the original screenplays for *The Black Marble* and *The Glitter Dome*, and penned several novels set in the desert, including *Fugitive Nights* and *The Secret of Harry Bright*. Although he was sidelined by a serious case of writer's block, which kept him out of the public eye for six years, Wambaugh has continued to delve into the workings of the criminal mind with his engaging, often humorous tales of law enforcement.

His influence has extended to TV, where he created the weekly anthology series *Police Story*, a warts-and-all progenitor of tough, sophisticated cop shows such as *Hill Street Blues*, *Law & Order*, and *Homicide*. They all owe a debt of gratitude to Wambaugh's courage for telling it like it is.

Funny Business

IT WAS A Hollywood meeting place born out of social necessity. Religious and ethnic discrimination had obligated members of this time-honored show-business fraternity to build their own country club, because, being Jews, they had been excluded from clubs in Los Angeles and Palm Springs.

The idea originated at the Hillcrest Country Club in Beverly Hills, where cackling comedians sat around noshing on corned beef, pastrami, and lox and bagels, while kibitzing about their early days in movies and vaudeville.

At lunch time, Al Jolson would hold court at the club's round table, where he was surrounded by Groucho Marx, Jack Benny, George Burns, Milton Berle, Eddie Cantor, and George Jessel, while producers, agents, lawyers, and accountants listened intently, afraid to go to the bathroom in case they missed an uproarious punch line.

Here, the members' metaphorical protective gloves were off, along with their garish makeup and costumes, which were kept in their dressing rooms. Here, they wore tailored suits, smoked cigars, and carried pocket watches. Jessel refused to call the Marx Brothers by their stage names, so he greeted Groucho, Chico, Harpo, Zeppo, and Gummo as Julius, Leonard, Arthur, Herbert, and Milton, the names printed on the brothers' drivers' licenses.

Comparisons between the male-dominated Hillcrest and the Algonquin Round Table in New York, where literary wits such as Alexander Woolcott, Dorothy Parker, and Robert Benchley congregated, were inevitable but superfluous. "It was strictly stag," recounted Harpo Marx, who was the only person to belong to both clubs.

Groucho was the heckler-at-large, his tongue as dangerous as a blowtorch. No one was safe from his verbal counterpunch. As for the rest, the jokes flew thick and fast, especially after a few drinks, when the humor would become vulgar. "The conversations at the Hillcrest comics' table were hilarious—sometimes funnier than the shows we put on in public," recalled Danny Thomas.

The group's discussion usually involved three subjects: girls, gags, and golf, which was as good a reason as any for the existence of Tamarisk Country Club, where so many Hillcrest members and their guests owned homes.

"The fancier clubs down there were restricted," said Harpo Marx. "We wanted to put up a course that would be the equal of any, but where everybody would have an equal right to play, regardless of his faith or the color of his skin." So they took a vote and built Tamarisk Country Club in Rancho Mirage. There, some of Hollywood's biggest and brightest stars had the times of their lives, hitting holes-in-one and cracking up at each other's risqué jokes.

■ ■ ■

IF LAUGHTER IS the best medicine, then the **Marx Brothers** must have taken an overdose. Not one but four of the show-business-raised brothers owned homes at Tamarisk, which opened in 1952. Each of these freewheeling merrymakers invested substantial money in the new development, to earn themselves a sizeable profit.

In fact, there's a street named after them, called Marx Road, though there has been some contention over whether it was dedicated to the comedians-in-residence or to the club's custom-home builder, Robert Marx, who, not surprisingly, was related to the boisterous team. The son of the fifth Marx brother, Gummo, who had been visiting Palm Springs for decades, Bob Marx saw an ideal opportunity to capitalize on the housing boom and, in partnership with architect Val Powelson and landscape designer Michael Mekjian, he set about constructing a selection of quality homes around the Tamarisk Golf Course.

The Marx brothers were not Bolsheviks or Communists, as their Russian-sounding surname might suggest. Nor were they certifiably crazy, as their antics often made them appear at first glance. But they certainly had their share of eccentricities. The brothers grew up impoverished in nineteenth-century New York. Their parents, Samuel and Minnie Marx, saved pennies to give their sons proper educations, but the boys wanted to do things their own way. They never finished high school and took menial jobs to support themselves while eking out a meager career in vaudeville.

Their family's abject poverty instilled a sense of economy and fair play in the brothers that followed them into adulthood, making them for the most part extremely practical and also sensitive about discriminating against others less fortunate than themselves. And of course laughter played a large part in their upbringing, an outlet that the brothers used to advantage in their riotous antiestablishment films *The Cocoanuts, Animal Crackers, Monkey Business, Horse Feathers,* and *Duck Soup.*

There was Groucho, the cigar-smoking ringleader and master of the putdown. Chico was his sly accomplice, tossing off non sequiturs in a fractured Italian dialect. Harpo was the girl-chasing mute, honking a tin horn and whistling to get attention. Zeppo was the well-mannered straight-shooter and ladies' man, though all of them possessed healthy libidos that needed exercising on a regular basis, both on and off the screen.

That probably explains the brothers' frequent marriages, especially in the cases of Groucho and Chico, who were dedicated womanizers. Harpo was the odd man out: he was a confirmed bachelor, or so he thought. Then he met a young actress named Susan Fleming, and they fell madly in love. Their engagement occurred during the brothers' sixth hilarious film, *A Night at the Opera,* and in 1936 Harpo and Susan exchanged wedding vows. They adopted four children, one of whom,

William Marx, grew up to become a musician and, as Bill Marx, composed and arranged two albums of harp music with his father.

A Night at the Opera was followed by *A Day at the Races, At the Circus, Go West,* and *The Big Store.* But after creating the madcap of *A Night in Casablanca* and *Love Happy,* the brothers split up. Older and richer, they wanted to go their separate ways.

In 1956, Harpo and Susan Marx retained the services of architect Wallace Neff to design El Rancho Harpo, an eight-acre spread located at 71–111 La Paz Road, where Harpo, who was reputed to have the highest IQ of all the brothers, embarked with Zeppo on a second career: growing and selling grapefruit. "Our new home, a timber-and-stucco house at the end of a long lane of oleanders, was finished in the spring of 1957," wrote Harpo, "and we moved in. The happy hooligans became desert rats."

In 1961, the normally silent third Marx brother published his autobiography, *Harpo Speaks,* in which he candidly discussed his career and the reasons for his move to the desert following three debilitating heart attacks, one of which occurred while he was shopping in downtown Palm Springs. He died of a fourth heart attack on September 28, 1964—the date of his twenty-eighth wedding anniversary—after undergoing surgery. He was 75.

"Although we are no longer there," reflected Susan Marx, who moved to larger premises at 37–631 Palm View Road, "our memories will always be with that wonderful time in our hacienda that had been designed just for us, by a man's genius that understood 'home' was the harmonious blending of a family's uniqueness within a living structure."

Chico Marx, who was the oldest of the five brothers, was never a homeowner in Tamarisk, even though he was photographed attending several local fund-raising events. His favorite pastime was playing pinochle at the Friars Club. "He never lived there," explained his nephew Bill Marx. "He was a gambler, not a golfer." Chico did stay at brother Gummo's home on the third fairway, however, during a brief visit in 1959.

A skillful pianist, Chico used to soak his hands in hot water to relax his fingers whenever he played the piano, which is how he was able to strike the keys in his unique "finger-pecking" style. He succumbed to a heart ailment in 1961 at the age of 74.

Meanwhile, their younger brother Groucho and his third wife, Eden Hartford, inhabited 36–928 Pinto Palm Way, where the loping, bespectacled comedian was living in 1966 after the cancellation of his Emmy Award–winning TV series *You Bet Your Life*—famous for its rhetorical question, "What's the secret word?"

Groucho's son, Arthur Marx, who was a frequent visitor, later detailed his father's strange sleeping habits. These included wearing a face mask, putting wax in his ears to keep out noise, and keeping a loaded BB gun by his bedside. If woken from his slumber, Groucho would not hesitate to fire off a few rounds at barking dogs or loud neighbors.

One time, Marx's producer-friend Irwin Allen, who had won an Oscar for his maritime documentary *The Sea Around Us*, was staying with Groucho for the weekend. He inadvertently got locked out of the house after the comedian plugged up his ears and went to bed. Without a key to let him inside, Allen, who had frantically banged on the windows to no avail, was forced to sleep in his car.

The misunderstanding didn't hurt their friendship; if anything it probably helped prolong it, or at least earn Allen some sympathy. He produced two films starring the team's acerbic leader, *Double Dynamite* and *A Girl in Every Port*, as well as the brothers' final film together, *The Story of Mankind,* in 1957.

The irascible Groucho, who was never seen without his cigar, was awarded a special Oscar in 1974. He passed away three years later at the very respectable age of 86.

Zeppo Marx, who lived at 37–791 Halper Lake Drive, was the spoiled baby of the family, though he had reached the spry age of 60 by the time his occupation was listed (jokingly) in the Palm Springs telephone directory as "fisherman." A former talent agent and part-time inventor, he patented a wristwatch that monitored the pulse rate of cardiac patients and also produced a clamping device that was used when the atom bombs were dropped on Japan in 1945.

Zeppo himself designed the home he shared with his second wife, fashion model Barbara Blakeley. Constructed in soft geometric contours, it included a "bump-free" 50-foot-long swimming pool that contained no nasty corners. A passionate golfer, he was a founding member of the

Tamarisk Country Club and could be seen on the links almost every day. He died in 1979 at the age of 78.

Nonperformer Gummo, who managed the team's business affairs, lived at 37–661 Golf Circle. A former garment manufacturer, he was only briefly associated with the brothers' stage act, back when they were still a singing group known as the Three Nightingales. He died at the age of 83 in 1977.

In her senior years, Harpo's widow, Susan, became the unofficial custodian of the Marx heritage, regaling journalists with humorous tales of her mischievous brothers-in-law. But this was no dotty celebrity living in the past. She remained active in the community, serving on local committees, and spent 35 years as a sitting board member of the Palm Springs Unified School District and the College of the Desert. She died at the age of 94 in 2002.

Somewhat eerily, Chico Marx's widow, Mary de Vithas, died the very same day. It was as if all the Marx brothers had come a-calling, asking their loved ones to join them onstage to take a well-deserved bow.

■ ■ ■

IN THE ANNALS of Hollywood moviemaking, few producers can hold a candle to **Hal B. Wallis**, a studious man with the penetrating gaze of a cobra who produced more than 400 films at Warner Bros., Paramount, and Universal. From 1930 until his retirement in 1975, Wallis turned out rip-roaring gangster tales, stark melodramas, and lusty historical epics in prodigious numbers.

He oversaw production of venerated classics such as *Little Caesar*, *I Am a Fugitive from a Chain Gang*, *42nd Street*, *Dames*, *Captain Blood*, *The Petrified Forest*, *Dark Victory*, and *The Roaring Twenties*. Along the way, he helped make stars of James Cagney, Bette Davis, Humphrey Bogart, and Errol Flynn. An avid theatergoer and art connoisseur, with an imposing air about him, Wallis imbued his films with grand style and rarified taste, often on tightly controlled budgets. A stickler for accuracy, he paid great attention to historical detail, especially period fashions and hairstyles. He critiqued each day's rushes and ordered retakes if he thought a scene could be done better. Wallis did not tolerate Flynn's lackadaisical behavior, for example, or Davis's tendency for overacting. He criticized Rosalind Russell's dowdy wardrobe and told Ann Sheridan to lose weight. If somebody did not please him, they either rectified the problem or were replaced.

A mark of the consistently high quality of his work: His movies *Jezebel, The Adventures of Robin Hood, The Letter, All This and Heaven Too, Sergeant York, The Maltese Falcon, Yankee Doodle Dandy, Kings Row,* and *Watch on the Rhine* all received an Academy Award nomination for Best Picture. *Casablanca,* his most famous film, won the Oscar for Best Picture in 1943. Wallis became known as "the man with the Midas touch" and he branched out into independent production, receiving additional accolades for his adaptations of acclaimed stage plays and bestselling novels.

If power is indeed the ultimate aphrodisiac, then Wallis must have been feeling pretty good about himself. He did not intend to run a casting couch or promote stars on the basis of their sexual abilities; still, he found it hard to resist the temptation when presented. Although Wallis reputedly enjoyed a solid marriage to actress Louise Fazenda, there were occasional rumors of infidelity. He was romantically linked to Lola Lane, one of the singing Lane Sisters, in whom he had a special interest, and he was sexually involved with French bombshell Corinne Calvert. He was also quite smitten with Italian actress Anna Magnani, but theirs was more an affair of the heart.

Indeed, apart from his unerring commercial instincts, Wallis's greatest attribute was his ability to spot a star and send it into ascendancy. He searched for actors and actresses he could put under personal contract and mold: Lizabeth Scott, a sultry blonde with a husky voice whom Wallis promoted as the next Lauren Bacall; Wendell Corey, a serious-looking stage actor who appeared in several Wallis films but whose career was compromised by alcoholism; Charlton Heston, who thankfully refused to change his first name to "Charles," as Wallis asked. Wallis's most contentious male discovery was Burt Lancaster, who strained their relationship with his bully-boy tactics. Their constant fighting even led some observers to speculate on a possible homoerotic attraction between the two men.

At the center of these disputes was Wallis's intent to make money and his actors' desire for creative control over their destinies. The task fell to Wallis to try and find the middle ground. He was mostly proud of the

President and Mrs. Ford
(Palm Springs Historical
Society)

President Lyndon Johnson
(Palm Springs Historical Society)

Arnold Schwarzenegger and Maria
Shriver (Hollywood Memories)

George Bush, Sr., Gerald Ford, and Bill Clinton
(*Palm Springs Life*)

Dunes gamblers
(Palm Springs
Historical Society)

The Dunes casino (Palm Springs Historical Society)

Romanoff's on the Rocks
(Palm Springs Historical Society)

Mike Romanoff and Frank Sinatra
(Palm Springs Historical Society)

William "Hopalong Cassidy" Boyd
(Palm Springs Historical Society)

Cathedral City intersection
(Craig De Sedle)

Amos 'n' Andy's Charles Correll
(Larry Edmunds Bookshop)

Carroll Baker topless (Movie Market)

Lalo Guerrero
with awards
(*Palm Springs
Life*)

Don Wilson and his wife
(*Palm Springs Life*)

Wilfrid Hyde-White
(Backlot Books
& Movie Posters)

Capone's desert hideaway
(Two Bunch Palms Resort & Spa)

Al Capone
(Larry Edmunds Bookshop)

John Jakob Raskob (Palm Springs
Historical Society)

Janet Gaynor and Paul Gregory
(Palm Springs Historical Society)

Pioneertown (Howard Johns Collection).

Jackie Cooper
(Backlot Books & Movie Posters)

Eric Burdon (Howard Johns Collection)

The Jeff Chandlers (Palm Springs
Historical Society)

Frank Morgan (Palm Springs
Historical Society)

Hardwicke's house (Craig De Sedle)

Cedric Hardwicke
(Larry Edmunds Bookshop)

Marion Davies
(Larry Edmunds Bookshop)

Dinah Shore Drive (Craig De Sedle)

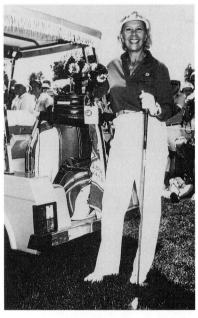

Kaye Ballard (Howard Johns Collection)

Shore and golf fans
(Palm Springs Historical Society)

Earle Hagen (*Palm Springs Life*)

Gene Barry and Carol Channing
(Larry Edmunds Bookshop)

Rod Laver (*Palm Springs Life*)

Darryl Strawberry
(Larry Edmunds Bookshop)

Telly Savalas (*Palm Springs Life*)

Don Drysdale (*Palm Springs Life*)

Newman's Own: Arthur, Patti,
and Paul (*Palm Springs Life*)

Mary Martin
(Larry Edmunds Bookshop)

Charles "Buddy" Rogers and
Mary Pickford
(Palm Springs Historical Society)

Jane Wyman, Ginger Rogers
and Olivia de Havilland
(Larry Edmunds Bookshop)

Lucy Ball's Palm Springs Home

Lucille Ball's house
(Palm Springs
Historical Society)

Lucy, Gary Morton, and
Jack Carter (Palm Springs
Historical Society)

Hoagy Carmichael
(*Palm Springs Life*)

Alice Faye and Phil Harris
(Palm Springs Historical Society)

Gerald and Betty Ford (*Palm Springs Life*)

Ginny Simms (Larry Edmunds Bookshop)

Ruby Keeler (*Palm Springs Life*)

Bing Crosby (Backlot Books & Movie Posters)

Crosby's house (Palm Springs Historical Society)

Joseph Wambaugh
(Larry Edmunds Bookshop)

Hal Wallis with Martha Hyer
(Larry Edmunds Bookshop)

The Marx Brothers: Chico, Zeppo, Groucho,
Harpo (Larry Edmunds Bookshop)

Groucho in old age
(Larry Edmunds Bookshop)

Jilly Rizzo and Joey Bishop
(Palm Springs Historical Society)

Danny Thomas
(Larry Edmunds Bookshop)

Marvin and Barbara Davis (*Palm Springs Life*)

Red and Georgia
Skelton (Palm Springs
Historical Society)

Danny Kaye (Backlot Books
& Movie Posters)

Gavin MacLeod
(Larry Edmunds Bookshop)

Walter and Lee Annenberg
(Palm Springs Historical Society)

Ronald and Nancy Reagan
(*Palm Springs Life*)

"Sunnylands"
(Palm Springs
Historical Society)

Frank Sinatra's
compound (Palm
Springs Historical
Society)

Mia Farrow with her cat
(Larry Edmunds Bookshop)

The Chairman of the Board
(Larry Edmunds Bookshop)

Frank and Barbara Sinatra
(Howard Johns Collection)

Jill St. John cooling off
(Movie Market)

Sinatra's
mountain
hideout
(Platinum
Properties)

The Sinatras: Nancy, Frank, Jr., Barbara, Frank, Sr., "Dolly," and Tina
(Howard Johns Collection)

Sinatra in decline
(Movie Market)

Johnny Cash (*Palm Springs Life*)

Elizabeth Taylor
(*Palm Springs Life*)

Liza Minnelli (Cinema Collectors)

Tony Curtis (Movie Market)

Robert Mitchum (Movie Market)

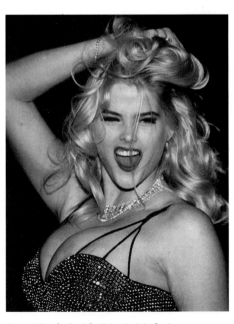

Anna Nicole Smith (Movie Market)

Chevy Chase (Cinema Collectors)

results, which affirmed his choice of actors, material, and his skills as a producer. Wallis's *Come Back, Little Sheba*, for example, won Shirley Booth an Oscar for Best Actress in her film debut. And few could fault him for one of his most profitable discoveries: the comedy team of Dean Martin and Jerry Lewis. The duo made nine films for the veteran producer, despite a rocky relationship with each other and with Wallis, who was often pushed to the breaking point by Lewis's spastic behavior on and off the set.

Perhaps his greatest unfulfilled discovery was rock 'n' roll singer Elvis Presley, who Wallis signed on "a hunch" after seeing Elvis do a television guest appearance, but long before Hollywood got a whiff of "the king's" pelvis-thrusting antics. Wallis saw tremendous film potential in Presley. But a business relationship that started out with the best intentions soon turned into crass exploitation, as Presley was shunted from one mediocre film to another. Incredibly, no one could agree on what the singer-turned-actor's image should be, so his talents languished in imbecilic plots involving girls, guys, racing cars, speedboats, carnivals, and other distractions.

Wallis's infallibility was also sorely tested when he signed Warren Beatty's older sister, Shirley MacLaine, to a long-term contract. "MacLaine had nothing good to say about Wallis," wrote Bernard Dick, "accusing him, among things, of chasing her around a desk, which Wallis denied in his autobiography—adding, however, that if he had, he could have caught her." MacLaine's complaint smacks of sexual harassment, which is probably why she bought out her contract for $150,000 and parted company with the producer. Those were the days before the feminist movement, and people were unused to dealing with allegations of sexual misconduct.

By then Wallis's career had mostly run its course, although his eye for attractive women was as clear as ever. He was boarding a plane from Los Angeles to New York for the gala premiere of *The Big Fisherman*, when he noticed a pretty actress named Martha Hyer waiting in line. He was still married, so he exercised discretion in courting her. But after his wife of 35 years, Louise Fazenda, died of a brain hemorrhage, Wallis proposed to Hyer, and they were married by a judge in Palm Springs on New Year's Eve 1966.

It was a joyous wedding. "Rarely does a man find the one right woman to marry," ruminated Wallis. "I was blessed. I found two." They settled at 70–649 Halper Lake Drive in a Santa Fe–style ranch house that was designed by architect Harold Levitt. It was called "Casablanca," in honor of Wallis's proudest achievement. The money Wallis made from movies helped decorate the home with valuable works of art, and the rooms were filled with artifacts of the Plains Indians and pre-Columbian sculptures.

Wallis's final two decades were spent in the glow of marital bliss and they were productive years. While living here, Wallis made *True Grit,* which won its paunchy star, John Wayne, an Oscar for Best Actor. He and Wayne also collaborated on the screenplay of the sequel, *Rooster Cogburn,* which Hyer wrote under a male pseudonym.

In 1981, Wallis was driving his car when he glanced down at the air conditioner and plowed into another vehicle. He was hospitalized with head injuries and diagnosed with diabetes, which necessitated the amputation of the toes on his left foot. Loss of circulation eventually required that his entire leg be removed, and Wallis realized the end was near.

The producer lingered on in the home he shared with Hyer, two gold Irving Thalberg Awards, and a million memories. He died in his sleep in 1986, at the age of 87.

■ ■ ■

RUSSIAN-BORN CINEMATOGRAPHER **JOSEPH Ruttenberg**, who was nominated for ten Oscars and won four—for *The Great Waltz, Mrs. Miniver, Somebody Up There Likes Me,* and *Gigi*—lived at 70–806 Halper Lake. Ruttenberg's career spanned practically the entire history of cinema, from silent films and the introduction of sound to early Technicolor and widescreen Cinemascope. He made a total of 134 movies, most of them for MGM.

A former newsreel cameraman who learned to get the shot in one or two takes, Ruttenberg possessed practical experience that proved invaluable on films such as the Marx Brothers comedy *A Day at the Races,* which was filmed on location at Santa Anita Park. He photographed Spencer Tracy's startling transformation from a civilized man into a wild beast in *Dr. Jekyll and Mr. Hyde,* the dangerous swordplay between Roman soldiers in Joseph Mankiewicz's film of *Julius Caesar,* and the choreographed ballet on heather-shrouded Scottish highlands in *Brigadoon.*

Ruttenberg's final film, *Speedway,* starring Elvis Presley and Nancy

Sinatra, took him back to his journalism roots: there he was, shooting from the sidelines as racing cars sped around Riverside International Raceway.

He died at the age of 93 in 1983.

■ ■ ■

WRITER **HARRY TUGEND** penned mirth-filled screenplays for films that starred irrepressible hams such as Bob Hope, Bing Crosby, Red Skelton, and Danny Kaye. He retired to 36–904 Pinto Palm Way in 1963, the year he also turned in the script for his 35th and final film, *Who's Minding the Store?* in which Jerry Lewis plays a klutzy department store worker attacked by household appliances.

Tugend's specialty was tailoring material to fit a comedian's style, and very often his contributions went unnoticed or were rewritten by others. Such was the case with *Take Me Out to the Ball Game*, which hit a home run for Gene Kelly and Frank Sinatra, and *Pocketful of Miracles,* which evoked both laughter and tears for Bette Davis, who played the movie's down-at-the-heels heroine. Adept at telling rags-to-riches stories, he worked on a spate of Shirley Temple dramas, including *Poor Little Rich Girl,* and he drew on his other great love, song and dance, for a bundle of Alice Faye musicals. In that spirited vein, Tugend produced *Golden Earrings*, a mysterious tale about gypsies that starred Ray Milland and Marlene Dietrich and launched the popular song of the title.

He died in 1989 at the age of 92.

■ ■ ■

MGM PRODUCER **Lawrence Weingarten** supervised more than 35 films, including the company's first talking musical, *The Broadway Melody.* He also assumed control of the seventh Marx Brothers movie, *A Day at the Races,* after Irving Thalberg, who had been in charge of production, died midway through the filming.

Weingarten, who resided at 70–418 Tamarisk Lane, went on to produce acclaimed movies such as *Adam's Rib, The Tender Trap, I'll Cry Tomorrow,* and *The Unsinkable Molly Brown.* He was nominated for an Oscar for Best Picture for his daring screen treatment of Tennessee Williams's celebrated play *Cat on a Hot Tin Roof.*

Weingarten was married to Irving Thalberg's sister, Sylvia, and during the course of their marriage he was promoted from studio publicist to production supervisor. He then divorced Sylvia and married Jessie Marmorston, a New York doctor who specialized in endocrinology. She subsequently became studio boss Louis B. Mayer's personal physician, fueling rumors that they were having a love affair. Weingarten, in fact, was concerned about his wife's fidelity when she doted on Mayer after the film honcho injured himself falling off a racehorse at his Perris ranch—she advised him on all manner of pharmaceutical treatments.

Ten years later, when Mayer's health sharply declined, she administered Vitamin B-12 shots, and in 1957, Marmorston was at Mayer's bedside when he received multiple blood transfusions for leukemia. The ailing mogul passed away a few months later.

Weingarten outlived Mayer by two decades. In 1974, Katharine Hepburn, who starred with Spencer Tracy in two of Weingarten's films, *Without Love* and *Pat and Mike*, presented the respected producer with the Irving Thalberg Award. He died the following year at the age of 77. Weingarten's widow, who continued to live in her husband's house, passed away five years after that, at 79.

■ ■ ■

THEY WERE THE most popular female singing group in the nation. They were the **Andrews Sisters**, three grinning, finger-snapping siblings whose catchy songs sent American servicemen and teenage jitterbuggers into frenzies whenever they performed at army canteens or nightclubs during World War II.

Not only could these girls sing and dance up a storm, they radiated homespun charm and wholesome sex appeal. The youngest of the group was Patty, a loud and energetic blonde who was also the group's lead vocalist. The middle sister, Maxene, was a brunette whose harmonic range sounded like four voices instead of three. And the eldest member of the trio, Laverne, was a strong-willed redhead with a sense of humor and an eye for fashion. Together they belted out some of the most beloved songs of the era, including their first big hit, "Bei Mir Bist Du Schon," which stayed at #1 on the Billboard charts for five weeks in 1937.

That success was followed by the bouncy, Oscar-nominated song

"Boogie Woogie Bugle Boy" from the film *Buck Privates,* the breezy romantic ballad "Don't Sit under the Apple Tree," and the rhythmic Latin number "Rum and Coca Cola." The girls earned $20,000 a week, making them among the biggest moneymakers for Decca Records.

The sisters became so popular that they were imitated and even parodied (on occasion they were unflatteringly portrayed as three singing horses). But their close harmonizing and clever musical arrangements, by Victor Schoen, set them apart from the competition. Their brassy, high-spirited recordings of "Pistol Packin' Mama," "Don't Fence Me In," "Rhumboogie," and "Beat Me Daddy Eight to the Bar," as well as lively cover versions of Fats Waller's "Hold Tight," "Oh, Johnny," and "Beer Barrel Polka" were big favorites. All in all, their songs earned a total of nine gold records and sold nearly 100 million copies.

But heartbreak and unhappiness lurked behind the fame.

Although each of the sisters was married (and Patty and Maxene were divorced), they were never far apart, and there were the inevitable tensions that frayed nerves and threatened to destroy their bonds. "We dressed together, we slept together, we roomed together, we went shopping together, and of course we rehearsed together. We never separated," said Maxene Andrews. By 1953, Patty Andrews had had enough of their quarreling and abruptly left the group to launch a solo career. Maxene and Laverne continued performing as a duo, but their success was limited. Then, a few years later, the sisters reunited and signed a new recording contract with Capitol Records.

In 1967, however, Laverne died of cancer, and the remaining sisters searched in vain for a suitable replacement. Devastated by the loss of their oldest sibling, and discouraged that they couldn't find anyone to take Laverne's place, the remaining Andrews sisters reluctantly broke up the act. Patty continued touring the country and making TV guest appearances. For Maxene, it was time for a change. She dipped into her savings and purchased the house at 70–890 Tamarisk Lane, where she reevaluated her life and career; the intersecting street, Andrews Circle, is named in her honor. She became Dean of Women for Tahoe Paradise College, where she taught speech and drama.

Nobody expected the remaining two sisters would ever get back together. But when Bette Midler's recording of "Boogie Woogie Bugle Boy" became a surprise hit in 1973, Maxene suddenly found herself in demand. She and Patty were offered starring roles in the Broadway musical *Over Here!* and played to sellout crowds for one year. Buoyed by the enthusiastic reaction, Maxene embarked on a solo career, although she put her plans on hold after she suffered a heart attack in 1982 and underwent a bypass operation. But she recovered and released an album of new songs called *Maxene: An Andrews Sister.*

In 1995, she toured in the musical revue *Follies '95* and appeared on Broadway in *Swingtime Canteen.* She was a big success, and at the age of 79 this chipper performer seemed poised to embark on yet another comeback. Tragically, it never happened. Maxene died of a heart attack, leaving Patty, the last Andrews sister, to grieve alone.

■　■　■

HE WAS LIKE a character straight out of a Damon Runyon story—a real wise guy. "You hadda be tough. You rode your bicycle and carried a baseball bat," said **Jilly Rizzo**, the one-eyed, broken-nosed, eighth-grade dropout and best pal of Frank Sinatra, who followed the singer everywhere.

"Frank wouldn't go to the bathroom without Jilly," confided a friend. And it was the truth. As Sinatra's major domo, he traveled around the world with the singer, peeling off hundred-dollar bills to tip waiters and bartenders, and keeping fans at a respectable distance. "From the mid-sixties on, no one was around Frank more than Jilly, and no one could get to Frank unless they passed through the massive wall of protection he constituted," said Shawn Levy.

Rizzo spoke like a punch-drunk ex-prizefighter. "Toots' Shor with an Italian accent," wrote Jerry Hulse. He was the man Sinatra leaned on for muscle and, depending on the singer's mood, to fetch a glass of water or a shot of bourbon during a performance. They traveled to Europe, South Africa, and Australia, winging across three oceans and racking up hundreds of thousands of air miles.

"Jilly was the brother my father never had," admitted Tina Sinatra. Their mutual affection was like the love between those mythical twins Romulus and Remus: Sinatra would do anything for the balding Rizzo, and Jilly would do anything for his toupee-wearing boss—even take a bullet if needed. "He'd die for him," admitted Rizzo's press agent with a flourish.

The two men had met when Rizzo operated Jilly's New York nitery, a piano bar at 256 W. 52nd Street in Manhattan that was renowned for its stiff drinks and tasty Chinese food. Everyone went there: Louis Prima, Judy Garland, Gordon MacRae, Jack Jones, Alan King, Soupy Sales. Jilly's was the favorite hangout of the Rat Pack in their barhopping days. Writer Gay Talese described the place as "swinging with rhythm and crawling with celebrities." Sports figures Sandy Koufax and Leo Durocher converged on the bar for lunch and dinner. So, too, did entertainment columnists Earl Wilson and Leonard Lyons.

A special booth and a private telephone were reserved for Sinatra. In return, the chairman of the board insisted that scenes for *The Manchurian Candidate, Come Blow Your Horn, Tony Rome, The Detective,* and *Lady In Cement* be filmed there as a favor to its pug-faced proprietor. In 1968, Sinatra and Rizzo opened Jilly's in Palm Springs, so their cronies from the East Coast could have a familiar place to pass the time in the desert. Rizzo decided to stay and bought a house for himself and his blue-haired wife, Honey, whom Sinatra nicknamed the "Blue Jew," at 70–940 Tamarisk Lane. From that point on, the two men were inseparable.

Rizzo was with Sinatra the night of Dean Martin's forty-ninth birthday party at the Beverly Hills Hotel, when the rowdy group ordered drinks in the Polo Lounge. When another customer, Fred Weisman, who was president of Hunt's Foods, complained about the noise, Sinatra threw a telephone at him, knocking Weisman unconscious. An ambulance rushed Weisman to Mt. Sinai Hospital, where he was listed in critical condition with a skull fracture and amnesia. He recovered and was dissuaded from taking legal action.

Jilly was also there the night Frank berated Mario Puzo in front of customers at Chasen's, until the bestselling author of *The Godfather,* who had allegedly based one of his characters on the mob-connected singer, got so fed up with Sinatra haranguing him that he left the restaurant. "Choke!" Sinatra yelled after him. "Go ahead and choke, you pimp!"

Rizzo came to Sinatra's rescue when a stalker infiltrated the singer's hotel room in Melbourne, Australia—the same place where Sinatra incurred the wrath of the country's union leaders when he launched a verbal assault against members of the press. Rizzo walloped the intruder over the head with a large standing ashtray, almost killing him. And Rizzo was there the night Sinatra and his pals were eating spaghetti at the Trinidad Hotel in Palm Springs and beat up an inebriated male customer in the cocktail lounge. The man sued them for $2.5 million in damages. Rizzo denied the charges, although his fingerprints were all over the guy. The case was settled out of court.

At parties, Sinatra often did a perfect imitation of Rizzo. Mussing his hair and pretending to have only one eye, Sinatra would curl his lip and snarl, "I smashed the rat bastard in the mouth and the cock-sucking motherfucker went down." Everyone cheered, especially Jilly, who thought it was the funniest thing he'd ever seen. If the expression "What goes around comes around" has a modicum of truth, then what happened to Rizzo on the eve of his seventy-fifth birthday, when his life was suddenly snuffed out like candles on a cake, may have been swift justice.

Much fuss has been made of that fateful evening of May 5, 1992. Rizzo had borrowed a friend's Jaguar XJ and planned to drive from his house to Mission Hills Country Club to pick up his own car, in anticipation of the following day's celebratory activities with Sinatra, who lived a few blocks away. Rizzo had also sent his friend Artie Funair out to buy a copy of the *Racing Form,* so he could check on the odds. Satisfied that the odds were in his favor, Rizzo reminded himself to place a bet on the next race, grabbed the car keys, and said "See ya later." He turned the Jaguar onto Los Alamos Road and traveled north until he reached the intersection of Gerald Ford Drive.

He had no idea that his bell was about to toll a few minutes after midnight. Blind in one eye, Jilly never saw what happened next. As the Jaguar idled outside the guard gate on Inverness Drive, he suddenly felt the car reverberate from a heavy crash, and then there was a loud explosion as the rear fuel tanks ignited. A Mercedes Benz 300 had rammed the Jaguar at a high rate of speed. A 28-year-old driver, later identified as Jeffrey Perrotte, jumped out of the Mercedes seconds before the Jaguar was engulfed in flames. Trapped inside, Rizzo pounded on the blackened windows, screaming in terror as he was consumed by fire.

When told his best friend had died, Sinatra dropped to his knees, sobbing uncontrollably, and banged his fists on the floor. Some accounts say that he had to be heavily sedated, others tell of his being placed in a strait-jacket for his own safety. There were fears that Sinatra might suffer a heart attack, and concerns that a contract would be taken out on Jilly's killer. These stories, if not true, are indicative of the unbreakable bond between two former street kids who had the world on a string. They were so close that Sinatra reportedly included a $100,000 bequest to Rizzo in his will. Had Rizzo lived, that amount undoubtedly would have been even higher. But the ultimate test of their friendship was laying Jilly to rest in the Sinatra family plot.

Jeffrey Perrotte was charged with second-degree murder and sentenced to fifteen years to life in state prison. He had been intoxicated and also stoned on marijuana at the time of the fatal accident. Guilt-ridden and remorseful, he sat in a jail cell for the next decade and contemplated his uncertain future.

Five days after the remake of the Rat Pack classic *Ocean's Eleven* opened in theaters nationwide, a group of investors, including rubber-faced, *Saturday Night Live* comedian Joe Piscopo, and Wally Rizzo, son of the late pub owner, reopened Jilly's at a new location: 41 West 58th Street in New York. (There's also a Jilly's in Chicago.)

In 2002, Nancy Sinatra wrote a heartfelt letter to Chuckawalla State Prison, requesting that the killer of her late father's best friend be denied parole. "Mr. Perrotte made a weapon of his car and used it to kill Mr. Rizzo," she said. "The terrorists of 9/11 have nothing on Mr. Perrotte. They used airplanes. He used his car." Her letter concluded, "Please make the punishment fit the crime of murder."

If the Sinatras have their way, Jeffrey Perrotte will be denied his freedom. An eye for an eye.

■ ■ ■

HUSKY AMERICAN LEADING man Kiel Mueller went from repertory theater to films in 1968, the year he met Claudia Martin, the daughter of Dean Martin. They subsequently married and raised a baby girl named Jesse. Henceforth known as **Kiel Martin,** he landed major roles in several praiseworthy movies. He was a desperate junkie in *The Panic in Needle Park* and a backwoods moonshiner in *Moonrunners*, which was later adapted for TV as *The Dukes of Hazzard*.

Martin's most impressive prime-time TV assignment, however, was portraying Detective John "J. D." LaRue, who foiled robbers and rescued hostages, among other acts of bravery, in the Emmy-winning NBC police drama *Hill Street Blues*. In an off-screen parallel to that tough but sensitive on-screen character, Martin, who resided at 71–129 Patricia Park Place, was a recovering alcoholic.

He followed his six-year run on *Hill Street* with a less successful stint on the Fox-TV sitcom *Second Chance,* playing Matthew Perry's guardian angel. But after that, Martin's health began to fail, compromised by many years of heavy drinking and smoking, and he only worked sporadically. He died of lung cancer at the age of 46 in 1990. Breast cancer claimed Claudia Martin at 56 in 2001.

■ ■ ■

LOVE HIM OR hate him—and many did—**Marvin Davis**, who resided at 71–070 Fairway Drive until his death at 79 in 2004, was the embodiment of Hollywood megalomania. A self-made billionaire whose net worth was estimated to be $5.8 billion by *Forbes* magazine, he was the single wealthiest man in Los Angeles for much of the last two decades, outtalking, outbidding, and mostly out-paying everyone. Standing six-feet four-inches tall and weighing 300 pounds, he was as imposing as a grizzly bear lumbering through the woods and just as unpredictable, according to those who met him.

Known throughout the Corn Belt as "Mr. Wildcatter," Davis amassed a fortune in oil, which gushed with such frequent regularity that he complained he could never rub the black stuff off his hands. He made so much money from oilfields in Colorado, Louisiana, Oklahoma, Wyoming, and Texas that he was propelled to buy things that most people only dreamed about. Over the years he bought and sold golden real estate properties such as the Beverly Hills Hotel and the Pebble Beach golf course. He also owned the Aspen Ski Company and its three mountains: Snowmass, Breckenridge, and Buttermilk, along with 200 miles of trails and the luxury hotel Little Nell. Davis reportedly laughed every time someone fell in the snow. To him, the world was his playground, and he was a carnival operator selling giant bags of cotton candy. The "deal" became his all-consuming passion, and it drove him to own as much as he could cram into his seven-days-a-week work schedule.

In 1981, Davis rocked Hollywood when he purchased 20th Century-Fox Film Corporation, one of the biggest old-time studios, for $720 million. A big movie fan, he nagged executives with suggestions to remake his favorite films or make sequels of others, including *The Sound of Music*. Producers disagreed with him. Nevertheless, under Davis's reign the company experienced some of its biggest box-office hits of the decade. They included *Porky's*, *Return of the Jedi*, *Romancing the Stone,* and *Cocoon*. But there were also costly flops such as *Rhinestone* and *Enemy Mine*, which caused him to sell off the studio—and pocket $350 million—after four years at the helm.

For years, Davis sponsored the glittering Carousel Ball in Denver, at one time the single biggest fund-raiser in the entire country. Noted for his generous charitable contributions, he and his wife, Barbara Levine, gave extravagant parties at their Beverly Hills home that were attended by Hollywood's A-list. Indeed, the couple was the town's premier party-givers. "They never stopped entertaining," said Dominick Dunne. "I remember nights there when violinists in red jackets stood playing on every step of the curved stairway in the marble front hall."

Davis certainly had an uncanny knack for knowing when it was time to buy or sell. The sale of Pebble Beach to a Japanese consortium, for example, was one of his greatest accomplishments, netting him a profit of $841 million. His chief philosophy was "never fall in love with any asset."

And his assets were choice. His investment portfolio included the $75-million Santa Monica Water Garden complex and the 34-story Fox Plaza, which Davis built in Century City. President Ronald Reagan kept offices there after leaving the White House, and Bruce Willis held terrorists at bay there in the explosive action thriller *Die Hard*.

"Even when he was out of the entertainment business," observed the *Los Angeles Times*, "Davis maintained strong ties and a keen interest in the industry." The paper noted that he was close friends with his Tamarisk neighbor Frank Sinatra, as well as with prominent political figures such as former president Gerald R. Ford and former secretary of state Henry

Kissinger.

An appreciative visitor to Davis's desert home was producer Robert Evans, who once played tennis and swam on the two-acre property while pitching a script that he wanted his younger brother, Charles Evans, to produce for another studio, Columbia. The film was *Tootsie* and it grossed $95 million.

But not everyone was a fan. An old adversary, Barry Diller, called him "that fat Marvin Davis," which got an unexpected laugh from the man himself, who on doctor's orders shed 130 pounds in an effort to ward off heart disease. Although Davis always thought big, he sometimes acted small, offering low bids for companies he thought were in financial trouble. It earned him a reputation as a tire kicker—someone who liked to look something over without paying for it.

In 2002, he tried and failed to buy the entertainment assets of Vivendi Universal, including its famed movie studio and theme park. His $13-billion bid was rejected as too low; the winning bid came from General Electric Company's NBC. Davis had played his last hand of poker. He cashed in his chips and never played again.

■ ■ ■

RICHARD "RED" SKELTON, America's most beloved clown, earned his nickname from the color of his hair. A goofy grin and a battered porkpie hat were his comic trademarks. He had the rare ability to make people laugh without uttering a word. But when he did speak, whether as Freddie the Freeloader, Clem Kadiddlehopper, or any of his cross-eyed, inebriated, stuttering characters, the laughs turned to howls of approval.

The mugging and the merriment took Skelton from stage to radio and ultimately to Hollywood, where he starred as accident-prone naïfs in the delightful comedies *Whistling in the Dark, Merton of the Movies, A Southern Yankee, The Fuller Brush Man, Watch the Birdie,* and *Excuse My Dust.*

But behind the comedy was a disquieting soberness. Orphaned by his father before he was born, Skelton was raised in unrelenting poverty. He spent his less-than-happy childhood selling newspapers on the streets of rural Indiana, literally clowning around in order to feed himself. He quit school at the age of ten and left home to become a teenage performer in burlesque and vaudeville, where he developed a donut-dunking routine that became his calling card. Another of his popular routines, called Guzzler's Gin, was based on one of his early bouts with alcohol.

In 1945, Skelton met and married his second wife, Georgia Davis, a demure young actress who had played bit parts in several films. The couple raised two children, Valentina and Richard, and they seemed like the happiest family on earth, until a doctor diagnosed their son with leukemia, and their world collapsed. Red refused to believe the worst, and they sought every cure, traditional and unorthodox, in a desperate effort to save the boy's life.

Both parents sought comfort in drinking, to cope with the stress of taking their dying son on an endless round of medical examinations and blood transfusions. Nothing helped. The plucky nine-year-old youngster gasped his last breath in 1958. The Skeltons were devastated by the tragic loss of life. Red promised to give up drinking and never touched hard liquor again, but Georgia found it difficult to stop. Misplaced feelings of guilt or remorse may have compelled her to reach for the bottle; whatever the cause, as her husband tried to pull his life together, she fell deeper into depression and became hooked on sleeping pills. Indeed, Red's line "Good night and God bless," at the end of *The Red Skelton Show* every week, took on renewed significance as the heart-broken comedian rushed from the studio to his Bel Air home to check on his frequently unconscious wife.

Four years after their son had been laid to rest in the family mausoleum, Skelton's friend and admirer Jack Entratter convinced Red to rid himself of the gloomy mansion and start looking for a new home not far from where Entratter lived in Rancho Mirage. (Red later sold the Bel Air house to Berry Gordy, president of Motown Records, for $600,000.) The Skeltons and their friend walked around Tamarisk Country Club looking at different houses. One day the three of them were standing chatting on the sixteenth fairway, when Red and Georgia both thought they saw the ghostly figure of a small boy with Richard's face playing and laughing on the lawn of a beautiful U-shaped home with a swimming pool. The address was 37–715 Thompson Road. Skelton knocked on the door and asked if the house was for sale. It wasn't, but he convinced the widowed owner, whose husband, Edgar Richards, had engaged the architect Wallace Neff to design it, to accept a cash payment of $150,000.

After moving in, Skelton, who had become enamored of Oriental mysticism, built a Japanese-style garden and tea house on adjoining land. There he could go to meditate or sleep, or write and rehearse comedy skits for his TV show. Skelton also purchased a small house for Georgia's parents, Mr. and Mrs. Mack Davis, and he bought a house in Palm Springs for his mother, whom he saw on a regular basis until she died of cancer in 1967.

One of his favorite hobbies was cultivating bonsai plants, and he would spend hours trimming the roots of small pine trees and twisting wire around their branches to get the proper shapes. His closest non-human companion in those difficult years was Gauguin, a rainbow-colored macaw that he carried with him everywhere. He often carried the bird on his arm during the closing monologue of his TV show.

The peace and serenity that Red had craved were at last realities. He was so happy puttering around his new home that he only left it for the weekly 130-mile-drive to the CBS studios, where he put on a hobo costume and greasepaint. Then it was back to the desert and his other life as Farmer Red, driving a red tractor around the grounds. He took up portrait painting and taught himself to create lifelike images of circus clowns. He experimented with still-lifes, landscapes, and watercolors of birds and animals. It seemed that the older Red got, the younger he became—or maybe he was merely channeling the ghost of his dead son.

Only his wife's drinking interfered with Red's recovery. As her alcoholism escalated, and Red absorbed this emotional trauma, the peace he had so painstakingly acquired began to slip away. He developed anxiety and then paranoia. Believing that his house was being watched by burglars, he would park his four Rolls Royces in the driveway to scare them away. He feared that a nuclear missile attack was imminent and began to hoard food.

One time, Irwin Allen, who was a frequent houseguest of Groucho Marx, walked into a local grocery store and was amazed to find its shelves empty.

"Going out of business?" Allen asked the proprietor.

"No," the proprietor replied. "Red Skelton was just in here. He backed a truck up to the front of my store and bought out the whole place, lock, stock, and barrel."

Convinced he was going to be robbed, Skelton hired a private security firm to patrol his house. He and Georgia slept with loaded .38 caliber revolvers under their pillows. He also carried large sums of cash—sometimes as much as $10,000—in case of an emergency.

It was around this time that Skelton began suspecting his wife of having an affair with his business manager, Chuck Luftig. Red fired him and hired their neighbor, Jack Entratter, who was president of the Sands Hotel in Las Vegas. But Entratter was too busy to do everything the comedian wanted of him, so he brought in an attorney, Joe Ross, to handle Skelton's business ventures. Ross's duties included writing checks for Irwin Allen's *Lost in Space* TV series, which Skelton had helped finance, and paying the comedian's bills.

It wasn't long, however, before Red had visions of his wife and Entratter sunbathing by the swimming pool and making love in their bedroom. So Red went out and began an affair of his own. The convenient woman was Lothian Toland, the 32-year-old daughter of Oscar-winning cinematographer Gregg Toland, of *Citizen Kane* fame. They met when Frank Sinatra, who was also a member of the Tamarisk Country Club, introduced Skelton to composer Frederick Loewe, for whom Lothian worked as a secretary.

Some people thought Skelton was the villain; others sympathized with his moral dilemma. Either way, his decision to stray must have weighed heavily on his conscience, for he knew his marriage was headed for disaster. "Georgia's drinking and her addiction to pills continued to be the one trouble spot Red couldn't cope with," said Arthur Marx. "She was on booze or pills or both most of the time. Like most alcoholics, she refused to recognize her problem, and as a result nobody could do anything to stop her."

During a nightclub engagement at the Sands in 1966, Skelton was informed by the staff that Georgia had attempted suicide; she had shot herself in the chest in their hotel suite with the same gun she kept at home to ward off prowlers. (The official version called the shooting an accident.) She was also ordering pitchers of ice water from room service, replacing the water with gin, and bribing waiters to refill her water glasses with gin at lunch and dinner, even though her husband had strictly forbidden them to do so.

Trusting no one, Red fired Entratter and Joe Ross, whom he incorrectly believed were colluding to take his money and, he thought, sleeping with his wife. He also started firing writers from his Emmy Award–winning TV show, prompting one disgruntled employee to quip, "Who does he think he is, Bob Hope?"

Skelton finally cracked under the strain of maintaining a suicide watch over Georgia, who was in a drunken stupor more often than not. By then, Lothian and Red were having sex in the same house where Skelton's wife lay passed out on the floor beside her empty gin bottles. Once, he managed to get her bathed and dressed for a Christmas photograph of them standing next to one of his prized Rolls-Royces, which had a wreath attached to the front bumper. But in her inebriated condition, and from his bedraggled appearance, the photo looked like the aftermath of bereavement more than the occasion for a blessing.

When Georgia refused to give him a divorce, he filed a petition himself at Indio courthouse, citing "irreconcilable differences which have caused a breakdown in our marriage." He tried to hang on to all of his estate, which, Red boasted to a friend, was worth $15 million. But when the divorce was finally granted in 1972, everything was split between the former husband and wife, down to the last penny.

Their troubles were far from over, however.

After Skelton and Lothian were married, they moved to a ranch in Anza. Georgia stayed on at the Thompson Road house, where she required a full-time, live-in nurse, because years of drinking had destroyed her health. Even apart, the Skeltons thought a great deal about their son, who would have turned 18 in 1976. On the afternoon of his birthday, Georgia asked her nurse to fix her a light meal. She poured herself a drink and ate in silence, like a prisoner on death row awaiting execution. Then she got up from the table and walked into the garden.

Standing under a grapefruit tree, Georgia reached into her dress and pulled out the .38 revolver, admiring its silvery glint in the deepening twilight. Then she put the barrel of the gun in her mouth and closed her eyes. There was a sharp crackle as the gun went off, and she fell in a crumpled heap on the lawn. The nurse found Georgia's body a few minutes later and notified the police.

Skelton arrived soon after. Fighting back tears, he went to his 54-year-old former wife, who lay on an ambulance stretcher covered in a white sheet, and told her how much he loved her, for better or for worse, until death did them part. Then he drove back up the hill to his other home and continued with his life.

Red kept performing in clubs and TV comedy specials until his farewell concert at Carnegie Hall in 1990. Seven years later, the little ghost appeared at his bedside and told him it was time to join his mother in eternal twilight. Skelton smiled for the last time and bid good night. He was 84.

■ ■ ■

ON TV, ACTOR **Gavin MacLeod** played Captain Merrill Stubing in the hit series *The Love Boat*, sitting at the captain's table and gloating over the romantic entanglements aboard the luxury ocean liner *Pacific Princess*. In real life he waged a private battle with obesity and alcoholism.

While MacLeod was playing cupid to star-crossed TV lovers and dispensing advice to the lovelorn, his own marriage was about to run aground. Despite the worldwide fame and financial security the top-rating sitcom brought him, MacLeod sank deeper and deeper into depression. "It's very trying on a marriage when you're doing a one-hour show week after week after week," he explained. Gavin's second wife, Patti Steele, hoped her husband would be able to control his temptations, but the problem was more difficult than either of them imagined.

MacLeod had waited years for this big break, marking time portraying sadistic killers and drug peddlers in various films and TV series. Then he became a household name as frumpy, balding, news writer Murray Slaughter on *The Mary Tyler Moore Show*. (Interestingly, Moore also battled alcoholism, as did her previous TV co-star, Dick Van Dyke.) When MacLeod was offered the starring role as the ship's kindly captain on *The Love Boat*, he grabbed the brass ring with both hands and refused to let go. "It was the greatest thrill of my life," he recalled.

Practically anyone who was anyone guest-starred on the ship-to-shore series, from old-time Hollywood stars Don Ameche, Ethel Merman, and Vincent Price to modern-day entertainers Sonny Bono,

Suzanne Somers, and Billy Crystal. Even underground pop artist Andy Warhol made an appearance. Oddly, this was MacLeod's fourth assignment to a ship's bridge—or the rudder. He had already played a submarine crewman in *Operation Petticoat*, a patrol boat member in *McHale's Navy*, and a merchant mariner in *The Sand Pebbles*.

But his resolve to stay off the booze crumbled in the face of a lucrative contract that took him around the world, to shoot episodes of *The Love Boat* in exotic countries such as Mexico, Australia, and China. Unable to reconcile their differences, MacLeod and Steele eventually separated, and they were divorced during the show's fifth season. The actor's beaming smile, which he flashed from under his white-and-gold captain's hat, concealed the heartbreak of a desperately lonely man who missed his wife and children.

Patti must have been suffering, too, because eventually, determined to strengthen their personal lives, Gavin and his ex-wife were reunited. They wrote about their struggles in *Back on Course: The Remarkable Story of a Divorce That Ended in Remarriage*. By that time, *The Love Boat* had sailed into history, and the MacLeods, who paid $290,000 for a retirement home at 70–070 Frank Sinatra Drive, next door to Nancy Sinatra's house in Tamarisk Villas, couldn't be happier.

■ ◻ ■

LIBERACE'S PERSONAL MANAGER **Seymour Heller**, who handled the posturing concert pianist's business affairs and transformed "Mr. Showmanship" from a highbrow Carnegie Hall attraction to a razzle-dazzle Las Vegas phenomenon, resided at 70–112 Frank Sinatra Drive for 20 years.

As the obsequious entertainer's prime mover and shaker, Heller was privileged to know intimate details of Liberace's private life, including his many homosexual affairs with good-looking younger men, whom he instructed Heller to put on the payroll as bodyguards, chauffeurs, and secretaries. (This fooled no one about the sequined, brocaded star's sexual proclivities.) Indeed, Heller, who was a happily married man with three children, was in a position of influence and trust that extended far beyond the boundaries of a normal working relationship.

"Heller was one of Lee's few close heterosexual associates," said Scott Thorson, who launched an unsuccessful gay palimony suit against Liberace for $100 million. (The lawsuit was settled out of court for $95,000.) "Businesslike and pragmatic, Heller made the ideal foil for Lee," Thorson explained. "Heller played hardball when negotiating contracts, while Lee played the smiling, agreeable 'anything goes' entertainer."

Heller had begun his career at the powerful talent agency MCA, where he booked the big bands of Tommy Dorsey, Glenn Miller, Guy Lombardo, and Paul Whiteman. When World War II arrived, he became an advance man for the U.S. Coast Guard stage show *Tars and Spars*, which featured muscle-bound actor Victor Mature, comedian Sid Caesar, and dancers Gower Champion and Bob Fosse.

In 1947, Heller teamed with agents Dick Gabbe and Sam Lutz to form their own personal management firm, Gabbe, Lutz & Heller. Their talent roster included Lawrence Welk, Frankie Laine, Al Martino, and Lyle "Skitch" Henderson. Heller signed Liberace, who became his biggest moneymaking client, in 1950, and for the next 37 years, he represented the flashy performer in all facets of show business, including his record-breaking performances at Caesars Palace and Radio City Music Hall.

It was Heller who ran media interference when news of Liberace's failing health first broke in 1986. The agent issued a strong denial, saying his most valuable client was suffering from emphysema, heart disease, and anemia—everything except the naked truth. By the time newspaper headlines screamed LIBERACE VICTIM OF DEADLY AIDS, Heller had circled the wagons and was firing off press releases like shotgun pellets. He kept issuing denials and even conspired to have the death certificate altered to keep the real cause of Liberace's illness a secret. It did him no good.

After Liberace died of AIDS early in 1987, Heller found himself on the receiving end of his former employer's vitriol. Heller alleged that Joel Strote, the entertainer's lawyer, had coerced Liberace to approve a hastily rewritten Last Will and Testament that the terminally ill star signed thirteen days before his death. Previous wills had named Heller; the new document removed Heller from Liberace's will and named Strote as sole executor and trustee of his $20 million estate. But Heller's legal battle against Strote was unsuccessful, and eventually he became just another former employee who was plum out of luck—and out of a job. He died in 2001 at the age of 87.

Strote now represents pop singer Britney Spears.

■ ■ ■

HOWARD W. KOCH, who was vice president in charge of production for Sinatra Enterprises, once owned the home at 70–122 Frank Sinatra Drive. The company produced six films starring the volatile singer and occasional actor, including the controversial political thriller *The Manchurian Candidate* and the Rat Pack's gangster spoof, *Robin and the 7 Hoods*. (Koch is not to be confused with the Howard Koch who wrote the Oscar-winning screenplay for *Casablanca*; they are unrelated.)

Koch and Sinatra's professional and personal lives had long been intertwined. In 1964, they were filming *None but the Brave* in Hawaii, when Sinatra and the producer's wife, Ruth Koch, were swept out to sea by a strong wave. Actor Brad Dexter saw the couple drowning and rescued them; after that, Koch, his wife, and Sinatra were inseparable. Subsequently Koch began a long and profitable association with Paramount Pictures where, as head of production, he oversaw the making of four Neil Simon comedies, including *The Odd Couple* and *Plaza Suite*.

This was the era when stars, writers, and directors were considered a film's biggest assets—not computer-generated special effects or an overly inflated budget. Koch's films, which ran the gamut from comedies and romantic dramas to Westerns and war adventures, reflected his genuine faith in the movie business. In that vein, Koch independently produced the hugely successful *The Other Side of Midnight, Airplane!*, and the love story *Ghost*—his sixty-first and final film. The philanthropic Koch received the Jean Hersholt Humanitarian Award, as well as the Directors Guild of America Frank Capra Achievement Award in 1991.

Interestingly, Koch lived at the Sinatra Drive address while producing the third of eight Academy Awards ceremonies, in 1975. Three years later he produced the star-studded fiftieth Academy Awards celebration, hosted by Bob Hope, who, gazing up at a staircase lined with some of Hollywood's biggest names, memorably quipped, "Welcome to the *real* Star Wars!"

Koch died at the age of 84 in 2001.

■ ■ ■

ON AUGUST 8, 1986, a brief obituary tucked away in the back pages of the *Los Angeles Times* told a remarkable story:

AGENT WHO DISCOVERED GABLE DIES

Minna Wallis, 92, the talent agent generally credited with discovering Clark Gable, died at her home in Rancho Mirage on Sunday. Miss Wallis began as a secretary to Jack L. Warner. She recommended that Warner hire her brother to manage the old Garrick Theater at 8th Street and Broadway in downtown LA which the Warner Brothers owned, thus launching his career in the film industry.

Miss Wallis progressed from secretary to agent, joining Famous Artists before branching out on her own in 1950. Over the years, she was associated with Greta Garbo, Myrna Loy, Cary Grant, and Gable, whom she met after his first wife, Josephine Dillon, taught him film acting.

For once, the Hollywood hyperbole was true, even if it wasn't the whole truth. The coquettish **Minna Wallis**, who had followed her younger brother to the desert in 1968 and purchased a home at 70–138 Frank Sinatra Drive, had indeed discovered the swaggering matinee idol that set women's hearts aflutter. But she also carried a torch for her secret love and held a grudge for never receiving the credit she felt was overdue.

Her famous brother, Hal Wallis, the "big producer" as she called him, saw his name flash repeatedly across the screen. Minna had to contend with anonymity, toiling away in the backroom of Hollywood casting offices like a dollar-a-day seamstress. She resented her brother and took every opportunity to remind the famous producer that it was *she* who had made it possible for *him*.

In her sunset years she exacted revenge, demanding that Hal take care of her. He did, grudgingly, inviting his sister for cursory visits to his home. "Being 'family,' Minna expected to be treated accordingly—which meant dinner, if not every night, then on a regular basis," said Bernard Dick. The task fell to Wallis's wife, Martha Hyer, to play chauffeur, picking Minna up and taking her home after a night spent watching a movie together.

It was a claustrophobic relationship that lasted until Minna's death. She was rumored to have been the lover of Clark Gable, but she never married him or anyone else. She remained a defiant martyr to the end, like the title character in one of her brother's films, *The Old Maid*.

Then, in 2003, the reason Wallis never married was finally revealed. It wasn't because she carried a torch for Gable; it was because she was a lesbian. Once, while staying at Frank Sinatra's house in Palm Springs, she had engaged in a *ménage à trois* with Garbo, who was her client, and with Marlene Dietrich. Minna and Garbo were lying naked by the pool, smoking cigarettes, when Dietrich started kissing Greta's lips. According to Sinatra's butler, who witnessed the event, Marlene slid her hand between the actress's legs and fondled her clitoris. Wallis lay next to them while the women pleasured each other. When their feverish lovemaking was interrupted by a nearby coyote's yell, the three women took their lovemaking inside, to a bedroom.

■ ■ ■

MAKE ROOM FOR Muzyad Yakhoob! No, somehow it just doesn't have the same ring as *Make Room for Daddy*, the top-rated family sitcom that starred much-loved American Lebanese comedian, better known by his adopted stage name: **Danny Thomas**.

Sporting a cigar only slightly larger than his prominent nose, Thomas assailed nightclub audiences with his witty monologues and schmaltzy songs, and over-emoted in the saccharine Hollywood musical biography *I'll See You in My Dreams* and a 1953 remake of *The Jazz Singer*. Thomas eventually found his niche as the durable star of his own TV series, for which he won an Emmy Award in 1954, five years before he purchased the home at 70–400 Frank Sinatra Drive. He also owned a 116-acre farm, which he christened Big Muz Ranch (after his Arab name). It served as his weekend retreat in the nearby city of Beaumont, and there he rode horses and baled hay when not rehearsing a show.

Thomas, along with neighbors Sinatra, Jimmy Durante, Sophie Tucker, Tony Martin, and Nat "King" Cole, were among the pioneering entertainers in Las Vegas, where casinos were controlled by the mob. But the mob's influence extended further than Vegas, as Thomas himself rudely found out.

When the up-and-coming comedian accepted an engagement at New York's famed Copacabana Club, but was inadvertently booked into a rival nightclub as well, the Copa's owner, Jules Podell, called Thomas an "asshole." Thomas kept his cool, but a short time later the promising stand-up comic received a phone call from mobster Frank Costello, who had money invested in the Copa, and told him there was a bet riding on whether Thomas would perform there or not. Costello had his hand in several East Coast nightclubs and casinos and was partners with Meyer Lansky in the Piping Rock near Sarasota Springs. Thomas, who understood the implication of Costello's phone call, reassured him that he had every intention of fulfilling his part of the agreement. One day, during his stint at the Copa, Thomas was eating a late breakfast in Lindy's Restaurant, the fabled showbiz hangout, when he was approached by a well-tailored man in a gray flannel suit. It was Costello, who politely thanked him for resolving the "incident."

It was not the only time Thomas crossed paths with the mob. In Chicago he made the acquaintance of the Fischetti brothers. Charles, Rocco, and Joseph Fischetti were "made" men in mafia parlance; they had taken the blood oath of eternal brotherhood and sworn to uphold the dark code of silence in the ancient society of La Cosa Nostra.

Charlie was the mob's political fixer in Chicago, Rocco ran the syndicate's gambling concessions there, and Joe helped out wherever he was needed. Among other things, they controlled the private gambling room at Chez Paree, another nightclub where Thomas worked. The brothers requested that the popular entertainer tell jokes at the wedding of Charlie Fischetti's sister and sent a limousine to ensure he would show up. "Sometimes they scared me, but mostly they couldn't have been nicer," Thomas confided about the mobsters he ran across. "And sometimes my dealings with them were like scenes out of *The Godfather* movies."

Supposedly, Thomas was Frank Sinatra's favorite comedian, and the singer often attended Danny's late-night shows. He'd sit at a back table so he wouldn't be recognized, a glass of Jack Daniels within easy reach, and try to analyze what made Thomas's jokes so funny. (The men were so close, in fact, that Thomas was godfather to Sinatra's son, Frank, Jr.)

But Thomas didn't always want to be at the beck and call of others, whether in nightclubs or on television. So he branched out into producing TV himself, financing *The Real McCoys* and partnering with actor-producer Sheldon Leonard on *The Dick Van Dyke Show, The Andy Griffith Show, Gomer Pyle,* and *The Joey Bishop Show.* After Leonard left to produce *I Spy,* Thomas and Aaron Spelling made *The Mod Squad* together, a venture that helped turn both men into multimillionaires.

Thomas wasn't only a taker; he was also a big giver, generously donating his time and money to build St. Jude Children's Research Hospital in Memphis, Tennessee, and roping in other celebrities such as Dinah Shore and Bob Hope to pass the hat around.

There was one child, however, whom he couldn't save: Rusty Hamer, who played his son on *Make Room for Daddy.* Hamer had lost his real father at an early age, so Thomas became the boy's surrogate dad, playing baseball and football with him and trying to make the boy feel loved. One day Hamer threw his arms around Thomas and wept, "You're the only Daddy I have now." It nearly broke the actor's heart. After Hamer grew up, however, he dropped out of sight, and years later Thomas was thunderstruck to pick up a newspaper and read that Hamer had committed suicide by shooting himself in the head.

Thomas had always realized how precious his own two children were to him, but Hamer's sad end strengthened his feelings. Danny's daughter, Marlo Thomas, who married talk-show host Phil Donahue, became a star in her own right as TV's first independent woman in *That Girl.* Her younger brother, Tony Thomas, became the producer of numerous sitcoms, including *The Golden Girls.*

In 1991, Danny Thomas had just made a guest appearance on *Empty Nest,* which Tony had produced, and he was looking forward to filming a TV movie with his daughter, when he was stricken with a fatal heart attack. He was 77.

■ ■ ■

SPEAKING OF THE mob, it's interesting to note that **Jack Entratter**, the former bouncer for the Stork Club and the Copacabana, where Danny Thomas had his memorable run-in with Jules Podell and where Frank Costello interceded on his behalf, later owned Thomas's home at 70–400 Frank Sinatra Drive. What are the odds of that being a coincidence and not part of a bigger plan?

A six-foot-three-inch bear of a man, Entratter was adored by the stars that played the Sands Hotel, which he fronted for his boss, Frank Costello. After all, Entratter offered them high salaries and deluxe accommodations. "He was our love," said comedian Jerry Lewis. "We wouldn't go anywhere in Vegas except where Jack was."

Billed as "A Place in the Sun," the Sands Hotel was the smartest and sexiest of the casinos on the Strip. It's where Entratter, in his tailor-made suits with French cuffs, was lord and master. When other hotels refused to sell black entertainers a room, the Sands gave keys to Herb Jeffries, Nat "King" Cole, and Sammy Davis, Jr.

Entratter had worked his way up the mob ladder from Stork Club doorman to president of the Sands. It was said he feared no one, except perhaps Frank Sinatra on a drunken night. Their wary friendship was put to the test in the fall of 1967, when Sinatra was lured away from the Sands with the promise of a $3-million contract to play the newest hot spot in town, Caesars Palace. When the Sands did not make a counter offer, Sinatra was incensed by their apparent show of disloyalty—and began drinking and gambling heavily. Drunk, he started breaking up furniture in his private suite, and after learning that the hotel had cut off his credit to protect him from himself, Sinatra went crazy, screaming profanities and accosting the staff. He commandeered a baggage cart and drove it, like a drunken stuntman, through a plate-glass window.

At dawn, Sands casino manager Carl Cohen stormed down to the damaged lobby, where he and the red-faced singer, who had played there to packed houses for 15 years, faced off like two boxers in front of scared restaurant employees. When Sinatra threw a handful of betting chips at Cohen and called him a "kike," the manager responded with a right hook to Sinatra's chin, splitting his lip and breaking two of his front teeth. The singer's bodyguard, Jilly Rizzo, made like he was about to pull a gun, but he was stopped by a burly security guard. Cornered, Sinatra picked up a chair and smashed it over another guard's head. He then ran pell-mell out the front doors and down the street, with Rizzo chasing after him.

Many people found Sinatra's loutish behavior and cowardice despicable. "After Carl Cohen punched him out and Frank left the Sands, Sinatra never spoke to Jack again," said Phyllis McGuire. "And Entratter lived next door to him in Palm Springs!"

The stress finally caught up with Entratter, who suffered a cerebral hemorrhage in 1971, two weeks after his fifty-eighth birthday. His widow, Corinne Cole, a former Playboy Playmate of the Month, later married George Sidney, who had directed Sinatra in *Anchors Aweigh* and *Pal Joey*.

■ ■ ■

TONGUE-TWISTING, LIMB-CONTORTING COMEDIAN **Danny Kaye** could have been a cat in another lifetime. He certainly was as dexterous as a feline, and seemed to possess nine lives and at least as many personalities. His physical agility and split-second timing were marvels to behold; whenever he took the stage, his voice quivering, arms flailing, and legs wobbling, it looked as though he was about to launch himself into orbit.

His breathless recitation of the names of 54 Russian composers, which he delivered in 38 seconds in the number "Tchaikovsky," during the Broadway musical *Lady in the Dark*, caused so much gleeful pandemonium in the audience that it stopped the show at every performance. His nonsensical song patter, such as "Git-gat-gittle with a geet-ga-zay" from "Melody in Four F," and "The Lobby Number," an absurd parody of coming attractions that he performed in his film debut, *Up in Arms*, left moviegoers in stitches.

Kaye's scatterbrained, whimsical characters, whether hypochondriacs, milquetoasts, or daffy army colonels, caused gales of laughter in *Wonder Man*, *The Secret Life of Walter Mitty*, and *The Inspector General*. And they all had one thing in common: they were daydreamers just like Kaye. But this schizophrenic performer was not who he appeared to be onstage or in the movies. In real life he was an unhappy, sexually repressed man trapped in a loveless marriage.

It probably would have been better if he had divorced his songwriter-wife, Sylvia Fine, whom he had married in 1940 when they were young lovers. Instead, seven years later, Kaye walked out on his wife and nine-month-old daughter, Dena, for actress Eve Arden, who had left her husband to be with Kaye. But Fine refused to let him go, and she waited patiently for his affair with Arden to reach its end.

Thus began a pattern of blame and forgiveness that continued throughout the Kayes' contrived marriage; he played the role of concerned husband, she played his loving wife, even though they slept in separate beds and often in different homes. By *On the Riviera*, his seventh film, Kaye had embarked on another affair, this time with dancer Gwen Verdon.

There were more romantic interludes with more actresses and chorus girls. Sylvia would take her revenge by refusing to write new songs or special material for Kaye; Kaye would repent; they'd go back to displays of public kissing and hand-holding for another six months, when the vicious cycle would start again.

In 1952, Kaye tackled his most challenging role, the introverted Danish folk hero Hans Christian Andersen in an elaborate Technicolor musical composed by Frank Loesser. Kaye cut his hair and wore hand-stitched vests and quilted pants in an attempt to capture the childlike aspects of the fabled writer of children's fairytales. It was an uncharacteristically subdued role for Kaye, devoid of his usual firecracker humor. Perhaps he was trying to find himself. If so, he may have been surprised to learn that the real Andersen, for all his infantile qualities, was actually a practicing homosexual.

A portion of Kaye's $200,000 salary from the top-grossing film went toward purchasing a four-bedroom home on the club's fifteenth fairway, at 70–710 Frank Sinatra Drive. There the enervated comedian took up golf and rested from the stress of concert tours and personal appearances. He would often follow Jack Benny around the course, telling jokes.

The few times that Sylvia Fine showed up on weekends, Kaye sped off in his golf cart to who-knows-where and did not return until sunset. Their marital charade fooled no one.

Interestingly, whenever his private life was in turmoil, Kaye made a public spectacle to divert attention from his troubles. For example, he developed a strange habit of wearing female drag at costume parties where other people showed up dressed as gangsters and pirates. To the astonishment of the guests, Kaye would arrive in high heels and flowing chiffon. At one benefit he was introduced as Kay Thompson, the mannish cabaret singer who was the godmother of Liza Minnelli. In Kaye walked, wearing an exact copy of Thompson's clothes, clutching a cigarette holder, and blowing kisses to the crowd. "Hello, darlings!" he gushed in a falsetto voice.

Kaye's fondness for cross-dressing reached its dizzy limit in the 1954 box office hit *White Christmas,* in which he and Bing Crosby put on women's makeup and lip-synched to Vera-Ellen and Rosemary Clooney's perform-ance of "Sisters." "Crosby was very uncomfortable with this," said biogra-pher Martin Gottfried, "and Kaye had to talk him into doing the number." After a few shots of whiskey, Crosby and Kaye sashayed onto the stage wear-ing tiaras and bracelets and waving feather fans in the air, all the while mouthing the words to the campy song. Their antics, replayed on hundreds of TV broadcasts, have inspired several generations of drag queens.

Kaye's lack of good taste notwithstanding, he was given an honorary Academy Award in 1955 for his unique talents and service to the motion picture industry. He and Sylvia reconciled again, and they put the fin-ishing touches to the film that would become his most popular and enduring work of cinematic art. "The pellet with the poison's in the ves-sel with the pestle. The chalice from the palace has the brew that is true." The words were Sylvia's but the clever intonation was pure Kaye in *The Court Jester.* It represented the pinnacle of his movie career.

There were more films, TV shows, and variety specials. But Kaye found his life taking a new direction. The gradual transformation from filibuster-ing funnyman to globetrotting UNICEF spokesman relegated his acting career to the sidelines. He grew his hair long, stopped wearing double-breasted suits, and put on floppy white golf hats, sweaters, and space shoes.

One day a smiling fan came up to him on the green at Tamarisk Coun-try Club. "Say, didn't you used to be Danny Kaye?" he asked. Kaye made the face of a gargoyle and walked away.

Over the next three decades, he exorcised some of his demons and ful-filled several long-held desires. He taught himself to become a master chef and cooked up eight-course Chinese banquets that included beef with onion rings, "banjo" duck, beer-battered scallops, and stir-fried oysters.

He earned his pilot's license and flew a McDonnell Douglas DC-10 airliner from New York to Athens, Greece. He wore a doctor's surgical mask and gown, made a stitch, and tied the suture during an anes-thetized hospital patient's heart-valve operation. And he achieved his greatest ambition: he picked up a baton and conducted the New York

Philharmonic Orchestra.

It was like a dream come true. He really *was* Walter Mitty.

But not all the demons were gone. He and Sylvia still fought like cat and dog. Kaye sought affection in the willing arms of ever-younger girlfriends such as Marlene Soroksy and Joanna Simon, a 28-year-old opera singer whose younger sister, Carly Simon, was married to singer James Taylor.

Kaye was awarded a second Oscar in 1982. And then it happened. He developed leg trouble, experienced chest pains, and was diagnosed with an irregular heart rhythm. He underwent quadruple heart-bypass surgery, but there were complications. His bladder ruptured. He was given multiple blood transfusions and contracted Hepatitis C. People said he had AIDS.

Two months after his seventy-fourth birthday, in 1987, Kaye died of a heart attack brought on by internal bleeding and post-transfusion hepatitis. Sylvia Fine sold the Rancho Mirage house and moved to a spacious apartment overlooking Central Park in Manhattan. She died from emphysema at the age of 78, in 1991.

■ ■ ■

THE CURRENT OWNER of Danny Kaye's former home, at 70–710 Frank Sinatra Drive, is Hollywood talent agent **Norby Walters**, who throws the annual "Night of 100 Stars" Oscar-viewing party at the Beverly Hills Hotel. According to tax records, he paid $105,000 for the house when it was listed for sale in 1994.

A *Sports Illustrated* article published in 1987 stated that Walters's business activities were under investigation by the FBI and a federal grand jury in Chicago. "He has made enemies, headlines and mistakes in profusion, prompting urgent calls by both sports and government officials for reform of the sports-agent game to protect athletes from his supposedly dangerous ilk," the magazine reported. In his defense, Walters replied he was the innocent victim of jealous, rumor-planting rival agents, sensationalizing reporters, and unscrupulous colleagues who had robbed him blind. Be that as it may, he sold his talent agency in 1990.

■ ■ ■

IF THE LIFE of **Walter Annenberg** is ever made into a film, the movie will require an actor of the caliber of Kevin Costner or Tom Hanks, and a director with the gravitas of Martin Scorsese. The title would need to be explicit, even daring: *The Racketeer.* The movie would be full of political intrigue, corruption, and scandal. It would not be a pretty story, but then neither was the life of this billionaire publisher, former ambassador, and philanthropist.

Annenberg wasn't always a slouching, white-haired, grandfatherly figure. In his younger days he was a charming and eloquent businessman who wore tailored three-piece suits, drove Packard roadsters, and romanced movie stars. Walter came of age in the wild and wooly 1920s, when the mob controlled the Chicago waterfronts and booze was illegal. A second-generation newspaper man, he witnessed his father's struggles to protect his growing empire during the bloody circulation wars, when rival groups fought for distribution territory and there were contract killings and other violent crimes.

His dad, Moses "Moe" Annenberg, owned *The Philadelphia Inquirer, Daily Racing Form,* and two raunchy men's magazines, *Baltimore Brevities* and *Click,* that were banned in some states. He also owned General News Bureau, a racetrack betting wire service deemed illegal by the authorities.

It was rumored, but never proven, that Annenberg had made a sweetheart deal with the mob, cutting them in on a piece of the action in return for their help in taking the wire service nationwide, as well as into Canada, Cuba, and Mexico. "Despite the respectable façade, Moe Annenberg did business with racketeers as an equal," stated Laurence Bergreen. "Indeed, he was, according to some accounts, the most powerful non-Italian racketeer in the nation."

Walter looked up to his dad with the same reverence as a kid watching his favorite baseball player hit a home run. But this was no game. When the elder Annenberg tried to force his wire service competitors out of business, his plan backfired, and Moses found himself a marked man. He fled the Windy City and relocated to Florida, where he bought the *Miami Tribune* and reportedly paid $1 million in annual protection money to keep his enemies off his back. Despite his best efforts, Annenberg came under increased scrutiny from the government, and in 1939 he was indicted by a federal grand jury for income tax evasion.

Walter, then 31, was charged with aiding and abetting his dad, which was not surprising; he was being groomed to take over the family business. Frightened that he would lose his livelihood, the older Annenberg plea-bargained to drop the charges against his son, in return for a guilty plea for himself.

But the trap snapped shut on him anyway. He was ordered to pay $9.5 million in back taxes and penalties and was sentenced to three years in federal prison. By the time he was released, Annenberg's spirit was broken. He died of a brain tumor in 1942 at the age of 65.

His heir apparent stood ready to assume the crown—and to avenge those who had wronged his father. But Walter realized it would take more than muscle to finish the job. Something else was needed, he told himself: respectability. Toward that end, the younger Annenberg worked to create a new image for himself, and in the process he redefined the relationship between government and free enterprise.

"Sunnylands," the 266-acre fairytale estate that was Annenberg's impenetrable fortress at 71–800 Frank Sinatra Drive, might be termed "the House that *TV Guide* built." Named after the winter retreat that Moe Annenberg owned in the Poconos, this ornate temple of media worship, in which every brick was bought and paid for by magazine subscriptions, is as much a tribute to the racketeer's son as Xanadu was to the fictional Charles Foster Kane.

Hidden from prying eyes by rows of eucalyptus trees, oleanders, and tamarisks, this man-made oasis is protected by armed guards and surrounded on four sides by an electrified wall, where offending trespassers, both human and animal, have been known to take a well-aimed bullet within seconds of violating the perimeter. Designed by architect A. Quincy Jones, the pink and orange, contemporary, Mayan-themed residence contains 32,000 square feet of polished living space, including a two-bedroom main house and a four-bedroom guest wing surrounded by arcades, loggias, terraces, and a porte-cochere. The property's total acreage, including an adjoining 658-acre tract of undeveloped land acquired by its industrious owner as a buffer zone, is a whopping 933 acres—10 percent more land than New York's Central Park and minus the crime or congestion.

Annenberg began the home's three-year construction in 1963, because he was tired of waiting for tee times at Tamarisk Country Club, he said, and wanted to get on with playing the game instead of talking about it.

He instructed Jones and golf-course designer Dick Wilson to build him a house on a course but with one major difference: he didn't want to see a grain of sand anywhere except in the sand traps. Interior decorator William Haines, famed for his work on the homes of Carole Lombard, William Powell, and Norma Shearer, chose the furnishings.

A former actor, Haines had been the #1 box office star in 1930. But his career had been ruined by homosexual scandal, and he was forced to reinvent himself as Billy Haines, "decorator to the stars." He lived openly with another man, James Shields, for almost 50 years, plying his newfound trade as a "fluffer" to the rich and fatuous. Among Haines's most important commissions was restoring the U.S. ambassador's three-story Georgian mansion in Regent's Park, London. But Sunnylands remains his greatest achievement.

Beyond the marbled patios, swimming pools, and botanical gardens extend manicured English lawns, duck-filled lakes with bubbling waterfalls, and a nine-hole golf course, where Annenberg would chip several rounds with desert neighbors Bing Crosby and Bob Hope, who was so nervous his ball ended up in the lake.

First-time visitors to Annenberg's plush estate were often astounded by the sheer grandeur and opulence of these kingly premises, which left some people totally in awe and others perturbed by the ostentatious display of wealth. Like Kane's Xanadu, there was no shortage of valuable works of art; Impressionist and post-Impressionist paintings hung on every wall, T'ang Dynasty tomb figures crowded the floors, and Steuben crystal pieces adorned cabinets and bookshelves.

And like Kane, who maintained a private zoo filled with alligators and monkeys, Annenberg possessed a collection of exotic birds, which he followed about the grounds like an ornithologist, watching them through his ever-present binoculars and pursing his lips to imitate their calls.

Invited guests to Sunnylands—for there is no other kind—first have to pass a security check at the main gate, where their personal identification is reviewed by guards in blue uniforms and their vehicles are searched for weapons. They are then escorted up a half-mile-long driveway, their movements monitored by closed-circuit TV cameras that are mounted between the trees, until they come to the grandiose main entrance. There, 60 trained staff thoroughly briefed on protocol aim to fulfill their every pleasure.

Annenberg's heavily fortified compound, where he entertained presidents, foreign heads of state, and royalty, might never have seen the light of day, however, had it not been for a small red-and-white paperback that was bought and read in more than 20 million households each week. It is incorrect to say that Annenberg invented *TV Guide*—he didn't. What he did was amalgamate several publications into one periodical that dominated the marketplace. He eliminated the competition, just as Moe had tried to do and failed.

Perhaps that is why Annenberg usually favored the underdog. He believed that America was a land of opportunity where, if you worked hard and conquered adversity, and used whatever means were at your disposal, you could make a fortune. Through the various publications that he either acquired or founded, including *Seventeen*, a glossy magazine for debutantes, Annenberg sought validation from officials and gained access to high places.

His second marriage, to Leonore Cohn, the stylish niece of Columbia Pictures's foul-mouthed mogul Harry Cohn, was a case in point. "Lee," as she was called, had previously been wedded to Beldon Katleman, the owner of El Rancho Vegas, and to former bootlegger Lewis Rosentiel, the head of Schenley Industries.

When Sunnylands was completed in 1966, Walter and Lee Annenberg threw a lavish New Year's Eve party to celebrate. In true, upwardly mobile Annenberg fashion, what began as a small dinner and a movie for 20 people soon mushroomed into an annual gala for 100 special friends, who occupied reserved seats, wore tuxedos and ball gowns, ate pheasant off exquisite Flora Danica china, and drank Dom Perignon champagne in Baccarat crystal.

Many lasting friendships were made over drinks and dinner with the Annenbergs. Walter and Lee supported Richard M. Nixon in his second presidential campaign and threw a victory party for him at the estate after his 1968 election.

Nixon was the most awkward of the U.S. presidents, a shifty-eyed, sweating, nervous hand-wringer prone to fits of depression and emotional outbursts. How he convinced the American people to entrust him with the highest office in the land remains a baffling mystery. And yet, Annenberg liked him.

And his devotion was rewarded when Nixon, while staying at Sunnylands, offered Walter the coveted position of ambassador to the Court of St. James's in London, England. Annenberg held the post for six years.

One person who abused his welcome at Sunnylands was Nixon's secretary of state, Henry Kissinger, a frequent desert visitor. Kissinger apparently had no qualms about calling the ambassador's foreign office to schedule a weekend stay at Annenberg's home as if it were a private hotel. "That he [Kissinger] had no professional respect for Walter and denigrated him behind his back, yet was more than willing to accept his hospitality was part of his deeply ingrained tendency toward deceit," accused political journalist Christopher Ogden.

When Nixon was drowning in the scandal of Watergate, and was forced to resign from the highest office in the land, Annenberg threw the shunned ex-president a much-needed life preserver: a five-year contract at $60,000 a year to be a consultant in international diplomacy and economics at the Annenberg School of Communications.

England's Prince Charles was also pleasurably seduced by Annenberg's avuncular goodwill. On the prince's first visit to Sunnylands, Charles, a non-golfer, careened down Walter's fairways playing golf-cart polo, with his host in friendly pursuit. It was something the prince could never have done at Windsor Castle. Charles, who had a rocky relationship with his parents, found Walter a receptive listener, especially after the death of his great-uncle, Louis Mountbatten, who was assassinated by an IRA bomb in 1979.

At the royal wedding of Prince Charles and Lady Diana Spencer in 1981, the Annenbergs, along with several of the prince's former girlfriends (including Camilla Parker-Bowles, with whom Charles was secretly in love), were given reserved seating in the front pews at St. Paul's Cathedral. Charles later confided to Walter and Lee about his troubled marriage, which was rumored to have been arranged by his mother to offset the bad press surrounding Charles's frequently embarrassing amorous conquests.

Walter's close friendship with actor Ronald Reagan, who appeared twice on the cover of *TV Guide*, was useful on several levels. The friendship brought the newspaper magnate Reagan's understanding ear when the actor became president of the Screen Actors Guild, and the connection was also helpful when Reagan was elected governor of California and subsequently became president of the United States. Walter endorsed his friend "Ronnie's" presidential run—the only time he ever publicly backed a political candidate—when Reagan sought the Republican nomination in 1980.

Indeed, the two men kept up a written correspondence for more than 40 years, and their wives behaved more like sisters. Lee and Nancy Reagan telephoned each other on a weekly, sometimes daily, basis, and Nancy never forgot Lee's birthday or anniversary.

When Reagan was elected the nation's fortieth president in 1981, Annenberg went out of his way to uphold the noble Spanish tradition of *mi casa es su casa*. The president's colleagues and friends were flown in for annual parties at Sunnylands. New York socialites Jerome Zipkin and Brooke Astor could be seen gossiping in one room, while U.S. Secretary of Defense Casper Weinberger and Secretary of State George Shultz debated foreign policy in another.

Annenberg couldn't pass up the opportunity to goad England's reigning monarch, Queen Elizabeth II, when she visited Sunnylands with the Reagans in 1983. He gave her a guided tour of his home by golf cart, pointing out the ducks and birds while an army of groundskeepers, cooks, maids, butlers, and gardeners smiled and waved at her.

After she left, Walter told an associate, "I just wanted to show Her Majesty how the average American lived." The queen, who was barely able to conceal her envy of such blatant extravagance, counted the pieces of bone china on which a regal luncheon was served and remarked in her cultured voice, "Walter has more than I do."

In 1988 Annenberg finally sold Triangle Publications, the company that had made him a billionaire. He drove a hard bargain; it cost Australian media baron Rupert Murdoch $3.2 billion, at that time the largest price ever paid for a publishing property.

Annenberg rolled over some of the money from the sale to buy more art, spending $28 million on fifteen paintings, including five Renoirs, a Matisse, a Gauguin, and three Cezannes. In 1989, he paid more than $40 million for one painting alone: *Au Lapin Agile*, a self-portrait of Picasso dressed as a harlequin. Another painting he especially liked was Van Gogh's *Vase of Roses*, which he bought for the modest sum of $2.5 million and hung over the fireplace.

Although Walter and Lee were extremely fond of flowers, they also liked portraits, including one of Annenberg dressed as a monk that he commissioned from the artist Andrew Wyeth. It was displayed at Sunnylands in the Room of Memories. Annenberg's eyes turned moist whenever he talked about his art collection, and he frequently addressed the paintings by individual names, as if they were his adopted children.

In a sense, they were. Annenberg's only son, Roger, had been schizophrenic and committed suicide in 1962 at the age of 22, leaving Annenberg's daughter, Wallis, to carry on the line. (Wallis Annenberg owned Fredric March's former home in Beverly Hills, which Brad Pitt and Jennifer Aniston later bought for $13.5 million.)

A head-count of the Annenberg art collection revealed 53 paintings worth more than $1 billion—not a large collection, perhaps, but an extremely valuable one. That is why Annenberg took great care deciding which museum would take them upon his death. He finally selected the Metropolitan Museum of Art in New York, much to the consternation of other museums that felt jilted by his promises of financial bequests.

In 1998, Lee Annenberg sent a private plane to bring Nancy Reagan and Betsy Bloomingdale to Sunnylands to celebrate Walter's ninetieth birthday. By then the New Year's Eve parties had run their course. Most of the guests were too old or infirm to travel long distances; others were dead. Parties wound down before the stroke of midnight, and guests were bid a hurried good-bye and shoved out the front door by the servants. "May you get everything you deserve and more," said Annenberg, squeezing hands and blowing kisses.

In his dotage, his precious energies expended and his vital signs waning, Annenberg retired to his bed. A conqueror at the end of a long battle, he was finally vanquished in 2002 at the age of 94.

He reportedly gave away $2 billion in his lifetime but still had $4 billion to his name. His will provided $10 million to each of his four grandchildren, $2.6 million to a stepdaughter, plus an additional $17.4 million to three step-grandchildren.

Four days after he died, Annenberg's body was interred in an elaborate steel and marble mausoleum at Sunnylands, the only home in the Coachella Valley with its own legally authorized cemetery. His widow will eventually be buried alongside him.

The Sins of Frank Sinatra

IT'S NO COINCIDENCE. The bitter estrangement of singer Frank Sinatra from his second wife, Ava Gardner, the sultry, blaspheming actress who matched him cigarette for cigarette, drink for drink, and fight for fight, signaled the most productive phase of his career.

He went from being a doting husband and affectionate father to his three children—Nancy, Frank, Jr., and Christina—to a free-spirited, swinging, independent bachelor, during what the press nicknamed the "ring-a-ding-ding" years. The split from Gardner ushered in the era of Sinatra's greatest popularity, when he made the most films, sold the highest number of records, and reaped the biggest financial rewards of his success, all while living in Rancho Mirage. On those rare occasions when he wasn't onstage or in a recording studio, he could be found soaking up the sun on his two-acre property at 70–588 Wonder Palms Road, cooking homemade pasta for invited guests, and showing them movies in his private cinema.

It was his escape from the world—from memories of the mean streets of Hoboken, New Jersey, where he was born and grew up, and from the mansions of Beverly Hills, where people often had more money than taste. He had loved his first house in Palm Springs, with its piano-shaped swimming pool, but it contained too many distressing memories of when he was down and out. Now, with his career on the upswing again, he wanted to remember only the good times.

And he didn't want those good times to end.

So in 1954 he separated from Gardner, whom he loved with all his heart, but with whom he could not live—their personalities were just too destructive (they divorced in 1957). He packed his belongings, invested in real estate at Tamarisk Country Club, and started a new life. He would reside at Tamarisk for the next 40 years.

"Frank was the perfect host," said actress Valerie Allen, who had a prominent role in *The Joker Is Wild*. "He thrived here," she said, recalling her carefree days as his houseguest in the desert. Here, for the most part, the reed-thin, lovesick Romeo avoided social convention and hung around in his favorite summer garb—straw hat, shirt, and shorts—smoking his pipe and driving a Buick station wagon.

But when the lights were on, and the orchestra was playing, Sinatra was either headlining at the Desert Inn in Las Vegas, where he'd performed since 1951, or singing for his supper at the Sands Hotel. The Sands, with its world-famous line of costumed Copa girls, was the city's newest casino when it opened in 1952. A veritable cornucopia of slot machines, blackjack, and other risky games, it was the domain of casino boss Carl Cohen, who treated gamblers to dancing showgirls, flaming chateaubriand, flowing Dom Perignon, and hand-made Cuban cigars. The Sands quickly became the top nightspot in the city.

And when Sinatra walked out on center stage, the audiences went wild. There he stood, immaculately groomed in a neatly pressed Sy Devore suit or a gleaming tuxedo, wearing black patent-leather pumps, the smoke from a freshly lit Lucky Strike wafting up from his left hand, and the glare of the spotlight reflecting off his gold signet ring.

But attaining his dream of professional accomplishment and personal happiness came at a high cost. From here on, whether Sinatra bestowed unending generosity on his family and friends, or extended his vicious wrath to those whom he felt had wronged him, his life would be mired in private misery and public controversy.

His raw emotions were best expressed in the plaintive words to the romantic ballads he crooned for top-selling records and in standing-room-only nightclubs: "Young at Heart," "Learnin' the Blues," "Love and Marriage," "The Tender Trap," and "All the Way." His favorite song, the one that always gave him goose bumps when he sang it, was Cole Porter's "I've Got You under My Skin." A self-described "18-carat manic-depressive," Sinatra's mood swings ran from uncontained euphoria to suicidal despair.

His nervous anxiety had begun when he was a skinny crooner with Tommy Dorsey's Orchestra; it had traveled with him to Hollywood, where he was signed by MGM, and then it nearly rose to uncontrollable heights when MGM, believing him a box office loser, had dumped him. Sinatra spent years clawing his way back, taking movie roles he deemed unworthy of his talents. Then he won an Oscar for Best Supporting Actor for his performance as the murdered army private, Angelo Maggio, in *From Here to Eternity*, and his life slowly turned around.

And in his fraternity with the Rat Pack he found a healthy compromise that satisfied his inner devils, permitting him to work and play at the same time. More than anything, perhaps, life with the Rat Pack symbolized Sinatra's move to the top.

On a typical Rat Pack excursion, the whirring propellers of Sinatra's $100,000, twin-engine Martin Convair aircraft, christened "Eldago," sputtered to life at Palm Springs Airport, and the orange-and-white plane taxied along the tarmac, picking up speed and barreling down the runway, past sage, smoke trees, and desert flowers, until its metal belly lifted into the air. The plane's customized interior, which had cost Sinatra $300,000, contained a large bar, a hi-fi system and a piano, and a galley-style kitchen. There were restrooms, a telephone, and mood lighting. "What a gasser!" Sinatra often exclaimed as the plane sped upward, leaving the craggy San Jacinto Mountains behind.

And when the plane landed, the Las Vegas strip never looked better. There were gold-flecked swimming pools and Amazonian showgirls decked out in blue-tinged ostrich feathers, rhinestones, and sequins. Huge neon signs and flashing lights brightened the night, and everywhere was the sound of jangling coins. Most important, glistening on the giant marquee of the Sands, in twenty-inch-high black letters, were the names:

FRANK SINATRA

DEAN MARTIN

SAMMY DAVIS, JR.

PETER LAWFORD

JOEY BISHOP

The Rat Pack had arrived.

At the Sands, Jack Entratter couldn't resist the temptation to spotlight each of them onstage twice every night, for four weeks. After all, the five performers were in the midst of shooting their introductory film, *Ocean's Eleven.*

Newspaper headlines were ablaze with the upcoming Paris summit between presidents Eisenhower, Khrushchev, and De Gaulle. "Let's have our own summit," Sinatra suggested—and they did. "It was the hottest ticket in town," recalled former Palm Springs resident Kirk Douglas, who was there with desert neighbors Lucille Ball, Tony Martin, and Martin's wife, Cyd Charisse. "The only person who's not here tonight is Bing Crosby," cracked Bob Hope.

Night after night, the pack told jokes, traded insults, and toasted each other with a cocktail or two—or three or four.

"Everyone hates a smart ass, Frank," Martin kidded.

"But everyone loves a lover," Sinatra shot back.

Sinatra owned a piece of the Sands; the Copa Room, people pointed out, had been built for him. Frank had the first steam room ever installed in town, they reported, where he rested his voice before each show. Each night, 1,200 people bought tickets, and another 800 were turned away. The cover charge was $5.95, which included dinner. Sammy Davis, Jr., "one of the great Jewish Mau Mau dancers," as he unashamedly described himself, could do no wrong. "You can get swacked just watching this show," he told the audience.

Peter Lawford, wearing a bowler hat and carrying a dancer's cane, hid his deformed right arm, the result of a childhood accident, behind his back or in a trouser pocket whenever he performed. But he could still put on a helluva show, people said.

One night, Joey Bishop, tired of Sinatra's constant ribbing, said, "Don't sing anymore, Frank. Tell the people about the *good* work the Mafia is doing." Everyone laughed except Sinatra. He hated the way people talked about him like he was some kind of petty criminal. His rumored association with the mob was always a sore point with him. Why couldn't people accept him for who he was? It made him so mad he wanted to go out and punch somebody.

Thankfully for Sinatra, audiences only saw his happy-go-lucky side. They were spared his mockery, spitefulness, and cruelty. A clue to his precarious state of mind could be found at the front gate to his home, where a large brass sign announced: IF YOU RING THIS BELL, YOU BETTER HAVE A DAMN GOOD REASON.

He was riddled with physical insecurities, not the least of which was the abnormal size of his penis, which was the topic of many crude jokes. Even in its flaccid state, its length was so noticeable that the oversized appendage had to be strapped tightly against his groin with an elastic undergarment. Most men would be proud; Sinatra was dismayed.

Another of Sinatra's anxieties was his creeping baldness. Each morning, his valet, George Jacobs, used a can of brown spray paint to conceal the shiny, hairless patch on the back of his scalp, which also required hand-stitched toupees and, eventually, full-size wigs that he kept on hat stands in an air-conditioned room.

But his most abhorred defect, in his mind, were his dark facial scars, two thick grooves of torn skin left from a doctor's forceps when, during Sinatra's difficult birth, his infant's purple head was yanked from his mother's swollen uterus. The offending scar tissue, which ran vertically along one side of his face, from his misshapen left ear down the carotid muscles of his neck, had to be covered daily with flesh-colored makeup. Sinatra applied it himself, dabbing the scars with a sponge.

No wonder Sinatra was angry with the world.

"Frank was not put on earth to be an exemplar of serenity," commented Armand Deutsch, the erudite Sears Roebuck heir who was Sinatra's friend and desert neighbor. "But he has always been at his easiest when his Palm Springs gates closed behind him." That is why he insisted on spending so much time eating, sleeping, and sunbathing here. On appointed days he would be pampered with a full-body massage, have his skin exfoliated, and receive a manicure and a pedicure.

It was also here, behind the opaque curtains of this well-protected abode, that Sinatra shed his tight-fitting underwear and made passionate love to some of Hollywood's most beautiful women: Lauren Bacall, Angie Dickinson, Juliet Prowse, and Jill St. John, among others. Their captivating faces and perfectly proportioned bodies aroused his primal instincts.

The California-ranch-style house contained 6,000 square feet of space, and sported five guest cottages, two swimming pools, a Jacuzzi, and tennis courts on the seventeenth hole. It was often so populated with movie stars, gangsters, and politicians, that it resembled a Holiday Inn during Spring Break. These guests, however, were not noisy kids but gorgeous men and women.

For them, life at the Sinatra compound was heaven on earth.

Every bedroom had his-and-hers bathrooms, with matching closets that offered new pairs of slippers and fresh bathrobes. The guest suites had hotlines to the full-service kitchen, which was open 24-hours a day, and a Pullman kitchen in each bedroom was fully stocked with food and liquor. And as one guest famously remarked: "Never a bill in sight!"

One holiday season, for example, Sinatra's honored guests were Armand Deutsch and his wife, Harriet Simon, sharing a cottage with Random House publisher and *What's My Line?* panelist Bennett Cerf, whom Sinatra teasingly called "the Bookmaker."

In another cottage was Leland Hayward, the Broadway agent-turned-producer of *Mister Roberts* and *The Sound of Music*, and his wife, Pamela Digby, who formerly had been married to Randolph Churchill, son of British prime minister Sir Winston Churchill. A confirmed nudist, Pamela Hayward would drop the towel from around her trim waist and sit naked in the Jacuzzi, the dark triangle between her legs provoking more than men's curiosity. After Hayward's death, she married Averell Harriman, formerly U.S. ambassador to Great Britain and governor of New York. (Sinatra, a habitual night owl, reportedly spied on his randy guests with a pair of infrared binoculars.)

Opposite the main house stayed celebrated stage and film actress

Rosalind Russell, who would talk the leg off her long-suffering husband, Frederick Brisson, who had produced *Damn Yankees*.

Down the way lolled another famous Hollywood couple, Claudette Colbert, of the constant left profile and short bangs, and her husband, Dr. Joel Pressman, a Beverly Hills physician. Around the corner, were William Goetz, the former head of production at 20th Century-Fox and Universal Pictures, and his wife, society hostess Edith Mayer.

Yet another cottage held veteran film producer Arthur Hornblow, Jr., who had brought the Broadway musical *Oklahoma!* to the screen, and next door to him was the near-sighted playwright Harry Kurnitz, who wrote *Once More with Feeling*. Kurnitz's roommate was bald-pate actor Yul Brynner, who strutted about Sinatra's compound like a prized peacock, as befitted his regal status in *The King and I*.

Guests came and went, no matter what the season. Some strutted; others skulked like hunted rats. Sam Giancana, the short, shifty-eyed Mafia boss of Chicago was such a person. A former chauffeur and bodyguard for Anthony Accardo, who was the undisputed leader of La Cosa Nostra, Giancana was "the pimple on the ass of America," according to federal law enforcement, which devoted hundreds of trained personnel and thousands of man hours to keeping track of his whereabouts.

For some inexplicable reason, Sinatra went out of his way to entertain Giancana, purchasing expensive linens and soaps, importing Beluga caviar, and hiring mariachis to serenade the gangster whenever he visited. Sinatra employed additional staff, inspected their hair, fingernails, and teeth, and made sure they were fully versed in the correct etiquette for serving pasta, Chianti, and Italian espresso.

On the appointed day, Sinatra's valet, George Jacobs, would meet Giancana's plane as it touched down at Palm Springs Airport. There, the little man shuffled off the plane in his dark glasses, silk suit, matching hat, and alligator shoes, looking like someone's inconspicuous Florida uncle, and slid into the backseat of Sinatra's car, while Jacobs piled Giancana's heavy suitcases, containing who-knows-what, into the trunk.

When Giancana, described by authorities as a cold, brutal killer, arrived at the Sinatra compound, the nervous singer, his hair freshly combed and his body doused in cologne, would practically fall to his knees in slavish devotion, actions that the FBI documented by situating multiple telephoto lenses atop utility poles and in nearby trees on the Tamarisk Country Club golf course.

Debunking the myth that Sinatra, in his own words, "never associated with mobsters," Jacobs later admitted driving Giancana around Palm Springs to pick up other visiting mafiosi who were staying at the gated mansions of various business tycoons and were invited for lunch or dinner at the singer's home. Any number of mobsters might be there and often were: Frank Costello, Mickey Cohen, Johnny Roselli, Joseph Fischetti, Johnny Formosa, and Paul "Skinny" D'Amato, who sat around playing gin rummy. The conversation was friendly, spirited, and ribald.

While these men smoked cigarettes and told jokes, Sinatra's chef busily fixed à-la-carte meals in the kitchen: eggplant parmesan, fettuccine Alfredo, and linguine with clams (each tasty dish was prepared with the freshest ingredients). As Jacobs, who was intimidated by the sight of so many "hoods," explained, sometimes the menu required improvisation. "There were no fresh clams in Palm Springs in those days," he recalled, "so I got canned ones and prayed to God the boys were drunk enough not to care about the difference."

The gangsters were often so hungry they ate everything on their plates. After dinner, groups of attractive young women would be flown in or driven onto the grounds to provide entertainment. Singer Phyllis McGuire, who was involved with Giancana, was one of the women regularly seen socializing in these men's company on Sinatra's premises.

Sinatra spared no effort to ensure his guests had a good time, even providing golf carts, caddies, and ice-cold refreshments so his friends from Chicago, whom songwriter Jimmy Van Heusen immortalized in the emblematic tune "My Kind of Town," would feel right at home.

Giancana loved playing golf and would hit the ball all over the course. He was quite a sight, his pants bulging with rolls of dimes and quarters that he used to make long distance calls from nearby pay phones, a star-sapphire ring clearly visible on his little finger as he dialed the ten-digit numbers he kept in a small pocketbook.

Gangsters were one thing; politicians were another, although, as Sinatra discovered, not necessarily better behaved for all their supposed merits. No worse example of ingrained corruption and blatant crudeness existed than Joseph Kennedy, the yellow-haired, 70-year-old patriarch of the powerful Bostonian family and a former ambassador to Great Britain. This mangy, bespectacled titan berated Sinatra's servants, called blacks "sambos" and Native Americans "savages," and told anti-Semitic jokes that made even Sinatra blanch with embarrassment.

"What's the difference between a Jew and a pizza?" asked Kennedy.

"I dunno, Joe," Sinatra groaned.

"The pizza doesn't cry on its way to the oven," he guffawed.

He had made his illegal fortune as a bootlegger and he had hit an even bigger financial jackpot as an inside trader on Wall Street, a stint that led to his ignominious appointment as head of the Securities and Exchange Commission. He had no hesitation about grabbing anything he could get for free, including his pick of numerous hookers that Sinatra offered like mints on a hotel guest's pillow.

"Dirty old Joe," as the overworked household staff called the shambling guest behind his back, took a particular delight in the nubile charms of a Catholic call girl who could easily have passed for a nun, except for one particular talent. Judith Campbell, the alluring ex-wife of actor William Campbell, had given Sinatra such a good blow job that he had kept her phone number.

Whenever he had important visitors, Sinatra invited Campbell over to demonstrate her oral aptitude, at which there was no doubting she was an expert. Campbell took Joe Kennedy by the hand and led him to a bedroom, where she unzipped his pants and went to work fellating his wrinkled penis until he quickly climaxed—shouting obscenities.

Joe found the experience so monumental, that the first thing he did when he returned to Hyannis Port was call up his favorite son, John, whose abnormally high libido gave him excruciating headaches unless his urgent sexual desire was immediately relieved. The father told him in pornographic detail about the girl who had given him the best blowjob of his life.

By the time both Kennedys hung up the phone, the son had a splitting migraine.

The horny Massachusetts senator, who had been chosen to be the Democratic Party's nominee in the forthcoming 1960 presidential election, wasted no time arranging a cursory visit to Sinatra's compound.

"What a beautiful home," Kennedy complimented him.

"Thank you," Sinatra blushed.

It was, indeed, beautiful. Comfortable armchairs and sofas were arranged around a large, gray, stone fireplace; a card table and upright piano stood in one corner, and Oriental *objets d'art* in another; there were a remote control television set, tape recorder, and record player, floor-to-ceiling bookcases, model cars and trains. Contemporary paintings adorned several walls: abstract, splashy, and orange—Sinatra's favorite color. The soothing chords of orchestral music by Vaughan-Williams filled the air-conditioned room.

As always, Sinatra's valet dutifully took drink orders, returning with crystal goblets filled to the brim with the best liquor. Grinning mischievously, Sinatra introduced Jacobs to Kennedy and, in a prearranged joke, suggested the senator ask his black manservant about civil rights. "I don't like blacks," kidded Jacobs, feigning a look of disgust. "The Mexicans smell, and I don't like them either."

Sinatra and Kennedy doubled over with laughter.

Later, they stood gazing out a window at the aquamarine pool, the tennis courts, and the gazebo. Kennedy sipped his drink. "You live in paradise," he told Sinatra.

"It's better than Hoboken," Sinatra confessed.

Then Sinatra welcomed Judith Campbell, who made her entrance in a stunning cocktail gown, her hair lacquered and her lips frosted pink. Kennedy was mesmerized. After a six-course Chinese banquet, they sat on the patio smoking cigars and drinking brandy under the stars. Then Kennedy and Campbell retired to a guest suite, where they awoke the next morning, their naked bodies tightly entwined.

Kennedy made four documented visits to Palm Springs throughout his political career, and most likely there were clandestine trips that went unrecorded. Veteran journalist James Bacon, who accompanied JFK to the desert at different times, recalled that "it was New Year's Eve every night he was in town."

Like his filthy-minded father, who had little respect for women, Kennedy liked to talk dirty, and the raunchier the better. It seems both men were more interested in discussing sexual matters than affairs of state. Even today, it still shocks to learn prurient details about Kennedy's obsession with the female anatomy. Once, while getting a massage, he asked Sinatra if Shirley MacLaine had red pubic hair. Another discussion centered on Juliet Prowse's shaved *mons veneris*.

But the biggest shocker, not made known until 2003, was the revelation about Kennedy's hardcore drug use. On several occasions in Palm Springs, Sinatra's valet observed Jack Kennedy and actor Peter Lawford, who was married to JFK's younger sister, Patricia Kennedy, crouched over a table snorting cocaine.

What a scary thought: here was the future leader of the free world inhaling a mind-altering drug and powerful aphrodisiac with Lawford. The two of them were often in a stupor, telltale specks of white powder stuck to their noses.

But getting high didn't hurt Kennedy's election chances; if anything, it probably gave him the ego boost he needed to carry him to victory, though it was the smallest recorded win in U.S. history. A mere 118,550 votes put him ahead of Republican candidate Richard M. Nixon, out of the nearly 69 million ballots cast.

Sam Giancana, who reportedly swung the election by pressuring Chicago West Side syndicate members to vote *en masse* for Kennedy, bragged to Judy Campbell, "Listen, honey, if it wasn't for me, your boyfriend wouldn't even be in the White House."

To express her gratitude for his help, Campbell thanked him the only way she knew how. Campbell had no idea, however, that she was the object of FBI surveillance during her sessions with Giancana at Sinatra's home. What's more, she was still sleeping with Kennedy and trading pillow talk between the two men.

Finally, Campbell realized that she was swimming in deep waters and broke off the affair with Kennedy. In 1996, Campbell told *Vanity Fair* that she ended the relationship because she grew tired of being the other woman. Pregnant by JFK, she had the child aborted.

By that time, the man who had brought her to JFK's attention had passed out of her life. In 1961, Joe Kennedy was playing golf in Palm Beach, Florida, savoring the memory of his latest carnal pleasure, when he was literally struck dumb by a massive stroke that rendered him speechless.

Whatever he had done to deserve such a horrible fate, the Kennedy patriarch's retribution was punishment of biblical proportions. He spent his final eight years in a vegetative state, tended by a battery of nurses and doctors who administered to his declining physical condition.

Maybe out of a profound sense of guilt, or misguided loyalty to his family, JFK's brother Robert Kennedy, the new attorney general, went on a crusade to clean up the White House. After all, his coke-sniffing brother was taking strange phone calls from suicidal women and having lunch with socially undesirable men, whose only relationship with the newly elected president was a common need for instant gratification.

Ironically, the man who was given the job of troubleshooting whatever problems came up concerning the president and his female "constituents" was Peter Lawford, who had precious little time for acting anymore. He was too busy arranging parties that all too often degenerated into orgies.

Even Lawford's marriage, which had been written up in newspapers and magazines as a fairytale union between the golden-haired Hollywood actor and the beautiful Boston debutante, had become a sham. He played house with Pat Kennedy, the mother of their four children, but slept in a separate bed, where he sucked down booze and popped pills to help him cope with the lack of morality in his life.

Their Santa Monica beach house, which Lawford had purchased from the late MGM movie mogul, Louis B. Mayer, became a notorious rendezvous for illicit sex. There were so many helicopters landing and taking off at all hours of the day and night, and secret service agents swarming the hallways, that songwriter Sammy Cahn dubbed it "High Anus Port." Lawford's main occupation was paying off whores and drug dealers with personal checks (he was later reimbursed from the Kennedy payroll).

Pat Kennedy, who was forced to endure this domestic travesty, was thoroughly disgusted at having her home, where her kids played, turned into a brothel where naked call girls fornicated with men by the swimming pool and where used contraceptives were tossed like candy wrappers onto the floors.

Not that Sinatra was free of blame either. He enabled the president's long-running affair with Judy Campbell by providing them a safe desert haven, and he aided and abetted Kennedy's extramarital flings with Marilyn Monroe, whose personal life had hit rock bottom and who was disheveled and incoherent most of the time. Sinatra felt sorry for Monroe, whom he genuinely liked. But he complained to those near and dear to him that he felt like a pimp, setting up dates for her with influential men who wanted nothing more than a roll in the hay with the bosomy actress, who was considered by many to be the embodiment of sex appeal.

Sinatra himself was not above taking advantage of Monroe's charms, as part of a political *quid pro quo*. He got and gave, having instigated Monroe's involvement with JFK, whom she met through Sinatra at exclusive parties in Los Angeles and New York.

During the Democratic Party's national convention, JFK and Marilyn had been seen dining together at a corner booth in Puccini's, an Italian restaurant owned by Sinatra and Peter Lawford in Beverly Hills. It was clear from the tender expressions on their faces that the chatty couple was more than just good friends.

The Kennedy and Monroe affair, one of the great romantic tragedies of its time, played itself out for several rapturous days at Sinatra's Wonder Palms home, where Marilyn hid her pale face and sagging bust line under a striped parasol while dipping her painted toenails in the pool. The all-consuming lust she felt for the newly elected president burned like a raging fire within her, making every extremity of her voluptuous body sensitive to human touch. She grew so responsive to his uninhibited lovemaking, which left her sobbing from multiple orgasms, that she was unable to sleep or eat for days.

Monroe was even willing to overlook JFK's embarrassing premature ejaculations, which happened with such alarming frequency, she told George Jacobs, that the actress became convinced it was the result of her feverish kisses and not because Kennedy lacked self-control.

The president's chain-smoking wife, Jacqueline Bouvier, who had full knowledge of the affair, categorically refused to be seen in their company and boycotted Kennedy's visits to California—routinely called "pleasure trips" by the press. "Jackie knew what was going on, and confided as much even to certain administration officials such as Adlai Stevenson," recounted Sally Bedell Smith. "But publicly she stoically chose to ignore her husband's infidelities, which gave her greater latitude in her own life of fox-hunting and hobnobbing with jet-set friends in Europe."

Like Sinatra, Lawford, and many others, Monroe had been seduced to join the Kennedy political bandwagon in hopes that it would lead to something better than just another Hollywood premiere. Stars always had one eye on their careers and another on the future, that inevitable day when their popularity would be usurped.

Kennedy was above suspicion in this sordid game; Monroe was not. Their feverish coupling in hotel suites around the nation, when they devoured each other's orifices at every available opportunity, was little more than a political distraction for JFK, despite his reputed promise to divorce Jackie and marry Marilyn. Any rational person should have realized such a promise was pure nonsense.

But Monroe's desperation to escape the sad reality of her own life had led her down the wrong path, a path that her presidential lover was unwilling or unable to rescue her from. The widespread knowledge that she had whored all over town, sleeping with just about anybody in the hopes of advancing her career, had tainted her name and marked the comely actress as a high-class prostitute, albeit a famous one.

Addicted to booze and pills, the once-glamorous blond bombshell was puffy-eyed and overweight, and depended on cash handouts from friends and the fleeting love of strangers to assuage her feelings of worthlessness.

It was a pitiful sight.

"She was frequently too depressed to bathe or wash her hair," said George Jacobs, adding, "she ate in bed and slept among the crumbs and scraps, and would wear the same stained pants for days."

The presidential escapades had to stop sometime, somehow, and this time Robert Kennedy himself would apply the coup de grâce. In the spring of 1962, the FBI briefed Bobby about Sinatra's dubious relationship with Sam Giancana and warned about its impact on the president. RFK began cracking down on organized crime. After meeting with the FBI's powerful director, J. Edgar Hoover, Bobby nixed a forthcoming JFK visit to Sinatra's compound because, in Lawford's words, "it was virtually a case of the President going to sleep in the same bed that Giancana, a man whom his brother is investigating, vacated only weeks before."

Sinatra was already in the midst of renovating his Rancho Mirage home for Kennedy's arrival, converting the four-bedroom guest wing into lodgings for the Secret Service, and installing a 25-line, state-of-the-art telecommunications system. He had built a formal dining room with a cathedral ceiling that could seat 40 people, made the kitchen into a butler's pantry, and had added a larger, restaurant-style kitchen.

He turned the guestroom into a library, pushed the living room and the bar walls out, and brought in large boulders and cactus plants to separate the pool from the adjacent golf course. Although never officially asked to perform this gargantuan task, Sinatra had workmen pour a huge concrete heliport and erect a tall metal pole for the presidential flag.

"Frank spared no expense on this project and paid hundreds of thousands of dollars in overtime to get the job done in a hurry," according to Kitty Kelley. He even had a solid gold plaque inscribed and hung on the wall: JOHN F. KENNEDY SLEPT HERE.

On the eve of JFK's intended visit, the phone rang at Sinatra's house, and Frank picked it up. It was Lawford calling with bad news: the president was canceling his trip. Well, not exactly canceling the *trip*. He was still coming to the desert, but he had chosen to stay someplace else.

"Where?" demanded Sinatra.

"At Bing Crosby's house in Palm Desert," Lawford answered.

Sinatra went berserk. He smashed the phone against the wall and ran from room to room, screaming like a disobedient child throwing a temper tantrum. He kicked in bedroom doors, pulled clothes out of closets, bent golf clubs in half, hurled ashtrays and bottles, and shattered mirrors. Then he ran outside, grabbed a workman's sledgehammer and started smashing holes in the helipad.

At the same time that JFK was withdrawing from Sinatra's hospitality, his affair with Monroe started on its downward spiral. At Bobby's urging, Kennedy had tried to break it off. But she kept calling him up and begging to see him. The president, still smitten, made plans to meet her at Crosby's house, for an assignation that Sinatra was bound to hear about sooner or later and which no doubt would annoy him even more.

On the day of their appointed meeting, Lawford picked up Monroe at her Brentwood home. She had overslept as usual and was rummaging through the kitchen cabinets looking for an alcoholic beverage. But Monroe quickly pulled herself together, hiding her blond hair under a black wig and headscarf. She then grabbed a pair of sunglasses, and they jumped into Lawford's Dual Ghia and sped to Palm Springs, where JFK was waiting in bed.

That night witnesses saw her with the president, who was wearing a turtleneck sweater, sitting outside enjoying the moonlit evening together. He was very talkative, and she was under the influence of liquor; he clutched her hand, and she gazed into his eyes. No one had any inkling that Monroe would soon be front page news. But she had been fired from her latest film, *Something's Got to Give,* and was suffering from severe mental depression after Bobby Kennedy secretly insisted that she end her romance with JFK.

On the morning of August 5, 1962, Marilyn was found dead in her Brentwood home. Her naked body was discovered facedown in bed, and she was clutching a telephone receiver in one hand. Fifteen medicine bottles were reportedly found on her nightstand, including an empty bottle of Nembutal, a powerful barbiturate that had been prescribed by a doctor.

Most people who knew Monroe were hardly surprised. Sinatra was suspicious, however, of the Kennedys' possible involvement in her demise, especially after the coroner was unable to find any drug residue in her system. Lawford, too, was alarmed at the prospect of a political conspiracy. He had been the last person to talk to Monroe on the fateful night of August 4, before she permanently lost consciousness. Whatever she confided to him, or whatever he may have surmised from her last garbled conversation, haunted him for the remainder of his life.

Joe DiMaggio never forgave Sinatra for passing his former wife around, in the words of one acquaintance, like "a platter of hors d'oeuvres" and promptly ended their friendship. DiMaggio was so sickened by Bobby Kennedy's callous treatment of Monroe that he barred both him and Sinatra from the funeral.

Lawford, drunk with grief at having lost both Monroe and Sinatra, who ostracized him from his inner circle in revenge against the Kennedy family, was allowed to be a pallbearer. But he was so overcome with emotion that he leaned on the coffin more than carried it.

No sooner had Sinatra recovered from the shock of Monroe's mysterious death than he found himself mired in another tragedy: the gruesome assassination of President Kennedy, who on November 22, 1963, was gunned down in Dallas, Texas, in broad daylight, before thousands of horrified bystanders.

Sinatra literally went to pieces, like a fallen house of cards. The color drained from his face, and his normally cocky demeanor became a picture of contrition. For three days, Frank locked himself in the bedroom of his Wonder Palms house, drowning his sorrows in bottle after bottle of Jack Daniel's, throwing up in the bathroom, and shaking uncontrollably like a junkie.

He couldn't eat, he couldn't sleep. He sat in a bathrobe, staring red-eyed at the TV. Like millions of other Americans, he watched slack-jawed as Jack Ruby pointed a pistol at Lee Harvey Oswald and fatally shot him in the stomach in the basement of a Dallas police station.

Sixteen days later, Sinatra was just getting back in the swing of things, when the phone rang and he dropped to his knees, shrieking in pain. His only male heir, Frank Sinatra, Jr., had been kidnapped at gunpoint. The singer's son had been eating dinner in his hotel room at Harrah's Lodge in Lake Tahoe, where he was performing with his own band, when two men in ski parkas, one of them brandishing a .38 revolver, burst into Frankie's room, blindfolded the terrified young singer, and stole him away into the night.

The first phone call Sinatra made after regaining his composure was to Attorney General Bobby Kennedy, who in turn notified the FBI. Fifty-four nerve-wracking hours later, Frank, Jr., was found alive and well, and three men were arrested for the crimes of kidnapping and extortion. Sinatra was so overjoyed by the safe return of his son that he called Chasen's and ordered enough food and liquor for a three-day party, which coincided with his own forty-eighth birthday.

In a cynical turn of events, it was later reported that the kidnapping was a hoax to garner free publicity for Frank Sinatra, Jr.'s singing career. Sinatra's family was furious and sued the offending source of the rumor, but many people remained skeptical. Sinatra himself was so afraid of being a target of a stalker that he took to carrying a .38 Smith & Wesson, which he wore in a specially tailored shoulder holster under his jacket.

On May 10, 1964, Sinatra did cheat death, but not from a bullet—in the ocean. He and Ruth Koch, the wife of producer Howard Koch, were swept out to sea off the coast of the Hawaiian island of Kaui and nearly drowned. Sucked underwater by a strong riptide, they were turning blue from lack of oxygen when actor Brad Dexter and two surfers braved the crashing waves to rescue them.

Later, back on dry land but weak from his life-threatening ordeal, Sinatra sat shivering under a blanket and acknowledged he was lucky to be alive; his brush with mortality made Sinatra realize that he had to grab every opportunity, no matter how fleeting, and live every day as if it was his last.

To help him realize that dream he sought the company of young women who were less worldly than he and totally devoted to him—father-daughter relationships that also provided the sexual ingredients he craved.

Sinatra's romantic encounters, which made him the Don Juan of the spaghetti set, had followed him from adolescence into his senior years with no apparent drain on his considerable sexual energies. But his strong sexuality seemed to arouse the jealousy of people in power. According to his daughter Tina Sinatra, her father blamed many of his early troubles on the so-called "garter-belt Mafia," homosexual men like FBI director J. Edgar Hoover, sharp-tongued Hearst columnists Westbrook Pegler and Lee Mortimer, whom, it was said, were infatuated with the exceptionally well-hung singer but publicly discriminated against him because he would not reciprocate their advances. Nor would he humor them, as is common among many of today's more sexually liberated entertainers.

One thing was for sure: Sinatra could never be accused of being gay, unlike flamboyant concert pianist Liberace or gyrating rock 'n' roller Elvis Presley. The heartthrob of teenagers from coast to coast, Presley was rumored to have been physically compromised early in his career by a homosexual blackmail plot—supposedly engineered by Presley's manager, Colonel Tom Parker—to keep the singer enslaved to a lifetime contract.

Sinatra, although very accepting of blacks and other racial minorities, showed disturbing signs that he was intensely homophobic. If a friend held a cigarette a certain way, for example, or spoke French, or ordered a bottle of wine instead of hard liquor with a meal, that person was immediately labeled a "fag" and humiliated in front of other guests. Sinatra would often poke fun at homosexuals, lisping and flipping one wrist to parody their behavior, especially when he was onstage. The bit always got a big laugh from the audience. "Anything that smacked of worldliness, culture, or sophistication," said George Jacobs, "was a 'fag thing.'"

Still, for some reason, Sinatra went out of his way to be friendly to Robert Wagner, Hollywood's newest "dreamboat." The son of a wealthy Detroit steel executive, Wagner got his start in movies by caddying at the Bel Air Country Club for the promiscuously gay actor Clifton Webb. Obsessed by Wagner's pretty-boy looks, the queenly movie star with the pursed lips and effeminate mannerisms arranged for Wagner to be represented by the powerful Hollywood agent Henry Willson, who had discovered Rock Hudson, the biggest gay movie star in the world.

Indeed, despite his apparent dislike of homosexuals, Sinatra maintained ongoing friendships with closeted gay stars such as Yul Brynner and Laurence Harvey, whose careers would have been in jeopardy had their private lives been revealed to the public. Sinatra worked with both of these actors, whom he totally respected. British musical performer and playwright Noel Coward, whose campy, extroverted behavior precluded him from attending many normal social gatherings, was a much-coveted New Year's Eve guest at the entertainer's desert home.

It could be argued that Sinatra's domineering maleness, his complete insistence on all things *macho*, hid a deep-seated insecurity—a fear of his own sexuality perhaps—which is possibly why he performed so strenuously with willing female partners in the boudoir.

His second wife, Ava Gardner, whose taste in men ran from handsome bandleaders to Spanish bullfighters, proudly defended Frank's deceptively skinny appearance by stating that he was "all cock." Gardner candidly admitted, "The problems were never in the bedroom. We were always great in bed. The trouble usually started on the way to the bidet."

Chauvinistic in his treatment of women, his favorite terms of endearment for the fairer sex were "dames," "broads," and "dolls." Grace Kelly, his alluring co-star from *High Society*, wanted nothing to do with him, though she later changed her opinion. When he did play the role of the ardent lover, he dismissed such amorous conquests as "mercy fucks." But he certainly had his favorites. Judy Garland was an old flame, who, between taking uppers and downers, needed a shoulder to cry on. Then there was Dorothy Provine, who had the looks, if not the talent, to tickle his fancy. To Sinatra's surprise, he even had erotic fantasies about Katharine Hepburn, whom he once regarded as a sexless tomboy but came to admire as the hottest fifty-something star in the business.

And when legendary movie tough-guy Humphrey Bogart died of cancer, Sinatra offered his grieving widow, Lauren Bacall, the free run of his Wonder Palms house for two weeks, while she quietly mourned the loss of her husband. Their commiseration over Bogie's death soon turned into a romantic courtship, which made a scintillating newspaper headline: SINATRA TO MARRY BACALL.

They were seen together in Hollywood, Palm Springs, and Las Vegas, cuddling like teenagers on their first date. But at the last moment, Sinatra got cold feet and dumped Bacall because, he said, she was too pushy. They didn't speak to each other again for six years.

"Actually," Bacall reflected, "Frank did me a great favor; he saved me from the disaster our marriage would have been. But the truth also is that he behaved like a complete shit."

Approaching the big "5–0," Sinatra thought he had found his perfect match in the beguiling Mia Farrow, whom he first spied on a Hollywood sound stage. He was filming interior scenes for the movie *Von Ryan's Express;* Farrow was starring as Alison Mackenzie in the TV series *Peyton Place.* Sinatra was striding across the 20th Century-Fox back lot with cinematographer William Daniels, when the frail-looking, 19-year-old actress, who had survived a childhood bout of polio, ran in front of him and asked if she could go on his plane to Palm Springs. Sinatra was momentarily stunned. "Sure," he replied. Farrow was so happy she hugged him and went to fetch her tote bag.

It was an interesting attraction. Sinatra resembled her balding father, John Farrow, who had directed both Ava Gardner and Frank in various films and who, before his untimely death, had witnessed the effect Mia's budding sexuality had on men considerably older than his daughter.

Most people found the 30-year age difference between Farrow and Sinatra laughable. "I've got Scotch older than Mia Farrow," quipped Dean Martin. "Frank didn't have to buy Mia a diamond ring," joshed Eddie Fisher. "He gave her a teething ring." But the worst reaction came from Ava Gardner. "Ha!" she scoffed. "I always knew Frank would end up in bed with a little boy."

They certainly were an odd couple. There was Sinatra, his thinning hair combed forward, wearing a Nehru jacket and love beads, and there was gloriously young Mia in her transparent sundress and sandals. Their love affair blossomed at Sinatra's home, where he stripped down to his shorts and caressed Mia's naked, waiflike body. She kissed him with such passion, and he held her so tightly, that some observers found their lovemaking almost indecent.

Brad Dexter was appalled by Sinatra's behavior. "Frank, let me tell you something. I know the kind of women you like. You like a woman with breasts and a nice ass. Every girl you've ever known has been a beauty," said Dexter, gritting his teeth.

Sinatra glared at him.

"Frank, this girl has no tits, no ass, and when you hold her in your arms—you're holding Frankie, Jr. You should go to a psychiatrist. Instead of getting married, why don't you go get some analysis or something?"

Sinatra saw red. He smashed glasses, busted lamps, and turned over tables. Then he raced out of the room, grabbed Mia, and ran off with her to the Sands Hotel to get married. Even Sinatra's family thought he was nuts, especially his bewildered son, who couldn't understand his father's actions.

It was a classic midlife crisis.

After Farrow moved to Sinatra's home, she converted the guestroom into her dressing room and had it painted pink. She also brought her favorite feline companion, Malcolm, a large, white, Angora cat that she thought was deaf. Mia would spend hours sitting cross-legged on the floor communicating in sign language to her cherished pet. Frank's impatience with Mia's childish games finally boiled over, and one day he exploded a cherry bomb next to the cat's food bowl. It ran off into the bushes and was never seen again.

Sixteen months after exchanging wedding vows, Farrow felt the full brunt of Sinatra's anger when she refused his demand to break her contract for the upcoming film *Rosemary's Baby*. To walk off the heralded film and make another less important one, just to appease her jealous husband, would have seriously damaged her career.

Sinatra didn't give a damn. He sued Farrow for divorce, pushing the emotionally distraught actress almost to the brink of suicide. Then, in a complete about face, he invited her to spend Christmas at the compound while he handed out expensive gifts to his grateful cronies. Confused, she fled to India and sought spiritual comfort in the arms of Maharishi Mahesh Yogi.

Sinatra's crudeness reached new levels when he invited a busty prostitute to his hotel room on the set of *Lady in Cement*. The next morning, Frank called up room service and ordered ham and eggs, which he then ate off the naked woman's chest with a knife and fork. The film's director, Gordon Douglas, said there was almost a lawsuit over the incident, but it was settled out of court.

Actress Jill St. John, who briefly dated Sinatra, took his behavior in her stride. The foxy redhead was the type of girl that usually appealed to the horny, middle-aged singer: she was bold, brassy, and available. And she had no problem doing whatever was required to advance her career. Sinatra introduced St. John to Sidney Korshak, the slick attorney revered by the nation's gangsters for his ability to solve their problems, whether transportation disputes or criminal investigations, in just a couple of phone calls.

Both men became interested in her welfare and advised St. John to divorce her second husband, Woolworth heir Lance Reventlow, and pursue an acting career. Grateful for their advice, she dumped Reventlow and became a star.

Other hopefuls looking for Sinatra to give them a leg up on the ladder to stardom did not always fare so well. A 43-day engagement between Frank and South African–born dancer Juliet Prowse fizzled when she asked him to meet her family. Actress Shirley MacLaine managed to hold onto his friendship longer by keeping a safe distance. "If you got too close to him," warned an ex-girlfriend, "you were sure to get your fingers burned."

Sinatra's bad rap was seemingly well deserved. In addition to being an adulterer, he had a widespread reputation as an aggressor, who would throw the first punch and then blame someone else for the ensuing brawl. His reputation for violence, especially if he was drinking, hovered dangerously close to the surface.

One time, at a party in Palm Springs, Sinatra was so intoxicated that he shoved a young woman through a plate glass window, nearly severing her arm. Broken glass and blood were everywhere. Jimmy Van Heusen had the presence of mind to take the injured girl to the hospital, where she received emergency treatment. Sinatra paid the girl off, and the whole thing was hushed up.

Comedian Shecky Greene, who was Sinatra's opening act at the Fontainebleau Hotel in Miami, Florida, invoked the singer's wrath when he started telling embarrassing jokes about him. Jackie Mason also tempted fate with off-color humor that involved Sinatra's toupees and dentures, and Mia Farrow's braces. Both comedians were badly beaten up by anonymous assailants, reportedly on Sinatra's orders.

Sinatra's violent actions were tempered to some extent by the news of Senator Robert Kennedy's assassination in 1968. Although he didn't like the former attorney general for hurting his friendship with JFK, Bobby's needless slaughter at the hands of a crazed killer, a mere five years after the assassination of the president, threw Frank for a loop.

But the heavy drinking and the freewheeling sexual escapades soon picked up again. One Sunday morning, Dean Martin stopped by Sinatra's home after playing a few rounds of golf and found Frank, his best friend, Jilly Rizzo, and composer Jimmy Van Heusen passed out from too much revelry, each man sharing a bed with one or two naked hookers. Martin shook his head and let himself out the side door.

Another time, Sinatra, Elizabeth Taylor, and Richard Burton were boozing it up at Ruby's Dunes in Palm Springs when Jay Sebring, dubbed "the hairdresser to the stars," who trimmed Steve McQueen's locks and was the inspiration for Warren Beatty's skirt-chasing hairdresser in *Shampoo*, arrived at the restaurant with a fashion model of Amazonian proportions.

Sinatra wasted no time getting to their booth, where he proceeded to wiggle underneath the red-and-white linen tabletop, kiss the inside of the model's long thighs, and according to an eyewitness, making her moan in ecstasy from his audacious hanky panky. Sinatra's father would have turned over in his grave at the prospect of seeing his son give cunnilingus to a girl in public. Then again, maybe not. Father and son had much in common: both were natural-born fighters with powerful sexual urges; both sought strong, opinionated women to bring order to their lives. Drinking was Martin Sinatra's outlet, as it was for his son.

Frank idolized his dad, who had been a fire captain in Hoboken, New Jersey. When Frank was a boy, his parents ran a tavern during Prohibition. "The Sinatras needed liquor for their bar and they needed protection, services only gangsters could supply," stated Anthony Summers.

When a rival bar owner jilted the Sinatras out of money that was owed to them, Marty took revenge. He bought an old horse, shot it dead in the other man's barroom, and left the rotting carcass there for the owner to dispose of.

In Marty Sinatra's book there was no more honorable profession than that of saloon owner. He would have preferred for his son to take over that line of work than end up singing in nightclubs, and when they locked horns over the issue, Marty became so angry that he kicked Frank out of the house. But ultimately he was proud of his son's success.

As for Frank, when his dad, who suffered from emphysema and heart trouble, died in 1969, Sinatra raised more than $800,000 for the Martin Anthony Sinatra Medical Education Center within Desert Hospital in Palm Springs.

After his dad was buried, Frank begged and pleaded with his mother, Natalie Sinatra, a one-time abortionist whom everyone called "Dolly," to move to Palm Springs so she wouldn't be alone. He knew she wasn't happy living in Fort Lee, New Jersey. But outspoken, tyrannical Dolly refused to give in; she was too proud to leave her old friends, many of whom she had known before her son was born.

Still, Frank was so determined to get his mom to stay with him that he flew out to the East Coast in his private Learjet to see the silver-haired dowager. He showed her the blueprints for the remodeled four-bedroom house he had purchased for her exclusive use at 70–670 Wonder Palms Road, next door to his compound. He boasted that the home's previous owner had been prominent Beverly Hills furrier Abe Lipsey, and that singer Keely Smith had lived there in the 1960s following her divorce from singer-husband Louis Prima. To sweeten the deal, Sinatra even promised to move his dad's remains to Desert Memorial Park in Cathedral City, so Dolly could place flowers on his grave.

Finally she relented and packed her bags.

It would prove to be the biggest mistake of his life. Call it payback, call it superstition, but after Dolly arrived, Sinatra began to think that someone was trying to get even with him for all the sins he had committed. It wasn't anything tangible, but he sensed a strange presence looking over his shoulder.

The first sign of something wrong was that his left hand developed a painful condition known as Dupuytren's contracture, which made it difficult for him to hold a microphone. Then there was his severe hair loss; he was now practically bald. He also felt tired and could barely summon the vocal energy needed to perform a two-hour concert.

In 1971, he was awarded an honorary Oscar that he displayed in his home office, along with shelves of other shiny awards, citations, and certificates. That same year, Sinatra, sounding hoarse, hung up his graying toupee and decided to call it quits.

The Chairman of the Board penned his "resignation," as he called it, while standing waist-deep in his swimming pool—the perfect environment for him to collect his thoughts. The last song he recorded before his self-imposed exile was appropriately titled "My Way," and he meant every word of it. But Sinatra's retirement didn't last long.

In 1973, President Richard M. Nixon convinced Frank to perform at a state dinner for President Giulio Andreotti of Italy. Worried that he was not in the best of voice, Sinatra painstakingly rehearsed until he was convinced he could fulfill Nixon's request. He completed the concert, but that night his eldest daughter, Nancy Lambert, who was pregnant with her first child, miscarried, and Sinatra sunk into one of his customary blue moods.

As the months passed, he ate so much pasta that he steadily gained weight. He would begin cooking in the early morning, simmering pots of ripe tomatoes, garlic, and oregano, and adding fresh pork chops and sausages, and he would feast well into the night. He also started drinking more heavily, putting away numerous bottles of Jack Daniel's and Stolichnaya. As always, the cocktail hour had no time limit. Mexican entertainer Lalo Guerrero, who played at Las Casuelas Nuevas in Rancho Mirage, where Dinah Shore, Red Skelton, Hoagy Carmichael, Alice Faye, and Phil Harris regularly ordered margaritas in the fancy cantina-style restaurant, was told not to approach Sinatra whenever the truculent singer stopped in for a drink.

Then one evening, Sinatra asked Guerrero to play a love song by Agustin Lara: "Solamente una Vez" ("You Belong to My Heart"). Next, he requested "Veracruz" and "Farolito." "When I turned to leave," said Guerrero, "he came over and shook my hand. And he left a crisp, brand new $100 bill in it!"

Despite his unpredictable nature, Sinatra was consistently a big tipper. Waiters, bus boys, and car hops were always well rewarded by the singer's generosity. He never carried a wallet or a credit card, just a set of folded C-notes in a gold money-clip. If more cash was needed, he'd snap his fingers, and Jilly Rizzo would materialize like a one-eyed tooth fairy and hand Sinatra another roll of bills.

Sinatra's barhopping knew no bounds: Jilly's for a couple of drinks, followed by dinner with the "boys" at Sorrentino's Restaurant, more drinks at Ruby's Dunes, a song or two at Ethel's Hideaway, and a nightcap at Melvyn's. Very often by the time he weaved his way home, he couldn't drive in a straight line, much less walk one. But he was never arrested for public intoxication or drunk driving.

His only nonalcoholic exercise was golf, which Sinatra played with friends like the disgraced vice president, Spiro Agnew, whom he publicly defended against people's better advice. He and Ted, as he called his vice presidential golfing buddy, would hit the links after lunch and often play through until sunset. One day a suspicious-looking package arrived at Sinatra's home, and the FBI was notified of its contents. A threatening letter demanded that Sinatra publicly denounce Agnew, or he would be blinded by a chemical substance transmitted by an African bushman's blowing tube.

"Your famous Blue Eyes are in jeopardy," the message warned. "Think about it. Which is better: keep the friendship of Agnew or spend the rest of your life in complete darkness." Luckily for Sinatra, it was a cruel practical joke. As he had first sensed when his mother moved to the desert, the singer had the uncomfortable feeling that he was being watched.

There were some bright spots. The street on which he had lived since 1954 was renamed Frank Sinatra Drive, and he was made an honorary mayor of Cathedral City in 1973, the same year that his adopted township of Rancho Mirage, which he called home, was incorporated as a city.

Gossip abounded about which rising new female star the footloose Sinatra was dating, and if and when he would tie the knot again. But

Frank had them all fooled; the woman he was secretly meeting for love in the afternoon was none other than his first wife, Nancy Barbato.

Whenever they got the chance, the two childhood sweethearts would meet. Sinatra's favorite place to romance Nancy was in the two-story mountain cabin he had built for himself off Highway 74 in Pinyon Crest, located 20 miles above Palm Desert and overlooking the San Bernardino National Forest. Frank had constructed the five-acre retreat in 1969 as a place he could get to in a hurry, by helicopter if needed, and hide out from pursuers in the event of trouble. It was definitely rustic, something Al Capone would have preferred to the smooth plaster walls of his Chicago hotel rooms.

Frank and Nancy had weathered so many storms together that their mutual love transcended words. They would sit in front of the brick fireplace, holding hands, and enjoy a cocktail without being interrupted by children or annoying phone calls. No one knew they were there, not even the forest rangers who patrolled the tinder-dry wilderness from a fire station below.

If time permitted, Frank and Nancy would stay at his cabin for four or five days, fixing antipasto and cooking meatballs, just like they did when they were a young married couple. Then, after taking a relaxing bubble bath, they would retire to his colonial-style bedroom, with its billowing curtains and hardwood floors, and make love by candlelight, holding onto each other, the rapturous strains of one of Sinatra's timeless ballads playing in the background. Their passion for each other still burned fiercely.

Fifty years after they first discovered the magical lifestyle of Palm Springs, Nancy bought a condominium at Tamarisk Villas, formerly Wonder Palms Hotel Guest Ranch, at 70–070 Frank Sinatra Drive, within easy walking distance of the compound. Ten years later, she was joined by her daughter, singer Nancy Sinatra, who still resides next door to her mother.

Once a week, her first and only husband, Frank, whose framed photographs and letters she kept close at hand, would saunter up to her front door, ring the bell, and be let inside. If anyone had been peering over the neatly trimmed hedges, they would have seen Sinatra, holding fresh flowers, plant a kiss on her cheek as the front door closed behind him.

But a second marriage between the two devoted lovebirds was out of the question. There had been too much water under the bridge for that to happen. Besides, Sinatra relished his freedom. But that was about to change.

Her name was Barbara Blakeley, and she was a tall, bleached-blond, Las Vegas showgirl who was married to Zeppo Marx. They lived across the seventeenth fairway from Sinatra in a home that the resourceful comedian had designed himself, outfitting the house with the latest appliances and gadgets.

"No one knew better than Barbara the power of illusion in catching and keeping a man, as she later proved so clearly," observed the fashion designer and critic known simply as Mr. Blackwell, for whom she worked as a model. Whenever there was a tennis game at Sinatra's home, Barbara would show up with Dinah Shore, and they would play mixed doubles with Frank and Spiro Agnew. One Saturday, after a grueling day on the court, Sinatra noticed Barbara giving him a sexy look.

Overcome with lust, Sinatra led his well-stacked opponent into the kitchen, backed her up against the wall, and gave her a slow, hard kiss that nearly made her ears fly off. They dropped their tennis rackets on the floor. It was like a reenactment of Lana Turner's seduction of John Garfield in *The Postman Always Rings Twice*, only with Frank as the patsy.

"I don't want no whore coming into this family!" yelled Dolly Sinatra when her embarrassed son informed her about his hot-and-heavy fling with Barbara Marx. Frank's friends were aghast that he was seeing a married woman, especially the wife of his longtime neighbor. "Poor Zeppo. He had no idea what was going on," said a close friend. "Barbara would make dinner for her husband, kiss him good night, then run across the golf course and jump into Frank's bed."

Their pattern of errant behavior went on for several years, with neither Sinatra nor his married girlfriend caring one iota for other people's opinions. How Zeppo Marx tolerated his wife's infidelity can only be attributed to his very compliant nature; any other husband would have beaten Sinatra to a pulp.

But Barbara had her share of staunch defenders.

They claimed that Zeppo, who was old enough to be her father, was sick all the time and that she was, after all, a healthy young woman in her sexual prime. Why wouldn't she find Sinatra a big turn-on—and vice versa?

Dolly was so troubled by her son's gauche behavior that she talked to a priest. Sinatra's grown-up children shook their heads in disbelief. But nobody could bring Frank to his senses. He ached for Barbara's delicate touch with every fiber of his 60-year-old body. It was his last big romantic hurrah, and he intended to go out with a bang.

Even though he was almost totally deaf, Zeppo, who sat at home, pining for his missing wife, finally got the message loud and clear. The former beauty contestant, who had once been crowned Miss Scarlet Queen, served the jilted, fourth Marx Brother with divorce papers thirteen years after he had begun caring for her and her son, Robert Oliver, from her first marriage. "She left me with a deck of cards and an old Sinatra album," a heartbroken Zeppo told his nephew, Arthur Marx.

Barbara, however, was overjoyed to be getting a new lease on life. She didn't walk, she ran into the arms of the bald, paunchy, blue-eyed crooner, who stood waiting at the front gate with a cocktail in one hand and a cigarette in the other. They couldn't wait for the big day when he would take her as his fourth wife and she would legally change her name to Barbara Sinatra.

The bride and groom were married on July 11, 1976, at the palatial estate of Walter Annenberg, a former ambassador to Great Britain and the publisher of *TV Guide*. The best man was actor Freeman Gosden, from Sinatra's favorite radio show *Amos 'n' Andy*. The matron of honor was Beatrice Korshak, wife of powerful mob attorney Sidney Korshak.

When the judge asked Barbara, "Do you take this man for richer or poorer?" Sinatra, biting his fingernails, nervously interrupted, "Richer, richer." The comment got some laughs, but people who knew the lovesick singer sensed he was scared—so scared, in fact, that he had asked the indispensable Korshak to ensure that his wife-to-be sign a prenuptial agreement, or no wedding. Barbara wasn't happy, but she had no choice.

After the emotional ceremony, 125 guests attended a reception at Sinatra's home. Ronald and Nancy Reagan, Gregory and Veronique Peck, and Kirk and Anne Douglas were among those friends who sampled a four-tiered wedding cake and watched Frank give his blushing bride six yellow roses and a blue Rolls Royce. Barbara's gift to her new husband was a green Jaguar.

Six months later, Sinatra was set to open at Caesars Palace in Las Vegas when a big storm whipped up blinding snow and rain in the San Gorgonio Mountains, reducing visibility for aircraft taking off from Palm Springs Airport. The Learjet carrying Frank and his wife made it over the jagged summits just in time, but the next flight out, a plane that carried Dolly Sinatra, disappeared shortly after take off.

It took three days for rescuers to find the wreckage. There were no survivors; Dolly's bloodstained muumuu dress was spotted hanging in a tree. Frank was so overcome with grief that he almost fainted. This was the black day he had long dreaded—the premonition of death that he had feared ever since his mother had moved to the desert.

Sinatra buried his mother with a requiem mass at St. Louis Catholic Church, where she had prayed every Sunday. He laid her to rest alongside his father in Desert Memorial Park. Jimmy Van Heusen, Dean Martin, Leo Durocher, Pat Henry, and Jilly Rizzo carried the coffin.

Sinatra felt strangely alone. He still had the love and support of his first wife, Nancy, and their three children, to whom he spoke almost every day. And he had his new wife, Barbara. But he no longer had a strong authority figure to keep him in line the way Dolly did. She had stood up to him, told him off, clipped him across his one good ear, pinched his cheek, slapped his ass, stomped on his foot, and made him laugh—all on account of the tremendous pride she felt for her only child.

More than one person has remarked that the shocking death of Sinatra's mom, whose body was torn to bits in the exploding plane crash, turned Frank into a zombie. Once he used to throw plates of food, pick up chairs, and break things; now he pouted, sulked, and hid in his room. At the same time, the Mafia juggernaut, at whose feet he had knelt in his pursuit of stardom, was hurtling toward its doom. In 1975, amid a U.S. Senate Select Committee investigation into a CIA-Mafia plot to assassinate Cuban dictator Fidel Castro, two of the alleged conspirators, Sam Giancana and Johnny Roselli, whom Sinatra had personally entertained on a regular basis, were both murdered.

Before Giancana had a chance to testify, he received seven .22-caliber bullets in the back of his head while cooking up a midnight snack of sausages in his Oak Park, Illinois, home. After Johnny Roselli took the stand, his asphyxiated body was found floating off the coast of Key Biscayne, Florida, in a 55-gallon drum. He had last been seen on a boat owned by Santo Trafficante, a co-conspirator in the Castro plot.

If Sinatra ever feared being rubbed out, he never let on, although that secret worry might explain why he was so irritable and jittery a lot of the time.

The truth was that much of his bad press resulted from the singer's long-standing Mafia connections. He always denied that New Jersey mobster Willie Moretti, for example, had strong-armed bandleader Tommy Dorsey and forced him to tear up Sinatra's lifetime singing contract, a one-sided deal that Frank admitted, in a rare moment of candor, was "slavery."

Sinatra steadfastly refuted allegations that he had served as a mob courier in 1947, delivering $2 million in "suitcase money" to narcotics kingpin Charles "Lucky" Luciano in Cuba. Years later, Sinatra was staying at the Excelsior Hotel in Rome, Italy, when he entered his suite and nearly dropped dead from fright: there, sitting in the darkened room on a plush velvet chair, was Luciano. The murderous old man stood up, put his arms around Frank, and kissed him.

Near the end of his lifetime, Sinatra confided to his daughter Tina that he once served as a courier, not for the mob as she might have expected, but for the CIA and the State Department. "But you can't tell anybody about it," he insisted. Was it the truth or just his attempt to pacify her latent curiosity?

Closer to home, a federal wiretap of the Rancho Mirage home of Sinatra's friend Tommy Marson recorded Marson talking to Gregory DePalma, the man linked to New York mobster Carlo Gambino, whose family ran the Westchester Premier Theater in Tarrytown, New York. The 3,500-seat venue had become the target of a federal criminal investigation after it was learned that the Mafia had skimmed as much as $9 million from ticket sales—of concerts by Sinatra, Dean Martin, Steve Lawrence, and Eydie Gormie—and forced the theater into bankruptcy. Sinatra copped a lot of flack over an infamous photograph of him smiling with Marson, DePalma, and Gambino in the singer's dressing room when he had performed at the Westchester Premier Theater in 1976.

It is little wonder that Sinatra, overwhelmed with this self-induced stress, sought to lessen his guilt through drinking, a feat at which Barbara, like Ava Gardner years before, could match her husband shot for shot. Their marriage quickly degenerated into a verbal slugging match—a home version of *Who's Afraid of Virginia Woolf?* They'd have a couple of drinks and start hurling abuse. He'd call her "a no-talent gold-digger," and she'd call him "a washed-up has-been." Then each of them would storm out of the room, slam the doors, and spend the night in separate beds.

If this was retirement, Sinatra didn't want any part of it. Better to be on the road singing, he felt, than fighting at home. So Frank packed his tuxedos, his patent leather shoes, and his wigs and went back to work.

He didn't need the money; he had plenty of that stashed away. Sinatra not only derived a six-figure income from singing, he also had substantial financial investments. He owned a Budweiser distributorship in Long Beach, a trucking company, an aircraft hangar in Palm Springs, a building in New York City, a wine distributorship, and water wells in Palm Springs. He also held valuable shares in movie, record, and publishing companies, and earned another $60,000 a month in music royalties.

Still, unaccountably terrified he would lose everything, Sinatra kept accepting gigs in faraway places that singers half his age would have turned down. He would look at a map and stare in bewilderment at the vast distances he had decided to travel, like Santa Claus contemplating a marathon delivery of toys. He played 65 concerts in 1990, 73 in 1991, and 84 in 1992. In one year alone, he appeared onstage in 17 countries, from Ireland and Sweden to Australia and Japan.

But something wasn't quite right. Sinatra had always been quick on the draw, spoiling to get into the ring like an angry prizefighter, calling male journalists "fags" and their female counterparts "two-dollar hookers." Now he looked dazed, as though he'd gone too many rounds with Mike Tyson. Onstage he stammered, stumbled, and slurred his words. Was this the same man who had once skipped across the stage with Sammy Davis, Jr., sung a duet with Peter Lawford, and told jokes with Dean Martin?

It was as if his body had been removed and replaced by a *doppelganger*— or a bad Sinatra impersonator whose voice was sometimes off-key, couldn't hold a note, and frequently missed the downbeat. Part of the problem's source was the very things he was running from: home and

Barbara. In an attempt to control his dangerous mood swings, which brought on violent tendencies, Barbara had seen that he was prescribed a range of mind-altering drugs, which left him mentally confused. Each afternoon when he awoke from his previous night's drug-induced slumber, he took half-a-dozen medications, including a diuretic, a sleeping pill, a barbiturate, and Elavil—an antidepressant.

Because his memory was failing, sometimes he would pop two pills instead of one, and if the dose was too strong, he occasionally would pass out in the middle of a performance. Finally doctors prescribed Antivert, to counteract the effects of the other drugs. Clearly he was never quite himself.

And then came the blackest day he had experienced since his mother's death. On May 6, 1992, Jilly Rizzo died. Sinatra received the terrible news that his best friend had been killed by a drunk driver. Sinatra's anxious doctors stood ready and waiting with pills and syringes, while he howled and punched the air with his fists, staggered like a wounded bull, and collapsed in shock on the floor of his home. It was a miracle he didn't have a fatal heart attack on the plush carpet. It took several days for him to regain the use of his diminishing faculties.

His final years were a blur. Fans screamed and hollered like the old days, but the object of their adulation was distinctly out of step. He couldn't see and he couldn't hear; concert promoters held their breath that he would show up and then held their breath that he could still sing.

The lyrics to songs he'd sung hundreds of times were printed in large letters on TelePrompTers that were displayed like blinking traffic signals around the stage. In one instance, he was reportedly fed a song, word by word, through a concealed hearing aid, and he repeated the sounds like a mechanical robot: "That's why . . . the lady . . . is a tramp!"

In the end, it was just too much of a strain for him to concentrate on singing anymore. Accepting a lifetime achievement award at the 1994 Grammy Awards telecast, he appeared disoriented and rambled on until someone, mercifully, cued the orchestra to cut him off.

His last public performance took place at Marriott's Desert Springs Resort & Spa in Palm Desert on February 25, 1995. He strolled out looking like he was on the moon, improvising lyrics and singing to his own beat. "Thank you," he bowed. "Thank you very much."

There was no encore.

Instead, Barbara Sinatra announced they were selling Frank's beloved desert home and moving to Beverly Hills to be closer to his children. The decision was made for him; he had no say in the matter. Uprooting Sinatra from his familiar desert surroundings was a traumatic blow to his fragile well-being, and he stalled the moving date for as long as possible. But finally the home's exasperated new owner, Canadian businessman James Pattison, who had paid $4.3 million for the house with its art studio, theater, model train set, and 12-car parking facility, demanded to take possession.

In December 1995, Christie's auctioned 200 of Sinatra's most-treasured belongings, including jeweled and enameled Fabergé boxes, gold and silver cigarette cases, and paintings by Grandma Moses, Andrew Wyeth, Rouault, and Bonnard. Also sold were Frank's German Bosendorfer grand piano and '76 green Jaguar, his wedding gift from Barbara. The sale netted $1.9 million, which thrilled Barbara but left Frank in one of his reported funks.

On the twentieth anniversary of their marriage, which many people thought had been 20 years too long, Sinatra was discovered lying on his bed and looking up at the ceiling, his arms crossed on his chest like a man waiting to be given the last rites. "What the hell have I done?" he bawled. Frank called up his first wife, Nancy, and begged her forgiveness; he did the same with his kids.

A short time later he suffered a heart attack and was admitted to Cedars-Sinai Medical Center for eight days. There, thin and anemic, he puffed on a cigarette even though he knew it wasn't good for him. Back at his Beverly Hills home, he snacked on nuts and candy bars and watched his old movies on TV.

On the night of May 14, 1998, millions of TV viewers were tuning in to the finale of *Seinfeld* and laughing at the crazy exploits of Jerry, Elaine, George, and Cosmo. Meanwhile, in a semidarkened bedroom in Beverly Hills, Sinatra woke up screaming as apparitions of Dolly, Marty, and Jilly swirled around him. His lips turned blue, his pallor was gray. A female nurse called 911, and an ambulance rushed the quivering 82-year-old singer to the hospital where, two hours later, he joined his parents in the hereafter.

Long before that fateful night, the battle lines had been drawn between Sinatra's kids and their stepmom, whom they resented for trying to control their dad's life and profit from his death. At stake were matters involving his financial assets, joint tenancy, rights of survivorship, and most important of all, product-licensing—worth its figurative weight in gold.

The Sinatras may have been a dysfunctional family but they had no intention of giving away the store, especially to a non-blood relative such as Barbara, who, little by little, was twisting the arms of lawyers and accountants to make sure she came first. Even Frank, his mind eroded by senile dementia, had sensed trouble and tried to head it off. "Get a good lawyer," he had instructed his kids.

In the end, Sinatra's street smarts saved them all and kept the delicate peace between warring family members. One month after he was buried next to his parents, after piles of damp earth had been shoveled on top of the mahogany coffin that contained a roll of dimes and a small bottle of Jack Daniel's, Sinatra's melodic voice spoke, if not sang, from beyond his freshly dug grave.

The late singer's exhaustive, 21-page, Last Will and Testament was read aloud in a special hearing attended by all relevant parties, who hid their faces behind dark glasses and dabbed their runny noses with Kleenex. The legal document, signed in Sinatra's shaky hand, warned that anyone who contested his will would be disinherited. "Does that mean the performance will be canceled?" someone joked, attempting to inject levity into the otherwise somber proceedings.

Everyone was given a Photostat copy of the will, which they opened to the first page. It stated that Sinatra, who had married four times, bequeathed $250,000 to his first wife, Nancy Barbato; $200,000 and real estate holdings to each of his three children; and $1 million in trust for his grandchildren.

He willed his fourth wife, Barbara Sinatra, his homes in Beverly Hills, Malibu, Rancho Mirage, and Cathedral City, along with the silverware, books, and paintings from those residences and remaining assets worth approximately $3.5 million. Sinatra also left $100,000 to his stepson, Robert Marx.

In addition, Barbara Sinatra was left the entertainer's Trilogy master recordings and all related music rights and royalties, and son Frank

Sinatra, Jr., inherited his dad's entire collection of sheet music.

He acknowledged having been married to Mia Farrow but did not leave her anything. His second wife, actress Ava Gardner, had died in 1990.

Wherever Sinatra's spirit was, he was no doubt smiling as his family mopped their brows and sighed with relief that everything was not a whole lot worse. One of the late singer's talismans was a hand-stitched pillow on his living room sofa, which he liked to display for fun. It read LIVING WELL IS THE BEST REVENGE.

Barbara Sinatra must have taken her dead husband's words to heart. In 2000, she paid $1.25 million for a three-bedroom home in the Club at Morningside, where she lives today. So far, she has not remarried.

Under the Influence

"**M**Y NAME IS **Betty Ford,** and I am an alcoholic and an addict!" Those thirteen words, bravely spoken by the wife and former first lady of the thirty-eighth president of the United States, Gerald R. Ford, did as much to break down the social stigma of alcoholism as the fall of the Berlin Wall did to undermine communism. Ford's confession was not an excuse to reap hundreds of thousands of dollars in commercial endorsements or profit from exclusive tabloid compensation. They were heartfelt words spoken by someone who had been to hell and back.

As early as 1964—ten years before her husband occupied the White House—Mrs. Ford had been hospitalized for alcohol-related problems. A doctor had advised her, "Stay on the other side of the room from the bar." She didn't listen.

She took pills—mostly Valium—to ease the discomforts of arthritis and a pinched nerve in her neck. She took pills to relieve the immense responsibilities of being first lady of the land. And whenever she popped a pill into her mouth, she washed it down with a good, stiff drink. It was no big deal; everybody drank, especially in Washington, D.C., at five o'clock in the afternoon. It was a ritual.

"I'm a very controlled person," Ford once reflected about days spent watching her husband sign bills in the Oval Office. "And I was never out of control."

Or so she thought.

The myth espoused by victims of this insidious disease, which affects an estimated 15 million Americans, is that alcoholics are never wrong. Believing their behavior to be justified by those around them, they are always in denial. Ford was no different, except that her husband was president and he was an enabler. Also, she had received a great deal of sympathy for having suffered from breast cancer and undergone a mastectomy. "Jerry had no idea about alcoholism," she said. "He felt I was just sick and that was the way I was going to be the rest of my life." But when the couple left 1600 Pennsylvania Avenue for a new life in the desert, both husband and wife had to face that Betty Ford's drinking was spinning out of control.

The Fords built a house at Thunderbird Country Club next door to their good friend Leonard Firestone, the former president of Firestone Tire & Rubber Company of California.

Settling in with this hard-drinking community, Betty Ford was like a kid in a candy store. Only two weeks after moving into their dream home, the family's visions of blissful retirement were splintered by the rattling of ice cubes and the breaking of well-drained liquor bottles. Ford's concerned husband and four children—Michael, John, Steven, and Susan—confronted their inebriated mother. "I'll never forget the moment my denial was shattered," said Ford. She checked herself into Long Beach Naval Hospital and underwent treatment. Terribly ashamed, she did not go out in public for three years.

While Ford struggled to regain her sobriety, her neighbor Leonard Firestone was suffering hangovers and alcohol-induced blackouts. It was almost like a scene from *The Lost Weekend*, where Ray Milland pawns his typewriter to buy a quart of whiskey, then imagines he sees bats flying around his living room. Except in Firestone's case, he was guzzling gin. From 1965 to 1975, he had never touched a drop of the stuff; then he fell off the wagon. "After 10 years," he said, "I decided I could handle alcohol. Fact was, I couldn't."

Eventually, Ford and Firestone both got sober. If they stayed that way, they reasoned, there would have to be a greater purpose than their own temperance. So they established the Betty Ford Center for the treatment of alcoholism and drug addiction, on the campus of the Eisenhower Medical Center in Rancho Mirage.

Eisenhower Medical Center is a state-of-the-art facility. Named after the thirty-fourth president, who was a valley resident, it stands at the corner of Bob Hope Drive and Country Club Drive, on the former site of Bob Hope's date ranch, a spread that once occupied 80 acres. The comedian generously donated the land, which was valued at $4 million, and ground was broken in 1968. Hope received a whopping tax break, but not the swollen pride of seeing the building named the Bob Hope Medical Center. These days, it is Betty Ford—not Hope and not Eisenhower—who possesses the greater name recognition around these parts.

From the street, Betty Ford Center's glimmering 100-bed, inpatient treatment facility looks like a five-star hotel or an expensive country club. And it might as well be, considering the price tag. Admission is voluntary—there's usually a two-week wait to get in and you can leave any time you please. But once there, an average monthly stay costs around $21,000—or $700 a day. There is no minibar and no maid service in these rooms. And chocolate mints on the pillow? Forget about it.

Instead there is a routine: up at 6:15 A.M. for breakfast, menial chores, and a brisk walk around the grounds. At 8:45 A.M., there's a lecture; at 10:00 A.M. there's group therapy. Then lunch at noon, followed by individual exercise programs and educational groups. Dinner is served at 5:15 P.M. and followed by an evening lecture or an AA meeting and written assignments. Lights have to be out at 10:00 P.M.

In Hollywood, the Center is the most trusted place for movie stars, young or old, to "dry out" without being hounded by the media. Hospital employees sign mandatory confidentiality agreements to protect the privacy of patients, some of whom are literally at death's door when admitted. But the tabloids have spies everywhere, so protecting people's identity is essential, if bothersome.

Ironically, although the Center has treated more than 40,000 patients in its well-publicized history, less than one percent of its clientele have been *bona fide* celebrities. For the record, that's approximately 400 familiar faces—or an average of 20 each year.

Some of those beloved countenances were barely recognizable when they strolled, shuffled, or limped through the front doors, their faces hidden under a variety of floppy hats, sunglasses, and, on occasion, fake beards and mustaches.

Barnaby Conrad, the acclaimed author of *Matador* and a recovering alcoholic, thought he had seen a mirage when he first set eyes on the Betty Ford Center. In the heat of summer, its shimmering concrete edifice seemed to float on a sea of grass. "It looked like an elegant clubhouse in need of [golf course architect] Robert Trent Jones," said Conrad. "There were four other one-story buildings behind it, and off to the left was a large pond with three swans gliding gracefully on it."

That's also the serene view that greeted Oscar-winning screen legend **Elizabeth Taylor**, who squealed with delight at the sight of those regal birds when she checked into the Center's main residential complex on December 5, 1983. Taylor's decision to commit herself after months of prompting by her best friend, actor Roddy McDowall, merely confirmed what the rest of the world already knew: The beautiful international star was slowly destroying her looks and her health through a daily intake of Percodan, Demerol, Tylenol with codeine, and other painkillers, mixed with potentially lethal quantities of vodka.

After signing in at the front desk, Taylor was shown to her room, a Spartan cubicle that contained two beds, two desks, two chairs, and two dressers. The 51-year-old movie queen, who, as Cleopatra, had been carried by Nubian slaves on a gold-plated barge to meet Roman general Mark Antony, was horrified to discover she would be sharing a bedroom and a bathroom with another woman!

Taylor threw a royal fit and was ordered to spend the night with three other women in a detention room called the "swamp," until she cooled off. A few days later, she was introduced to her support group of retired businessmen, middle-aged housewives, and long-haired students—a mix of recovering addicts that could have been found at a casting session for one of her movies. Each person had been interviewed, and each had seen their personal belongings searched for hidden drugs—even for tobacco, aspirin, and mouthwash, which contains an alcohol base.

At the center, patients are required to do their own housekeeping, including laundry. They are barred from leaving the hospital grounds, and the use of telephones is allowed only on weekends. Visitors are allowed only on Sundays. Attendance is required at all meals and lectures, as well as at group therapy sessions, where patients are expected to confess their addictions. The treatment program is based on five of the 12 steps of Alcoholics Anonymous, which advocates abstinence and prayer among its teachings.

Taylor's five-week stay would become the focus of intense media speculation about her physical appearance and emotional state. Her recovery was not made easier when visitors to other patients snapped photographs of the overweight actress making beds, emptying trash cans, and doing water exercises in the heated swimming pool, though rumors that she'd been put on "toilet detail" as punishment for bad behavior were grossly exaggerated. (After the photographs appeared, the Center instituted its strict privacy policy.)

"They'd never had a celebrity before," Taylor told *Vanity Fair*. "The counselors told me later, they didn't know what to do with me, whether they should give me sort of special isolated treatment. They decided to lump me in with everyone else, which of course was the only way to do it."

Despite a lifetime of play-acting, Taylor was unprepared for the frank discussions of her private life and personal relationships. "Christ!" she quipped. "I need a drink!" She was much happier commiserating with the other patients during these healing sessions, holding hands, and offering encouraging words.

It was two weeks before Taylor could muster the courage to tell an assembled group what Betty Ford had already confessed: "My name is Elizabeth Taylor, and I am an alcoholic and a drug user." Nobody was surprised. A two-year investigation by California's attorney general, John Van de Kamp, into the pharmaceutical practices of three of Taylor's physicians, found the drug-addicted actress had been given thousands of prescriptions for opiates, hypnotics, painkillers, tranquilizers, antidepressants, and stimulants. "Enough medication," said an investigator, "to fuel an army."

In 1981, Taylor had received three hundred different prescriptions for various ailments. In 1982, during one 17-day stretch that coincided with pop star Michael Jackson's birthday party, Taylor had been prescribed at least 600 pills. Whether the pills were for Taylor or her friends, many of whom were gay and dying of AIDS, has never been determined, claimed biographer C. David Heymann.

Confronted by the overwhelming evidence of substance abuse, Taylor responded, "A drunk is somebody who drinks too much. Somebody who takes too many pills is a junkie. There's no polite way of saying it."

■ ■ ■

WATCHING TV COVERAGE of Taylor's drug treatment from his West Hollywood home was actor **Peter Lawford**, who had been battling his own devils for more than 20 years. Lawford and Taylor had appeared together in *Julia Misbehaves* and *Little Women,* when they were both child stars at MGM.

Lawford's fourth wife, Patricia Seaton (not to be confused with Patricia Kennedy, who divorced Lawford in 1966), had been 17 when they first met. She decided that if Betty Ford could help Elizabeth Taylor kick a drug habit, it could do the same for her alcoholic husband. They flew to Palm Springs and were met at the airport by a monogrammed courtesy van.

When Lawford, hopelessly intoxicated, gazed out the plane's window and saw the van from the Betty Ford Center on the tarmac, he thought he was going to have lunch with the former president and his wife. "Are we going to visit her?" he asked. "I've always liked Betty."

Once inside the treatment center, however, his demeanor quickly changed. He was resentful of authority and refused to participate in any planned activities. "The only activity Peter performed with any relish at all was vacuum cleaning," said his wife. "He'd never operated a vacuum cleaner before, and the appliance intrigued him. He would vacuum for hours, even after he left the hospital and returned home."

After Taylor and Lawford were reunited, his lack of commitment to the recovery program threatened her delicate sobriety. He sent out to a Longs Drug Store for two cartons of Salem cigarettes, her favorite brand, as well as for Max Factor pancake makeup and deep olive eyeliner, so that Taylor could make herself look prettier.

When Lawford was subdued by guards for not following protocol, the struggling actor angrily replied, "She's only a Hollywood actress, but I'm the former brother-in-law of President John F. Kennedy!"

As the symptoms of his withdrawal worsened, Lawford went looking for a liquor store and even tried to score hard drugs. Somehow, he managed to contact a cocaine dealer, who arranged for a helicopter to fly in and land on an empty lot near the center. The actor sneaked outside, met his contact, snorted a few lines of coke, and then strolled back into the facility as though nothing had happened.

In another embarrassing incident, *The National Enquirer* bribed Lawford with $4,000 to smuggle in a photographer so they could take pictures of him and Taylor having a fake romance. Betty Ford was reportedly infuriated at the breach in security, which she believed threatened the Center's entire operation.

Taylor eventually relapsed after being sober for less than a year. Lawford's alcoholism was so entrenched that he was beyond help. Destitute, he lived in appalling squalor in a rented apartment inundated with cat feces. He died of acute liver and kidney disease on Christmas Eve 1984, at the age of 61. His body was cremated the following day, and his ashes were interred in Westwood Mortuary, near his close friend Marilyn Monroe.

Four years later, Lawford's funeral expenses, which totaled $10,000, were still unpaid, and his widow, who was virtually penniless, was asked to settle the outstanding bill. Someone—perhaps the Kennedy family, possibly Taylor—paid the debt to avoid unfavorable publicity, and Lawford's ashes were removed from the mortuary and scattered in the Pacific Ocean.

Barnaby Conrad, who followed Elizabeth Taylor's history-making visit to the Betty Ford Center, where stories abounded about the pampered star getting preferential treatment, conceded that the risks of relapsing are great. But, he always added, so are the benefits for those who have the will and ability to overcome their addiction.

■ ■ ■

ONE WHO MADE a valiant attempt was country music legend **Johnny Cash**. A child of the Great Depression, he grew up in his adopted state of Tennessee, poor and often drunk on moonshine. He was cut from the same cloth as Memphis singing discoveries Elvis Presley and Jerry Lee Lewis, contemporaries of Cash and working-class heroes who, in spite of winning international fame, never quite conquered their private fiends.

Cash's singing career, throughout which he moaned and groaned like a wounded panther, ignited in 1956 with "Folsom Prison Blues" and his first #1 hit, "I Walk the Line." In prison at various times on charges of drunkenness and buying illegal drugs, the singer finally broke out of the slammer with two electrifying concert albums, recorded live in true Blues Brothers style at Folsom Prison and San Quentin, where one of the well-behaved inmates reportedly was Merle Haggard.

The prison albums, Cash hoped, would mean good-bye to his starving past and hello to a rosy future. But he was unprepared for the trappings and temptations of success. Living on the road and working one-night stands, Cash became hooked on barbiturates and amphetamines. His monster 1963 hit, "Ring of Fire," with its searing refrain of "burn, burn, burn," was a major crossover hit whose irony was not lost on the frequently high singer. Fame, he said, "was hard to handle. That's why I turned to pills."

In 1964, two days after a Nashville recording session, he crashed a borrowed Cadillac into a utility pole, causing $2,000 damage to the car and several minutes of power failure to the surrounding neighborhood. The following year he was so strung out on amphetamines that he ditched a friend's automobile at the Farmer's Market in L.A., where it was later found with a dead battery and the keys still in the ignition. His bad habit of crashing and abandoning vehicles while in drug-induced frenzies threatened his own safety and made him a danger to those around him.

In 1965, Cash overturned a tractor at his five-bedroom ranch in Casitas Springs, near Ventura. That same year, while fishing in the Las Padres National Forest, he stalled his camper in the sand near the edge of a creek. In frustration, he kept revving the engine, until the overheated exhaust pipe started a wildfire that decimated 500 acres. It took 450 firefighters to put out the blaze, and the federal government sued Cash for more than $125,000. Two years later, the case was settled for $82,000.

It all took a toll on his career and ended his first marriage, to Vivian Liberto, in 1966.

But Cash was in denial. Most people would have called his actions a nervous breakdown; artists are more likely to label them "a creative dry spell." Whichever description best applied to Cash, he was experiencing a severe personal crisis. To cope with the pain, he drove out into the desert, where he drew figures in the sand and talked to himself. Was he mad? No, just angry.

"Sometimes he'd even dress in antique Western clothes with a gun strapped to his leg," related Cash's biographer, Steve Turner, "and spend a few nights in an abandoned ranch in Maricopa, California—with nothing but candles for light and a wood-burning stove for heat—hoping to find his inspiration."

It seemed that Cash was destined to burn, as in the song. But at the last minute, as he later described it, he saw the light. By 1968, the "Man in Black" had found religion, given up pills, and married the woman who made it all possible: June Carter of country music's esteemed Carter family.

All his life needed was some tender loving care. At the end of his biggest year, 1969, Cash had sold more records than the Beatles, and his popularity rivaled that of the Rolling Stones and the Beach Boys. There were movies, TV specials, and more hit records. The biggest thrills of his life were being inducted into the Country Music Hall of Fame and traveling with the Highwaymen, a quartet of grizzled country performers that included Willie Nelson, Waylon Jennings, and Kris Kristofferson.

By the early 1980s, Cash had almost beaten his drug habit, when several incidents triggered a major relapse. A pet ostrich on his property in Henderson, Tennessee, kicked him in the stomach and broke two of his ribs. The force of the attack knocked Cash to the ground, and he cracked three more ribs and required emergency medical treatment.

Then a Christmas dinner in Jamaica turned into a near-catastrophe when Cash, Carter, and a group of their friends were ambushed by three men who invaded the house where Cash was staying. Armed with a machete, a knife, and a gun, they held the terrified group captive for four hours while they ransacked the place. One of the gang was later caught and killed by authorities when he attempted to board a plane at the airport. Two others were jailed and then shot when they tried to escape. But the worst was yet to come.

In a hotel room in Nottingham, England, on the tenth stop of a 12-show European tour, Cash began hallucinating from a combination of drugs and alcohol. When his bed wouldn't budge for some reason, Cash began punching the wall in annoyance, driving his fist through the plaster and badly cutting his hand. The injury required immediate surgery, and that's when doctors discovered internal bleeding, which necessitated the removal of part of the singer's spleen, stomach, and intestines. Morphine was prescribed to dull the pain, and Cash, not surprisingly, suffered a chemical overload.

At the urging of his doctors, family, and friends, the over-medicated singer checked into the Betty Ford Center in late 1983, to spend the next 43 days being cleansed of his addictions both physically and spiritually. He celebrated his newfound sobriety with a Western-style feast at the Gene Autry Hotel in Palm Springs, where he ordered iced tea instead of bourbon.

Five years later, he had heart-bypass surgery. "He was very stoic," said musician Rosanne Cash, the singer's daughter from his first marriage. "He was from the old school, where you suffered, and it was, you know, like an *art*. You just did it—you didn't talk about it."

In 1997, the 11-time Grammy-winning icon was diagnosed with Parkinson's disease, which made his hollowed face take on the appearance of a malnourished convict. He was hospitalized in 1998 with severe pneumonia, which damaged his lungs, and although he continued to make recordings, it was the end of his performing career.

Two years after she had a pacemaker implanted, June Carter underwent heart surgery in 2003 but failed to regain consciousness; she was 73. Johnny Cash, her soul mate and husband of 35 years, passed away less than four months later, at the age of 71, from complications of diabetes and eventual respiratory failure.

■ ■ ■

BEING THE TALENTED daughter of Judy Garland was probably a curse as well as a blessing for **Liza Minnelli**, the three-time Tony Award–winning Broadway performer, for she has battled many of the same addictions that killed her mother in 1969, at the age of 47. Ironically, Minnelli traces her chemical dependency back to the aftermath of

Garland's funeral, when a well-meaning doctor prescribed Valium to help Minnelli cope with the loss.

Liza never had a normal childhood. She grew up to become the Next Big Star, but nobody taught her how to deal with overnight success or its psychological effects. She was still a chubby two-year-old in diapers when Garland dressed her in a frilly costume and gave her to co-star Van Johnson to hold in the finale of *In the Good Old Summertime*. Minnelli remembers the moment with a mixture of sentiment and sheer terror—a perfect description of her life in the public eye.

At nineteen, she met the New York fashion designer Roy Halston, who introduced the young actress to the world of sex and drugs. Halston was a self-made man: rich, talented, and gay. And thus began Minnelli's recurring physical attraction to homosexual men, which sometimes resulted in incompatible marriages and created further emotional problems.

In this respect, Minnelli was also imitating her mother. Garland, suffering from the same psychological hang-up, had affairs with gay or bisexual actors such as Peter Lawford, Dirk Bogarde, and Mark Herron. There even were rumors that Garland's second husband—Liza's father, Vincente Minnelli, a former Broadway set designer and director—had been gay.

By the time Garland died, Liza had already had intimate relationships with French lounge singer Charles Aznavour, whom she regarded as a father figure, and with profligate British comedian Peter Sellers, who was heavily into drugs. Garland introduced her teenage daughter to the gay Australian pop star Peter Allen, with whom Garland herself was reputed to have had a romantic involvement (Allen and singer-songwriter Chris Bell were Garland's opening act at the Hong Kong Hilton in 1964). Minnelli and Allen were married in 1967 and divorced in 1974. He died of AIDS in 1992.

By the time Minnelli and Allen split, she had made a career transition from the shy schoolgirl of *The Sterile Cuckoo* to the vamping nightclub entertainer in *Cabaret,* a bravura role that won her an Oscar. The film's obsessive director, Bob Fosse, snorted cocaine throughout the three-month production, and there were strong rumors that Minnelli did, too.

Her second husband was Jack Haley, Jr., whose father had co-starred with Garland in *The Wizard of Oz*. Newspapers treated their wedding as a joke: DOROTHY'S DAUGHTER MARRIES TIN MAN'S SON.

It seemed Minnelli was unable to attain true happiness, but she certainly ran herself ragged trying to find it. During the late 1970s, she became part of Andy Warhol's fashionable circle and frequented Studio 54, the trendiest nightclub in New York City. It was the height of the disco craze, and Minnelli and Halston, once again Minnelli's main escort, made the scene practically every night, along with novelist Truman Capote and model Bianca Jagger.

Minnelli had begun dating Martin Scorsese, and one evening, Halston, in a show of affection, gave Liza a box that contained cocaine, marijuana, Valium, and Quaaludes—to kick-start the affair. Another time, witnesses saw her on her knees in the club's VIP room, administering fellatio to Russian ballet dancer Mikhail Baryshnikov.

But as with so many addicts, the wild times proved too much for Minnelli, who started missing performances of her critically acclaimed musical revue *The Act*. The more shows she canceled, the more intense the media scuttlebutt that she was about to follow her mother to an early grave.

By 1984, Minnelli was so strung out on pills and booze that she committed herself to the Betty Ford Center for seven weeks. Sympathetic telegrams arrived from Bob Fosse, Sammy Davis, Jr., Chita Rivera, and Dudley Moore, her co-star from *Arthur*. Gene Simmons, lead singer of the super rock band *KISS*, with whom Minnelli had been briefly involved, was among those concerned friends who paid her a weekend visit.

At the Betty Ford Center, part of the healing process involves a patient writing an intensely private letter to the one person who has made the biggest impact on his or her life. In Minnelli's case, that person was obvious. Liza picked up a ballpoint pen and slowly, painfully, wrote the words "Dear Momma" on a sheet of paper.

What followed was a personal conversation with Judy Garland, whom Liza truly loved but toward whom she harbored fierce resentment. Her mother had been both insensitive and self-destructive, and Liza was imitating that behavior in her own battle with addiction.

Unfortunately, the treatment did not take. In 1986, one month before she turned 40, Minnelli was readmitted to the Center for additional care—what is known as a "retread." The exhausted star, who had endured multiple surgeries to repair damaged vocal chords and knees injured by dancing, and undergone two hip replacements, told friends she wanted to strengthen her resolve and stay off drugs.

But she also had another deeply personal reason for reentering the Center: to make peace with her dying father. Liza wanted Vincente Minnelli to know that she would get better once and for all. When they hugged for the last time, he prayed to God she would keep her promise.

Sadly, her newfound commitment came too late to help the most important men in her life: Fosse suffered a fatal heart attack in 1987; Halston, like Allen, perished from AIDS; and Jack Haley, Jr., died in 2001.

■ ■ ■

NOT MANY ACTORS get second chances, but **Robert Mitchum** got a lot of them, perhaps because he was a force to be reckoned with. An irascible man, with the strength of a bull and the striking power of a rattlesnake, he was well known in Hollywood circles as someone not to be crossed, drunk or sober.

Early in his career, Mitchum had been arrested for possession of marijuana and handed a 55-day jail sentence. The 1948 newspaper headline, ROBERT MITCHUM DRUG BUST, made the event sound like a major smuggling operation. But it was just a bunch of Hollywood pals smoking reefers in a Laurel Canyon house, raided by police who had received an anonymous tip.

Mitchum could easily have bought his way out of the problem. Instead he opted to take the punishment. Rather than hiding his head in shame, he served his time at a prison farm in Northern California and walked away a bigger star than before. He flaunted his time-served like a champion prizefighter in the ring.

But then, Mitchum always thumbed his nose at social convention. His cocky, don't-give-a-damn attitude, droopy eyes, and mumbling voice were unmistakable, whether onscreen or in person. Years later, when a curious fan inquired of him, "Aren't you Robert Mitchum?" the craggy actor replied, "I never touch the stuff!"

That bad-boy reputation was well deserved. A problem childhood had left him cynical and suspicious of the world. He didn't trust anyone and was reluctant to tell the truth, and when he did, he made it sound like a big joke.

True, the humor concealed heartbreak; his father, a railroad brakeman, had been crushed to death between two locomotives when Mitchum was a kid. His mother had to take a job as a typesetter to support her two orphaned sons.

But as a teenager, Mitchum was already on the road to trouble. At 16 he was charged with vagrancy and wound up on a Georgia chain gang, from which he escaped. Then he rode freight trains and box cars around the country in search of odd jobs as a day laborer or mechanic. He turned to acting, he always said, because it was easier than working for a living.

During that teenage roaming, Mitchum developed what would become the lifelong habit of smoking marijuana, which grew in abundance by the side of the railroad tracks. "After much practice," said biographer Lee Server, "he claimed to be able to taste the regional characteristics in any sampling—Georgia hemp from Louisiana shitweed from California Red, and so on—at a single toke, blindfolded."

Mitchum's other vice was whiskey, and throughout most of his life he was a heavy drinker, which probably accounts for his perpetually dazed look. His famous walk—listing to one side, neck pulled back, gliding across the floor—was the result of nearly constant inebriation.

Onscreen, in gritty detective films such as *Out of the Past* and *The Big Steal,* the characters he portrayed were mostly loners—misfits who bore strong similarities to himself. When he convincingly played a murderous priest who chases two children in *The Night of the Hunter,* or a serial rapist who gives a black eye to a female prostitute in *Cape Fear,* it was sometimes too close for comfort.

He did practically anything that was asked of him in the movies, including wearing drag; during one scene in the Western comedy *Girl Rush,* he sat at a bar in a gingham dress and bonnet, pretending to be cute (the scene ended in a full-scale brawl). He never took himself too seriously. "I'm the biggest whore in town," he once boasted. "I work cheap and do my own stunts."

In 1982, Mitchum was 65 and still in great demand. Unlike his graying contemporaries, he never seemed to age; paradoxically, as he got older, his fans got younger. His career particularly received a boost when he starred as Victor "Pug" Henry, the victorious naval captain in the 1983 TV miniseries *The Winds of War* and its sequel, *War and Remembrance.*

Around this time, however, he first exhibited the symptoms of alcoholism. He had always kept his drinking under control, but slowly it had begun to affect his work and his health.

By 1984, the actor's worried family—his wife, Dorothy Spence, and their sons, James and Christopher—were pleading with him to get professional help for his alcohol addiction. Mitchum laughed at them as he poured another drink, but he agreed to seek treatment.

He was unprepared, however, for what lay in store at the Betty Ford Center. It wasn't the menial chores—he could handle those. "No hardship," he said; "I made my bed all through the army." It was Mitchum's emasculation by doctors and nurses, who saw him shivering in his underwear, which wounded his pride.

"He was not happy to be there and he made it quite clear," a source was quoted as saying. "One time we were getting him into the swimming pool with the other patients and he didn't want to go. So he peed in the pool in front of everyone."

The day of his release from the Center, Mitchum stopped at the Beverly Hilton Hotel on his way home. He ambled up to the bar, ordered a drink, and said, "Fuck 'em all." He continued to drink and to smoke a pack of cigarettes a day until his death from lung cancer in 1997, one month before his eightieth birthday.

■ ■ ■

MARY TYLER MOORE considered her drinking problem hereditary. "The Queen of Denial" would have been an apt description for this brave soul, for her Mary-Sunshine face hid a heart that was breaking from feelings of guilt and remorse.

"Drinking during the day had been my mother's trait. It was the source of greatest fear and shame for me—so when I looked at myself," she said, "I could no longer pretend that I wasn't really an alcoholic. I was my mother."

An actress skilled in the art of emotional concealment, Moore had been able to hide her secret for 15 years. All through *The Dick Van Dyke Show*, she would chain-smoke Marlboros at rehearsals and get snookered at the end of each day's filming, yet still show up for work the next morning.

When her 17-year marriage to TV executive Grant Tinker ended in divorce, her alcoholism worsened. It hardly seemed possible that the actress who had played a shy flapper in *Thoroughly Modern Millie* and a timid nun exchanging chaste kisses with Elvis Presley in *Change of Habit* could be a raging drunk. But that was Moore when the cameras stopped rolling.

Not that anyone suspected her tipsy secret. Unlike other stars with the same problem, she mostly drank at home; every day at five o'clock, "two fishbowl-sized glasses of vodka on the rocks" made all her problems go away. Her drinking probably would have gone on undetected for a good deal longer if a tragic event had not pushed her over the edge. In 1980, Moore's 24-year-old son from her first marriage, Richard Meeker, Jr., shot himself one month after the film premiere of *Ordinary People*, in which Moore played a frigid mother coming to terms with the accidental death of her oldest son and the suicide attempt of his guilt-ridden younger brother.

Talk about life imitating art.

Whether deliberate or accidental, her son's senseless death almost destroyed her. Hooked on Valium, Moore locked herself in her New York apartment and drank enough margaritas, she said, to incapacitate a horse. "A quarter of a blender of bottled mix, one-quarter of ice, one-half of tequila, and shake it up baby! It had the consistency of a milk shake and the effect of morphine," she said.

Realizing that it was her only option, Moore sought a cure and found one 2,500 miles away at the Betty Ford Center.

Like an unemployed actress begging for a job, she was asked to come in the next day and, in a sense, audition. The staff confiscated her medicines, including thyroid pills and insulin for her diabetes (later returned). Then they showed her to a small room with a patio, which would be her home for the next five weeks.

One week later, however, the round-the-clock regimen and daily chores took their toll on the six-time Emmy Award–winning actress. Frightened, Moore packed her bags and took off in the middle of the night. Then, after checking into a nearby Marriott hotel, she contemplated her fate and reluctantly contacted Betty Ford herself, who asked Moore to reconsider joining the program.

It was not the first time they had talked. The two women first met when Mrs. Ford made a guest appearance on *The Mary Tyler Moore Show* in 1976. The sitcom had filmed a scene in the White House, and ironically Betty Ford had seemed oblivious to the proceedings; she had sat on a couch, smiling broadly, her speech slurred from alcohol and pills.

On that day, Moore had helped the first lady get through a difficult shoot by feeding her lines until their scene was finished. Now it was time for Ford to help Moore in her own agonizing hour of need. "That phone call," Moore later said, "saved my life."

■ ■ ■

TONY CURTIS HAD more to lose from his addiction than did many patients who entered Betty Ford Center. He possessed tremendous good looks, a great physique, and worldwide fame. But by the age of 45, his career was slipping away. The handsome actor, who had starred in highly regarded films such as *Sweet Smell of Success*, *The Vikings*, and *The Defiant Ones*—for which he received an Oscar nomination for Best Actor—was no longer considered box-office magic. Was he destined for the same career fate as many "pretty boys" who neared middle age in Hollywood: fewer good parts, less recognition, and a nagging sense of self-doubt about their own dramatic abilities? Curtis wondered and worried.

In 1970, he was arrested at Heathrow Airport in London with a small amount of marijuana. Subsequently he snorted cocaine with his daughter, Jamie Lee Curtis, an action that shocked and appalled her mother, Janet Leigh, and their close friends.

Now Curtis was so stoned most of the time that people lost respect for him. His fear had become a reality, and he had to contend with films where he played the buffoon instead of the best man, acted stupid instead of smart, and pretended that the joke was on him when, in fact, he was often the whole joke.

One day Curtis woke up and saw the truth facing him in the bathroom mirror. He was no longer trim, taut, and terrific; he was a tired, bloated, middle-aged has-been. He started to drink more, began taking Dexedrine and Dexamyl to get him through the day, and one or two sleeping pills to knock him out at night.

Worst of all, he was confronted by every man's greatest fear: impotence.

"It took me a long time to figure out that a major cause and effect of drug abuse is sexual dysfunction," said Curtis. "You either come too quickly or you don't come at all." So he started taking cocaine and free-basing to get a better "high." To take the edge off coming down, he drank a lot of whiskey, which made him feel better but quickly got him drunk.

Then came a time when Curtis was so desperate for a hit of coke, he was filling his nasal passages with a few grams of white powder mixed with baby laxative and dextrose—and couldn't tell the difference. That's when he bottomed out.

Scared that he would wind up dead in an alley from a drug overdose, Curtis cried out for help, and his family heard him. His daughters Jamie Lee, Kelly, and Allegra, from his marriages to actresses Janet Leigh and Christine Kaufmann, confronted their father and told him that if he wanted to live he had to undergo treatment at a drug and alcohol reha-bilitation center.

Weeping and confused, he agreed to go.

"At the Betty Ford Center I found myself waiting on tables, cleaning up after lunch and dinner—part of their routinization," said Curtis. "I was sharing a room with another guy. No blinds on the window. I was unable to sleep, irritable, nervous. There was no effort to ease it for me. They gave some patients tranquilizers to calm them down. Not with me. Absolutely nothing. Cold turkey."

His counselor, Drew Anderson, gathered everyone at the center together so they could meet their boyhood idol. "Fellas, take a good look at him," Anderson told the assembled group, many of whom were diehard movie fans. "He's the worst fifty-eight-year-old fuck-up you'll ever meet." Nobody laughed; especially not Curtis.

He managed to kick the soul-destroying habit just in time. Unfortu-nately, Nicholas Curtis, the actor's oldest son by his third marriage, was-n't so lucky. The husky 23-year-old, who was hoping to break into movies, died from a heroin overdose in 1994.

■ ■ ■

COMEDIAN **CHEVY CHASE** has made no secret that he loves getting high one way or another. On TV's *Saturday Night Live*, he and his smirking co-stars, Dan Aykroyd, John Belushi, and Bill Murray, were always sniffing and sneezing between scenes. In films like *Foul Play, Caddyshack,* and *Fletch,* Chase always played accident-prone dorks whose minds seemed to be—well, elsewhere.

In 1986, Chase, who was earning an estimated $6 million per movie, checked into the Center to beat his addiction to the painkiller Percocet, which he claimed he began to take after injuring his back from too many pratfalls. Whatever the reason, his stay at the center proved ineffectual. In 1995, he was busted for drunk driving in Beverly Hills. The following year, a limousine driver on the Disney film *Man of the House* was arrested and later sued Chase, asserting that the actor had instructed him to drive across the U.S.-Canadian border to pick up a Federal Express package containing 100 Percocet pills.

Chase is not the only funnyman to undergo clinical treatment for drug problems, nor will he be the last. Fidgety, fumbling, stand-up comic **Richard Pryor** frequented many a rehab program, including the Betty Ford Center in 1990.

Pryor was black society's voice of discontent with his hilarious and often profane observations about the inequities of everyday life. His vulgar humor turned him into an unlikely movie star, and top-grossing films such as *Car Wash, Stir Crazy,* and *Bustin' Loose* gave the politically incorrect comedian an international platform for his unrestrained humor.

But behind the scenes lurked a deeply troubled man whose life was plagued by severe depression and marital infidelity. In 1980, a suicidal Pryor set himself on fire while freebasing cocaine. Some reports had him pouring a bottle of rum over his head and lighting a match. The event was labeled an "accident," but Pryor later confirmed that it was an unsuccessful suicide attempt, the circumstances of which he incorporated into subsequent comedy routines.

Sadly, Pryor conformed to the belief that most comedians are unhappy people. He inhaled vast amounts of cocaine, suffered three heart attacks, contracted multiple sclerosis, and eventually was confined to a wheelchair. In 2005, he died of a heart attack at the age of 65.

■ ■ ■

SINGERS AND MUSICIANS seem especially vulnerable to the wonders of drugs. Perhaps that's because of the hard lives many of them lead before they become famous, or the hardships of a career lived on the road.

Country singer **Tanya Tucker**, who scored a #6 hit on the country music charts with "Delta Dawn," which she recorded when only 13, required two stays at the Betty Ford Center to overcome her cocaine and alcohol addictions.

By age 15, Tucker had a Grammy Award nomination, a Greatest Hits package, and had appeared on the cover of *Rolling Stone* magazine. At 19, she became the second female country singer to have a #1 hit single as a teenager with the song "What's Your Mama's Name?"

By the time of her twenty-first birthday, Tucker fell prey to hard liquor and pills and was on the road to ruin, unable to alter the course of her disastrous life. It didn't help that Tucker's boyfriends during her drug-taking days included Don Johnson, Glen Campbell, and Merle Haggard, all of whom battled alcoholism.

But Tucker was able to rescue herself from the abyss and turn her life around, a lesson in prevention that hopefully will be heeded by young pop stars like Jessica Simpson, LeAnn Rimes, and Lindsay Lohan.

■ ■ ■

SINGER AND TEEN idol **Andy Gibb** was not so fortunate.

Andy was the youngest and sexiest of the Gibb brothers—Barry, Robin, and Maurice—who had achieved worldwide fame as the Bee Gees. While still a teenager, Gibb was the first male solo artist to score three consecutive #1 *Billboard* hit singles: "I Just Want to Be Your Everything"; "Love Is Thicker than Water"; and "Shadow Dancing."

But Andy's impressionable youth and extreme sensitivity was no match for the temptations of alcohol and drugs, which quickly robbed him of his stamina and the ability to write and perform his own music. He became a cocaine addict.

Close friendships with producer Robert Stigwood, singer Olivia Newton-John, and a well-publicized affair with actress Victoria Principal could not halt his rapid descent into drug hell. Nor could the well-meaning moralizing of the Betty Ford Center, where an emaciated Gibb was admitted in the mid-1980s. He died of heart failure, aggravated by a bout of heavy drinking, just five days after his thirtieth birthday in 1988.

■ ■ ■

Rock 'n' roll performer **Jerry Lee Lewis** was dubbed the "Madman of Music" for his lascivious piano playing, which he often executed standing up, gyrating his hips and banging his hands on the keyboard while howling the words to "Whole Lotta Shakin' Goin' On" and "Breathless." His crazed antics, which included jumping on top of the piano, sticking out his tongue, and making obscene gestures, made the demented musician look like Danny Kaye on drugs.

Legend has it that at the end of one manic performance of the song "Great Balls of Fire," Lewis squirted lighter fluid over a Steinway piano and set it on fire, laughing hysterically as the instrument was scorched by flames.

Lewis's flagrant disregard for social convention backfired, however, when it was revealed that the wild entertainer's third wife was actually his 13-year-old second cousin. That kind of marriage happened to be legal in his home state of Louisiana, except for the minor detail that Lewis had failed to obtain a divorce from his second wife.

Criticizing Lewis's cradle-robbing, incest, and bigamy, sanctimonious moralists called the singer a pervert, an accusation that sent Lewis into a tailspin of depression. Although he was still popular, his concert tours were canceled, radio stations refused to air his music, and he was reduced to playing one-night stands. It was 15 years before he had another hit record with "Chantilly Lace."

In 1973, Lewis, whose apt nickname was "The Killer," became drunk and despondent over the death of his teenage son, who was killed when he crashed his Jeep—a birthday present from dad. It was the second time that one of Lewis's children had died; his oldest son had drowned in a swimming pool when the boy was an infant.

After that, the tragedies seemed to pile up. Not long after the car crash, Lewis nearly died from a bleeding ulcer. Then his fourth wife drowned in a swimming pool under suspicious circumstances. Less than two years after that, his fifth wife was found dead at their home from a methadone overdose. Addicted to alcohol and drugs, Lewis checked himself into the Betty Ford Center, where he cleaned up his act.

In 1989, Lewis's tumultuous life story was filmed as *Great Balls of Fire!* It starred Dennis Quaid as Lewis, Winona Ryder as his child bride, and

Alec Baldwin as his sinful cousin, preacher Jimmy Swaggart, who was arrested by police for soliciting a female prostitute in Indio.

■ ■ ■

COUNTRY SINGER AND songwriter **Tammy Wynette** was justly famed for her poignant working-class anthems, notably "Stand by Your Man," one of the biggest-selling songs recorded by a woman in music history.

Wynette had endured an impoverished adolescence and a harsh life as a young married woman, all of which were reflected in her plaintive songs. Her father died of a brain tumor when she was an infant, and her third daughter suffered from spinal meningitis. She herself suffered from numerous physical ailments and was operated on for gall bladder, kidney, and throat problems.

Still, she seemed to overcome these challenges through her singing. Her first hit single was "Apartment #9," recorded in 1967. Its success was followed by three more #1 hits: "Take Me to Your World," "D-I-V-O-R-C-E"; and "Stand by Your Man," which Tammy said she wrote in fifteen minutes. In 1969, she had two more well-deserved #1 hits: "Singing My Song" and "The Ways to Love a Man."

Along with Loretta Lynn and Dolly Parton, Wynette drew attention to sexual discrimination against women with a mixture of wit and wisdom, sprinkled like gold nuggets among the lyrics of her songs.

But the quality of Tammy's love life did not improve despite many professional accolades and five marriages. Her third husband, country music singer George Jones, with whom she recorded many a duet, was a hopeless alcoholic.

In 1994, Wynette contracted a nearly fatal abdominal infection and lay in a coma for six days. She recovered, but underwent 26 major surgeries and deepened her addiction to painkillers, for which she was treated at the Betty Ford Center. Wynette passed away at the age of 55 in 1998.

■ ■ ■

ON OCTOBER 25, 1988, **Elizabeth Taylor** returned to the Betty Ford Center for a seven-week stay. Because of her bad back she was excused from regular exercise and instead was pushed around in a wheelchair by the male orderlies.

Taylor had been told by her nutritionist to stay off a fat-drenched diet of New York–style cheesecake and Haägen-Dazs ice cream, which Taylor craved almost on an hourly basis. So every chance she got, the high-strung actress lit up a cigarette and puffed on it until she was almost out of breath.

At the same time, Taylor's 93-year-old mother, Sara Southern, who lived in Rancho Mirage, was admitted to Eisenhower Medical Center with bleeding ulcers (caused no doubt by worrying about her daughter's health), a situation that probably intensified the actress's own stress.

Displeased by the unappetizing selection of food available in the Betty Ford Center's cafeteria, Taylor brought in her personal hairdresser, to fix her hair and makeup, and then devised a plan to visit her ailing mother and help herself to all the freshly baked goodies in the Eisenhower Medical Center's dining room. Cackling like Margaret Hamilton, who played the evil witch in *The Wizard of Oz,* and looking just as weird, she sailed into the food hall, her nose twitching at the sweet aromas, eyes bugging as she scanned the daily specials posted on the blackboard.

Medical staff could practically set their watches by Taylor's well-timed arrivals for lunch and dinner. There she was: ladling thick gravy onto plates of baked chicken and meatloaf, grabbing handfuls of French fries, and stocking up on sweet desserts. According to C. David Heymann, "Elizabeth often asked for seconds and supplemented her diet at night and at breakfast with secret stashes of fancy Italian chocolates."

By the time she left the Center on December 10, Taylor had put on 25 extra pounds—all of them fat. Along the way, she had also picked up other baggage that she could easily have done without: a tall, rugged, 37-year-old construction worker, who had been staring at her in group therapy sessions. Flattered by the attention, she had giggled and blushed and batted her violet eyes like a shy schoolgirl. As things turned out, he had an arrest record for drug possession and was on probation for three years for driving while intoxicated. "I drink and do a little coke now and then, but I don't smoke marijuana," he told the arresting officer.

Taylor couldn't take her eyes off him. She extended her clammy hand, and the furry man bent down and kissed it. "My name's Larry Fortensky," he announced, scratching his ear like a flea-bitten mutt in the dog pound.

"I'm Elizabeth," she replied in her best Blanche DuBois voice. "Perhaps you've heard of me."

"Yes, ma'am," he answered. "May I have the honor of pushing your wheelchair?"

"Why, I'd be delighted," she drawled, looking up at him.

It was love at first sight.

In 1991, Fortensky became the eighth Mr. Taylor. It was a marriage only Hollywood could dream up. Their union lasted nearly five years, and during that time many people questioned the aging screen diva's wisdom in hooking up with a fellow addict. They believed it was five years she could ill-afford to waste.

"Hell, if she wanted to have sex," opined a longtime friend, "there are plenty of male escort agencies in the phone book she could have called."

It would have been much easier and a whole lot cheaper.

■ ■ ■

TWO YEARS AFTER Taylor's relapse, her fourth ex-husband, **Eddie Fisher**, who had previously been married to Debbie Reynolds, enrolled at the Betty Ford Center to treat his cocaine addiction. A doctor had informed the jittery 62-year-old singer that if he didn't do something about his runny nose he'd be dead within a few months.

Funny how fear of one's mortality always makes a stronger impression than common sense; shaken by the shock diagnosis, Fisher immediately made an appointment

But he was a textbook example of uncontrollable human ego. He arrived at the center with a box of his CDs, ready to put on a show for the hell-and-back patients. Except of course nobody wanted to hear him sing "Anytime" and "Wish You Were Here," or listen to him talk about his former life with Cleopatra. Enough already, they groaned at the water cooler.

For Fisher it was a reality check—the one-time Coca-Cola Kid's final wake-up call.

The first week, he waited tables. The second week, he worked garbage disposal. The third week, he did laundry detail. Every day was difficult, he said, but every day things also got better.

The first chance he got, Fisher called his girlfriend, Betty Lin, who would soon become his fourth wife. "Betty," he blabbed, "in the middle drawer in your bedroom is an envelope with cocaine in it. I want you to open it up and throw it down the toilet."

"Oh, no, Eddie," she protested. "It's worth thousands of dollars."

"Down the toilet," he insisted.

After that sacrifice, there arrived an unexpected reward. Betty visited him for four hours one Sunday afternoon. He was as nervous as a kid on his first date, with an impatient erection in his khaki pants. "Just holding her hand sent a surge of sexual energy through my body. We were not supposed to bring anyone to our rooms," he admitted. "We couldn't get there fast enough. No one ever disturbed us."

Not even the smiling, solicitous Betty Ford.

Taking comfort in this newfound divinity, Fisher married his sweetheart in 1993. His nerves must have been sorely tested when she died of cancer in 2001. But four years later, after mourning her devastating loss, he was still sober.

■ ■ ■

NOT EVERYONE HAS been so lucky. **Margaux Hemingway** probably never stood a chance of shedding her inebriation, inherited from generations of Hemingways that came before her.

The fashion-model-turned-movie-star lived in the shadow of her legendary grandfather, Ernest Hemingway, the bearded, bearlike author of romantic novels such as *The Sun Also Rises, A Farewell to Arms,* and *For Whom the Bell Tolls.* A hard-drinking, boastful man given to paranoid delusions, he suffered from increasingly bad health caused by lingering physical injuries and from periods of mental illness. Eventually he committed suicide by kneeling over the barrel of a shotgun and pulling the trigger. Hemingway's father had also committed suicide; he aimed a Civil War pistol at his head and left a telltale splash of red on the walls.

Margaux's father, Jack Hemingway, the writer's son, hoped and prayed that the bad seed which had caused his male ancestors so much emotional misery would spare him. And it did, only to root itself in the brain of his second oldest daughter.

The bright-eyed youngster was born prematurely four months after her granddad's news-making death. She was named after the French Bordeaux vineyard Chateau Margaux, a naming that was both ironic and profound.

Like the lost generation about which Hemingway wrote with such flourish in his anguished books, Margaux was doomed to a fatal addiction:
alcohol.

An epileptic, she experienced her first seizure at the age of seven. Then,
during the onset of puberty, she underwent a growth spurt and reached
a height of six feet. The blossoming teenager developed an overbite and
a husky voice, uncommon characteristics that were extremely attractive
to admirers of both sexes but not, it seemed, to her.

Dyslexia prevented her from reading the novels that sat on her family's bookshelves in Ketchum, Idaho, like small tombstones in a miniature graveyard. Those books, she sensed, held the answers to a mystery
that plagued her in recurring erotic dreams that often turned into night-
mares. In them, Ernest would chase his mentally disturbed granddaughter, Joan, with a shotgun, while Margaux and her younger sister, Mariel,
ran after him with a butterfly net.

By the time she was 21, Hemingway's seductive face and svelte body
were plastered on magazine covers around the world. She starred in the
exploitative rape melodrama *Lipstick*, and signed a $1-million promotional
contract with Fabergé perfume. But the worldwide fame predicted for
her failed to materialize, and she started drinking heavily and gorging herself on fatty foods.

Depressed, Margaux drank Stolichnaya vodka to nurse herself through
a nearly fatal skiing accident and her second divorce in as many years.
After she almost bit off her tongue during an epileptic seizure triggered
by booze, she checked into the Betty Ford Center in 1988.

Reflecting on her chaotic life, she told *People* magazine, "I loved to dance
and went to Studio 54 at least twice a week. But I always felt nervous around
the people there. I was in awe of that whole Halston-Liza Minnelli crowd.
To me, they were the real celebrities and I was just a girl from Idaho. So I
drank to loosen up. I never thought then that alcohol would become a problem. In my grandfather's time it was a virtue to be able to drink a lot and
never show it. And like him, I wanted to live life to the fullest, with gusto."

On July 2, 1996, the 41-year-old model's inert body was found by
police in her second-floor Santa Monica apartment. She was sitting in
bed, her arms and legs stiff from rigor mortis, a book on her lap.

More than a month after Margaux's death, the Los Angeles County Coroner's Office confirmed that she had died of a drug overdose. Investigators found "a fatal dosage of Phenobarbital" in her system, enough to conclude that this descendent of the Hemingways had most likely killed herself.

Indeed, in a bizarre, almost surreal coincidence, her death had occurred on the thirty-fifth anniversary of her Nobel Prize–winning grandfather's suicide.

■ ■ ■

A MORE SUCCESSFUL candidate for the Betty Ford Center was *Miami Vice* star **Don Johnson**. He had once licked a serious booze problem. But he promptly fell off the wagon five years into his second marriage, to actress Melanie Griffith, his co-star in both *Paradise* and a 1992 remake of *Born Yesterday*.

Johnson's bad-boy image has been fodder for the tabloids for more than 30 years. Arrested for hot-wiring cars, and sent to reform school at the age of 12, Johnson first rode the wave to stardom as the straight friend of the well-known gay actor Sal Mineo, who got Johnson the role of the young inmate who is raped by a gang of male prisoners in the shocking play *Fortune and Men's Eyes*.

Nude photographs of Johnson displaying his manly assets ensured a loyal following, but they also spurred rumors about his private life that have hounded him to the present day, even though he has married three women, including actress Patti D'Arbanville, and is the father of four children.

In 1994, Johnson had a very public relapse, which led to a one-month stay at the Center. The actor told friends he was determined to control his demons and give up drinking once and for all, and after being released, his career bounced back with the TV series *Nash Bridges*.

Griffith, whom Johnson eventually divorced, has also wrestled with addiction, to both alcohol and prescription painkillers. Her wake-up call came in 1988, when she was so drunk on the set of *Working Girl* that her incapacity held up production. "I was my own worst enemy," said Griffith. The actress says she is now clean and sober after a lifelong addiction to booze and pills.

■ ■ ■

ANYBODY, IT SEEMS, can be an alcoholic. Take **Gene Autry**, Hollywood's first "Singing Cowboy," who galloped across the plains in nearly 100 films, from *Boots and Saddles, Carolina Moon,* and *Robin Hood of Texas,* to *The Strawberry Roan* and *Mule Train.*

Autry recorded more than 600 songs, almost half of which he had a hand in writing. Tuneful odes to the prairie such as "South of the Border," "Back in the Saddle," and "The Last Round-Up" sold more than 60 million copies, earning the smiling buckaroo more than a dozen gold records and a fortune in never-ending royalties.

Autry's most famous composition, "Rudolph the Red-Nosed Reindeer," is the second bestselling single of all time, and two other festive songs that he wrote, "Here Comes Santa Claus" and "Peter Cottontail," have become classics. The wide-eyed kids that hummed these playful tunes never suspected that their smiling, good-natured hero in the white Stetson and embroidered Western shirt battled a drinking problem.

The truth was, Autry loved to bend the elbow. The sad fact was that he couldn't stop.

"Drinking was a way to celebrate the end of a day or a deal," confessed Autry, who found his lips trembling at the sight of a frosty glass. "I reached a point where I felt I could have one drink and walk away from the bar. Some nights I didn't walk away and I wished I had."

Once voted the screen's #1 Western star, and acclaimed the fourth biggest box-office attraction in the nation after Mickey Rooney, Clark Gable, and Spencer Tracy (all of whom were heavy drinkers, too), Autry hid his craving for alcohol behind a polite, jovial façade. If he seemed just a little bit flushed in the afternoon, well, few people noticed.

"One reason Gene drank so much and so often," explained a longtime friend, "was that he had a lot of responsibilities in those days." Aside from acting, Autry produced and starred in the TV adventure series *The Gene Autry Show.* A lifelong baseball fan, he also owned the California Angels (now the Anaheim Angels). He had money tied up in oil wells and hotels, and in six TV and radio stations.

It was a heavy load for one man to carry on his shoulders. "I appeared on stage, a very few times, when I was less than cold sober," Autry recalled. "Socially, I said or did things that embarrassed me later."

After his patient and understanding wife of 48 years, Ina Spivey, died in 1980, Autry got lonesome and hitched up with a former vice president of Security Pacific Bank. "A real good looker," in Autry's opinion, Jacqueline Ellam was a stout, 37-year-old redhead whose comforting way with bank customers had impressed the 79-year-old widower. She had resigned her position, in fact, after an elderly customer died and left her some commercial property.

"Autry's fondness for the spirits was no secret," wrote Palm Springs journalist Allene Arthur, "and observers say she often matched him glass for glass." Their first date was at a New Year's Eve party, where they both got completely soused.

Among the other things the couple shared when they weren't drinking were riding horses and watching baseball. So after a whirlwind courtship, Gene and Jackie were married in 1981, and she became Autry's life and business partner in his multimillion-dollar empire.

Just as his investments were finally paying him huge dividends, Autry, on his doctor's orders, cut back on the booze and became what he preached in his movies: a good citizen. "You have to do the right thing if you want people to trust you," he advised his younger bride.

Jackie, however, had difficulty following that advice. One of Jackie's responsibilities, though it hardly amounted to much work, was counting the receipts at the Gene Autry Hotel in Palm Springs. Observing the employees and chatting with customers became a day-to-day affair, and the new Mrs. Autry could often be found at the bar, smoking and drinking with the best of them. And she couldn't stop.

Fearing she would lose her husband's love and respect if he found her passed out someplace, she decided to quit drinking. She called the Betty Ford Center and enrolled in a one-month program for the treatment of alcohol dependency.

Autry took the news with his customary politeness, though it was overheard around the hotel that he was displeased to see his wife's chronic drinking written up like a horse sale in the local papers. But he understood her need to take care of the problem, which included attending AA meetings two or three times a week.

When he died of lymphoma in 1998, at the age of 91, Autry possessed a fortune that *Forbes* magazine estimated to be worth $230 million. The longtime cowboy reportedly held his wife's hand as the sun was setting on his life. "You're a great gal," he said.

■ ■ ■

MANY SPORTSMEN HAVE also battled with their weakness for fermented spirits. National Baseball Hall of Fame legend **Mickey Mantle**, who scored 536 home runs in a spectacular 18-year career with the New York Yankees, was a patient at the Betty Ford Center in 1994, after he received a liver transplant for chronic alcoholism, cirrhosis, and hepatitis C.

Mantle hit the all-time World Series records for home runs (18), for runs scored (42), and runs batted in (40). He also did what every baseball player has dreamed about: he smacked a ball that traveled 565-feet through the air and across the roof of Griffith Stadium in Washington, D.C.

Mantle wasn't just a one-hit wonder. He walloped another ball that cleared the roof at Tiger Stadium in Detroit and traveled an estimated 643 feet. It was, admittedly, a tough act to follow, and Mantle had great difficulty living up to those superhuman feats of strength. In his final days, he became a born-again Christian, his weakened body at the mercy of his family, who loved him despite decades of alcohol abuse and its inevitable consequences.

Unfortunately, his health was too far gone for him to be saved from his destiny, and Mantle, his mind full of regrets but his heart comforted by people's forgiveness, died of liver cancer in 1995. He was 63.

■ ■ ■

ACTOR **GARY BUSEY** was nominated for an Academy Award for his star-making performance as the pioneering rock 'n' roller who dies in a plane crash in *The Buddy Holly Story*. The compelling film was the highpoint in Busey's troubled life, which has included police arrests for drug possession and domestic violence.

In 1988, the extroverted performer, who played edgy characters in *Big Wednesday, Eye of the Tiger,* and *Lethal Weapon,* was nearly killed in a motorcycle accident because he was not wearing a helmet. Busey's skull was fractured, and it was thought he suffered permanent brain damage. But the injured actor made a miraculous recovery.

Busey also was a heavy drug user, and a second brush with death occurred in 1995, when he almost died from a cocaine overdose. Only prompt medical attention saved his life, and he narrowly escaped going to jail. Busey claimed that he suffered a terrifying near-death experience during which he saw visions of hell and the devil—not surprising given his reckless past.

In 1997, a plum-sized tumor was removed from his sinus cavity, most likely the result of inhaling various toxic substances. After a trip to the Betty Ford Center he became a born-again Christian and joined a Colorado-based antidrug group called Promise Keepers.

■ ■ ■

ANNA NICOLE SMITH went from being an anonymous waitress to the nation's most talked-about sex symbol when she posed nude à la Marilyn Monroe in *Playboy* magazine. The ensuing publicity landed the voluptuous pin-up enticing roles in films such as *Naked Gun 33 1/3*, where she played a gangster's moll and seduces white-haired star Leslie Nielsen.

Smith later became an object of media ridicule over her failed legal challenge to inherit half of the $1.6 billion estate of her late 90-year-old husband, Texas oil billionaire J. Howard Marshall II, whom she had met when dancing at a topless bar in Houston. The horny nonagenarian forked over fistfuls of one hundred dollar bills to see Smith dangle her surgically enlarged, 42DD-cleavage in his salivating face.

Smith said Marshall had promised her half of his fortune if she married him. Her abject disappointment when he died nine months later without leaving her anything, even though she was his wife, caused the model to experience severe emotional stress.

Her weight soon tipped the scales at 200 pounds, the result, she stated, of difficulty contesting Marshall's will. She had also been heavily sedated and believed that the medication added to her depression. Eventually this nonstop party girl with a hearty appetite for food and liquor was hospitalized for an overdose of Xanax, Vicodin, and alcohol.

That didn't bring a halt to her exploits. In 1995, she was arrested for public nudity on a beach in the Bahamas. Smith then gate-crashed a Jewish boy's *bar mitzvah* at the Beverly Hills Hotel and performed a lewd dance for the shocked guests. The following year, she took another over-dose of pills and checked into the Betty Ford Center to cure her dependency on painkillers.

Marshall probably had no intention of leaving a nickel to the topless dancer, especially after giving her thousands of dollars for services rendered. Instead, he strung Smith along with the promise of more riches so he could take the memories of watching her strip and perform sex acts to his grave.

For that reason, Smith thought she could win a judgment against the dead man and gain what she believed was rightfully hers. But Smith's dear-departed sugar daddy wasn't as dumb as all that, and after five years of court battles his fortune remained intact. In 2001, a U.S. Court of Appeals ruled that the late oil tycoon's son, Pierce Marshall, was the sole heir to his father's fortune.

Smith did not walk away totally empty-handed, however. To capitalize on the continuing news coverage, E! Entertainment Television launched a weekly reality program called *The Anna Nicole Show*, which followed the buxom blonde on blind dates and shopping sprees.

■ ■ ■

FOUR-TIME EMMY AWARD–WINNING actor **Kelsey Grammer**, who played the bombastic psychiatrist Frasier Crane on the long-running TV sitcoms *Cheers* and *Frasier*, has more than one legitimate excuse for his mental depression and substance abuse: his father was murdered when he was 13; his sister was raped and killed after leaving a Red Lobster restaurant; and his twin half-brothers were mauled to death in a shark attack.

The one bright spot in all this tragedy was Grammer's salary for *Frasier*: $1.6 million per episode, which set a new record. The astronomical sum would seem to be enough to make anyone forget their troubles, except Grammer, whose private life has been mired by continued unhappiness.

At the top of the list was Grammer's second wife, a former stripper who tried to commit suicide while pregnant with their child and suffered a miscarriage.

In 1987, Grammer was charged with drunk driving and possession of cocaine. He was put on 90 days house arrest and then served 30 days in jail in 1991 for violating parole.

Adding insult to injury, the actor was accused of statutory rape by the parents of his daughter's underage babysitter, although the police found no evidence to support the accusation. After publishing his autobiography, presumably to clear up some of these misconceptions, he was sued by a former girlfriend for defamation of character and invasion of privacy.

Finally, in October 1996, Grammer was admitted to the Betty Ford Center after flipping his $66,000 Dodge Viper near his Malibu home and sustaining minor head injuries. Police charged him with driving while intoxicated and with an expired license. He is now sober.

■ ■ ■

THE LATEST BURNED-OUT star to relight their flame in the center's carpeted hallways is Grammy-winning singer-songwriter **Billy Joel**, who was a model patient there for one month in March 2005.

The self-styled musical genius, whose mega-hits include "Piano Man" and "Uptown Girl," checked into the center to be treated for alcohol abuse after experiencing severe gastrointestinal distress. Three years earlier, Joel had spent two weeks in a psychiatric hospital in Connecticut, where he also underwent treatment for substance abuse.

Joel's latest meltdown came after several decades of intense pressure.

Between 1974 and 1993, Joel placed at least one single in the Top 40 in every year but three. Thirteen of his 33 hits have made the Top 10, and three of them—"It's Still Rock and Roll to Me," "Tell Her About It," and "We Didn't Start the Fire"—reached #1.

On his third album, Joel stretched himself as a songwriter and stylist with a varied set that ranged from the Brill-Building pop of "Say Goodbye to Hollywood" to the cabaret-style tribute to his home turf, "New York State of Mind."

The 56-year-old performer has a long history of alcohol-related problems. In 2003, Joel careened his brand new Mercedes Benz coupe into a tree. The following year, he crashed his 1967 Citroen 2CV into an elderly woman's house.

A friend who saw Joel after he checked out of the Center said that he has completely sworn off booze. The strongest drink he now imbibes is coffee. Maybe one day Joel will write a song about it.

■ ■ ■

IN 2003, THE Betty Ford Center celebrated its twentieth anniversary. Six hundred guests in tuxedos and evening gowns streamed into the Hyatt Grand Champions Resort in Indian Wells for the gala event, while violins played, and waiters served nonalcoholic drinks and fat-free appetizers. The $1,000-a-plate dinner raised $1.6 million for the Center's financial assistance program.

CNN broadcaster Larry King was master of ceremonies. The featured performer was singer Josh Groban. There were glowing tributes, heartfelt thank-yous, and a few tearful farewells. Former first ladies Rosalynn Carter, Nancy Reagan, Barbara Bush, and Hillary Clinton were introduced while the orchestra played a stirring rendition of "God Bless America." President George W. Bush and first lady Laura Bush sent a videotaped greeting.

Those onstage were joined by the special guest of honor, Betty Ford, and the star-studded audience, which included Congresswoman Mary Bono, entertainer Merv Griffin, and actor Kirk Douglas, broke into loud applause.

Guests lingered late into the evening. As they left, Mrs. Ford gave each person a souvenir of the occasion: an inscribed music box that played "The Wind Beneath My Wings."

West Coast Camelot

AIR FORCE ONE, the president's customized four-engine, jet-propelled Boeing 707, touched down at Palm Springs Airport in brilliant sunshine. It was President John F. Kennedy's third of four trips to the desert and his second official visit since winning election to office.

His flight was met by a guard of honor from March Air Force Base and the U.S. Marine Band from Twentynine Palms, which played "Hail to the Chief" with a flourish of trumpets and drums as the nation's leader disembarked onto the tarmac.

This was the plane on which Lyndon B. Johnson would be sworn in as thirty-sixth president following Kennedy's assassination. It was also the plane on which Johnson's successor, Richard M. Nixon, would travel to China for a historic meeting with Chairman Mao Tse-Tung.

On this warm December day in 1962, however, Kennedy wore a dark business suit and struggled under the weight of his orthopedic back brace, which he wore beneath his shirt and jacket to correct spinal problems.

On the ground, five thousand men, women, and children lined the chain-link fence, waving small American flags and taking pictures with their pocket cameras.

Half a dozen Secret Service agents, carrying walkie-talkies and concealed handguns, kept a respectable distance. Brushing a strand of hair out of his eyes, Kennedy shook hands with well-wishers and smiled for photographers. He was then shown into an open Lincoln Continental sedan, which drove him from the runway and out a side gate.

Escorted by a fleet of California Highway Patrol cars and motorcycles, the president's sedan proceeded in an easterly direction along Highway 111 and, while Kennedy took in the passing scenery, continued without stopping for the next 12 miles until it reached Palm Desert.

This flat, irrigated basin was originally called Palm Village, a small community of livery stables and farms, one of which was owned by ventriloquist Edgar Bergen, who was among the most popular entertainers on radio and television. Bergen had invested heavily in real estate, often doubling and tripling his money. It was he who saw the potential of turning the underused land into a booming tourist haven.

"You gotta take a look at this place," Bergen urged his best friend, real estate developer Clifford Henderson, an early aviation pioneer with a gift for promotion. Henderson agreed it was a gold mine waiting to be discovered, so the two men teamed up together. They sank a well 600 feet into the ground and discovered, much to their surprise, a reservoir of artesian water. "This is it!" exclaimed Henderson. Plans were drawn up, and building soon got underway for the desert's newest resort. Called Shadow Mountain, this exclusive enclave of hotel bungalows, surrounded by a figure-eight swimming pool equipped with a diving pontoon, opened in 1948.

The presidential motorcade passed through sandy plains where Mexican laborers had once grown grapes, dates, and citrus fruit, the parched earth now covered with housing tracts. Kennedy looked out the window at Portola Avenue, which rose like a crest toward the Santa Rosa Mountains.

He knew the spot well.

Twenty years earlier, General George S. Patton, Jr., who commanded the Third Army Division, had taken over the surrounding land, where he conducted secret tank exercises in preparation for his North African campaign against Field Marshal Erwin Rommel.

"There," the new president informed his press secretary Pierre Salinger, who was in the backseat next to him, "is where 500 armor-plated tanks engaged in battle practice."

At the time, Kennedy had been serving as a lieutenant in the U.S. Navy aboard torpedo boat PT-109 when it was sunk by a Japanese destroyer in the Solomon Islands. The collision threw him across the deck, injuring his troublesome back. He spent six days adrift in the water before he and his crew were rescued.

Kennedy smiled at the irony. To think he had been rejected from the army because of his imperfect health, he told himself, only to be accepted by the navy, which nearly got him killed.

The CHP maintained a routine speed as they turned right and headed up the hill to Silver Spur Ranch. At the main gate Kennedy breathed in the crisp desert air and was reminded of the last time he had been here: almost nine months ago, for a secret rendezvous with Marilyn Monroe. He could still smell the fragrance of Chanel No. 5, which lingered on her neck and shoulders as she straddled his naked torso, pushing her hips down on him.

Monroe was so deeply in love with Kennedy that she had received hormone shots to increase her fertility and become pregnant, so that Kennedy would divorce Jackie and marry her. When confronted with the awful truth that "the Prez" as she called him had no intention of marrying her, Monroe couldn't live with herself anymore. Three months later she took a fatal overdose of sleeping pills.

Kennedy's car was escorted past the fence posts and ocotillo bushes to the majestic seven-bedroom home of **Bing Crosby** at 49–400 Della Robbia Lane, which the Kennedy entourage had rented for the weekend.

A fine-looking, California ranch-style house, Crosby's home had a master suite and six guest wings angled in a Y-shape around a heated swimming pool. The house could comfortably sleep 14 people, exactly the number of guests Kennedy had invited.

In the entrance hall, recessed near an antique front door, stood a three-foot-high porcelain figure of a mother and child, which had come from the Hearst Castle. The Crosby family crest was embedded in the white terrazzo floors, on which stood hand-carved Elizabethan furniture. It was a house fit for a king, and even Kennedy was impressed.

The magnificent place held special significance for the Crosbys: it was where Bing, an honorary mayor of Palm Desert, lustily carried his new bride, Kathryn, over the threshold to their candle-lit bedroom, in preparation for their big wedding night. One month later she found herself pregnant with his fifth son, Harry, Jr.; one year after that she gave birth to Mary; and two years after that, a sixth boy, Nathaniel, arrived.

Once Kathryn bore him children, however, Crosby treated her like a servant. And his new wife, who had thrown away a promising acting career playing the fairytale princess in *The 7th Voyage of Sinbad* to stay at home, grew resentful of his cavalier treatment. Despite Crosby's wealth, conservatively estimated at $150 million, they were not a happy family. Bing was extremely testy, and his four adult sons by Dixie Lee had emotional problems that were exacerbated by drinking.

Either Crosby didn't think anything of their troubles or he simply didn't care. In any case, he was frequently absent from the Palm Desert home, as was Kathryn Crosby during Kennedy's two visits. After the president arrived on Saturday afternoon, a phalanx of Secret Service agents was deployed to guard the property, and Kennedy retired to the master bedroom, where he couldn't wait to take off his clothes. "I have a really bad headache," he told Peter Lawford, who had followed the motorcade from Janet Leigh's house in Palm Springs, where he was staying with the actress (she was recently divorced from Tony Curtis). They had all been fervent Kennedy supporters, along with Frank Sinatra, Shirley MacLaine, Sammy Davis, Jr., Angie Dickinson, Milton Berle, and Judy Garland (but not Dean Martin, who preferred his home to political rallies).

Lawford knew what would cure Kennedy's headache, and it wasn't an aspirin. His job? To make sure there was food, liquor, and beautiful young women for the weekend. So he went from room to room looking for eligible candidates, until he found a pretty, long-legged girl in a bikini.

"Darling," Lawford slurred, "are you ready to do your job for national security?"

The girl gave him a strange look.

"Not me, stupid," he said, gesturing toward the hallway. "Him."

He took the girl by the arm and led her to Kennedy's room. Then he shoved her inside and closed the door. After a few more cocktails, Lawford staggered outside to the patio, where, it was observed, he propositioned an airline stewardess who rejected his advances.

Several eyewitnesses claimed the actor disgraced himself with his lecherous, intoxicated behavior. In all fairness, however, it may not have been entirely his fault, nor was he the only one to behave irresponsibly that night.

Dave Powers, the president's personal aide, was horsing around that night and got so drunk that he bent over and made an obscene gesture (within earshot of the president, he said, "Hey, pal, look at this!"). He also ran in and out of the house carrying armfuls of Crosby's suits, and jumped into the pool with them.

According to investigative reporter Seymour Hersh, "The party was so noisy that a group of California state policemen on duty at the front of the estate, which bordered on a desert wilderness area, assumed that the shouts and shrieks of the partygoers were the nighttime calls of coyotes."

By evening's end, there was still any number of couples, naked or otherwise, doing whatever felt good. Secret Service agents were told to look the other way, though one observer, when questioned, humorously remarked, "Nothing's happening out there, but one coyote is sitting on top of another one."

On Monday, at one o'clock in the morning, Kennedy secretly flew out of Palm Springs on Air Force One, bound for Washington, D.C. All in all, 30 police officers had been put on duty for the 36 hours that the president was at Crosby's house in Palm Desert.

The press reported that Kennedy was feeling "much refreshed" from his two-day stay.

As usual, Peter Lawford took all of the credit but accepted none of the blame for the president's transgressions. Congressman Patrick J. Hillings, who had supplied automobiles for Kennedy's visit, courtesy of his client, the Ford Motor Company, said, "We had a hard time finding all the cars when JFK returned to Washington. Eventually, we found many at the homes of movie starlets and girlfriends."

Kennedy's sexual excesses may have contributed indirectly to his death. He tore a groin muscle while frolicking next to the pool with a female partner on a third visit to Crosby's home in September 1963. The excruciating pain necessitated a second back brace, which Kennedy was wearing at the time of his visit to Dallas, seven weeks later.

Although the braces were meant to keep him in an upright position and protect him from further injury, they made it almost impossible for him to move in any other direction. He was virtually incapable of protecting himself when struck down by two sniper bullets, which came from the direction of the Texas School Book Depository during the final moments of his presidential motorcade.

The first shot that Lee Harvey Oswald allegedly fired into the president's neck was not necessarily fatal, but the second one, coming as rapidly as the first, struck Kennedy in the head and killed him because his upper body was totally immobile. In the words of one disgusted onlooker, "It was a first-class turkey shoot."

Texas Governor John Connally, Sr., who was sitting in the front seat of Kennedy's open limousine, was hit in the chest by a sniper's third bullet, apparently intended for the fatally injured president as the motorcade sped through Dealey Plaza.

In the aftermath of this devastating tragedy, temporary domestic tranquility slowly returned to Crosby's Silver Spur home, which had been dubbed by family and staff President Kennedy's "Desert White House."

But it didn't last very long.

In 1959, Bing's younger brother, Bob Crosby, a Dixieland bandleader, was stabbed by his wife, who claimed her husband had beaten her with his fists and broken one of her ribs. Bing's four boys, who had developed a nightclub act, began fighting among themselves and broke up. They were reunited—minus the eldest, Gary—at the Chi-Chi nightclub in Palm Springs. Following a jury trial, Dennis was found to be the father of a three-year-old daughter named Denise, who had been born out of wedlock, and he was ordered to pay child support to the mother. Indeed, Dennis and his twin brother, Phillip Crosby, were both divorced by their respective wives on the grounds of "extreme cruelty."

In 1961, Gary's wife took a near-fatal drug overdose. The following year, Lindsay's wife, who was eight months pregnant, attempted suicide and lost the baby (she subsequently filed for divorce). Lindsay himself suffered two nervous breakdowns and in 1963 was committed to a psychiatric hospital.

Along the way, Bing's infant son, Harry, Jr., was seriously injured in a car accident at their vacation home in Los Cruces, Mexico, and had to be flown back to Los Angeles for emergency medical treatment.

The ensuing years were hardly easier on Crosby's health and well-being. In 1970, his three youngest children were lucky to survive a car crash in Redding, California, that injured their grandfather and killed their grandmother. Crosby himself underwent numerous operations for kidney stones and was required to consume quantities of distilled water instead of Scotch, his preferred drink. Among his recurring illnesses were bursitis and pleurisy, which required the removal of a small portion of his left lung.

Life ended, as it almost had begun for Crosby, on a golf course. In 1977, he was chipping away in Madrid, Spain, when he felt a twinge of pain on the eighteenth hole. Photographers saw Crosby fall to the ground. He was pronounced dead of a massive heart attack at the age of 74.

There was no love lost for their father among the male-dominated Crosby clan. He was reviled as a monster by his four oldest sons, who blamed him for their misfortunes. In 1989, Lindsay shot himself to death, as did his brother Dennis two years later. Gary Crosby expired from cancer in 1995, and Phillip passed away in 2004.

In *High Society*, one of Crosby's most popular films, he sings a tipsy duet with Frank Sinatra, his one-time neighbor whose friendship succumbed to rivalry for the affections of a slain president. Attired in a smart tuxedo, Crosby grabs a champagne glass and waxes lyrical about his good luck, accompanied by his harmonizing rival. To paraphrase the song, "What a swell party it was!"

■ ■ ■

COMPOSER **JIMMY VAN Heusen**, who contributed some of the most scintillating popular songs of the last century, owned the home at 49–300 Della Robbia Lane, where John F. Kennedy's Secret Service agents stayed during the presidential trysts at Bing Crosby's home.

He and Crosby first met when Van Heusen was hired to write the score for *Road to Zanzibar*, the second of seven movies starring Crosby, Bob

Hope, and Dorothy Lamour, who was synonymous with another time-less Van Heusen composition, "Moonlight Becomes You."

Although Van Heusen was Crosby's next-door neighbor twice—he had previously lived a stone's throw from the crooner at Thunderbird Heights—he was considered one of Sinatra's best friends. The songwriter was allowed the special privilege of calling the singer "dago," and Frank addressed Jimmy by his real name, Chester.

Van Heusen and Sinatra had a brief cooling off period when the president's brother, Attorney General Robert F. Kennedy, squelched plans for JFK to stay with the singer, who was deemed a security risk for his reported association with mobsters. Sinatra screamed at Van Heusen, called him a traitor, and tore up pieces of sheet music. The composer weathered Sinatra's outbursts by playing golf until things blew over.

Indeed, the disagreement didn't seem to affect their working rela-tionship. Often in collaboration with lyricists Johnny Burke and Sammy Cahn, Van Heusen wrote hundreds of lively ballads that the tempestuous singer recorded: entertaining ditties such as "Love and Marriage"; "The Tender Trap"; "Come Fly with Me"; "The Last Dance"; "Only the Lonely"; "Ring-a-Ding-Ding"; and the show-stopping number "My Kind of Town," from the gangster spoof *Robin and the 7 Hoods*.

Their alliance was more like that of rival brothers. They boasted to each other about their sexual conquests and commiserated over each other's lost loves, especially Sinatra's distressing breakup with his second wife, Ava Gardner, who was considered the real love of the singer's life.

"It was at Van Heusen's New York apartment that Frank slashed his wrists over Ava's absence in 1953—one of many little incidents that the composer overlooked in the pursuit of a friendship built around Frank's singing his songs," according to Shawn Levy. Indeed, Van Heusen had har-bored Sinatra at his first Palm Springs home, located near the Racquet Club, when Frank stormed out of his own house after a drunken fight with Gardner—the first of many blowups.

Van Heusen's songwriting talents won numerous awards, including three Oscars for the surefire hits "Swinging on a Star" from *Going My Way*, "All the Way" from *The Joker Is Wild,* and "High Hopes" from *A Hole in the Head.*

It was in the house at Della Robbia Lane, when Van Heusen wasn't busy entertaining various shapely ladies, that he composed the score for the last Crosby-Hope film, *Road to Hong Kong.* There, too, he wrote the song for which he won his fourth Oscar: the wistful ballad "Call Me Irresponsible" from *Papa's Delicate Condition.*

Van Heusen had many interests apart from songwriting. He was an accomplished horseman and kept six thoroughbreds on 20 acres that he owned in Yucca Valley, a place that became his favorite retreat and to which he permanently moved in 1964, saying "the world is getting too small." He also was an experienced pilot who commuted regularly between Los Angeles and Palm Springs in a twin-engine Beechcraft and a Hughes helicopter.

When producer William Perlberg, who had made two films with Bing Crosby, *Little Boy Lost* and *The Country Girl*, passed away in 1968, his petite, dimpled widow, Bobbe Perlberg, formerly known as Josephine Brock of the singing Brox Sisters, married Van Heusen.

Their "sunset" union prompted the couple's longtime friends to rib them about the vast difference in their ages (she was 13 years older than he). The Van Heusens were unfazed; they drank a toast to love and stayed together for the next 22 years. Their final address was the Springs Club in Rancho Mirage, where Van Heusen died at the age of 77 in 1990. Bobbe followed him to his grave nine years later at the age of 98.

Around the corner from where Crosby lived, Alice Faye's husband **Phil Harris** kept a second home at 49–400 JFK Trail, so-named to honor the fallen president.

Naming this street after Kennedy seems almost lascivious in its pointed reference to the man's unbecoming conduct (the intersecting street is fittingly named Crosby Lane). There is no road dedicated to Van Heusen.

■ ■ ■

TODAY, PALM DESERT is among the most heavily populated of the desert cities, with 45,000 year-round residents. Its gleaming centerpiece is the 1,127-seat Bob Hope Cultural Center and the McCallum Theatre for the Performing Arts.

El Paseo, or "the Avenue," the city's major thoroughfare, contains some of the desert's swankiest boutiques, art galleries, and bistros. The fashionable boulevard came into being when Cliff Henderson, who built the ultra-modern Pan-Pacific Auditorium in Los Angeles, purchased 1,600 acres of land a few blocks south of the original Palm Village and planned a palm-tree-lined avenue as the centerpiece of a new residential development.

This homogenous city, where old money and new money exist side by side, was the longtime home of **Catherine May Bedell**, the first woman elected to Congress from the state of Washington. Bedell, a Republican, was elected in 1958 and served six terms in the House of Representatives.

An early women's rights activist, she worked to insure that a prohibition against discrimination based on gender would be included in the 1964 Civil Rights Act, and she supported the Equal Rights Amendment. In 1971, President Richard M. Nixon appointed her to the International Trade Commission, where she served a ten-year term, and after leaving that post, she was named by President Ronald Reagan to be a special consultant to the 50 States Project.

More recently, this smart political maven, who resided at 514 Sandpiper Street, was president of her own consulting firm. She died at the age of 90 in 2004.

■ ■ ■

VETERAN COMPOSER, SONGWRITER, conductor, and arranger **Adolph Deutsch**, who won three Oscars for *Annie Get Your Gun, Seven Brides for Seven Brothers,* and *Oklahoma!,* was a full-time resident of 1713 Sandpiper Street.

A graduate of the Royal Academy of Music in London, England, Deutsch orchestrated and conducted Broadway musicals for George Gershwin and Irving Berlin before being signed to a long-term Hollywood contract.

Once in Hollywood, Deutsch became musical director for more than 100 movies. He scored or orchestrated many fine atmospheric melodramas at Warner Bros., including *They Drive by Night, High Sierra, The Maltese Falcon, Across the Pacific,* and *Action in the North Atlantic* (all starring Humphrey Bogart). He composed the lush scores for several adventure movies starring Errol Flynn, Alan Ladd, and James Stewart. Then, mostly at MGM, he worked on expensive Technicolor attractions such as *Show Boat, Million Dollar Mermaid, The Band Wagon, Funny Face,* and *Les Girls.*

Because of his knack for imitating other composers' styles, Deutsch was often brought in to write incidental music or bridge additional scenes, most notably on *Gone with the Wind,* for which he took over the musical chores after Max Steiner left that history-making production to work on other films.

Deutsch's two last important films were the gangster spoof *Some Like It Hot,* with its fast-paced jazz riffs, and the romantic love triangle *The Apartment,* which featured a memorable piano solo.

Then Deutsch announced his retirement. He died of heart failure at the age of 82 on New Year's Day 1980, two days after the death of composer Richard Rodgers, his colleague on *Oklahoma!*

■ ■ ■

WESTERN CHARACTER ACTOR **George "Gabby" Hayes** made a career out of playing toothless old men, a neat parlor trick he performed by removing his dentures in more than 200 films, and particularly in 18 installments of the exciting *Hopalong Cassidy* series, in which he often rode shotgun with peacekeeping vigilante William Boyd.

His tattered appearance and his tendency to come out with catchy phrases such as "Yer durn tootin!," "Young whipper snapper," and "Yessir-ee Bob!" were often the highpoints of these boisterous outlaw tales. The camera lingered on Hayes sitting astride his tired horse and grinning shamelessly while tugging on his scruffy beard.

He supported singing cowboy Roy Rogers in more than three dozen films, including *Southward Ho, Nevada City,* and *Don't Fence Me In,* and he partnered John Wayne in several movies, among them *Dark Command* and *Tall in the Saddle.* "Gabby was wonderful, always with a yarn to spin," remembered Gene Autry, who used him as comedy relief in four films, including the all-star singing Western *Melody Ranch.*

Indeed, moviegoers were so fond of his eccentric behavior that from 1946 through 1951 he was voted Hollywood's third most popular cowboy star. And after the feverish craze for movie Westerns ended, the grizzled-looking actor hosted his own weekly TV series, *The Gabby Hayes Show,* and made many personal appearances.

In real life, Hayes was an intelligent, well-groomed gentleman whose knack just happened to be playing gummy codgers; he was virtually unrecognizable without his customary beard and floppy hat while living at 44–801 San Jacinto Avenue.

Hayes devoted the final years of his life to investments and caring for his wife of 42 years, Olive Ireland, who passed away in 1957. He died at the age of 83 in 1969.

■ ■ ■

Rock musician **James** **Gurley** played electric guitar with the San Francisco–based band Big Brother & the Holding Company, which he founded with fellow musicians Peter Albin, Sam Andrew, and Chuck Jones (later replaced by Dave Getz) during the Haight-Ashbury hippie movement. Gurley's passionate amplified guitar solos, on resonating songs such as "Ball and Chain," "Summertime," and "Combination of the Two," earned him the unique title, Father of the Psychedelic Guitar.

Big Brother was part of the history-making line-up at the 1967 Monterey Pop Festival, along with the Mamas & the Papas, Canned Heat, Simon & Garfunkel, Jefferson Airplane, The Who, and Country Joe & the Fish. They performed onstage with singer Janis Joplin, who died from a heroin overdose in 1970. Among the band's breakthrough albums were *Big Brother, Cheap Thrills,* and *How Hard It Is.* Big Brother officially broke up in 1972 but was reunited a decade later.

Gurley, who resides at 74–226 De Anza Way, is among several long-haired rock 'n' rollers who have inhabited the valley. Two of these validated artists are Glenn Frey, one of the founders of The Eagles, formerly of La Quinta, and Jack Russell, the tattooed lead singer of Great White, who lives in Palm Desert.

■ ■ ■

"Hi, this is Bob Hope reminding you hungry GI's that after dinner tonight they'll be dancing to the music of Les Brown and his Band of Renown. So grab yourself a pretty girl and enjoy the show!"

Hope leered, the boys cheered, and Brown appeared onstage grinning like a chipmunk with a baton, ready to get American servicemen returning from World War II, Korea, and Vietnam in the mood for two hours of swing and big band music.

A former saxophone player, conductor, and arranger, Les Brown formed his band in 1938 and used his extensive musical knowledge and training to imbue the group's performances with a light, catchy beat that appealed to GIs and their girls, college students and their parents.

In the band's regular lineup was bass trombonist **Clyde "Stumpy" Brown**, so named because of his diminutive 5-foot-1-inch size. For more than 50 years, Clyde Brown played at almost every performance and recording session of his older brother's band, often standing for a solo spot and occasionally taking the microphone himself.

Indeed, from the beginning, Clyde and his middle brother, Warren Brown, were permanent fixtures of Les Brown and his Band of Renown, all the way to the band's hit recordings of "Sentimental Journey" and "I've Got My Love to Keep Me Warm," and to Hope's Pepsodent radio shows, U.S.O. tours, and Chrysler TV specials.

Les Brown's original version of "Sentimental Journey," which was crooned by the band's former singer, Doris Day, remained the #1 song in the country for 16 weeks. The 18-piece swing band also scored major hits with "You Won't Be Satisfied," "My Dreams Are Getting Better All the Time," and "The Christmas Song"—all sung by Day.

Clyde Brown paid $177,500 for the home at 243 San Remo Street in Monterey Country Club, where he has resided since 1988. Les Brown died of lung cancer at the age of 88 in 2001.

■ ■ ■

SILENT SCREEN INGÉNUE **Patsy Ruth Miller**, who was enthusiastically hailed as one of Hollywood's emerging young stars but did not survive the medium's transition to talkies, once resided at 425 Sierra Madre North.

Miller played the gamine-like role of Nichette in the 1921 version of *Camille* starring Rudolph Valentino and Alla Nazimova. The film that transformed her into a star, however, was the lavish 1923 production of *The Hunchback of Notre Dame*, in which she played the dancing peasant girl Esmerelda, who brings water to the hideously deformed Quasimodo, portrayed by Lon Chaney.

Miller went on to star in more than 70 films, until she retired in 1931. Married three times, her husbands included MGM director Tay Garnett and the Oscar-nominated screenwriter John Lee Mahin. Miller's stardom allowed her to live in high style, driving a Pierce Arrow and giving her younger brother, Winston, a Stutz Bearcat that she had bought from Constance Talmadge.

Perhaps her sisterly affection helped turn Winston Miller into a successful writer of Westerns. His more than 40 screenplays included *My Darling Clementine* with Henry Fonda, as well as various films for Errol Flynn, Randolph Scott, and Ronald Reagan. He also produced the TV series *Ironside*, *It Takes a Thief*, and *Cannon*, all filmed at Universal on the same back lot where his sister had once shone. He died in 1994, one day before his eighty-fourth birthday. His sister outlived him by one year, passing away in 1995 at the age of 91.

■ ■ ■

TALL, SANDY-HAIRED ACTOR **Edward Faulkner**, who, along with Harry Carey, Jr., Ben Johnson, Bruce Cabot, and John Agar, comprised the mainline members of John Wayne's latter-day stock company, now resides at 271 Tolosa Circle. A former Air Force jet-fighter pilot, Faulkner played young military officers and soldiers in six of the Duke's final films, including *McLintock*, *The Green Berets*, *Hellfighters*, *The Undefeated*, *Chisum*, and *Rio Lobo*.

His large build, distinctive voice, and social affability assured him success in front of the camera whenever Wayne was around. It also didn't hurt that Faulkner could ride a horse or play chess, one of Wayne's preferred hobbies, or that the two men shared a happy-go-lucky temperament. "Ed's a very talented actor," praised Harry Carey, Jr. "He did his job very well, he always knew his lines and Duke was very fond of him."

Faulkner got to act in many noteworthy scenes with the 6-foot-4-inch cowboy legend, as well as with newcomers like the actor's handsome son, Patrick Wayne, and the perky brunette Stefanie Powers. Possibly even more to his liking, he shared several scenes with Wayne's favorite leading lady, Maureen O'Hara, who was reputed to be the actor's longtime sweetheart. "There was chemistry between Wayne and O'Hara," said Faulkner. They were "like Tracy and Hepburn."

■ ■ ■

BRIGHT-EYED ACTRESS **Patsy Garrett** first distinguished herself as a novelty singer with Fred Waring's orchestra on his weekly radio program *The Chesterfield Hour*. The plucky teenage performer was featured in national magazine advertisements as the uniform-wearing Chesterfield girl who holds a carton of gold-and-white cigarettes in her upraised palm.

Composer Cole Porter was so impressed by Garrett's vivacious personality that he requested she perform his song "Begin the Beguine" from the hit musical *Jubilee* to promote its reissue in the MGM film *Broadway Melody of 1940*.

It was a far cry from Porter, but one of Garrett's most famous performances was as the Purina Cat Chow lady in the popular commercials for that pet food: she danced the "chow-chow-chow," a variation of the cha-cha, with a delighted feline. Garrett's affinity for domesticated animals resulted in her being cast as Mary Gruber, the chatty housekeeper in the family movie *Benji* and its sequel *For the Love of Benji*, starring a talented part-terrier canine mix named Higgins.

In 1991, Garrett sold her home in Northridge and moved to 40–785 Posada Court (off Hovley Lane), where neighborhood fans often see her shopping at the local Vons supermarket.

■ ■ ■

THE LOVE SONGS of Italian American singer **Jerry Vale**, who resides with his wife, Rita Grable, in a two-bedroom condominium at 105 Verde Way, in Silver Sands Racquet Club, are as enjoyable to the ear as Italian food is to the taste buds. In fact, Vale's romantic ballads are often played at candle-lit restaurants where loving couples toast each other with glasses of Chianti.

Known for his delicate high-tenor voice, and a cherubic, dimpled face that has been pinched by hundreds, if not thousands, of adoring grandmothers, Vale is known for his renditions of some of the most emotion-filled songs of his generation. These include standards such as "Innamorata," "Volare," "Amore, Scusami," and the tune with which he is most identified, "Al-Di-La."

Vale's exalted rise as the prince of "pasta pop," as his music has sometimes been humorously described in the trades, came about by sheer luck

and happy coincidence. During high school, he took a part-time job shining shoes at a New York City barbershop and, to wile away the hours,
sang the traditional folk songs that his mother had sung to him. Pop
crooner Guy Mitchell heard his melodic voice and arranged for the
impish-looking teenager to make some demonstration records, which
found their way to Mitch Miller, the A&R manager at Columbia
Records.

In the snap of a breadstick, Vale was signed to a long-term contract and
pushed into the recording studio, where Miller surrounded him with
enough horns and strings to create the lush sound that became the singer's
trademark. His first records sold like homemade bottles of marinara
sauce: "You Can Never Give Me Back Your Heart"; "Two Purple Shadows"; "I Live Each Day"; and his biggest hit—"You Don't Know Me"—
arranged by Percy Faith.

In spite of his tremendous success, it took of a lot of persuasion on
Vale's part to convince Miller to do an authentic Italian-sounding album.
But the singer eventually got his wish with not one but three recordings:
I Have But One Heart, *Arrivederci Roma*, and *The Language of Love*.

The proudest moment of his blessed life occurred when Vale was
booked as the opening headliner at the world-famous Copacabana, a spot
he would hold for 10 years. He was following an illustrious line of showbiz legends, including Frank Sinatra, Tony Bennett, Dean Martin, and
Peggy Lee, and was understandably nervous. And, truth to tell, not everybody was a fan; Robert Goulet angrily jostled him, and Johnny Carson,
who was drunk, heckled from the sidelines.

He was also deep in mob-controlled territory, and at first Vale was
intimidated by the bluster of the Copa's menacing owner, Jules Podell,
who talked tough and wore a large diamond pinky ring. But Vale need
not have worried. When he completed his first season, Podell gave him
a new set of golf clubs and a $1,500 bonus.

Then Sinatra arranged for Vale to play the Sands Hotel, where the
Chairman of the Board was a part-owner. Vale was asked to show up on
a Friday, did as he was told, and netted a two-week gig in the lounge. Jack
Entratter heard him and was so impressed he extended the engagement
22 weeks. Every night Vale sang an encore of "Mala Femina" in Neapoli-
tan, then in Calabrese, and finally Sicilian, which brought down the

house. The gamblers loved him, and so did the men in dark glasses who counted the cash.

Vale credits TV with getting him more fans than he ever expected. After he appeared on *The Ed Sullivan Show* and sang "Have You Looked into Your Heart?" more than 45,000 copies of the tear-inducing record were sold the very next day!

It was inevitable that Hollywood would knock on his door. The question is why did it take so long? Jerry was 57 when Martin Scorsese asked him to play himself in *Goodfellas*. He put on his best suit and sang "Pretend You Don't See Her," much as his rival, Al Martino, had done when he performed "I Have But One Heart" in *The Godfather*.

Five years later, Scorsese asked Vale to squeeze into a ruffled tuxedo and croon "Love Me the Way I Love You" in *Casino*, Scorsese's glitzy homage to old-fashioned Las Vegas–style gambling. Perhaps that's why Vale was singled out with a few of his older counterparts to participate on a compilation CD called *Mob Hits*, which featured 22 Italian musical "hits."

Today, Jerry Vale is as much a part of the history of Sin City as roulette. Simply put, there is nobody quite like him. It's like comparing vermicelli to Velveeta.

■ ■ ■

FILM CRAFTSMAN **ALAN Crosland, Jr.**, a second-generation Hollywood director of more than 50 TV series, including several stand-out episodes of *The Twilight Zone*, *The Outer Limits*, and *The Wild, Wild West*, used to live at 74–458 Myrsine Street.

He edited 20 films at Warner Bros., the studio where his father, Alan Crosland, Sr., had previously helmed *Don Juan*—the earliest film with synchronized music—and *The Jazz Singer*, which was the first 100-percent talking picture. Unfortunately, Crosland, Sr., was killed in a Los Angeles car crash in 1936 (his wife, the silent screen star Elaine Hammerstein, would die 12 years later, also in an automobile accident).

But their son carried on the family's filmmaking tradition. Among the best examples of Crosland, Jr.'s superb "cutting" technique are *Deception*, *The Unfaithful*, *Adventures of Don Juan*, *Young Man with a Horn*, *The Flame and the Arrow*, *The Breaking Point*, *Operation Pacific*, *Come Fill the Cup*, and a 1953 color remake of his father's greatest triumph, *The Jazz Singer*.

Crosland, Jr., later joined Burt Lancaster's production company, where he worked on important films such as *Apache, Vera Cruz, Marty,* and *Sweet Smell of Success.* He died in 2001, at the age of 83.

■ ■ ■

VETERAN FILM EDITOR **Harold Kress**, whose masterful cutting of Civil War battle scenes and modern-day feats of heroism won him two Academy Awards, resided at 73–720 Sawmill Canyon Way in Palm Desert Greens Country Club. Kress spent a total of 30 years at MGM and Columbia studios, working his special magic as he labored over 50 movies and the millions of feet of exposed film that passed through his trusted Moviola.

Among the memorable scenes his hands shaped were Jeanette Mac-Donald and Nelson Eddy's spirited operatic duets in *New Moon,* Spencer Tracy's monstrous transformation in *Dr. Jekyll and Mr. Hyde,* Fred Astaire's expertly choreographed dance steps in *Silk Stockings,* and Jeffrey Hunter's painful crucifixion in *King of Kings.*

A six-time Oscar nominee, Kress won his first award for the three-screen Cinerama classic *How the West Was Won,* an assignment that required him to synchronize separately filmed images and match each one to its front, center, and right counterpart—not an easy task. From the superbly matched shots of interlocking clover-leaf freeways, to images of vast canyons, swollen rivers, and grain-covered plains, Kress demonstrated his full command of the film editing process.

His ability to suspend an audience's disbelief was put to its greatest test when Irwin Allen, who was both a dedicated movie buff and an inveterate showman, asked Kress to create hell upside down in his disaster film *The Poseidon Adventure.* As usual, Allen's edict was "Make it bigger!"—often easier said than done.

Combining live action, miniatures, and photographic effects, Allen had simulated an ocean liner capsizing under the force of a 90-foot tidal wave. Kress's job was to take the pieces of celluloid and create a believable sequence during which the ship rolls over, leaving its passengers literally hanging from the floor above them. But because the company ran out of money, the final scene—of survivors rescued from the ship's hull and hoisted to safety by a Coast Guard helicopter—was never completed.

Instead, Kress cleverly suggested it by showing an upturned model of the ship in the foreground.

Two years later, Allen called on Kress again, this time to edit the destruction of the world's tallest building as it burns to the ground in *The Towering Inferno*. Reportedly, this film gave the acclaimed editor his greatest anxiety. The bombastic Allen had promised moviegoers "more spectacle, more stars, and more suspense" than they'd ever seen in one movie, and Kress was hard-pressed not to let them down. From the film's atmospheric main titles, which were superimposed over a stunning, traveling, aerial shot of the San Francisco skyline, to the riveting sequences of the 138-story skyscraper being consumed by fire, to the climactic flood that doused the giant flames, it promised to be a Herculean editing task.

Over the course of four months, Kress and his son, Carl, who was as skilled as his father, edited more than 2 million feet of film photographed by eight different cameras. They whittled it down to a serviceable 165 minutes, during which time they added, trimmed, and enhanced scenes of extraordinary impact. The action had spread across 57 sets, on eight sound stages utilizing four complete camera crews, had required 200 dangerous stunts, and called for a million gallons of water to be dropped from a height of 40 feet and coincide with an explosive detonation that put the fire out. For this truly amazing feat, Kress earned his second Oscar and not a few gray hairs.

He was strong-armed by the impetuous Allen to do a third film—a humdinger about African killer bees called *The Swarm*, much of it filmed in slow motion to show millions of angry bees in frenzied flight. But after that assignment, Kress told Allen to buzz off and called it a day. Fittingly, Carl Kress was the editor of still another disaster film, *Meteor*, about a giant asteroid hurtling to earth.

In 1992, Harold Kress, who was described as a kind and humble man, accepted a well-deserved lifetime achievement award from his film editing peers. He died at the age of 86 in 1999.

■ ■ ■

HOLLYWOOD HISTORY IS littered with the bodies of both the famous and the forgotten, and their lives and deaths are often intermingled. Actress **Dorothy Arnold**, a once-promising movie starlet with a passing resemblance to Bette Davis, is an example of the latter—a pitiful casualty of her own fleeting fame.

Originally known as Dorothy Olson, she was a promising nightclub singer when Universal Pictures signed her to a movie contract. But under her new name, the blond, wide-eyed actress was rated the studio's fetching "Oomph Girl."

Arnold was third-billed after famous Hungarian horror film star Bela Lugosi in the 12-chapter serial *The Phantom Creeps.* She played the imperiled heroine so well that subsequently she was paired with William Gargan in *The House of Fear*, a baffling whodunit about a backstage murder.

Obsessively ambitious about her acting career, she would stick "her finger down her own throat, throwing up her dinner" in order to avoid putting on extra weight, said biographer Richard Ben Cramer. But films and potential stardom would quickly be forsaken for domesticity as the first wife of America's #1 baseball player, Joe DiMaggio, whom Arnold had met on the set of *Manhattan Merry-Go-Round.* According to newspaper reports, she was smitten by his lanky, bashful charm, and he, in turn, was strongly protective of her porcelain, doll-like beauty.

The actress was 21 and the great DiMaggio only 24 when they were married at Saints Peter and Paul Italian Church in San Francisco, on November 19, 1939. The marriage almost turned into a shambles, for the nervous couple was mobbed by 20,000 well-wishers outside the church.

It may have been an omen of things to come. The DiMaggios settled down to a life of marital bliss that produced a baby son, Joe, Jr., but their happiness was soon interrupted by Joe, Sr.'s frequent baseball contests and Dorothy's constant nightclub wanderings. After five years, they separated; they were granted a divorce in 1944. Arnold's career never recovered. She was labeled a scarlet woman for her rumored infidelity and mistreatment of her husband and their baby, who was raised in summer camps and boarding schools.

As for DiMaggio, the ace ballplayer was distraught when Dorothy remarried in 1946, because he was still deeply in love with her. Dorothy, he mourned, had promised to wait for him to return from his wartime stint with the U.S. Army Air Force. It was commonly believed, in fact, that DiMaggio always carried a torch for his ex-wife, and that its burning flame was not extinguished by his catastrophic marriage to Marilyn Monroe. That union ended after less than one year, with Monroe complaining to Robert Slatzer that all Joe did was talk about how much he missed Dorothy and that he cried himself to sleep.

Following a minor comeback in the 1957 film *Lizzie,* acting the mother of a mentally disturbed daughter (played by Eleanor Parker) who suffers from Multiple Personality Disorder, Arnold moved to Palm Springs and married her third husband, Ralph Peck of Cathedral City. They opened a small restaurant called Charcoal Charley, where the former actress serenaded bar patrons.

By 1984, Arnold was estranged from Peck and living alone at 73–193 Trail Circle. After being diagnosed with pancreatic cancer, she checked into LaGloria Clinic in Ensenada, Mexico, where she underwent alternative medical treatment. She died one week before her sixty-seventh birthday, although the details of her death were not made public.

DiMaggio, for his part, was devastated by the failure of both his marriages and the loss of each of his wives, and never remarried. In addition, his only son was unable to adjust to adult life and endured various hardships. They did not speak for many years.

Shortly after DiMaggio died of lung cancer in 1999, at the age of 84, tabloid reporters found Joe, Jr., living in a trailer and working in a junkyard near Sacramento. It was revealed that DiMaggio had left his destitute son a $20,000-a-year trust fund. But Joe, Jr., never lived to collect it. He died five months after his father from the long-term effects of drug and alcohol abuse. He was 57.

■ ■ ■

SOME OF TV'S most popular character actors have lived behind the bubbling fountains and picturesque rocks of Desert Falls Country Club, which hugs the border of Palm Desert. Dapper **Anthony Eisley**, who starred opposite Robert Conrad and Connie Stevens on the popular Honolulu-set detective series *Hawaiian Eye,* resided at 462 Ever Green Ash.

With his dark wavy hair and neatly trimmed mustache, the handsome Eisley was instantly recognizable. His looks served him well on *The Dick Van Dyke Show,* on which he played Dick's new next-door neighbor, a suave bachelor lawyer named Arthur Stanwyck.

But acting had been a second choice for this graduate of the University of Miami. Indeed, the poor man must have been desperately in need of money to have appeared in *The Wasp Woman, The Navy vs. the Night Monsters, Journey to the Center of Time, The Mummy and the Curse of the Jackals,* and *The Mighty Gorga,* which must rank among the worst sci-fi movies of all time.

Still, despite their flaws, Eisley's films have developed a strong cult following, and his performances are admired for their sincerity in the face of ridiculous scripts and laughable special effects. He died in 2003, one day after celebrating his seventy-eighth birthday.

■ ■ ■

EISLEY'S NEIGHBOR AT 487 Desert Falls Drive North was the gopher-faced character actor **Alvy Moore,** who played scatter-brained county agent Hank Kimball on TV's *Green Acres.* The wickedly grinning comedian with a crew cut was a genius at getting well-timed laughs and was often seen in major films, including *Gentlemen Prefer Blondes* and *There's No Business Like Show Business.* But there was more to him than met the eye.

Moore was a "hands-on" person who could play virtually any type of role, and often did, in 70 films and 65 TV guest appearances. He also was a producer. His off-screen interest in the occult led him to undertake several films on the subject, including *The Witchmaker,* co-starring his friendly neighbor, Anthony Eisley.

Later Moore formed a production company with fellow actor L.Q. Jones. They made two quirky films, *The Brotherhood of Satan* and the telepathic tale *A Boy and His Dog,* which enjoy minor cult status. He died in 1997 at the age of 75.

■ ■ ■

SILVER-HAIRED, NATIVE AMERICAN actor **Ned Romero,** who played the American Indian leader Chingachgook in two made-for-TV movies, *Last of the Mohicans* and *The Deerslayer,* lives at 249 Vista Royal Circle West.

Romero started out as an opera singer but wound up playing native warriors in *The Talisman, I Will Fight No More Forever,* and *Tales of the Nunundaga,* several decades before American Indians were portrayed as real people in *Dances with Wolves*. Romero also played the role of Krell in a memorable episode of the TV series *Star Trek*, in which William Shatner as Captain Kirk is bitten by a bearlike creature called a Mugatu. His other roles included Sergeant Joe Rivera in *Dan August* and assistant district attorney Bob Ramirez in *The D.A.* More recently, he was seen in several episodes of *Walker, Texas Ranger* and in the recurring role of River Dog in *Roswell*.

■ ■ ■

PRODUCER **WILLIAM T. Orr** is not someone whose name immediately springs to mind these days. But this former resident of the Lakes Country Club, at 220 Wagon Wheel Road, was highly influential in older, more established Hollywood circles, both as the son-in-law of Jack Warner, who was president of Warner Bros., and as vice president in charge of television at the company's Burbank headquarters.

Shrewd and debonair, the executive left his familiar, abbreviated moniker, Wm. T. Orr, scrawled across the end credits of 25 TV series, many of them based on successful films such as *Kings Row*, *Casablanca*, *The Roaring '20s*, and *Mister Roberts*, which had been churned out by the studio. But more important, it was Orr, a former actor, who convinced his obstinate father-in-law to break Hollywood's boycott against the burgeoning television industry.

It should be remembered that, at the time—1955—movies were losing a fortune because millions of people were staying home to tune in to weekly shows such as *I Love Lucy* and *The Honeymooners,* which they could watch in the comfort of their living rooms for free. In protest, Warner Bros. had refused to allow a TV set in any of their films, and plots assiduously refrained from mentioning this new medium. "Jack used to say, 'How can anyone watch a big picture on that little box?'" said Orr, who saw the future in clear, monochromatic tones.

Eventually the dam burst, and Warner Bros., under pressure from Orr, became the first movie studio to embark on regular TV production. Orr's groundbreaking distribution deal with ABC, in which the dominant studio supplied approximately one dozen half-hour and one-hour shows, pushed the fledgling network to the front ranks and opened the floodgates for Hollywood to produce films for television.

Of course, there were no guarantees of immediate success. *Kings Row* was deemed a failure. *Casablanca* did only so-so business. On the other hand, *Cheyenne*, which made a star of Clint Walker, was an unqualified success, igniting the fuse that fired up popular TV Westerns such as *Sugarfoot, Maverick, Colt .45, Bronco,* and *Lawman*—all of which Orr supervised. And when the genre appeared to be burned out, along came a clever spoof called *F Troop*, another of this smart man's top-line productions.

Too smart to put all his television series in one thematic basket, Orr also produced the slickly made, youth-oriented detective shows *77 Sunset Strip, Bourbon Street Beat, Hawaiian Eye,* and *Surfside Six.* Set in the exotic climes of Hollywood, New Orleans, Honolulu, and Miami, these programs not only offered enticing plots but also allowed for some titillating glimpses of scantily clad men and women.

Previously, in his movie work, Orr's knack for discovering new talent had brought forth Marlon Brando, Paul Newman, and James Dean, each of whom made their memorable film debuts at Warner Bros., although Newman's screen bow in a Roman toga and curled hair was anything but auspicious.

Now, faced with the TV revolution, Orr was picking up stars like freshly minted silver dollars. Merv Griffin, Debbie Reynolds, James Garner, Ty Hardin, Roger Moore, Troy Donahue, Robert Conrad, Connie Stevens—these were all performers whom Orr either discovered, put under contract, or had a hand in promoting. .

Orr also produced the provocative "adult comedy" *Sex and the Single Girl,* based on the racy bestseller by Helen Gurley Brown. The film, which co-starred Natalie Wood and Tony Curtis, was a tremendous success, even though Orr acknowledged that the studio had felt obligated to tone down the sexual innuendos, to avoid heavy censorship.

But Orr's enduring love was always the small screen, which others feared but he knew instinctively was here to stay. In fact, his proposed autobiography, which he never got around to writing, was to be called *TV . . . or Not TV.* He died on Christmas Day 2002 at the age of 85.

■ ■ ■

"CLAYTON FARLOW'S DEAD!" exclaimed surprised viewers of the long-running TV series *Dallas,* when a heavily promoted cast reunion featuring Larry Hagman, Linda Gray, Patrick Duffy, and Victoria Principal aired on CBS on November 7, 2004.

Noticeably missing from the impressive lineup at that evening's black-tie event was **Howard Keel,** who had portrayed the second husband of "Miss Ellie" for 10 years on the popular nighttime soap, matching wits with her unscrupulous son "J.R." Ewing, and sometimes trading punches with him. The reason for this absence was that Keel, who had taken over the grandfatherly role following the demise of family patriarch Jock Ewing (played by Jim Davis), had been pronounced dead of colon cancer in his home at 394 Red River Road, where he had lived at the Lakes since 1994. He was 85.

As millions tuned in to see their favorite stars dish each other on the *Dallas* special, CNN news bulletins broke the story of Keel's death, showing photographs of him in his white cowboy hat from *Dallas* and running film clips of him in younger days, when he was a handsome, grinning, barrel-chested hero of hit musicals.

The strapping, 6-foot-4-inch performer first caught people's attention more than a half-century earlier, when he played Billy Bigelow, the role created by John Raitt, in the original Broadway production of *Carousel.* Subsequently he starred as Curly in the first London outing of *Oklahoma!* His rich singing style caused so much buzz coast-to-coast that Warner Bros. gave him a screen test and, incredibly, turned him down. Their lame excuse, according to Palm Desert neighbor William Orr: they already had Gordon MacRae and Dennis Morgan under contract.

It was their loss. Producer Arthur Freed saw Keel's screen test and signed him to an MGM contract, where he was chosen to play sharp-shooter Frank Butler opposite Judy Garland in Irving Berlin's musical comedy *Annie Get Your Gun.*

Unfortunately, it proved to be a jinxed production. Keel broke his leg when his horse fell on him, and he spent the next six weeks on crutches. Actor Frank Morgan, who was all set to play Buffalo Bill, suddenly died and had to be replaced by Louis Calhern. Finally, Garland suffered a nervous breakdown, and her role was assumed by the tomboyish Paramount star Betty Hutton—not a popular choice. "They didn't want me," bemoaned Hutton. "It was the worst experience of my life." Still, the combination of Hutton and Keel made for a spirited duet of the tongue-twisting song "Anything You Can Do . . ."

If politics makes strange bedfellows, then the vagaries of show business are just as fickle. Despite its backstage drama, this knockout film was a certified smash hit and thrust the buckskinned Keel, in his polished Stetson, braided leather jackets, and rhinestone-studded boots, to the forefront of Hollywood stardom.

It was a big shock to him. The son of an alcoholic coal miner, who abused him physically, and a Methodist mother who forbade her son from having any entertainment, Keel had grown up shy and inhibited about his sexuality. MGM publicity handouts refrained from discussing his past, but it was later hinted that Keel was "befriended" by an influential sponsor who introduced the robust 20-year-old aircraft mechanic to music, which he came to love.

Keel always remained mum on the subject. He did confess to "making nine bucks a week parking cars in a lot across from the Paramount Theatre, Fred MacMurray's included," he said, and before that, digging up soil to plant lemon trees in a fruit orchard, a job that paid him three cents a tree, or two dollars a day.

So stardom must have hit him like a bolt of lightning. It's lucky for him he was a large man with a well-developed physique. He needed every ounce of strength to handle the transition from his stint as a singing waiter at the Paris Inn restaurant in Los Angeles to his lofty status as King of the MGM Musicals.

The movies, they just kept coming. Sporting a mustache and top hat, he serenaded Kathryn Grayson in *Show Boat* to romantic melodies such as "Make Believe" and "Why Do I Love You?" According to Keel, their attraction was the real thing. "Kathryn and I were mad about each other, and there was no way to stop it," he confessed. But Keel didn't want to create a scandal, so, except for a lustful one-night stand they kept a safe distance from each other. Still, he must have liked being reunited with Grayson for the bold and brassy *Kiss Me Kate*, in which they played feuding theatrical spouses, and sang the expansive "Wunderbar" and "So in Love."

As a clean-shaven Wild Bill Hickok, Keel matched Doris Day's brave Indian scout step-for-step in *Calamity Jane*, in which they performed the lively duet "The Black Hills of Dakota." He was paired with prim Ann Blyth in *Rose-Marie* and the mystical *Kismet,* swam alongside Esther Williams in *Pagan Love Song,* and acted Hannibal to her Amytis in *Jupiter's Darling.* And in *Seven Brides for Seven Brothers,* his all-time favorite film, Keel bellowed the joyful refrain "Bless Your Beautiful Hide" while asking for the hand of petite Jane Powell.

"He was a singing Clark Gable," said George Sidney, who directed the virile thespian in three films. His voice was extremely flexible, moving from a low C to a pure falsetto with ease. But it was his booming baritone, forceful yet sensitive, that entranced moviegoers. He would have kept singing for a lot longer, but the trend for movie musicals regrettably waned, and he found himself, quite literally, out of a job.

TV, nightclubs, and especially theater came to the rescue. There Keel received a new lease on life, piling up a résumé of stage musicals by touring in *Camelot, Man of La Mancha, Paint Your Wagon, I Do! I Do!, Gigi, Show Boat, Kismet,* and *The Fantasticks.*

Keel's off-screen life, if not as glamorous, was every bit as adventurous as his movies. He was married three times. In fact, he first visited Palm Springs when he honeymooned at La Quinta Hotel in 1949 with his second wife, Helen Anderson, with whom he had three children: Kaija, Kristine, and Gunnar.

Ten years later, he returned to the desert to play Saint Peter in *The Big Fisherman,* which was filmed at Lake Cahuilla. Then, in 1970, he married his third wife, Judy Magamoll, a former flight attendant with whom he had a daughter, Leslie.

The following year, it was reported that the couple had moved to a houseboat—a reflection of Keel's dwindling fortunes. Soon there were rumors that the singing actor had developed a drinking problem, which, if true, would hardly have been surprising, given the sorry state of Hollywood musicals at the time. But Keel, who valued his family too much to lose it in a whiskey bottle, quickly kicked the habit.

The dignified actor had reached the nadir of his career and was playing one of the fuddy-duddy weekly passengers on *The Love Boat,* when producer Leonard Katzman contacted Keel to replace terminally ill Jim Davis on *Dallas.* And as often happens in Hollywood, the one-time guest appearance generated so much fan mail that it turned into a long-term gig.

As one of the last of Hollywood's great musical stars, Keel was featured prominently in MGM's kaleidoscopic retrospective *That's Entertainment* and its two sequels, providing insightful commentary into what seemed a lost art form.

■ ■ ■

NOT EVERYONE HAS a mother like Cher's mom, **Georgia Holt.** Not only do mother and daughter have the same clear voice, high cheekbones, and willowy figures, but they have the same taste in men, too.

The child of a poor alcoholic father, Georgia grew up in rural Arkansas, where she sang in smoky honkytonks and gin mills while her dad collected tips. According to Holt, she had the natural talent but not the essential good looks to be a singer, so, when she was 18, she threw away her dream and married John Sarkisian. Their daughter, Cherilyn, would blossom into a woman who possessed both the looks and the talent to achieve Holt's long-held desire of stardom.

Georgia's happiness with Sarkisian was short-lived, and they divorced. She married Gilbert La Piere, and they had a daughter, Georganne, an actress who played a recurring role on the TV soap opera *General Hospital* for two years.

"I married three alcoholics and one drug addict," recalled Holt, who finally gave up on marriage. It wasn't until she was nearly 50 that this fiercely independent woman met the love of her life, a 27-year-old antique collector who swept the startled divorcee off her feet. "I told him, 'I can't marry you, you're too young,'" she said. Instead, they lived together as domestic partners for nine years.

Coincidentally, Cher married her first husband, a young song plugger named Salvatore Bono, when she was 18. Their marriage turned into one of the great success stories in American pop culture: Sonny and Cher. After their daughter Chastity was born, they were divorced, and Cher married rock musician Greg Allman.

But the man who really took her fancy was an aspiring actor named Robert Camilletti, 18 years her junior; it seems that mother and daughter prove true the wise expression "The older you get, the younger you like it!"

Today, Georgia Holt lives in quiet retirement at 81 Appian Way (Tierra Vista). Her home is filled with books, antiques, and photos of her daughters and grandchildren, who give her the greatest comfort.

When her life was at its lowest ebb, Holt said she contemplated suicide but, for the sake of her children, could never do it. Fortunately, after years of personal heartbreak and career disappointment, Holt found her calling, not as the singer she once dreamed of becoming, but as a writer. She wrote *Star Mothers*, a revealing look into the world of showbiz parents, including the doting moms of Tom Selleck, Goldie Hawn, Sylvester Stallone, Candice Bergen, George Hamilton, and Elizabeth Taylor.

■ ■ ■

FROM BUBBLE-HEADED BIMBO to successful businesswoman, there isn't much that comely actress **Connie Stevens** hasn't experienced in her lifetime. Stevens may have acted dumb, but she wasn't stupid. "An apple blossom with the wham of a bulldozer," proclaimed Hedda Hopper of this living Barbie doll with the shaggy blonde hair and squeaky voice.

Jerry Lewis realized her potential when he cast Stevens as the adoring girl-next-door who gives birth to quintuplets in his mixed-up comedy *Rock-A-Bye Baby*. Fans of classic TV have never forgotten her as the scatterbrained nightclub chanteuse "Cricket" Blake in the detective series *Hawaiian Eye*. Stevens's breathless adulation of Edd Byrnes, with whom she crooned "Kookie, Kookie (Lend Me Your Comb)" is either the high-or low-point of 1950s kitsch. She also recorded "Sixteen Reasons," "Why Do I Cry for Joey?" and "Let's Do It."

When Warner Bros. refused to give this hardworking star a pay raise, however, she hawked Avon cosmetics outside the studio commissary until her protest wore down frazzled executives. Through it all, Stevens smiled at her good fortune and kept putting money in the bank. At the height of her fame, she co-starred with lanky heartthrob Troy Donahue in four very popular films, including *Parrish*, *Susan Slade*, and *Palm Springs Weekend*, although the two actors reportedly didn't get along.

Alternately labeled a prima donna and a publicity hound, Stevens had her fair share of romantic entanglements. She dated actor Glenn Ford and singer Elvis Presley; one was a drunk, the other "a great kisser," she said. But choosing the right husband was a problem. Her first marriage, to actor James Stacy, ended in divorce in 1966, and not a moment too soon. Stacy, who lost his left arm and leg in a motorcycle accident in 1973, was later sentenced to six years in state prison for molesting an 11-

year-old girl, and in 1982 a warrant was issued for Stacy's arrest after he failed to appear in Indio Municipal Court on charges of assault and battery. Two weeks later, he was taken into police custody for investigation of public drunkenness and drug possession in Palm Springs.

Stevens's second husband, Eddie Fisher, was also a drug addict. But at least their turbulent marriage produced two daughters, Joely and Tricia, whom Stevens raised single-handedly and without much-needed child support following the couple's acrimonious breakup.

Stevens certainly endured tough times. Her Hollywood career dried up, and she was relegated to "has-been" status. Between films, she toured Vietnam with Bob Hope's U.S.O. show and also headlined in Neil Simon's comedy *Star-Spangled Girl* on Broadway.

But never one to give in without a fight, the struggling sex symbol remembered her Avon days and decided to try again. She mortgaged her house and went into the beauty business. For the past 16 years, Stevens, who lives at 311 Arrowhead Drive, has run her own cosmetics company, Forever Spring, which manufactures more than 400 beauty products. She also runs a day spa, the Garden Sanctuary, in Los Angeles.

These days, Stevens owns an $11-million Holmby Hills estate, as well as homes in Las Vegas and New York, a 100-acre retreat in Jackson Hole, Wyoming, and a beach house in Puerto Vallarta, Mexico. With a personal fortune estimated at $100 million, Stevens can well afford to give Hollywood the finger.

■ ■ ■

WHEREVER SHE HAS lived, whether it's New York, Las Vegas, or Palm Springs, tousle-haired comedienne **Rita Rudner** always sees the funny side of life. "I love the desert with all the lakes, flowers, bunnies and birds," the eight-year resident of 321 Tomahawk Drive enthused. "It's also the best climate for my hair, no frizz at either place."

Rudner can afford to laugh. The former Broadway dancer, who discovered she had a knack for tickling people's funny bones, was voted Best Comedienne in Las Vegas for two consecutive years. On top of that special honor, she also has a $1.2 million cabaret theater that was built for her at the New York, New York Hotel & Casino.

It's all quite an accomplishment for someone who is relatively new at the joke-telling game, unlike Bob Hope and George Burns who had been around it for 100 years—literally. Rudner did not aspire to be funny; it just happened that way.

This limpid performer was 25 when she decided to become a stand-up comic, talking into a microphone in front of inebriated nightclub patrons and waiting to hear their laughter. Her hushed, deadpan delivery bowled audiences over, and she wound up doing skits on the late-night talk-show circuit.

Rudner's comic talents have also been featured in several HBO specials, satirical books, and lighthearted films co-written with her longtime husband, Martin Bergmann. The movies include *Pete's Friends*, which was directed by Kenneth Branagh, and *A Weekend in the Country*, in which Rudner co-starred with the late Jack Lemmon.

When not working, the Bergmanns relax by playing golf or taking cross-country drives with their English sheepdog, Bonkers, formerly the high-jumping canine star of the animal act Super Dogs. But their life is not all fun and games. Rudner takes her status as a Las Vegas comedy queen seriously and maintains a busy work schedule. "I like to say I've been in more hotels than a hooker," she quipped.

■ ■ ■

FORMER WHITE HOUSE counsel **John W. Dean III,** who was charged with obstruction of justice and spent four months in prison for his role in the Watergate cover-up, was the unexpected target of strong media interest when he bought a Palm Valley Country Club home at 76–099 Palm Valley Drive in 1993.

Dean's close working relationship with President Richard M. Nixon, whom he represented from 1970 until Nixon fired him in 1973, earned the young legal advisor the dubious title "White House lawyer for a thousand days." In the finger-pointing that followed his dismissal, Dean alleged before the Senate Watergate Committee that he and former Attorney General John Mitchell, along with Nixon, covered up an attempted burglary of Democratic National Committee headquarters at the Watergate Hotel in Washington, D.C., in 1972.

The Watergate scandal was exposed by two newspaper reporters for *The Washington Post*, Bob Woodward and Carl Bernstein, whose nosy exploits were dramatized in the Oscar-winning film *All the President's Men* starring Robert Redford and Dustin Hoffman. The two reporters' relentless and dangerous search for clues was assisted by a confidential informant known as "Deep Throat." (Three decades later, that source was revealed to be W. Mark Felt, associate director of the FBI.)

Throughout the investigation, Nixon vehemently denied Dean's allegations that he authorized a cover-up. Many people believed him because there was no actual proof beyond scribbled notes Dean had taken in his meetings with the president. Not until the existence of secret White House tape recordings was made public, and those tapes were analyzed, were Dean's accusations proved to be correct.

Under questioning, Dean admitted supervising payments of "hush money" to the burglars, and that the chief perpetrator, CIA agent E. Howard Hunt, was one of several high-level operatives, including G. Gordon Liddy, whom the president had called upon to commit burglaries and install wiretaps. Dean also revealed the existence of Nixon's Enemies List, a collection of more than 500 names of political opponents that Nixon feared or loathed. Among the list was United Artists film executive Arnold Picker, actors Paul Newman, Jane Fonda, Steve McQueen, and Barbra Streisand, and liberal journalists Daniel Schorr and Mary McGrory. To avoid impeachment, Nixon resigned from office in the summer of 1974.

Thirty years after the Watergate crisis, Dean is still considered a controversial figure for his outspoken political views. In 1992, he filed a lawsuit against G. Gordon Liddy for defamatory comments Liddy made about Dean in his book *Will*. He also sued St. Martin's Press over their publication of the book *Silent Coup*, which claimed Dean masterminded the Watergate burglary to retrieve documents linking him and his wife to a prostitution ring.

Now an investment banker in Beverly Hills, Dean is the author of two Watergate memoirs, *Blind Ambition* and *Lost Honor*, as well as a biography of the late Supreme Court Chief Justice William Rehnquist.

Dean sold his Palm Desert home for $298,500 in 2001.

■ ■ ■

EMMY AWARD–WINNING COMEDIC actor **Peter Marshall** was the original, unflappable host of *The Hollywood Squares*. Marshall presided over

3,536 episodes of that riotous, often raunchy, tic-tac-toe TV game show, which pushed the boundaries of acceptable taste to score huge ratings. Today, Marshall resides at 38–029 Crocus Lane, where he spends most of his time playing on the golf course with his third wife, Laurie Stewart, or frolicking on the grass with their two dogs and three cats.

The outgoing, toothily grinning performer began his showbiz career as a young big-band singer. He later segued into films as half of an ersatz comedy team; the other half was Tommy Noonan, with whom Marshall appeared in the low budget movies *The Rookie* and *Swingin' Along*.

Marshall's quick wit, which was developed in smoky nightclubs and most famously onstage at the renowned Chi-Chi in Palm Springs, gave him the edge over other actors when he auditioned for the smiling emcee of a new quiz show called *The Hollywood Squares*. The show's concept was that celebrities would give true and false answers to confuse contestants, and the result, with Marshall on board, was a half-hour of inspired comedy *shtick* that often took precedence over the game itself.

Marshall never lost his cool, though he sometimes lost his composure, breaking into spontaneous laughter at the ribald humor of regular panelists such as Paul Lynde, Rose Marie, and Wally Cox. Many tapings of the program had to be heavily edited to censor offensive remarks.

According to participants on the show, alcoholic beverages were consumed during lunch breaks to help loosen people's inhibitions. Undoubtedly this helped raise the level of comedy between various guests, many of whom were visibly under the influence on occasion.

"The best bluffer I ever saw," revealed Marshall, "was Robert Fuller. After his answer, I'd be so sure he was right I'd barely glance at the card. When I'd look down and see that his answer was totally wrong, I was always amazed.

"The worst bluffer," he said, "was Kaye Ballard. She was so sweet she didn't want any of the contestants to lose, so if she tried to bluff, she'd actually end up telling them she was bluffing."

Marshall's sister was green-eyed actress Joanne Dru, who co-starred with John Wayne in *Red River*, *She Wore a Yellow Ribbon*, and *Wagon Master*. She died in 1996, at the age of 74.

■ ■ ■

FOR THE EMINENT wordsmith **Larry Gelbart**, telling jokes is no laughing matter. The two-time Oscar nominee takes his job as a top-of-the-line scriptwriter very seriously—so seriously in fact that he gets paid a minimum of $1 million per film to sit at his personal computer. For that high price, Gelbart's humor is topical, clever, irreverent, bitchy, and always right on the money. It needs to be if he is going to maintain the quality to which he has attained in witty scripts such as *The Notorious Landlady*, *The Wrong Box*, *Oh, God!*, and *Tootsie*.

Gelbart got his start writing gags for Danny Thomas, who used to get his hair cut by Gelbart's father at Harry Rothschild's barber shop in Beverly Hills. Thomas later quipped, "The haircuts were okay but the jokes were hilarious." With that kind of recommendation it wasn't very long before Gelbart was hired to supply punch lines for Bob Hope, Red Buttons, and Sid Caesar.

He quickly earned the respect of grateful performers and of fellow writers like Mel Brooks, who called the hardworking Gelbart "a real *mensch*." Still, rumor has it that when Hope noticed Gelbart buying a new Cadillac convertible, out of money that the wise-cracking comedian had paid him, Hope fired the young writer. But then, Hope was known to be not only cheap but also jealous of other people's success.

And success has followed Gelbart, who moved to a new home at 76–916 Coventry Circle (Regency Estates) in 1996. He collected Tony Awards for the Broadway farce *A Funny Thing Happened on the Way to the Forum*, starring Zero Mostel, and *City of Angels*, a musical spoof of old-time Hollywood. He garnered an Emmy Award for the TV series *M*A*S*H*, for which he contributed nearly 100 episodes.

His skewering of American politics in *Mastergate*, a biting satire of the Iran-Contra affair, and of corporate wheeling and dealing in *Barbarians at the Gate*, pushed his talents into a new stratosphere. These were followed by *Weapons of Mass Distraction*, about a battle royal between two feuding TV moguls reportedly based on Ted Turner and Rupert Murdoch.

But beware of comic writers; they usually get the last word. Although Gelbart clashed with star Dustin Hoffman during the making of *Tootsie*, the movie was a phenomenal success and is universally regarded as one of Hollywood's all-time funniest comedies. "Never work with an Oscar winner who's smaller than the statue," said Gelbart when it was all over.

■ ■ ■

IN 1988, NATIONAL Football League record holder **Thomas "Tom" Fears**, who was the first league player to catch a total of 400 forward passes, lived at 41–470 Woodhaven Drive East in Woodhaven Country Club.

Fears began his professional career in 1948, as a defensive back with the Los Angeles Rams. In his first game, he intercepted two passes, running one back for a touchdown, and was moved to offensive end. Fears led the league in his first three seasons, catching a total of 212 passes. He caught 18 passes against the Green Bay Packers during the 1950 season—a record that remains unbeaten—and he caught three touchdown passes against the Chicago Bears and a 74-yard touchdown against the Cleveland Browns in 1951.

In 1956, Fears retired after catching only five passes, his best games behind him, and twenty-four years later he was elected to the Professional Football Hall of Fame. He suffered from Alzheimer's disease and died at the age of 76 in 2000.

■ ■ ■

"DIRECTED BY **JOSEPH Pevney**" is a screen credit that may not merit the same importance as Alfred Hitchcock or Orson Welles. But it is a name that has been associated with some of Hollywood's most commercially successful and critically acclaimed films, even though many of Pevney's best works have curiously been ignored. Whether he did not seek recognition, or perhaps because he was conveniently overlooked by his more gregarious peers, there is no denying that out of nearly 80 films and TV series on which Pevney received directing credit, many are unsung classics awaiting rediscovery.

This ten-year resident of 43–705 Texas Avenue in Palm Desert Country Club developed a passion for the performing arts at an early age. By the time he was 13 he was appearing in vaudeville, and during the 1940s he acted in moody crime films such as *Nocturne, Body and Soul,*

The Street with No Name, and *Thieves Highway.* Then, seeking to work the other side of the camera, in 1950 he joined Universal-International Pictures, which was in the process of expanding its line-up from simple-minded comedies to socially relevant dramas and large-scale action-adventures.

With youthful enthusiasm and determination, Pevney rose through the ranks to become the studio's busiest workhorse, a no-nonsense director recognized for his uncanny ability to imbue a film, no matter how modest, with bravura acting performances and visually striking set pieces—and also bring it in on time and within budget. He did this not once but repeatedly during his long and abundant career, at the same time making genuine stars out of novice actors such as Rock Hudson and Tony Curtis, and reinvigorating the careers of former screen greats James Cagney and Errol Flynn.

Pevney's confident handling of Jeff Chandler, whom he directed in seven films, resulted in some of the actor's best work, including *Iron Man, Yankee Pasha, Foxfire,* and *Away All Boats.* Chandler also got to square off with Joan Crawford in the campy suspense thriller *Female on the Beach,* in which she tells him, "I wouldn't have you if you were hung with diamonds upside down!"

But Pevney's most noteworthy collaboration was with Tony Curtis, who had a lot to prove in four films that showcased his penchant for physical roles, including *Flesh and Fury, Six Bridges to Cross,* and *The Midnight Story.* "He was an excellent director in many ways," recalled Curtis. But he believed Pevney lacked ambition. "He hurt his directing career by not demanding the quality of production he really needed."

That may explain why the brass ring was always slightly beyond his reach. Still, people spoke superlatives about *Tammy and the Bachelor,* which contained Debbie Reynolds's most appealing performance, and about Cagney's *tour de force* as Lon Chaney in *Man of a Thousand Faces,* probably Pevney's best film.

There were other big names in other good films: Rock Hudson in *Twilight for the Gods,* Glenn Ford in *Torpedo Run,* James Garner in *Cash McCall.* Then Pevney moved into TV, where he handled many popular episodes of *Star Trek,* including "Arena," "Amok Time," "The Trouble with Tribbles," and "The Immunity Syndrome."

It was around this time that the director's career, which had finally built up momentum, was derailed. There were rumors of heavy drinking on the set, which Pevney always denied. But he could not deny the loss of his beloved wife, former child star Mitzi Green, who perished from cancer at the age of 48 in 1969. That, more than anything else, is probably what curbed Pevney's incentive to do better work. After all, why settle for second best?

■ ■ ■

AMERICAN TENNIS STAR **Alice Marble**, who won 12 U.S. Open Championships and five Wimbledon titles, and became one of the sport's earliest celebrities, resided at 77–300 Indiana Avenue, where she died at the age of 77 in 1990.

A highly competitive player, Marble used her powerful serves and volleys to dominate women's tennis throughout the late 1930s and early 1940s. She also created a stir by wearing baggy shorts on the court instead of the traditional pleated skirt. Indeed, Marble's straightforward style inspired a generation of sports-minded women to pick up a tennis racquet and prove that they could be just as proficient as, and sometimes better than, their male counterparts.

Alice's private life, however, was mired in personal tragedy. She had been raped at 15, and it was many years before she could overcome that psychological trauma, although it hardened her resolve both on and off the court.

As an example of her determination, on her first trip abroad she collapsed from tuberculosis and pleurisy, anathemas to a sports figure. But when she recovered her health, she turned professional, playing in exhibition matches around the country and demonstrating her athletic proficiency for servicemen at military bases during World War II.

In 1942, she married a soldier she had met on one of her tours. But that also tested her metal. A car accident caused her to miscarry, and then several days later, Alice learned that her husband's plane had been shot down and he had been killed.

The next chapter of Marble's life is worthy of a Hollywood movie. In response to her husband's death, she attempted suicide, but eventually, to overcome her feelings of worthlessness, she participated in an espionage plot for U.S. Army Intelligence. Facing considerable danger, she traveled to Switzerland to investigate the financial ledgers of a Swiss banker and ex-lover, who was suspected of harboring Nazi wealth.

Upon returning to civilian life, she wrote her autobiography, *The Road to Wimbledon*, and later coached promising tennis players such as Billie Jean King.

■ ■ ■

NEVER JUDGE A book by its cover—or an actress by her glossy 8x10 head-shot. If that warning could be applied to anyone, it would be **Rochelle Hudson**, who sounded like an old-fashioned glamour queen but in reality was a pretty-faced ingénue.

She started out playing Claudette Colbert's teenage daughter in *Imitation of Life* and Shirley Temple's older sister in *Curly Top*. Then she morphed into a polite leading lady and finally into a forthright character actress: she played Natalie Wood's mother in *Rebel without a Cause*. In real life, too, Hudson took on varying personas. During World War II, she worked for Naval Intelligence in Latin America, and after her acting career petered out in the 1960s she became a successful real estate broker.

But all was definitely not what it seemed. She was married and divorced three times, and along the way this once-beautiful actress developed a serious drinking problem. On January 17, 1972, Hudson was found dead in her club home at 77–038 California Drive. The cause of death was pneumonia brought on by a liver ailment. She was 58.

■ ■ ■

DIRECTOR **NORMAN TAUROG**, who won the Oscar for Best Director for *Skippy* in 1931, and was nominated a second time for *Boys Town*, which won Mickey Rooney the award for Best Actor, retired to 42–635 Tennessee Avenue.

The stocky, bespectacled Taurog looked more like a kindly druggist than a Hollywood film technician who spent 12 years at MGM. But "Taurog had a temper," confessed his nephew, the actor Jackie Cooper, who remembered his uncle using various tricks to get child stars to perform on cue. Taurog's favorite incentive was handing out chocolate bars; if that failed, he resorted to threats and intimidation.

He kept the overactive Rooney on the straight and narrow for six films, including *Young Tom Edison*, *A Yank at Eton*, and *Girl Crazy*, and handled Rooney's fragile co-star, Judy Garland, with kid gloves in the vehicles *Little Nellie Kelly* and *Presenting Lily Mars*.

When he moved to Paramount in 1951, Taurog hooked up with Dean Martin and Jerry Lewis, who persisted to tease and torment him through six movies, including *Jumping Jacks*, *The Stooge*, *Living It Up*, and *You're Never Too Young*. The team's antics were all in good fun, and Taurog, who apparently possessed a sense of humor behind those spectacles, enjoyed the levity.

Maybe because he demonstrated a propensity for unending tolerance, Taurog was deemed the perfect man to handle Elvis Presley, whom he coached to improve the nervous singer's hesitant acting in *G.I. Blues*—Presley's first film since his army demobilization. Their father-and-son style of partnership resulted in nine films, not all great, but most of them passable entertainment. The list includes some of Presley's biggest moneymakers: *Blue Hawaii; Girls! Girls! Girls!; It Happened at the World's Fair; Tickle Me;* and *Speedway*.

One thing Taurog couldn't control, unfortunately, was Presley's ballooning weight. Producer Hal Wallis ordered the guitar-strumming rock 'n' roller to shed a few pounds and get a suntan, but fans didn't seem to mind the extra pounds. So, in his remaining films, there are fewer shots of Presley in a bathing suit and more scenes of him dressed in a shirt, jacket, and tie.

After his retirement, Taurog taught film studies at the University of California at Los Angeles, while the more than 140 films he made were stored in film vaults, some to be revived on TV and videocassette. In the last decade of his life he went blind, and he died in 1981 at the age of 82.

VIP Treatment

JANUARY 15, 1947: It was a typical blue-gray dawn in smog-filed Los Angeles, the bustling metropolis known as the City of Angels. Detective Sergeant **Harry Hansen** of the Los Angeles Police Department was winding up another case when he received an urgent call over the police radio from Captain Jack Donahoe of Central Homicide.

"University's got a bad one, Harry. A girl cut in half around the middle, in a vacant lot. Stark naked and there's already photographs on it!" Hansen listened as the captain ordered a shutdown of the immediate area and instructed extra men to be posted at the crime scene. The radio crackled with so much static that it sounded like an S.O.S.

By the time Hansen and his partner, Finis Brown, made their way through the early morning traffic to the corner of 39th Street and Norton Avenue in Leimert Park, the area was filled with gawking neighbors and cars of sightseers craning their necks for a better view. Newspaper photographers were running across the empty lot, trampling the grass and throwing empty flashbulbs and cigarette butts on the ground.

Hansen gritted his teeth and pushed his way through the swelling crowd of excited onlookers. "Hell, the only thing missing here is a picnic basket," someone remarked as he passed by. Only this was no picnic.

Lying spread-eagled on the ground was the mutilated corpse of a 22-year-old woman named Elizabeth Short. She had been cut in half like a loaf of bread, her body drained of blood by her unseen killer, who, in his perverse gratification, had also shampooed her hair. Pieces of skin had been cut out of her face and legs, and there were knife marks across her wrists and feet. Hansen winced at the gruesome scene and ordered that the body be covered from the sun until the coroner arrived.

Short's dismembered corpse was transported to the city morgue, where it was placed on an autopsy table, and her disfigured features were stitched together so that photographs could be taken of her remains and distributed to cops throughout the city. At that time no one knew her name, so she was simply called "Jane Doe." Hansen was placed in charge of the investigation—the biggest story to hit the L.A. airwaves since the bombing of Pearl Harbor.

A postmortem showed that the young woman had been systematically tortured and had been forced to eat her own feces as some sort of cruel punishment by her killer, who took sadistic pleasure in his victim's slow and painful death. Then there was an unexpected medical bombshell: the unidentified woman was missing female genitalia, which meant she had not been able to fully consummate the sexual act.

Hansen thought he'd seen it all. Now he had a dead woman on his hands who wasn't really a woman at all—maybe she was a hermaphrodite. If so, Hansen theorized, he saw a possible motive for the ghastly crime. Perhaps the woman had encountered the unsuspecting man, and when he learned she was unable to have conventional sex, he killed her in a violent rage. At least that was one theory.

Fingerprints established her true identity, and Hansen delved into the girl's past. What he learned was hardly cause for jubilation. A product of a broken home, Betty Short had often been arrested for underage drinking. She had moved from city to city, soliciting men for money and companionship, until her travels brought her to Hollywood, where she hung out at nightclubs, bars, and hotels. She had a penchant for wearing dark clothes and makeup, and when the press learned that detail, they dubbed her the Black Dahlia, a name that came to symbolize both the murky crime and her own fatal attraction to the netherworld. The papers went crazy: STRANGE LIFE OF GIRL VICTIM OF WEREWOLF KILLER.

Hansen goaded himself for his toughest fight in more than 20 years on the LAPD, to solve a chilling murder that had more red herrings than an Agatha Christie whodunit. There were plenty of suspects: bums on skid row, perverts, crazies, wife beaters, thrill killers. More than 150 sex offenders were interviewed during the first night of Hansen's round-the-clock investigation.

Extra police were put on desk duty to handle the flood of information, which included 38 written confessions and 200 phone calls. One person mailed a package to the *Los Angeles Herald-Examiner* containing Short's missing social security card, birth certificate, photographs of her in the company of various servicemen, business cards, and claim checks for luggage she had left at the bus depot.

As the police dragnet widened, more than 750 investigators were assigned to the case, including 400 sheriff's deputies and 250 California Highway Patrol officers. Sixty detectives from the vice squad hit the streets of Hollywood, to canvas bars and restaurants looking for clues. Thirty officers were assigned to dig through trash cans in alleyways, and another 40 patrolmen went door-to-door in the neighborhood where Short's body had been found.

Hansen never rested. He remained on the case, probing every lead, investigating each clue, until his retirement in 1971. He smoked so many cigarettes and drank so much coffee that it's a miracle he didn't contract throat cancer or suffer caffeine poisoning from the high level of stress. It all added up to naught. The killer was never found.

"He didn't know it then, maybe none of us did," Finis Brown, the investigating officer, recalled, "but Harry had met his challenge with the Black Dahlia case. He'd met his goddamned Waterloo."

The ongoing public fascination with the morbid case resulted in several books and films, including *Who Is the Black Dahlia?*, starring Efrem Zimbalist, Jr., as Hansen, and *True Confessions*, written by John Gregory Dunne. Hansen assisted with them all, in hopes that the actual killer would be brought to justice.

Hansen retired to 73–207 Tumbleweed Lane in 1968, but it always bothered him that he was never able to crack the infamous case and walk into City Hall with the killer in handcuffs. Even in retirement, he was still pursued by cranks and the curious hoping to get some mileage out of the tarnished Dahlia legend. He received more than 400 written "clues" from people who all thought they knew who did it.

If Hansen was cynical about the likeliness of an arrest, he was still accommodating to the general public. But it was rumored that he had withheld one critical piece of evidence, which he never revealed to anyone. That way, he would know the killer's true identity if and when that time came. Alas, it never did.

In 1983, at the age of 80, Hansen died of a stroke.

■ ■ ■

GLOWERING ACTOR **BRIAN Donlevy**, whose masochistic streak and authoritative voice made him a memorable foe in more than 90 films— mostly playing crooked playboys, fearless gangsters, and glory-seeking martinets—imbibed excessively while residing with his third wife, Lillian Arch, at Sun Lodge Colony, 75–535 El Paseo (off Larkspur Lane).

The son of an Irish-whiskey distiller, Donlevy was a well-muscled teenager when he joined General John Pershing's Mexican border expedition against Pancho Villa as a bugler. Then in World War I he lied about his age and enlisted as a pilot with the famous Lafayette Escadrille.

Like fellow daredevil actor Errol Flynn, with whom he had much in common, Donlevy's real-life adventures inevitably led him to Hollywood, where he was snapped up by producers to play tough-talking, two-fisted characters. He could ride a horse at full gallop, wield a pistol or a sword, and lead a cavalry charge.

In 1939, Donlevy starred in six films, including *Jesse James, Union Pacific, Allegheny Uprising*, and *Destry Rides Again,* and that same year he received an Oscar nomination for Best Supporting Actor, for playing the sadistic army sergeant who orders his men to death in the foreign-legion adventure *Beau Geste*.

Soon, his energetic, snarling performances were so popular with wartime movie audiences that he received star billing in *The Remarkable Andrew* (as the ghost of Andrew Jackson), *Wake Island*, and *The Glass Key,* among other movies. At the peak of his Hollywood career he played the roguish title role in Preston Sturges's political satire *The Great McGinty*.

Aside from his impressive physical abilities, Donlevy was also a talented writer and poet. It seemed this artist could do no wrong. But the brawling actor's serious drinking problem caused him more than morning-after headaches, and he was eventually forced to work abroad in cheaply made science-fiction and horror films such as *The Creeping Unknown*, *Enemy from Space*, and *The Curse of the Fly*.

He died of throat cancer at the age of 71 in 1972.

■ ■ ■

ACTOR **WILLARD PARKER** and his wife, actress **Virginia Field**, who was previously married to actor Paul Douglas, owned and managed a bungalow motel called The Parkers at 73–929 Larrea Street. It was a handy place for out-of-town guests and obliged those Hollywood stars who wanted to protect their anonymity.

Lana Turner stayed at the Parkers' lodge after divorcing her fourth husband, Lex Barker, in 1957. Forthright and down-to-earth, Turner had been a close friend of Virginia Field, whom she called by her real name, Margaret. They'd known each other a long time, having met while under contract at different studios, when each played provocatively attired damsels in scores of melodramas and elaborate costumers.

Turner became the bigger star, romancing the likes of Clark Gable, Robert Taylor, and John Garfield. The demonstrative blond sex symbol soon cornered the market when it came to playing girls who entice men with the promise of a fun time and then deny it, a trick that Turner was good at both on and off the screen.

But Turner's success had no effect on her friendship with Field. On this particular visit to Field's bungalow, Turner was accompanied by a strapping young male protégé named Ralph Vitti, a baseball shortstop turned actor who would soon change his name to the mysterious-sounding "Michael Dante." And with them were Turner's impetuous 14-year-old daughter, Cheryl Crane, and Field's daughter, Maggie Douglas, who was a seventh grader at Crane's boarding school.

Turner and Dante took a poolside bungalow, where they spent the weekend swimming and tanning themselves in the sun, while Turner downed Blood Marys. The girls hung out around the pool and tennis courts at Shadow Mountain Club. All was going well until Cheryl innocently put her arm around Dante's shoulder, and her jealous mother gave the teenager a tongue-lashing. "You listen to me, young lady," she seethed. "Just because you got away with some things here this weekend, don't think I didn't see them."

Crane was crestfallen.

"What things?" she asked.

"The way you try to flirt with Michael."

Crane couldn't believe her ears.

"I saw you—and you've done it before," raged Turner. And then, in a bold moment straight out of one of her histrionic films, she slapped the shocked girl across the face.

Crane resolved to run away, and back in Los Angeles, she jumped out of a taxi and ducked into an alleyway. Turner, alarmed by Cheryl's disappearance, told the police that her daughter was missing, and the result was a massive, citywide dragnet that roused concern for the girl's welfare. Shortly before midnight, the police found Cheryl unharmed, and she returned to Turner the following day. But the girl's escapade made the front page of every newspaper in town: LANA TURNER'S RUNAWAY DAUGHTER FOUND.

Two weeks after the ordeal, Turner reported to work on her thirty-seventh film, *Peyton Place*, based on the bestseller about adulterous life in a small New England town. The emotional scene where Turner slaps her rebellious daughter, played by Diane Varsi, is always singled out for praise. But Crane always found the episode difficult to watch. It brought tears to her eyes.

■ ■ ■

FOR 30 YEARS, portly actor **Edgar Buchanan** commanded movie and TV screens playing curmudgeonly old-timers, judges, and doctors. Throughout that time he appeared in more than 100 films, in which he drank whiskey and chewed tobacco with some of the best actors in Hollywood.

There was no mistaking that chubby face and those whiskers, or the man's sly, quizzical stare, which hinted at dangers in "them-thar-hills" of the Old West. Depending on how much money a movie offered him, Buchanan was a natural at playing smart, dumb, or corrupt officials.

A second-generation dentist, he was the former head of oral surgery at Eugene Hospital in Oregon, where he performed hundreds of tooth extractions. During the day, he applied fillings, crowns, and bridges to his patients; at night he took acting classes. Buchanan's dental training later came in handy on the set of *Red Canyon* in Kanab, Utah, when co-star George Brent developed a swollen jaw and needed emergency treatment for an abscessed tooth. Buchanan pulled the infected tooth with a pair of pliers, and Brent made a swift recovery. In fact, Buchanan was so adept at handling mouth drills that he played dentists in several Westerns, notably *Texas*, one of a dozen films he made with longtime friend Glenn Ford. He also played doting fathers, uncles, and politicians in numerous comedies.

But those roles are not nearly as memorable as his scruffy appearances in Westerns like *Rawhide*, *The Big Trees*, *Shane*, *Destry*, *The Lonesome Trail*, *Wichita*, *Day of the Bad Man*, *The Comancheros*, and *McLintock!* All he had to do was wear a battered derby hat and fiddle with a pocket watch, and he'd steal the scene from any star he worked with.

In his senior years, Buchanan became a veritable fountain of rural wisdom as the bearded lawmaker in the weekly TV series *Judge Roy Bean*, and as Uncle Joe, co-owner of the Shady Rest Hotel, on the popular family sitcom *Petticoat Junction*. (The show's theme song was composed and performed by Curtis Massey, a resident of Indian Wells.)

Buchanan was almost 70 when his buddy Ford lured the semiretired actor back to work, to play a sheriff's deputy in the modern-day Western drama *Cade's County*. But serious health problems forced Buchanan and his wife, Mildred Spence, to move from their home in Los Angeles to a modest apartment at 73–835 Shadow Mountain Drive.

In 1976, he underwent surgery to relieve the pressure of spinal fluid on his brain, and three years later he was admitted to Eisenhower Medical Center for another operation and contracted meningitis. He remained in critical condition for two months until he died from pneumonia at the age of 76 in 1979.

■ ■ ■

A FEW BLOCKS up the hill from Edgar Buchanan's house is Shadow Mountain Golf Club, where glistening movie stars recline around the world-famous figure-eight swimming pool at the Shadow Mountain Resort & Spa, and where the diving tower is manned by lifeguards who keep one eye on the water and the other on the daily parade of bathing suits. The club's founder, Cliff Henderson, and his wife, **Marian Marsh,** moved into 73–597 Pinyon Street.

A native of Trinidad, West Indies, Marsh had been accorded the Hollywood glamour treatment during the transition from silent movies to sound; she starred opposite the mesmerizing John Barrymore in *Svengali*. Marsh had been cast for her startling resemblance to the fictional heroine of George du Maurier's novel *Trilby*, on which the film was based. The two actors' partnership was so successful, in fact, that Barrymore, who was then at the height of his career, and Marsh, who continued to radiate uncommon beauty, were reunited in *The Mad Genius*, another tale of unrequited love.

Marsh was also very effective as the unwitting victim of Edward G. Robinson's corrupt journalism in *Five Star Final* and fought off Boris Karloff's evil advances in *The Black Room*. She showed great compassion for Peter Lorre in *Crime and Punishment* and fell in love with Ralph Bellamy in *The Man Who Lived Twice*.

But she retired from the screen at the age of 30, believing that the roles she was being offered no longer measured up to her expectations. (By comparison, her older sister, Jean Fenwick, a well-known character actress who played in the grand costume dramas *Mary of Scotland, If I Were King,* and *Tower of London,* continued to work into the 1950s.)

Marsh and Henderson were married in 1960. He died at the age of 88 in 1984; Marsh, who turned 92 in 2005, still lives in the same house.

■ ■ ■

ACTOR **RALPH WAITE,** who resides at 73–317 Ironwood Street, could play practically any type of part, from farm laborer to president of the board. But his messy hair and craggy features are best identified with the fatherly role of John Walton, the patriarch with the stern voice and compassionate smile whom he played for 10 years on the Emmy Award–winning TV series *The Waltons*.

His ability to empathize with a character's moral dilemma and resolve an emerging crisis was the result of his real-life experience. Prior to becoming an actor he had been a social worker in New York State, a practicing Presbyterian minister, and ultimately a religion editor for what is now the publishing firm of HarperCollins.

He was also a recovering alcoholic, an aspect of his personality that gave him strong insights into other people's problems, especially difficulties involving willpower and dependency. Waite had appeared in Broadway plays and had been cast as sympathetic characters in several films before hitting the acting jackpot with *The Waltons*.

Interestingly, the role that finally brought him fame had originally been played by Henry Fonda in a 1963 film called *Spencer's Mountain,* and Waite's Palm Desert neighbor James MacArthur had played the sensitive son. In the TV movie *The Homecoming*, which evolved into the series, Andrew Duggan played the father. Both the 1963 film and the TV series were written by Earl Hamner, Jr., who had once penned a movie with a desert connection—*Palm Springs Weekend*.

After *The Waltons* ended its run, Waite married his third wife, Linda East, at La Quinta Hotel. Reverend Mark Armstrong, a Lutheran clergyman from the Betty Ford Center, performed the wedding ceremony, and the bride and groom toasted each other with glasses of iced tea.

It was very much a family affair. Actor-musician Jon Walmsley, who had played Waite's second oldest son, Jason Walton, in the TV series, provided dance music with his five-piece rock band at the reception in the Frank Capra Room. Waite, himself an ordained minister, had married Walmsley and his wife, Lisa Harrison, who had played Toni Walton during the show's final season.

After moving permanently to the desert, Waite immersed himself in local politics. He stumped for the Democratic Party and ran unsuccessfully against Republican congressman Al McCandless in 1990. The failed election bid cost Waite an estimated $300,000 and prompted him to return to acting; he appeared in *The Bodyguard* opposite Kevin Costner and in *Cliffhanger* with Sylvester Stallone. But soon he was back in politics. In 1998, he ran unsuccessfully against Mary Bono to fill the unexpired term of her late husband, congressman Sonny Bono, who had been killed in a skiing accident.

He had fought challenges all his life, but perhaps Waite's greatest test of his inner strength was the unexpected death of his younger brother, Don Waite, the proprietor of Don & Sweet Sue's Café in Cathedral City in 1998. Moments after speaking about his sobriety at a local meeting of Alcoholics Anonymous, Don Waite suffered a heart attack and collapsed. He was rushed to the hospital, but he passed away four days later, with Ralph at his side. The strong bond that the brothers shared was typical of Ralph's commitment to family and friends, qualities that he had drawn upon to make *The Waltons* such an unqualified hit.

In 2004, Waite's character, John Walton, Sr., was ranked #3 in *TV Guide*'s list of the "50 Greatest TV Dads of All Time."

■ ■ ■

AVIATION PIONEER **A. Harold Bromley**, who was the first person to attempt a long-distance flight across the Pacific Ocean, lived at 73–640B Golf Course Lane opposite the club's fifth fairway.

Bromley's flying career spanned 50 years. A native of British Columbia, he was hired as a test pilot by Lockheed Aircraft founder Allan Lockheed in 1928 and moved to Burbank, California, where he matched propellers with Wiley Post, Amelia Earhart, and Jimmy Dolittle on the Lockheed Vega. After flying from Tacoma, Washington, to Tokyo, Japan, in 1929, in a single-engine Emsco B-3, Bromley attempted to return in the opposite direction but encountered bad weather and mechanical problems. Thirty hours after takeoff, Bromley and his navigator, Harold Gatty, were forced to turn back when deadly carbon monoxide fumes from a broken exhaust line filled the plane's cockpit.

But that was simply an adventure to these aviation pioneers. Bromley flew mail and passenger planes from El Paso, Texas, to Mexico City, then established a regular service flying gold and silver out of isolated mining towns. Gatty, who was overcome with fumes on that historic Pacific flight, went on to fly around the world with Wiley Post in 1931.

After spending more than 20 years crisscrossing the nation's skies, and putting in time as regional director of the Federal Aviation Administration, Bromley retired to the desert township of Mecca, where he grew dates and grapes. Later, he opened a real estate office in North Shore.

He died in 1998 at the age of 99, at Monterey Palms Health Care Center.

■ ■ ■

SINGER, PIANIST, AND arranger **Buddy Greco** hasn't let old age get the better of him, despite a scarcity of nightclub bookings that almost sounded the death knell for his once-flourishing career.

Before Elton John, Barry Manilow, and Billy Joel were tickling the ivories, there was Greco. He hypnotized music lovers with his clever, improvisational versions of popular songs such as "The Lady Is a Tramp," which sold over one million copies. Critics praised his ad lib performing style and compared Greco's bop-inspired vocalizing to that of Nat "King" Cole.

It was beautiful music to the ears of this curly-haired native of Philadelphia, who became a star attraction in Las Vegas, Atlantic City, and Monte Carlo supper clubs, where he played piano and sang for nearly half a century. During that time, Greco released 70 albums and 126 singles, ranging from jazz to pop.

This witty, talented performer first made a big splash with his recording of Carmen Lombardo's "Ooh! Look-A-There, Ain't She Pretty?" Then, heard exercising his tonsils at Philly's Club 13 by Benny Goodman, who offered him a job, Greco joined Goodman's swing orchestra and accompanied the musicians on several tours. His flexible vocals graced Goodman sides such as "It Isn't Fair," "Don't Worry 'Bout Me," "The Land of Oo-Bla-Dee," and "Brother Bill."

In 1951, stardom knocked on Greco's stage door and he went solo, landing a regular spot on the TV variety show *Broadway Open House* and providing Coral Records with the hit single "I Ran All the Way Home." Hundreds of nightclub engagements followed, one of which generated the bestselling album *Buddy Greco at Mister Kelly's*, a fabulous record of his sellout appearances at the fabled Chicago club in 1955. Wherever he was, he closed every show with a powerful instrumental version of "MacArthur Park," guaranteeing him a standing ovation.

More recently, Greco toured with the Benny Goodman Tribute Big Band and performed with his own 18-piece orchestra at Trump Plaza in Atlantic City, where blasé gamblers momentarily stopped playing slot machines to hear his brilliant musical interpretations. Among Greco's own compositions, always performed with gusto, are "Make Up Your Mind," "El Greco," "Just Walk Away," and "Stay Warm."

When he turned 75, Greco was faced with the realization that he was no longer a big draw in Las Vegas, the city where he lived with his fourth wife, cabaret singer Lezlie Anders, and their menagerie of exotic pets. So, after eight years spent fighting increased traffic congestion and noisy building construction, the couple decided to get the hell out of town.

Reluctantly, Greco put his two-and-a-half acre Spanish Mission–style house on the market, and in 2005, he moved to Palm Desert, where he and Anders paid $600,000 for a much smaller home at 74–540 Monte Verde Way (off Deep Canyon Road). Not content to spend his days on the putting green, Greco decided to create a permanent venue for his talents and bought a commercial building in Cathedral City. Twelve months later, he opened Buddy Greco's Dinner Club, a 90-seat restaurant with a bandstand.

■ ■ ■

HE WAS WITHOUT doubt America's greatest film director. He was also a devout Catholic, a sentimental moralist, and a misogynist. "My name's **John Ford**. I make Westerns," he growled from behind a battered fishing cap, a black patch covering his blind left eye, and a half-smoked cigar sticking out of his wet mouth. A man of few words and simple tastes, he had a grand vision of America as the Promised Land, a theme that was reinforced in 145 films he directed over a 50-year period.

Ford was the quintessential Irishman, and that aspect of his personality found its way into the charming, often conniving characters that populated nearly all of his mostly male-dominated films. The men in his movies were shy when sober, boisterous when drunk, chivalrous in the company of women, and courageous in the face of danger.

This celebration of the human spirit, of its determination and self-sacrifice, was a hallmark of his best work, in which manly presences such as Victor McLaglen, John Wayne, Henry Fonda, and James Stewart wrestled with their consciences or sought solutions to overwhelming problems. They appeared in stories of families torn asunder by conflict, of battles fought between opposing armies, and bloody wars with rampaging Indians.

Ford became known for red-tinged panoramic vistas, many of which were filmed against the awe-inspiring backdrop of Monument Valley, Arizona. In richly detailed pictorial classics such as *Stagecoach*, *My Darling Clementine*, *Fort Apache*, *She Wore a Yellow Ribbon*, *Rio Grande*, and *The Searchers*, thirsty soldiers, tired horses, and lines of covered wagons were photographed on long, overland treks through spectacular scenery.

But Ford wasn't interested only in the Old West. He could easily whip up a devastating tropical storm in *The Hurricane* or plan a thrilling African safari in *Mogambo*. No matter what the subject matter, he was able to give the movie a look of quality and a sense of purpose.

Ford won his first two Oscars for *The Informer* and *The Grapes of Wrath*. He received his third Academy Award for the stirring mining saga *How Green Was My Valley* and a fourth for *The Quiet Man,* a welcome piece of blarney filmed on the Emerald Isle. Two of his wartime documentaries, *The Battle of Midway* and *December 7th*, which he made for the U.S. Navy, also garnered Oscars.

In filmmaking, Ford always had his eye on the dramatic moment.

When Carroll Baker was driving a buckboard that nearly overturned as she tried to cross a raging river in *Cheyenne Autumn*, Ford admonished her for not following the script but kept the unrehearsed shot in the finished picture. During a poignant scene in *How the West Was Won,* when George Peppard's character leaves home to join the army, a mongrel dog ran out of the crowd and unexpectedly chased Peppard's wagon up the road, much to Ford's delight (he kept it in).

He could also be practical. If a film's production was running behind schedule, he was known to tear pages from the script to make up for lost time. If someone was down on their luck and needed a job, Ford would put them on the company payroll. He could be cruel if provoked but was otherwise a loyal and dependable person.

His best friends were actors (he came from an acting family), and they trusted him. They knew that, whether the movies were heart-wrenching melodramas or whimsical fables, they connected with audiences who identified with the competitive rivalry, sense of honor, and feeling of achievement that was always part of "A John Ford Film." Inevitably, as his filmmaking career aged, so did he, and his daily intake of alcohol and tobacco rendered him a diabetic by his seventh decade. Ford attempted to hold his fear of death at bay, traveling abroad to make a documentary in Vietnam and attending film festivals in Europe.

But when Ford was diagnosed with incurable stomach cancer in 1971, he seemed resigned to his impending fate. He decided to move to Palm Springs—"the elephant's graveyard," as it's sometimes called— saying he had always liked the desert. He and his wife, Mary McBryde, who was in the early stages of Parkinson's disease, had recently celebrated their fiftieth wedding anniversary. Katharine Hepburn went looking for a suitable house for him to buy and found a cozy four-bedroom home at 74–605 Old Prospector Trail, near Shadow Mountain Golf Club, that she thought was "just darling."

"It was an incongruous kind of house for them," recalled Robert Wagner, whose older sister, Mary Lou Wagner, was the home's prior owner. "It was a Spanish-style home that Zane Grey would have owned, but not John Ford." Still, Jack took one wing, and Mary took the other, and so began the twilight of Ford's life, during which a long procession of co-workers, friends, and relatives made the pilgrimage to his house to say good-bye.

The grand old man of movies, whom his best friends called "Pappy," was confined to a bed, doped up on morphine, and puffing on a plastic bucket of cigar butts. Votive candles and a small statue of the Virgin Mary stood on a nightstand, and a silver-and-black saddle was mounted on a sawhorse at the end of the bed.

Hepburn spent many hours with him, looking out the window and talking about old times. William Wyler reminisced about their early days in Hollywood. Howard Hawks sat on a chair and told stories. John Wayne tried to put on a brave face as they joked, and Ben Johnson and Joanne Dru held back their tears. Even Henry Fonda, a man not known for his displays of emotion, was visibly moved after seeing him.

On the last day of August 1973, Ford was given the last rites. For six hours, Woody Strode, who had played the title role in *Sergeant Rutledge*, sat on the edge of the director's bed, holding Ford's cold hand until he slipped into a coma. He died a short time later, at the age of 79. "His sister and I took an American flag and draped him in it," said Strode.

"We got some brandy, toasted him, and broke the glasses in the fireplace."

A requiem mass was held for Ford five days later in Culver City. His coffin was covered in a tattered World War II flag, a Navy rifle squad fired a salute, and a bugler blew "Taps."

His wife and his daughter, Barbara Ford, a film editor, lived in the Palm Desert house until Mary Ford's death in 1979. Barbara, who was a close friend of the Ford scholar and independent filmmaker Peter Bogdanovich, for whom she edited *Mask*, died of cancer in 1985.

■ ■ ■

VERSATILE ACTOR **JAMES MacArthur**, whose face and name are synonymous with the role of plain-clothed police detective Danny Williams, which he played for 11 years on the groundbreaking TV series *Hawaii Five-O*, is happily retired. He basks in the glory of his well-deserved fame in the home he shares with his third wife, Helen Duntz, at 74–092 Covered Wagon Trail.

The fictitious crime-busting Honolulu police unit 5–0 (named after Hawaii's ranking as the fiftieth state), which regularly apprehended Communist spies, drug dealers, and kidnappers, was the tropical island's biggest advertisement for tourism since Dole pineapples went on the market. The show's kaleidoscopic opening montage, which was set to the pulsating drum rhythms of breaking ocean waves and included images of a hula dancer's swinging hips, flashing police lights, and a zooming shot of Jack Lord standing on the penthouse balcony of the 30-story Ilikai Hotel, on Waikiki Beach, gave viewers a healthy dose of eye candy.

MacArthur's participation as Lord's second-in-charge—hunting down leads, tailing suspects, and finally making arrests when his boss ordered, "Book 'em, Danno!"—provided rousing scenes in the weekly pursuit of lawbreakers who inhabited the scenic state, with its sandy beaches and red and yellow hibiscus blossoms.

But cast and crew had little time to savor the delights of this beautiful paradise. MacArthur worked six days a week, ten hours a day, often in torrential rain and gusty trade winds. He appeared in 260 out of a total of 278 one-hour episodes filmed between 1968 and 1980. His only day

Kelsey Grammer
(Cinema Collectors)

John F. Kennedy
(Palm Springs
Historical Society)

Silver Spur Ranch
(Craig De Sedle)

Marilyn Monroe
(Howard Johns Collection)

Jimmy Van Heusen
(*Palm Springs Life*)

Josephine Lombardo and Jerry Vale
(Howard Johns Collection)

Howard Keel in *Dallas*
(Backlot Books & Movie Posters)

Connie Stevens bares all
(Larry Edmunds Bookshop)

Cher (Movie Market)

Harold Kress
(*Palm Springs Life*)

Rita Rudner
(Howard Johns Collection)

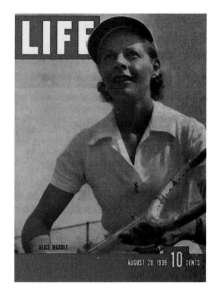

Alice Marble
(Howard Johns Collection)

Peter Marshall
(Backlot Books & Movie Posters)

Rochelle
Hudson
(Backlot
Books &
Movie
Posters)

The house
where
Hudson died
(Craig
De Sedle)

Black Dahlia Murder Investigator Dies
Ex-LAPD Sergeant Harry Hansen Was 80; Case Still Unsolved

Harry Hansen
of the LAPD
(Howard Johns
Collection)

Elizabeth Short's body (Howard Johns Collection)

Brian Donlevy (Backlot
Books & Movie Posters)

Clifford Henderson and Marian Marsh (*Palm Springs Life*)

Ralph Waite
(*Palm Springs Life*)

Waite's home (Craig De Sedle)

John Ford (Movie Market)

Anne Francis
(Howard Johns Collection)

James MacArthur and wife at a luau
(Hollywood Memories)

William Frye
(Larry Edmunds Bookshop)

Marrakesh
Country
Club (Craig
De Sedle)

"H.B" Haggerty
(Backlot Books & Movie Posters)

Carson Daly
(Howard Johns Collection)

Goldie Hawn
and Kurt Russell
(Movie Market)

Ray Ryan and
William Holden
(*Palm Springs Life*)

Gable's home (Becker & Becker Realty)

Clark Gable (Movie Market)

Fred and Virginia Waring (*Palm Springs Life*)

Rock Hudson near death
(Cinema Collectors)

Johnny Mann (*Palm Springs Life*)

Diahann Carroll and Vic Damone
(*Palm Springs Life*)

Ellen Drew (Larry Edmunds Bookshop)

Harry Oliver
(Palm Springs Historical Society)

Joanna Moore
(Backlot Books & Movie Posters)

Jack Jones (*Palm Springs Life*)

William and Meredith Asher
(*Palm Springs Life*)

Julia Roberts (Larry Edmunds Bookshop)

Dorothy Hamill (*Palm Springs Life*)

Joan Kroc
(Howard Johns Collection)

Bob Cummings
(Backlot Books & Movie Posters)

Lee Iacocca (Larry Edmunds Bookshop)

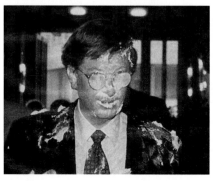

Bill Gates gets a pie in the face (CNN)

Ike and JFK (Palm Springs Historical Society)

John Conte
(Larry Edmunds
Bookshop)

LBJ and Ike (*Palm Springs Life*)

Randolph and Pat Scott
(Palm Springs Historical Society)

Anthony Accardo ran the Mafia
(Howard Johns Collection)

Merle Oberon
(Larry Edmunds Bookshop)

Oliver Stone in court (CBS)

Arthur Lake as Dagwood Bumstead
(Backlot Books & Movie Posters)

La Quinta Hotel (Howard Johns Collection)

Frank Capra (*Palm Springs Life*)

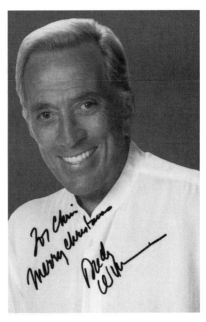

Andy Williams
(Howard Johns Collection)

Glenn Davis (Celebrity Books)

Pierre Cossette (*Palm Springs Life*)

Merv Griffin with Eva Gabor and her mother Jolie (*Palm Springs Life*)

Arnold Palmer (*Palm Springs Life*)

Cochran and Amelia Earhart (Howard Johns Collection)

Jackie Cochran
(Backlot Books
& Movie Posters)

Cochran's home today (Craig De Sedle)

Paul Genge and Bill Hickman (right) in *Bullitt* (Hollywood Memories)

General Patton (Backlot Books & Movie Posters)

Patton's tanks in the desert (Craig De Sedle)

James Dean (Howard Johns Collection)

William Devane
(Backlot Books & Movie Posters)

Al Adamson's death imitated his
films (Hollywood Memories)

Brian Aherne (Larry Edmunds Bookshop)

off was Sunday, when the actor would go surfing or host a barbecue at his beachfront home. Not surprisingly, his marriages to actress Joyce Bulifant and then to actress Melody Patterson, whom he wed during the show's third season, did not survive the rigorous schedule. Even MacArthur admitted that it was a tough slog, which is why he opted to quit the series before its historic 12-year run was over.

The adopted son of famous show-business parents, MacArthur grew up in a warm and loving household devoted to the arts. His mother was the celebrated stage actress Helen Hayes, the first person ever to win an Oscar, a Tony, an Emmy, and a Grammy Award in competitive categories; she won a second Oscar for Best Supporting Actress as the crafty stowaway in *Airport*. His father was the acclaimed playwright Charles MacArthur, who collaborated with Ben Hecht on several plays, including *The Front Page*, and a number of films. MacArthur and Hecht were twice nominated for Oscars, notably for their screenplay of *Wuthering Heights*.

The MacArthur's two children, James and his sister Mary, both trained in summer stock theater, and James also appeared on "live" television. Tragically, the husky, freckle-faced actor made his film debut as a confused teenager in *The Young Stranger* the same year that his father died of a heart attack. MacArthur went on to play conflicted young men in films such as *The Light in the Forest*, *Kidnapped*, and *Swiss Family Robinson*. He graduated to more mature roles in *The Interns*, *The Bedford Incident*, and *Battle of the Bulge*, a reenactment of a World War II military campaign.

Although much fuss was made over Jack Lord's rampant egotistical behavior during the making of *Hawaii Five-O*, MacArthur managed to escape criticism whenever Lord sparred publicly with journalists and network executives. If he found the shooting schedule demanding, he made up for that by enjoying himself the rest of the year. In his spare time, he scaled the Matterhorn in Europe, climbed Ayers Rock in Australia, and traveled by Land Rover across the deserts and jungles of South Africa.

Following the death of his mother in 1993, MacArthur sold the family's 22-room mansion in Nyack, New York, to talk-show host and comedienne Rosie O'Donnell for $770,000, and he moved to Palm Desert with his wife, who is a professional golfer.

■ ■ ■

HE MAY HAVE been a small and unassuming man, but **Lew Landers**, who lived for six years at 73–347 Tamarisk Street, enjoyed a giant reputation as the unofficial "King of Low Budget Horror Films."

Landers began directing one-hour programmers at Universal Pictures under his birth name, Louis Friedlander, calling the shots on fast-paced 1930s serials such as *The Vanishing Shadow, Tailspin Tommy,* and *Rustlers of Red Dog.* His first feature, however, was *The Raven,* a blood-curdling classic starring Boris Karloff and Bela Lugosi, and with that he started a trend. Over the next ten years, he churned out creepy thrillers such as *The Boogie Man Will Get You, The Return of the Vampire, The Mask of Dijon,* and *Inner Sanctum,* which played on people's fears of electric chairs and mental asylums.

Landers also proved equally adept at telling rousing pirate stories and colorful fairy tales, which brought out the kid in him, judging by their imaginative titles: *Law of the Barbary Coast, Davy Crocket—Indian Scout, Last of the Buccaneers, The Magic Carpet, Aladdin and His Lamp,* and *Captain Kidd and the Slave Girl.*

His efficiency and speed made him a natural for TV, where he used to shoot two episodes of *The Adventures of Superman* back-to-back in a single week. He also directed various episodes of such family favorites as *The Cisco Kid, Kit Carson,* and *Rin-Tin-Tin.*

He died in his sleep at the age of 61 in 1962.

■ ■ ■

CINEMATOGRAPHER **WILLIAM H. DANIELS**, one of Hollywood's most distinguished cameramen, photographed an astounding 162 films, from Erich Von Stroheim's silent epic, *Greed,* to *Dinner at Eight, The Glenn Miller Story, Cat on a Hot Tin Roof,* and *Valley of the Dolls.* He resided at 73–363 Goldflower Street.

The white-haired, pink-cheeked Daniels was known as "Garbo's cameraman," because he carefully lit and photographed virtually all her films, including *Mata Hari, Grand Hotel, Queen Christina, Camille,* and *Ninotchka.* He insisted that Garbo's scenes be shot on closed sets with no one in attendance except the director and himself, and Daniels was held in such high esteem that producers acquiesced to his request.

He also photographed ten films starring his friend and associate Frank Sinatra, among them *Ocean's Eleven, Robin and the 7 Hoods,* and *Von Ryan's Express,* which necessitated arduous location shooting in the Italian Alps. Sinatra was said to be very sensitive about his physical appearance, in particular his receding hairline and deep facial scars (the result of a surgeon's forceps when the singer was born), and through careful lighting and photography, Daniels camouflaged these flaws.

Daniels won an Oscar for Best Cinematography for his hundedth film, *The Naked City,* which was shot on the streets of New York. He died in 1970 at the age of 69.

■ ■ ■

HOLLYWOOD SONGWRITER **MORT Greene** penned sheets of lyrics for more than 35 films, but he is probably best remembered as the man who created the humorous musical theme for *Leave It to Beaver,* the classic TV sitcom that starred Barbara Billingsley, Hugh Beaumont, Tony Dow, and Jerry Mathers as "the Beaver."

Greene began his career as a lyricist of patriotic songs and romantic ballads, often teaming up with composer Harry Revel to work on films such as *Moonlight Masquerade, Four Jacks and a Jill,* and *The Big Street.* Their composition "There's a Breeze on Lake Louise," from the George Murphy musical *The Mayor of 44th Street,* was nominated for an Oscar for Best Song.

Greene also collaborated with the composer Leigh Harline, and together they wrote the title songs for three successful postwar melodramas: *From This Day Forward,* starring Joan Fontaine; *Nocturne,* with George Raft; and *The Velvet Touch,* featuring Rosalind Russell. In addition to writing music, Greene contributed comedy scripts for *The Red Skelton Show,* writing "The Silent Spot," a regular segment of pantomime that Skelton performed at the end of his weekly show. He was also the producer of *My Hero,* starring Robert Cummings, and worked with several Las Vegas acts.

A desert resident since 1983, Greene resided at 72–890 Deer Grass Drive, where his *cordon bleu* cooking skills were recognized by *Sunset* magazine, in which he was named Chef of the West five times. He died in 1992 at the age of 80.

■ ■ ■

MARRAKESH COUNTRY CLUB was developed by Johnny Dawson, whose other projects included Seven Lakes and the Eldorado and Thunderbird Country Clubs. Their elegant fairway homes were designed by Los Angeles architect John Elgin Woolf, who was renowned for the Hollywood Regency–style residences of actors such as Loretta Young, Cary Grant, and Myrna Loy.

It was certainly an appropriate address for veteran Hollywood production designer and art director **Henry Bumstead**, who once resided at 47–037 Marrakesh Drive.

This vigorous artisan entered the movie business in 1937 by apprenticing as a draftsman to the German-born art director Hans Dreier. During his long career he won two Oscars for Best Art Direction, for his authentic re-creation of rural Alabama in *To Kill a Mockingbird* and then for bustling 1930s Chicago in *The Sting*. He also collaborated on eleven films with Clint Eastwood, including *Unforgiven, Midnight in the Garden of Good and Evil, Space Cowboys, Mystic River,* and *Million Dollar Baby*.

Wherever possible, Bumstead tried to convince moviegoers that what they are seeing is real, whether it's a frontier-style saloon, a hospital emergency room, or the flight deck of a NASA space shuttle. Most of his settings, however, were crafted from balsa wood and plaster lathe on the back lots of Paramount, Universal, and, most recently, Warner Bros., where he has lent his stylish touches to more than 100 films. A highpoint at these studios: four fruitful collaborations with legendary director Alfred Hitchcock, including *The Man Who Knew Too Much* and *Vertigo*. The low point: six comedies with Dean Martin and Jerry Lewis.

A highly disciplined craftsman, Bumstead lamented the absence of modern-day glamour in an industry that's become all business and no show. But he acknowledged that computer graphics have made his job a lot easier. "A picture like [Hitchcock's] *The Birds* would now be a cinch to make, and it would be an altogether different type of picture," he said. He died of prostate cancer at the age of 91 in 2006.

■ ■ ■

WHEN FILM CRITICS speak of beautiful blondes they invariably mention Marilyn Monroe, Kim Novak, Jayne Mansfield, and Carroll Baker. Rarely do they talk about the talents of sultry actress **Anne Francis**, who graced many movies and TV series with her elegance and poise.

This talented actress had both beauty and brains, as she tried very hard to convey throughout her ingénue roles in *Elopement, Lydia Bailey,* and *Dreamboat,* made while under contract to 20th Century-Fox. But this was the era of publicity shots of scantily-clad girls in bathing suits, and Anne's trim physique kept getting noticed more than her IQ.

So she switched to MGM, where for a while she was cast in dramatic roles in serious films: *Bad Day at Black Rock,* starring Spencer Tracy; *The Blackboard Jungle,* with Glenn Ford; and the science fiction classic *Forbidden Planet*—one of her most popular films—in which she played opposite Walter Pidgeon, Leslie Nielsen, and Robby the Robot.

Still, frustrated by the lack of challenging roles, Francis sought to change her image in her next film, *Girl of the Night,* about a prostitute who undergoes psychoanalysis. "It was a character study and the most demanding role I've ever done," she stated.

But, producers continued to look at this excellent actress and see a sex symbol. At the height of the James Bond craze, Francis donned black leather and stiletto heels to play the role of *Honey West,* a female detective with a pet ocelot, a skill for judo, and an arsenal of gadgets that included a radio transmitter disguised as lipstick. The campy TV series became an instant hit with baby boomers.

A regular visitor to Palm Springs, she found herself in the Indian Canyons and at various locations along Highway 74, making a high concept thriller about germ warfare called *The Satan Bug,* with George Maharis. The locations were not far from the site of Francis's future Marrakesh Country Club home at 47–464 Maroc Circle, where one day she would plant portulacas and zinnias and watch hummingbirds drinking from the feeders on her property.

There just were precious few good films. Her experience making *Funny Girl,* a musical based on the life of Fanny Brice, in which Barbra Streisand re-created her star-making Broadway role, was the epitome of Hollywood nepotism and back-biting. Francis, who was fourth billed as Ziegfeld Follies dancer Georgia James, watched in horror as her part was cut down to almost a walk-on, allegedly because her scenes competed with Streisand's for audience sympathy. The unfair treatment resulted in

Francis reportedly filing a breach-of-contract lawsuit against Columbia Pictures. "The flashy role, along with the drunk scenes (which hit the editor's floor) pretty much cinched the prospect of a supporting nomination with the Academy that year," the bitterly disappointed actress stated in an open letter to Streisand that was published in 2002.

Today, Francis is philosophical about the loss. At the time, however, the intense animosity and rivalry between the two headstrong actresses could have started a forest fire. The hot embers of their dispute left Streisand, who won the Oscar for Best Actress, feeling victorious, while Francis, who was left empty-handed, felt victimized.

■ ■ ■

HOLLYWOOD BON VIVANT **Armand Deutsch**, who survived a childhood murder plot to become a well-known movie producer and confidant to some of the nation's top actors and politicians, lived in the same club at 47–466 Maroc Circle.

The oldest grandson of Julius Rosenwald, the chairman of Sears, Roebuck & Company, Deutsch used his heavy-duty social caché to barnstorm his way into a film career. Among his producing credits were the Western *Ambush*, starring Robert Taylor; *Carbine Williams,* starring James Stewart; and a romantic adventure called *Green Fire* that starred Grace Kelly.

As a precocious 11-year-old, Deutsch was selected to be the original kidnap victim of thrill-seeking murderers Nathan Leopold and Richard Loeb, on May 21, 1924. But when they were unable to abduct him, another wealthy schoolboy was snatched and later killed. Deutsch dined out on the story for years, but preferred to count his blessings rather than dwell on the sordid details of the murder.

His reputation as a ladies' man was chiefly derived from his two showbiz marriages, to Broadway musical comedy star Benay Venuta, with whom he fathered two children, and Harriet Berk Simon, the young widow of film executive S. Sylvan Simon, who produced the snappy comedy *Born Yesterday.*

Deutsch's classy nature and easy affability made him a fixture at Hollywood dinner tables. He befriended songwriter Frank Loesser, sponsored filmmaker Stanley Kramer, and enjoyed the hospitality of Frank Sinatra, but never criticized him. "Ardie" as he was often called, was part of the inner circle that entertained and endorsed the political career of Ronald Reagan.

But if Deutsch, a one-time Democrat, harbored any political ambitions, he preferred to keep them to himself. He shared a box at Dodger Stadium with Jack Benny and then with Walter Matthau, traveled the world with publisher Bennett Cerf, lunched regularly with director Billy Wilder, and had dinner every Christmas for years in the Beverly Hills home of James Stewart.

Ultimately, his taste for the finer things in life precluded him from undertaking any serious involvements; he was happiest in a tuxedo at cocktail parties telling stories over a tumbler of Chivas Regal. Deutsch succumbed to pneumonia in 2005, at the age of 92; his wife, Harriet, died of complications from a stroke at the age of 89, three weeks later.

■ ■ ■

HIS NAME SOUNDED British, but he wasn't. **Rowland V. Lee** was a stage-trained actor from Ohio, who followed his dream of becoming a Hollywood director. During the era of silent films and into the period of the first talkies, Lee showed great versatility, covering almost every genre, from romantic melodramas to musicals, Westerns to horror films.

His most entertaining work was steeped in the classics and often involved historical reenactments. Strongly influenced by the German expressionist style, he copied it with Gothic flair in dark and forbidding tales such as *Zoo in Budapest* and *Son of Frankenstein,* which starred Boris Karloff in his third and final outing as the monster.

Seeking autonomy, Lee frequently doubled as his own producer, memorably in the 1935 version of *The Three Musketeers,* and in *Service de Luxe* and *Tower of London*—another of his macabre stories—in which he got to direct two of his favorite actors, the great Karloff and Vincent Price. But he was at his popular best with swashbucklers like *The Count of Monte Cristo* and *Captain Kidd,* a stirring depiction of the pirate legend.

After a long period of inactivity, Lee attempted a major comeback in 1959 with *The Big Fisherman,* a grandiose adaptation of a book by religious scholar Lloyd C. Douglas, about the life of Saint Peter (played by Howard Keel). But the film's limited production values, a largely uninspired cast, and the huge competition from another biblical epic, *Ben-Hur*, which had been released the same year, brought the curtain down on Lee. His final residence was 47–047 Kashbar Drive; he died at the age of 84 in 1975.

■ ■ ■

VETERAN FILM AND TV producer **William Frye** brought a touch of old-style Hollywood glamour back to the movie business with his assemblage of geriatric stars, namely Gloria Swanson, James Stewart, and Olivia de Havilland, whom he gathered together in the harrowing aviation calamities *Airport 1975* and *Airport '77*.

Frye's ability to sweet-talk former clients and friends such as Swanson, Myrna Loy, Dana Andrews, and Joseph Cotten into being pummeled by wind and drenched in water—all in the name of entertainment (if not art)—says a lot about his powers of persuasion. The frantic results, already ripe for parody when these films were produced, have since taken on a mythic quality as classic examples of "they-don't-make-movies-like-that-anymore."

Twenty years on, however, those stars were a distant memory, and Frye and his assistant producer and longtime partner, James Wharton, packed their bags and moved to Ironwood Country Club, where they bought a two-bedroom home at 49–215 Quercus Lane.

A former MCA talent agent, Frye had worked with the likes of Cary Grant, Irene Dunne, and Ronald Colman, whom he befriended, both on radio and TV. He produced two tongue-in-cheek "spiritual" comedies starring Rosalind Russell in a nun's habit, *The Trouble with Angels* and *Where Angels Go, Trouble Follows*, both of which have since developed a cult gay and lesbian following. Frye then hit upon the idea of hiring his over-the-hill buddies for a series of movies of the week about various people in jeopardy. The concept was a good one and led to his being anointed by Universal vice president Jennings Lang to take over as the producer of the *Airport* movie franchise. The promotion made Frye a kind of corporate combatant against rival filmmaker Irwin Allen, who had been crowned Master of Disaster for filming unparalleled feats of heroism aboard an upturned ocean liner *(The Poseidon Adventure)* and atop a burning skyscraper *(The Towering Inferno)*.

The second and third *Airport* installments were rushed into production to capitalize on the first film's $80-million gross. With these two sequels—one set in the air, the other in the ocean—Frye reached his apotheosis as the Master of Camp. After all, who else could have envisioned granite-jawed Charlton Heston and nervy Jack Lemmon as pilots? Or buxom Brenda Vaccaro and cross-eyed Karen Black as stewardesses?

But while some stars jumped at the opportunity to be drowned or roasted alive, others balked at such distasteful theatrics, as Frye learned the hard way when he produced *Raise the Titanic!* A $36-million leviathan, minus Frye's usual coterie of senior citizens, it sank like a stone at the box office. Its failure is one reason why stars like Cary Grant and Irene Dunne took early retirement; they would never have condescended to appear in such motley disaster films.

As a kind of consolation prize, Grant gave Frye two decoupage lamps, and Colman (who had already played a memorable airplane crash scene in *Lost Horizon*) offered him an ornamental Kuan Yin statue, both of which now proudly reside in Frye's home.

■ ■ ■

SPEAKING OF DISASTER, **Jennings Lang**, the man who authorized the *Airport* movies, spent the final decade of his life suffering from the aftermath of a paralyzing stroke, under a doctor's care in Palm Desert.

Lang had a big hand in creating a disaster epic that nearly leveled the city of Los Angeles. The film was *Earthquake*, one of those watch-them-die movies where some of Hollywood's biggest stars of yesteryear grimace in the face of horrible tragedy, this one a .10 magnitude tremor that strikes the overpopulated city in broad daylight, sending thousands of screaming extras and tumbling stuntmen fleeing for their lives.

"If you throw the pills in the toilet, you might at least flush it," Charlton Heston tells his dissipated wife, Ava Gardner, a few seconds before things start rattling.

Like Frye, Lang had also come up through the ranks of MCA, which had a stranglehold on talent. His instinct for moneymaking was right on the nose; *Earthquake* was a huge success, grossing almost as much bling as *Airport* and winning Oscars for Best Sound and Best Visual Effects. Lang knew he was onto a good thing and kept trying to make lightning strike twice. But his mania for costly remakes and cheap sequels proved to be burdensome, and he was eventually done in by his own cleverness, along with a strong desire to live life on the edge. The man simply loved to court danger.

Back in 1951, twelve days before Christmas, he had taken a bullet in the right testicle from producer Walter Wanger, who had been spying on the dapper young agent and discovered him shacking up in a hotel apartment with Wanger's actress-wife, Joan Bennett. The producer pulled a .38 revolver and ambushed both of them in the MCA parking lot.

Lang's first wife, Pamela Friedheim, nursed him back to health after the shooting but died from an overdose of sleeping pills five days before her forty-first birthday. Lang's second wife, band singer Monica Lewis, was made of stronger stuff. The first singer to record the song "Put the Blame on Mame," she had been a well-known cabaret performer and was also the animated voice of the Chiquita banana lady for 14 years. Lewis demanded and got roles in her husband's movies: *Charley Varrick, Earthquake, Airport '77, Rollercoaster,* and *The Concorde: Airport '79.*

That last film had also been written by her overzealous producer-husband, and it wasn't good. Nor were subsequent enterprises, for Lang continued dipping into the evaporating well of his imagination with mind-blowingly bad films like *Little Miss Marker* and *The Sting II.*

Thankfully Lang never got a chance to make another movie. He died at Manor Care Nursing Home, Palm Desert, in 1996, one day after his eighty-first birthday.

■ ■ ■

STRADDLING THE MONOLITHIC rocky outcrops that rise above State Highway 74 in Palm Desert is the entrance to Santa Rosa & San Jacinto Mountains National Monument. This scenic route, descriptively labeled on tourist maps as the Pines-to-Palms Highway, takes visitors through thousands of acres of high country, including nearby Anza, where the late Red Skelton maintained his ranch and art studio.

Sharp-eyed movie fans will recognize the two-lane road on which Elvis Presley, a part-time desert resident, drove a Model-T Ford on his way to the village of Idyllwild in the boxing saga *Kid Galahad.* It is one of many famous scenes that have been filmed here. In the heat of July

1962, for instance, five 1948 Chevrolets were pushed off Highway 74 for the opening sequence of *It's a Mad, Mad, Mad, Mad World*. In that remarkable episode, Jimmy Durante crashes his car and "kicks the bucket," sending Milton Berle, Sid Caesar, Buddy Hackett, Mickey Rooney, Phil Silvers, and Jonathan Winters on the greatest treasure hunt in movie history.

Five months later, Durante was arrested in Chicago when his erratic driving caused a real three-car collision on a busy expressway. He was charged with having no driver's license, driving too close to another vehicle, and damaging city property.

Highway 74's precarious turnouts have also appeared in several other noteworthy films. In 1965, special agent George Maharis combed the nearby roadside for a deadly toxin in *The Satan Bug*. Thirty years on, retired cop Edward James Olmos followed Sean Young in a dangerous car chase along the same highway in the suspense thriller *Mirage*.

■ ■ ■

RUDY GALINDO, the first openly gay Mexican-American figure skater, whose sexual frankness helped other gay athletes gain acceptance and turned him into a poster boy for gay sports heroes, spent several warm winters with his dogs and cats at 73–271 Riata Trail.

In 1996, the smiling, athletic Galindo became the first Latino to win a gold medal at the National Figure Skating Championships. That same year he also took home a bronze medal at the World Figure Skating Championships.

Galindo's openness about his homosexuality earned him both notoriety and acclaim. He appeared on such top-rated TV sitcoms as *Will & Grace* and did a weeklong stint as a contestant on the game show *Family Feud*. His brilliant exhibition skating, for which he wore elaborate costumes, waved rainbow-colored flags, and performed dramatic pirouettes to the disco music of the Village People, drew sellout crowds. Critics have applauded his intricate skating maneuvers, which involve elaborate, precisely timed multiple spins, as well as varied leg positions that are unmatched among current professional male skaters.

In addition to holding national titles in singles skating he also won two awards in pairs, most notably with 1992 Olympic champion Kristi Yamaguchi. They performed a difficult side-by-side triple-flip jump sequence that brought audiences to their feet.

In 2000, Galindo contracted pneumonia and tested positive for HIV, which had already claimed two of his coaches and a brother, George, who died of AIDS. He told *USA Today,* "I took care of my brother and saw every day what he went through, and that was a nightmare, although I knew he didn't take care of himself. And I think of that sometimes, but then I tell myself that it's different now, and the medicine is better and that I am very different from my brother. Still, you don't think it's going to happen to you, and now it has."

Neither the losses nor his own affliction have dampened his love of performing. After regulating his health, he returned to a national tour of *Champions on Ice.* He developed hip problems that required a major operation to replace both hips with ceramic implants, but the 36-year-old skating star made a complete recovery and was soon on the ice again, performing his famous triple jumps.

In 2004, Galindo toured in the successful musical extravaganza *Broadway on Ice* with Olympic figure-skating gold medalist Oksana Baiul and Emmy Award-winning entertainer Leslie Uggams. He now resides in Reno, Nevada.

■ ■ ■

AMID THIS COLONY of artists and athletes lived a man whose normal appearance belied his provocative reputation as a first-class pervert. His friendly basset-hound face and jug-handle ears made him look like an average Joe to the neighbors. Only a few select visitors to the home of the writer, producer, and director **Russ Meyer,** at 72–550 Sundown Lane, knew of this man's uncontrollable fetish for women's gigantic breasts.

Meyer was one of the top glamour photographers of the 1950s; he lit and photographed thousands of half-naked strippers and actresses whose big bosoms gave him an instant hard-on as he peered through the camera lens. Anita Ekberg, Joan Collins, Lili St. Cyr, Mamie Van Doren, Gina Lollobrigida, Barbara Eden, and Jayne Mansfield—these were only some of the women whom he posed provocatively.

Meyer's erotic fantasies, in which he imagined he was being smothered by monster-sized bosoms, fueled his total obsession with the female anatomy. It wasn't long before he escaped from his darkroom and began to cruise the streets of San Francisco and Los Angeles with a movie camera, looking for participants willing to show off their pendulous assets. The results were a shocking progression of cheaply made skin flicks. Beginning with *The Immoral Mr. Teas,* Meyer portrayed women as sexual aggressors and men as their helpless victims, all-too-frequently devoured by these lusty beasts. The titles alone served as a warning: *Eroticon, Eve and the Handyman, Naked Gals of the Golden West,* and *Europe in the Raw.*

Meyer's stag films evolved during the same era of sexual repression that produced another dedicated breast fetishist, Hugh Hefner, who launched *Playboy* magazine in 1953. Hefner stirred up controversy by selling centerfolds; Meyer needled his critics by filming buxom housewives and waitresses jiggling their boobs or exposing their derrières.

What set Meyer apart from other pornographers, however, was his flashy camera style, which combined fast cutting, loud music, and silly narration—a heady mixture that resembled obscene parody. Many of these films featured seminude women climbing oil rigs, lying on top of Cadillacs, and dancing provocatively near railroad tracks.

For *Motor Psycho!*—a tale of sexual revenge—Meyer took his overheated cast and crew to Blythe, on the California-Arizona border. According to biographer Jimmy McDonough, "Meyer charged around the desert like a pirate, a cigar in his mouth and a .45 on his hip." For *Mondo Topless,* he shot nude footage of busty stripper Darlene Gray frugging in the wilderness beneath the Chocolate Mountains near Indio.

This fanatical filmmaker's salacious influence extended far beyond the raincoat brigade that guaranteed Meyer strong ticket sales; in subsequent decades his movies were embraced by university students and devoted cineastes who reveled in his adolescent debauchery. Two of Meyer's prominent films have become a part of the music lexicon. A grunge rock band took the title of the obscene backwoods drama *Mudhoney!* for their group's suggestive name. The violence-filled *Faster Pussycat! Kill! Kill!* inspired the sleazy Hollywood metal band Faster Pussycat, which had a Top 40 single called "House of Pain."

"I love to put sex in outrageous situations. Up a tree. In a canoe.

Behind a waterfall," proclaimed Meyer, who was dubbed King Leer for his crass exploitation of unconventional lovemaking in such R-rated drive-in favorites as *Vixen* and *Cherry Harry and Raquel.* "Screwing under tremendous odds strikes me as both erotic and funny."

At least one important film critic came to Meyer's defense when he was under heavy attack from politicians and feminists. "If there was an auteur working in American commercial film-making during the 1960s—a man totally in control of every aspect of his work—that had to be Meyer," said Roger Ebert, who co-authored Meyer's preposterous morality play, *Beyond the Valley of the Dolls.*

This kinky, highly profitable 1970 sequel to the Susan Hayward film *Valley of the Dolls* helped stave off 20th Century-Fox's angry creditors, following a string of flops at the renowned studio. The trashy movie also ushered in a new era of permissive cinema involving lesbianism, homosexuality, and transvestism. Unfortunately for Meyer, he never again enjoyed such gushing success and spent the next three decades trying to reclaim his past glory. He divided his retirement between a house in the Hollywood Hills and Palm Desert, where he shared his bed with a hugely endowed stripper named Melissa Mounds, whom he had first met in 1988 and whose enormous breast implants he generously paid for.

Here, for ten years, surrounded by walls covered with movie posters and tables spilling over with film equipment, Meyer got drunk on cheap booze and carried on with his mistress while taking photographs of her in the nude. Mounds wasn't the only big-time stripper Meyer fondled in this house. He also entertained oversized adult-film performers such as Kitten Natividad and Pandora Peaks, who had a brief role in the Demi Moore film *Striptease.*

In 1998, police were called to Meyer's home, where they found an intoxicated Mounds sitting outside by the swimming pool with a loaded gun. She informed the two officers that Meyer had threatened her with a weapon from his private stash and then fled the house in his GMC Suburban. One year later, when Meyer refused to give the inflated star the money to buy a truck and a mobile home, Mounds clobbered him, sending Meyer to the hospital and landing her in court. She was charged with three counts of domestic violence and sentenced to 60 days in jail.

When their relationship ended, Meyer gave her the house where they had fornicated as a farewell gift. Mounds sold the three-bedroom home for $500,000 in 2000, the same year Meyer published his exhaustive 1,213-page autobiography titled *A Clean Breast*.

Throughout his life, Meyer always feared insanity. He was petrified he would end up in a psychiatric hospital like his mother and sister, both of whom had been institutionalized. His fear almost became a reality when Meyer was legally declared to be suffering from dementia, and in 2000, following an investigation by the California Department of Social Services, a conservator was appointed to manage Meyer's business and personal affairs. But in 2004 he died at his Hollywood Hills home of complications from pneumonia. He was 82.

■ ■ ■

GRAMOPHONE SINGER **IRVING Kaufman** was one of the most prolific recording artists of the twentieth century. His clear tenor voice was heard on more than 6,000 acetate recordings for major record companies such as Edison, Columbia, Victor, Brunswick, and Aoelian, as well as hundreds of smaller labels.

His specialty was crooning the love songs and dance numbers that were all the rage early in the jazz era, when discs were made acoustically, with the performers singing directly into a horn without the use of a microphone. Kaufman's melodious tones were ideally suited to this simple device, because he could project his voice and make all the words audible to listeners. Between 1914 and 1930, he was in such high demand singing popular songs under his own name that he resorted to using pseudonyms to avoid saturating the market. Thus many of his songs were credited to fictitious singers such as Frank Harris, Noel Taylor, George Beaver, and Pete Killeen. "I had so many different voices that half of the time my wife would say, 'Who are you going to be today?' I would say, 'I won't know until I get to the studio.'"

Although Kaufman was never associated with one particular song, his records were big sellers. They included the 1927 hit "My Dream of the Big Parade," about World War I, and "Since Movies Learned to Talk," which laments the fate of stars of the silent screen. Another popular favorite was his tearful recording of "Sonny Boy," which outsold Al Jolson's version ten to one. Alas, Kaufman was paid a flat fee each time he recorded and never earned any royalties. In the 1930s, Kaufman made fewer records but worked regularly in radio, a medium that took full advantage of his talent for changing voices and imitating dialects. He was less in demand after studios converted to electronic recording.

Kaufman retired in 1949 following a heart attack, and by the early 1960s he and his wife, professional pianist Belle Brooks, became desert residents, first in Palm Springs, then Rancho Mirage, and finally in Indian Springs Mobile Home Park at 49–305 Highway 74. He died in Indio in 1976, one month before his eighty-sixth birthday.

■ ■ ■

CHAMPIONSHIP WRESTLER **DON "Hard Boiled" Haggerty**, who was instantly recognizable by his shiny bald head, handlebar mustache, and ever-present grin, which could convey friendship or anger, used to live at 48–959 Sunny Summit Lane (Indian Hills).

A gifted athlete, he played professional football under his real name, Donald Stansauk, for both the Green Bay Packers and Detroit Lions, and at the time was the largest player in the NFL. He became known as "Hard-Boiled" Haggerty when he entered Pro Wrestling during the 1950s and 1960s—taking advantage of his charisma and stage presence, the promoters made him a villain in the wrestling arena. Don quickly gained a reputation as one of the toughest wrestlers in the world, drawing international crowds that became enthralled by his antics both in and out of the ring. He was United States Heavyweight Champion and held several World Tag Team titles.

Haggerty began his acting career in the 1960s and made his movie debut as one of the gold miners in *Paint Your Wagon*, starring Clint Eastwood and Lee Marvin. He went on to make 22 motion pictures, more than 100 TV shows, and 35 commercials. Among his memorable film roles was the bad-tempered pool player told by off-duty policeman George Kennedy that "the shot didn't count," after a violent tremor shook a downtown Los Angeles bar in *Earthquake*.

But it was growling and flexing his muscles that got Haggerty the most attention. He played the menacing wrestler Billy Kiss, who slugs it out with Jackie Chan in *The Big Brawl* (the Hong Kong martial arts star's first English-speaking film). Haggerty's other bare-chested roles include Mr. Clean in the wrestling drama *Mad Bull,* with Alex Karras, and Captain Nemo in the wrestling comedy *The One and Only,* opposite Henry Winkler.

Haggerty was inducted into the Stuntmen's Hall of Fame and was the winner of the "Iron" Mike Mazurki Award (given in honor of the late actor and wrestler) from the Cauliflower Alley Club, the association of retired wrestlers and boxers. In 2003, he suffered a broken neck, and he died from a series of strokes the following year, at the age of 78.

■ ■ ■

"MOST REQUESTED" MULTIMEDIA personality **Carson Daly** knows he always has a comfortable bed ready for him whenever he drops in to visit his mother, Patti Daly, and his stepfather, Richard Caruso, in their four-bedroom home at 72–970 Carriage Trail.

Carson, voted the Sexiest Broadcaster in America by *People* magazine, is the former host of MTV's *Total Request Live,* where he introduced music videos from Times Square while being mobbed by clamoring teenage fans. The news-making video deejay, or veejay, began his career behind the microphone at radio stations in Palm Springs, San Diego, and Los Angeles. Currently, however, he hosts the late night talk show *Last Call* on NBC, which is less stressful but still leaves him open to occasional outbursts from swooning women in the audience.

Daly takes it all in his stride. The brown-haired, blue-eyed broadcaster dated *Party of Five* TV star Jennifer Love Hewitt for two years, until her mushrooming movie fame and his busy work schedule put an end to their romance. Then he was linked to *American Pie* actress Tara Reid, but the couple broke off their engagement after one year.

Carson has also had to be careful that he doesn't leave his laundry unattended. A recent burglary of his home resulted in an obsessed fan stealing clothes, awards, and photographs which soon were posted for sale on eBay. Was it a childish prank or a publicity stunt? It seems some people don't know when to leave a person alone.

■ ■ ■

ACTRESS **GOLDIE HAWN** started out as the zany, ding-ding blonde with the high-pitched giggle who chimed "Sock it to me!" on the award-winning TV comedy show *Rowan & Martin's Laugh-In*. Hawn had male viewers drooling over her painted, half-nude body as she gyrated to disco music while reading profane cue cards that made her hysterical with laughter.

This talented go-go dancer always had trouble being taken seriously as a performer. The truth was that she hated dancing and especially despised the demeaning behavior of patrons who saw her at bars and strip clubs in New York and Las Vegas. One man exposed himself and another masturbated in front of her while she was onstage. So she fled to Los Angeles, only to be employed as a chorus girl and specialty dancer in television variety specials.

Then fate intervened and she joined the original cast of *Laugh-In* with Lily Tomlin, Henry Gibson, and Ruth Buzzi. Goldie's flair landed her some acting auditions, and she was cast in her first major film, *Cactus Flower*, as the mistress of Walter Matthau. To her complete surprise, she won an Oscar for Best Supporting Actress. It was the ticket to stardom that Hawn had always dreamed about, and she rode the bus all the way to the last stop.

Still, no matter how hard moviegoers laughed at her antics in side-splitting films such as *Shampoo*, *Foul Play*, and *Private Benjamin*, she was far from happy in real life. Her choreographer-husband Gus Trikonis was chronically unemployed and, tired of being the breadwinner, Hawn divorced him and married actor-musician Bill Hudson, with whom she had a son, Oliver, and a daughter, Kate. Then *he* grew jealous of her fame, and they divorced; he later sued her for alimony.

Bitter and resentful, Goldie vowed never to marry again. She threw herself into more heartwarming comedies: *Seems Like Old Times*, *Best Friends,* and *Protocol*. In between, she dated French actor Yves Renier, Chevy Chase, and Tom Selleck. It wasn't until she was teamed with former Walt Disney child star **Kurt Russell** in *Swing Shift* that Hawn realized she had found the perfect match. Russell, who is six years younger, had matured from a gangly teenager into a chunky leading man with an impish grin, and he literally swept her off her feet.

On their first date, he took her to the Playboy Club and booked a hotel room where they stayed overnight in 1983. Goldie compared their lovemaking to a wildfire, and they were soon cohabiting at her Pacific Palisades home, where she regularly gave herself pregnancy tests. To celebrate their commitment to each other, Goldie announced she had conceived a son named Wyatt, who was born in 1986.

Hawn insisted that Russell give up smoking, and he joined an aerobics class to stay in shape. His new, slimmer look helped foster his reputation as a major sex symbol, and to cash in on their newfound popularity, Hawn and Russell co-starred in the raucous boating comedy *Overboard* and combined their two real-life families, including Kurt's son, Boston, from his failed marriage to actress Season Hubley.

After they had become a hot item, the press bombarded Hawn with questions about impending marriage. But the loving couple has stated that they have no intention of exchanging wedding vows, because they don't want to complicate their lives. Russell, however, certainly assumed the role of working dad, starring in the blockbusters *Backdraft*, *Stargate*, *Executive Decision*, and *Breakdown*. Goldie on the other hand became the stay-at-home mom in T-shirt, jeans, and sandals, preparing meals for their four children, two of whom have since embarked on their own acting careers. Hawn seemed content to spend time at their 72-acre ranch at Old Snowmass near Aspen, Colorado, where the family rides horses and ropes cattle. They also own a huge mansion in Vancouver, Canada, and maintain a summer residence in the Muskoka wilderness of Ontario, where Kurt hunts deer, elk, and other game.

But Hawn couldn't stay away from movies for long. Proving she hasn't lost her goofy sense of humor, she starred in *Death Becomes Her*, a comedy about transfiguration, and played an aging actress not unlike herself in *The First Wives Club*. She also poked fun at her nice-girl image in *The Banger Sisters*.

In 2003, Hawn and Russell purchased a luxury four-bedroom Tuscan-style villa with views of the twelfth green at 534 Mesquite Hills in Bighorn Golf Club, where they can occasionally be seen enjoying barbecues.

■ ■ ■

FLASHY PROMOTER **JERRY Weintraub**, who booked sellout concerts for Elvis Presley, Frank Sinatra, Bob Dylan, and Led Zeppelin, and produced the all-star remake of the Rat Pack classic *Ocean's Eleven,* along with its 2004 sequel, *Ocean's Twelve,* currently resides at 632 Pinnacle Crest. Commenting on his new home, where he moved in 2004, Weintraub remarked, "It's a peaceful place to sit and drink my vodka in the evening." This glittering showplace, bought and paid for by the loot he's collected from his top-grossing films, boasts seven bedrooms, 11 bathrooms, a 30-foot waterfall, a bar designed as a facsimile of an English pub, and 35 big screen plasma TVs, so Weintraub can roam his modern castle and never lose sight of football touchdowns or baseball home runs.

Jerry got his start as a film producer when George Bush, Sr., then ambassador to the United Nations, asked him to invite fellow U.N. delegates to a John Denver concert. His wife, singer Jane Morgan, threw a party and invited *M*A*S*H* director Robert Altman, who pitched Weintraub the script for *Nashville.* Intrigued by Altman's offbeat story about the music business and politics, Weintraub decided to make the film. "I take a lot of heat for being a Republican in Hollywood," said the producer, whose conservative views are matched only by his bullish optimism.

He followed that critical success with *Diner,* which helped launch newcomers Kevin Bacon, Mickey Rourke, and Steve Guttenberg, and he revived the career of octogenarian entertainer George Burns in *Oh, God!* His most commercially successful films were *The Karate Kid* and its three sequels. Of course, lumped together with these profitable hits were a few painful misses: the unfunny Barbra Streisand marital farce *All Night Long;* and *The Specialist,* a dull Sylvester Stallone action-thriller. A lame big-screen remake of *The Avengers,* starring Ralph Fiennes and Uma Thurman, also bombed at the box office (deservedly).

Weintraub's biggest embarrassment, however, was *Cruising,* a violent, homophobic film starring Al Pacino as a cop-turned-murderer. The film portrayed gay men in such an unflattering light that it caused widespread protests and inspired several copycat killings. This odious piece of celluloid depravity is noticeably absent from Weintraub's résumé.

■ ■ ■

GLAMOROUS TV FASHION accessory **Mary Hart**, the beaming, relentlessly perky host of *Entertainment Tonight,* which touts itself as "the most-watched entertainment news program in the world," resides at 197 Metate Place in Bighorn Golf Club.

Hart has been dishing the dirt on what's hot in movies, TV, music, and fashion for the past 24 years. During those rapidly changing years, people have demanded a more probing glimpse into the lives of the rich and famous, and that's what *E. T.*, which made its debut in 1981, gives them, in a news format transmitted by satellite every 24 hours to stations around the globe.

It was a move destined to change the face of news reporting and has resulted in this top-rated program becoming the media-savvy cornerstone of American pop culture. Among the show's in-depth cover stories have been exposés of stars' private lives, while other stories have included "first" interviews with Nancy Sinatra after the death of her father, Frank Sinatra; Kirk Douglas during his recovery from a major stroke; and Annette Funicello, who is bravely fighting multiple sclerosis.

But not everybody has enjoyed Hart's verbal gyrations. In 1991, it was reported that a 45-year-old woman suffered an epileptic seizure when she heard Hart chirping away during a broadcast. Think what you may, but this really happened. According to the *New England Journal of Medicine*, the sound of Hart's shrill voice caused the female viewer to experience mild seizures, nausea, and headache. Tests by her doctor established that Hart's unusual voice frequency set off abnormal electrical discharges in the woman's brain. When she stopped watching the show, the seizures stopped. The unusual medical condition has been dubbed Mary Hart Syndrome.

But neither the embarrassed woman nor Hart is laughing. The incident made them both the butt of many jokes and even turned up on an episode of *Seinfeld*, when Cosmo Kramer, played by Michael Richards, collapsed after hearing Hart's voice emanating from his TV.

These days, Hart and her producer-husband Burt Sugarman, who paid $4 million for their 7,000 square-foot home in 2000, are very happy with their newfound lifestyle. They golf, hike, and swim on weekends, with hardly a care in the world. And, for their own peace of mind, they keep the TV turned off.

■ ■ ■

THURSDAY, JULY 23, 1970, began like any other day for bearded Hollywood composer **Leith Stevens**, a six-year resident of Pinyon Crest, where he lived in a two-story chateau in the mountains near Idyllwild, approximately 45 miles from Palm Springs.

A former child prodigy, Stevens was best known for his thrilling and evocative music for science-fiction classics such as *Destination Moon, When Worlds Collide,* and the colossal alien invasion, *War of the Worlds.* One afternoon, he was going over music charts for *Mission: Impossible, The Brady Bunch,* and *The Odd Couple* in his office at Paramount Pictures in Los Angeles when the telephone rang.

"This is Mr. Stevens," he answered, fingering a music cue sheet.

His face suddenly froze and he dropped the music on his desk.

"Oh, my God," he wailed, "this can't be true."

Sadly, it was.

Police informed Stevens that his 59-year-old wife, Elizabeth, had just been killed in a horrific automobile accident on the edge of the San Bernardino National Forest. Apparently she had lost control of her vehicle while traveling on Highway 74, south of Palm Desert. The car tumbled end-over-end down the 150-foot mountainside, crushing her body in a landslide of tangled metal and rocks. Miraculously, their three pet dogs, also inside the car, escaped unhurt.

The distraught composer listened to the police description of the terrible accident. He replaced the phone in its receiver and buzzed his secretary on the intercom to tell her the grim news. He would have to notify friends, relatives, make funeral arrangements; his mind whirled, and he suddenly grew faint, like an electric cord that has been unplugged from its power socket. Stevens struggled for breath. He loosened his tie and staggered toward the office door. Then his legs gave out, and he fell to the floor dead.

The story was splashed across newspapers and TV stations:

SHOCK OF WIFE'S DEATH KILLS COMPOSER
Leith Stevens, 60, dies from heart attack.

Stevens had been nominated for three Oscars for Best Music for *Julie, The Five Pennies,* and *A New Kind of Love.* As head of the music department at Paramount, he was responsible for supplying music for three-and-a-half hours of television each week. This included three regular series, eight specials, and nine pilots. In 1954, he was credited with being the first composer to introduce an entire jazz score in a movie—*The Wild One,* starring Marlon Brando as the leader of a motorcycle gang. That year Stevens also became the founder and first president of the Composers and Lyricists Guild of America. His wife, Elizabeth Stevens, was a native of Australia. She was an outstanding equestrian and kept her quarter horse mare, Princess, at the Smoke Tree Stables.

His was a tragic end to a brilliant musical career, as well as a heart-wrenching dissolution of a marriage that friends said had been made in heaven.

Mob Scene

O N OCTOBER 18, 1977, a pow- erful bomb exploded in the parking lot of the Olympia Health & Beauty Resort in Evansville, Indiana, blowing apart a Mark-V Lincoln Continental. It threw the car's hood 150 feet into the air—higher than a two-story building—rocked neighboring businesses, damaged nearby automobiles, and knocked out power to sections of this town of 122,000 people for more than three hours.

Spa employees braved thick smoke and roaring flames to reach the vehicle's driver and pull his burning body from the tangled wreckage. But he died moments later. Evansville Police Chief David Jackson said the slaying of the man, who always visited the health club twice a week for a two-hour workout, had the "earmarks of a gangland killing." Jackson revealed that several sticks of dynamite had been fastened under the right side of the car, where the 73-year-old man usually sat when his chauffeur and bodyguard drove. That day, however, the man had been alone.

There were no witnesses to the explosion and no immediate suspects.

But the victim provided investigators with plenty of clues, beginning with his name—**Raymond J. Ryan**—and an out-of-town address—84–136 Avenue 44, Bermuda Dunes—which was sixteen miles from Palm Springs. As investigators would later discover, the dead man also maintained ten addresses at home sites in nearby Indian Wells, where he was a property developer. The killing occurred less than one month before Ryan, a multimillionaire investor in oil and real estate, was to appear in a Washington, D.C., court on charges of fraud and tax evasion. The IRS had been trying to collect $6 million in back taxes dating from 1958 to 1965.

Ryan was the son of a Watertown, Wisconsin, general contractor. As a teenager he had drifted south after briefly studying at a local college. Tall and pudgy, with the youthful optimism of a man determined to succeed on his own, he resembled not so much a tycoon-in-the-making as a big, friendly turtle. In the small town of Tyler, Texas, the enterprising Ryan became involved in the oil leasing business with money he had made selling pipe and chewing tobacco. In 1939, he bought an oil lease near Crossville, Illinois, paid $10,000 for two arid fields totaling 100 acres, and borrowed the money to start drilling. Almost immediately, guided by his instinctive hunches, he struck it rich.

Ryan Oil Company, the firm he established in Evansville, drilled more than 1,000 wells in sixteen states and poured out 3,000 barrels a day. Its biggest operations were in Texas, where Ryan became associated with Harold Hunt, Clint Murchison, and other high-risk entrepreneurs. Even the coming of World War II didn't stop this investor. Quite the contrary. Ryan owned a California machine factory that supplied parts for the Air Force, a deal that brought him additional income, which he reinvested in his oil-making enterprises.

It all provided Ryan with the large sums of cash that he needed to indulge his first love: gambling. While drilling oil, he would keep one eye on the gushing derricks and another on a desert road map, which frequently guided him west to the new gambling mecca of Las Vegas, Nevada. There he quickly developed a reputation for being a well-dressed high roller who shelled out thousands of dollars at poker and blackjack, a character profile he did nothing to discourage. There were tales of how he won $243,000 in a gin rummy game while crossing the

Atlantic Ocean and how once, on a single Saturday, he put $50,000 on each of 12 college football games. Ryan never denied the stories. All he wanted to do was gamble, make money, and gamble some more, and given his lucky streak, that seemed easy enough.

From the moment Ryan first arrived in Palm Springs in the mid-1940s, and inhaled the aroma of unsullied land and fresh air, he saw the desert's potential to become America's winter playground. Marveling at the vastness that stretched before him, and yearning to have a piece of it for himself, Ryan paid $1.4 million for the 300-room El Mirador Hotel, a sprawling complex of chandeliered rooms, gardens, and swimming pools that had been converted into Torney General Hospital for the use of convalescent troops during the war.

He spent another $5 million to give the landmark a much-needed facelift, and the remodeled hotel became Ryan's flagship. He threw lavish banquets for foreign dignitaries, business tycoons, and chummy Hollywood stars like Danny Thomas, Red Skelton, and Debbie Reynolds, whom he entertained in his zebra-themed Safari Room. Musicians played bongo drums, while waiters dressed as African slaves served the Hollywood faithful.

"Those were glorious, glamorous years," recalled society maven Hildy Crawford. "I can still see Ray and Lily Pons in red and blue royal robes as they reigned supreme over the fabulous Beaux Arts Ball, which was held each year at El Mirador." It was like a sight from the film *Decameron Nights*. "Louella Parsons wearing ostrich plumes, Nina Anderton dripping diamonds, and other great women of the era were all fixtures at Ray's great festivals."

During the late 1940s, Ryan sensed the time was right to expand into the entertainment industry, so he founded a production company called Screen Associates. In 1948, he reached an agreement with Hollywood agent Abbey Greshler to sign moneymaking clients Dean Martin and Jerry Lewis to a seven-picture deal. Ryan's intention: to make money from the nation's emerging #1 comedy team and set himself up as a film producer.

But Ryan did not count on the interference of Hal Wallis, a crafty independent filmmaker who had already signed the clowning duo to a long-term contract. Further complicating matters, Martin and Lewis were in the midst of forming their own production company, which would effectively split everything three ways. When Screen Associates realized that Martin and Lewis could not possibly deliver what they had foolishly promised, Ryan, who was the godfather of Martin's son, Dino, decided to cash in on the high grosses of the team's third film, *At War with the Army*, and he hit all the parties with lawsuits. Rather than face the cost of litigation, Martin and Lewis gave up their majority interest in the film to Ryan and parted company as wary friends. The boys continued on their profitable way; Ryan picked up some hefty pocket change.

Not all of Ryan's deals ended on such a high note, however. In 1952, Ryan, Chicago mail-order tycoon Ralph Stolkin and Stolkin's father-in-law, Abraham Koolish, formed a syndicate and put up $7 million to buy RKO Radio Pictures from Howard Hughes. But *The Wall Street Journal* broke the news (reportedly planted by Hughes himself) that Ryan and the other buyers were involved with "organized crime, fraudulent mail-order schemes, and big-time gambling." Hughes canceled the deal, and this time it was Ryan who lost out. His syndicate forfeited their $1.5 million down payment, and among other things, the world learned that one of Ryan's business partners was New York Mafia boss Frank Costello. But that was not the kind of setback that deterred Ryan. He may have been considered a fast-talking interloper in New York, but in Palm Springs people treated his money with the utmost respect.

Just as Ryan had wanted to be part of Hollywood, so he yearned to be part of the desert's future. He began buying up land with all the zeal of a bookmaker taking bets on the next horse race. Now, in addition to operating El Mirador, he owned nearly 400 acres of land adjacent to the Palm Springs Airport and acquired large holdings in Indian Wells. But unlike land investors who merely want to turn a quick profit, Ryan intended to cover his grainy sand traps with high-class residential developments. And thus it was that in 1955, Ryan and Ernest Dunlevie built the 18-hole championship Bermuda Dunes Country Club on the outskirts of Indio.

How to attract buyers? In what must have seemed like the public relations ploy of the 1950s, Ryan and Dunlevie gave away a four-bedroom house to actor **Clark Gable** as a way of luring other movie stars to purchase second homes in their brand-new development. Known to be as tight with a dollar as he was with a right hook to the jaw, Gable gladly accepted Ryan's gift of a house that bordered the sixth fairway, and the three men—two developers and a movie star—huddled together for a commemorative photograph as Ryan handed over the keys to 79–842 Ryan Way. "Now everybody, smile!" coached photographers. "No false humility, thank you."

And Gable did smile—dentures and all. His real teeth had rotted years earlier, and he was about to endure that very same fate. Only nobody knew it except him. His doctors had told him to cut down on smoking and drinking, but he had waved them away with large, gnarled, nicotine-stained hands and lit up his tenth Kent cigarette of the morning.

Gable's imbibing of Scotch and brandy was as common a sight as a fifth grader munching an apple during lunch. He started drinking at breakfast and continued through dinner, holding his own while drooling co-stars fell off their barstools or passed out in their dressing rooms. After leaving MGM, which had provided him with a cocoon for 23 years and given him blockbusters such as *Red Dust, Mutiny on the Bounty, San Francisco*, and *Gone with the Wind*, he had branched out on his own, looking older and heavier, but still the undisputed King of Hollywood.

He was not a wealthy man in comparison with other, newer stars; most of his film career had been spent in servitude, signed to a negligible contract. It was calculated that his films grossed $500 million at the box office, but he received none of the profits. Gable's standard weekly rate had been $7,500—barely enough to buy some dame a bag of trinkets, he once complained. So was he frugal? Yes. Frivolous? No. He had wisely invested his meager income in common stock: American Home Products, Bethlehem Steel, Caterpillar Tractor, DuPont, Florida Power and Light, Goodyear Tire, Reynolds Tobacco, Standard Oil. In other words, he was not without money in the event of sudden unemployment.

Besides the offer of a free Bermuda Dunes home, Gable had another reason to smile: he had just married his fifth wife, Kay Williams, a blue-eyed divorcée with the body of a swimsuit model and a net worth of $550,000 (plus a million-dollar trust fund for each of her two children by wealthy third husband Adolph Spreckels, he of the granulated sugar fortune). Kay was so in love with Gable that she couldn't keep her manicured hands off him, and pawed his meaty thighs and buttocks until he was forced to take cold showers.

Gable's impressive sexual endowment was well known in the bedrooms of Hollywood; his agent, Josephine Dillon, had literally gone down on her knees and begged to become his first wife. Joan Crawford, one of his most ardent lovers, wrote in her diary that she could hear the weight of his balls knocking together whenever he walked. Indeed, as late as 1958, when Gable moved into his new home, he was observed wearing specially tailored pants to accommodate both his outsized genitals and expanding girth.

Overweight and with a severe drinking problem, he was by this time subsisting on a diet of broiled steak, tomatoes, and cottage cheese in order to reduce from a bloated 230 pounds to 195. He had become so big, in fact, that he drove a silver-colored Mercedes Benz SC with gull-wing doors that opened upward instead of out, because his weight made it difficult for him to hop in and out of standard vehicles.

And yet he possessed infinite sex appeal. Biographer Lyn Tornabene almost melted at the sight of Gable's elephantine charms on the set of his final film, *The Misfits*. "The pants are cut looser than the jeans worn by most of the other guys around," observed Tornabene of male cast members' attempts to best Gable by not wearing underwear. But Gable was in a class by himself. "Kings don't compete in such games," Tornabene said. "Kings are kings."

By then his complexion was ruddy and covered with unsightly blemishes, his skin was tanned like beaten leather, and his knotty eyebrows were so wiry they had to be plucked with large tweezers to remove the thorny bristles from his brow. But no one, not even Gable, seemed to care that good living had gotten the best of him.

He had already suffered at least two heart attacks. At Bermuda Dunes, Gable had a coronary while swinging a club on the golf course; his face turned gray, and he slumped over like a wounded soldier. But he seemed to recover and continued to imbibe at a reckless pace that endangered his life and prevented him from getting medical insurance. When journalists asked him to comment about rumors that he'd been told to give up his wanton ways, Gable smirked through his dyed brown mustache. "Yeah, I heard about it," he said. "I was having a highball at the time."

The Misfits was a severe trial for him. He had insisted on performing dangerous stunts such as roping wild horses, which raised concern about his blood pressure—already too high. The physical exertion was not helped by co-star Marilyn Monroe, who was constantly groping him.

Shortly after Kay Spreckels announced she was pregnant with his only son, John, Gable underwent full cardiac arrest one week before Thanksgiving Day, 1960, and died without regaining consciousness. He was 59.

■ ■ ■

GABLE'S WAKE WAS a happy affair. There was much laughter and imbibing of distilled spirits. "Here's to the King," toasted Ray Ryan, raising his whiskey glass with a group of inebriated friends, including the actor William Holden.

"Long live the King," crowed Holden. "It's too bad he can't go on any more safaris with us."

The resort community of Bermuda Dunes might never have become a reality if Ryan had not made Holden's acquaintance. Ryan was always seeking business partners. The charismatic actor, ever on the lookout for good investments, became the fast-talking gambler's front man, opening doors that otherwise might have stayed closed. In the late 1950s, Ryan, Holden, and Swiss banker Carl Hirschmann had founded the Mount Kenya Safari Club in Africa. Located 140 miles north of Nairobi, outfitted with well-appointed rooms, an open-air restaurant, and a plantation bar, and accessible only by private plane or truck, it was the only sportsmen's club of its kind anywhere in the world.

Movie stars, heads of state, royalty—they all wanted to belong. The club's active members included Bob Hope; Red Skelton; John Ford; Walt Disney; Joan Crawford; Lily Pons; Jack Dempsey; Conrad Hilton; Norman Vincent Peale; Sir Winston Churchill; Alexander Montagu, the tenth Duke of Manchester; and Prince Bernard of the Netherlands. In 1961, Ryan was made an honorable chief of the Kikuyu tribe, which lived a short distance from the club. He received the distinction in a five-hour ceremony that paid him tribute for providing tribesmen with the funds to build a modern village, thereby raising their standard of living. Ryan told Holden that the honor meant more to him than all the money in the world.

Perhaps. Back home, Ryan's gambling had become an all-consuming passion. He would bet money on just about anything if he thought the odds were in his favor. "I remember a $10,000 bet Ryan made with a man he met in a bar," recalled former Palm Springs Mayor Frank Bogert. "The guy claimed he could toss a key into a door lock at least twice out of ten tries. The guy did it, and Ray paid right up." To keep pace with his gambling, Ryan upped his investments. Ryan and Ginny Simms's husband, Donald Eastvold, spent millions of dollars developing the 1,000-acre North Shore Beach Yacht Club and Marina, which could accommodate 400 boats, and offered a luxury hotel and private homes at Salton Sea, 30 miles south of Palm Springs.

Ryan's real estate holdings weren't limited to the U.S.A. Off-shore investments included a $2-million canal on three miles of oceanfront in Jamaica's Montego Bay, and farther away, 72 miles of waterfront property on the Adriatic Sea in Yugoslavia. But over the course of several decades, the friendly turtle had become a sitting duck, as international governments and high-ranking criminals studied his movements. Blithely unconcerned by the ever-present threat of danger, Ryan preferred to believe the odds were still in his favor. Unfortunately for him, they weren't.

Mobsters had been keeping score of Ryan's growing fortune. In their view, it added up to a lot of payoffs, and they intended to collect what they felt he owed them. Their representatives tailed Ryan and compiled a dossier on their latest mark. If Ryan had been keeping his own tally, he would have remembered that his troubles with the mob began at El Mirador Hotel. There, one day in 1963, he received a call from Marshall Caifano, a prominent member of the Chicago Mafia who identified himself on the phone as John Marshall.

The rumpled-looking Caifano was a professional hit man, bank robber, and bookmaker. Among the crimes in which he was suspected of playing a prominent role, according to an Associated Press report, were the slaying of a Chicago policy rackets figure that had killed Caifano's brother, and a mobster girlfriend who was bludgeoned, burned, and stabbed with an ice pick. California authorities listed Caifano as a top lieutenant in the Chicago crime syndicate run by Indian Wells resident Anthony Accardo, who was Al Capone's successor and "a suspected underworld muscle and triggerman." It was alleged that Caifano was the brains behind the fatal car bombing of Hollywood extortionist Willie

Bioff, a panderer and labor racketeer.

So when Ray Ryan answered the phone on that ill-fated day in 1963, he broke out in a cold sweat even though it was 80 degrees in the shade. After introducing himself, Caifano calmly informed Ryan that they had some unfinished business, and if he knew what was good for him, he would meet him in the hotel lobby.

Ryan nervously replied that he had no idea what Marshall was talking about.

"Yes, you do," Caifano sniggered, "and it'll cost you $60,000 a year to make me forget about it."

"You're crazy," said Ryan, wiping the perspiration from his face, and he hung up. He went to the liquor cabinet and poured himself a stiff drink; then he called his attorney and described the reason for Caifano's threatening call. It was like a movie flashback, with the screen going blurry and Ryan's voice echoing as though he was falling down a well. When everything came into focus, Ryan was sitting at a gambling table with a big stack of chips in front of him.

Ryan's problems apparently stemmed from a high-stakes poker game he had played 13 years earlier with Nicholas "Nick the Greek" Dandolos at the Thunderbird Hotel Casino in Las Vegas. These cagey adversaries were accustomed to playing for six figures, and they played sometimes up to five or six hours a day. Their marathon game lasted over a week and finally ended with Dandolos losing more than $500,000 and writing a personal check to Ryan to cover the loss.

The men's friendly smiles turned to contemptuous sneers, however, when Dandolos learned that Ryan had supposedly paid a confederate $20,000 to monitor the game using binoculars. Supposedly Ryan was being informed of his competitor's hands through a hidden short-wave device. Dandolas confronted Ryan, who claimed to be outraged by the suggestion that he had cheated. He refused to pay up.

When the flashback evaporated, Ryan asked his lawyer why the mob had waited so long to get even with him. Why now?

That's the mob's way, his attorney told him.

Ryan reluctantly went downstairs and met Caifano, who was wearing a dark blue suit and sunglasses. They got in the backseat of a rental car driven by Miami, Florida, mob associate Charles Delmonico and tooled around the neighborhood looking at different houses. To protect himself, Ryan had the hotel bell captain and a stewardess follow him in another car. Occasionally, the gambler and the mobster stopped and admired the painted fences and neatly trimmed hedges. "Look," Caifano explained, his small brown eyes boring into Ryan, "we know you stiffed Dandolos, so it's gonna cost you $60,000 a year plus $15,000 to make sure nothin' happens to you."

When Ryan objected, Caifano raised his right arm and struck him hard across the chest, warning him, "That's just to show you we mean business."

Frightened, Ryan asked to be let out of the car, and he was driven back to the hotel, where he went to his office and vomited. He washed his face and fixed himself a drink. It was the wrong thing to do, he knew, but he had no choice: he called the FBI and informed them about the extortion, saying he refused to be shaken down by a bunch of crooks. Ryan's only option, the Bureau explained to him, was to press charges in federal court. He decided to mull things over during a business trip to the Desert Inn in Las Vegas. But Caifano intercepted him and suggested they take a car ride in the desert. That's when Ryan knew it was time to take action. He bolted out the door and started running down the street, afraid he would be shot in the back.

"Go ahead and shoot me," he yelled. "That's how you guys do business."

"You're a dead man, Ryan," Caifano warned.

Ryan no longer had any hesitation about taking the stand; the decision had been made for him. The FBI gave Ryan round-the-clock protection, and he hired an armed bodyguard who followed him everywhere. Nothing deterred him, not even warnings from gangsters Johnny Roselli and Sam Giancana that, if he persisted in his court action, they would alert the IRS to go after him.

During the ensuing trial, Ryan testified that he believed he was the victim of a setup. He made sure everyone clearly understood: he would not pay protection money to the mob, no matter what the consequences. He had been the object of shakedowns in the past, Ryan told the court, but he had never paid anyone a penny. The judge believed him. For their part in the Ryan extortion case, Caifano received a 10-year sentence and Delmonico got five years. The two men went to prison in 1966.

You would think the mob would give up, but no.

Dandolos filed a civil suit against Ryan, seeking $1.5 million in damages for allegedly "welching on a poker bet." The case was thrown out of court, and Dandolos died shortly after. But Ryan's troubles were far from over. He soon found himself the target of an IRS investigation, and in 1968 a federal grand jury indicted him on charges that he conspired to obstruct justice through the alleged destruction and falsification of records from the Mt. Kenya Safari Club.

In 1970, a California judge sentenced Ryan to three years in prison and fined him $5,000 for allegedly altering club membership records. Freed on $50,000 bail, he said hundreds of Hail Marys, and in 1971 a higher court overturned his conviction, citing insufficient evidence. According to Frank Bogert, Ryan never denied he altered the records. He claimed that he destroyed the membership cards to prevent embarrassment to club members such as then-President Lyndon B. Johnson, actor John Wayne, and Illinois Senator Everett Dirksen.

Ryan returned to federal court the following year, indicted on four counts of failure to file foreign investment reports with the IRS on his business dealings in Jamaica. Again, a federal judge dismissed the charges, telling prosecutors that they had failed to prove any criminal offense. Was somebody in the federal government protecting a man who had helped put two mobsters away?

Ryan may have eluded prison, but by 1973, Caifano was out and bent on revenge. And as old-time Mafiosos like Frank Costello, who had known Ryan, relinquished their posts or were exterminated, Ryan found himself alone and vulnerable. He told an employee, "They'll get me some time, I know it."

But for all his concerns, Ryan was not the type of man who lived in fear. William Holden once walked into Ryan's hotel suite in Dallas, Texas, as Ryan was opening a suitcase on the king-size bed. Inside were stacks of crisp one hundred dollar bills—$400,000 worth.

"My God, aren't you worried about carrying around all that money?" Holden asked him.

"Yeah, it does get a little heavy," Ryan replied with a sheepish grin.

Still, Ryan now carried a gun for protection, and he traveled to most places under an assumed name or with a bodyguard.

The day of his death, Ryan got a massage and an alcohol rubdown near his company's headquarters in Evansville. He left the health club feeling happy and relaxed, and got into his car. When he turned the key in the ignition, there was a blinding flash followed by total blackness. In that brief instant, Ryan knew his life was over.

Authorities suspected Ryan had been followed for several days, perhaps even longer, while his killer learned the wealthy investor's daily routine. The FBI believed the bomb was planted by an out-of-state hit man, and touched off by a timing device or a remote-controlled detonator. When word reached Caifano that his nemesis had been rubbed out, the gray-haired mobster made the sign of the cross and spat a large gob of spit on the ground.

In 1979, Caifano was arrested for transporting stolen stock certificates and received a 20-year prison term—unofficial payback for Ryan's unsolved murder. He spent the next decade languishing behind bars, but showed no remorse for his actions. He was paroled in 1991 and retired to Fort Lauderdale, where he died in 2003 at the age of 92.

■ ■ ■

THE KEY MAN behind the Bermuda Dunes Country Club was gone, but the development he had spearheaded was prospering.

There was only one thing that Pennsylvania bandleader **Fred Waring** liked better than leading his 55-piece orchestra, The Pennsylvanians, and that was hitting a golf ball! The straitlaced Waring, whose syncopated rhythms were all the rage of 1930s American ballrooms and radio broadcasts, was one of the earliest members of the Bermuda Dunes Country Club, where he purchased a condominium in the Colony. Whenever he wasn't performing his lively song and dance music at sold-out concerts and parties, Waring could be found at 42–360 Adams Street, swinging a five-iron instead of his familiar baton.

Known as "The Man who Taught America How to Sing," Waring was the country's foremost conductor of choral music, complete with strings, horns, percussion, his harmonizing glee club, and pretty stage dancers. His musical finesse was equal parts Carnegie Hall and Coney Island. He was also one of Hollywood's earliest cinematic attractions, appearing with his band in many early talking shorts, as well as RKO's first feature film release, *Syncopation,* and the college musical *Varsity Show.* He always had moviegoers tapping their feet to his catchy jazz rhythms.

Waring's spectacular shows were just that: a cavalcade of light, sound, and song that inevitably began with the lush refrain "I Hear Music," followed by merry hits such as "Button Up Your Overcoat," "I Love My Baby (My Baby Loves Me)," and "Love for Sale." Each show ended with his theme song, "Sleep," which he had first recorded in 1923.

A successful entrepreneur as well as a talented showman, Waring was among the first of the twentieth century's pioneering musicians to earn money from sales of his recorded music. He also showcased a line of household appliances, including the famous Waring Blender, which revolutionized food preparation. When television became the preferred form of mass entertainment, Waring jumped feet first into the new medium, packaging his choral music for a new generation of bobbysoxers and debutantes. They crowded around TV sets to watch *The Fred Waring Show*, which ran for six years on CBS.

For 37 years, Waring held summer choral workshops at his Pennsylvania headquarters in Shawnee-on-the-Delaware, where his son William, one of three children by Waring's second marriage, managed his father's historic 80-room waterfront inn. It was at Waring's hotel and golf course that Jackie Gleason learned to play the sport that would become a personal obsession, and where Arnold Palmer met his first wife, Winnie Walzer, whom he married in 1954.

Young musicians from all over America enrolled in the choral sessions and were taught to sing with precision, sensitivity, and enthusiasm by the meticulous Waring, who insisted that every syllable of a song's lyrics be as audible as the music. In 1957, past the acme of his popularity but still a well-known entertainer, Waring and his orchestra played at the White House, charming England's Queen Elizabeth II and Soviet Premier Nikita Khrushchev with spirited harmonies.

Waring never tired of performing; by 1980, he had recorded over 1,500 songs on more than 100 albums, and he toured well into his final decade, often logging some 40,000 miles a year on the road. But the highpoint of his career and indeed his life, according to family and friends, was receiving the Congressional Gold Medal, the nation's highest honor for a civilian, presented to him by President Ronald Reagan. He was also handed an unexpected tribute when 44th Avenue, which extends from Palm Desert to Indio and is one of the valley's longest streets, was renamed Fred Waring Drive.

In 1984, Waring was about to close on a new desert home with his third wife, concert pianist Virginia Morley, when he suffered a fatal heart attack following his eighty-fourth birthday. The end came moments after he finished videotaping a TV concert with his ensemble, the completion of his summer choral workshop in Pennsylvania. Like the consummate showman he always was, Waring smiled and took a dignified bow.

■ ■ ■

ANOTHER EARLY RESIDENT of Bermuda Dunes was actor **William Gargan**, who lived at 79–461 Bermuda Dunes Drive. Gargan established himself on Broadway in the critically acclaimed play *The Animal Kingdom*. Its success led him to Hollywood, where he played energetic leading roles in *Rain*, *You Only Live Once*, and *They Knew What They Wanted*, the movie that netted him an Oscar nomination.

Gargan later became an early TV star in *Martin Kane, Private Eye*. In fact the hard-drinking actor had just resurrected the series in 1957, when he was diagnosed with cancer of the larynx. His vocal chords were removed, ending his career. Two years after losing his speech, he gave his final performance, portraying a mute clown on TV in *King of Diamonds*, starring Broderick Crawford.

Throughout his physical ordeal, Gargan kept a low profile, but he was unexpectedly swept up in a miniscandal involving presidential nominee John F. Kennedy. In 1960, Gargan had rented a hotel apartment in Hollywood and was living one floor below rooms owned by Jack Haley. One afternoon, Gargan was reading a script when he heard a loud noise and went out into the backyard. He looked up just in time to see a naked man carrying a pair of swimming trunks shimmy down the fire escape.

This, however, was no ordinary man. This was JFK, the nation's future president, caught in the buff. Gargan watched in disbelief as Kennedy put on his trunks, climbed over a back fence, and disappeared.

Within minutes of the escape of the president-to-be, the apartment complex was overrun with policemen and TV cameras, as reports of a grinning, blond-haired prowler circulated all over the city. Columnist Walter Winchell picked up on the story and speculated that the nation's future leader was having a little precelebration dalliance the very day of his party's nomination. Gargan told Associated Press reporter James Bacon, "I thought I'd seen it all," and then added "Now I have!"

During Gargan's recovery from lifesaving surgery, he learned esophageal speech and subsequently taught it for the American Cancer Society, where he became a fierce opponent of smoking. He died in 1979 at the age of 73.

■ ■ ■

"HEEEEERRRRE'S JOHNNY!" WAS without a doubt the most famous introduction ever heard on television. For 30 years, announcer Ed McMahon used those drawn-out words to bring on *The Tonight Show*'s cheerful host, Johnny Carson, who stepped out from behind a curtain to wild applause while Doc Severinsen and his orchestra played the show's theme song.

The man whose trumpet often dominated those joyful musical interludes, which punctuated Carson's jokes and the outbursts of audience laughter, was jazz musician **Secundo "Conte" Candoli**, who joined the band in 1969 and continued to play trumpet when the show moved from New York to Los Angeles in 1972.

Candoli had begun his performing career at the age of 16 with Woody Herman's Thundering Herd, and he had developed a taste for jazz that never left him. Other early influences were swing era trumpet players like Harry James and Roy Eldridge. But his greatest influence was Dizzy Gillespie, who inspired him to try improvisational jazz.

Candoli worked with a succession of bandleaders, including Chubby Jackson, Stan Kenton, and Charlie Barnet, and eventually formed his own musical group. He toured Europe with saxophonist Gerry Mulligan and often played in partnership with his younger brother, Pete Candoli, whose trumpet licks could be heard on the TV series *Johnny Staccato* and *Peter Gunn*. A studio musician as well as a live performer, Candoli was heard on hundreds of recordings for interpretive singers such as Frank Sinatra, Bing Crosby, Sammy Davis, Jr., and Sarah Vaughan.

But it was his regular place on the bandstand with Doc Severinsen that earned him the adulation and respect of his colleagues. And there he remained until Carson's retirement in 1992, when Candoli also stepped down. He always said that the security which the well-paying job provided had encouraged rather than detracted from his love of playing jazz. Two years later, Candoli moved to a three-bedroom cottage at 78–420 Runaway Bay Drive, where this revered performer, whose nickname was the "Count," continued to be in strong demand for a variety of jazz concerts and recordings.

In 2000, Candoli's innovative CD titled *Conte-nuity* was named best straight-ahead jazz album of the year by the British magazine *Melody Maker*. In 2001, he died after a short bout with cancer, at the age of 74.

■　■　■

THE BIOGRAPHY OF popular 1950s actor **George Nader** should be subtitled "The Man Who Led Two Lives." It certainly would be a fitting description of this dark, handsome, blue-eyed hunk, whose career spanned stage, film, and TV, including two popular network series—*Ellery Queen* and *Man and the Challenge*—in which he played quick-thinking investigators.

Viewers had little conception that behind Nader's smiling gallantry was a man whose deceptive actions would have caused his fans to express outrage and condemn what, given the times, they would have seen as his questionable morality. For more than 30 years, Nader lived in the shadow of his best friend, Rock Hudson, who was Hollywood's reigning pretty-boy and the star of monumental box-office hits such as *Magnificent Obsession*, *Giant*, and *Pillow Talk*.

Hudson and Nader, who were both built like Greek gods, became fast friends when they were still relatively unknown performers hoping to make it big in Hollywood. They enjoyed a love of acting and a passion for the great outdoors. They also shared a deep, abiding secret: both of them were gay. "We lived in fear of an exposé, or even one small remark, a veiled suggestion that someone was homosexual. Such a remark would have caused an earthquake at the studio," said Nader, who was under contract to Universal, where the brawny Hudson became the top male star.

On their days off, the two men would often take trips together, chaperoned, as was studio policy, by perky young starlets whose job it was to create the illusion that the two men were at least lusting after women, if not in love with them.

Sometimes it worked; other times it didn't.

Robert Harrison, a New York–based publisher of sleazy men's magazines such as *Titter* and *Wink*, began fishing around for information on Hudson's private life for a tell-all story in his top-selling scandal sheet, *Confidential*. Hudson's agent Henry Willson was tipped off by an informant and quickly swung into damage-control mode.

A notorious homosexual who knew the monetary value of male pulchritude, Willson had a talent for taking tightly muscled, well-hung busboys and carhops and transforming them into statuesque movie idols. Among his star discoveries were Guy Madison, Tab Hunter, Troy Donahue, John Saxon, and James Darren. Not wanting to lose his most valuable client, Willson and Universal struck a deal with the muckraking tabloid: Rory Calhoun, a lesser star from the same studio, whom Willson also managed, had served time for burglary and auto theft when he was younger. To avoid a scandal that would have destroyed Hudson faster than a gunshot, the agent revealed Calhoun's unsavory past, and the magazine received a sizable sum of money to squelch the Hudson story.

Confidential ran the tacky piece on Calhoun, complete with prison mug shots of him as a pimply-faced youth. But the fallout was nowhere near as shocking as it would have been had Hudson been "outed" to the world. To make doubly certain the gay rumors did not spread, Hudson was talked into marrying Willson's secretary, Phyllis Gates, to protect his "straight arrow" image. Nader was advised to do the same for his own safety. But George, who was conflicted in his emotions, said he couldn't go through with a bogus marriage, and his career ultimately suffered for it.

Actress Joanna Moore professed that the real reason Nader didn't become a bigger star was that he was shy and not as confident as Hudson. But, she pointed out, such comparisons had nothing to do with George's acting ability. "I don't want to discuss what really happened," said Moore, shortly before her death from lung cancer in 1997. "But you know what I'm talking about."

Her intimation validated long-standing rumors, including the allegation that Hudson, in order to promote his career, had engaged in fellatio with Universal-International Pictures executive Edward Muhl, who was in charge of production. It was said that Muhl reportedly kept a stack of film scripts on his desk—scripts such as *All That Heaven Allows* and *Written on the Wind*—and that he asked Hudson to choose one in exchange for services rendered on the influential executive's casting couch.

It would certainly explain why Hudson was offered more important roles than Nader, who was relegated to cheap B-movies like *Congo Crossing* and *Joe Butterfly,* which gave him little chance of making the necessary leap to the front ranks. Nader was no stranger to playing the "star" game, however, and like Hudson, he often went out on prearranged dates. As Debbie Reynolds, who was a friend of Hudson's, later explained, "The publicity department would say, 'We'd like you to go out with Rock.' The limousine would pick him up and pick me up and we'd be off to an opening at the Cocoanut Grove or Grauman's Chinese Theatre."

One of those arranged dates brought Nader and Hudson to the desert, where they went water skiing on Salton Sea and picnicking in Andreas Canyon for a magazine layout. On that trip, which occurred in 1956, Hudson brought his wife, Phyllis, and Nader was accompanied by actress Mara Corday. The cameras clicked away as the grinning foursome carried picnic baskets, clambered over fallen trees, and snoozed under the palms. A third man, who was seen hovering in the background, and whom most people mistook for a studio driver, was in fact Nader's male lover, Mark Miller.

It was a nearly perfect image of normalcy: happy stars and their spouses. "Sex with Rock was always passionate; he knew all the right moves," recounted Phyllis Gates. "But it was usually brief. I didn't complain." Gates believed that "Rock would learn to please me as well as himself." Hudson's marital charade was bound to be discovered sooner or later, and after his wife became the recipient of strange phone calls from effeminate young men looking for her husband, their marriage ended in divorce in 1958.

Nader, craving the privacy that Hollywood didn't offer, purchased a home at 42–521 Stardust Place, Bermuda Dunes, where he and Miller swam and listened to their favorite records on weekends. The contem-

porary house, which overlooked the golf course, would figure prominently in Nader's friendship with Hudson when it was learned that the
Oscar-nominated actor had contracted AIDS.

Publicly, the aging matinee idol denied having the disease, but privately
he was devastated. George and Mark were shocked but pledged their support. "What can I do?" Nader asked. "Silence," replied Hudson. They
made one concession: an anonymous note, which Nader wrote from his
desert home and mailed from the local post office, informed Hudson's
last three sexual partners that his blood was contaminated and that they
should be tested.

It was while living at Stardust Place that Nader and Miller, who had
taken a job as Hudson's private secretary, would put the terminally ill star
on a plane to France, where he could receive a new, experimental drug
that might prolong his life. In the meantime, they fretted over Hudson's
worsening health.

In 1985, Hudson called Nader and asked if he could visit over the
Easter weekend. It was the first time George had seen his dying friend
since Hudson had visited the desert one year earlier with his blond, bisexual lover, Marc Christian. "George had been warned that Rock looked
poor," explained biographer Sara Davidson. "But the sight of Rock's face
was still a jolt. It was hard to believe it was the same face that George had
known for three decades, the face that the camera had loved."

Miller picked Hudson up from Beverly Hills in his Jeep Wagoneer, and
they drove to Nader's home. The two men hugged, and they all went out
to a quiet dinner at Shame on the Moon. The next day the three men
lounged by the pool. Rock, who was covered in itchy sores, wanted to
take off his shorts because the sun made him feel better, and he lay naked
on a beach towel in the backyard. In high spirits, they drove to Joshua
Tree National Park and went rockclimbing. On their way home, they
turned on the car radio and listened to Patti Page, who had once been
a resident of Bermuda Dunes, singing "Mockin' Bird Hill," which Hudson had loved to hear when he first arrived in Hollywood.

On the last day of his farewell visit, Hudson sat in the living room
doing needlepoint with Miller, while Nader quietly read the newspaper.
No spoken words were necessary to describe their intimate friendship.
Hudson died six months later at the age of 59; he was cremated, and his

ashes were scattered at sea.

In 1986, Hudson's longtime companion Tom Clark, a film publicist who had worked for MGM and Walt Disney, occupied the house while writing his autobiography, *Rock Hudson: Friend of Mine*, one of several books that were published about Hudson after his death. Clark's intimate memoir revealed the closeness of their personal relationship, which had lasted 17 years. He also wrote about his profound sadness at being estranged from Hudson when the actor died.

In the meantime, Christian sued Hudson's estate, claiming that he was put at risk by the actor's bad health, which had been kept a secret from him. He testified in court that he and Hudson had lived together, shared the same bed, and had sex on more than 160 occasions. After months of listening to medical evidence and sworn testimony from witnesses, a jury voted to award Christian $14.5 million in damages against Rock Hudson. Two days later the judge awarded a further $7.25 million in punitive damages against Mark Miller, for refusing to tell Christian that Hudson had AIDS. In total, Christian had been awarded nearly $22 million. The defense immediately moved for a mistrial and a reduction in the amount of damages. Two months later, the damages were reduced to $5.5 million on appeal.

For their peace of mind, Nader and Miller moved to Hawaii and lived there until 1991, when they returned to the desert and purchased a house in Palm Springs. Clark, who had undergone a 12-step program for the treatment of his alcoholism, died in 1995 at the age of 64. Nader passed away in 2002. He was 80.

■ ■ ■

BENJAMIN "BUGSY" SIEGEL was a personal friend of staccato-voiced actor George Raft, who used to introduce the narcissistic gangster as "my good friend, Benny." Siegel dined with Mary Pickford and Douglas Fairbanks, Jr., and lived in Holmby Hills, the neighborhood where Humphrey Bogart, Judy Garland, and Bing Crosby resided.

It was said that Siegel possessed the energy of a rutting deer and could make love for hours on end without tiring himself. But he was considered too dangerous and unpredictable for most people to allow into their homes, so these marathon bedroom trysts were confined to hotel rooms and rented bungalows. According to Dan Moldea, "The stars seemed to enjoy having the friendship of a gangster; it was their version of a walk on the wild side. Jack Warner frequently boasted about his friendship with the mobster."

In 1946, Siegel built the Flamingo, Nevada's first big hotel and casino. One day, in a typically cocky mood, Siegel told Del Webb, the Phoenix building contractor (and future Palm Desert developer) who had constructed the Flamingo, that he had killed 12 men. Webb blanched. "But don't worry," laughed Siegel, "we only kill each other."

And steal from each other. It was estimated that Siegel skimmed as much as $3 million from the Flamingo's gambling tables. The handsome tough-guy received his comeuppance when two steel-jacketed slugs from an army carbine rifle were fired through the living room window of Siegel's girlfriend, Virginia Hill, while he was home alone reading a newspaper on her chintz sofa. One shot hit him in the face and the neck, and another blew out his right eye, which was found 15 feet from his body.

Webb, who was rumored to be an associate of numerous crime figures, apparently had no need to worry about his own safety, even though, along with his generous building contract, he also received a 10 percent interest in the Flamingo. Later he built and owned the Sahara Hotel in Las Vegas, as well as other casinos in Las Vegas, Reno, and Lake Tahoe. Webb never revealed how he was able to snag so many building contracts, but during the Great Depression, when other construction firms went bust, his company had rapidly expanded into a multimillion-dollar operation.

According to Webb, checks bounced back then, and he was often left holding the bag. But somehow he always turned a profit. By 1945, he had made so much money that he bought the New York Yankees baseball team and three stadiums. One of his biggest clients was Howard Hughes. Webb did more than $1 billion worth of business with the eccentric aviator and hotel owner, after Hughes moved to Las Vegas and installed himself in the penthouse at the Desert Inn.

Webb began constructing retirement homes in 1960, when he built the first Sun City in Arizona, followed by other planned senior communities in Nevada and California. In 1976, Frank Sinatra purchased a

5 percent interest in the Del Webb Corporation, which built Sun City in Palm Desert. The ever-watchful Nevada Gaming Commission prohibited Sinatra's unlicensed involvement, but his attorney Mickey Rudin had no such problem and was appointed to the board of directors.

By 1978, four years after Webb's death from lung cancer, his company was the largest gaming employer in Nevada with more than 7,000 workers, which is probably why Sinatra, who had learned a valuable lesson from his mob bosses, wanted a piece of the action.

■ ■ ■

MUSICIANS DON'T COME more conservative than Grammy Award–winning composer, arranger, conductor, and recording star **Johnny Mann**. His group of male and female singers, dressed in long white pants and blue skirts, red V-neck sweaters and white turtlenecks, challenged American audiences who objected to the Vietnam War to *Stand Up and Cheer*—the jingoistic title of his popular TV variety show, which enjoyed a solid three-year network run.

It may have been the era of Woodstock, but not everybody was smoking marijuana and taking off their clothes. Mann certainly wasn't. "My family's always been very pro-American," recalled Mann, who was appalled by flag burnings and student demonstrations. So he put together a choral group that sang patriotic songs and wore red-white-and-blue costumes. The result was a hit record: *This Is My Country*.

Mann had begun his musical career as a trombone player and singer with the U.S. Army Field Band. His musical ability soon took him to Hollywood, and there he arranged the music scores for seven movies at Warner Bros., 20th Century-Fox, and Columbia Pictures. He then became the choral director for the *NBC Comedy Hour*, which led to the formation of the Johnny Mann Singers and a contract with Liberty Records, where he racked up 39 top-selling albums.

Over the years, he worked with George Gobel, Johnny Mathis, Nat "King" Cole, Dean Martin, Frank Sinatra, Julie London, and Steve Allen, and he was Danny Kaye's musical conductor on a 12-week tour. He was invited by President Richard M. Nixon to perform twice at the White House, where he entertained Imelda Marcos, first lady of the Philippines, and Leonid Brezhnev, general secretary of the U.S.S.R.

One of Mann's less well-known talents is his clever ability to imitate funny voices. When Ross Bagdasarian, a songwriter with Liberty Records who had a huge hit with "The Flying Purple People Eater," came up with the novel idea of the Chipmunks, a group of singing rodents, he asked Mann to be the group's musical director and sing the voice of Theodore to the Chipmunks' lead singer, Alvin.

In 1994, after living in the San Fernando Valley for 40 years, Johnny and his wife, Betty Mann, purchased a house at 78–516 Gorham Lane in Del Webb's Sun City. (Prior to that, the couple had maintained a home in Indian Wells for ten years.) They still believed staunchly in God and country and old-time values, but conservatism did not always do right by them. When Kelsey Grammer was in drug rehab at the Betty Ford Center, Mann, who was a big fan of the TV series *Cheers*, approached the bullish actor, who'd been known to hum a tune now and then, and asked him to record an album of nostalgic favorites, among them "I Wonder Who's Kissing Her Now" and "The White Cliffs of Dover." Mann's enthusiasm couldn't overcome the project's limitations. In a recent interview with *Smoke* magazine, Grammer dismissed the CD as a collection of "old fart songs." The CD was never released.

In 2005, the Mann's sold their home for $675,000, more than twice what they paid for it.

■ ■ ■

HOLLYWOOD IS FULL of beautiful women who gave up budding careers as actresses and models to become the dedicated wives of top agents and producers.

One person who fulfilled these requirements was **Elinor Donahue**, a one-time child actress who played the sympathetic role of Betty Anderson, Robert Young's sensitive teenage daughter on the popular TV sitcom *Father Knows Best*. The cute, but sometimes cloying, weekly series, in which Young always called his daughter "Princess," reaffirmed old-style family values and ran for 203 episodes, until CBS pulled the plug in 1962. Donahue then shed her ponytail and jumped into another top-rated show, playing Ellie Walker, the enticing Mayberry pharmacist who catches the eye of widowed Sheriff Andy Taylor on *The Andy Griffith Show*.

But Donahue's prim and proper image did not survive the social upheaval of the 1960s, which changed the face of television. So she swapped acting for real-life domesticity as the second wife of producer Harry Ackerman, who was 25 years older than she. Ackerman, however, was no elderly codger sitting by the pool blowing smoke rings from his cigar. He helped create *I Love Lucy* and *Gunsmoke*, and also put *Leave It to Beaver* on the air. Later, as vice president in charge of production at Screen Gems, he gave the green light to TV classics such as *Bewitched, Gidget,* and *The Flying Nun.*

And Donahue, as it turned out, could not stay away from acting forever. She returned to television as Felix Unger's steady girlfriend in the hit sitcom *The Odd Couple,* and decades later, still turning heads, she was cast as Jane Seymour's older sister on *Dr. Quinn, Medicine Woman.*

Following Harry Ackerman's death at the age of 78 in 1991, Donahue married her third husband, Louis Genevrino, a wealthy building contractor, and they purchased their current home at 78–533 Sunrise Mountain View.

■ ■ ■

RETIRED PHOTOJOURNALIST **BILL Kobrin**, who is a resident of 78–332 Silver Sage Drive in Sun City, worked for the Associated Press and *Look* magazine, shooting thousands of rolls of film of news-making events like the Harlem riots of 1942 and General Douglas MacArthur's retreat from Inchon. Kobrin took his historic photographs with his trusty Speed Graphic camera with the Bellows Lens and screw-in flashbulbs. When he got tired of shooting serious stuff he turned to cheesecake, staking out Miami Beach for potential models like Bunny Yeager, who posed nude along with some of her friends.

One of his easier gigs was being the New York location shooter for 20th Century-Fox, when he would be stationed on street corners and park benches photographing cast members during rehearsals for the company's upcoming releases. In 1954, Kobrin spent a warm summer night at Lexington Avenue and 52nd Street shooting Marilyn Monroe and Tom Ewell in the famous billowing-skirt scene from *The Seven Year Itch.*

Billy Wilder, who was directing the risqué comedy, was so frustrated by Monroe's erratic behavior that he had to shoot the same scenes over and over; Kobrin didn't mind one bit. His shot of Monroe's skirt being blown upward by a blast of air from beneath a subway grating has been a source of gossip and innuendo for half a century. It's been said—sworn-to by countless witnesses, in fact—that Monroe was not wearing underwear. Her jealous husband, Joe DiMaggio, who was watching the racy scene from across the street, was so repulsed by his wife's exhibitionism that he filed for divorce.

For the record, Monroe was definitely wearing panties that night—a double layer. Kobrin's photos of that unforgettable event don't lie.

■ ■ ■

HAZEL-EYED ACTRESS **ELLEN Drew** had a strong affinity for desert living. It's where the brunette leading lady with the enchanting smile moved with her fourth husband, Motorola executive James Herbert, when he retired to Palm Desert in 1971. It's also where, 32 years later, she returned to spend her final days.

Drew was "discovered" while working in an ice cream parlor on Hollywood Boulevard. Actor William Demarest saw her, and Paramount Pictures signed her to a seven-year contract and gave her the big buildup. They had her nose bobbed, her teeth capped, and they gave her testing roles in dozens of films, to demonstrate her acting talents. Her career finally took off when she played Fred MacMurray's sweetheart in *Sing You Sinners,* with future desert neighbor Bing Crosby. That same year, she also played the dramatic role of Huguette, the honest girl who falls in love with Ronald Colman in *If I Were King.* She held her own opposite Dick Powell in the Preston Sturges comedy *Christmas in July* and was a memorable foil for Jack Benny's cowboy antics in the Western spoof *Buck Benny Rides Again.*

Her career was briefly interrupted by two short-lived marriages, to Hollywood makeup man Fred Wallace and then to scriptwriter Sy Bartlett, the father of her son. Her battles with a third husband, Chicago millionaire William Walker, sometimes made headlines.

Although Drew's forte was comedy, she proved she could handle meatier assignments such as the classic B-movie *The Monster and the Girl,* about a young woman sold into prostitution, and the spooky chiller *Isle of the Dead,* in which Boris Karloff accuses her of being a female vampire. Before leaving Paramount for RKO, she filmed *The Remarkable Andrew*, in which she portrayed William Holden's fiancée and is infuriated by his conversations with the ghost of President Andrew Jackson, whom she cannot see until the end.

Aside from Holden, with whom she worked twice, Drew had the good fortune to share screen time with two other well-known desert actors. She played Randolph Scott's wife in *China Sky*, the love interest of George Montgomery in *Davy Crocket—Indian Scout*, and the schoolmarm who wins Scott's heart in *Man in the Saddle*.

In 2003, at the age of 88, Drew died of a liver ailment at the home of her son, David Bartlett, who resides at 78–250 Estancia Drive in Sun City.

Thousand Palms

The tiny oasis of Thousand Palms, eight miles north of Bermuda Dunes, has barely enough shade for its 5,000 residents, many of whom are elderly or live on fixed incomes. But that hasn't prevented the likes of bandleader Lawrence Welk from pitching the place's sedate appeal to elderly citizens, whom he implored to move to Ivey Ranch Country Club, a nearby community for seniors.

Small though Thousand Palms may be, it has attracted a select few who have called it home. The boyishly charming actor **Robert "Bobby" Agnew**, who starred in more than 60 silent and sound film comedies, from *Bluebeard's Eighth Wife* opposite Gloria Swanson to Blanche Sweet's first talkie, *The Woman Racket,* and the all-star *Gold Diggers of 1933*, once resided at 73–523 Algonquin Place in Tri-Palm Estates Country Club. He died there at the age of 84 in 1983.

Then there was bearded Hollywood art director **Harry Oliver,** who received Oscar nominations for *Seventh Heaven* and *Street Angel*, starring Janet Gaynor and Charles Farrell. An early convert to the desert, he built an adobe home that he christened Fort Oliver in 1946. Between 1919 and 1938, Oliver's extensive list of credits included *Little Annie Rooney* and *Sparrows,* both with Mary Pickford, and *Lucky Star* and *Liliom*, which reunited Gaynor and Farrell. Oliver's sets were renowned for their rustic look, and for faithfully duplicating the interiors of haylofts and wood-framed hotels.

In addition, Oliver was art director on the Harold Lloyd comedy *Movie Crazy* and worked at MGM on memorable films such as *Dancing Lady*, *White Woman*, *Viva Villa!*, and *The Good Earth*, a film that called for a devastating plague of locusts. But moviemaking was only one of Oliver's talents. In 1921, he designed one of Los Angeles' most popular tourist attractions: the off-kilter Beverly Hills house shaped like a witch's cottage that belonged to Irvin Willat, a silent-screen cameraman, director, and producer who was married to the actress Billie Dove. Years later, in 1948, Oliver also designed and constructed a spectacular outdoor stage for the first Arabian Nights Pageant at the Indio Date Festival (cost: $25,000).

Back in Thousand Palms at his homemade "fort," Oliver edited, printed, and distributed a pocket-size quarterly titled the *Desert Rat Scrapbook*, which he mailed all over the country. He died at the age of 85 in 1973. Harry Oliver Trail, which is located off Varner Road and Monterey Avenue, north of Interstate 10, is named in his honor.

Billionaires' Row

DISCRIMINATION IS ALIVE and well in the wealthy enclave of Indian Wells—but only if you're rich. Dubbed "CEO Heaven" because of the high-powered executives who own homes here, Indian Wells has the highest number of millionaires per capita of any city in the United States. A bastion of political conservatism, this planned urban development occupies 13-and-one-half square miles of some of the most valuable land in the entire country.

On this land, which derives its name from the fresh-water wells that quenched the thirsts of Native Americans centuries ago, live approximately 4,500 prosperous residents, sitting on their precious investments like fat geese incubating golden eggs. There is no crime, vagrancy, or noise pollution, only the idling motors of stretch limousines, the buzz of electric gates, and the rhythmic irrigation of Rainbird watering systems on golf courses.

The city won't allow poverty—it's that simple. The Indian Wells Redevelopment Agency even tried to transfer its housing funds to nearby Coachella, a largely impoverished Latino community. But the State Department of Housing and Community Development ruled the transfer was illegal, stating that "Indian Wells has the obligation to use 20 percent of its annual property tax increment for affordable housing within its borders."

It's not the first time these overfed birds at Indian Wells have received a swift kick to the tail. In the early 1980s, Superior Court Judge Fred Metheny squelched an initiative to install border guards and issue identification cards, to prevent unwanted people from infiltrating this posh neighborhood.

Originally, the majority of residents didn't even want a city, because they were so happy living it up inside their guarded and gated mansions and swank condominiums. But Riverside County officials warned that if they didn't comply with incorporation they would be annexed, which meant running the risk of no public services or, worse, being absorbed by another city.

So in 1967, Indian Wells became the four hundredth incorporated city in California and the sixteenth city in the fruit-laden county that already includes the neighboring municipalities of Palm Springs, Rancho Mirage, and Palm Desert.

■ ■ ■

CALEB COOK, THE former president of the Coachella Valley Date Growers Association, built one of the city's earliest adobe homes on 20 acres of land along what is now Deep Canyon Drive. He was one of several ranchers, including James Arkell of the Beechnut Chewing Gum Company, who owned property along Highway 111.

When real estate developers began subdividing the adjacent land, date growers and residents alike did not want to see a shanty town spring up out of the harvested remains of Deglet Noor and Medjool Palms. So they banded together in an effort to oppose the building of trailer parks and other low-income abodes.

Their gambit was successful. Not only did their strategy make a strong environmental impact before such concerns gathered widespread momentum, it also kept real estate prices at a premium, thus averting crass exploitation at the hands of merciless businessmen.

The tactics did not prevent Indian Wells from promoting itself as a world-class destination resort with a host of five-star amenities, including the Hyatt Grand Champions Resort & Spa, the Renaissance Esmeralda, and the Indian Wells Tennis Garden, a $75-million, 16,000-seat sporting arena that opened in 2000. Highway 111 is lined on both sides with country clubs, hotels, and restaurants.

As for Caleb Cook, he died from accidental cyanide-gas poisoning in his Indio date-packing factory. But the good people of Indian Wells are forever in Cook's debt; they named the four-lane street that separates Indian Wells from Palm Desert after him.

■ ■ ■

AT THE CITY's hub is the Desert Horizons Country Club, where popular nightclub, TV, and recording star **Vic Damone** and his fourth wife, the respected stage and film actress **Diahann Carroll**, owned a fairway home at 44–816 Del Dios Circle.

One of the preeminent Italian American crooners of the twentieth century, Damone's dark and expressive features perfectly matched his strong, smooth baritone. That voice launched him onto the music charts with passionate love songs such as the 1949 smash hit "Again" and "You're Breaking My Heart," which sold over a million copies. His follow-up song, "My Heart Cries for You," made it to the Top Five.

At that point MGM signed the handsome lothario to an exclusive film contract, and he was showcased in the Technicolor musicals *Rich, Young and Pretty; Athena;* and *Deep in My Heart,* in which he cradled Jane Powell while wearing his customary double-breasted tuxedo and French cuffs. The couple worked so well together that they appeared in *Hit the Deck* (this time Damone wore a white sailor suit). Then, from beneath a jeweled turban, he played the mischievous Caliph in MGM's last big musical, *Kismet,* an Arabian Nights fantasy in which Vic passionately crooned the melodic song "Stranger in Paradise" with co-star Ann Blyth.

Away from the movies, the singing heartthrob returned to the Top Five with a successful cover version of Guy Mitchell's "My Truly, Truly Fair," and weeping fans rushed to local record stores to buy his version of Al Martino's "Here in My Heart," which made it to the Top Ten. His LP *That*

Towering Feeling!, on which he recorded his powerful rendition of the Lerner and Lowe song "On the Street Where You Live," reached the Top 20 (the song was his third to sell a million copies).

Like Frank Sinatra, with whom he has sometimes been compared, Damone's popularity temporarily suffered from the emergence of rock 'n' roll. He had only one more Top 20 hit, Harry Warren and Harold Adamson's song "Our Love Affair," from the 1957 Cary Grant weeper *An Affair to Remember.* After Sinatra left Capitol Records to form his own company, Damone was recruited to fill the void left by the problematic singer. Although he tried to emulate Sinatra's sound with the snappy LPs *On the Swingin' Side, Linger Awhile,* and *The Lively Ones,* his efforts mostly fell flat. A 1965 album titled *You Were Only Fooling* provided Damone with another hit single.

After that, Damone worked mostly in Las Vegas, where he and Sinatra became fixtures at the casinos, their songs of unrequited love placating the late-night drunks and gamblers who frequented the Strip. Unlike Sinatra, however, who earned millions of dollars a year, Damone was unable to afford the expensive trappings of his fading stardom, and in 1971 he claimed bankruptcy.

That was an unhappy year for Damone. His first wife, actress Pier Angeli, committed suicide with an overdose of barbiturates, and Damone divorced his second wife, Judith Rawlins. (Three years later she, too, would die of a drug overdose, although it would be labeled accidental.) With Angeli, Damone had a son, Perry Damone, now a radio disk jockey at KEZ 99.9FM in Phoenix, Arizona. With Rawlins, Damone had three daughters: Victoria, Andrea, and Daniella.

Nearly twenty years later, Damone's personal life apparently improved. In 1987, he married actress and singer Diahann Carroll, who shared his appreciation of music, and they moved to Indian Wells. It seemed to be the marriage that both had dreamed about: two performers with the mutual love and respect needed to sustain a relationship. Carroll had made her film debut in Otto Preminger's version of *Carmen Jones,* had appeared on Broadway in *House of Flowers,* and won a Tony Award for her performance in the Richard Rodgers musical *No Strings.* She had starred in the groundbreaking TV series *Julia,* which earned her an Emmy nomination and a Golden Globe Award for Best Actress, and she received an

Oscar nomination for her heartwarming performance in the love story *Claudine,* co-starring James Earl Jones.

But after nine years of marriage to Damone, years marred by his inability to make a successful comeback, the couple separated, and they were divorced in 1996. Their home in Indian Wells sold for $345,000 in 1997—the same year Damone gamely poked fun at himself in the film comedy *Money Talks,* in which Chris Tucker poses as his son.

The traumas of four failed marriages and a faltering career caused the 72-year-old Damone to suffer a mild stroke in 2000, interrupting his final concert tour. But Vic's fifth wife, fashion designer Rena Rowan, the co-founder of Jones New York, helped her husband recover from his terrible ordeals, and one year later he gave a moving farewell performance in West Palm Beach, Florida. He is now retired.

■ ■ ■

SEXY BLOND ACTRESS **Joanna Moore** played smoky-voiced temptresses in a variety of Hollywood films, pouting her luscious lips and thrusting her pointy bosom, snaring one famous husband and garnering an avalanche of free publicity.

Moore first gained artistic recognition in Orson Welles's masterpiece *Touch of Evil,* in which she played the grieving daughter of a murdered big-shot who is blown to bits by a car bomb at the start of the movie. It was Moore's third film of the half dozen she made for Universal Pictures, where she was forced to undergo silicone injections in her face to enhance her beauty and was prescribed amphetamines to lose weight.

Moore showed her dramatic flair as the mentally retarded prostitute Miss Precious in *Walk on the Wild Side* and, always sexy, she portrayed flirtatious vamps in two Walt Disney films, *Son of Flubber* and *Never a Dull Moment.* She is probably best remembered, however, as Nurse Peggy McMillan during the third season of *The Andy Griffith Show.*

Soon after that stint, Moore became involved with actor Ryan O'Neal. They were married in 1963 and had two children, Tatum and Griffin O'Neal. But the marriage proved tempestuous. Ryan and Joanna divorced in 1967, and subsequently Moore suffered severe depression and became addicted to alcohol and drugs. There were embarrassing stories about her living on communes with hippies and foraging in trash cans for food.

Indeed, Moore was not heard from for several years, until she was dis-covered living at her former husband's Palm Springs condominium in Deepwell Ranch. By then she had retired from films; her last important role was a doomed zeppelin passenger in the 1975 movie *The Hindenburg*.

Bad luck has stalked the Moore-O'Neal families. Ryan O'Neal was briefly married to actress Leigh Taylor-Young and subsequently lived for 17 years with Lee Majors's ex-wife, Farrah Fawcett. Recently Ryan underwent treatment for leukemia.

As for Ryan's and Joanna's children, Tatum and Griffin O'Neal inher-ited their parents' acting talent but were ill-prepared for the stardom that came with it. In 1987, Griffin, who starred in *The Escape Artist* and *Hadley's Rebellion*, was charged with manslaughter in the boating death of Giancarlo Coppola, the 23-year-old son of director Francis Ford Coppola. Tatum O'Neal won a well-deserved Oscar for portraying the smart-talking orphan in *Paper Moon*. She married champion tennis player John McEnroe and bore him three children, but they divorced in 1994.

As for Joanna, addictions cost her dearly. She was arrested five times for drunk driving and lost three fingers on her left hand when she crashed her Jeep on the Pacific Coast Highway. A heavy smoker, she was diagnosed with lung cancer. In the late 1990s she rented a house at 74–994 Tahoe Circle (off Cook Street), and there hospice nurses cared for her until she died at the age of 63 in 1997, with her tearful daugh-ter at her bedside.

■ ■ ■

DROOPY-EYED ELECTRIC GUITARIST and songwriter **Brian Setzer** had adolescent girls screaming his name when he fronted the popular 1980s rock band Stray Cats. Their breakthrough album *Built for Speed* produced two Top 10 hits, "Rock This Town" and "Stray Cat Strut," both of which reached #3 on the music charts.

In his glittering jackets, stovepipe trousers, and suede shoes, Setzer resembled a cartoon version of Elvis Presley. But Setzer has his own trade-marks: a thick blond pompadour and long sideburns that are nearly as rec-ognizable as his musical arrangements, which are an infusion of hardcore swing, jump blues, and rockabilly rhythms. In the 1990s, Setzer fueled a big-band comeback when he formed the Brian Setzer Orchestra, a hybrid musical group in the style of Gene Krupa and Benny Goodman that has played to enthusiastic applause all over the world. The orchestra had a major hit with "Jump, Jive and Wail," which, along with renewed interest in Frank Sinatra and the Rat Pack, helped launch a big swing revival. But Setzer's zest for big things got him into big trouble in 1995. He was arrested and charged with driving under the influence one block from his home at 75–355 Stardust Lane, off Rancho Palmeras Drive (Rancho Palmeras Estates). He pleaded guilty and received three years' probation. Since then, Setzer has only met with success. After cutting an album of cover tunes, he went back into the recording studio and produced *Guitar Slinger*, a mixture of jump blues and Texas blues. That was followed in 1998 by the CDs *Dirty Boogie* and *Vavoom!*

In 2004, Setzer was nominated for a Grammy Award for Best Pop Instrumental Performance. The reason? His Palm Springs–inspired single "Rat Pack Boogie"—an ode to the plaid and polyester that symbolizes desert chic.

■ ■ ■

SMARMY ACTOR **GEORGE "Skip" Homeier**, who graduated from juvenile leads to starring in *Dan Raven,* where he played an L.A. county sheriff solving crimes on Hollywood's Sunset Strip, is a full-time resident of 75–381 Desert Valley Lane.

Homeier began his acting career when he was a youngster performing onstage and on the radio (that's also when he won the nickname "Skippy," which he later shortened). He first impressed critics with his histrionic performance as a Hitler Youth in the 1944 film *Tomorrow, the World!* and the die was cast: he portrayed spoiled teenagers and cocky young adults throughout his skinny adolescence and early adulthood.

One of his best dramatic roles was the trigger-happy soldier in *Halls of Montezuma* opposite Richard Widmark. He was Gregory Peck's treacherous killer in *The Gunfighter* and a violent bank robber who holes up at preacher MacDonald Carey's homestead in *Stranger at My Door*. Firmly typecast, he portrayed braggarts, ne'er-do-wells, and callous lawbreakers in numerous Westerns, including *Ten Wanted Men, The Tall T,* and *Comanche Station,* often engaging in furious gun battles with his Indian Wells neighbor Randolph Scott.

Occasionally Homeier got the chance to break out of his bad-guy movies, notably when he made an imposing foil for timid geek Don Knotts in the haunted house comedy *The Ghost and Mr. Chicken*. When he turned 50, however, Homeier decided he'd had enough of playing disreputable foes and retired from acting. He purchased this three-bedroom home in 1990.

■ ■ ■

BOUNCY, ENERGETIC **PEGGY Ryan** was a talented child performer who was literally breast-fed on the milk of show business. By the age of three she was dancing in her parents' vaudeville act and she rarely slowed down, except to take a bow, for the rest of her life.

When she wasn't on stage, much of Ryan's time was spent in Hollywood as the dancing partner of Donald O'Connor. They were Universal Pictures's answer to MGM's Judy Garland and Mickey Rooney: two naïve kids who expressed their joy and sorrow through song and dance. Ryan and O'Connor were such a popular team that Universal paired them in 12 movies over the course of three years.

Their first joint screen appearance was as part of a teenage dance troupe called the Jivin' Jacks and Jills in the minimusical *What's Cookin'?* starring the Andrews Sisters. It was followed by Ryan's "zoot" dancing with O'Connor in *Private Buckaroo*, also with the Andrews Sisters. Next came *Get Hep to Love,* in which Ryan sang "Let's Hitch a Horsie to the Automobile," and *When Johnny Comes Marching Home*, a patriotic salute to World War II troops that ended with the whole cast singing "The Yanks Are Coming." *Chip Off the Old Block* featured some rapid-fire tap dancing from the nimble duo, whose final film together was *Patrick the Great*.

Ryan was then teamed with boyishly handsome dancer-actor Ray McDonald in three films, among them *Shamrock Hill* and *All Ashore*— described as a poor man's *On the Town*—with Mickey Rooney, Dick Haymes, and McDonald as sailors on leave.

In 1953, McDonald and Ryan were married and they moved to 31–663 Avenida Paloma, where Peggy taught dancing when the couple wasn't touring in a nightclub act. Career uncertainties caused the couple to split, however, and in 1959 McDonald, who had divorced Ryan two years earlier, choked to death on a piece of food in a New York hotel.

For the remainder of her life Ryan alternated between Hawaii, where she lived with her third husband, Honolulu newspaper reporter Eddie Sherman, and Las Vegas, where she ran a dance studio and performed into her seventies with a group of old-timers called the TNTs.

In 2002, she predicted her own death, telling a reporter, "This is my big finale! My tombstone will say, 'Tapped out.'" She continued dancing until two days before being hospitalized for the stroke that finally stilled her hoofer's legs in 2004, at the age of 80.

■ ■ ■

MOVIE STARS DON'T just happen; somebody usually discovers them. That's what occurred when producer **Irving Asher** auditioned a leonine young man of Australian origin and international sex appeal whose real name just happened to be Errol Flynn.

In 1934, Asher was the head of production at Warner Bros. First National Studios in Teddington, England, when he signed the enthusiastic newcomer to a $150-a-week film contract. Asher personally cabled Jack Warner in Burbank, alerting him to their latest find. The result: Flynn fortuitously replaced Robert Donat in the title role of *Captain Blood*, the movie that launched the handsome actor from Down Under on a long and successful Hollywood career.

A native of San Francisco, Asher began his film tenure in 1919. As the managing director of British projects for Warner Bros. from 1931 to 1938, he oversaw the production of more than 100 films, including five critically acclaimed melodramas by the highly imaginative director Michael Powell. As the world headed toward war, Asher's timely movies included *The Spy in Black* with Conrad Veidt and *Q Planes* starring Laurence Olivier. He also was associate producer on Alexander Korda's stirring epic *The Four Feathers*.

When England entered World War II, Asher returned to Los Angeles and took a job at MGM, producing the 1941 remake of *Billy the Kid,* starring Robert Taylor, and the Greer Garson tearjerker *Blossoms in the Dust*. The latter film earned him an Oscar nomination for Best Picture.

In 1953, Asher's loudly trumpeted production of *Elephant Walk*, which was being filmed among the tea plantations of Ceylon (now Sri Lanka), made headlines when Elizabeth Taylor replaced Vivien Leigh, who had suffered a nervous breakdown. The film, which was released in 1954, was widely publicized for its climactic elephant stampede, which destroyed a lavish, two-story tropical bungalow.

In 1970, Asher and his longtime wife, silent-screen actress **Laura La Plante**, moved to 75–600 Debby Lane. In her heyday, La Plante had been a style-setter. She sported a shingled hairdo that never changed, even when she was scared out of her wits in the haunted-house thriller *The Cat and the Canary* (though she did wear ringlets as Magnolia in the first film version of *Show Boat*). She also graced a popular nail-biter called *The Last Warning*, as well as the early, two-strip Technicolor film, *King of Jazz*.

Neighbors had no idea that the silver-haired couple greeting visitors at their front gate was so famous, nor did they know that Asher had discovered Flynn. But that didn't seem to bother Asher and La Plante, who spent their final years in relative obscurity, overlooked by film historians in their rush to chronicle the achievements of influential producers, writers, and directors who comprised the golden years of Hollywood.

In 1985, Asher was admitted to John F. Kennedy Hospital in Indio, where this once formidable moviemaker died after a long illness at the age of 81, leaving his wife, who had kept a bedside vigil, sorrowing at her loss. She succumbed to Alzheimer's disease in 1996, at the age of 91.

■　■　■

THE SUGARY LYRICS that invited passengers to come aboard this luxury ocean liner as it set sail for fun and romance on the high seas, said it all: Love, "exciting and new," was expecting you. Yes, it was TV's biggest wallow in nostalgia, courtesy of Aaron Spelling. And no, it wasn't *Dynasty* or *Beverly Hills 90210*, which he also produced. It was *The Love Boat*.

And do you know who gets the most credit, if not the largest amount of fan mail, for making *Love Boat* one of the most popular TV shows of all time? Singer **Jack Jones**, who crooned the title song's lyrics about love being life's "sweetest reward." If you let it flow, he suggested, it will float back to you. How corny can you get? As corny as you want, if the Nielsen ratings for this smash hit were anything to go by. From 1977 to 1986, the ABC television network kept people glued to their sets, watching gangplanks of movie stars look for love on the high seas aboard the *Pacific Princess*. Nowadays, Jones can afford to smile at the memory, but back then it was considered a career-killer to sing the theme song of a TV show, especially if it was a schmaltzy sitcom.

Then again, Jones has always taken chances as a singer. He had already recorded the title songs for prudish films such as *A Ticklish Affair, Love with the Proper Stranger,* and *Where Love Has Gone.* And when everyone else was gyrating to rock 'n' roll numbers, he was delving into the great American songbook to record his versions of time-honored numbers by George and Ira Gershwin, Cole Porter, Harold Arlen, Sammy Cahn, Jimmy Van Heusen, Michel Legrand, and Alan and Marilyn Bergman.

He didn't sing those songs because his father, Allan Jones, had warbled "The Donkey Serenade" in the Jeanette MacDonald musical *The Firefly,* or because his mother, actress Irene Hervey, made GIs stomp their feet in approval at her revealing skirts and tight corsets in *Destry Rides Again.* No, Jones sang those tunes because he liked them, which is as big a recommendation as you can get.

When Bob Hope asked Jones to accompany him on a U.S.O. tour of Vietnam, he jumped at the opportunity, even though the war was unpopular at home. Jones's two Grammy Awards for Best Male Vocalist, for "Wives and Lovers" by Hal David and Burt Bacharach and for the saccharine "Lollipops and Roses," chauvinistic songs that most likely wouldn't get recorded today, are proof of the singer's courage under critics' fire, as well as his enduring popularity.

At a recent concert, Jones headed-off feminists' attacks over Bacharach's politically incorrect "Wives . . ." anthem, which he sings at every show. "Women beg me not to sing this song," Jones stated, "but it was my hit and I'm gonna sing it until I die." So there. Prematurely gray but always handsome, he had a well-publicized romance with actress Susan George, starred in the cult horror film *The Comeback,* and was briefly married to Jill St. John (now Mrs. Robert Wagner).

Still in demand, Jones continues to perform and record CDs, and he grants interviews from his home at 75–825 Osage Trail, where he lives with his fifth wife, Kim Ely, teenage daughter, Nicole, their extended canine family of Buddy, Max, and Haley, and their two cats, Tux and Sassy.

■ ■ ■

IF HEREDITY IS ANYTHING to go by, then baby-faced writer-director

William Asher (no relation to Irving Asher) should have made horror movies instead of comedies. His father, Ephraim Asher, was an executive at Universal, where he produced *Dracula, Frankenstein,* and *Murders in the Rue Morgue,* among other creepy entertainments.

William would visit his father on the famous back lot where Erich Von Stroheim played foppish Prussian military officers and Lon Chaney, made up to look like a monster, scared hundreds of extras with his grotesque appearance. When his dad died of a stroke in 1937, William dropped out of school. Forced to fend for himself, he scrounged for food and stole whiskey for his alcoholic mother. It was, he always remembered, a terrible childhood.

Bill finally took a job in the mailroom at Universal and taught himself how to write scripts. After a brief stint in the army, he moved to the Salton Sea near Indio and became a full-time writer. But his troubles weren't over; an uncle, an aunt, his sister, and his mother all committed suicide. No wonder he yearned to hear the sound of laughter!

Asher's first film assignment was the low-budget boxing drama *Leather Gloves,* which he wrote, directed, and produced in collaboration with actor Richard Quine. That's how Asher got the reputation of being a "triple threat," industry jargon for a filmmaker who can do it all.

After that, it was on to comedy. In 1952, he was hired to direct the pilot and first ten episodes of the TV sitcom *Our Miss Brooks,* starring Eve Arden. Desi Arnaz was so impressed that he asked Asher to take over the directing chores on *I Love Lucy* for its second season, and Asher was so tickled, he stayed with the historic show for the remainder of its run, directing 103 of 179 episodes.

Bill's favorite memories of working with Lucille Ball were of the comedienne getting hilariously drunk on Vitameatavegamin, stuffing her face while impersonating an assembly line worker in a chocolate factory, and accidentally setting her fake nose on fire while wearing a disguise to elude actor William Holden. Another memorable episode featured Lucy and Harpo Marx reenacting the classic mirror sequence from *Duck Soup.* Sadly, the rigorous filming proved too stressful for Harpo, who was semiretired because of a heart ailment, and he suffered a heart attack right after the show.

During his first summer hiatus from the hugely popular series, Asher directed the pilot and most of the first year's episodes of another land-mark sitcom, *Make Room for Daddy,* starring Danny Thomas. After *I Love Lucy* went off the air, Asher brought his comedic touch to *The Patty Duke Show.* But his proudest achievement was a funny series about the super-natural that was inspired by the play *Bell, Book and Candle.*

Originally called *The Witch of Westport,* the new series contained the leading role of a suburban housewife with magical powers. Asher thought the part would be perfect for his second wife, fair-haired actress Eliza-beth Montgomery, and that's how the popular TV show *Bewitched* came into existence. It won Asher a well-deserved Emmy Award for Best Comedy Direction.

The heartwarming sitcom changed their lives forever, for both good and ill. When Asher, Montgomery, and their three small children—William, Jr., Robert, and Rebecca—went out of town to a hotel on weekends, they would be mobbed by fans. Back home, however, the marriage showed the strain of 254 episodes. When the show ended in 1972, Asher and Mont-gomery divorced, and the director blamed himself, saying, "I was an ass. I worked too much." Montgomery died in 1995 of colorectal cancer.

When not directing television, Asher helmed movies and started another trend: those silly, youth-oriented films about Southern Califor-nia's thriving beach culture. *Beach Party, Beach Blanket Bingo, How to Stuff a Wild Bikini*—they all reflected the man's fondness for hot rods and surf-ing, and he had a lot of fun making them during his summer vacation.

In 2004, Asher paid $779,000 for a four-bedroom home at 75–497 Painted Desert Drive, where he currently resides with his fourth wife, Meredith Coffin, a 1965 graduate of Palm Springs High School.

■ ■ ■

OSCAR-WINNING *ERIN BROCKOVICH* star Julia Roberts has been a famil-iar face around Indian Wells since her betrothal to motion picture cam-eraman Daniel Moder, the son of veteran Hollywood producer **Mike Moder**, who lives at 75–621 Painted Desert Drive.

Roberts met Moder's handsome young son when he was a camera operator on *The Mexican.* She was chatting with co-star Brad Pitt on the film's set when her eyes caught sight of a bare-chested blond hunk with six-pack abs. Friends said it was love at first sight, and within a couple of weeks they were a hot item—even though Moder was already married to makeup artist Vera Steimberg.

The National Enquirer broke the story: JULIA ROBERTS RUNS OFF WITH MARRIED MAN. One week before the September 11, 2001, terrorist attacks, Roberts flew into Ontario, California, where Danny Moder picked her up at the airport in his truck and drove her to his family's mountain cabin at Lake Arrowhead. According to news reports, Mike Moder was suspicious of the *Pretty Woman* star's motives. But he warmed up to her over a cup of hot cocoa when she professed her overwhelming love for his son and her strong desire to have children.

It was an uncharacteristic declaration for Roberts, who has a reputation as a heartbreaker. Julia walked out on her first husband, country singer Lyle Lovett, after 21 months. On the eve of her wedding to Kiefer Sutherland she left him for actor Jason Patric, and then she dumped *him* for *Law & Order* star Benjamin Bratt. After four years, she was taking up with Moder.

An incensed Vera Steimberg waged a vitriolic public campaign against Roberts, whom she called a husband-stealer. Roberts responded by strutting up and down the street in a T-shirt emblazoned with the words A LOW VERA. Not to be outdone, Steimberg wore her own T-shirt, with the slogan PRETTY UGLY WOMAN printed on the back. The feud didn't end until Roberts offered the scorned wife a financial settlement of $400,000, which she accepted, giving Moder his belated freedom.

In 2002, Roberts and her newest man were married in a lavish July 4, Southwestern-style fiesta at the actress's $2-million 40-acre ranch in Arroyo Seco outside Taos, New Mexico. The ceremony was arranged hastily, before the bride and groom could get cold feet, so there was no best man, maid of honor, flower girl, or ring bearer. Among the few guests who made the pilgrimage to the secret wedding were actor Bruce Willis and director Steven Soderbergh, who had helmed *Ocean's Eleven*. Roberts's frequent squeeze, George Clooney, was unable to attend because of the funeral of his aunt, singer Rosemary Clooney, in Kentucky.

In 2004, Roberts gave birth to a twin boy and girl. But soon she was seen kissing men other than her husband, and it wasn't long before the tabloids were predicting the end of Moder's marriage. Only time will tell.

■ ■ ■

ACTOR **TAYLOR NEGRON** has been a familiar sarcastic face in scores of film comedies that require his spicy mixture of Puerto Rican and Jewish temperaments. He can be counted on to play flamboyant, sexually ambiguous men who are at their flippant best when things are in utter chaos. Moviegoers first caught a glimpse of Taylor's acerbic brand of humor when he played the slightly perturbed young man who delivers a pizza to longhaired Sean Penn in the classroom of *Fast Times at Ridgemont High.* Then there was the comic role of Julio, the nervous groom who marries Rodney Dangerfield's teenage daughter in *Easy Money.* He also made cameo appearances in the cult 1980s films *Better Off Dead, One Crazy Summer,* and *River's Edge.*

Taylor honed his performing skills in comedy clubs, where he learned to get laughs by poking fun at everyday things—valuable training for when he acted one of the eager hopefuls in *Punchline,* a valentine to stand-up comedians starring Sally Field and Tom Hanks.

The first cousin of Chuck Negron, lead singer of the rock band Three Dog Night, Taylor regularly stops into town to see his debonair father, former Indian Wells mayor and city councilman Conrad Negron, Sr., who resides at 75–665 Painted Desert Drive.

■ ■ ■

AMERICAN FIGURE SKATING champion **Dorothy Hamill** was 19 years old when she won a gold medal at the 1976 Olympic Games in Innsbruck, Austria. It was a thrilling accolade for the shy teenager, whose famous "wedge" hairstyle started a fashion craze. Overnight, her name and her innocent face were plastered all over glossy magazine covers, and she became a media darling, eagerly sought to endorse beauty products such as Clairol and to star in her own TV special for ABC. She became the first female athlete to sign a $1-million-a-year contract with the Ice Capades.

The skating star's well-coiffed head was soon spinning as fast as her feet did pirouettes on the ice. In public, she exuded grown-up confidence, but at heart she was just a big kid. "I was really a spoiled brat when I was a kid skating," she said. "Meals are cooked for you, you are driven to the rink, and they make costumes for you. You don't have to think about anything but skating. I used to have terrible tantrums. Actually, what I needed was a swift kick in the pants."

To her thousands of fans Hamill could do no wrong. Mistress of skating artistry and technique, she performed risky triple jumps with ease and flowing grace. She even invented her own unique move, the "Hamill Camel," during which she moved quickly from a camel spin into a sitting spin. All too soon, however, people discovered she was not as pure as the driven snow—or the ice on which she counted for her livelihood. Although she was one of the most popular performers in the nation, her private life was far from happy as she searched in vain for the right husband and struggled to maintain her top ranking in a highly competitive sport.

In 1982, the "Ice Tyke," as the media nicknamed her, married Dean Paul Martin, the actor, tennis player, and the son of the famous entertainer who lived in Palm Springs. It was a marriage made with the best of intentions but for all the wrong reasons. Two years later the couple divorced, and Martin, a pilot in the California Air National Guard, was tragically killed in 1987 when his jet crashed in the San Bernardino Mountains.

Hamill remarried a year after Martin died, and her second husband, Dr. Kenneth Forsythe, eventually bought the Ice Capades and completely revamped the show, turning it into a story ballet with top skaters. Despite elaborate productions of the fairy tales *Cinderella* and *Hansel and Gretel*, the revised format did not produce a hit. The Ice Capades was sold, and shortly afterward Hamill asked Forsythe for a divorce, alleging that he had been unfaithful throughout their marriage.

Hamill was learning the cruel lessons that often come with fame and fortune: first, said the disillusioned ice queen, that "You can't trust anyone"; and second, that "Money is evil." Unable to sustain heavy financial losses, Hamill filed for bankruptcy in 1996. She had been on top of the world and now she seemed to be sliding faster than an ice skater taking a spill. At the age of 40, doctors diagnosed her with osteoarthritis, a degeneration of the cartilage surrounding the joints. Hamill was convinced that her skating career was finished.

But the figure skater responded well to medical treatment. Returning to the ice, she competed in the 2000 Goodwill Games and performed with a new touring show, *Champions on Ice*. In 2004 her former home at 75–490 Fairway Drive sold for $800,000.

■ ■ ■

NO ONE EVER accused **Robert Cummings** of being subtle. This smug-looking actor was prone to pulling faces and chewing the scenery if left unsupervised. But he had a genuine talent for comedy, and a definite flair for ingratiating himself with his leading ladies, from Deanna Durbin in *Three Smart Girls Grow Up*, which made him a star, to Jean Arthur in *The Devil and Miss Jones* and Barbara Stanwyck in *The Bride Wore Boots*.

These were the sort of bland, innocuous films that focused on the trials and tribulations of romantic courtships—the kind of movies in which Cummings, at his best playing lovesick fops intent on marrying the right girl, excelled. Occasionally he would tackle a dramatic role. He matched grins with Ronald Reagan to portray an idealistic young blade in the small-town melodrama *Kings Row*, and he played an innocent man wrongly accused of a crime in *Saboteur*. But comedy, not drama, was his true forte.

Cummings thought so too, which is why he was rarely caught being serious on or off the screen. "A well-seasoned ham," one critic called him; "Heavy on the glaze." A self-confessed faker, he went by many different names and affected a range of accents to break into show business, and when he got there he was determined not to lose his grip. Obsessed by his physical appearance, he went to extremes to preserve his boyish good looks. He was 50 and still playing cute as the skirt-chasing photographer in the TV sitcom *The Bob Cummings Show*, considered risqué for the times. In *My Living Doll* he created a female robot, played by the pneumatic Julie Newmar.

The godson of pioneering aviator Orville Wright, who had taught him to fly, Cummings served in World War II and was a pilot in the United States Air Force Reserve. He flew his own plane most of his life, preferring to touch down at small airports rather than valet his car.

He was 60 and had divorced his third wife, Mary Elliott, the mother of his five children, when he took up residence at 76–297 Fairway Drive with his fourth spouse, Regina Fong. In typical fashion, the time and date of their marriage were set by Cummings's astrologer. Was he superstitious? Maybe. "If I have a problem, I get expert counsel then ask the opinion of a good psychic," he declared. That wasn't his only idiosyncrasy.

A health food devotee, he attributed his glowing looks and vitality to natural foods and vitamins, which he consumed in enormous quantities.

He also experimented with homeopathic remedies and alternative medicines decades before they became popular. Alas, his regimen did not stave off the inevitable decay, and Cummings got a rude shock when he reached an important milestone, his seventy-fifth birthday. Doctors discovered that he was suffering from Parkinson's disease, and his youthful appearance withered away like the decaying portrait of Dorian Gray. He died of kidney failure at the age of 82 in 1990.

■ ■ ■

HE MIGHT HAVE bad skin and dandruff (or so it's been claimed), but **William H. Gates III,** or Bill Gates, as he is more commonly referred to by thousands of loyal employees of the Microsoft Corporation, the worldwide leader in computer software and Internet technology, can afford to thumb his nose at social conventions.

Gates, the chairman and chief software architect of Microsoft Corporation, the company he founded with Paul Allen in 1975, is the richest man in the world. As of 2005, his net worth was estimated to be $46.5 billion—equal to France's military budget. Gates's immense wealth, and the power that goes with it, have instilled millions of people around the globe with respect for and fear of his company's far-ranging technological capabilities. That's why Gates is often portrayed in the media as a super-intelligent megalomaniac bent on world domination, someone with elements of Blofeld, Goldfinger, Drax, and other James Bond villains thrown in for good measure.

It's easy to forget in the rush to judgment that Gates is in fact human and has a wife and three children, not to mention some of the most astronomical tax bills on the planet. He also has a history of behavioral problems and was sent to a psychiatrist while still in his teens. In 1977, he was arrested on a traffic violation in Albuquerque, New Mexico, and in his police mug shot he looks like the classic computer nerd: scruffy hair, bottle-bottom glasses, and a nylon sweater. His bedraggled appearance belied an important fact: Gates was on the threshold of a discovery that would revolutionize the future of people everywhere. His invention—software for desktop office and home computers—replaced typewriters and yellow legal pads, and effectively destroyed the paper-and-pencil domain of scholars that dated back to the papyrus of the ancient Egyptians.

Gates could not have helped but calculate the vast sums of money to be made from such a product and from licensing it to other companies. His investment of time, cash, and technical know-how resulted in the biggest retail boom since the invention of the electric lightbulb.

The success of Microsoft allowed Gates to live in the style to which he had become accustomed, whether he chose to get a haircut and wear fashionable clothes—or not. Mindful of his newfound status, Gates embarked on a buying frenzy as though he were a thief with a stolen credit card, only this gold card seemingly had no limit.

First there was a $166,000 bachelor pad in the Leschi neighborhood of Seattle, Washington, where he paid for live-in housekeepers to take care of shopping, cleaning, and other mundane chores. In 1983, he fixed his myopic eyes on a house for sale in Laurelhurst, a half-mile from the Seattle home in which he had grown up and which his parents still occupied. Gates snapped the place up for $889,000 with the proceeds from a stock deal. He ordered a huge bathtub so he could multitask while the water was running (it's been said he often neglected to wash himself thoroughly, although how anyone knew for sure remains a mystery).

Still a bachelor, he was infamous for his "virtual dates," during which he would correspond with an unknown woman in another city and discuss the latest movies and music. Then there was the story of the $240 pizza, which Gates reportedly ordered from Domino's one night after the local outlet of the pizza-delivery giant had closed. He and some friends were hungry and, with no food in the house, decided to send out for a pie, whether the joint was closed or not. At that price, Gates and his pals must have asked for a lot of extra toppings. Another time, someone spilled Dom Perignon champagne on the floor at a party, and Gates was supposed to have joked, "That's a five dollar puddle." It's a small clue to the bizarre sense of humor of this computer geek, whose favorite non-alcoholic drink is Diet Orange Crush.

After Laurelhurst, Gates's next home, which he called "Gateaway," was in exclusive Hood Canal, one hour by car from Seattle. At a cost of $650,000 he bought three-and-a-half acres, on which he erected a tennis court, a spa, and four separate houses that doubled as corporate retreats. When Gates wanted to laugh, he invited *Far Side* cartoonist Gary Larson to visit. When he wanted a singer, he hired Kris Kristofferson. But it wasn't all fun and games. His mother, Mary, was the victim of an attempted kidnapping, and Gates himself would later become the target of an extortion plot. He felt compelled to find a more secure address.

Not wanting to attract attention, he deployed a front man to act as the real estate buyer, ostensibly to keep the transaction a secret but also to prevent a seller from jacking up the price. Perhaps as a diversion, he plunked down $8 million on the former home of Jack Sikma, an all-star basketball player for the Seattle SuperSonics.

Eventually, however, Gates completed construction on an impregnable, electronically monitored, $113-million fortress in Medina, Washington, where he now resides with his wife, Melinda French, and their young daughters, Jennifer, Rory, and Phoebe. According to *Vanity Fair*, Gates spent an additional $14 million buying up 11 properties adjoining his lakeside estate, which is reputed to have a beach of polished white sand imported from Lanai, Hawaii.

When his growing family feels the need to take a vacation, they will soon be able to fly to the desert, where Gates paid almost $1.3 million for a three-quarter-acre parcel of land at 49–826 Hidden Valley Trail. There he intends to build a second home. He will not be far from his biological father, William Gates II, a Seattle attorney who retired from practicing corporate law and in 1992 paid $1.6-million for the home at 46–309 Jacaranda Court, where he resides in the Vintage Club.

Should less fortunate people think that Gates is only concerned about making huge profits and building enormous houses, his company is quick to emphasize their founder's many good deeds, especially the Bill and Melinda Gates Foundation, which has an endowment of $27 billion. For the record, Gates gives away approximately $1 billion to humanitarian causes every year.

■ ■ ■

AMERICAN INDUSTRIALIST **LEE Iacocca** saved the Chrysler Corporation from near-bankruptcy and became an unlikely media celebrity in one of the great comeback stories of the 1980s.

Ten years after retiring as Chrysler's battle-weary chairman in 1992, Iacocca, a part-time resident of 75–252 Pepperwood Drive, was back in the automotive fray, peddling a range of electric-powered bicycles and cars for the baby boomer generation. It was a dramatic contrast to the days when Iacocca was promoting the assembly line of gas-guzzlers that nearly put his company under, and many people were skeptical. Others believed Iacocca was doing penance. After all, the man had spent 46 years touting motor vehicles with toxic emissions that have been blamed for everything from a spike in birth defects and cancer to global warming.

Iacocca had few such concerns when he started out. He joined the Ford Motor Company as an engineer, quickly moved up the ranks to sales, and was promoted to product development. In 1964, he launched the Ford Mustang, which proved to be a winner, and six years later, in gratitude for his loyalty and service, the board of directors made him president of the company. But Iacocca's apparent impatience and arrogance, and contempt for people who didn't share his vision of producing compact cars and minivans, caused the company's chairman, Henry Ford II, to fire him in a rare fit of pique.

Chrysler, jumping at the opportunity to corner the growing market for fuel-efficient vehicles, snapped him up, and with good reason. The company was in serious financial trouble. Its showrooms were overstocked with expensive, low-mileage cars, debt was spiraling out of sight, and hundreds of factory layoffs were imminent. When Iacocca became CEO in 1979, Chrysler was on the verge of going out of business.

Iacocca summoned his courage and asked Congress to guarantee a $1.5-billion loan to bail out the distressed automaker. He figured it was a gamble neither the company nor the federal government could afford to lose; the country was in economic turmoil, and Washington needed to spur national confidence in the automobile industry. Congress agreed to the proposal.

Iacocca's next step sent shockwaves through corporate boardrooms. The new CEO did what few highly paid executives have ever done: he took a pay cut, reducing his salary to one dollar a year. Can you imagine any of today's executive fat cats working for one dollar a year to save their employees' jobs?

Of course, Iacocca's gesture was mostly a symbolic one, for he received an income from stock options and other investments. But this token sacrifice was needed to convince labor unions and employees of his good intentions. And as he had proved in Washington, he wasn't shy about asking or accepting help. "Bob Hope came to see me," he recalled of the comedian's offer to pitch his product. "Frank Sinatra wanted to help, too."

But it was Iacocca, with his graying, neatly combed hair, steel-rimmed glasses, and air of saintly benediction, who became Chrysler's most popular pitchman in those dark days. He'd point his finger at the TV camera and say, "If you can find a better car, buy it!" He reserved his disdain for the extravagant lifestyle of competitor Henry Ford, who, according to Iacocca, "made the head of General Motors look like he was on welfare."

Ford's lack of interest in selling cheaper cars was ultimately Chrysler's gain. Within two years, the company was back on its feet. They released the K-car series and the Chrysler minivan, and acquired the AMC Jeep. But Iacocca's personal triumph was tinged with tragedy. His second wife, Mary McCleary, died of complications from diabetes in 1983, and his third marriage, to Darrien Earle, ended in a costly and bitter divorce.

Now in his senior years, he is back where he started: selling cars. In 1997, he founded a new company, E. V. Motors, to market electric bicycles, and he branched out in 2001 with Lido Motors, a partnership that builds so-called neighborhood electric vehicles, or NEVs. The fiberglass-bodied, battery-powered Lido (the first name on Iacocca's birth certificate) is a street-legal, emission-free car. Western Golf Car manufactures the shiny four-wheeled vehicles in their factory in Desert Hot Springs.

■ ■ ■

PHILANTHROPIST **JOAN KROC** was the third wife of McDonald's co-founder Ray Kroc, who popularized fast food meals through his signature red-and-yellow restaurants, which serve 45 million people in 120 countries. Kroc owned the home at 47–675 Vintage Drive East, which she purchased for $4.6 million in 1998.

According to *Forbes* magazine, the bouffant-haired widow was worth $1.7 billion in stock and other investments, which she inherited from her husband, who died in 1984 at the age of 81. The former milkshake salesman met Joan Mansfield, whom he called "the love of his life," in a restaurant (not McDonald's) in 1956. They both had other spouses at the time, but they were finally married in 1968. He continued to run McDonald's, and she went on to found and head Operation Cork, a national program that helped the families of alcoholics, of whom, it was alleged, her husband was one. The Krocs moved from Chicago to San Diego in 1976, two years after buying the Padres baseball team and preventing the team's planned move to Washington. Although it was rumored that Joan Kroc didn't know one end of a baseball bat from the other, she quickly became a dedicated and passionate fan of the sport.

Then, unexpectedly, Ray Kroc suffered a stroke in December 1979 and soon afterward entered an alcoholism treatment center in Orange, California. "I am required," he admitted, "to take medication which is incompatible with the use of alcohol." He didn't say if he had also been told to abstain from eating his company's fatty hamburgers and french fries. Kroc's health continued to decline, however, prompting speculation that maybe his food wasn't what it was cracked up to be—a charge that company officials, in the face of widespread criticism about the high levels of cholesterol in junk food, vehemently denied.

After her husband had been laid to rest, Joan Kroc decided to spread the wealth they had reaped from selling high-priced franchises, and she began donating large sums of money to various institutions. Among the causes that topped her list of priorities were world peace, education, health care, cancer research, and the fight against AIDS.

When 21 people were killed in 1984 during a shooting rampage at a McDonald's in San Ysidro, Kroc started a relief fund for victims' families, personally donating $100,000. The corporation pledged $1 million—a smart public relations move. But Joan Kroc did not give everything to charity. A shrewd businesswoman in her own right, in 1990 she unloaded the San Diego Padres for $75 million, to an investment group led by Tom Werner, whose company, Casey-Werner, produced *The Cosby Show* and *Roseanne*. That sale apparently signaled a turning point in her life. Instead of watching a bunch of men hitting a ball and running around a stadium, she spent more and more time with her grandchildren.

Kroc died of brain cancer in 2003 at the age of 75. Unlike many other rich people, who would take their money with them if they could, she was more than happy to leave her fortune to those whom the money could truly benefit. Among her bequests were $1.5 billion to the Salvation Army and $200 million to National Public Radio, reportedly the largest monetary gift ever received by an American cultural institution.

■ ■ ■

SELF-MADE BILLIONAIRE **ALEXANDER "Gus" Spanos** amassed a large fortune by building and selling affordable new homes to thousands of working-class families in Northern California.

Spanos was a poor Greek American baker with a pregnant wife and a young son to support when he grew tired of making pastries and borrowed $800 to start a catering business. He knew many local farmers, so he bought a truck and began delivering homemade sandwiches to feed their Filipino and Mexican workers. The farmers eventually paid him to cook and serve three meals a day; the cost of each meal was deducted from workers' wages, and Spanos pocketed the profit.

During the yearly harvests, he found himself recruiting *braceros,* or migrant workers, from border towns like El Centro and delivering them to the fields to pick crops, thus doubling and even tripling his food sales. This rapid progression led him to provide cheap housing for hundreds of workers, who ordinarily would have congregated in unsanitary labor camps.

In 1960, he formed A.G. Spanos Companies to oversee the construction of apartment buildings in his hometown of Stockton, as well as in Modesto and the surrounding cities of Fresno, Sacramento, Antioch, and San José. Within a few years, Spanos became, in his own words, "the number one builder of apartment complexes in America." In emerging towns like Tracy and Gilroy, he erected shopping centers and office buildings that often won awards for their environmental and architectural features. The money and prestige that Spanos derived as a builder enabled him to take an early retirement, and at the age of 33 he took up golf, which became his all-consuming passion (he has a five handicap).

"But there's little glamour, publicity or fame in construction," he lamented, so he sought the friendship of people that could provide him with that recognition. Meeting Bob Hope at the Eldorado Country Club, when they played in a foursome against Bing Crosby in 1969, changed Spanos's life. Despite the 20-year discrepancy in their ages, the two men hit it off, and they formed a lasting friendship.

Hope, however, may have had a more pragmatic reason for taking a shine to the entrepreneur than just their mutual love of golf. Spanos owned several planes that he flew cross-country to attend business meetings and oversee construction projects. Hope took full advantage of his new buddy and received free rides to golf tournaments and charity shows.

In return, Hope gave professional tap-dancing lessons to Spanos, until his star-struck admirer was able to perform a buck-and-wing wearing a straw hat and twirling a cane. In fact, Hope and Spanos sang and danced together at numerous fund-raisers all over the country, donating their time and money to a host of worthwhile causes.

In 1981, Spanos and his wife, Faye Papafaklis, paid $335,000 for a three-bedroom home at 75–177 Kavenish Way, where they serve ouzo and baklava to their family of four children and 15 grandchildren. Spanos also purchased the San Diego Chargers football team, which was founded by Barron Hilton, the son of hotelier Conrad Hilton and the grandfather of fashion models Paris and Nicky Hilton.

From tasty gyros to generous financial grants for medical research and education, Spanos has helped spread the wealth that he created half a century ago. In 2004, *Forbes* magazine listed his net worth at $1.1 billion.

■ ■ ■

DURING THE CIVIL War, sorting wheat from chaff enabled feed supplier William Cargill to build a financial empire that stretched across the Midwest and eventually around the world. His timely merger with the MacMillan grain-harvesting family of Minnesota created one of America's great farming dynasties and the largest privately held company in the world: Cargill Incorporated. Today, Cargill has 105,000 employees in 59 countries. In 2005, this prosperous global company, which provides a vast range of agricultural products and services, posted revenues of $71.1 billion. And that's no bull.

Although Cargill's original founders are long buried, their third- and fourth-generation descendants still draw upon the income generated from feed, soybean processing, and vegetable oil. The surviving heirs— Duncan MacMillan, Whitney MacMillan, who ran the family business for nearly 20 years before retiring in 1995, and their brother, **Cargill MacMillan, Jr.**, who currently resides at 74–705 Wren Drive—are the last of the family's management team. With an estimated personal worth of $975 million each—that's right, each—the three men are tied for the position of fifth richest Minnesotan, according to *Forbes* magazine.

But silver spoonfuls of nutritious cereal aside, these human, grain-fed links to the past are acutely aware of their unique place in history, its risks as well as its rewards. For years, the family has been tight-lipped about long-rumored domestic problems such as alcoholism and drug addiction. "My grandfather hated getting his name in the paper," Duncan MacMillan recently commented. "*Time* magazine once printed an article criticizing the company, and his way of commenting was to call up and cancel his subscription. . . . We don't talk about the family, period."

For the most part, the present-day MacMillans have followed the path set by the Astors and the Rockefellers, who were well known for their philanthropy. Recently, for example, this close-knit family donated $20 million to Brown University in Rhode Island. It's one of many financial contributions they have made without attracting unnecessary fuss. On all levels the Cargill motto still seems to be "Our Word Is Our Bond."

■ ■ ■

RETIRED AEROSPACE CEO and champion horse breeder **Allen Paulson** sounded like two different people. In fact the executive and the horse devotee were one and the same—living proof of this man's determination to mix business and pleasure, and make money from both enterprises.

A former commercial pilot who flew for Trans World Airlines, in 1951 Paulson started his own aviation company. In 1978 he founded Gulfstream Aerospace Corporation, which manufactures the small, white private jets much favored by business tycoons, rock stars, and Paulson himself. From June 1987 to February 1988, Paulson established 35 international speed records during two around-the-world flights in Gulfstream IVs. His aviation accomplishments made him the winner of the Wright Brothers Memorial Trophy and the Howard Hughes Award for Aviation.

His love of flying was almost equaled by his affection for horses. His career as an owner and breeder began in 1980, and he quickly rose to the top ranks. His first champion was the great grass mare Estrapade in 1986, and his last was the classy mare Escena in 1998. He bred at least 85 stakes winners and owned, alone or in partnership, over 100. Indeed Paulson is ranked as the number one owner of Breeders' Cup starters: 33. And he has had at least one starter in each of the last 16 runnings. His best known horse was no doubt the great Cigar (named, like several of his horses, for an aviation checkpoint), which in 1995–96 tied the modern record for consecutive wins and set a record for lifetime earnings at $9,999,815.

When he was diagnosed with cancer in 1999, Paulson chose not to tell anyone except his wife, Madeleine, and his three sons, Richard, Jim, and Mike. But he quietly sold off many of his possessions, including his home at 47–355 Las Cascadas Court, which fetched $5.6 million. His prized racehorses, however, were not part of the sale. He died in 2000 at the age of 78.

■ ■ ■

THE ELDORADO COUNTRY Club was founded in 1957 by W. Clarke Swanson, the president of Swanson Frozen Foods, and by Los Angeles businessman Robert McCulloch, founder of McCulloch Motors Corporation. Named after the mythical city of gold, the Eldorado has long been an apt haven for America's moneyed elite, who often seek relief at the bar and in the clubhouse's glass-walled dining room, which was designed by architect William F. Cody.

President **Dwight D. Eisenhower** became so identified with the Eldorado that the mountain overlooking the club was christened Mount Eisenhower.

Few presidents alive today can hold a candle to the humility and self-lessness of Eisenhower. His achievements as supreme commander of the Allied forces in Europe during World War II, when his efforts brought about the surrender of Nazi Germany, and his two popular terms as the nation's thirty-fourth president, are a distinguished record of service. No matter what his flavor of politics, Eisenhower, or "Ike," as he was fre-quently called by the voting public, was the living embodiment of cap-italism; and no greater example of that existed anywhere in the world than in the U.S.A. during the 1950s.

He was 70 by the time he returned to civilian life, but seemed at least a decade older. War and the presidency had taken their toll on Ike's health, and he probably knew his days were numbered. But he didn't let on; he was always cheerful, ready with a lame joke or a bit of friendly advice.

Eisenhower had first toured the valley when he was still president. During a visit to dedicate the La Quinta Country Club, he had stayed at the home of Mississippi businessman George E. Allen and spent a long golfing weekend with mutual friends (and the Secret Service, always one golf cart behind). After cutting the ribbon, Eisenhower grabbed an 8 iron and hit a ball 125 yards down the middle of the fairway, surprising onlookers as much himself. (When he left the presidency, Avenida Serra, the original street where the club grounds were located, was renamed Eisenhower Drive.)

On that historic trip to the valley, newspaper columnist James Bacon received a hurried telephone call summoning him to an important "presidential meeting." Bacon raced to Allen's home, and Ike asked if it was possible to get an autographed picture of the singing group called the Lennon Sisters. His request was happily obliged; clearly Ike liked the neighborhood.

Bob McCulloch, whose company manufactured chainsaws and other outdoor power tools, built a contemporary three-bedroom home at 46–300 Amethyst Drive, overlooking the club's eleventh green. Eisenhower, to whom McCulloch granted exclusive lifetime use of the property, wintered here from 1961 until his death eight years later. The Secret Service stayed in a guest house next door.

Architect Welton Beckett, who had designed the Bullock's department stores, equipped the home with many handy features, including a private office with a library, where the former president could receive important guests and keep up his daily correspondence. For Eisenhower, now in his twilight years, this was a time of both elated joy and profound sorrow.

Ike had experienced his first heart attack in 1955, and he never felt completely well afterward. He had recurring intestinal problems and suffered a mild stroke in the Oval Office in 1957. Although he enjoyed playing golf, doctors warned him about the dangers of exerting his weakened heart. In 1965, he had a second heart attack, followed by a third debilitating attack three days later. He was put on a low-cholesterol diet that he disliked and was soon back to his old ways, grilling steaks and cooking up greasy plates of prime rib with sauerkraut that he served to his Eldorado neighbor Freeman Gosden and his family.

While the Eisenhowers may not have been health conscious, they were certainly money conscious. Mamie Eisenhower, who still liked pink dresses and wore her dyed red hair in bangs, would comb the supermarket aisles looking for specials. While shoppers watched in disbelief, the former first lady would squeeze the tomatoes to test for ripeness and thump the watermelons. She even saved discount coupons, which she personally clipped from newspapers and magazines and presented to the cashier with her weekly purchase of groceries.

After months spent resting up, Ike's health seemed on the mend, so he plunged back into golf, swinging and chipping away at the ball with the enthusiasm of a man half his age. Although pale and weak, he matched clubs with champion golfers Ben Hogan and Johnny Dawson. In 1968 he hit his first and only hole-in-one on the thirteenth fairway of the Seven Lakes Country Club in Palm Springs. Three months later, he had his fourth heart attack. Three more attacks followed within two months, bringing the total number that he had suffered to eight. His once healthy body, which had weighed 176 pounds when he was elected president, shriveled to less than 120 pounds by the end of the year. He had little strength and virtually no appetite.

Mamie took the train from Indio to be at his bedside at Walter Reed General Hospital in Washington, D.C., where Ike was given round-the-clock medical care in a lavish five-room suite on the third floor. There he remained under careful observation for the final ten months of his life; electrodes were taped to his chest, and he breathed through a tube. His wife slept next door in her own room, painted pink, and the night staff could occasionally hear her sobbing.

The sun rose and set 600 times while Eisenhower lay in bed thinking about his family: their firstborn child, who had died at the age of three; their son, John, who served in the army and was appointed U.S. ambassador to Belgium; grandson David, who surprised them all when he married Richard M. Nixon's daughter Julie. Sometimes Ike dreamed he was fishing and had caught some bass, which he cleaned and then cooked on an open fire. Those had been happy days, and the memories made him smile. At other times, the shock of smoke-filled battlefronts, screeching army tanks, and exploding shells woke him from his slumber.

In 1969, on the occasion of his seventy-eighth birthday, the hospital chefs baked him a huge cake, and the United States Army Band stood outside beneath his window and played "Happy Birthday." Mamie blew out the candles. Eisenhower had grown too weak even to read the Bible, which had always comforted him. His face was a death mask, his voice a whisper. As Mamie sat numbly, watching her husband of 52 years lie dying, he uttered his final words. "I want to go," he said. "God take me."

Ten years later, it was Mamie Eisenhower's turn, and she was ready, if reluctant, to make the journey. Rumors of alcoholism dogged her final years; at their summer home in Gettysburg, Pennsylvania, it seemed that she couldn't stand up without falling over. Critics charged that she was habitually drunk—nipping at bottles she kept in the kitchen and the lavatory. She always denied it. The official medical diagnosis was vestibulitis, a condition of the inner ear that produces dizziness, nausea, and vomiting. She lost 30 pounds, and her bones were as brittle as matchsticks. Confined to her own bed by this time, she couldn't tolerate one drop of alcohol, let alone a full bottle. She died in her sleep, two weeks shy of her eighty-third birthday, in 1979.

■ ■ ■

THE ACTOR **RANDOLPH Scott**, whose Southern charm, gentlemanly ways, and fast draw were a staple of movie Westerns for three decades, proved that a man can be both fearless and polite in the face of danger. Even when armed with a gun, Scott talked like a preacher. This was not surprising; he had grown up in the Bible belt, and his saintly face and mellow voice reflected that righteousness in more than 90 films.

He began his career in light-hearted movies, playing eligible bachelors in two musicals that headlined Fred Astaire and Ginger Rogers: *Roberta* and *Follow the Fleet*. Mae West ogled him as though he was a plate of succulent roast beef in *Go West, Young Man*, and Irene Dunne eyed him when he played a farmer in the aptly named *High, Wide and Handsome*.

But Scott made his best impression on horseback, chasing outlaws and upholding justice in *Frontier Marshal*, *Virginia City*, *When the Daltons Rode*, *Western Union*, and *Belle Starr*. He also donned a military uniform for a string of World War II flag-wavers that reaffirmed his law-abiding image and strong masculine presence.

Speaking of which, there has been a lot of scuttlebutt about Scott's much-rumored homosexual fling with Cary Grant, with whom he and Dunne co-starred in *My Favorite Wife*. It has been suggested that the two attractive men, who at one point were roommates, shared the same bed. But this sounds more like unsubstantiated gossip than proven fact. Still, when both men were between marriages and renting a house together, their friendship started tongues wagging all over Hollywood. Director George Cukor called Scott and Grant "the handsomest couple I ever saw," while Carole Lombard wryly commented, "Their relationship is perfect. Randy pays the bills, and Cary mails them."

Whether Scott ever slept in the same bed as Grant is unimportant in light of more perplexing allegations about other stars' private lives. In actuality, both these actors were wed more than once; Grant, in fact, was married five times. Each was also betrothed to independently wealthy women: Scott to Marion DuPont and Grant to Woolworth heiress Barbara Hutton. Scott's unwillingness or inability to father children didn't stop him from taking a second wife, Patricia Stillman, in 1944 and adopting two children.

Scott's highly profitable business partnership with Palm Springs producer Harry Joe Brown resulted in a total of 19 films which, if not Scott's best, were a testament to his immense popularity and cinematic longevity. As he aged, his face hardened, and he took on the roles of sheriffs and vigilantes who apprehended bank robbers and hunted down killers. His films with Brown included *Man in the Saddle, The Stranger Wore a Gun, Ten Wanted Men, Decision at Sundown, Ride Lonesome,* and *Comanche Station.*

Whatever his screen image, Scott was mostly the opposite. In real life he never carried a gun or a whip, nor did he hold a grudge. But he did love to ride horses. He boarded his favorite mare, Stardust, a large Palomino with a flowing white mane and tail, at Silver Spur Ranch, and every weekend he and his teenage son, Christopher, took their horses and went for a ride.

The Scotts were regular desert visitors. Randy, as his friends called him, liked the dry heat so much that he bought cottage #36 at 46–000 El Dorado Drive, where he could play golf. He had an excellent swing and could be seen practicing daily in the sand traps.

But riding and golfing were about as extroverted as he got. Out of the saddle and off of the course, he was quite shy. He preferred to stay home with Pat, who answered his never-ending fan mail, and eat a quiet dinner with their neighbors, Freeman Gosden and his wife, Jane Stoneham.

Scott's well-known dislike of big parties emerged from a genuine physical handicap. He suffered from acute deafness, caused by numerous gun
shots going off near his head during filming. Both ears sustained extensive nerve damage, and he was forced to use hearing aids. The deafness
hampered his enjoyment of social gatherings and even prevented him
from going dancing. "I think he felt uncomfortable in noisy environments
because of his hearing," revealed Chris Scott. "The din of the voices in
the room coupled with loud music made it very difficult for him to hear
with or without the hearing aids that he hated wearing." That may be
the reason he slowed down in later years.

Scott finally hung up his saddle after *Ride the High Country*, in
which he and Joel McCrea played aging gunslingers. Why did he stop
making films? Most people assumed it was because he had lost interest, but actually Scott enjoyed keeping busy; he did not like to remain
idle for long periods of time. A possible motive for Scott's early retirement can be found in his application to join the Los Angeles Country Club. The actor's Beverly Hills home bordered on the club, which
repeatedly turned him down as a member, as it did Bob Hope and
Bing Crosby.

Speculation exists that the club did not want to encourage actors, who
supposedly lacked the necessary social pedigrees. It is alleged that Scott
was prevailed upon to change his occupation to that of "oil investor" to
merit the board's approval of his application, and that his decision to retire
from films was based on that tacit agreement.

One of Hollywood's wealthiest actors, Scott had accumulated an estimated $100 million in his lifetime from canny investments in oil wells,
real estate, and securities. He certainly didn't need to work, and so, in light
of these events, he might have weighed the pros and cons and decided
"to heck with it."

In his sunset years, he refused all interviews and avoided film retro-
spectives. Like New York Yankees baseball star Joe DiMaggio, who also
dropped out of sight, Scott became a symbol of lost innocence, his independent persona best summed up in the Statler Brothers' country-and-
western hit "Whatever Happened to Randolph Scott?"

A touching footnote to his career purportedly occurred in the 1970s,
when the maitre d' at the Beverly Hillcrest Hotel said he noticed Scott

and Cary Grant sitting together in the back of the restaurant. They were holding hands.

Three months before he died of a heart ailment in 1987, at the age of 89, Scott had an emotional reunion with his adult son, Chris, who had been undergoing treatment for manic depression. Chris had been discharged from the hospital and was taking a regular dosage of 800 milligrams of Lithium to ease the mood swings and restore his equilibrium. Father and son hugged in a tearful farewell that could have been the last scene from one of his old movies.

Ten years later, Scott was posthumously honored at the 1997 Golden Boot Awards. Scott's widow, Pat, who continued to live in the house she had shared with her husband, passed away in 2004. She was 85.

■ ■ ■

ACTOR **JOHN CONTE** cut a dashing figure in Hollywood as the well-tailored host of NBC's *Matinee Theater*, a showcase for his dark good looks and *basso profundo*. The show was one of the first color programs to broadcast choice adaptations of literary classics "live" on TV. Conte's flattering introductions of each week's impressive guest stars, enunciated in letter-perfect diction, often camouflaged his own list of accomplishments, which were considerable in television, on the stage, and in film. Among his leading movie roles was turban-wearing Prince Ramo in the Abbott and Costello comedy *Lost in a Harem*, co-starring Marilyn Maxwell, a brassy showgirl who became Conte's off-screen wife.

It was a short-lived union, but it kept newspaper columnists busy on both coasts with the latest exploits of this perennial ladies man. Three years later, after Conte was drafted into the army, the couple divorced. Maxwell's name was subsequently linked to comedian Bob Hope, who took her on his U.S.O. tours.

Conte was not lacking for female companionship. After Alice Faye divorced her first husband, Tony Martin, in 1940, she was briefly involved with Conte, who pursued the blond singer in New York and Hollywood, where he performed second duty as the radio announcer on the *Burns and Allen Show*. The press even considered him the odds-on-favorite for Faye's next husband. Their prediction proved incorrect, however; she married Jack Benny's bandleader, Phil Harris, instead.

The daily scribes should have been paying more attention to Conte's regular gig as the announcer of *Maxwell House Coffee Time*, which starred the beloved American comedienne Fanny Brice as Baby Snooks. That show was more famous for what went on behind the scenes than what occurred in front of the microphone. Most listeners were unaware that Brice and Conte, who was more than 20 years the actress's junior, were engaged in a four-year love affair. "Part of John's appeal was the way that he made Fanny feel young," commented biographer Herbert Goldman. "They would go fishing, and do other things. Sex, as such, was not the only issue." But their vast age difference proved an obstacle as far as marriage was concerned, and the romance petered out. "Fanny took the end of her affair with Conte stoically," said Goldman.

Thanks to Brice's influence, however, Conte's career gained momentum. Composer Richard Rodgers, who had seen the handsome performer in an out-of-town play, asked John to take over the role of the villain Jigger Craigin in *Carousel* for the remainder of its Broadway run, and he played the lead in another Rodgers and Hammerstein musical, *Allegro,* as well as in *Arms and the Girl* with Nanette Fabray. Conte's fame peaked in a selection of lavish TV color spectaculars, in which he sang and acted with confident aplomb in the light operas *Naughty Marietta* with Alfred Drake, *The Merry Widow* opposite Anne Jeffreys, and *The Desert Song,* starring Nelson Eddy. He also hosted the popular half-hour musical series *Mantovani*, which was filmed in England.

In 1965, Conte married his third wife, Sirpuhe Philibosian, and they constructed a home at 75–600 Beryl Lane. There, in between eating his wife's Armenian delicacies, he embarked on a second career as a broadcast media owner. Noticing there was no local TV station serving the Coachella Valley, Conte founded the NBC affiliate KMIR, which began broadcasting in 1968. At the same time, Bob Hope announced a rival venture, but whether he intended to go the distance or merely wanted to spoil Conte's chances is unknown, for Hope quickly dropped out of the affiliate race.

Conte's victory over Hope was bittersweet. The ABC affiliate KPLM (now KESQ) went on the air one month earlier, beating him to the punch. But Conte was unfazed. He hired Jack Latham, long a fixture on Los Angeles news shows, as his anchorman, and then brought in Don Wilson, whom he had known from his radio announcing days, to run a daily interview program called *Town Talk*. The start-up cost was $4 million, but when it came time to sell the station in 1999, the 84-year-old media owner stepped out of the spotlight with a handsome profit.

■ ■ ■

DRUG WARS ARE not only fought in the jungles of Colombia, they are also fought in corporate boardrooms across America, between powerful conglomerates competing for lucrative pharmaceutical contracts. One of those rivalrous companies was Kansas City–based Marion Laboratories, whose founder and chairman, **Ewing M. Kauffman**, resided at 75–650 Beryl Lane.

Kauffman developed his interest in medicine when he was 11 years old and caught a cold that wouldn't go away. Soon after, he was diagnosed with a heart ailment that could only be cured, in the doctor's opinion, by complete bed rest. So for twelve months, the young Kauffman was confined to his bed and not allowed to move, for fear that otherwise he would never be able to play football or baseball.

As a young adult, Kauffman worked as a retail salesman for Lincoln Laboratories. After realizing the vast amount of money to be made from selling drugs, he quit his job, raised $5,000, and started his own pharmaceutical business in 1950. He reportedly chose his middle name, Marion, for the enterprise so that the company would not appear to be a one-man operation.

One of his earliest products was Os-Cal tablets, a calcium supplement made of oyster shells that he introduced in 1951. He went on to build his small drug-making business into a diversified health care company with $1 billion in annual sales and a workforce of 3,400 employees. Among Marion Laboratories's best-known products were the Cardizem family of cardiovascular drugs, the nonsedating antihistamine Seldane, and Carafate, an antiulcer product.

Kauffman's vast fortune allowed him to indulge his passion for sports, and in 1968, at the urging of his wife, Muriel McBrien, he purchased the Kansas City Royals baseball team. He proved to be as smart at owning a major league club as he had been at steering a pharmaceutical corporation. During his tenure, the Royals won six division titles and two league championships. Their biggest win was the 1985 World Series, when they defeated the St. Louis Cardinals.

As an indication of just how far Kauffman had come, in 1989 Marion Laboratories had estimated revenues of $930 million. The following year it merged with Merrell Dow Pharmaceuticals (now part of Aventis).

Sadly, all the money and drugs in the world could not relieve the excruciating pain that overtook Kauffman as his body was slowly ravaged by bone cancer. He died in his sleep at the age of 76 in 1993. One month before his death, Royals Stadium was renamed Kauffman Stadium in his honor.

■ ■ ■

ACTOR RUSSELL WADE, who played gallant young men on land, sea, and air in popular RKO wartime attractions such as *Bombardier*, *Tall in the Saddle*, *The Bamboo Blonde*, and *Shoot to Kill*, relishes his cozy retirement at 47–255 Crystal Loop, where he moved in 1984. It's about as far away from Hollywood as this self-conscious matinee idol could get without ending up in total oblivion.

Wade made more than 50 movies between 1933 and 1948, but today Wade is best-known for playing opposite Richard Dix in the fog-bound thriller *The Ghost Ship* and for extricating himself from Boris Karloff's evil clutches in the medical chiller *The Body Snatcher*. The actor's tendency toward blandness always caused him to disappear from view. What Wade lacked in style, however, he made up for in substance. When this lenient performer sensed his acting career was going nowhere, he retired from movies and went into real estate, selling Trousdale Properties in the San Fernando Valley and Westwood.

He and his wife, Jane, moved to Palm Springs in 1946 and became involved with the development of Deepwell Ranch Estates, Tahquitz River Estates, and Southridge Estates—posh neighborhoods that attracted many movie stars. Wade and his associate, Lew Levy, negotiated the first 99-year Indian land lease in Palm Springs. They represented the sales of homes in the celebrity havens of Thunderbird Country Club and Thunderbird Heights, in Rancho Mirage; sold the acreage for Ironwood Country Club in Palm Desert; and handled the sale of the land on which the city of Indian Wells was built, to become a temple for millionaires.

Wade has maintained an office at the Eldorado Country Club since its inception, and he also has represented home sales for the Vintage Club. These lasting achievements proved much more satisfying to this visionary developer than his fleeting cinematic fame—and certainly more profitable.

■ ■ ■

IN KEEPING WITH its desire for exclusivity, Indian Wells has always courted investors with deep pockets and big ideas. One of the prominent checkbooks belonged to actor **Desi Arnaz**, the political refugee from Cuba who distinguished himself as a nightclub performer and, with his wife, Lucille Ball, as a TV producer.

In 1955, Arnaz and a small group of investors, including Paul Prom, Eddie Susalla, Milt Hicks, and John Curci bought 50 acres of land and earmarked it for the desert's third country club. That winter, the men broke ground on the Indian Wells Country Club, and twelve months later, an 18-hole championship golf course and a brand-new $300,000 clubhouse designed by Val Powelson were completed. Arnaz also built the Indian Wells Hotel, which was the epitome of *nouveau riche* luxury when it opened in 1957.

Not surprisingly, the stress of acting, producing, and running the hotel soon got under Desi's skin. "He was drinking quite a bit then," recalled director William Asher, who was a frequent guest, "but he was a jolly drunk. Everybody in Indian Wells paid court to him as a celebrity but it wore off after a while."

Arnaz's reputation as a boozer sometimes attracted the wrong kind of attention. One night, Frank Sinatra stopped in to give the inebriated entrepreneur a piece of his mind about the way Italian gangsters were being unflatteringly portrayed in the TV series *The Untouchables*, a Desilu Production. Sinatra, who was feeling no pain after a night on the town with his girlfriend Dorothy Provine and chum Jimmy Van Heusen, told his friends, "I'm going to kill that Cuban prick!"

Unconcerned, Arnaz smiled and called out, "Hi ya, dago," which only pushed Sinatra's mercury further toward the boiling point. He stood there, fists clenched, spoiling for a fight. But Desi refused to take the bait and simply walked away.

■ ■ ■

IN 1929, FILM editor **Robert Carlisle** worked with Edward L. Cahn on the early sound musical *Broadway,* the start of a long association with the man who would become a prolific director at Universal. That collaboration was followed by *All Quiet on the Western Front*—regarded as the granddaddy of all war movies for its realistic battle scenes—which the pair co-edited without receiving screen credit and which went on to win the Oscar for Best Picture in 1930.

All together, Carlisle edited more than 50 sound films, including the classic murder mystery *The Last Warning,* directed by Paul Leni, and the two-strip Technicolor musical revue *King of Jazz.* One of his widely seen efforts, hardly appreciated, was the novelty film series *Speaking of Animals.* But his cleverest work was the classic Three Stooges short, *Punch Drunks,* in which Moe plays a boxing promoter whose prizefighter, Curly, goes bananas every time he hears Larry play the tune "Pop Goes the Weasel."

Carlisle reunited with Cahn for the director's last six films, which revolved around such tried-and-true storylines as a stagecoach hold-up in *Gun Fight,* a botched robbery in *Boy Who Caught a Crook,* and the classic fairytale *Beauty and the Beast.* Carlisle died at the age of 92 in 1998.

■ ■ ■

NEWSPAPER OBITUARIES WERE strangely subdued about the passing of one of America's most powerful crime figures, Chicago Mafia boss **Anthony Accardo,** a longtime resident of 76–841 Roadrunner Drive.

Dubbed "Big Tuna" by the headline-hungry press, who marveled at his ability to keep swimming in a sea of sharks, the wily Accardo was the last link between Al Capone and Prohibition. At the time, he had excelled as Capone's fearsome bodyguard, often wielding a baseball bat as his weapon of choice. Accardo's preferred nickname, in fact, was "Joe Batters," because of a famous incident involving two Sicilian contract killers named Alberto Anselmi and John Scalise. When Accardo learned they were plotting to kill Capone, he allegedly clubbed the two men to death and calmly dumped their bodies in a ditch.

After Capone's successor, Frank "The Enforcer" Nitti, committed suicide in 1943 (rather than take the rap for his crimes), Paul Ricca, a former gangland waiter, assumed control of the mob. Accardo was promoted to his second-in-command. When Ricca was sent to prison for three years, Accardo ran the day-to-day operations from outside but deferred all decisions to his boss on the inside. Ricca was apparently so grateful that, when he got out of prison, he put Accardo in charge of the mob's wire operations and betting parlors.

Accardo fought to gain control of the Nationwide News Service, which had been owned by Moses Annenberg and was taken over by James Ragen after Annenberg was sent to prison. But when Ragen refused to cut Accardo in on a share of the profits, the stubborn wire owner found himself the victim of a drive-by shooting, which he miraculously survived only to be poisoned, reportedly on Accardo's orders. Clearly Accardo was not to be trifled with.

By 1950, he controlled more than 10,000 Chicago gambling dens, ranging from cigar stands to pool rooms. Later, under his leadership, the Chicago outfit expanded its territory to include Las Vegas, which they took away from the New York mob as well as the rest of the United States. For much of this time, Accardo ran his betting empire, which the Kefauver Senate Committee had called "the life blood of the outfit," from a black marble bathtub in the opulent home that served as his unofficial command post. Indeed, throughout his reign, Accardo boasted that he had never spent a night in jail, even though he was indicted several times between 1948 and 1982 for various crimes, including income tax evasion.

He was briefly forced to relinquish his leadership to Sam Giancana, when adverse publicity about Accardo's grandiose lifestyle made the headlines in 1962. But he was reinstalled four years later when Giancana did a yearlong prison stretch for refusing to testify before a federal grand jury. From 1979 until his retirement, Accardo served as the mob's chairman emeritus, living in the desert and overseeing business from Indian Wells, while younger men carried out his orders back in Chicago.

Trouble finally caught up with him in his final years, when he was besieged by legal and personal problems. Only through his body's inevitable demise, as he slowly succumbed to advancing heart disease and cancer, was the ailing gang leader able to escape prosecution for his crimes. He died at age 86 in 1992.

■ ■ ■

WORLD WAR II fighter pilot **Robert Prescott** earned the peacetime admiration of the nation's corporate sector as founder and president of Flying Tiger Line, which pioneered air cargo transportation. He resided at 76–742 Iroquois Drive.

Early in the war he had participated in five major campaigns while serving as a flight leader for the American Volunteer Group—popularly known as the Flying Tigers—which flew medical supplies and other precious cargo over China. When the AVG was disbanded in July 1942, Prescott returned to the United States and began flying with the Intercontinental Division of Trans World Airlines. He was a copilot on the famous Mission to Moscow flight of Ambassador Joseph E. Davies in 1942, and later that year he returned to China as a captain with the China National Aviation Corporation, flying military supplies into China from India over the famous "Hump." He completed more than 300 flights over that treacherous Himalayan route.

Back in the United States in 1944, he took a trip to Acapulco, Mexico, and met a group of Los Angeles businessmen associated with Samuel Mosher, the Los Angeles oil pioneer and magnate. Mosher and his associates were exploring the possibility of establishing an air freight line along the west coasts of the United States and Mexico. Prescott convinced them that a better idea would be a route across the United States. They agreed to match whatever capital he could raise, and Prescott was appointed to find aircraft and set up the airline.

He found 14 Navy-surplus Budd Conestoga cargo aircraft and collected $89,000 from friends who had flown with him in China; Mosher's group put up an equal amount. A month or so later, he landed his first three consignments: a planeload of grapes from Bakersfield to Atlanta, flowers from California to Detroit, and furniture from New York to California. And that's how, in 1945, Prescott founded the Flying Tiger Line.

A four-year fight for official government certification ended in 1949 with approval of the nation's first commercial all-cargo route. Twenty years later, in mid-1969, Flying Tiger Line was awarded the first scheduled transpacific all-cargo route, and in 1977, Congress and President Carter approved the deregulation of the air freight airlines, which then enabled Flying Tiger to offer expedited freighter service to all 50 states, Puerto Rico, and the Virgin Islands.

One year later the adventuresome Prescott died of cancer. He was 64.

■ ■ ■

SPINDLY ACTOR **ARTHUR Lake** was best known for his screen character Dagwood Bumstead, the bow-tie-wearing, squeaky-voiced, idiot husband in the *Blondie* film and TV series. But all that was behind him when he retired to 76–829 Iroquois Drive, his third desert home.

Despite appearing in more than 140 silent and sound films, including the sparkling comedy *Indiscreet* and the ghostly fantasy *Topper*, Lake remained convinced that he was typecast and sought refuge in a drink or two at the end of each day on the set. "When I don't play a dope, I don't work," he lamented. Thirty years later he was still getting fan mail addressed to "Dagwood," which both surprised and annoyed him. Whenever he put on his coat and tie and made a personal appearance at a reunion with a bunch of kids dressed as Baby Dumpling and Cookie, someone inevitably presented him with a mountainous Dagwood sandwich. He couldn't eat it because he was on a strict diet.

Lake was a real, honest-to-goodness show business baby. The son of circus acrobats, he had started performing on the stage as an infant and graduated to juvenile roles. He matured into a tall, lanky young man, and his future seemed uncertain—until he met and fell in love with William Randolph Hearst's young niece, Patricia Van Cleve.

Their meeting was serendipitous. Lake was starring in the *Blondie* films; Lake had become friendly with Hearst's sons, whose father's newspapers ran the *Blondie* comic strip. Van Cleve had been a singer with the Russ Morgan band and bore a striking resemblance to Hearst, with whom she was often seen at family gatherings.

Their 1937 storybook wedding at the Hearst castle at San Simeon was an elaborate affair—and the only matrimonial ceremony that took place on those hallowed grounds during Hearst's lifetime. The teary-eyed grand old man of newspaper publishing threw a huge party for the newlyweds, although guests had to toast the bride and groom without the customary champagne, because "W.R." forbade liquor to be served; he feared that his guests would become intoxicated.

The Lakes had two children: Arthur Jr.; and a daughter they christened Marion, in honor of Hearst's alcoholic mistress and moral champion, Marion Davies (the ban on liquor had no effect on her—she smuggled her own stash into the castle). It was Davies in fact who welcomed the young son-in-law into the gloomy Hearst fold and made sure he was treated like one of the family. More than sixty years later, the reason for her demonstrative behavior became all too clear.

It seemed that the family harbored a dark secret, which Davies and Hearst made Arthur Lake and his wife promise not to reveal. Lake, who died of a massive heart attack at the age of 81, took the secret with him to the grave. But in 1993, when she was dying of lung cancer, Patricia Van Cleve Lake gathered her children to her bedside and informed them that it was time to tell the world her secret.

She wasn't a Van Cleve, as people had been led to believe so many decades earlier. She was the love child of William Randolph Hearst and Marion Davies.

Gasping for breath, she explained what had really happened. Davies had become pregnant by Hearst in the fall of 1918 and had given birth the following summer to a healthy, blond-haired baby girl. To avoid a scandal that would have ruined all their lives, the parents handed over the precious bundle to Davies's sister, Rose Douras, a chorus girl whose own child had died in infancy. According to Patricia's amazing story, the birth certificate was altered, and the little girl was raised as the daughter of Rose and her husband, George Van Cleve. Hearst paid for her education at private schools in Boston and New York, where she was introduced to café society as Hearst's niece. The public was fooled; hardly anybody suspected the charade. Then, on her wedding day, W.R. took his "niece" aside and broke the news that she was really his daughter. Pat looked at her father and she knew, and they hugged each other and cried tears of joy.

After finishing her heart-breaking confession, Patricia Van Cleve Hearst Lake fell silent, although her wan face was smiling. She died shortly after. Various reports gave her age as 70, but her social security card didn't lie: she was actually 74.

Six months later, Arthur Lake, Jr., whom Hearst had nicknamed "A.P." after the abbreviation used in newsrooms for the Associated Press, was speeding along Highway 111 when his car crashed near the city of

Blythe and he was killed. He was 51. His funeral took place the following week at Hollywood Memorial Park, two days before what would
have been his late father's eighty-ninth birthday.

■ ■ ■

THE SPECTER OF death clung to Oscar-nominated cinematographer
Lucien Ballard, who was a resident of 46–420 Blackhawk Drive. Ballard
was renowned for his sumptuous photography on nearly 130 films, starting with Ernst Lubitsch's *The Love Parade* and continuing with Josef Von
Sternberg's *Morocco* and *The Devil Is a Woman,* both of which starred Marlene Dietrich. The German-born actress, who wanted to look ten years
younger than she actually was, trained Ballard in the subtle art of lighting.

Ballard remembered that lesson when it came time to photograph
Merle Oberon in 1944 in *The Lodger.* The British-Indian actress had sensitive skin that had been severely damaged by cosmetics. In 1937, she had
sustained facial scarring in a near-fatal car crash in London during the
making of *I, Claudius,* which was produced by her former husband, Hungarian movie mogul Alexander Korda. Ballard devised a special spotlight
to reduce unflattering lines and shadows on Oberon's face. He mounted
the device, which he called an "Obie," next to the camera, so that in close-
ups Oberon's skin defects would be minimized by the filtered light.
Oberon was so grateful for Ballard's kindness that she married him, and
he performed the same magic on her next three films.

After they divorced in 1949, Ballard was kept busy lighting and photographing many large-scale productions. There were Technicolor epics
such as *Prince Valiant, White Feather,* and *Seven Cities of Gold*, which benefited from his unerring ability to render a stately pictorial quality, and
there were tense, smaller dramas such as *Don't Bother to Knock, The
Killing,* and *A Kiss Before Dying.* His expertise at capturing panoramas
resulted in some of the best-looking Westerns of the period; snow-
capped mountains, sun-dappled forests, and raging rivers draw the eye in
The Sons of Katie Elder, Nevada Smith, and *Will Penny.* There was also *True
Grit* with its famous autumn showdown between John Wayne's one-eyed
sheriff and Robert Duvall's posse on horseback.

Ballard particularly enjoyed the camaraderie of pistol-packing director Sam Peckinpah, with whom he worked on five films. Peckinpah was

a bloodthirsty martinet who demanded realistic violence in *Ride the High Country, The Wild Bunch, The Ballad of Cable Hogue, Junior Bonner,* and *The Getaway.* Ballard indulged him with close-ups of gaping bullet holes, knife wounds, and spurts of blood so realistic that audiences feel squeamish. "I want to contribute to a picture," he said, "not just work on it. I'm their man if they want more than a cameraman."

In 1988, that realism would come back to haunt him when Ballard was fatally injured in a local traffic accident, dying a hero's death as he reportedly tried to avoid colliding with another vehicle. He was 84.

■ ■ ■

COLD, CALCULATING, AND always pushing the bounds of controversy, writer, director, and producer **Oliver Stone** has made a career out of selling conspiracy theories to the masses. It seems that audiences are eager to believe in corruption at the highest levels, whether in Cuba, Vietnam, or Washington, D.C.—places that have been touched by Stone's vivid re-creations of political history.

Even his most recent film, *Alexander,* about the Greek conqueror that cut a swathe through much of the ancient world, seemed less a re-creation of one man's life than a reinvention of it to fit the mood of the times—a one-man crusade against tyranny retold as a modern-day political allegory. His right-wing critics may call him paranoid, but Stone, who has labored for decades to bring his pet subjects of high-level scandals and intricate cover-ups to the screen, would probably be much happier with the all-encompassing title of cinematic provocateur.

Stone won an Oscar for *Midnight Express,* for which he wrote a pulsating screenplay about Billy Hayes's true-life arrest and imprisonment in a Turkish jail for smuggling hashish. Impressively acted by the late Brad Davis, who succumbed to AIDS, it was the first mainstream film to deal head-on with the horrors of drug-related incarceration in a foreign prison.

Unfortunately, Stone's next two screenplays, for *Scarface* and *Year of the Dragon,* were lambasted by critics for their sexism and violence. If these films had a point of view that was intended to demonstrate the vagaries of crime, Stone's cocaine binges, which allegedly fueled his imagination, detracted from the finished product. He fared better with his personal vision of a soldier's hell in *Platoon*, the first of his three films dealing with the atrocities of Vietnam, where he had served a tour of duty prior to his filmmaking days. Stone's uncompromising movie won him an Oscar for Best Directing, as did his emotional follow-up about the plight of returning servicemen, *Born on the Fourth of July*. The last entry in Stone's war-torn trilogy was *Heaven and Earth*, which was based on the memoirs of a Vietnamese survivor, Le Ly Hayslip.

Moving from the killing in Vietnam to people who make killings in the stock market, Stone engineered a surprise hit with *Wall Street*, an exposé that was released on the eve of the 1987 global recession. The movie's star, Michael Douglas, won the Oscar for Best Actor for his ferociously intimidating performance as Gordon Gecko, whose "Greed is Good" motto became the mantra for junk-bond traders and get-rich-quick entrepreneurs.

But it was while living at 46–522 Arapahoe that Stone embarked on some of his most groundbreaking and disturbing films. Lobbing the first volley with *The Doors*, the fearless director offered up a psychedelic retelling of the life of legendary rock 'n' roll singer, songwriter, and poet Jim Morrison, who died of a heart attack most likely precipitated by a drug overdose.

His next movie proved even more provocative. Stone had always identified strongly with social martyrs, so it was fitting that he should take up the subject of President John F. Kennedy's assassination for *JFK*, a stunning visual paean to the fallen king of Camelot. But so much of the three-hour marathon was deemed a suspicious concoction of fact and fiction that wags christened its politically obsessed creator "Oliver *Stoned*."

He must have ignored the hint and said to hell with the critics, because he really tripped out during his next cause célèbre, *Natural Born Killers*, about a pair of hallucinating lovers who go on a cross-country crime spree. Stone's repellent film inspired a copycat shooting that left a female convenience-store clerk a quadriplegic and resulted in a multimillion-dollar lawsuit against the director.

Unfazed, Stone followed with *Nixon*, which attempted to portray the much-maligned president, who had resigned from office over the Watergate scandal, in a sympathetic light. This latest take on the abuse of power garnered Stone his eleventh Oscar nomination, although there were still detractors who accused him of playing fast and loose with the truth.

Bowing to media pressure at long last, Stone finally chose a less controversial topic for the introspective character study *U-Turn,* about an unlucky gambler whose car breaks down in the sweltering desert. The stylish Sean Penn film was released in 1997—the same year Stone quietly sold his Indian Wells Country Club home.

Two years later, in one of those surreal "life-imitates-art" moments, Stone was arrested for drunk driving and possession of hashish when police stopped his swerving car late one night in Beverly Hills. But where Billy Hayes, the drug-smuggling hero of Stone's *Midnight Express* was beaten and raped at the hands of his Middle East captors, Stone was spared those atrocities by the LAPD. He pled "no contest" to drunken driving and drug possession, and entered a drug rehabilitation center for treatment. He paid a token fine and was allowed to go home with his celebrity status intact.

So much for the evils of democracy!

Famous Liaisons

I T WAS EITHER fortuitous or foolish; he wasn't quite sure which. But Walter Morgan of San Francisco, whose wealthy father, John S. Morgan, owned the Morgan Oyster Company, felt compelled to spend $150,000 to construct a 20-room, hacienda-style hotel in a sheltered spot called Marshall Cove, 18 miles east of Palm Springs.

The year was 1925, and nothing existed in that part of the land except for a shallow dirt road and a few isolated watering holes. Morgan didn't care. Like a gold prospector suffering the effects of sunstroke, he staked his claim and was determined to strike it rich. Morgan had been imbued with this peculiar vision of a "home-on-the-hill" since encountering a rancher who described a big house surrounded by cottages that he had seen on a vacation to rural Mexico. The place had been named "La Quinta."

Morgan envisioned creating a secluded getaway similar to the one that had been described to him and with that in mind he purchased 1,400 acres of land in Happy Hollow, as the Cahuilla Indians called the place.

The sand, he had been told, was the bottom of an ancient lake, and fossilized prehistoric shells could be glimpsed in the hardened clay at the base of the Santa Rosa Mountains, where native tribes combined the red substance with water to make earthenware pots, or ollas.

Morgan's sense of pride propelled him to hire the best architect that his money could buy, and the person in whom he had the greatest faith was a man named Gordon Kaufmann. Within a few years, Kaufmann would become a leading practitioner of California-Spanish architecture—an eclectic, freely interpreted, Mediterranean-style of design that would prove ideal for the climate and habits of Southern California. But for now, Morgan's hotel was the architect's first important commission.

Morgan and Kaufmann conferred many long hours over the hotel's construction, to ensure the best possible layout and design for its interweaving concourse of buildings and pathways. Mexican laborers crafted more than 100,000 adobe bricks, along with 60,000 roof tiles and 5,000 floor tiles, handmade from clay and fired in glowing kilns at the construction site.

Designed around three stone courtyards, 20 cottages were arranged in concentric circles and named alphabetically after Spanish patron saints: San Anselmo, San Benito, San Carlos, San Dimas, San Jacinto, San Lucas. . . . The list went on.

Whenever Morgan needed inspiration, he would walk into a nearby field and turn his head to the heavens—or so it was said. Then he would nod in mute understanding, as though he had heard a voice, and return to the hotel to continue his work. Even the hotel's name was carefully chosen to reflect Morgan's belief in a higher power. According to Spanish legend, La Quinta, which means "the fifth," is the customary day of rest for overland travelers. Morgan wanted his hotel to be known as a place of rest.

For Morgan, however, there was little relaxation. He had planned the grand opening for Christmas 1926, but had to delay the debut for two months in order to finish decorating the hotel and stocking it with the provisions needed to meet his stringent demands. No sooner had the rooms been painted and furnished, than an influx of visitors descended on the cozy inn, pulling up to the curb in shiny roadsters and passing through the blue-and-white double doors into the lobby.

Among the auspicious names on the first season's guest roster were

Senator Robert Taft's brother, Charles Taft, and San Francisco railroad magnate William Crocker, who were served plates of fresh rock oysters and chilled magnums of French champagne. Although Morgan abhorred publicity, he wasted no time promoting his hotel to Hollywood's newest stars. Greta Garbo, Ronald Colman, Marlene Dietrich, Clark Gable, Joan Crawford—they came by car and train to Palm Springs, where they were escorted to the hotel.

"La Quinta Hotel in the 1930's was notorious for having more celebrity, political and royal guests than any other hotel in the world," said nationally ranked tennis player Fred Renker, whose name graces one of the hotel's swimming pavilions. "While working there as a tennis professional, I had the privilege of teaching many of these famous people."

Morgan, however, never lived to see these impressive results. In 1931, he was found dead, a victim of carbon monoxide poisoning. In a suicide note to his wife, Elizabeth Sheard, he lamented his family's dwindling fortune and his personal health problems, which would have required that he be committed to a sanitarium. He was cremated, and his ashes were scattered among the date groves and flower gardens of the hotel he loved.

In succeeding years, a change of management brought renewed luster to the stately white adobe compound, with its 125-foot flagpole, visible from several miles away. "I'm off to La Quinta," a beaming Bette Davis told reporters between takes on the set of *Jezebel*. She had good reason to smile—the film was being directed by her effusive lover William Wyler and would win the melodramatic star a second Oscar for Best Actress. Davis holed up at La Quinta for weeks at a time, often studying the script for her next film, marking the pages with a red pencil, and going through so many cigarettes that puffs of smoke wafted up from her bedroom window.

But the majority of stars, who toiled on Hollywood sound stages under hot lights for twelve hours a day, six days a week, found La Quinta was not so much a source of inspiration as a place to discover some isolation. The elusive Garbo, for example, nearly always traveled under the cover of darkness, and she insisted on using pseudonyms, one of which was Harriet Brown.

Legend has it that Garbo's first visit to the hotel was at the suggestion of her agent Harry Edington, who, with the help of his chauffeur, rescued the world's most admired actress from a phone booth where she was being surrounded by a mob of clamoring fans.

"Where to, boss?" the chauffeur asked.

"Do you have a full tank of gas?" asked Edington.

"Yes," he replied.

"Then don't stop until we get to La Quinta."

Retired bellboys, who said they were generously tipped by Mrs. Brown, stated that she and her roguish co-star John Gilbert, who registered as Mr. Brown, were frequent guests during their real-life love affair. The couple also supposedly leased "La Casa," a private home built in the late 1920s on the hotel's southwest corner, next to the house later occupied by the lesbian Hollywood director Dorothy Arzner.

When Garbo bowed to studio pressure and reluctantly broke off the tumultuous affair, Gilbert was so devastated that he began drinking heavily. He died of a heart attack in 1936.

Hollywood stars were not the only celebrities to seek refuge from the outside world at La Quinta. Well-known industrialists like the DuPonts, the Gianninis, and the Vanderbilts also vacationed there. "If it's far from the maddening crowd you want to be," wrote Cornelius Vanderbilt, Jr., "there's no better place to be than at the exclusive La Quinta Hotel."

Film and theater composer Irving Berlin, whose multitude of hits include the movie *Top Hat* and the Broadway show *Annie Get Your Gun*, is said to have written the song "White Christmas" while staying in one of La Quinta's cottages, where he puffed on a cigar while pounding on an upright piano.

■ ■ ■

CERTAINLY NO GREATER example of the desert's power for divine intervention exists than the fruitful collaboration of two highly creative men whose personalities and styles were wildly different.

The films of Italian-born director **Frank Capra** and New York screenwriter Robert Riskin rank among the best examples of traditional American cinema. Their buoyant optimism and devoted belief in the cornerstones of democracy formed the basis of their heartwarming films.

Capra and Riskin first experienced the charms of La Quinta Hotel in 1933 when the pair settled down in one of the cottages to write *Lady for a Day*, based on a Damon Runyon story about a bunch of hoodlums who turn a penniless old woman into a society dame. Riskin wrote the script in six weeks, and its basic premise became the template for what critics referred to as "Capra Corn": the director's special brand of idealism, a film in which the little guy or girl gets a chance to beat the system.

It spurred the myth that Capra was a writer, which he was not; he was an ideas man, a role he had taken as far back as the silent-film era, when he used to devise gags for the *Our Gang*, Harry Langdon, and Mack Sennett comedies. Riskin typically wrote his first draft while sitting in the sun on the verandah outside his office at Columbia Pictures. Then he and Capra would travel to La Quinta and rewrite scenes and dialogue until they had a finished script. The whole process took approximately three months.

That's how they came up with the zany comedy *It Happened One Night*, which starred Clark Gable and Claudette Colbert. It was originally a short story called "Night Bus," about a runaway heiress who falls in love with a newspaper reporter. Capra read the tale in *Cosmopolitan* magazine, while getting a haircut at a Palm Springs barbershop, and thought it would make a good movie. The film swept the 1934 Academy Awards, winning an unprecedented five Oscars for Best Picture, Actor, Actress, Writer, and Director—the only quintuple win until *One Flew over the Cuckoo's Nest* more than 40 years later.

After the film's big success, Capra and Riskin considered La Quinta their lucky writing spot, and each year they returned to the hotel at 49–499 Eisenhower Drive to spin more movie magic. Their collaborations included the good-natured racetrack fable *Broadway Bill*, which was followed by the endearing antics of *Mr. Deeds Goes to Town* and the search for utopia in *Lost Horizon*. Their final two scripts, which Capra acted out while Riskin typed, revolved around the exploits of a greedy family in *You Can't Take It with You* and a newspaper hoax that almost ends in tragedy in *Meet John Doe*. These cinematic treats were all written in Capra's favorite *casita*, #136.

Riskin authored nine screenplays for Capra, and the director based four other films on Riskin's material, including two remakes. The resulting films won Capra two more Oscars for Best Director, bringing his combined award tally to three. It was, by and large, a happy partnership.

"Riskin brought to Capra a slangy, down-to-earth humor, almost a cracker-barrel philosophy, which worked well with Capra's style," marveled Sidney Buchman, who wrote *Mr. Smith Goes to Washington*. The moral qualities extolled in Capra's populist films were not empty gestures;

he carried them over into his private life.

For instance, he was modestly proud of his professional achievements and he was embarrassed about sexual matters, professing that he had been a virgin until about the time of his first marriage, which ended in divorce after four years. For almost two years he was deeply in love with actress Barbara Stanwyck, whom he directed in five films. But their affair was fraught with her overwhelming neuroses and his personal hang-ups, and their passion for each other gradually abated.

As much as Capra realized he needed the love of a strong woman, he was afraid he couldn't satisfy her emotional and physical needs. No matter how attractive a woman's figure or her virtues, he always considered himself to be a "wash-out" in bed. Privately, Capra anguished over his slight physical appearance and claimed he was sexually dysfunctional, the result of being beaten as a young child by his abusive mother and homosexually molested as a youth.

Somehow none of that affected his second marriage, to Lucille Rayburn, and they formed a lasting union. The couple raised three children: Frank, Jr.; Lulu; and Thomas. A third son, John, was born deaf and subsequently died while undergoing a tonsillectomy. The loss had a profound effect on Capra. Afterward, his films took on a darker tone, particularly in his despairing Christmas tale, *It's a Wonderful Life*.

Not surprisingly, the melancholy film, in which James Stewart wails about his misfortunes, was a box office failure. It wasn't until 25 years later, when the movie began attracting renewed interest through frequent TV showings, that this fable about a suicidal father whose life is saved by a guardian angel found a new audience ready to accept its message of hope. The film's assertion that family is everything was pure Capra, and it's a message in which he truly believed. Nothing mattered more to him than spending time with his family.

He took them to La Quinta at every opportunity. "The whole family would move into the hotel when dad was writing," recalled Tom Capra. "Dad and Bob Riskin would write every morning, and every afternoon they swam or played tennis." The kids rode horses and explored the desert, and meanwhile composer Dmitri Tiomkin would be picking out a tune on the piano for Capra's next movie.

Capra tradition dictated that the entire family should spend a week at

La Quinta Hotel between Christmas and New Year's Day. "We'd have all the Christmas decorations from our house in L.A. brought down and set up in our hotel room," Tom Capra said. By the end of 1945, Hollywood's connection with La Quinta was so entrenched that the hotel was bought by Chicago businessman John Balaban, whose brother Barney Balaban was the president of Paramount Pictures. It became a place to send valuable stars like Gary Cooper, Joel McCrea, and Charlton Heston for rest and relaxation.

Capra continued to stay at the hotel, but Riskin was no longer able to keep up the pace the collaborators had set during the previous decade. The grind of making movies, no matter how profitable, affected his health, and in 1950 he suffered a stroke that left him an invalid. Rancho Mirage residents Harpo and Susan Marx were among the first people to visit the paralyzed writer at home. Capra, curiously, was not among the well-wishers.

Riskin died in 1955 at the age of 58. His widow, actress Fay Wray, who gave an unforgettable performance as the screaming heroine abducted by a giant ape in *King Kong*, survived him by 49 years. She died at the age of 96 in 2004.

As for Capra, when he no longer felt the burning desire to create works of cinematic art, he retired to a sprawling hillside ranch in Fallbrook near San Diego, where he worked 30 acres of lemons, four acres of limes, and 52 acres of avocados. Predating the agricultural endeavors of another great Italian director, Francis Ford Coppola, with whom he had much in common, Capra also cultivated 105 acres of olive trees. For several years he operated a mail-order business that sold olive oil in bottles labeled "Produced by Frank Capra."

But the unpredictable nature of farming proved financially draining, and when Capra found himself in need of cash he sold the ranch for $2 million, which was a lot more money than he had ever seen from any of his films. "I wasn't really wise financially—I'm probably the poorest director you ever saw," Capra complained. In fact, the director was worth around $5 million, much of it from investments in land and blue-chip stocks.

La Quinta Hotel continued to be a popular weekend getaway. After the Balaban family sold the hotel and its surrounding acreage to Chicago financier Leonard Ettelson, the historic lodging expanded and added an 18-hole championship golf course.

■ ■ ■

OF MAJOR INTEREST was the opening of La Quinta Country Club in 1960, which attracted an influx of well-heeled members, including Conrad Hilton, founder of Hilton Hotels, and Washington attorney Edgar Eisenhower, President Dwight D. Eisenhower's older brother, who celebrated his eightieth birthday at the club.

In 1970, the Capras retired to a white ranch-style home at 49–280 Avenida Fernando, on the tenth fairway. The energetic director put the finishing touches to his autobiography, *The Name Above the Title,* and golfed with Senator Barry Goldwater and President Gerald R. Ford. Capra also served as committee chairman for the fund-raising drive to build St. Francis of Assisi Church, a full-scale replica of an eighteenth century chapel at 47–225 Washington Street. The spectacular Romanesque church, which took ten years to complete, was designed by famed Italian opera director Franco Zeffirelli, who is best known for the films *Romeo and Juliet* and *Endless Love.*

For the most part Capra was happy basking in his glory. The thrill of filmmaking now gone, he learned to live vicariously through other people's achievements. Then suddenly, after years of being ignored, he found himself the recipient of numerous awards, and there was even talk of a comeback. But Lucille, who had witnessed her husband's greatest triumphs as well as his biggest disappointments, pleaded with him for peace and tranquility in the sunset of their lives. After ten years they sold the house and leased a three-bedroom bungalow at La Quinta Hotel. The arrangement was far from perfect, but Capra had little choice; his wife was dying of lung cancer. She had been told to give up cigarette smoking back in 1963, but she continued to puff away on as many as three packs a day until she contracted emphysema, which killed her in 1984.

After she died, Capra became sullen and withdrawn. When Universal proposed a TV movie called *It's Still a Wonderful Life,* with James Stewart and Donna Reed reprising their original film roles, Capra, still smarting over the failure of his last movie, *Pocketful of Miracles,* bitterly replied, "They can go fuck themselves."

His dark moods were not helped by failing eyesight, which prevented him from reading books and driving a car, and made him a virtual prisoner in his own home. The resulting nervous tension caused him to suffer a devastating series of strokes, much like those that had crippled his former writing partner Robert Riskin. According to Capra's biographer, Joseph McBride, "He spent his declining years in a condominium at the Santa Rosa Cove, a security complex next to the La Quinta Hotel, in a becalmed, passive state, eating and sleeping and watching television in the company of his nurses and family."

Jimmy Stewart was shocked to find Capra in this vegetative state when he visited his old friend for the last time in 1988. Mercifully, the director's deteriorating condition didn't last too long; Capra died in his sleep of a heart attack in 1991, at the age of 94, and was laid to rest beside his wife of 52 years in Coachella Valley Cemetery.

The following year, La Quinta Hotel was purchased by KSL Resorts and renamed La Quinta Resort and Club. Today La Quinta is the only incorporated city in the United States named after a hotel, a little-known fact that brings immense pride and satisfaction to the city's 30,000 residents and innumerable visitors.

■ ■ ■

PEOPLE DRIVING PAST the front garden of the tile-and-stucco home of **Dorothy Arzner**, who resided at 49–800 Avenida Obregon, had no idea that the hunched lady occasionally seen trimming roses in the backyard was Hollywood's first woman director.

Despite having made more than 20 widely acclaimed feature films, she had managed to go unnoticed during her retirement, until several well-deserved tributes brought her newfound attention late in life. Arzner characteristically took it all in her stride, as she had way back in the silent era when she first joined Famous Players-Lasky (later Paramount Pictures) as a dependable typist in their secretarial pool. Her keen intellect and strong work ethic took the talented young employee to the editing department, where she used her cutting and pasting skills to edit the Rudolph Valentino bullfighting drama *Blood and Sand* and the 1923 Western epic *The Covered Wagon*.

Those were prestigious films in their day, and the fact that Arzner, who labored for long hours on their production, was not overawed by their importance or her responsibility, impressed the studio brass. She soon assumed the even more important position of script writer, and at the age of 28 she wrote and edited the exciting seagoing adventure *Old Ironsides*, which was directed by her mentor, James Cruze.

The results proved so impressive, she was handed her first directing assignment, the racy comedy *Fashions for Women* starring Esther Ralston, who had been dubbed "the American Venus" for her voluptuous good looks. From then on Arzner helmed many scenarios that dealt with the battle of the sexes. Arzner's timing was fortunate: most of her best films were made before the introduction of the Hays Code, which imposed strict censorship on the movies. The young director was able to depict many vices, including drug addiction and prostitution, that a few years later would be taboo.

In that vein, she directed Paramount's first talking picture, *The Wild Party*, starring Clara Bow as a good-time girl, along with *Sarah and Son*, the tale of a dedicated mother searching for her abused son; *Anybody's Woman;* and *Working Girls*, about the plight of women during the Great Depression. One of her most poignant films was *Merrily We Go to Hell*, in which an heiress squanders her affections on an alcoholic playwright. Arzner's outspoken behavior on the set sometimes peeved male chauvinistic executives, but it endeared her to many of the actors and actresses in these films, notably Ruth Chatterton and Fredric March, who were allowed to stretch in challenging roles.

After leaving Paramount, Arzner freelanced at different studios, including RKO and Columbia. She helped launch the career of Katharine Hepburn, whom she directed as a liberated aviatrix in *Christopher Strong*, cast Rosalind Russell as a materialistic spouse in *Craig's Wife* (the picture won Arzner an Oscar nomination for Best Director), and gave Lucille Ball a rare leading part as the gruff burlesque dancer in *Dance, Girl, Dance*.

Each of these films represents strong feminist values at a time when most women's roles on the screen were subordinate to those of their leading men. This ability to package her heartfelt message as glossy entertainment, while not diluting its social relevance, was quite a feat. If the subject matter of Arzner's films was considered heavy stuff to some observers, her appearance was just as formidable. She dressed like a man, close-cropping her hair and often wearing a business suit and tie. If a producer gave her any flack she would stop filming, pick up the script and head for the parking lot." "Get yourself another boy," I used to tell them."

It has long been rumored that Arzner was romantically involved with Joan Crawford, whom she directed with typical sassiness as the poor girl who makes good in *The Bride Wore Red*. After joining the board of Pepsi-Cola, Crawford personally requested Arzner's services to make a batch of film commercials promoting the popular soft drink. Arzner obliged, although one can hardly imagine the director rubbing her hands together with glee at the prospect.

For much of her life, this no-nonsense director lived with Marion Morgan, a writer and choreographer who had once worked for Mae West. Arzner devoted her final years to teaching screenwriting and directing at UCLA. She died at the age of 82 in 1979.

■ ■ ■

POUTING ACTRESS **TIFFANI-AMBER** Thiessen, who played the conniving vixen Valerie Malone on *Beverly Hills 90210* for five seasons, is one of the new breed of young Hollywood stars who are desert-bound.

The former teenage cover girl and winner of Miss Junior America got her big break playing the popular cheerleader Kelly Kapowski on the NBC family sitcom *Saved by the Bell*. Her firm breasts and shapely legs stirred the first awakenings of sexuality in millions of pubescent school boys and undoubtedly in many infatuated girls who watched the weekly series.

Thiessen eventually bid farewell to TV and moved to the big screen, where she landed fetching roles in the adolescent comedies *Love Stinks,* with French Stewart, and *The Ladies Man,* opposite Tim Meadows. She was then chosen to play a buxom actress who seduces Woody Allen in the funny romantic tale *Hollywood Ending*. Not surprisingly, the full-figured actress has a long list of handsome suitors. She lived with her *90210* co-star Brian Austin Green for several years and was engaged to actor Richard Ruccolo from Fox TV's *Two Guys, a Girl and a Pizza Place*.

In 2001, Thiessen paid $525,000 for the home at 49–442 Avenida Obregon, where she is a frequent visitor with her current fiancé, actor Brady Smith, and their two dogs and cats.

■ ■ ■

HUNGRY DINERS NEVER lost their appetite for the tangy breakfasts that executive chef **Peter Marsoobian**, who resided at 78–975 Via Trieste, created for the International House of Pancakes.

A culinary-arts graduate of Le Cordon Bleu in Paris, and three times a national gold-medal winner for his famous pancake mix, Marsoobian helped revitalize that traditional menu item by filling it with exotic spices and adding rich, flavorful sauces. In 1958, IHOP cofounder Al Lapin, Jr., who, with his younger brother, Jerry, established the blue-roofed restaurant chain in Toluca Lake, California, hired Marsoobian to create the company's signature line of pancakes and crêpes.

The restaurants became a pancake fanatic's delight. Diners feasted on German griddlecakes with lemon butter, French crêpes with orange sauce, Swedish pancakes made with lingonberries and dripping with lingonberry butter. The tables offered pitchers of boysenberry, blueberry, and strawberry syrups, which most people at that time had never tasted. The delectable combinations, coupled with a carafe of freshly brewed coffee, ensured a memorable dining experience.

Marsoobian, the man who revolutionized American breakfasts, died in 2003 at the age of 82.

■ ■ ■

THEY SOUNDED LIKE a vaudeville team: the Touchdown Twins. But their talent wasn't singing or dancing; it was playing football. Their names were Felix Blanchard and **Glenn Davis**, and they were a rough-and-tumble fullback and halfback, whose speed and agility on the field made them the most famous running-back combination in the history of college football.

The two young men had met at the U.S. Military Academy in West Point, which produced an unbeatable Army team that dominated college football after World War II. Blanchard was the bigger of the two, so he kept to the inside, and Davis was quicker on his feet, so he stayed on the outside. They could do it all: running, passing, and blocking; defense and offense.

The "twins" played together for three exciting seasons, leaving crowds cheering in the stands, and each winning the Heisman Trophy for their efforts. Davis scored 59 touchdowns, Blanchard 38. In his final game for Army, played against Navy, Davis made a leaping, left-handed interception and returned it for a touchdown. Although they both had the right moves, most of the news coverage focused on Davis's athleticism and good looks. *Time* magazine said he possessed "a special kind of speed that is all his own . . . he simply leans forward and sprouts wings."

Wings or no wings, it wasn't enough to prevent a near-tragedy. When Columbia Pictures offered the duo $20,000 each to star in *The Spirit of West Point*, a nine-minute short that was filmed at UCLA, their big break turned into heartbreak: Davis severely twisted his right knee and collapsed on the field with torn ligaments. "It was the end of me," Davis said. He joined the infantry; Blanchard became a jet pilot in the Air Force.

Photographers thought they had a bonanza when Davis, on furlough in 1948, met Elizabeth Taylor, who was then a ravishing young starlet, and a romance blossomed. Their famous embrace, when he returned from Korea on leave and *Life* magazine ran a photo of Taylor wiping lipstick from his handsome face, was a publishing coup—the Brad Pitt–Angelina Jolie romance of its day.

Like so many celebrity flings, however, this one didn't pan out, and Davis married the baby-faced actress, Terry Moore, an alliance that ended in divorce. Davis tried a sports comeback with the Los Angeles Rams, where he played for two seasons, taping and bracing his badly damaged knee, but he was no longer football's wonder boy. Davis finally took a job at the *Los Angeles Times,* where he worked until his retirement in 1987. After the death of his second wife, Harriet Slack, in 1995, he married Yvonne Ameche, the widow of 1954 Heisman Trophy winner and NFL player Alan Ameche, and they moved to 47–650 Eisenhower Drive in La Quinta Country Club.

In a cruel irony, Glenn's real-life twin brother, Ralph Davis, who played varsity football but never received much public recognition, moved to Joshua Tree and lived there in modest obscurity until he died in 2005. By that time, Glenn was battling prostate cancer, which claimed him two months later. He was 80 years old.

■ ■ ■

ANY SINGER WHO has enjoyed the longevity of **Andy Williams** is bound to run the risk of being ridiculed by people who are envious of his talent. Like Johnny Mathis and Dionne Warwick, whose popularity defies criticism, Williams is occasionally called "Mr. Musak" because his soothing tenor can be heard emanating from car radios, office elevators, and doctors' waiting rooms.

The ever-smiling Williams, who first hit it big with Top 10 easy-listening favorites such as "Butterfly," "Are You Sincere," "Lonely Street," and "Can't Get Used to Losing You," is no doubt grateful for the continuing recognition; it has brought him millions of record sales during more than 45 years and made him a wealthy man.

But Williams might never have made it to the top of the fiercely competitive record industry if not for the chance to perform the Oscar-winning ballad "Moon River" from the film *Breakfast at Tiffany's*, which he sang to thunderous applause at the 1962 Academy Awards. His friendly and relaxed singing style captivated millions of viewers, and the next day they besieged record stores to buy his latest album, which luckily featured the newly recorded song. "We did it in like ten minutes," he explained, and the day after the Oscars "we sold about 400,000 albums."

Is that what you call a lucky break? His record label, Columbia Records, in fact worked hard for that golden opportunity. Williams's career took off, and he never looked back. The following year, lightning struck twice when he recorded another movie theme song, "Days of Wine and Roses," which topped the album charts. Williams became the foremost interpreter of composer Henry Mancini's music.

What Sinatra and Tony Bennett were to the hip '50s, Williams was to the swinging '60s, often appearing in turtleneck sweaters and football jerseys, and sitting on a stool crooning love songs in front of a log fire. Certainly that is the image TV viewers remember from the three-time Emmy Award–winning musical variety series *The Andy Williams Show*, which aired on NBC for nine years. His fans grew in number, and he had top-selling albums with "Where Do I Begin?" from *Love Story* and "Speak Softly Love" from *The Godfather*. In 1973, he had another hit album with his recording of the Neil Sedaka song "Solitaire."

Williams spends nearly every winter at 49–035 Cedros Circle in La Quinta Country Club, where he has lived since 1965. He bought the four-bedroom home with his music royalties, and on the days when he isn't working the silver-haired singer can be found reclining on the living room sofa in his favorite yellow-and-white sweatsuit and matching sneakers. Life with his second wife, Debbie Haas, and their three German short-haired pointers is a model of tranquility.

But things were different when Williams was married to French-born singer Claudine Longet, who co-starred with Peter Sellers in the improvisational comedy *The Party*. Williams was literally swept off his feet by her large brown eyes and soft, childlike voice. Their courtship began when she was 18, and their hasty marriage produced three children before they separated and were divorced.

It was a love affair that was played out in the tabloids, with Williams portrayed as the classic older man chasing after a naïve young girl. Later, however, their roles were reversed when Longet shot and killed her handsome boyfriend, Vladimir Sabich, in a ski chalet in Aspen, Colorado, in 1976. The bizarre shooting made headlines around the world. Apparently Sabich was disrobing in the bathroom of their home when Longet picked up a German Luger .22-caliber pistol, and it mysteriously fired, killing him.

Williams, who still carried a torch for Longet, rushed to her side, and they were photographed holding hands as she wept over the death of her handsome lover. But the press hinted at dark goings-on in the snow-covered mountain resort, often referred to as "the cocaine capital of the U.S.," where wife-swapping couples made plays for each other.

Was this murder or a crime of passion or temporary insanity? There were rumors of drug traces found in blood tests, and an incriminating diary that was illegally seized and not admitted into evidence, and later purportedly burned. But no one believed the weepy chanteuse was a cold-blooded killer. After a highly publicized murder trial, Longet was convicted of criminal negligence and sentenced to 30 days in jail. Four years later, she married her defense lawyer, Ron Austin.

Left out in the cold again, Williams went on his merry way. In 1999, he found himself back on the music charts in England, where he has always enjoyed a strong following. The song, a re-release of his earlier recording of "Music to Watch Girls By," was a Top Ten hit—his first in more than a decade.

Williams now owns and manages the Moon River Theater in Branson, Missouri, where he can be found four months out of the year onstage with an 11-piece orchestra, serenading tourists.

■ ■ ■

CANADIAN PRODUCER **Pierre Cossette** is inexorably linked to the annual Grammy Awards telecasts, which rival the Oscar ceremonies as a TV ratings staple, deliver flotillas of narcissistic actors, wigged-out rock stars, botched facelifts, bad fashion statements, barbed political jokes, and other newsworthy fodder, most of it scripted, some of it not.

Cossette has been at the producer's helm for 35 years of shows, planning lists of Grammy Awards presenters, watching nervous recipients make expected faux pas, and listening to guests bitch about backstage screw-ups. The satisfaction he gets from all this turmoil comes from the worthy achievements of those people who have dedicated their lives to the pursuit of their musical art and are generously rewarded with an inscribed gold gramophone for their home or office.

ABC agreed to televise the first Grammy Awards ceremony in 1971, but only if Frank Sinatra, Dean Martin, or Andy Williams would host the event. Cossette delivered Williams, his La Quinta neighbor and golfing buddy, and changed the course of television history.

Cossette had plenty of experience working behind the scenes to pull off this difficult task. The chunky Quebec native has been listening to the demands of interfering network executives and mollycoddled celebrities ever since he started in the entertainment industry 50 years ago. He produced *The Andy Williams Show*, *The Sammy Davis Jr. Show*, *The Glen Campbell Show*, and *Sha Na Na*. More recently he produced the six-time Tony Award–winning Broadway musical *The Will Rogers Follies*, starring Keith Carradine, as well as *Tommy Tune Tonite!* and *The Scarlet Pimpernel*.

In 2001, Cossette paid $1 million for a three-bedroom home at 49–350 Avenida Anselmo, where this nimble 82-year-old showbiz veteran, who can still run rings around most other so-called producers, retired after producing the forty-seventh Grammy Awards in 2005.

■ ■ ■

WITH HIS BROTHER Himan Brown, who resided at 49–335 Rio Arenoso, filmmaker **Mende Brown** brought his talent for mystery and imagination to the popular, ominous-sounding radio and TV series *Inner Sanctum*. The Browns, whose independent films mimicked the European *cinema vérité* style, also collaborated on the innovative second features *That Night* and *The Violators*, which were filmed on location in New York City and directed by John Newland, a specialist in the documentary genre.

In 1970, Mende Brown moved to Sydney, Australia, where he wrote, produced, and directed *The Evil Touch*, a half-hour TV series about ghosts, monsters, and witchcraft in the style of *The Twilight Zone* and *Night Gallery*. This eerie late-night anthology was hosted by British actor Sir Anthony Quayle and featured notable guest stars such as Leslie Nielsen, Darren McGavin, Carol Lynley, Harry Guardino, Kim Hunter, and Vic Morrow, who was decapitated in a helicopter accident on the set of *Twilight Zone: The Movie* in 1982. Brown also produced the thriller *And Millions Die!* starring Richard Basehart and Susan Strasberg, which was filmed in Sydney and Hong Kong. His final cinematic enterprise was *On the Run* starring Rod Taylor, which he produced and directed in 1983.

While Mende was producing internationally, Himan was stateside, producing and directing the Peabody Award–winning CBS Radio Mystery Theater, which aired from 1974 to 1982. He was subsequently inducted into the Radio Hall of Fame.

After living abroad for 20 years, Brown returned to the United States and moved his family to Malibu. In 2002, he was visiting his brother at Himan's La Quinta home when he collapsed and died of a heart attack at the age of 81.

■ ■ ■

WRITER AND PRODUCER **Andrew J. Fenady** was responsible for the resurgence of the machismo Western, a type he helped propagate on TV during the 1960s with top-rated weekly series such as *The Rebel* starring Nick Adams, *Branded* with Chuck Connors (a former Palm Springs resident), and *Hondo* featuring Ralph Taeger. Fenady's timely Western revival culminated in the rowdy, gun-blazing films *Ride Beyond Vengeance* and *Chisum,* in which John Wayne played a bombastic cattle baron, his seventy-eighth starring role. An aficionado of the Old West, Fenady both wrote and produced this sprawling epic, which became one of Wayne's most successful films during the last years of his career.

A part-time resident of 51–351 Avenida Navarro, Fenady and his wife, Mary Dolan, are the parents of six children, including a son, Duke, whom they named after Wayne, their good friend and favorite actor, who lost a long battle with cancer in 1979. In addition to his fondness for Western folklore, Fenady loves to spoof the modern detective genre. Adapting his own novel for the screenplay of *The Man with Bogart's Face*, Fenady had Humphrey Bogart look-alike Robert Sacchi filling the shoes of the legendary tough guy. Fenady was also responsible for Robert Mitchum's reprise as a trench-coated sleuth in *Jake Spanner, Private Eye* and for *A Masterpiece of Murder*, which featured Bob Hope as an aging gumshoe.

His latest novel is *The Rebel: Johnny Yuma*, a continuation of the popular TV series. He penned the lyrics to the title song "Johnny Yuma," which was recorded by country singer Johnny Cash.

■ ■ ■

SONGWRITER **ALAN O'DAY**, who wrote of love, heartbreak, and loneliness in a collection of memorable pop songs that culminated in the smash hit "Angie Baby," resides at 77–271 Calle Durango in La Quinta Cove.

A former student at Coachella Valley High School, Alan loved to play piano and spent most of the 1960s traveling with a four-piece band. In his twenties, he teamed up with actor-musician Arch Hall, Jr., scored Hall's film *Wild Guitar*, and even appeared on *The Ed Sullivan Show*. But he felt his career was going nowhere.

"When I was twenty-eight years old, I was completely miserable," O'Day said. "I couldn't see what my future would be. I'd been playing in bars and clubs with various groups for years, waiting for that break that would catapult me to stardom."

Then in 1971 he wrote "The Drum," which became a hit single for Bobby Sherman, and he followed that success with a trio of poetic songs: "Train of Thought," recorded by Cher; "Rock 'n' Roll Heaven," cut by the Righteous Brothers; and "Angie Baby," which was written in a Palm Springs hotel room.

"Angie Baby" told the mysterious tale of a woman living in a world of make-believe. Alan read the first draft to the hotel's proprietor, who liked it, and when he completed the song, his publisher offered it to Cher. She turned him down, and it was her loss. Helen Reddy ultimately recorded the legend of Angie, "a special lady," and it became her third consecutive hit and biggest-selling record when released in 1974. O'Day credits much of the song's success to Reddy's strong vocals, good studio production and distribution, and of course, frequent air plays, which, as all composers know, are crucial to a record's success.

Three years later, O'Day wrote and sang "Undercover Angel," which reached #1 on the *Billboard* music charts. The catchy song, which he described as a "nocturnal novelette," sold more than 2 million copies and earned him a gold record. A follow-up single, "Skinny Girls," became a #1 hit in Australia in 1980, and in 1981 Alan cowrote "Your Eyes" with singer-songwriter Tatsuro Yamashita, which was a big hit in Japan. O'Day was invited to Tokyo to cowrite six more songs with Yamashita for his award-winning album "Big Wave."

Alan next teamed up with singer-songwriter Janis Liebhart, to write children's songs for the animated TV series *Jim Henson's Muppet Babies*. Eight years on, they had written almost 100 clever tunes for this Emmy Award–winning Saturday morning program, which is syndicated worldwide.

■ ■ ■

ACTRESS **ALISON LOHMAN** portrayed Michelle Pfeiffer's troubled teenage daughter in *White Oleander* and drew rave reviews as Nicholas Cage's undisciplined kid in *Matchstick Men*. She resides with her non-showbiz parents, Gary Lohman, who builds custom homes, and Diane Aston, who owns a French bakery, at 78–551 Deacon Drive East in Tradition Golf Club. Built in 1996, the clubhouse is situated on the spacious grounds of "Hacienda del Gato," formerly the home of Los Angeles businessman William Rosecrans, whose oil-rich family is descended from a famous Civil War general and U.S. congressman of the same name.

As for Alison, this graduate of Palm Desert High School has made a profitable career playing girls that are almost half her age. In her first film, *Dragonfly*, with Kevin Costner, the talented 26-year-old performer shaved her head for her role as a cancer patient, a part that unfortunately for Lohman was cut from the film, because it wasn't contributing enough to the story. That's show business!

It didn't stop Lohman from getting noticed in other films, however. She made quite a splash in *Big Fish,* in which she played the young Sandra Bloom while Jessica Lange took on the role of Sandra all-grown-up. In Lohman's follow-up film, *Where the Truth Lies,* she closed the age gap with her adult portrayal of a journalist who investigates a murder, and she has played leading parts in the family film *Flicka* and the offbeat drama *Delirious.*

■ ■ ■

SPORTS ICON **ARNOLD PALMER**, the undisputed king of golf who swung, pitched, and putted his way to seven major championships, including the Masters (four times) and the British Open (twice), is now semiretired. He watches the sunsets from his living room window at 52–123 Dunlevie Court.

Palmer's luxury home is a short drive from his latest business endeavor, Arnold Palmer's Restaurant (78–164 Avenue 52), which serves hearty fare like Crackling Pork Shank with Applewood bacon, corn, and black beans. The restaurant's rooms are papered with memorabilia from the golfing legend's 50-year career.

The lanky Pennsylvanian first achieved national prominence when he won the U.S. Amateur Championship in 1954. His natural charm, intelligence, and humor helped popularize golf for a new generation of television viewers—and potential players—much as Bob Hope and Bing Crosby's obsession with the game brought it widespread attention in their day. Palmer's most successful years were the early 1960s, when he won 29 tournaments, including the Palm Springs Golf Classic, and his name appeared in advertisements for everything from fast cars and fashionable clothes to films.

But behind the victories, Palmer was fighting to control addictions that threatened his health. He struggled for years with a two-pack-a-day smoking habit, which left him fatigued—a serious impediment for a champion golfer.

"After I turned 40, I quit smoking and began paying more attention to what I eat and how much I exercise," said Palmer, who also battled excess weight and waged a successful fight against prostate cancer.

Palmer's greatest challenge, however, was holding on to his golfing crown. Although his unbeaten record was eventually broken by rival Jack Nicklaus, who surpassed him in actual tournament wins, Palmer won a PGA tour every year until 1970, and the following year he enjoyed a spectacular revival, winning four events. Throughout the 1980s, Palmer demonstrated his outstanding skill during the Champions Tour, winning ten events, including five senior tournaments. Even after his winning streak was over, Palmer has remained one of golf's biggest money-earners because of his enduring appeal to sponsors and the public.

In 2004, Palmer competed in the Masters for his fiftieth and final time, marking the end of a brilliant career that had spanned half a century.

In addition to his restaurant, Palmer has other business interests that keep him busy during his retirement. For instance, he owns the Bay Hill Club and Lodge in Orlando, Florida, a regular venue on the PGA Tour and the place where Tiger Woods won the Bay Hill Invitational four years in a row.

■　■　■

YOU HAVE TO HAND IT to veteran film producer **Mike Medavoy**: he always seems to be in the right place at the right time. As chairman and co-founder of Phoenix Pictures, which produced hits such as *The People vs. Larry Flynt, Apt Pupil, The Thin Red Line,* and *Urban Legend,* he certainly knows how to pick a winner. Of course, taking credit for a hit is easy. The hallmark of a really smart producer and studio head is to know how to keep your distance from a box office flop. That's a skill Medavoy also possesses.

Medavoy started his career by sorting letters in the mailroom at Universal. Then he became an agent and the vice president of International Famous Agency. Before United Artists was gobbled up by MGM, Medavoy was appointed senior vice president in charge of production and oversaw the making of *One Flew over the Cuckoo's Nest, Rocky,* and *Annie Hall,* each of which won the Oscar for Best Picture.

When UA's management team of Arthur Krim and Robert Benjamin left to form Orion Pictures, Medavoy joined them, and the result was a veritable parade of critical and commercial winners: *The Terminator, Amadeus, Platoon, Robocop, Dances with Wolves,* and *Silence of the Lambs.* Medavoy's influence was not always central to a film's production; an executive's input rarely is. Mostly he tended to peripheral elements, bringing together the writer, director, and star in order to give a film, like a newborn baby, its best chances at survival.

From Orion he went to TriStar Pictures, where, as chairman, he was involved with the making of blockbusters such as *Philadelphia, Sleepless in Seattle, Cliffhanger,* and *Legends of the Fall,* an impressive list of hits in a decade strewn with scores of casualties. Of course, nobody can claim to be infallible, and Medavoy is no exception. He fired the talented young director Steven Spielberg, for example, when Spielberg was just starting out in TV, and he rejected a bunch of scripts, including *All the President's Men* and *Good Morning Vietnam*, that proved to be gold mines for other studios. In Medavoy's case, however, people tend to remember the hits more than the misses.

But movies are just one facet of Medavoy's life. When not attending high-level meetings, he unwinds at 80–135 Via Valerosa in Mountain View Country Club. An enthusiastic Democrat, he co-chaired Gary Hart's 1984 presidential campaign and he was among the first Hollywood players to introduce Arkansas governor Bill Clinton to the movie industry; he participated in Clinton's successful 1992 and 1996 presidential election campaigns.

Certainly Medavoy is not one to shy away from a fight. In 2003, Medavoy made headlines when he and his fifth wife, actress Irena Ferris, who played Tammy Miller in the TV series *Dallas*, sued Botox manufacturer Allergan, claiming she suffered serious side effects from an injection of the wrinkle-reducing drug.

■ ■ ■

STYLISH ACTOR **HAL LINDEN** was nominated seven times for an Emmy Award for his humorous portrayal of a New York police captain trying to keep law and order in his neighborhood precinct. The star of the long-running TV series *Barney Miller* owns a four-bedroom home at 54–099 Southern Hills in PGA West, where he has lived since 1991.

Linden began his performing career as a wavy-haired clarinet player in dance bands and orchestras. He studied music at Queen's College in New York City and trained in voice and drama at New York's American Theatre Wing. His first Broadway musical was *Bells Are Ringing,* in which he understudied the show's lead actor, Sydney Chaplin, who now resides in Rancho Mirage.

In 1970, Linden won a Tony Award for Best Actor for his starring role in the musical *The Rothschilds.* He also was seen in Alan Jay Lerner's *On a Clear Day You Can See Forever* and appeared in major revivals of *Three Men on a Horse, The Pajama Game,* and *Cabaret.*

Recently, Linden returned to Broadway to headline in the acclaimed dramas *I'm Not Rappaport* and *The Gathering.* But when he is not acting, he joins his wife, Frances Martin, for some golf on PGA West's magnificent courses.

■ ■ ■

ALA-KAZAAM! Master magician **Marvyn Roy** has led a fascinating life. For half a century, he toured the world performing breathtaking illusions, combining traditional sleight-of-hand with the powerful effects of electric light at New York's Latin Quarter, the London Palladium, and Gorky Park in Moscow.

During the 1950s and 1960s no variety performer was considered more unique than Roy and his ambidextrous assistant, Carol Williams. Their artistry has been described by one critic as "arguably the finest magic act ever conceived." Billed as "Mr. Electric," Roy had audiences at the MGM Grand and Radio City Music Hall gasping in wonderment at his miraculous ability to pull a strand of more than 20 illuminated light bulbs out of his mouth. One of his most potentially dangerous stunts was the "Lighting of a 300-Watt Bulb," in which he illuminated an electric light that he held in his hand—by secretly touching his shoes to a metal plate hidden in the floor of the stage.

Over the course of many demonstrations, he perfected this illusion until he was able to light specially made bulbs of varying intensities. He performed this hazardous trick six times on *The Ed Sullivan Show* and on tour with Liberace for seven years.

Born Marvin Levy, the magician had already perfected one of the greatest sideshow acts of all time when he was only a youngster. Calling himself "Marvin, the Magic Silk Merchant," he conjured up brightly colored silks, writhing serpents, and glowing lights with his fingers while dressed like an Arab in the marketplace.

Roy went to painstaking lengths to perfect these illusions and reportedly purchased the rights to a number of electric tricks from retired Canadian magician Bobby Arren, who was known professionally as Voltaire. This mixture of stagecraft and modern science culminated in Roy being called "The Man Who Lights a 1,000-Watt Light Bulb with His Bare Hand."

His magic almost proved fatal, however, when the eight-year resident of 54–229 Oak Hill was nearly electrocuted during a performance at the Fabulous Palm Springs Follies. Moments before going onstage, a short circuit caused his costume to ignite. Luckily, nervous chorus girls smothered the fire with their feather boas, and Roy managed to unplug himself only seconds before somebody doused him with a champagne bucket full of ice.

■ ■ ■

HIS PHYSICAL APPEARANCE has been compared to Lurch, the cadaverous butler in *The Addams Family,* and to Richard Kiel, the steel-toothed villain called "Jaws" in the James Bond movies. Only there is nothing quite that freakish about **Anthony Robbins**, whose telepathic ability to inspire millions of disenchanted people to change their lives has made him one of the greatest motivational speakers of his times.

Glib, grinning, and yes, gigantic, Robbins has the power to turn the biggest skeptics into true believers with his emotion-charged rallies. "Stand up and cheer!" he urges his excited audiences, waving his hands and smiling like a big kid. "The power is within you," he tells them. "Go on, you can do it!"

His endorphin-charged rhetoric—friendly, loud, and uplifting—is delivered with all the zeal of a Hollywood movie director, or a football coach at the Super Bowl. No wonder he has amassed an international following, and been called upon to advise and counsel the rich and famous, who can well afford his premium service charges.

When President William J. Clinton was mired in the Monica Lewinsky scandal, and his irate wife, Hillary Clinton, forced him to sleep on the White House couch, the chastened world leader reportedly sought Robbins's advice.

"Tony?"

"Yes."

"This is the president."

"Hi, Bill."

"Hillary's mad at me."

"No problem."

Needing some self-help tips, Olympic gold medalist André Agassi and two-time U.S. Open champion Greg Norman gladly dialed his number to ask how they could improve their tennis and golf games. He has addressed members of the British Parliament and Harvard Business School, given pep talks to NHL and NBA sports teams. He has even talked to the U.S. Army about improving morale. Robbins's message is the same, no matter how elite that person or group may be: take control of your life.

He uses every medium available to him. Never one to turn down a chance to spread the good word, he appeared in films such as *Reality Bites,* with Ben Stiller, and *Shallow Hal,* opposite comedian Jack Black, offering these two screen "losers" some tips on how to succeed. His classes in self-empowerment and career turnaround, through which he helps individuals and business companies reach their maximum potential, are the equivalent of learning to walk barefoot on hot coals.

A strong proponent of mind over matter, he is the bestselling author of three titles published in 14 languages: *Unlimited Power, Awaken the Giant Within,* and *Giant Steps.* He has produced the biggest-selling personal development audio series of all time, *Personal Power,* which sold 24 million audiotapes in less than five years.

And yet, somehow, all this positive thinking couldn't save his 15-year marriage, which ended in a highly publicized divorce in 2000. Robbins's wife, Becky, an educator whom he met at one of his "peak performance" seminars, gladly quit-claimed the home they occupied at 56–525 Riviera in PGA West and signed it over to her philosophical ex-husband.

Today, Robbins is happily married to his second matrimonial disciple, Bonnie Humphrey, and the power couple commutes by private jet between La Quinta and a luxury home in Del Mar near San Diego, and the Fijian island of Namale.

■ ■ ■

ONE OF LA QUINTA'S most visible residents is entertainment kingpin **Merv Griffin**, who can be seen at all hours of the day and night spinning through town in a white GMC Yukon with his two dogs—Patrick, an Irish setter, and Lobo, half malamute and half wolf—nuzzling him as he waits for the traffic lights to change. If he looks a trifle impatient, it's because Griffin is not used to waiting around. At 81, this human dynamo still has plenty of energy to burn. Even a recent bout with prostate cancer hasn't slowed him down.

The term multimedia could have been invented for Griffin, whose creative versatility as an actor, singer, bandleader, talk-show host, game-show inventor, hotel owner, horse breeder, and arts patron pretty much runs the gamut of show business possibilities. There isn't much his pudgy hands haven't touched, though he is understandably reluctant to reveal all his secrets for fear of harming his reputation. He is, after all, a major Hollywood player and has been around far too long to let his tongue dig his grave. Even at the height of his celebrity status on *The Merv Griffin Show*, when he wore a coat and tie, grinning like a Cheshire cat while a gaggle of stars giggled, gushed, and guffawed, he wisely kept his mouth shut.

Sure, he could whoop it up with the best of them, if he wanted, but as Griffin knew only too well from his early Hollywood days, the perfect party host never drinks even if his guests are completely smashed. Someone has to be in charge, and Griffin made up his mind long ago that the "someone" would be him.

As a young, overweight, acne-faced singer with the Freddy Martin Orchestra, he had few illusions about his own potential, despite the successful novelty song "I've Got a Lovely Bunch of Coconuts," which reached #1 on the Hit Parade.

Movies didn't light his fire, especially after he saw the rushes of *So This Is Love*, starring Kathryn Grayson, and *Phantom of the Rue Morgue*, which starred a rampaging gorilla—two of a handful of minor films he made under contract to Warner Bros. He was much more interested in playing tennis with studio boss Jack Warner, and picking his brains about how to become a producer, than in playing inferior roles in poor scripts. So he took a different tack and decided to make a lot of money.

Benefiting from his talks with Jack, he went to work and established himself as a smart interviewer in the emerging new vogue of current affairs. On TV he always played it straight, looking into people's eyes and smiling when they did or pretending to be sad when someone told a poignant story.

Knowing that controversy sells, Griffin booked topical guests such as journalist Adela Rogers St. Johns, futurist Buckminster Fuller, writer Norman Mailer, and critic Malcolm Muggeridge. His was also among the first talk shows to feature radical comedians like Dick Gregory, Lily Tomlin, Richard Pryor, and George Carlin. It was loads of fun, and Griffin lapped up the applause.

But he kept getting distracted by trivia questions and true or false answers that took root in his mind. A habitual puzzle-solver, Griffin had often toyed with the idea of turning his favorite morning pastime of crosswords into a TV series. After all, he told himself, it had never been done.

So in 1964, he invented the game show *Jeopardy!* He also created *Wheel of Fortune*, where players compete to guess the letters of a mystery word, and at the height of the disco craze, he launched *Dance Fever*, an amateur dance contest where well-known judges chose the most talented performers.

After collecting 15 Emmy Awards in almost as many years, Griffin finally realized his dream to be a media mogul: he sold his company, Merv Griffin Enterprises, to Columbia Pictures, then owned by Coca-Cola, for $250 million. At the time, it was the largest acquisition of an entertainment company that had been owned by an individual. Johnny Carson may have been the "King of Late Night TV," but it was Griffin who, like Liberace, laughed all the way to the bank.

In 1998, *Forbes* magazine ranked Griffin among America's 400 richest people. Worth more than a billion dollars today, he comes in slightly below music producer David Geffen and *Star Wars* creator George Lucas in personal wealth. But trouble was brewing.

The wily entrepreneur, who had managed to avoid the usual quota of tacky scandals, became the scuttlebutt of jokes about his sexuality. And he wasn't helped by his flagrant adulation of legendary gay icons like Judy Garland and Tallulah Bankhead; about whom he relished telling off-color stories at parties. It was clear that he adored the semitragic figure of Garland, whose cloying songs could often be heard wafting through his house, and a misty-eyed Griffin would frequently join her tremulous disembodied voice for a spooky duet, a glass of wine in one hand and a lit Benson & Hedges cigarette in the other.

His message seemed to be: You don't have to be gay to like Judy Garland. Critics might add: Yes, but it helps.

His defenders maintain that Griffin can't be gay because he was married for 17 years to Julann Wright—the mother of his son Tony—whom he divorced in 1976. It should be remembered, however, that Liberace and Rock Hudson, both of whom were gay, were also married and divorced. For more than 15 years, Griffin dated Eva Gabor, the youngest and prettiest of the campy Gabor sisters. Rumors abounded that she was merely his "beard," but people close to him noticed there was genuine affection between them. "Eva truly was my best friend," he said after she died of respiratory failure in 1995, at 76.

In 1991, Griffin's former secretary, driver, and companion Brent Plott brought a $200-million palimony suit against his tubby employer, alleging the two men were lovers. Griffin denied the charges, saying he was the victim of extortion. That same year, Deney Terrio, the former host of *Dance Fever* and the man who taught John Travolta some convincing dance moves for his star turn in *Saturday Night Fever*, filed an $11.3 million sexual harassment suit against Griffin, whose lips remained sealed. Luckily for him, a judge dismissed both lawsuits.

Driving around Palm Springs, Griffin is obviously in his element. He has helped professional figure skater and actor Jonathan De Paz, who lives in a waterfront home at 79–915 Via De Sol a Sol, in the Palmilla subdivision of La Quinta. Griffin recognized the 35-year-old skater's artistic talents and helped him get a toehold in the entertainment business. But Griffin also talks about the old days, when he went to the Racquet Club and saw Dinah Shore, Marilyn Monroe, and Elizabeth Taylor, and he offers his opinion on the city's revitalization.

"There are a lot of gay people—not wildness or anything," he recently told *Vanity Fair*, "except on the night of their White Party, but they come in and fix up the houses and straighten the furniture."

Given that environment, La Quinta seemed an odd choice of locale for Griffin to build his retirement home, but that's where he chose to erect a faux Moroccan ranch with eight guesthouses, on 240 acres located at 81–345 Avenue 54. He also has a tile-covered stable where 52 racehorses are boarded, and a private lake named Merveilleux with a 50-foot high fountain.

One week before he was due to move in, however, an electrical fire burned the main house to the ground. Griffin was in New Jersey at the time, but he watched the "live" news coverage of his smoldering home on CNN. Like a phoenix rising from the ashes, Griffin's king-size palace was totally rebuilt, right down to the French limestone floors, 12-foot-high French windows, and antique tapestries. There are lots of pinks and greens in the color scheme, and the walls are decorated with French impressionist and colorist paintings.

Among Griffin's regular houseguests are veteran character actor Robert Loggia, of *Big* and *Independence Day*, who has known Griffin for more than 40 years. Visitors want for nothing when they arrive at his home for the weekend—not even hand-milled soaps and ivory toothbrushes, of which there are plenty to go around.

Ronald and Nancy Reagan stayed there for one week in the months preceding the public disclosure in 1994 that the former president was suffering from Alzheimer's disease. Unlike her Presbyterian, churchgoing husband who strongly disapproved of homosexuality, Nancy Reagan has always enjoyed the company of gay men.

When Reagan became too ill to go out in public, Griffin escorted Nancy to lunch at Griff's, his jungle-themed restaurant in the Beverly Hilton Hotel. The media tycoon purchased the hotel for $100 million and opened the dazzling Coconut Club, a showplace for the music of yesteryear, where couples danced to big band music in a tropical setting complete with toy monkeys clinging to gold and silver palm trees. (The club closed when Griffin sold the hotel for $130 million in 2003.)

Wherever there's a piano, in fact, Griffin can easily be coaxed to perform with the likes of Johnny Mathis and Michael Feinstein, or sing along gamely with actors Tony Danza and Steve Guttenberg, just as he did on TV when confronted by a choice of talented guests all those years ago. Nowadays, Griffin divides his time between La Quinta, a winery in Carmel that specializes in Sauvignon Blanc (its private label is Mont Merveilleux), and a getaway in the Bahamas, where he cruises the blue waters in his $7-million yacht, *The Griff.*

He also owns St. Clerans, an eighteenth-century Georgian manor house that formerly belonged to the egalitarian movie director John Huston, in Galway, Ireland. They met when Huston, ever the raconteur, regaled Griffin with tales of fox hunts and grouse shooting on the Limerick isle. That is, after all, how this talk show host met a lot of rich and powerful people, including Presidents Nixon, Ford, Carter, and Reagan, whose extensive showbiz résumé filled him with both awe and nostalgia. As the former president slipped further away from the world, Griffin commiserated with Nancy on the telephone, and they cried together over the gradual loss of her beloved husband and his friend. And he was there for her when Ronnie, ill with pneumonia, stopped breathing in 2004 at the age of 93.

At Nancy's personal request, Griffin was an honorary pallbearer at her husband's sunset burial, when four Navy fighter jets flew overhead, and a military honor guard cocked their rifles and fired a volley of shots into the air. Griffin bowed his head as a bugler played "Taps" and Reagan's mahogany casket was interred in a garden crypt at the Ronald Reagan Presidential Library in Simi Valley, California.

Secret Dates

INDIO, THE OLDEST and at one
time the most profitable of the
desert cities, celebrated its seventy-
fifth birthday in 2005. With that
milestone came the realization that
the antiquated city, located 20 miles from Palm Springs, was in need of
a makeover. Time had not been kind to this bustling agricultural center,
which teetered on the brink of change but clung to its history-laden past.

Indio recently endured a setback that was a particularly uncomfortable reminder of its advancing years: Hotel Indio, built in 1925 and the
city's oldest lodging—a place where presidents and heads-of-state once
stayed in well-furnished suites—was gutted by fire. Many other fine-
looking buildings, their facades weathered by the unkind ravages of
time, have also gone, either by sheer accident or design.

In 1930, when Indio was founded, its population was 1,875. But the
city soon lost its virginity to Southern Pacific railroad engineers, migrant
farm workers, and army servicemen, who pilfered the abundant sources
of food and water.

Today the city has more than 55,000 inhabitants. According to the U.S. Census Bureau, 75 percent of these residents are Latino, but there are also Japanese and Armenian communities. This diversity is represented by an abundance of yearly celebrations: the Southwest Arts Festival, the Riverside County Fair/National Date Festival, Coachella Valley Music and Arts Festival, the Salsa Festival, and the Tamale Festival. Demonstrations of the city's supposed vitality, these colorful attractions are designed to entice merchants and customers.

But there is a nagging concern among Indio residents that all is not as it should be.

The recent sale of Shields Date Gardens was seen by many citizens as a portent of things to come. A 40-foot-tall knight in sheet-metal armor, outside the Shields factory store at 80–225 Highway 111, used to urge motorists to stop and sample date shakes or purchase boxes of fruit. But even the company's alluring red-and-blue signage, which beckoned visitors to witness the "Romance and Sex Life of the Date," was not enough to prevent the 80-year-old business from shutting its doors when the store changed hands in 2005. The longtime owner said the economic impact of low-price supermarket chains was just too great, and he was closing shop.

As luck would have it, the new owners decided to reopen—at least for the time being—and try to save existing jobs. But the future of Shields and its competitors, Hadley Date Gardens in Thermal and Sun Date in Coachella, is far from guaranteed. It would appear that the desert's economic future will be more dependent on large-scale urban expansion and less on concentrated growth.

This will not sit well with the descendants of those pioneers who toiled for years to carve out comfortable lives for themselves and made Indio the agricultural hub of Riverside County, producing millions of dates, table grapes, and citrus fruit.

■ ■ ■

THE FIRST TIME the distinguished American aviatrix **Jacqueline Cochran** saw the city of Indio was from 20,000 feet in the air, when she was flying across the Southern California desert from San Diego in the mid-1930s.

Cochran, who in her lifetime held more speed, altitude, and distance records than any other pilot, male or female, in aviation history, almost stalled the engine of her two-seater airplane when she looked down and saw the copper-toned mountains and sandy plains spreading out beneath her. Jackie Cochran's flying career spanned 40 years, from her news-making debut in 1934 as a racing pilot flying coast-to-coast, through World War II and into the jet age, when she became the first woman pilot to fly faster than the speed of sound. Dubbed the "Golden Girl" because of her striking physical appearance, she would go on to conquer a man's world without ever once compromising her values or her femininity. At the height of her fame, she was voted one of the ten best-dressed women in America.

When she landed at Coachella Valley Airport, between Highway 111 and Van Buren Street, the record-breaking pilot was convinced she had found home. "I lost no time in buying twenty acres," said Cochran, who fell in love with the desert's splendid charms on that unforgettable day. "Under the sun's glare, deep colors shrink into pastels and the limitless white of the sands merges into the grays, greens, and purples of the sage, the desert holly, the yucca and the ocotillo, the mesquite and smoke trees," Cochran wrote in her diary. Over the next 40 years, Cochran would make many more acute observations of life among the coyotes, lizards, and rattlesnakes of her adopted Indio home.

Cochran's Indio investment would soon be more than matched by that of her husband, Wall Street financier **Floyd Odlum**, whose purchase of additional land brought their combined ownership to 800 acres. But it was Jackie's favorable first impressions of this palm-fronded oasis that firmly cemented their lives.

They had met at a society party in Miami, Florida, in 1932. Cochran was a fluffy, blond-haired, brown-eyed beautician, who dreamed of marrying a millionaire. Odlum, who was already married, was bald, freckle-faced, and wore horn-rimmed spectacles that hid the glint in his lascivious eyes. They bantered for several hours, and when the evening was over arranged to meet again. So began a tentative courtship that blossomed into a full-blown affair.

From the start, Odlum insisted on absolute discretion, for their illicit relationship carried enormous risk. Odlum's wife, Hortense McQuarrie, was the president of Bonwit Teller, one of New York City's most prestigious department stores, and one of the many companies that he owned. Odlum was one of the ten richest men in the United States. Before the stock market crashed in 1929, he had wisely converted his paper investments into a cash value of $14 million. When other millionaires lost everything and started jumping from office buildings or blowing their brains out, Odlum was tripling the value of his money. He controlled, managed, or reorganized companies in every conceivable industry, including banking, public utilities, motion pictures, department stores, railroads, aircraft, oil, and mining. He owned RKO Pictures, Convair, Atlas Industries—and a host of other businesses.

A scandal involving the mild-mannered millionaire and his ambitious young mistress was the last thing he needed. Cochran maintained she had no idea he was worth so much money. But the late Sydney Guilaroff, who was the longtime head of MGM's hair and makeup department, told a very different story. Guilaroff claimed to have known Cochran when she was a manicurist at Antoine's Beauty Salon in Saks Fifth Avenue and Guilaroff was working there as a stylist.

According to the hairdresser and makeup artist, Cochran overheard Odlum's wife, who was getting a beauty treatment, mention that she and her wealthy overworked husband were having marital problems and were planning a relaxing ocean cruise. Guilaroff said that Cochran booked herself on the same cruise, seduced Odlum, and extracted a promise of marriage.

Clare Booth Luce reportedly used Guilaroff's story as the basis for her hit Broadway comedy *The Women*, which was later adapted into a film starring Joan Crawford as husband-stealing Crystal, the character Jackie Cochran allegedly inspired. Whether Cochran did, in fact, set a trap to catch the unsuspecting millionaire (which would seem to suggest more guile on her part than is truly believable), her romance with Odlum flourished, and they headed for the altar.

It was Odlum who, hearing Jackie's ambition to sell beauty products in retail stores across the nation, recommended she get a pilot's license—an odd suggestion for most women but not for Cochran, who immediately saw the wisdom in his idea. Odlum realized she would need to be able to travel at a moment's notice; what better way to service her growing list of clients than to take to the skies? It would certainly keep her ahead of the competition.

No wonder they fell in love. Odlum was the ideal person to make the young woman's dreams come true, and she adored him for it. His divorce finalized, Odlum and Cochran were married in 1936. Not long after that happy day, Jackie's bicoastal visits brought them to the desert, where they remained for the rest of their lives.

The Cochran-Odlum ranch stood on a grassy knoll overlooking the surrounding countryside, its red terra cotta roofs shimmering under the desert heat that ripened thousands of fertile Egyptian date trees. Guests entered the property at 49–599 Monroe Street, pausing momentarily between two arched gateposts that bore the C-O brand name in wrought-iron letters above their heads, and continued down a long, gravel driveway, where they were met by the home's smiling owners.

The 30-acre estate was conceived, designed, and constructed by Stephen Griffith, who had created the famed Lido Isle in Newport Beach. The 8,000-square-foot main house, an example of the Spanish Mission–style that was prevalent up and down the West Coast, was built to withstand the 130-degree summer temperatures. Before the advent of household air-conditioning, its reinforced, two-feet-thick adobe walls maintained a cool temperature indoors. Raised plaster ceilings contained hundreds of massive, hand-hewn wooden beams, and the floors were inlaid with thousands of handmade clay tiles.

The living room fireplace, where guests gathered for nightly cocktails and after-dinner cigars, was made of solid uranium rock that glinted from the light of burning logs. The home's Olympic-size swimming pool, reputedly one of the first heated pools ever installed in the valley, also doubled as an irrigation reservoir for the newly planted lawns, date gardens, and citrus groves.

During and after World War II, Floyd and Jackie's parties attracted some of America's top military brass: General Carl Spaatz, who commanded the U.S. Air Force's strategic bombing missions in Germany and Japan; Rear Admiral Alan Kirk, the former ambassador to Moscow; General Hoyt Vandenberg, the former U.S. chief of Military Intelligence. They shared the same dinner table with VIPs such as Senator Stuart Symington of Missouri, movie producer Samuel Goldwyn, chemicals heiress Marion DuPont, industrialist Henry Kaiser, and test pilot Chuck Yeager.

■ ■ ■

ONE SPECIAL PERSON who made a lasting impression on her generous hostess was the pilot **Amelia Earhart**, who first met Cochran in 1935. The boyish-looking Earhart had been the first person to fly solo across the Pacific Ocean from Hawaii to California. She also flew unassisted from Los Angeles to Mexico City and back to Newark, New Jersey. Earhart was awarded the Distinguished Flying Cross and the French Legion of Honor for attempting to duplicate Charles Lindbergh's epic flight across the Atlantic Ocean from New York to Paris. But bad weather, which would prove troublesome on future record attempts, caused her to touch down in Northern Ireland.

Earhart's personal bond with Cochran, with whom she was frequently seen, both on the ground and in the air, sparked rumors of a lesbian affair. In December 1936, they flew together in Amelia's $50,000 Lockheed Electra from New York to Amarillo, Texas, and on to Burbank, California. That Christmas, the two women bunked together at Cochran's newly completed ranch, while awaiting the arrival of Earhart's husband and flying patron, New York publisher George Putnam.

Despite Cochran's dictum that "guests stayed in the guest houses," of which there were several equipped with their own kitchens and bathrooms, Amelia was considered much more than a guest. So even though there was only one bedroom in the main house, Cochran offered to share it with Earhart, who happily accepted the invitation. She stayed at the ranch for 14 days, and the two women went horseback riding and swimming together.

Floyd Odlum, meanwhile, was ensconced in New York, running his profitable Atlas Corporation, and presumably oblivious to his wife's attentiveness to the shy pilot with the bobbed hair. Syndicated Hearst journalist Adela Rogers St. Johns, who later interviewed Cochran, made a veiled reference to their lesbian attraction. "Amelia Earhart, who was her idol, always looked like Lindbergh's younger brother when she wore flying togs, or even street clothes," the journalist said, adding, "She looked like a pilot; Jackie Cochran doesn't."

On Earhart's first visit to the ranch, Cochran showed her around, and they admired the beautiful wildflowers and then stood, their cheeks flushed, watching the desert sunset. Jackie felt an overwhelming compulsion to take Amelia in her arms and kiss her, but she didn't. Instead, the two women sat in front of the fireplace and played mind games, variations on the mental telepathy that Cochran had been practicing for several years. That night, as they talked candidly about each other's lives, Jackie experienced a strong psychic connection.

On the radio that evening they listened to a news report about a missing Western Airlines flight that had crashed somewhere between Los Angeles and Salt Lake City. Earhart sat transfixed as Cochran communed with some paranormal source and eventually offered the location of the downed aircraft. When they relayed the map coordinates to authorities, it turned out there was nothing but banks of snow in that area. But three days later, when the snow melted, the missing plane was located two miles from where Jackie had visualized it.

Another intriguing evening occurred after Earhart's first attempt to circumnavigate the earth, a hazardous 27,000-mile adventure that abruptly ended when she encountered engine trouble off Hawaii. Amelia wanted to give it another try; Cochran wasn't so sure it was a good idea. Their debate took place at Cochran's ranch, where they were sitting around eating and drinking while going over details of the proposed trip. Odlum, who was present that day, voiced his concerns as well. Amelia listened and said she would think things over.

Several weeks later, Earhart was back with a new idea: she would fly in the opposite direction, which she thought would be easier. She brought maps and drawings and spread them in front of the fireplace, and the threesome huddled in deep conversation until dawn. This time there was no talking Earhart out of her perilous journey; her mind was made up. So they wished her well for the history-making flight, which would surely put Amelia's bold achievement in the record books.

The Odlums were driving to Palm Springs from their ranch one afternoon when Jackie became upset: she had seen the engine of Amelia's plane catch on fire. Hours later, this accident, which had occurred at Tucson and which Jackie had foreseen in her mind, was broadcast on the radio. The mechanical problem was repaired, and Earhart took off from

San Francisco and headed across the Pacific Ocean. On July 2, 1937, Putnam called Cochran to tell her that Amelia had not arrived at Howland Island, the next destination on her world trip.

Cochran went into a semitrance and saw the plane floating in the ocean, where it had crash-landed hundreds of miles from land. Earhart was at the controls, her copilot seriously injured from a gash in his forehead. Cochran identified an American freighter and a Japanese fishing boat that were nearby, but she was unable to pinpoint the exact location.

Three days later, Jackie started sobbing uncontrollably for her lost friend, whom, she suddenly realized, had perished in the sinking plane. Amelia's last words, heard over shortwave radio were, "Circling . . . cannot see island . . . gas running low."

In her memoirs, Cochran described her strong feelings for Earhart. "She was a beautiful person," said Cochran. "That's why I loved her. It wasn't her achievements or the glamour surrounding her that caught me. It was her personality."

Flying wasn't Cochran's only passion.

Her other great interest—one that she turned into a successful business enterprise with the founding of Jacqueline Cochran Cosmetics in 1935—was the manufacture and sale of beauty products. This little-talked-about aspect of Cochran's life has been submerged by her piloting skills, but both deserve equal recognition.

Dorothy Gray, Helena Rubenstein, Elizabeth Arden, Jacqueline Cochran—they were true pioneers of the American cosmetics industry, researching and developing beauty products that are still in use today. Cochran was among the first manufacturers of custom-blended cream bases for makeup, antiperspirants, and do-it-yourself hair dyes. "Chestnut brown" and "topaz blond" hair dyes were introduced by Cochran. Her most famous invention was Flowing Velvet, a soothing moisturizer that she developed after experiencing problems with her skin when flying at high altitudes and over long distances.

But perhaps her most useful invention was Lipsaver, a clear protective lipstick for chapped lips that she initially created for her husband. "[Floyd] used to be troubled by dry, cracked lips which would only get worse when he'd visit the California ranch," explained Cochran. "I asked my laboratory to make up several lipsticks minus their color pigments.

"Finally," she said, "I changed the ingredients a little, put them into a line of men's cosmetics I was developing, and called it Lipsaver." She also designed Marilyn Monroe's lipstick gloss for the film *Gentlemen Prefer Blondes*, which gave the well-contoured actress a luscious look by keeping her lips shiny and moist.

One of her proudest innovations was the Jacqueline Cochran "Perk-Up" Cylinder, a three-and-a-half-inch-long stick that separated into six compartments. Ideal for traveling, it would fit anywhere and contained everything: cleansing cream, special foundation cream, eye shadow, rouge, a solid stick of perfume, and a little sifter for face powder.

These products were formulated during the time she lived in Indio and tested on many of the visitors to her home. Everyone from professional golfers to airplane pilots benefited from her ingenuity. She was living proof that necessity is the mother of invention.

■ ■ ■

ANOTHER OUTSTANDING AVIATOR who was frequently seen at the Cochran-Odlum ranch was **Howard Hughes**, whose attempts at record-breaking flights received almost as much press attention as Amelia Earhart's.

Hughes had set several speed records, including his famous New York-to-Miami dash in Cochran's Northrop Gamma, which he talked her into leasing to him, with an option to buy. He may even have had a crush on Jackie, to whom he would sometimes place calls late at night, when he was soused, and prattle on about aeronautics.

Hughes's eccentric lifestyle was full of cloak-and-dagger intrigue. He changed cars and clothes several times each day, stayed in out-of-the-way hotels, repeatedly took hot and cold showers to ward off germs, and cadged money from strangers to use pay-toilets and make phone calls. His habits would have been laughable if he hadn't believed they were necessary to protect him from the dangers he imagined in the outside world.

The billionaire was considered an oddball even before his famous mental crack-up, when he crashed his experimental XF-11 airplane into three houses in Beverly Hills (one of which belonged to the actress Rosemary DeCamp) and narrowly escaped death. His favorite topic of conversation, when he wasn't hunched over a drawing board looking at the latest design specs for airplanes, was explaining the ideal shape and size of women's breasts to his incredulous employees.

Hughes and Odlum, who maintained a polite respect for each other, were close business associates for more than 25 years. "Both men were reclusive multimillionaires with an eccentric reputation," said Richard Hack. "Odlum conducted his business while floating on an inner-tube in his heated pool, while Hughes sweated in wool slacks and a well-worn long-sleeve shirt, watching dates fall from the palm trees."

At least Odlum's behavior was justified. He had begun to show the effects of chronic arthritis in 1941 and was soon relying almost totally on a wheelchair. The desert air helped to soothe his aching joints, which is why he liked to keep close to the pool.

It was common for board meetings to be held poolside. Odlum would have the board of directors of one company sitting at one end of the pool, and another group at the other end, all with their shoes and socks off, wiggling their toes in the water.

In the middle of the pool would be Odlum, sitting on a rubber tube in a bathing cap and swimming trunks, a 100-foot-long telephone cord strung between him and the "shore" while he talked to his accountant in New York.

Even before the onset of his illness, Odlum hated the sterility of offices and didn't believe in desks. "A storehouse for junk, bad for posture and a setting for cold conversation," was how he described the world of his corporate counterparts. If Odlum were alive today, he would no doubt have embraced laptop computers and cellular phones.

When Hughes came a-calling, he would often arrive at the ranch unannounced, having hitched a ride on a grapefruit truck, and he would sit at the kitchen table swatting imaginary flies. His behavior was extremely troubling, but Odlum was not the least bit distracted. He knew Hughes wanted something—something probably involving money.

"Would you like a sandwich, Howard?" Odlum used to ask.

Hughes would scrutinize his wristwatch.

"Not now. Maybe tomorrow," he would answer.

At other times, Hughes would inspect the house, opening and closing all the doors, looking behind curtains and under beds to make sure people were not spying on him. Once he showed up for dinner with Rita Hayworth, then sat at the table and refused to eat anything. The time he visited the ranch with teenage actress Terry Moore, she was too terrified to eat even a handful of peanuts, because she knew Hughes didn't want her to get fat. She hid them under the cushions of Odlum's leather couch.

But where money was concerned, the checks never bounced.

In 1948, Hughes authorized the payment of $8.8 million to purchase 929,000 shares of RKO Radio Pictures from Odlum, who managed to get his old friend to pay more than one dollar above the market price for each share.

At the time, RKO was third in the studio pecking order, lagging behind MGM and Warner Bros. The company had a checkered history of boom-and-bust movies, everything from Orson Welles's vanity productions to *Dick Tracy* serials. "Odlum," commented Lee Server, "was a businessman, not a picture maker, and had never been seduced by the creative or hedonistic pleasures of the film industry." What Hughes bought, in fact, wasn't much: the company offices in Hollywood, 26 soundstages, a ranch in the San Fernando Valley where Westerns were filmed, and a chain of 124 movie theaters in 12 states. Immediately after the deal was closed, and Odlum deposited Hughes's check, the value of the studio went down, largely because of the screwball reputation of its new owner.

Producer Dore Schary saw the writing on the wall when he subsequently took a meeting with Hughes, not in an office, like other moguls would have required, but in a rented beach house with the lights turned off. Schary knew his time was up when his sweaty boss greeted him from the corner of an unfurnished room, where he was helping a naked woman with a large cleavage hook up her bra.

Things went from bad to worse until Odlum, who had been personally hired by Hughes to run the organization, was forced to sue him. The increasingly addled Hughes, his mind distracted by various nubile women, kept reneging on his contractual responsibilities.

After posting heavy losses, Hughes began selling off RKO in 1952. Three years later it was bought by the General Tire and Rubber Company, and in 1958, Desilu Productions took over the studio.

The last time the two men spoke was when Hughes telephoned Odlum in the middle of the night with an urgent request. He wanted to know if he could borrow a mattress with a hole in the middle. Odlum was perplexed. "Why?" he asked. "Because," Hughes whispered, "I have a really bad case of hemorrhoids and I can't sleep."

Three weeks after Hughes's death in 1976, scores of people descended on Odlum's home, claiming to be business representatives and relatives looking for Hughes's missing will, which he had purportedly hidden somewhere on the ranch. Their search always came up empty.

Indeed, more than 30 versions of Hughes's Last Will and Testament, all laying a claim to his $1.5 billion fortune, were eventually submitted to Nevada and Texas probate courts, although all of the documents were declared to be fakes.

For years it has been speculated that a fortune in uranium ore, Federal Reserve currency, or even gold bullion lies buried somewhere on Odlum's property, most likely under the groves of date trees where workers once labored in the broiling sun. Or, rumor has it, perhaps the missing loot is stashed somewhere in the walls and roof of the house itself, awaiting the day when it will be discovered, like the riches of King Tutankhamen's tomb.

Odlum was always as mystified as everybody else.

■ ■ ■

WITHOUT A DOUBT, Howard Hughes was the strangest man Odlum encountered, but he came into contact with many other fascinating people.

Presidents Herbert Hoover, Franklin D. Roosevelt, and Harry S. Truman all called on the feisty millionaire for assistance during their terms in office, and were warmly welcomed to the ranch both during and after their administrations. The Eisenhowers, whom he liked, spent many Christmases at the ranch. But Odlum had a strong mistrust of the Kennedys, going back to John F. Kennedy's father, Joe.

During Odlum's negotiations to buy Paramount Pictures, he learned that his business associate Joseph P. Kennedy, who enjoyed a long flirtation with Hollywood, was trying to louse up the deal for him, and he promptly told Joe where to go. Odlum was so annoyed by Kennedy, he told the *New York Times,* that he didn't mind being remembered as "the man who fired Joe Kennedy."

President **Dwight D. Eisenhower** and Odlum's wife were very close friends. Jackie Cochran attended his first inauguration and sat with Mamie Eisenhower in the presidential box next to General Hoyt Vandenberg, chief of staff of the United States Air Force. The Eisenhowers and the Odlums enjoyed a down-to-earth rapport, whether in Washington, D.C., or Indio, where Ike and Jackie played golf together.

After leaving office, Eisenhower sometimes became exasperated by having to be seen at various functions that he would rather not have attended, especially when his health was failing. His home at Eldorado Country Club was often besieged by the media, and he found it increasingly difficult to get the peace and quiet his doctors had prescribed for him.

Cochran, sensing his growing frustration, offered Eisenhower the use of the C-O ranch. "We converted one of the guest cottages into an office," Jackie said. "It was quiet and the lawn around it was spacious and you could see the mountains fifty miles distant." There, with no distraction other than the sound of Odlum splashing in the pool, the former president wrote a big chunk of his memoirs.

Cochran could see him from the kitchen window. "He had injured his knee playing football and would wear one shoe with lead in the sole, cross his legs, and swing the bad one up and down." Very often he would sit there for as many as five hours, dictating to his secretaries and exercising his leg. At other times, he would gaze at the mountains with a look of deep concentration on his moon-shaped face.

Probably no other person gathered as much inner strength from the desert as Eisenhower. But he was a sick man, ravaged by heart disease and burdened with an alcoholic wife, and both of them constantly required medical attention. Now, in his greatest hour of need, he was dodging the protection of the Secret Service to sit under a pecan tree at Cochran's home and eat a chilled grapefruit—and loving every minute of it.

It was at the C-O ranch, in cottage #2, that famed journalist Walter Cronkite conducted his probing TV interview of Eisenhower, asking the man who had commanded the D-Day invasion of Europe, and presided over America's postwar economic boom, to reflect on his achievements.

When the interview aired, Jackie threw a dinner party and served roast beef, chicken cooked on a spit, and spare ribs. Comedian Bob Hope, who sat in the living room next to Eisenhower that night, cracked, "Well, General, you had fifteen million people in the palm of your hand for an hour and not one single laugh in the whole lot of it." It broke the tension, and everyone laughed.

Eisenhower, who was on a strict diet, would periodically get up from his chair and tip-toe into the kitchen, where he would help himself to dishes that were frequently off limits: mashed potatoes, thick gravy, and homemade chocolate-cream pie.

■　■　■

ODLUM APPRECIATED HIS wife's friendship with Eisenhower; he was less captivated by her fondness for President **Lyndon B. Johnson**, whom he called a blabbermouth because the tall Texan never stopped talking. Once, at a private dinner in the White House, Johnson snuggled up to Cochran and, following dessert, kicked off his shoes and rested his head on her lap. It was all purely innocent fun, which is why they liked each other.

One day Johnson paid a surprise visit to the ranch, barely allowing Cochran enough time to wash and set her hair. Two cars pulled up, one with LBJ wearing his white Stetson, the other filled with Secret Service men. In the backseat of Johnson's bulletproof car sat Eisenhower, grinning about this bit of subterfuge. Their arrival thrilled Jackie, and she nearly hugged them both, but then thought better of it.

The two men had been playing golf. Eisenhower, ever the gentleman, took off his spiked shoes before entering the house, but Johnson barged right in, golf shoes and all. The household staff was thunderstruck at the sight of two presidents standing next to each other in the same room, both prattling on about their score cards while Cochran asked the maid to prepare afternoon tea. Odlum, who had no idea what was going on, casually strolled in from the pool in his bathing suit and changed into a terrycloth robe. Tea was served, and everyone sat down to continue their discussion.

As Jackie remembered, "Lyndon did all the talking. He kept going on and on about Vietnam. At one point he asked Eisenhower, 'What do you think?' The general said, 'I don't see how you could have done it any other way.' "

On the spur of the moment, Johnson asked Cochran to give him a guided tour of the ranch. Before the Secret Service had a chance to object, LBJ had grabbed Jackie's arm, and they were bounding down the back stairs to the president's car. Then, to her complete astonishment, he said, "You can drive," and got in the front seat next to her. They sped out the gate and down the road, pursued by Secret Service.

She proudly showed him around her horse stables, date farm, and private, 9-hole golf course, where players scattered as the presidential car came whizzing by. Back at the ranch, Eisenhower took Cochran to task for breaching protocol and putting LBJ's life at risk.

"No private citizen ever drives the President of the United States anywhere," Eisenhower said, "and you just did."

"Well, goddamn it," she fumed, "Lyndon got in the car and he didn't have to."

It was one security lapse that didn't do any harm. Ike understood and smiled.

But the next week, news of the presidential joyride hit the fan. One stunned golfer named Ray Rummonds mailed a letter to *The Desert Sun* recounting his brush with history:

"I was standing on a green at the Cochran-Odlum golf course last Sunday afternoon, about to hit my ball, and I'm here to tell you that the President of the United States and Jacqueline Cochran came by in an automobile. Jackie rolled down the window and said to me, 'Don't you dare hit that golf ball. The President of the United States is in this car.' And I'll be darned if it wasn't Lyndon B. Johnson himself who shook my hand."

Despite Odlum's worsening arthritis, he kept up a vigorous schedule of phone calls and business meetings until his retirement in 1960. He was devoted to Cochran, who was 14 years his junior and often absent from home, flying cross-country. If he sometimes referred to their union as a "long distance" marriage, that was a term of endearment as well as light mockery of their arrangement.

They led such busy lives that there was precious little time for them to get on each other's nerves, and when they were living together at the ranch the relationship was by all accounts blissful. She cared for him as he shrunk to the size of a wizened deity, unable to move without two muscular male nurses to lift his crippled body out of bed and carry him to the front porch. There he would sit in bathrobe and slippers, reading the stock market results in the *Wall Street Journal*. Occasionally the nurses would gently lower him into his heated pool, so he could relieve the burning pain of his arthritic joints.

As for Cochran, eventually she had to suspend flying; she had a weak heart, and doctors inserted a pacemaker to keep her alive. Jackie's wings had been clipped, and she consoled herself by following other people's attempts to best her speed records, living through their achievements while she increased her daily consumption of gin.

Cochran used to peddle around the grounds in a big three-wheeled bicycle, picking vegetables and fruit. But when neither she nor Odlum was able to care for the ranch any longer, she reluctantly packed their belongings, including framed photographs of her secret love, Amelia Earhart, and of Howard Hughes, her one-time suitor, and she and Odlum moved across the street to a smaller house.

It was a decision that was as inevitable as it was symbolic. Unfortunately, in his infirmity, Odlum unwisely entered into a business deal with his only son, **Bruce Odlum**, to build 150 residential homes on the land that he and Jackie owned. Letting his guard down, Floyd literally bet the ranch and lost it. The housing project went bankrupt, and Odlum was as furious with himself as Jackie was with him.

As for Bruce, he was unable to deal with the messy aftermath and committed suicide in 1974, shooting himself in the mouth with a .38-caliber revolver. He left a suicide note addressed to his wife, telling her where to find his body, which was recovered a short distance from their home on the property.

It broke Floyd Odlum's heart to end his days in such disgrace. The public never knew the full measure of his personal devastation, but it was a profound loss from which he never recovered. Jackie was particularly troubled by her husband's grief, for it accelerated his decline. Two years after the suicide, the Associated Press teletype machine printed out this short obituary:

INDIO, Riverside County, June 18, 1976. Industrialist and financier Floyd B. Odlum, founder of the Atlas Corp., a giant holding company, died yesterday at his home here. He was 84. Odlum had suffered from arthritis for many years and was bedridden at his ranch.

He and his wife, aviator Jacqueline Cochran, had hosted many famous persons, including President Dwight D. Eisenhower. . . .

In 1980, when she was 74, Jackie Cochran joined her husband. The simple funeral was held at Coachella Valley Cemetery, where her pine coffin adorned with yellow roses was lowered into the ground.

Ironically, the housing development in which Cochran lived alone during her last four years, adjacent to the land which she had first seen from the air on that bright summer's day, has subsequently prospered as Indian Palms Country Club.

In 2004, Cochran was the deserving recipient of a posthumous honor: Desert Resorts Regional Airport in Thermal was renamed Jacqueline Cochran Regional Airport. The ribbon-cutting ceremony included a dazzling aerial display of vintage planes, high-speed jet demonstrations, and a colorful parachute jump by more than 20 skydivers.

As Cochran herself would have noted with smiling approval, there wasn't a cloud in the sky.

■ ■ ■

ACTOR AND STUNTMAN **Bill Hickman** demonstrated his nerves of steel as the man behind the wheel of some of the movie industry's most hair-raising car chases. He also doubled for some of the most famous actors of all time, performing dangerous leaps and taking bone-crunching falls without audiences ever suspecting the clever deceptions.

With his tall physique, menacing features, and cool demeanor, it was natural he would be earmarked to play cowboys and assassins. But it was his unequalled reputation as "the best wheelman in the business" that kept him employed for 20 years, risking his life in front of the cameras. Wearing black-rimmed spectacles and leather gloves, Hickman first impressed moviegoers as a professional hit man in *Bullitt*. His moment of cinematic glory: the now-legendary scene where he drives a black Dodge Charger being pursued by police detective Steve McQueen in his green Ford Mustang, the two cars thumping up and down the bumpy streets of San Francisco at speeds approaching 110 mph.

During the high-speed chase, Hickman crashes the Charger into a parked car, collides with a concrete wall, loses several hubcaps, passes a speeding truck, and scrapes a metal guard rail, while his accomplice blasts McQueen's Mustang with a pump-action shotgun. The getaway car eventually runs off the highway, leaps a fence, and plows into a gasoline station, finally to explode in a giant ball of fire. The thrilling ten-minute action sequence took two weeks of careful planning and filming.

Because of his well-earned reputation on *Bullitt*, Hickman was hired to stage a similar car chase on the crowded streets of New York City for *The French Connection*. Doubling for the film's star, Gene Hackman, Hickman drove a brown Pontiac Lemans at speeds up to 90 mph in the famous scene where Hackman, pursuing an armed killer who has hijacked an elevated train in Brooklyn, nearly runs down a female pedestrian.

Before becoming a movie stuntman, Hickman drove midget race cars and rode motorcycles. The son of film director Charles Hickman and actress Virginia Cantrell, he broke into movies as a talented extra and worked his way up. He played Clark Gable's mechanic in the racing drama *To Please a Lady* and a prison guard who whips Elvis Presley in *Jailhouse Rock*. He also performed stunts for Dean Martin in *Rio Bravo*, was Robert Mitchum's stand-in in *El Dorado*, doubled for longtime friend George C. Scott in *Patton*, and played the role of Patton's Army driver.

But it was Hickman's off-screen friendship with James Dean that created the most media interest when the two actors, who had first met in 1951, became car-racing enthusiasts. The credo "Live fast, die young, and leave a good looking corpse" seems to have been invented for Dean, who did his utmost to fulfill that morbid promise, partaking in risky stunts and courting death with a devilish grin. Hickman, by contrast, was more cautious in the face of danger and never took unnecessary risks.

In March 1955, with starring roles in *East of Eden* and *Rebel without a Cause* to his credit, and a third film, *Giant*, in production, Dean entered his Porsche Speedster in the Palm Springs Road Races. The two-day event was his first competitive race, and he was in a jubilant mood. He won the preliminary, which qualified him for the finals, and finished in third place behind Ken Miles and Cy Yedor (he was moved to second place after Miles was disqualified on a technicality).

Over the next few months, Dean competed in two more races, in Bakersfield and Santa Barbara, but because of film commitments missed upcoming events at Torrey Pines and Hansen Dam as well as a second race in Santa Barbara.

On September 30, 1955, Dean drove his brand-new silver Porsche Spyder from Los Angeles to Salinas to compete in the annual Sports Car Road Races.

He never made it. On Highway 46, between Bakersfield and Paso Robles, his car collided with a Ford coupe traveling in the opposite direction. The deadly collision, which occurred at twilight near the intersection of Highway 41, in the township of Cholame, broke Dean's neck and seriously injured his German mechanic, Rolf Wutherich.

Hickman, driving the Ford station wagon and trailer that normally hauled Dean's racing car, was the first person on the scene of the shocking accident. He ran to the wreckage where the 24-year-old actor lay fatally injured. "I pulled him out of the car, and he was in my arms when he died," Hickman said. "I heard the air coming out of his lungs." The memory of that moment haunted him forever.

Hickman continued to perform car-driving stunts in popular films such as *The Great Race*, *The Love Bug*, *Vanishing Point*, and *Diamonds Are Forever*. But after injuring his tailbone in a boating mishap off Santa Catalina Island, he retired from films. His last stunt was doubling for Elliott Gould in a 100 mph car chase in the gripping thriller *Capricorn One*.

In 1982, Hickman decided it was to time to stop tempting fate. He gathered his belongings, revved his car's engine, and moved to Indio. He spent the last three years of his life in seclusion at 82–317 Lancaster Way (Indian Palms Country Club), where he died of cancer at the age of 65 in 1986.

■　■　■

A FEW STARS were lured to Indio by daydreams of becoming farmers—tilling the fields and harvesting crops—though the reality was often vastly different from what they imagined. Drought and extreme temperatures, which ruined so many harvests, was an ever-present threat, and flying insects and other pests frequently ravaged orchards and vegetable crops. But these hardships did not deter all comers.

When **Jack Benny**, the skinflint comedian whose "slow burn" drew unending laughs on radio, films, and television, moved to Palm Springs, he and his longtime friend George Burns investigated buying a date ranch. They were sitting around Tamarisk Country Club with Leonard Firestone when Burns, who was the more industrious of the two entertainers, proposed going into business together. "Jack," he said with a puff of his cigar, "everybody in Palm Springs has a ranch except us. All you do is tell jokes and play the fiddle. All I do is tell jokes and sing a song. We ought to have a ranch."

Benny threw Burns a quizzical look, as if to say "You're kidding me." Then Firestone, who was warming to the idea, said he knew of 180 acres for sale in Indio. So the three men hopped in Burns's car and drove out to a pile of sand dunes with a real estate agent, who convinced them they could grow oranges, cotton, and dates.

Benny, who was notoriously cheap, didn't bat an eye. He looked out the car window and said, "Fine, let's buy it."

They all shook hands and became ranch owners.

But the comedians were too busy being funny to pay close attention to planting and harvesting. Eventually they sold their stake.

■ ■ ■

APART FROM AGRICULTURE, Indio's other claim to fame is its barren topography, which has been featured in countless films and TV series when an authentic-looking Middle Eastern flavor is required by cost-conscious Hollywood producers. Indio's empty plains have witnessed horses galloping into the hot wind, and armored tanks rolling across scorching sand to the call of "action!"

During World War II, in fact, the U.S. government requisitioned 200,000 square miles of desert terrain, a human deathtrap that stretched from Pomona, California, to Phoenix, Arizona, and Boulder City, Nevada, so that **General George S. Patton, Jr.**, could prepare troops for the desert campaign against Field Marshal Erwin Rommel. Called the Desert Training Center, its command post was located 30 miles east of Indio at Chiriaco Summit, a desolate outcrop of rock and sand where the inhabitants were mostly scorpions, rattlesnakes, and tarantulas.

The first troops to arrive at the Desert Training Center described it unkindly as "the place God forgot." But desolate or not, it became the training ground for more than one million troops in seven armored and

13 infantry divisions. Soldiers began training the first day they arrived; one month later they were expected to be able to run a mile in ten minutes while carrying a full backpack and a rifle.

General Patton arrived with his wife, Beatrice, and they stayed in a rooftop suite at the Hotel Indio, at 45–077 Smurr Street in "old downtown."

Four days after his arrival, the general's troops took their first desert march. Within 23 days Patton had conducted 13 tactical exercises, including several nighttime armored-tank exercises. Wearing his metal army helmet and swinging a riding crop, Patton told his men, "If you can work successfully here, in this country, it will be no difficulty at all to kill the assorted sons of bitches you meet in any other country."

In spite of the primitive living conditions, and Patton's characteristically brusque manner, it's been said his troops respected, admired, and even loved the raspy-voiced general, who spent more than three months eating and sleeping in field tents with the thousands of men. Many troops reportedly felt bitter when the War Department designated the Desert Training Center command post "Camp Young," after a high-ranking army chief of staff, instead of after Patton, whom they thought more deserving of the accolade.

Following its dedication, however, Camp Young became the scene of a Hollywood-style grand opening when master of ceremonies Edward G. Robinson, pianist Victor Borge, tap dancer Ann Miller, and the Los Angeles Philharmonic Orchestra conducted by Leopold Stokowski welcomed the new recruits with a spectacular outdoor concert.

Within a few weeks there were U.S.O. stations, Red Cross depots, and observation towers throughout the city of Indio. Thermal Army Air Base was established as a backup facility to March Field in Riverside, and a Naval Auxiliary Air Station was built in Twentynine Palms.

The desert was doing its part for the war effort.

Sixty-two years after General Patton stayed at the Hotel Indio, the historic two-story building, which had welcomed movie stars and presidents, mysteriously caught fire and burned to the ground. The devastating blaze occurred less than one week before Christmas 2004.

Firefighters from Indio, Palm Desert, Desert Hot Springs, and Coachella responded to the blaze. Glass windows exploded, flames raced across the roof, and floors collapsed as fire crews pulled back to avert casualties. They doused surrounding buildings with water, and watched the brick and wooden structure writhe and groan in its final, agonizing moments.

One week later, yellow plastic tape stretched across the sidewalk to prevent trespassers. The acrid smell of burning embers still hung in the air as bulldozers moved into position, their hydraulic blades poised to remove the blackened debris. The burned-out remains of the famous hotel, where history had been written by the man called "Old Blood and Guts," had been marked for demolition.

■ ■ ■

ONE WONDERS WHAT General Patton, who had once stood at the top of Chiriaco Summit squinting through his binoculars, would think if he had seen a motor home driven by Elizabeth Taylor's former husband **Larry Fortensky** barreling down Interstate 10, with a woman trapped inside the speeding vehicle screaming for help.

In 1998, Fortensky and his unidentified girlfriend were driving from Phoenix to San Juan Capistrano when they started an argument in the motor home. Their dispute quickly escalated into a shoving match, and Fortensky began hitting his girlfriend and pulling her hair. When they stopped at a gas station, the hysterical woman jumped out, ran to a pay phone, and dialed 911.

Riverside County Sheriff's deputies arrived on the scene to find the couple sitting outside the motor home. Fortensky was taken into custody and booked in Indio jail on charges of felony spousal abuse.

It was not the first time abuse charges had been brought against Fortensky. Six months earlier, he was accused of beating his live-in girlfriend, Kelly Matzinger. In 1988, he had been convicted of drunk driving and had checked into the Betty Ford Center, where he met pampered screen legend Elizabeth Taylor. The alcoholic duo fell in love, and they were married in 1991 at Michael Jackson's Neverland Ranch in the Santa Ynez Valley, recently the focus of a criminal investigation into allegations of child sexual abuse against the pop star. (Jackson surprised media pundits when he was acquitted of the charges.)

After separating from Taylor in 1996, Fortensky was twice arrested for various offenses, including suspected drug use. He and Taylor were divorced in 1997.

■ ■ ■

SOME VETERANS OF World War II felt a special bond with the desert and later retired to the Indio area. One such person was **Colonel Mitchell Paige**, who resided at 80–071 Palm Circle Drive, in nearby Westward Isle, on the border of La Quinta and Indio. As a loyal and dedicated platoon sergeant, Paige had been awarded the Medal of Honor by President Franklin D. Roosevelt for acts of valor during the bloody fighting on Guadalcanal.

On October 26, 1942, every member of Paige's platoon was either wounded or killed battling 2,700 Japanese soldiers. The only marine still able to fight, although his face was bloodied and his hands were scraped raw from warring in the treacherous jungle, Paige held opposing forces back, using several of the dead Marines' machine guns until reinforcements appeared. He then assembled another line of men and led them in a lethal bayonet charge against the advancing Japanese.

Paige received a battlefield commission to lieutenant and later achieved the rank of colonel. He died at the age of 85 in 2003.

■ ■ ■

INDIO CRAVES RESPECTABILITY, BUT it has earned a reputation for recklessness, the result of lawless behavior by famous people who should have known better but did not feel the need to set good examples.

High-profile criminal trials involving the likes of actors Tom Neal, Trini Lopez, and Robert Downey, Jr., have been held at Indio Court, which is located in the Larson Justice Center. They are certainly not the first, nor will they be the last, of the offenders that Indio has seen. Who knows which stars will be making court appearances there in the future?

In 1948, **Frank Sinatra** and **Ava Gardner** went on a drunken spree in downtown Indio, shooting out street lights and damaging store windows. The two stars had spent the night carousing at Sinatra's Palm Springs home, then grabbed two .38 pistols from the singer's bedroom dresser and decided to go on a midnight joyride. They took off in Sinatra's Cadillac with Frank behind the wheel and Ava riding shotgun. The couple drove around in the dark taking potshots at road signs; one bullet accidentally hit a bystander, and when the cops were called Sinatra gave himself up, and the couple was hauled off to jail.

Worried about the legal consequences, Sinatra called his press agent

Jack Keller from the police station, while Gardner took a nap in the squad room. Keller borrowed $30,000, chartered a plane, and flew to Indio, where he met with the police chief, who already had toted up a list of the charges.

"Okay Chief, let's get down to business. How much to keep this whole thing quiet?" he asked.

They figured $2,000 for the two policemen who made the arrest, $2,000 to repair the damage that had been done to city property, $1,000 to destroy the hospital records of the man who'd been shot, and $5,000 for the chief to bury the whole sorry mess.

Buying off the frightened man who had received a superficial bullet wound to his stomach cost them another $10,000.

Altogether, Sinatra's dangerous escapade totaled $20,000. But that was better, he reasoned, than defending a headline-making scandal.

■ ■ ■

ASSEMBLIES OF GOD televangelist **Jimmy Swaggart,** who, like his famous cousin, singer Jerry Lee Lewis, learned only too well the consequences of playing with fire (or in Swaggart's case, prostitutes) met his deliverance in Indio.

The publicity-seeking Swaggart stirred up plenty of controversy when he lambasted his rival, Praise-the-Lord-Ministry Bible-thumper Jim Bakker, accusing him of sexual misconduct and telling CNN's Larry King that Bakker was a "cancer in the body of Christ."

Swaggart's religious ranting didn't stop there. Among his outrageous pronouncements were the statements that sex education promoted incest and that pornography was as addictive as drugs. His irresponsible comments should have tipped off a few of his clergy to what would soon become a well-known fact: their moneymaking man-of-the-cloth was a porn-addicted pervert.

When Swaggart's hypocritical hounding got New Orleans preacher Marvin Gorman defrocked for being caught in an extra-marital affair, Gorman decided to get even with Swaggart and he hired a private investigator to stake out the sex-obsessed sermonizer.

The incriminating photos of Swaggart, with his pants down and his pride up in a seedy motel room with an open-legged Louisiana prostitute, were too much for AOG members They demanded a public apology and Swaggart's removal from the pulpit. What they got instead was the sacrilegious Swaggart sobbing uncontrollably on national TV. "I have sinned against you, my Lord," he bawled, "and I would ask that your precious blood would wash and cleanse every stain until it is in the seas of God's forgetfulness, never to be remembered against me."

Translation: he hoped they would let him do it again.

In 1989, Bob Guccione broke the story in *Penthouse* magazine that Swaggart had hired the services of another willing prostitute, Debra Murphree, to whip his naked body with a riding crop—presumably as punishment for his earlier sins. Murphree also revealed that Swaggart had sexual fantasies about raping her nine-year-old daughter.

As penance for his latest indiscretion, Swaggart drove his white Jaguar to Indio in 1991, where he solicited the services of a third prostitute, Rosemary Garcia, whom he intended to take back to his hotel room so she could give him some much-needed physical discipline.

But as luck would have it, he was stopped by police for a traffic violation in a red-light district before he had a chance to do the deed. It was later revealed that Swaggart had visited an adult bookstore near Palm Springs and purchased several pornographic magazines. Fumbling through a slew of excuses, he finally begged police, "Gimme a break, I'm a preacher."

The cops were not impressed by his cries of hell and damnation, nor were his colleagues and former disciples. This time there was no easy way out of Swaggart's dilemma. He was forced to resign from his ministry and seek professional counseling.

In a moment of divine revelation, however, he said God told him to return to the pulpit—presumably so he could commit these offenses all over again.

■ ■ ■

THE PROVERB "THOSE that live by the sword shall die by the sword" is aptly applied to **Al Adamson**, a sneering, amoral independent filmmaker whose tasteless horror-and-sex films exploited broken-down actors, drugged-up bikers, and drunken bimbos.

"Trash" would be a good word for the lewd and amateurish movies such as *Half Way to Hell, Satan's Sadists,* and *Blood of Dracula's Castle* that were the hallmark of Adamson's cost-cutting style. These and other film titles, which promised more than they delivered, should have forewarned moviegoers about the peril of spending hard-earned cash to see the decrepit likes of Lon Chaney, Jr., and J. Carrol Naish writhing about in mock agony, sporting dollops of tomato ketchup to simulate gore.

A Hollywood *schlockmeister* with unfulfilled artistic pretensions, Adamson was little more than a con man who extracted money from investors, always promising to share the profits from multiple showings of his cheaply made films at suburban drive-ins and country movie theaters.

Adamson directed 30 films, produced 17, acted in eight, and wrote three. Yet there is not one film among them with any discernable merit. Did he really believe that he was creating works of art, or like a junk peddler did he think that people deserved nothing better than what he was offering? Not only did Adamson defraud theater owners by repeatedly selling them the same film—he released *Horror of the Blood Monsters* under as many as 15 different titles—he duped ticket buyers into believing they were getting professional entertainment when they were really getting home movies on a big screen. Then he'd take the money and run.

His films set records for awfulness previously only accorded the likes of Ed Wood, Jr., who had a reputation for turning out some of Hollywood's worst. (Wood had talked Bela Lugosi into an embarrassing comeback after the former *Dracula* star had been discharged from a psychiatric hospital for drug addiction.) Adamson's behavior ran a close second. He hired the partially disabled John Carradine, whose limbs were crippled by arthritis, for minimum wages, and enticed Scott Brady and Lon Chaney, Jr., both of whom were alcoholics, with bottles of booze.

A habitué of Palm Springs, Adamson had owned or leased as many as three separate homes there, including Harold Lloyd's former estate, where Adamson photographed some of the nude sex scenes for *Blazing Stewardesses*. Needless to say, he worked fast, often under cover of darkness, employing nonunion labor and forgoing the proper film permits.

Although Adamson was tight with a dollar, especially when it came to making movies, he had plenty to show for his thriftiness: seven luxury automobiles; real estate holdings that stretched across five states; a 52-foot yacht, which was moored in Hawaii; and time-shares in Australia and New Zealand.

Until recently, Adamson resided in a two-story Regency-style home in Las Vegas, which he occupied with his young girlfriend, Stephanie Ashlock, a topless dancer who also worked as a roller-skating waitress at Hooters. But they had separated, and Adamson had moved to Indio, where his questionable tactics finally caught up with him. (His wife, Regina Carrol, a busty actress in the Jayne Mansfield mold, had died of cancer.)

In 1995, Adamson's sixty-sixth birthday had come and gone, when his brother, Ken Adamson, became concerned that he had not heard from the pornographer in nearly five weeks. Maybe Al was out of town—or in hiding someplace. He kept calling Adamson's home at 80–950 Avenue 49, on a dirt road between the Empire Polo Club and the Desert Aire R.V. Park, and leaving frantic messages on the answering machine. But his calls were never returned.

In exasperation, Ken Adamson filed a missing persons report with the Indio Police. But when uniformed officers checked the house, they saw nothing out of the ordinary except a dismantled Jacuzzi that had been removed from a small mirrored room adjoining Adamson's bedroom. Concrete had recently been poured, and tile had been laid on the floor.

During Adamson's last phone conversation with his brother, the budget-minded filmmaker had complained that his live-in contractor had run up $4,000 of unauthorized charges on his credit cards. "If he doesn't pay it," said Adamson, "I'm going to put him in jail."

Contractor Fred Fulford, the man whom Al was griping about, was nowhere to be found. He had last been seen two days after his employer disappeared, handing a presigned check to the driver of a Redi-Mix truck that delivered four tons of wet cement to Adamson's home. The police summoned two city workmen with jackhammers, and they started excavating the concrete slab beneath the Jacuzzi, where Adamson liked to sit naked and read pornographic magazines, while the hot bubbles soothed his lower back and legs.

After nine hours of drilling, the rancid smell of rotting flesh suddenly filled the room. A human rib cage was partially detected sticking out of its concrete grave.

Investigators had found their missing man.

Adamson would have relished this moment, perhaps even filmed it for posterity, if he could have hired a cameraman with a strong stomach to do the job. As workmen drilled the concrete slab into smaller pieces, the form beneath the cement took on a ghastly appearance, more horrific than any scene in Adamson's films.

In a macabre twist worthy of Edgar Allan Poe, the slain director was starring in his own posthumous biopic. There, crouched before the group of appalled onlookers, in nauseating color, was Adamson's rapidly decomposing corpse, his eyes missing from their sockets, his brain liquefied, and his battered skull leering at them like a murdered pirate.

His revolting demise would be remembered by the sensational hyperbole: HORROR FILM DIRECTOR BURIED ALIVE. If it was a slight exaggeration, the wording was not nearly as misleading as Adamson's voyeuristic films, and much more authentic than the atrocities he so enjoyed depicting.

Five days after Adamson's putrefying remains were exhumed from his makeshift tomb, Fulford, who had disposed of the body and then fled the state, was arrested at the Coral Reef Motel in St. Petersburg, Florida. He was charged with first degree murder, forging 25 of Adamson's personal checks, and the theft of four of the director's cars, which the murderer had intended to sell.

Everything went into foreclosure: cars, houses—even Adamson's boat. His saddened girlfriend tried to rationalize the brutal death. "He'd do anything to save a buck," she said. "That's what killed him."

Fulford's lame defense consisted of a not-guilty plea. In desperation he insisted that it wasn't Adamson's body but someone else's buried under the old Jacuzzi. Fulford claimed Adamson had simply vanished and that he was being framed for a murder that never happened.

Producer Sam Sherman, who had been Adamson's business partner for 32 years, put forward another theory: the unlucky contractor had stumbled across the dead director, panicked, and concealed the body. Desperate for money, he had ransacked the house and fled the scene of the crime.

But police investigators didn't buy either of these half-baked explanations, nor did a jury. In 2000, an Indio court found Fulford guilty of second-degree murder, and he was sentenced to 25 years to life in prison. On the witness stand, Fulford said Adamson had owed him money for the remodeling work he had done. He admitted to forgery, perjury, and taking money from Adamson but repeatedly denied killing him. "I didn't do it!" he whined.

It was a classic doom-filled scenario. All it needed was the sardonic, sonorous voice of Vincent Price, in all his ruffled finery, to give the finale an element of class—if Al Adamson, the eternal cheapskate, would have been willing to pay him for it.

Thermal

A deceptively nonchalant star with a yen for the simple life—that was debonair, mustachioed, British leading man **Brian Aherne**, who cultivated 160 acres of seedless grapes on his ranch at 81–770 Avenue 58, Thermal.

Aherne, who was nominated in 1939 for an Oscar for Best Supporting Actor in *Juarez*, in which he portrayed Emperor Maximilian, moved there in 1955 following the end of his six-year marriage to actress Joan Fontaine. Onscreen and off, he epitomized the gentlemanly consort with impeccable manners, a man who always had a cigarette within easy reach of his manicured fingers.

Many of his early roles in *The Constant Nymph, Sylvia Scarlett,* and *The Great Garrick* required Aherne to be supercilious. In real life, he was an extremely practical fellow. Among his nonacting business ventures was an Arizona land deal he entered with other movie-industry people. The large tract of desert land was developed as an airport for training civilian pilots, and during World War II it was leased by the U.S. government for Thunderbird and Falcon landing fields.

To underwrite the cost of these financial endeavors, Aherne appeared in prestigious films such as *I Confess, Titanic, Prince Valiant,* and *The Swan* and continued to play well-tailored roles in *The Best of Everything, Susan Slade,* and *Rosie.* In 1971, Aherne was replastering the adobe walls of his home when he received a surprise visit from his longtime friend George Sanders. The caddish actor was dropping by with his new bride, Magda Gabor, whom he had recently married in Indio.

Sanders said he was despondent over his failing health and inability to live "up" to his responsibilities as Gabor's fifth husband. Aherne tried to console his old pal, but his words had no effect. Six weeks after they had exchanged wedding vows, the Sanders-Gabor marriage was annulled, and poor George was left alone and depressed.

The following year Aherne picked up a newspaper and was shocked to read that Sanders had committed suicide by taking an overdose of sleeping pills. "I feel I have lived long enough," read the note Sanders left behind on his bedside table. "I leave you all in your sweet little cesspool and I wish you luck."

Aherne put down the paper and his eyes filled with tears. He died at the age of 83 in 1986.

■ ■ ■

ANOTHER FAMOUS BRITISH expatriate who lived and worked here was the acclaimed playwright **John Van Druten**, whose sophisticated comedies and dramas rank among the most performed literary works of the twentieth century.

A fall from a horse in Mexico in 1936 left the London-born dramatist with a permanently crippled arm. Seeking relief from his persistent discomfort, he visited Palm Springs and purchased the former A.J.C. Ranch at 83–260 Avenue 61, where he spent the remaining 20 years of his life.

Van Druten wrote many of his best known plays in a small study just off the main house, laboring on his typewriter from early morning until late afternoon to create *Old Acquaintance, The Voice of the Turtle,* and *I Remember Mama,* all of which were performed on the stage and then became highly successful films.

Among his other popular plays were *Bell, Book and Candle* and *I Am a Camera,* the latter was partially the source for the Broadway musical *Cabaret* and the film starring Liza Minnelli. The evocative cinematic portrait of Berlin between the world wars garnered a total of eight Academy Awards.

The ranch also was a working farm for Van Druten, who, despite his physical handicap, grew self-sustaining crops. Maintaining a quiet existence, he was rarely seen in public except on periodic excursions to Indio, a trip he made in a farm truck and later by automobile.

Still, while harvesting vegetables he continued to turn out memorable screenplays for classics such as *Night Must Fall, Parnell, Raffles,* and *Gaslight,* which combined dramatic suspense and romantic intrigue.

"I would not have thought in those days," contemplated Van Druten in his autobiography *The Widening Circle,* "that I would live in country like this. There is great beauty where I live," he explained, "and there is great variety."

He died in 1957 at the age of 56.

■ ■ ■

IT WASN'T ACTING that brought **William Devane** to the desert; it was polo. The two-time, Emmy Award–nominated actor, who impersonated President John F. Kennedy in *The Missiles of October* and portrayed black-listed writer John Henry Faulk in *Fear on Trail,* first came to Indio more than 15 years ago, when Stefanie Powers invited him for a game of stick-and-ball at the Empire Polo Club.

Polo may be considered the sport of kings, but in the Coachella Valley it's mostly played by athletic movie stars, fashion models, and media moguls, although England's Prince Charles did play one charity match there.

Devane was so captivated by the friendly atmosphere and wide open spaces that he decided to stay and bought himself a 140-acre property at 84–383 Avenue 61. He named it Deer Creek Farms, after his mountain spread in Utah, and fashioned it after the Argentine and Mexican *estancias,* or polo ranches, that he's played on throughout the years.

When he first arrived in town, Devane was in the middle of his 10-year stint as the enigmatic tycoon Gregory Sumner, on the CBS-TV prime-time soap *Knots Landing.* On that top-rated series, his wolfish grin made him a popular rival to Blake Carrington and J.R. Ewing, known as "the men you love to hate."

Devane's homestead is traditional California-Spanish, decorated with sienna-colored tiles and with Hopi artifacts on the walls. He spends as much time here as possible, tending to his grazing horses or keeping in practice at the polo fields, where he enjoys a one-goal handicap.

Although a relative newcomer to the desert, Devane has substantial valley ties: his father Joseph Devane was Franklin D. Roosevelt's personal chauffeur when FDR, whose family regularly vacationed in Palm Springs, was governor of New York.

Devane himself has been privileged to work with several directors who spent considerable time in Palm Springs. They include Alfred Hitchcock, who directed Devane in the occult thriller *Family Plot*, and the late John Schlesinger, who featured the actor's devilish smile in *Marathon Man*, *Yanks*, and *Honky Tonk Freeway*.

In 1991, the hardworking actor and gourmand opened Devane's Restaurant, serving New York Italian cuisine at 80–755 Highway 111, West Indio. When he's not performing onstage or in films, Devane can normally be found in the dining room assisting his wife, Eugenie, and their two sons, Joshua and Jacob, who manage the restaurant when their dad's away.

■ ■ ■

PIONEERING DATE GROWER **Lionel Steinberg,** who was also one of the desert's foremost producers of table grapes, owned the 1,300-acre grape ranch at 57–800 Fillmore Street, off the old State Highway 99.

Steinberg cultivated a wide variety of grapes, including Thompson Seedless, Perlettes, Cardinal Beauty Seedless, and Exotics. He once recalled planting his first table grape vineyard in 1952, "on the raw desert sand along the Thermal slope."

Not content to be only a farmer, Steinberg also was active in state and federal politics. A liberal Democrat, he served as agricultural advisor and Central California campaign manager for Adlai Stevenson during the Illinois governor's failed runs for the presidency in 1952 and 1956.

In 1960, California Governor Edmund "Pat" Brown appointed Steinberg to the California State Board of Agriculture, of which he later became its president. He served on the White House Food for Peace Council under President John F. Kennedy and advised his successor, President Lyndon B. Johnson, on agricultural issues.

Steinberg ruffled industry feathers when he signed the first table grape contract with Cesar Chavez and the United Farm Workers, whose members had been on strike for higher wages. Chavez had gone on three hunger strikes over poor working conditions and led a boycott against growers' use of harmful pesticides.

The two men became allies and friends, for Steinberg believed in the right of workers to earn a fair living as well as the right of farmers to make a profit. But Steinberg wasn't only concerned with grapes. He also invested heavily in real estate, and he owned a valuable art collection with his second wife, Katrina Heinrich.

He died of kidney failure in 1999 at the age of 79.

■ ■ ■

INDIO IS TRYING its hardest to catch up with the future. Nowhere is this more noticeable than in Indian gaming, which is already a big revenue raiser for other desert cities. In 2002, Donald Trump entered into a leasing agreement with the Twentynine Palms Band of Mission Indians to manage the Spotlight 29 Casino in Coachella.

The deal called for Trump Hotels to use the company's expertise and run the gaming facility but put tribal members in key positions. In true Donald Trump fashion, however, the New York hotshot demanded that the name be changed to Trump 29 Casino, and he flew in by private plane to monitor the situation.

Latin pop star Marc Anthony agreed to be the first headliner at the revamped $60-million casino, as "a favor to Trump," a close personal friend. Other big-name acts that have played there include Englebert Humperdink, Art Garfunkel, Tony Bennett, and Bill Cosby.

In 2004, the casino hosted a twenty-seventh anniversary rock 'n' roll tribute to Elvis Presley, starring Paul Casey, who was billed as "The Official Elvis of Las Vegas." The show featured the Sweet Temptations, announcer **Al Dvorin**, former entourage member Ed Bonja, and friends and colleagues of Elvis such as Patti Parry, Cynthia Pepper, and the Stamps Quartet. But lady luck wasn't smiling on them that song-filled night.

After the musical acts had been put through their paces, the sweating, white-jump-suited Casey took his final bow and exited the stage. Dvorin closed the show with his famous announcement, "Ladies and gentlemen, Elvis has left the building. Thank you and good night." The nostalgic crowds dispersed, and the elated performers rejoiced with a backstage party.

Several hours before dawn, the exhausted group loaded their musical instruments and costumes into a convoy of cars and vans and headed across the Mojave Desert to Las Vegas. Dvorin was recalling one vivid moment in Presley's career when the car he was traveling in at high speed hit a bump in the road near Ivanpah and swerved out of control. Suddenly there was an agonizing sound of squealing tires as the vehicles slammed on their brakes to avoid a collision. Dvorin, who was not wearing a seat belt, was ejected from the passenger seat and landed in the yucca-filled desert. The driver and Ed Bonja ran to help the 81-year-old announcer, but he was already dead. Dvorin, like Presley before him, had not only left the building, he had permanently exited the planet.

Salton Sea

Many actors received their first taste of the desert while filming war films and biblical epics that have utilized the Indio hills and the briny Salton Sea for backdrops. These action scenes have ranged from the U.S. Marines' heroic defense of a Pacific atoll in *Wake Island* to the fictitious attack of prehistoric giant mollusks in the B-movie classic *The Monster That Challenged the World*.

This vast so-called sea, which covers an area of nearly 400 square miles, is the largest lake in California. It was formed a century ago when heavy rainfall caused the Colorado River to burst its banks, flooding the town of Salton, 26 miles from Indio, and creating a vast reservoir of trapped water.

Over the course of 50 years, however, the rising salinity and the lack of drainage gradually have altered the water's chemical balance. What was once a shimmering lake is now a quagmire of green algae and harmful bacteria that have decimated local fish and birds.

The surrounding landscape was used to simulate an apocalyptic world in *Damnation Alley* and a desert planet in *Dune*. Here, second-unit cinematography of navy ships stranded in the water created the revelatory climax of James Cameron's blockbuster sci-fi hit *The Abyss*, which won an Oscar for Best Visual Effects.

Perhaps most appropriately, in the 2002 film *The Salton Sea*, actor Val Kilmer went undercover to bust a drug ring that was responsible for the murder of his wife. The movie's title was a metaphor for the absence of life along the lake's empty shore.

Once a popular boating and swimming destination for weekend vacationers, who dubbed it the "beach in the desert," the Salton Sea also provided Los Angeles fish markets with a fresh supply of mullet, corvina, and tilapia.

Today, however, the fish are diseased or dying. Suggested remedies for this environmental disaster have included the construction of desalination plants, evaporation ponds, pipelines to the ocean and causeways with underwater filters. Congressman Sonny Bono once asked the U.S. government to fund a massive cleanup campaign. But when Bono was killed in a skiing accident in January 1998, many people believe the idea died with him, despite the best efforts of his widow, Mary Bono, who assumed his congressional seat and continued the fight. (In 2001, 40 miles of Interstate 10 were dedicated as the Sonny Bono Memorial Freeway.)

One of the latest plans, proposed by the Salton Sea Authority in early 2006, involves a residential development of 200,000 homes, a tax base that would be used to pay for a new saltwater dam.

It remains to be seen if and when an antidote will be found for this massive pool of floating toxicity. More than impassioned speeches and budget proposals will be necessary; major government intervention and scientific assistance will be required to repair the ecological damage.

A better solution might be to drain the whole stinking mess and start again. The problem requires someone with a lot of money and imagination to transform this modern Dead Sea into a profitable hotel casino or aquatic resort—somebody like Bill Gates, Donald Trump, Merv Griffin, or Oprah Winfrey. Somebody with the ability to make it happen.

Dominick Dunne has observed, "Hollywood forgives lies, cheating, forgeries, even murders on occasion. But never your failures."

Perhaps redemption is at hand.

Bibliography

Aherne, Brian. *A Dreadful Man*. New York: Simon & Schuster, 1979.

Autry, Gene, with Mickey Herskowitz. *Back in the Saddle Again*. New York: Doubleday & Company, Inc., 1978.

Bacon, James. *Hollywood Is a Four Letter Town*. Chicago: Henry Regnery Co., 1976.

Baker, Carroll. *Baby Doll: An Autobiography*. New York: Arbor House, 1983.

Ball, Lucille. *Love, Lucy*. New York: G.P. Putnam's Sons, 1996.

Ballard, Kaye, with Jim Hesselman. *How I Lost 10 Pounds in 53 Years*. Boulder, CO: Argent Books, 2004.

Bergen, Candice. *Knock on Wood*. New York: Simon & Schuster, 1984.

Bergreen, Laurence. *Capone: The Man and the Era*. New York: Simon & Schuster, 1996.

Blackwell, Mr., with Vernon Patterson. *Rags to Bitches*. Los Angeles: General Publishing Group, 1995.

Burke, Anthony. *Palm Springs, Why I Love You*. Palm Desert, CA: Palmesa, Inc., 1978.

Callow, Simon. *Charles Laughton: A Difficult Actor*. New York: Grove Press, 1987.

Carmichael, Hoagy, with Stephen Longstreet. *Sometimes I Wonder*. New York: Farrar, Straus and Giroux, 1965.

Channing, Carol. *Just Lucky I Guess*. New York: Simon & Schuster, 2002.

Clark, Tom, with Dick Kleiner. *Rock Hudson: Friend of Mine*. New York: Pharos Books, 1989.

Cochran, Jacqueline, and Maryann Bucknum Brinley. *Jackie Cochran: An Autobiography*. New York: Bantam Books, 1987.

Conrad, Barnaby. *Time Is All We Have: Four Weeks at the Betty Ford Center.* New York: Arbor House, 1986.

Cooper, Jackie, with Dick Kleiner. *Please Don't Shoot My Dog.* New York: William Morrow & Co., 1981.

Cramer, Richard Ben. *Joe DiMaggio: The Hero's Life.* New York: Simon & Schuster, 2000.

Crane, Cheryl, with Cliff Jahr. *Detour: A Hollywood Story.* New York: Arbor House/William Morrow & Co., 1988.

Crosby, Kathryn. *My Life with Bing.* Wheeling, Illinois: Collage, Inc., 1983.

Curtis, Tony, with Barry Paris. *Tony Curtis: The Autobiography.* New York: William Morrow & Co., 1993.

David, Lester, and Irene David. *Ike and Mamie.* New York: G.P. Putnam's Sons, 1981.

Deutsch, Armand. *Me and Bogie.* New York: G.P. Putnam's Sons, 1991.

Dick, Bernard F. *Hal Wallis: Producer to the Stars.* Lexington, KY: University Press of Kentucky, 2004.

Elder, Jane Lenz. *Alice Faye: A Life Beyond the Silver Screen.* Jackson, MS: University Press of Mississippi, 2002.

Evans, Robert. *The Kid Stays in the Picture.* New York: Hyperion, 1994.

Feuer, Cy, with Ken Gross. *I Got the Show Right Here.* New York: Simon & Schuster, 2003.

Fisher, Eddie, with David Fisher. *Been There, Done That.* New York: St. Martin's Press, 1999.

Freedland, Michael. *The Secret Life of Danny Kaye.* New York: St. Martin's Press, 1985.

Gilmore, John. *Severed: The True Story of the Black Dahlia Murder.* Los Angeles: Amok Books, 1998.

Goldman, Herbert G. *Fanny Brice: The Original Funny Girl.* New York: Oxford University Press, 1992.

Gottfried, Martin. *Nobody's Fool: The Lives of Danny Kaye.* New York: Simon & Schuster, 1994.

Griffin, Merv, with David Bender. *Merv: Making the Good Life Last.* New York: Simon & Schuster, 2003.

Grudens, Richard. *Jerry Vale: A Singer's Life.* Stony Brook, NY: Celebrity Profiles Publishing, 2000.

Guerrero, Lalo, and Sherilyn Meece Mentes. *Lalo: My Life and Music.* Tucson, AZ: University of Arizona Press, 2002.

Guiles, Fred Lawrence. *Marion Davies.* New York: McGraw-Hill Book Company, 1972.

Hagman, Larry, with Todd Gold. *Hello Darlin'.* New York: Simon & Schuster, 2001.

Hersh, Seymour M. *The Dark Side of Camelot.* New York: Little, Brown and Company, 1997.

Herz, Peggy. *La Quinta Country Club: Silver Anniversary 1959-1984.* La Quinta, CA: La Quinta Country Club, 1984.

Heymann, C. David. *Liz.* New York: Birch Lane Press, 1995.

Higham, Charles. *Merchant of Dreams: Louis B. Mayer, MGM and the Secret Hollywood.* New York: Donald I. Fine, 1996.

Hillings, Patrick J., with Howard Seelye. *Pat Hillings: The Irrepressible Irishman.* Harold D. Dean, 1993.

Hiney, Tom. *Raymond Chandler: A Biography.* New York: Atlantic Monthly Press, 1997.

Hinton, Gregory. *Cathedral City.* New York: Kensington Books, 2001.

Hodel, Steve. *Black Dahlia Avenger.* New York: Arcade Publishing, 2003.

Hudson, Rock, and Sara Davidson. *Rock Hudson: His Story.* New York: William Morrow & Co., 1986.

Iacocca, Lee, with William Novak. *Iacocca: An Autobiography.* New York: Bantam Books, 1984.

Jacobs, George, and William Stadiem. *Mr. S: My Life with Frank Sinatra.* New York: Harper Entertainment, 2003.

Jurow, Martin, as told to Philip Wuntch. *Marty Jurow Seein' Stars.* Dallas, TX: Southern Methodist University Press, 2001.

Kanfer, Stefan. *Ball of Fire.* New York: Alfred A. Knopf, 2003.

Kashner, Sam, and Nancy Schoenberger. *Hollywood Kryptonite.* New York: St. Martin's Press, 1996.

Kavieff, Paul R. *The Purple Gang: Organized Crime in Detroit.* New York: Barricade Books, 2000.

Keel, Howard, with Joyce Spizer. *Only Make Believe: My Life in Show Business.* Fort Lee, NJ: Barricade Books, 2005.

Kelley, Kitty. *His Way: The Unauthorized Biography of Frank Sinatra.* New York: Bantam Books, 1986.

Kuntz, Tom, and Phil Kuntz, Eds. *The Sinatra Files.* New York: Three Rivers Press, 2000.

Laflin, Patricia B. *Coachella Valley, California: A Pictorial History.* Virginia Beach, VA: Donning Company, 1998.

Lamparski, Richard. *Whatever Became Of...?.* New York: Crown Publishers, Inc., 1968.

Leigh, Wendy. *Liza: Born a Star.* New York: Dutton, 1993.

Levy, Shawn. *Rat Pack Confidential.* New York: Doubleday, 1998.

Lewis, Alfred Allan, and Constance Woodworth. *Miss Elizabeth Arden.* New York: Coward, McCann & Geoghegan, Inc., 1972.

MacShane, Frank. *The Life of Raymond Chandler.* New York: E.P. Dutton, 1976.

Manes, Stephen, and Paul Andrews. *Gates.* New York: Doubleday, 1993.

Marlow-Trump, Nancy: *Ruby Keeler: A Photographic Biography;* McFarland & Company, Inc., Publishers, Jefferson, North Carolina, 1998.

Marshall, Peter, and Adrienne Armstrong. *Backstage with the Original Hollywood Square.* Nashville, TN: Rutledge Hill Press, 2002.

Martin, Mary. *My Heart Belongs.* New York: William Morrow & Co., 1976.

Marx, Arthur. *Life with Groucho.* New York: Simon & Schuster, 1954.
————. *Red Skelton.* New York: E.P. Dutton, 1979.
Marx, Harpo, with Rowland Barber. *Harpo Speaks!.* New York: Bernard Geis Associates, 1961.
McBride, Joseph. *Frank Capra: The Catastrophe of Success.* New York: Simon & Schuster, 1992.
————. *Searching for John Ford: A Life.* New York: St. Martin's Press, 2001.
McDonough, Jimmy. *Big Bosoms and Square Jaws: The Biography of Russ Meyer, King of the Sex Film.* New York: Crown Publishers, 2005.
McDougal, Dennis. *The Last Mogul: Lew Wasserman, MCA and the Hidden History of Hollywood.* New York: Crown Publishers, 1998.
McGilligan, Patrick. *Alfred Hitchcock: A Life in Darkness and Light.* New York: Regan Books, 2003.
Moldea, Dan E. *Dark Victory: Ronald Reagan, MCA and the Mob.* New York: Viking, 1986.
————. *Interference: How Organized Crime Influences Professional Football.* New York: William Morrow & Co., 1989.
Moore, Clayton. *I Was That Masked Man.* Dallas, TX: Taylor Publishing Company, 1996.
Moore, Mary Tyler. *After All.* New York: G.P. Putnam's Sons, 1995.
Morella, Joe, and Edward Z. Epstein. *Jane Wyman: A Biography.* New York: Delacorte Press, 1985.
Mungo, Ray. *Palm Springs Babylon.* New York: St. Martin's Press, 1993.
Nass, Herbert E. *Wills of the Rich and Famous.* New York: Warner Books, 1991.
Neff, Wallace, Jr. *Wallace Neff: Architect of California's Golden Age.* Santa Barbara, CA: Capra Press, 1986.
Ogden, Christopher. *Legacy: A Biography of Moses and Walter Annenberg.* New York: Little, Brown and Company, 1999.
O'Neal, Tatum. *A Paper Life.* New York: Harper Entertainment, 2004.
Pejsa, Jane. *Romanoff: Prince of Rogues.* Minneapolis, MN: Kenwood Publishing, 1997.
Quirk, Lawrence J. *Paul Newman.* Dallas, TX: Taylor Publishing Company, 1996.
Rogers, Ginger. *Ginger: My Story.* New York: HarperCollins Publishers, 1991.
Saroyan, Aram. *Rancho Mirage.* New York: Barricade Books, 1993.
Scott, C.H. *Whatever Happened to Randolph Scott?* Madison, NC: Empire Publishing, Inc., 1994.
Scully, Frank. *This Gay Knight: An Autobiography of a Modern Chevalier.* Philadelphia: Chilton Books, 1962.
Server, Lee. *Robert Mitchum: "Baby, I Don't Care."* New York: St. Martin's Press, 2001.
Shapiro, Marc. *Pure Goldie: The Life and Career of Goldie Hawn.* Secaucus, NJ: Birch Lane Press/Carol Publishing Group, 1998.
Shepherd, Donald, with Robert F. Slatzer. *Bing Crosby: The Hollow Man.* New York: St. Martin's Press, 1981.

Sikov, Ed. *On Sunset Boulevard:The Life and Times of Billy Wilder.* NewYork: Hyperion, 1998.

Sinatra,Tina, with Jeff Coplon. *My Father's Daughter.* NewYork: Simon & Schuster, 2000.

Smith, Sally Bedell. *Grace and Power:The Private World of the Kennedy White House.* NewYork: Random House, 2004.

Spada, James. *Julia: Her Life.* NewYork: St. Martin's Press, 2004.

———. *Peter Lawford:The Man Who Kept the Secrets.* NewYork: Bantam Books, 1991.

Spanos, Alex, with Mark Seal and Natalia Kasparian. *Sharing the Wealth: My Story.* Washington, DC: Regnery Publishing Inc., 2002.

Spoto, Donald. *A Passion for Life:The Biography of Elizabeth Taylor.* NewYork: HarperCollins, 1995.

Steen, M. F. *Celebrity Death Certificates.* Jefferson, NC: McFarland & Company, Inc., 2003.

Sudhalter, Richard M. *Stardust Melody:The Life and Music of Hoagy Carmichael.* NewYork: Oxford University Press, Inc., 2002.

Summers, Anthony. *Goddess:The Secret Lives of Marilyn Monroe.* NewYork: MacMillan Publishing Co., 1985.

Tannen, Lee, *I Loved Lucy.* NewYork: St. Martin's Press, 2001.

Thomas, Danny, with Bill Davidson. *Make Room for Danny.* NewYork: G.P. Putnam's Sons, 1991.

Thorson, Scott, with Alex Thorleifson. *Behind the Candelabra: My Life with Liberace.* NewYork: E.P. Dutton, 1988.

Tornabene, Lyn. *Long Live the King:A Biography of Clark Gable.* NewYork: G.P. Putnam's Sons, 1976.

Turner, Steve, *The Man Called Cash.* Nashville,TN:W Publishing Group, 2004.

Wallis, Hal, and Charles Higham. *Starmaker:The Autobiography of Hal Wallis.* NewYork: Macmillan Publishing Co., 1980.

Watters, James, and Horst P. Horst. *Return Engagement.* NewYork: Clarkson N. Potter, Inc., 1984.

Wayne, Jane Ellen. *Gable's Women.* NewYork: Prentice Hall Press, 1987.

Whitfield, Eileen. *Pickford:The Woman Who Made Hollywood.* Lexington, KY: University Press of Kentucky, 1997.

Williams, Esther, with Digby Diehl. *The Million Dollar Mermaid.* NewYork: Simon & Schuster, 1999.

Windeler, Robert. *Thunderbird Country Club 50th Anniversary History.* San Bernardino, CA: Crown Printers, 2002.

Wray, Fay. *On the Other Hand.* NewYork: St. Martin's Press, 1989.

Index

Index

Index